Routing and Dimensioning in Circuit-Switched Networks

André Girard
INRS-Télécommunications

ADDISON-WESLEY PUBLISHING COMPANY

Reading, Massachusetts • Menlo Park, California • New York
Don Mills, Ontario • Wokingham, England • Amsterdam • Bonn
Sydney • Singapore • Tokyo • Madrid • San Juan

This book is in the **Addison-Wesley Series in Electrical and Computer Engineering: Telecommunications**

Library of Congress Cataloging-in-Publication Data

Girard, André, 1944-
    Routing and dimensioning in circuit-switched networks / André
Girard.
        p.   cm.
    ISBN 0-201-12792-X
    1. Telecommunication--Switching systems--Mathematical models.
I. Title.
TK5103.8.G57   1990   89-17531
621.382--dc20   CIP

This book was processed through a Sun Microsystems Sparcstation 1 from tape files composed by the author using Donald Knuth's TEX typesetting system.

Preface

Objectives

The objective of this book is to provide an overview of traffic engineering for circuit-switched telecommunication networks. Circuit switching is generally identified with telephony and telephony is often considered a well-known field where most problems have already been solved. This book takes a different view on both counts.

The recent evolution of telephone networks towards digital transmission and switching systems has brought a new set of network management and design problems for which the previous planning tools are not well suited. The introduction of new services in the integrated networks now being proposed will only aggravate this problem. There has been a burst of activity in the design of planning methods over the last few years and it will continue in the future. Hence the need to have a sound theoretical understanding of the current methods and how they can be extended to these new cases.

It is also clear that the new multi-service networks of the future will operate on a virtual circuit mode. Because the fundamental differences between packet and circuit-switched networks are very small, at least as far as traffic engineering is concerned, the proper management and design of virtual-circuit networks will have to rely on the current circuit-switching tools or their extensions. This is the second reason why a sound understanding of these methods is needed.

Contents

Because of the wide scope of traffic engineering, the book concentrates on those areas that are amenable to mathematical analysis. Even so, the range of topics is so large that it would be impossible to cover them all in detail within a book of reasonable size. A selection had to be made and this was done more on the subjective basis of the author's preferences than on any objective "value" attributed to the selected topics. It is still possible that relevant material has been left out, however, and the author would appreciate any suggestion from readers aware of interesting subject matter.

The first chapter is a general discussion of telecommunication networks and of the planning process. This is followed in the next chapter by a qualitative description of routing methods currently used in or proposed for circuit-switched networks. The next two chapters are fundamental. Chapter 3 covers the standard teletraffic theory, and Chapter 4, the basic methods for network performance evaluation. The fifth chapter is a description of practical methods usable on real networks, and Chapter 6 covers the case of networks with adaptive routing. Chapter 7 deals with the optimization of routing, and Chapters 8 and 9 with the optimization of the transmission systems in networks. Finally, the last chapter gives a short introduction to multi-service networks, and to their relation with circuit switching and with the topics discussed in the book.

Intended Audience

The book is intended for first-year graduate students in engineering and operations research as well as for practicing engineers having to deal with network planning problems. Queuing theory and mathematical programming are heavily used in the text and the reader should have a good basic knowledge of these two areas.

This text has a double function. It can serve as the basis of a one-semester course in traffic engineering of circuit-switched networks based on Chapters 1, 2, 3.1, 4, 6, 7 and 8. These chapters cover the fundamentals of the subject in a simplified form. The objective here is to give some understanding of the principles used in routing and dimensioning networks without paying much attention to the practical problem of applying these methods to real cases. The other parts, on the other hand, deal with more practical problems. In these other chapters, algorithms that are used on real network problems are described with as much detail as possible, paying attention to all aspects of a working algorithm. These sections should interest the practicing engineer, since they give explicit descriptions of working methods that can be used in practice. They also show how the simple theoretical models of the other sections have to be modified to make them usable in real cases.

Acknowledgements

Many thanks go to the external reviewers of this book: Dr. K.R. Krishnan, Bell Communications Research, Prof. Kumpati S. Narendra, Yale University, Dr. Brion Feinberg, AT&T Bell Laboratories, and Dr. Peter O'Reilly, GTE Laboratories. I would also like to thank colleagues that have offered many useful suggestions: Dr. Zbigniew Dzion, Warsaw University of Technology and Dr. Brunilde Sanso, Centre de recherche sur les transports de Montréal, as well as the students that have take the network planning course based on this material.

Prof. Michael Ferguson, of INRS-Télécommunications, who provided an extensive set of TeX macros with graphic capabilities and much time in solving the various problems that arose during the preparation of the manuscript, deserves my gratitude.

The work of the editorial staff at Addison-Wesley has been very useful, and they should be thanked for it. Needless to say, whatever errors remain in the text are the sole responsibility of this author.

Quebec

A. G.

Contents

CHAPTER 1

Introduction

Since the early 1960s, the world of telecommunications has undergone dramatic changes, which will continue to accelerate. Twenty-five years ago, there were only two distinct telecommunication networks, each geared to a particular type of service. The telegraph network transmitted information in digital form, operated in a store-and-forward manner via message-switching techniques, and was dedicated to the transmission of written information. The telephone network transmitted information in analog form, operated in a circuit-switched mode, and was used exclusively to transmit voice. Each network served a well-identified need, and there was relatively little interconnection between them. As with many other technology-dependent areas, telecommunications started to change with the arrival of computers in the early 1960s.

Computers had a double impact on telecommunications. First, the communication requirements between computers themselves created a new class of user that was not well served by either of the existing networks. The transmission of digital information requires a low probability of error, which the analog telephone network was not designed to provide. Also, interactive computer use entails relatively long periods of inactivity between requests for transmission, which means that the line is not used efficiently and can remain idle for a substantial fraction of a call's duration. The digital telegraph network, on the other hand, was too slow for computer communications.

At the same time, it became obvious that in addition to using telecommunication networks, computers could be used within these networks to carry out many of the management and planning functions required to operate them smoothly — in particular, switching messages within the network. With the combination of computers and the increased use of digital transmission, there soon emerged a new class of telecommunication network designed specifically for the need of a new type of customer, the remote interactive computer user. The growth of these specialized networks has been dramatic; within the last few decades, they have appeared in all industrialized countries.

Telephone networks have been similarly transformed. Most of the switching is now done by computers, as opposed to wired-logic electromechanical devices, and transmission systems are increasingly being converted to the digital format.

1

While the dichotomy between the voice and data networks still exists, the distinction is becoming less sharp. Both networks use digital transmission methods, at least in the transport network; in both, computers are responsible for switching information through the network. This trend is becoming more pronounced as the demand for digital services such as facsimile increases and as new, high-capacity services such as low- or high-speed video services are introduced. Since all these services will be digital, the concept of a unique network carrying all types of information in the form of bit streams immediately comes to mind; clearly it is only a matter of time before the two networks are merged into one.

In the 1990s network planners will be engaged in designing such integrated networks. Because planning techniques are evolutionary in nature, the new planning techniques will be based on current methods, modified to handle the new problems arising in an integrated environment. Thus it is necessary to understand the methods developed for the existing networks before embarking on the development of new tools for more complex systems.

Planning telecommunication networks is a complex process, drawing on the techniques of electrical engineering, economics, probability theory, and operation research. Many elements of this process, such as forecasting or transmission engineering, are not specific to telecommunication networks, but occur in many other areas of engineering or economics. One specialized part of planning, however, is closely related to the particular nature of the network: *traffic engineering* as it is traditionally called. Because it is so specialized, traffic engineering is not treated outside the telecommunications area.

The telephone network has been in existence for nearly a century, and there exists a large body of information on the subject of modeling and planning these networks. This information, however, largely confined to telephone companies, is reported at little-publicized conferences such as the International Teletraffic Congress. In comparison, a very large body of information on models and planning techniques is available about data networks, although they have existed for less than 25 years. This information is widely published in the open technical literature. This book collects and synthesizes the known planning methods that are specific to the traffic engineering of circuit-switched networks.

The emphasis is on mathematical models, not only with respect to the current network, but, more importantly, with a view on potential generalizations applicable to the integrated network case. First, however, we must describe the contents of the book in relation to other areas of telecommunication network planning. We do this from two points of view. In Section 1.1, we describe a standard hierarchical model of telecommunication systems, using it to show where the problems addressed in the book appear in this hierarchy. In Section 1.2, we relate this model to current switching techniques, and in Section 1.3, we consider the planning of networks in general, showing at which points in this process it is important to take into account that we are dealing with a telecommunication network operating in a particular mode.

1.1   The OSI Layered Architecture

The transmission of information between widely separated points is a complex process that requires the cooperative operation of a large number of systems. Designing and implementing these systems is much too difficult to be tackled in a single stage, and a systematic approach is required. The organization of cooperating processes is not specific to the world of telecommunications, but is found in computer science, operations management, and engineering, among other areas. There are many ways to organize cooperating processes efficiently to achieve some end; although the centralized approach is conceptually the simplest, other organizations such as sequential or network modes are also used.

One type of organization is based on the notion of a layer. Briefly stated, a layer at level n is defined by a set of processes called *peer processes*, a set of functions that can be performed by these processes, and by a set of rules, also called *protocols*, that govern the actions in question. Each layer is responsible for a precise subset of the operations required to perform the global task. These functions are implemented by sending requests for service to lower layers, which provide services to the layers above them. The usefulness of the layered approach comes from the requirement that the operation of a layer must be independent of the other layers; the implementation must also be independent from one layer to the next.

In general, the actions and the protocol are defined at level n in such a way that the user has no indication as to how these functions are actually carried out. This specification is done in terms of functions of layer $n - 1$, but is of no interest to the user of layer n, and in fact is carefully hidden from him or her. Hiding the implementation of the function — an essential feature of the layered approach — offers a measure of independence between processes that would otherwise be seen as strongly coupled.

As an example, consider the user of electronic mail on a computer. The processes could be the mail processes, with the corresponding actions of reading, sending, and copying mail. The protocol for this layer is a set of rules that specifies how the messages are to be organized, for instance, the format of the addresses and the meaning of the sender, recipient, and copy fields. The only concern of the mail user is to construct each mail message according to these rules. Once the message is ready, the user requests that it be sent to its destination. The layered architecture guarantees that whatever operations are required to send the mail are totally invisible to the mail user. The user

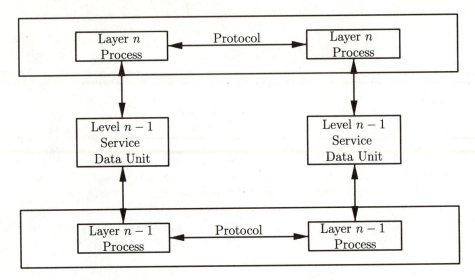

Figure 1.1   The Layer Organization of Cooperating Processes

has no knowledge about the way the message is transmitted to the destination, whether by a virtual connection over a public packet-switched network, a telephone connection over the public telephone network, or some other means. The obvious advantage of masking functions in this way is that the mail-level functions remain unchanged even if the transport function is implemented differently.

To repeat, there are two types of communication in the layered approach. The communication between peer processes is regulated by the protocol at the level at which the process operates. The communication is logical in the sense that the exchange of information between the peer processes, although appearing to be a direct exchange, is actually carried out by a series of requests to lower levels. This communication between adjacent levels is done via rigidly defined formats called *service data units*, which serve to mask implementation issues to the user of level n. This distinction is illustrated in Fig. 1.1 for levels n and $n - 1$.

The *International Standards Organization* (ISO), in collaboration with the *Comité Consultatif pour le Téléphone et le Télégraphe* (CCITT), has sponsored studies in defining such a layered model applicable to telecommunication systems. This model is known as the *Open System Interconnection* (OSI) model. Although not the only one in use, the OSI model provides a good basis for discussing various communication techniques. It includes most of the features found in commonly used systems such as DECNET or SNA, even though the

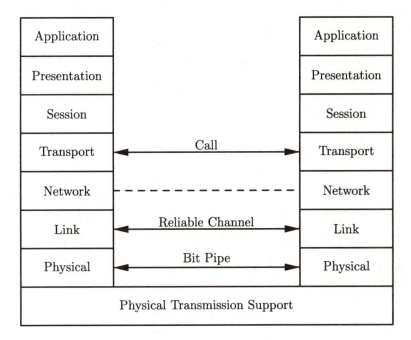

Figure 1.2   OSI Seven-Layer Model

layers of these implementations may not match the layers of the OSI model precisely. The first seven layers of the OSI model are shown on Fig. 1.2. We explain the functions of only the first four levels, however, since they are the levels relevant to this book. More detailed descriptions appear in [1,2,3].

Point-to-Point Layers

The first two layers of the OSI model deal with communication between two points connected by some transmission system. The service offered at the physical layer is the transmission of bits between the two points by the use of electrical signals. This service is implemented in devices such as modems, which are responsible for the electrical transmission of digital information. The nature of this transmission — for instance, whether it is synchronous or asynchronous — is not relevant to this discussion. The physical-layer service is often called a "bit pipe" since this is its appearance to the level-one user.

Nowhere in the level-one service is there any guarantee that data being transmitted in the bit pipe will be received correctly at the other end. This is the preoccupation of the level-two service — the reliable transmission of blocks of data over the pipe — which is done by known methods of error detection and error correction. These methods are the subject of much of information theory; numerous excellent references exist [4]. In practice, the level-two service adds information to the data being offered by the upper layer that is used by the peer process at the other end to detect and correct errors, if necessary.

Although other functions, such as link flow control, may be added at the level-two layer, the level-two service is succinctly described as a *reliable channel* for the point-to-point transmission of information. This function is the one we consider in the remainder of this discussion.

Transport Layer

The level-three and level-four layers, more complex than the point-to-point layers, are called the network layers for reasons that will become obvious shortly. To clarify the respective roles of layers three and four, we first offer two examples of telecommunication applications and show how they are related to the level-four services. The level-three functions are then presented as intermediate stages between levels four and two. It should be noted that the description here is somewhat simplified; a full description of the network layers appears in [1,2,5,6].

Consider the user of the computer system of a company connected to some local network, say in North America, who wishes to communicate with another computer of the company, say in Europe. The user issues a command to his or her local network requesting the connection and, if it is granted, proceeds with the terminal session exactly as if connected to the local computer. The actual transmission of information and control required to achieve this connection is totally invisible to the user, and is carried out by other lower levels of the OSI model.

Next consider the case of long distance telephone calls. Here, too, the user requests a connection by sending a number of digits to the local telephone office. Again, if the connection is made, the exchange of information proceeds exactly as if the user were directly connected to his or her correspondent, without any knowledge of the intervening stages in the connection or transmission process.

The similarity between these two modes of operation is not coincidental since both are functions of level four of the OSI model. In fact, at this level, the examples are indistinguishable, except perhaps for the fact that the connection request is being made using different signaling techniques: the ASCII (or EBCDIC) code for the first one, and pulse or tone dialing for the second. In both cases, the user is given a "pipe" between two points that can be used to transmit whatever is desired; at this level, the system look like a direct connection between the origin and destination terminals.

With these examples in mind, we can now describe the main function of level four. It provides the user with a connection, sometimes called a *virtual circuit*, from one point to another, that can be used to transmit blocks of

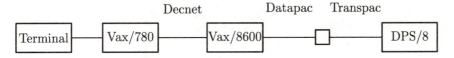

Figure 1.3   A Multisystem Connection to a Remote Host

information. More precisely, the transport layer provides a full duplex channel for the transparent transmission of normal data of unlimited size, as well as priority control data of limited size. This layer also provides independent flow control and a grade of service that can be parametrized. A connectionless version of the transport layer is currently under study in the CCITT but plays no role in the discussion that follows; see [1].

Although conceptually the level-two and level-four functions are similar, there is a crucial difference: In general, in level four, a direct physical transmission system need not exist between the two points. Logically, however, the requirements are the same: There may be delay constraints, maximum permissible error rates, a requirement for maintaining the order of blocks of information, flow control, protection or security requirements, and so on. In fact, many of the level-four techniques for error control and recovery, flow control, and sequencing are identical to those used within level two. Again, this is not surprising in view of the logical similarity between the functions of the two layers.

Network Layer

The transport-layer service provides a virtual circuit that meets the requirements of the user, without any indication as to how this is actually carried out. In principle, the user of a virtual circuit should be unable to decide whether he or she is directly connected to the destination or whether a more complex arrangement is required, and how this is carried out. In practice these more complex arrangements are often required, as in the preceding examples. In the case of this author, the connection to a remote computer in France looks like that of Fig. 1.3: It goes through the local area network, then through the packet-switched network of the country of origin, then the packet network of the destination country, and finally the local network of the destination computer. The same is true for the telephone users, with the national telephone networks at both ends and their local area networks replacing the local area networks of the computer user.

In both cases, the connection is made through a number of telecommunication systems, each of which implements the first three layers of the OSI model (see Fig. 1.4). In order to provide the virtual circuit, a number of physical

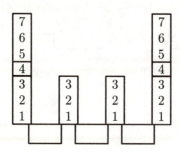

Figure 1.4   Telecommunication Systems in the OSI Model

devices must be made to operate cooperatively. The functions of the level-three layer are those required to implement this cooperative operation of the telecommunication systems. Network-layer protocols, responsible for setting up, maintaining, and clearing connections, provide independence to the functions of the higher layers from the data transmission and switching technology. The network layer includes a number of features worth explaining.

One difference between the network layer and the transport, link, and physical layers is that no single pair of peer processes operates at the end of a virtual connection. Instead, a multiplicity of processes must exchange information within the layer in order to establish and maintain the connection. As a consequence, the network layer is generally distributed geographically in many processes, often one such process per switching point along the connection.

The network layer may have many of the functions of the transport layer already implemented in it. A well-known case is the X.25 recommendation for packet-switched networks, which provides a virtual circuit between a pair of nodes with all the functions of the transport layer already implemented at the network layer. In this case, the distinction between the two layers becomes blurred; in practice, the two levels are merged into one. In fact, the two layers are in many ways redundant; one may ask why they have been defined this way. One plausible explanation, frequently denied by the standards organizations, is that the transport layer was the realm of the data processing organizations, while the network layer belonged to the telecommunication people. Even if not the case, it is still convenient to view the two layers this way because the redundancy becomes more natural (especially when considering the strict separation between data processing and telecommunication organizations when the standard was initiated in the mid-1970s.)

For the purpose of this discussion, we maintain a sharp distinction between the two layers, with the transport layer in charge of the virtual call and the network layer responsible for setting up, maintaining, and clearing the call through a number of telecommunication systems. Making this separation gives a unified view of switching methods and describes network functions in terms of resource allocation to the calls (see Section 1.2).

Other Layers

We have examined the first four lower levels of the OSI model in the context of an interactive session on a remote computer, or a long distance telephone call. Three additional levels are currently provided for by the OSI architecture. The session layer provides services required for setting up a session: directory assistance, access rights, and so forth. The presentation layer processes information before it enters the virtual circuit, whether for encryption, data compression, or code conversion. Finally, the application layer is defined as the functions that are required beyond those provided by the other six layers. These upper layers are not discussed any further since they play no further role in this book. Again, the interested reader can find more information on this subject in the references; see [1, 2, 3].

Traffic and Layer Coupling

The OSI model has been constructed in such a way that the interprocess communication at a given level is completely isolated and independent from the processes at the other levels. This does not mean, however, that the various layers are not related in other ways. In fact, a major problem of traffic engineering is to study this dependence and to determine to what extent it can be ignored — or how to take it into account when it cannot be ignored. The coupling comes from the particular mode of operation between layers, where a service request at one layer generates one or more requests at the layer immediately below.

Returning to our electronic mail example, the requests for sending messages arrive at random, according to some stochastic process. Suppose that a user requests that the same message be distributed to all the members of a mailing list. Assume that each message is sent by opening a virtual call to the destination. The generation of a mail request in the mail level produces in turn a number of requests for connection in the transport level, below it. Similarly, once a virtual connection is established, it generates a number of requests to the network layer to transmit the information, either in packet form or as an ordinary call. This process repeats downward until the physical level is reached. This increasing cascade of service requests is one of the two forms of coupling between the layers that must be taken into account in conducting a performance analysis of the network.

The second form of coupling operates in the other direction, from the lower to the upper levels. This type of interlayer coupling occurs because some of the decisions that must be taken at a given level depend on the state of the level immediately below. In our example, a request to distribute a message over a mailing list may be refused, or postponed, if the number of virtual calls currently open exceeds some threshold above which the quality of operation in the computer would be degraded unacceptably. Similarly, a particular request to open a virtual call may be denied if the network level is experiencing a high level of delay or loss. Finally, the path chosen by the network level to connect a call depends to a large extent on the state of congestion of the link level throughout the network.

A major task of traffic engineering is to compute whatever quantities are of interest at a given level, for instance the probability of blocking for a call, from the quantities available at the lower level — say the probability that the individual links in the network are fully occupied when a call arrives. For circuit switching, the interrelation between the transport and link layers is fundamentally important, and will be the subject of a large part of this book. From the brief description just given, we can see the types of disciplines that are relevant to traffic engineering. Because of the statistical nature of the requests at each level, the methods of probability theory must be used for the analysis. Also, because of the coupling between the levels, decomposition methods and their counterparts, iterative solution techniques, also play a fundamental role. Optimization techniques are also used because most of the problems relate to the synthesis of systems.

1.2   Switching Methods

The description of network operation in terms of the OSI model is useful to classify the various functions that are required in this process. The OSI model also provides a synthetic view of the system, which in turn can be used to relate some aspects of networks that were previously seen as distinct. A case in point is the so-called switching methods used in telecommunication networks today — which, as we now see, are not really switching methods, but rather different types of processes for allocating resources to calls.

Current telecommunication networks fall into two very general classes: circuit switched and packet switched. These classes are often presented as totally different, and their modes of operation distinguished in such a way as to make it difficult to take a synthetic view of the two switching methods. Here we show that, within the context of the OSI model, packet switching and circuit switching share some underlying features, at least from the point of view of the transport and network layers, but also have some essential differences. In addition to giving a clear picture of the similarities of and differences between the two switching techniques, this unification provides a framework in which to classify the new switching methods that are currently being proposed for new services (see Chapter 10).

We have seen that the network functions are responsible for connecting and maintaining calls between two processes operating in the transport layer that is within and between the telecommunication systems used to carry the information from one end of the network to the other. In other words, when a call request is set up, the network makes a commitment to have some resources available for use by the call if and when they are required. In this sense, the network layer protocols are responsible for allocating transmission resources to the call. The particular way in which this allocation is made is the fundamental difference between the switching methods, and is determined to a large extent by the characteristics of the call.

In our discussion of the OSI models we gave two examples of calls: (1) an interactive session on a remote computer and (2) a long distance telephone call. Other examples are a file dump from a computer on a line printer, a teleconference, and the transmission of a still picture. In general, the flow of information within the call is not constant, but comes in bursts of various lengths. For instance, for the interactive computer user, there will be short bursts corresponding to the typing of commands, rapidly followed by longer responses from the computer, then followed by quiet intervals corresponding to the "think time" of the user. In this case, the utilization, defined as the ratio of busy time to the total duration, is often quite low. On the other hand, calls corresponding to a file transfer have a short burst corresponding to the request followed by a long continuous stream of activity; the utilization will be quite high. Finally, telephone calls have a utilization that falls in between, typically around 50%, and other types can have utilizations that range from zero to one. The utilization factor is one of many parameters used to describe a call. Others are the origin and destination, bandwidth (average, peak, or other), delay constraint, and admissible error rate. The common features of switching techniques come from the realization that whatever the method, the same three decisions must be made; these decisions are arrived at in the same way, based on the call parameters and the current knowledge of the network state.

The first decision to be made is access control, that is, whether to accept the call or not. Then, if the call is accepted, what telecommunication systems should be used to connect it must be determined. This is the resource-allocation process mentioned before, and it is here that the two switching methods differ. Note that these two stages are interrelated since the decision whether to accept a call may very well depend on the path used to carry the call if it is accepted. This, as we said before, is what provides the coupling between the two levels. Finally, flow control is the process that ensures that the call parameters remain within the specified values. This process is relevant only for virtual circuit switching, where the connection request may specify a maximum instantaneous bandwidth that the call will use during its duration. Once the call is set up, the network must make sure that the call does not exceed this threshold by sending a large burst of packets in a very short time. This is particularly important for new services, such as video, where the process by which packets are generated within a virtual call is highly bursty. We now discuss how the first two stages are carried out for the two switching methods, indicating how flow-control issues may arise in these systems.

Circuit Switching

Every time a connection request is made, the requirements in terms of bandwidth, duration, utilization, and so on are known. A simple allocation strategy is to reserve immediately all the resources required in all the telecommunication systems that link the origin to the destination, and to keep them reserved for the complete duration of the connection. This is the essence of circuit switching. The task of the network-layer processes is first to determine whether such an allocation is possible. The decision rule may be that the call is accepted whenever there exists a path in the network with sufficient bandwidth to meet the call requirement, or it may be based on more complex measures of the future impact of accepting this call at the present time. If the call cannot be accepted, it is said to be blocked, and either can be made to wait until the resources become available, or can be cleared. If the call is accepted, the network processes must make sure that the reservation of capacity is correctly carried out along the selected path. Here again, the routing rules may be quite simple, such as to take the first path available from a fixed list, or may depend on a more complex measure of the network state, such as taking the path with the largest expected residual capacity. After this connection stage, the network processes have very little work to do while the call is in progress except to ensure that capacity is correctly released when the call terminates. Because of the complete reservation inherent in circuit switching, the transmission systems are already available whenever the call has something to transmit.

Circuit switching has traditionally been used for telephony, where a physical connection between the two ends of a call was established using a real circuit through mechanical relays. With the advent of frequency and time division multiplexing, this circuit is now replaced by a frequency band or a time slot. Conceptually, it is the same as traditional circuit switching in the sense that the particular band or time slot is not available to anyone else as long as the call remains connected.

Because there is an allocation of physical resources, circuit switching is well suited to calls with a high utilization, such as file transfer or uncoded voice, as well as to calls that require little or no delay in the transmission of information, such as voice or real-time applications. The only delay is caused by propagation in the medium, generally negligible except perhaps when satellite links are involved. Also, because of the minimal amount of work necessary to maintain the connection, a large number of calls can be processed through a given switch, as in large public telephone networks. Finally, circuit switching provides complete isolation between customers after the calls are set up, making flow control within the call unnecessary.

Circuit switching as it currently exists also has a few disadvantages, some more important than others. Most frequently mentioned is the impossibility of tailoring the bandwidth allocated to the instantaneous requirements of the call and the ensuing poor utilization of bandwidth for some types of applications. The importance of this defect depends on the relative costs of bandwidth and switching; it is rapidly becoming less relevant with the advent of very large-capacity optical transmission systems. More important are the long set-up times, of the order of seconds or tens of seconds, which prevent the use of circuit switching for applications with stringent real-time constraints.

Another defect of circuit switching appears when considering calls with large bandwidth requirements. Current switching systems were designed primarily for voice communications, and can switch only calls having the bandwidth of a single voice call. As a consequence, wide-band calls cannot be switched as a single entity, but must be demultiplexed into individual voice calls, switched, and then remultiplexed into the wide-band call. This procedure is quite complex and requires additional multiplexing in the switches, making the use of circuit switching for wide-band applications less attractive. These last two defects cannot easily be eliminated with current switching technology. Preliminary work on fast circuit switching and bulk switching in cross-connect switches, however, indicates that these capabilities are feasible and could become available in the next generation of switches.

Packet Switching

For calls with a low utilization factor, circuit switching is inefficient — the allocated resources are used only a small fraction of the time. Packet switching is designed specifically for such calls. Currently packet switching is used primarily for computer communications. The call is generally accepted when it arrives, although in many networks the call can be rejected if the network is congested. The difference from circuit switching is that no physical resources are allocated until there is actually something to transmit. When there is, the information to be transmitted is divided into subunits, called *packets* or *messages*, and network resources are allocated for individual packets, and only for the duration of the transmission from one switching point to the next.

Here the network processes must first determine whether the call should be accepted, as with ordinary circuit switching. The decision rule may be a threshold for the expected transit delay across the network at the time the call request is made, or may depend on other parameters, such as average or peak bandwidth. Then the routing decision must be made for accepted calls. Again, this could be based on an estimate of the network state, on characteristics of the available paths, and on the call parameters. Typically, the call is connected on the path with the shortest expected end-to-end delay within a given list of available paths.

So far, this procedure is conceptually identical to the access control and routing for circuit switching, the only difference being the particular choice of call parameters and network states used to reach a decision. The main difference between the two modes is that, at this stage in packet switching, *no physical resources are allocated to the call*. This allocation is made every time there is something to transmit within the call, and only on a point-to-point basis, that is, at the link level. Thus the work to be done by the level-three processes during the duration of the call is significantly greater than in the case of circuit switching. On the other hand, this procedure is clearly more efficient than circuit switching in terms of bandwidth utilization. Also, flow control within the call must be provided to ensure that a user does not exceed his or her allocated bandwidth or some other parameter associated with the call.

A Unified View of Switching

We can now express more clearly the difference between circuit and packet switching as viewed from the network and transport layers. In circuit switching, a network-wide resource allocation is made for the complete duration of the call (i.e., at the transport level), while in packet switching, a step-by-step allocation is made as packets progress within the network on a need basis (i.e., at the link level). For circuit switching, there is a real commitment of resources at call connection, while for packet switching, this commitment is only virtual. Put another way, the allocation of resources to a circuit-switched call is deterministic; to a packet-switched call, it is stochastic. Nevertheless, even with this probabilistic allocation, the process of call acceptance and routing for packet-switched calls is very similar to the corresponding processes for circuit-switched calls: The statistical effect of the allocation can be calculated, at least in principle, whenever the characteristics of the call and the network state are known. The result can be used for access control and routing decisions based on the consequences of this virtual allocation of resources to the call and its impact on the performance of the network, just as with circuit switching.

For example, from the knowledge that the call request is for an interactive session on a remote computer, it is possible to compute the average bandwidth required for this call on some path in the network. Accepting this call means that the network must be prepared to allocate this much bandwidth *on the average* to this call on the path selected to route the call. This in turn increases the expected delay on this and other network paths, information that can be used to decide whether to accept the call and where to route it. Average delay is only one of many parameters that can be used. Other measures of network utilization are available, such as a percentile on the delay distribution, although most such measures are more difficult to compute than the average.

This decision process is conceptually identical to the connection process for ordinary circuit switching, except that the call and network state parameters are different and that expected instead of deterministic values are used. The unifying view comes from the fact that even though one method uses a real allocation of resources while the other uses only a virtual one, the call-connection process as viewed from the transport layer is fundamentally the same, and can in principle be described very similarly for both switching techniques. For this reason, much of what will be said in this book should apply equally well to the routing of virtual calls and to traditional circuit switching.

Finally, note that the policy used in the presence of call blocking is in no way a characteristic of the switching method. Although it is customary to use a blocked-calls-lost policy for circuit switching, and a blocked-packets-delayed policy for packet switching, this distinction is irrelevant to the switching method used. Current telephone switching machines can make blocked calls wait, a process known as *call queuing*. The other possibility, that of packet switching with blocked packets lost, is a perfectly legitimate mode of operation for information that can tolerate loss, such as voice, although apparently this method has not been used much. A notable exception is the knockout switch, where a small packet loss probability is tolerated in return for a large increase in throughput [7, 8].

Scope of Circuit-Switching Methods

As its title indicates, this book is about circuit switching, that is, about levels four and three of the OSI architecture. Most of the theory expressed here comes from the area of telephone network operation and planning, which use ordinary circuit switching. This may seem to limit the scope of the techniques discussed to telephony. We expect, however, that circuit switching will be used for quite some time for voice, as well as for new networks. In the first case, the large base of installed equipment used for telephone service will remain in place for at least the medium term; the shift to new integrated networks must be evolutionary. In the longer term, it is not clear whether a synchronous mode of transfer such as circuit switching or an asynchronous mode of the packet-switching type will be used in the integrated transport network.

Another possibility, which seems increasingly attractive, is a unique hybrid switch, capable of both circuit and packet switching. Circuit-switching methods would continue to be used for a significant fraction of the traffic. There is also an emerging consensus that if the new networks are of the packet-switching type, this will be done in a connection mode. As the discussion in this chapter indicates, many of the results of classical and more recent circuit-switching methods will become relevant to these virtual circuit-switched networks. As shown in the discussion of the OSI model in Section 1.1, the methods of circuit switching can be applied much more widely than merely for telephone service; they apply to the transport layer of *any* network operating in a connection mode. The reasons should be obvious by now: The access control and the routing decision are the same in both cases; they depend both on the parameters of the call and on the state of the network.

For circuit switching, a call is blocked if the resources are not available at the time of the request. For packet switching, the call is rejected if accepting the call is *expected* to degrade the network performance beyond a certain value. This decision also depends on the call parameters and the network state. Also, the routing of an accepted call can be made to depend on the call parameters and network state in a similar way for both methods. The decision rule is the same in nature; only the call and network parameters used to reach the decision are different.

As of today, this integrated view of access control and routing has not been used in planning and analyzing telecommunication networks. Telephone networks and data networks have evolved separately, using routing and control techniques that are on the surface quite distinct. With the advent of integrated transport networks, a wide variety of virtual calls will have to be served by the same network. Some of these calls will have characteristics that make them suitable for packet switching, while others will be ideally suited to circuit switching. In this case, more complex admission-control and routing techniques for virtual calls than the ones currently used may be required, independently of the actual policy used for allocating resources by the network layer. A unified view of access control and routing through the generalization of the results of classical circuit switching would become necessary; this is the subject of current research. Let us now examine another aspect of this work and its relation to the planning process for telecommunication networks.

1.3   The Planning Process

In this section, we give a short description of the traditional view of the planning process of telecommunication networks and its relation with the contents of this book. As with any decision process, to arrive at its results network planning relies on external information. In case of telecommunications, the forecast of the demand for services over some horizon drives the evolution of the network. Some economic information concerning the cost structure of the elements making up the network is also required. There exist numerous methods of forecasting and engineering economics [9,10] to obtain these values, which are not specific to the field of telecommunications and thus are not discussed here. Another requirement is some knowledge about the technical capabilities of the available systems, which may limit the options available for the design. Although this aspect is more specific to the planning of technical systems, we again assume that it is given as input to the planning process; it is therefore not the subject of decision.

The planning problem can now be stated as follows: to implement the first four layers of the OSI model and to provide the required physical support. This must be done in such a way as to keep track of the evolution of the demand for services, while also ensuring that a satisfactory grade of service is maintained at all times. The knowledge required for this task spans a variety of scientific disciplines. At one extreme, the definition and implementation of peer processes and protocols is an area of computer science. At the other extreme, the design and implementation of point-to-point transmission systems is a subject of electrical engineering and physics. Network planning as we understand it in this book is the intermediate stage in which these elements are connected in such a way that the OSI model becomes operational.

Assuming that all the protocol issues have been settled and that the transmission technology is known, what remains is a complex, distributed, and dynamic capacity-augmentation problem. Because of its complexity, the problem cannot be solved in a single stage — the traditional, and only feasible, approach is through decomposition. We identify four interrelated stages in the planning process, each with an increasing level of detail in cost and structure.

The first stage is the design of a topological structure for the network: where to place the components and how to interconnect them, subject to connectivity constraints. Here we use the methods of topological optimization and graph theory. At this stage, the cost information is simplest. All information about the transmission network is summarized into a fixed interconnection cost per unit length between offices. Typically, this is a single value calculated from the capacity of the transmission systems actually installed in the network; the actual cost is proportional to the distance between offices. Similarly, the switch costs are given and can take only a limited set of values, one for each switching technology available; these costs do not depend on the traffic volume through the switches. The output of this step is a connectivity matrix and, in some cases, the optimal location of switches or concentrators.

The network-synthesis problem uses this information to calculate the optimal size of components, that is, the transmission and switching systems, within the topology specified by the result of the topological optimization stage, and subject to grade-of-service constraints on network-performance measures such as transit delay or loss probability. A linear cost model and fractional sizes for the network components are used. Because the constraints are not linear, the methods of nonlinear optimization are most frequently used at this stage. The network synthesis is made up of two distinct and interrelated subproblems: traffic routing and dimensioning. The routing problem is to determine how to connect calls as they arrive, given the topology and size of the transmission and switching equipments. Conversely, the dimensioning problem is to determine these sizes given a particular routing method, taking into account some constraints on the grade of service (GOS) that must be met by the network. The output of the synthesis stage is a route plan and a set of logical links between nodes, that is, the requirements for transmission facilities between switching points.

The logical links express a requirement for transmission equipment between two points but do not specify the particular technology used to implement the requirement. This is done in the network-realization stage, often called the circuit-routing stage, or sometimes simply the routing stage. Network realization determines how to implement the capacity requirement computed by the synthesis stage using the available components such as a cable of copper wires, a frequency division multiplexed coaxial cable, or a digital transmission system. Each component has a different cost/capacity characteristic function and comes in different modular sizes. The circuits in the copper and coaxial cable can be allocated one unit at a time, while those in the digital system must be used in large blocks, typically of 24 or 30 circuits at a time. Also, the marginal cost of these systems may be different — for instance, because of the A/D conversion equipment that may be required in some cases, depending on the type of switch to which the transmission system is connected. Similar situations hold for the start-up cost of a new system and for the incremental cost of providing a new capacity module. The usual solution is *not* to route all the demand on the cheapest transmission technology between two points. Systems are subject to failures, microwave systems can be sensitive to weather conditions, and people have the bad habit of digging out telephone cables while in the process of construction. For reasons of reliability, a circuit demand should not be routed on a single system, and conditions should be placed on the solution to force multipath routing in such a way that a minimal grade of service is maintained in case of failures. All these elements are taken into account in the circuit-routing stage. The problems to be solved are generally of the multicommodity flow type, with modular and nonlinear cost functions and with reliability constraints.

Obviously, these four stages are interrelated and the planning process is iterative, embedded with many levels of iteration (see Fig. 1.5). The output of the circuit-routing stage yields detailed information on the actual transmission cost between two switches. Given the current size of the logical link, a new value can be computed for the average cost per circuit, which can be used as input to another synthesis stage. Similarly, after this synthesis-routing process has converged, new values for the interconnection costs are computed, and a new topological optimization step can be performed.

In practice, only a few iterations are required before a satisfactory solution is found, and not all steps of this process need be performed each time. The topological structure of a network is not changed very often, especially that of

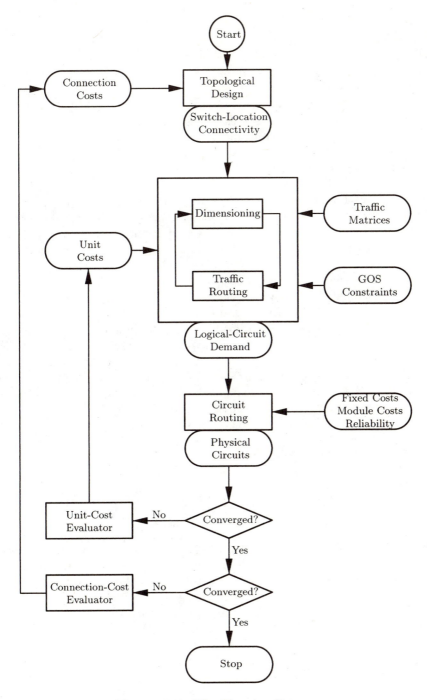

Figure 1.5 The Planning Process

a long-established network such as the telephone network. Similarly, the *type* of routing used in the network is not changed often — typically once every 20 or 30 years. The component sizes, such as trunk group capacity, change more frequently, typically every year and sometimes more often in the case of demand servicing. This time scale is likely to become smaller with the introduction of dynamically rearrangeable networks using slow switches, which allow a network to be reconfigured on a demand basis. Finally, on a shorter time scale still, the parameters of a particular routing method may change on an hourly basis, and, in the case of fast adaptive methods, on a call-by-call time scale in some cases.

A dynamic element is often required in the planning process. In such a case, the evolution of the demand is predicted for a number of years, and an evolution strategy must be mapped over this horizon. The process is still represented by the diagram of Fig. 1.5, but with an explicit dependence on time. Although the problem is conceptually not very different, the numerical difficulty is much greater; as a consequence, the planning process may be simplified even more.

The topological design and circuit-routing stages arise in many areas besides telecommunication networks, such as transportation and power networks. There is an abundant literature on this subject, most of which applies to the telecommunication network problem [11,12,13]. Because of the traffic-routing component, only the network-synthesis stage is specific to telecommunications, and the particular models and techniques used to solve it depend to a large extent on the switching method. The synthesis problem for packet-switched networks has been amply studied and documented in the open literature; there are many good references on the subject [2,3,14].

The synthesis problem has also been solved very efficiently for conventional circuit-switched networks, but, as stated earlier, this information is scattered in a number of conference proceedings and is generally not as easily accessible. Therefore we provide a more synthetic view in this book.

1.4   Notation

We are now ready to begin an in-depth study of circuit switching. First, however, there are a few points about the notation used throughout the book. Of principal importance is the distinction between variables representing quantities defined across a network (e.g., the average time for a message to go from its source to its destination node) from quantities that are defined for the two ends of a link (e.g., the average time for a message to be transmitted from point a to point b over some transmission system).

As a rule, superscripts such as i, j, and k denote end-to-end variables, while subscripts such as s and t refer to variables related to a particular link. We use equivalently a two-or one-index notation for double-index variables. It is assumed that there is a mapping $o(k), d(k)$ that gives the number of the origin and destination nodes o and d for a given value of the single index k, and conversely that there is a mapping $k(o, d)$ that yields the index for any origin-destination pair. With this notation, the probability that a telephone call from an office i to an office j cannot be connected is represented by $L^{i,j}$, or equivalently, by L^k, where $k = k(i, j)$. This is defined even when no direct link exists between nodes i and j. The probability that a particular link s of the network is blocked when a call attempts to use it is given by B_s, or equivalently by $B_{m,n}$. This convention is used consistently throughout the book.

Other indices besides those denoting the origin and destination are introduced in some cases. This is done in such a way that the use of subscripts and superscripts follows this convention whenever the distinction is meaningful. In other cases, the precise meaning of the index should be clear from the context. A detailed list of the symbols used in this book can be found in Appendix C.

References

[1] Stallings, W., *Data and Computer Communications*, Macmillan, 1985.

[2] Schwartz, M., *Telecommunication Networks: Protocols, Modeling, and Analysis*, Addison-Wesley, 1987.

[3] Bertsekas, D., and Gallager, R.G., *Data Networks*, Addison-Wesley, 1987.

[4] Gallager, R.G., *Information Theory and Reliable Communication*, Wiley, 1968.

[5] Green, P.E., *Computer Network Architectures and Protocols*, Plenum, 1982.

[6] Green, P.E., "Protocol conversion," *IEEE Transactions on Communications*, vol. 34, pp. 257–268, 1986.

[7] Eng, K.Y., Hluchyj, M.G., and Yeh, Y.S., "A knockout switch for variable-length packets," *International Conference on Communications*, pp. 794–799, 1987.

[8] Yeh, Y.S., Hluchyj, M.G., and Acampora, A.S., "The knockout switch: a simple, modular architecture for high-performance packet switching," *IEEE Journal on Selected Areas in Communications*, vol. SAC-5, pp. 1274–1283, 1987.

[9] Smith, R.L., "Optimal expansion policies for the deterministic capacity problem," *The Engineering Economist*, vol. 25, No. 3, pp. 149–160, 1980.

[10] Luss, H., "Operations research and capacity expansion problems: a survey," *Operations Research*, vol. 30, pp. 907–947, 1982.

[11] Frank, H., Frisch, I.T., Van Slyke, R., and Chou, W.S., "Optimal design of centralized computer networks," *Networks*, vol. 1, pp. 43–57, 1971.

[12] Yaged, B., "Minimum cost routing for static network models," *Networks*, vol. 1, pp. 139–172, 1971.

[13] Yaged, B., "Minimum cost routing for dynamic network models," *Networks*, vol. 3, pp. 193–224, 1973.

[14] Hayes, J.F., *Modeling and Analysis of Computer Communications Networks*, Plenum, 1984.

CHAPTER 2

Routing Techniques and Models

The performance of a network depends on such factors as the network configuration, the offered load, and the network management methods. An important element of network management, called *network routing*, consists of the decision rules used to connect the calls as they arrive at the network; a variety of methods are now possible. We describe in depth some of the methods that are currently in use or proposed for implementation in large circuit-switched networks. We also introduce useful graphical models to represent these methods, and briefly cover some mathematical models that can describe them. The question of evaluating the performance of a particular network operating under one of these algorithms is discussed in Chapter 4; the question of choosing the optimal routing method, in Chapter 7.

2.1   Definition of Routing

Consider the real-time operation of a network. Whenever a new call arrives at an office, we must determine whether there exists a path on which the call can be connected to its destination. If a path is found, we must decide whether to use it or not; if there is no available path, we must decide what to do with the call. Each of these steps is related to a different aspect of routing.

The selection of an available path constitutes the routing problem in the strict sense, requiring the paths available for each stream to be defined — an important part of the specification of a routing technique. This definition could be the set of all paths permitted by the network structure or, more simply, some convenient subset. It must also include a description of a procedure for finding such a path and for selecting which path to use if more than one is available.

The decision of whether or not to connect a call on an available path is often called *flow control*. Flow control can be viewed as a special case of routing, where lost calls are routed on a fictitious path of infinite capacity. Although the flow-control problem has been extensively studied for packet networks, no comparable work exists for circuit networks. In this book we do not consider the flow-control problem, but rather assume that a call that can be connected always will be connected.

The last step of call routing deals with handling blocked calls, that is, those for which no path is available. In general, we assume that such calls are lost and do not return. This implies that the call-retrial rate is negligible — probably accurate for a network with a low blocking rate. In networks with high blocking, for instance in the case of failure or overload, call reattempt can be significant. The blocked-calls-lost option is not the only option available: Many networks, mostly private ones, may operate on the basis of blocked calls delayed. We shall not consider this case any further since the corresponding models are much more difficult than those in this book, involving complex protocol issues that cannot be considered here.

Note that call termination has not been mentioned as part of the routing problem. We assume that a call that terminates has no effect on calls already in progress, and that it can influence future calls only by freeing up a path in the network. This is equivalent to saying that there is no rearrangement of calls in progress in the network. Although this option has not been implemented in any real network and is still the subject of research, it is becoming a possibility with the advent of faster switches.

Given these considerations, let us define more explicitly what we mean by a routing technique (sometimes called a routing algorithm or method), or, using the terminology of optimal control, a routing policy. A routing technique is a set of rules that specifies, for each new call arriving in the network, on what path to route the call, and the data required to make that choice; it is the same as the definition of a process in computer science terminology.

We do not claim to present a complete classification of routing methods. There is no consensus on the precise meaning of many of the terms used to characterize routing, and another attempt at this topic would probably lead far from our objective. It is more important to obtain a clear understanding of the operation of the routing methods that are effectively used in networks than to set up a very general framework that attempts to cover all potential cases of routing but is of little practical use. The concepts of dynamic and adaptive routings, however, appear often enough that we should discuss their meanings in this book.

In this book, a dynamic routing is one where a part of the routing varies over time, while an adaptive routing is one where some part of the routing is a function of some estimate of the network state at the time a decision must be made. The point is that a dynamic routing is not necessarily adaptive; in fact, one dynamic routing method currently being implemented in a real telephone network does not use state measurements and would not be classified as an adaptive method here. The converse is somewhat more unlikely. An adaptive routing is normally dynamic unless the network is so quiet that the state is not changing at all. Furthermore, implicit in the notion of adaptive routing is the notion of measurement of the network state, which is not required for purely dynamic routings.

Both dynamic and adaptive routings have some time-varying component: the path-selection rules, the data for the algorithm, or both. To further complicate matters, a given routing method may be viewed as static or dynamic, depending on which parts of the routing algorithm are used to characterize it. A case in point is the old alternate routing method, which, although generally considered static, can be viewed as an adaptive method if the actual paths selected are used as a criterion for deciding whether the algorithm is dynamic or not. Although these issues appear primarily semantic, they appear sufficiently often that the distinction between dynamic and adaptive routings should always be made explicit. In particular, saying that an algorithm is static or dynamic does not mean much by itself. One should specify with respect to which component of the routing such a statement is made, since some parts may be dynamic, while others may be static or adaptive. The examples presented in Section 2.4 will clarify these points.

2.2   The Continuous-Time Markov Process

Routing algorithms are frequently described qualitatively and thus are subject to ambiguity and do not lend themselves to quantitative analysis. There is, however, a well-known framework within which all these notions can be made more precise: the theory of continuous-time Markov processes and of Markovian decision theory.

The Markov model for circuit-switched networks follows from two standard assumptions about external traffic: (1) the calls arrive according to independent Poisson processes, and (2) the call-holding times are independent, exponentially distributed random variables. To simplify notation, the time unit is assumed to be equal to the mean holding time. Thus both the arrival and the service processes are memoryless stochastic processes; provided we can define a state space and a transition matrix, a continuous-time Markov process formulation of the network operation is possible. This approach would seem promising in view of the large body of knowledge on Markov processes. It is used mostly for theoretical understanding, however, since it is impractical for analytical or numerical calculations when considering networks of realistic sizes. In this section, we first review some of the elements of Markov theory using the notation of [1,2]. Then we show how the general theory can be used to describe the routing of calls in circuit-switched networks, also indicating the practical difficulties encountered.

Continuous-Time Markov Processes

The finite state continuous-time Markov process is defined by a set of states labeled $i = 1, 2, \ldots N_s$ and a transition-rate matrix $Q_{i,j}$ defined for each pair of states i, j, $i \neq j$. The transition-rate matrix is such that the probability of occurrence of a transition from i to j in a small time interval dt is precisely $Q_{i,j}dt$. The diagonal element is defined by $Q_{i,i} = 1 - \sum_{j \neq i} Q_{i,j}$. Suppose now that the system is started in some state k. The probability of being in state i at time t depends on k, t, and Q. To simplify the notation, we assume that k is given and known and thus drop this index from the notation. The probability of being in state i at time t is then denoted $p_i(t)$. It is given by the matrix differential equation

$$\frac{dp_i(t)}{dt} = \sum_l p_l Q_{l,i}. \tag{2.1}$$

It is well-known that these probabilities take an asymptotic value p_i that depends only on the initial state; they are given by the equation $\mathbf{p}Q = 0$. There is such a probability vector $\mathbf{p}$ for each initial state, and we define the probability matrix S such that its ith row is made up of the $\mathbf{p}$ vector corresponding to starting the system in state i. There are as many distinct $\mathbf{p}$ vectors as there are irreducible classes of states; in particular, the S matrix has all rows identical if there is only one such class.

It is sometimes useful to place a value on a Markov process. This is done via the transition values $r_{i,j}$, which are the revenue produced by a transition from state i to state j. In addition, there may be some value to simply being in a state. We define the value of a state $r_{i,i}$ as the *rate* at which revenue is generated while the system is in state i. Note that $r_{i,j}$ and $r_{i,i}$ have different units: the former is a revenue; the later, a revenue per unit time. Finally, the earning *rate* of the process in state i is defined by $q_i = r_{i,i} + \sum_{j \neq i} Q_{i,j}r_{i,j}$. The quantities of interest are the total revenue expected from operating the system until time t, given that the initial state was i. These quantities, called the value of state i, are represented by $v_i(t)$. It is not hard to show that the value vector $\mathbf{v}(t)$ is given by the differential equation

$$\frac{d\mathbf{v}(t)}{dt} = \mathbf{q} + Q\mathbf{v}(t).$$

This equation can readily be solved in the Laplace transform domain. We have

$$\mathbf{v}(s) = \frac{(sI - Q)^{-1}}{s}\mathbf{q} + (sI - A)^{-1}\mathbf{v}(0),$$

and it can be shown that

$$(sI - A)^{-1} = \frac{1}{s}S + T(s),$$

from which we get the asymptotic value

$$\mathbf{v}(t) = \mathbf{g}t + \mathbf{v},$$

where

$$\mathbf{g} = S\mathbf{q}$$
$$\mathbf{v} = T(0)\mathbf{q} + S\mathbf{v}(0)$$

In these equations, the T matrix is the Laplace transform of the transient terms of the differential equation (2.1). The vector $\mathbf{g}$, called the gain or rate vector, denotes the rate at which the system is generating revenue for all initial states. This is obviously the quantity of interest since it determines the long-term value of the system. It is the natural objective to maximize in those cases where there exists a possibility of choosing such parameters of the process as the transition-rate matrix or the revenues.

Application of the Markov Model to Routing

Following the work of Beneš [3], let us now examine how the Markov model can be used to represent routing in circuit-switched networks. In the following, we assume that all the paths between each origin-destination pair are known and listed in some fixed order. This amounts to saying that $\mathcal{I}$, the arc-path incidence matrix for the network, is given; we denote a column of this matrix by the vector $\mathbf{a}$.

First we define the state space. Using the standard multicommodity flow representation, let $x_m^{o,d}(t) =$ number of calls in progress on the mth path between nodes o and d at time t. These variables are constrained to take integer values only. A state is defined as a path-flow vector $\mathbf{x}(t)$ that specifies the number of calls on each path in the network at time t. We use the notation $\mathbf{x}_j$ to denote a particular state vector, and the scalar x_i^j for the number of calls in progress on the ith path of the network for this particular state j. Here $\mathbf{x}_j$ denotes a *state*, that is, a complete multicommodity flow in the network, with the specification of calls carried on all the paths. On the other hand, x_i^j is defined for a particular state j and is a scalar depending on the particular path chosen in this state. Although the dependence on the state is included in the notation, in practice the state index is omitted whenever there is no ambiguity as to the state in question; this allows us to simplify an already complex notation.

The state variables are constrained by the equations $\mathcal{I}\mathbf{x} \leq \mathbf{N}$, the capacity constraints on the number of calls on each arc. The state $\mathbf{x} = 0$, called the empty state, is denoted $\emptyset$. Equivalent representations are also possible (see Problem 2.2). An auxiliary quantity of interest is $n_j(t)$, the total number of calls in progress when the network is in state $\mathbf{x}_j$; this is given by $n_j(t) = \sum_l x_l^j(t)$.

Denote the state space $\mathcal{S} = \{\mathbf{x}_j\}$. An arbitrary state i is connected to the empty state $\emptyset$ since it is always possible to empty the network by a sufficient

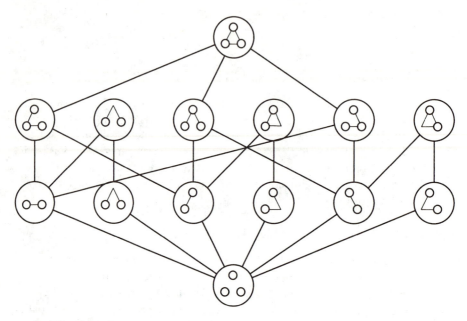

Figure 2.1   Hasse Diagram for Three-Node Network, Single Link per Arc

number of call terminations. The converse is not true, however, since starting from ∅ it may be impossible to reach some state j, either because this is not permitted by the routing rules or because there is no external traffic between some origin-destination pairs. Let $\mathcal{S}'$ be the set of states i that can be reached from ∅. $\mathcal{S}'$ forms an irreducible, aperiodic class, while its complement $\mathcal{S} - \mathcal{S}'$ forms a set of transient states. (In fact, these states will never occur if the network is started from ∅; otherwise they will eventually disappear and never reoccur.) For the sake of simplicity, we assume from now on that the transient states have been removed from consideration and that $\mathcal{S}'$ is the state space. In this case, the system is ergodic and has a single set of stationary state probabilities. From these, we can compute, for each origin-destination pair (i, j), the fraction of the time during which no path is available to connect a call. Called the *end-to-end loss probability* and denoted $L^{i,j}$, this important measure of network performance is discussed in later chapters.

The Hasse diagram provides a useful graphical representation of the partial order between states. The example shown in Fig. 2.1 corresponds to the three-node network with a single two-way trunk between each node. In this diagram, the states are ordered in layers, with the states in one layer produced from the states in the layer below by the addition of a single call. Each state is

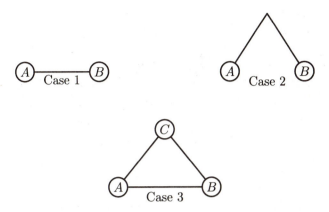

Figure 2.2   Description of Network States

represented by the graph of the network, with each call in progress in the state indicated by an arc in this graph. The various state configurations have the following interpretation. A direct call between nodes A and B is represented by the first case of Fig. 2.2, and a tandem call between these two nodes via node C by the second case. Note that in this case, the node C is not shown on the graph, in contrast to the case of three direct calls (A, B), (A, C), and (B, C), where node C now appears in the graph (see the third case in Fig. 2.2).

Potential transitions between states are indicated by an arc linking the large nodes. Whether such an arc represents an actual transition depends on the particular routing method used. In fact, the specification of a routing is equivalent to the selection of the set of arcs that appear in the transition diagram.

This set contains a unique aperiodic recurrent class; as a consequence, there is a *unique* set of stationary state probabilities p_i independent of the original state, which can be found by the standard equation $\mathbf{p}Q = 0$. Thus there is a *unique* average blocking probability. The fact that these probabilities are unique is important because of the behavior of real networks operating under simplified routing rules. Such networks seem to operate as if there were effectively more than a single value for these probabilities. This behavior is described in more detail in Section 4.4, where a plausible explanation is offered for the observed results.

Having defined the states of the Markov process, we now need the transition-rate matrix to compute the state probabilities. The transition-rate matrix can be constructed according to the following rules. For simplicity, we assume that a call is connected whenever a path is available for it at the time of its arrival. Because of the second-order effect of simultaneous events, transitions can occur only between adjacent states, that is, for states $\mathbf{y} = \mathbf{x} \pm \mathbf{e}$, where $\mathbf{e}$ is an elementary vector in the space of multicommodity flows.

1. For a call departure, j contains exactly one call less than i between some pair of nodes o and d. Assuming that a call termination does not cause any rerouting of calls in progress, $Q_{i,j}$ is effectively the rate at which a connected call will terminate.

$$
Q_{i,j} = \begin{cases} \dfrac{\displaystyle\sum_k x_k^{o,d}}{\displaystyle\sum_{(o,d)} \sum_k x_k^{o,d}} \times Q_{dep} & \text{if } \mathbf{x}_j = \mathbf{x}_i - \mathbf{e} \\ 0 & \text{otherwise} \end{cases} \tag{2.2}
$$

where Q_{dep} is the transition rate of call terminations in the network. Because we assume that call-holding times are independent and exponentially distributed, we can write

$$
Q_{dep} = \frac{n_i}{n_i + \gamma}. \tag{2.3}
$$

Here γ is the total arrival rate of new calls into the network and is given by $\gamma = \sum_l A^l$.

2. For a call arrival, j contains exactly one more call than i, between nodes o and d. Q is then the rate at which an (o,d) call will arrive, which is known from the traffic matrix

$$
Q_{i,j} = \begin{cases} \dfrac{A^{o,d}}{\displaystyle\sum_{m,n} A^{m,n}} \times Q_{arr} & \text{if } \mathbf{x}_j = \mathbf{x}_i + \mathbf{e} \\ 0 & \text{otherwise} \end{cases} \tag{2.4}
$$

where Q_{arr} is the overall arrival rate for new calls in the network and is given by

$$
Q_{arr} = \frac{\gamma}{n_i + \gamma}. \tag{2.5}
$$

The construction of the transition-rate matrix is subject to constraints that reflect the nature of the system and show up as the *if* statement in the first part of Eq. (2.4). The first set of such conditions simply reflects that a transition cannot be made if the total number of calls in progress on all links exceeds the number of circuits on that link. These conditions can be expressed, with the aid of the arc-path incidence matrix, as

$$
\mathcal{I}\mathbf{x}_j(t) \le \mathbf{N}, \quad j \in \{\mathcal{S}\}, \ \forall t, \tag{2.6}
$$

where $\mathbf{N}$ denotes the vector of arc capacities. The second set (the most important one, from our point of view) is any other set of conditions that can be imposed on the connection process. These conditions are generally expressed by some rule or by a verbal description. Because such rules determine the transition matrix, this matrix is the mathematical object that corresponds to these routing rules, to the extent that the matrix *is* the routing. In other words, knowledge of the matrix determines completely how new calls are to be connected for any state. Conversely, if we have described the routing by some rule, then the matrix must be constructed in such a way that only those transitions permitted by the rule, and all of these, are found in the matrix. Which of these methods we choose is irrelevant from a theoretical point of view, since they produce the same effect. This dual way to represent the routing is in fact a result of the Markov process representation we are using for the network operation — no surprise to the reader who is already familiar with Markov decision theory, since it corresponds to the specification of a *policy*, which can be done equally well by a rule or a transition matrix.

Given the state space and the transition matrix, we can, at least in theory, compute the state probabilities of any network given the input values such as the means of the arrival processes and the size of the groups. This in turn yields the end-to-end loss probabilities and the carried traffic, which are the measures used most frequently of a network's performance. In some cases, we may want a more flexible performance measure; we can do this by giving a value to the Markov process.

There is a great deal of latitude in selecting a value for the process that describes the operation of a network. A simple case is to take $r_{i,j} = 0\ i \neq j$, and $r_{i,i} = n_i$ as the rate of reward for having n_i calls in progress in the network. Under this condition, we have $q_i = n_i$; since there is only one set of probabilities, there is a single gain g given by $g = \sum_i p_i q_i = \bar{n}$. As expected, the gain of the network — that is, the rate at which reward is being incurred — is simply the expected number of calls in progress in the network. This is a reasonable measure of network efficiency and a reasonable objective for maximization. More complex revenues can be defined that may correspond to the actual monetary value of a call carried in the network; such revenues may be chosen artificially in order to perform some management function. Some applications of these revenues are given in Chapter 7, where we discuss the optimization of routing.

The Markov model for routing requires a very detailed description of the network state; the amount of information required for this formulation grows very quickly with the size of the network. As an example, consider the networks shown in Fig. 2.3. The first three have identical traffic between all pairs of nodes and a single two-way trunk between each node. The fourth network has a single destination node D, three traffic streams, and N_{o,T_1}, N_{o,T_2}, $N_{T_1,d}$, and $N_{T_2,d}$ trunks. These values are indicated in Table 2.1, which shows the number of states for each case. It is quite obvious that attempting to use this model for performance evaluation or routing optimization entails the manipulation of some very large matrices, which soon becomes infeasible for any network larger

Number of States with n Calls	Network 1	Network 2	Network 3	Network 4 (3,4,12,10)	Network 4 (3,4,7,10)	Network 4 (3,4,12,7)
0	1	1	1			
1	6	13	20			
2	6	44	128			
3	1	44	319			
4	-	13	319			
5	-	1	128			
6	-	-	20			
7	-	-	1			
Total	14	116	936	2070	1170	1380

Table 2.1   Number of States for Small Networks

than a few nodes. Nevertheless, the Markov models have their use. They clarify the nature of some concepts such as routing by putting them in the familiar framework of a transition-rate matrix. They also indicate the complexity of such problems as network performance evaluation and routing optimization, showing that approximations are absolutely essential and that exact solutions are infeasible. Finally, the Markov models can act as the framework in which these approximations can be constructed systematically, instead of ad hoc, as has generally been the case.

Multicommodity Flows

The Markov description of the network is too complex to be used for practical cases. The fact that the system we are studying has a network structure suggests that other, more compact representations could be used for numerical and analytical calculations. We already suggested this in defining the states in terms of integer multicommodity flow vectors. These flow models occur in many areas of engineering; in some simple cases, they lead to some of the most efficient optimization algorithms known. It therefore seems that a flow description of the network could also lead to efficient numerical methods.

First we must define an expanded network. Assume that each node i that receives external calls is split into two nodes i_1 and i_2, and that these two nodes are connected by an arc with infinite capacity. Calls of stream l arriving at node i enter the expanded network at node i_1 and begin service immediately. Let $y^l(t)$ be the number of calls of stream l in progress on link i_1, i_2 at time t. The $\mathbf{y}(t)$ process generates calls at node i_2 that have exactly the same statistics

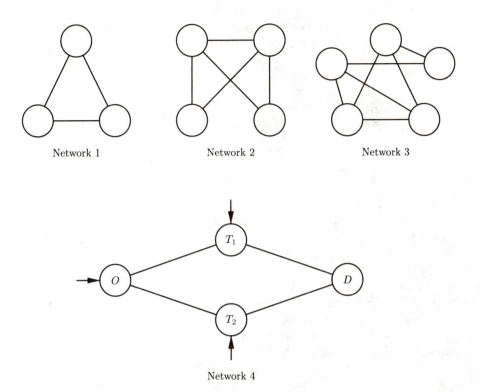

Figure 2.3   Networks for Markov Model Examples

as the external calls in the real network. In particular, we have $\bar{y}^l = A^l$. The calls that arrive at node i_2 are treated exactly as if they were the true external calls, some of which are routed through the network and some of which are rejected. Assume further that the calls rejected at node i_2 remain on link i_1, i_2 for the normal duration of their service time. Within this augmented network, we now have the following set of linear inequalities:

$$\mathcal{I}\mathbf{x}(t) \leq \mathbf{N} \quad \forall t \geq 0 \tag{2.7}$$

$$y^l(t) \geq \sum_m x_m^l(t) \quad \forall t \geq 0 \tag{2.8}$$

Equations (2.7) and (2.8) are very similar to those defining a multicommodity flow, the only difference being the inequality condition in Eq. (2.8); they define a stochastic multicommodity flow. Because they are linear, we can take the expectations on both sides, obtaining a *deterministic* multicommodity flow corresponding to the *expected* values of the number of calls carried in the network. We have

$$\mathcal{I}\bar{x} \leq \mathbf{N} \tag{2.9}$$

$$\bar{y}^k = A^k \geq \sum_m \bar{x}^k_m, \tag{2.10}$$

which we can rewrite

$$\bar{y}^k = L^k A^k$$

$$\mathbf{x} \geq 0,$$

where L^k is defined as the end-to-end blocking probability of stream k and x^k is the vector of *carried traffic* on the network paths for the stream k. Note that both x^k and L^k are functions not only of the network parameters such as the offered traffic and the group sizes, but also of the routing. A major topic of this book is the calculation of these quantities and their optimization with respect to some of these parameters. There will be many occasions to return to these flow models in later chapters.

Because of the complexity of the Markov model, routing algorithms are generally more simple than the full description of the transition matrix, or than a policy described in terms of the complete state space. The simplification takes three forms. First, the set of paths available is reduced considerably from the full set allowed by the network topology. Second, the path-selection rules are changed so that some transitions possible in the full Markov description are forbidden. Finally, the states are merged into aggregates, thus reducing the amount of information available for the routing decisions. We now describe some of the more widely used techniques, as well as some proposed ones that are likely candidates for implementation in future networks.

2.3   Load Sharing

The first routing policy we examine, called *load sharing*, is not implemented in any network and is not very efficient. Load sharing is described here, however, because it is the policy for which we have the largest collection of theoretical results. Also, it has some nice mathematical properties that will be quite handy in our discussion of numerical methods for performance evaluation and optimization of more realistic policies.

In its simplest form, load sharing works as follows. For traffic stream k, a set of R_k paths is given that constitute the only paths available to route the calls of stream k. The stream is partitioned into R_k substreams, where the calls

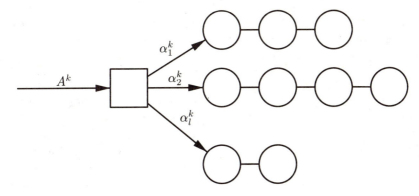

Figure 2.4　Graphical Representation of Load Sharing

from substream l are offered to path l. If the path is not free, the call is lost. In practice, this separation can be done by drawing from a uniform distribution with probabilities $\alpha_l^k, | \sum_l \alpha_l^k = 1$ whenever a new call arrives from stream k. In this way, the statistical properties of the real stream are maintained in the substreams — in particular, if the arrival is Poisson in the real stream, then so are the arrivals in the substreams. Graphically, load sharing in represented by giving, for each stream k, the list of paths available. As shown in Fig. 2.4, the separation of the original stream is represented by a square node.

The advantages of this method are that the probabilities belong to a compact set and that optimization can be carried out using standard nonlinear programming methods. Also, as we shall see later, the sharing coefficients need not be fixed, but may be made to depend on state measurements.

2.4　Alternate Routing

An obvious defect of load sharing with fixed coefficients is that once the identity of a path is drawn, there is no possibility of selecting any other path. If the selected path turns out to be unavailable, the call is lost, although another path may be free that could be used to connect the call. For this reason, pure load sharing is not a very good routing algorithm and must be improved to be usable in real networks. The improvement is to provide, for each call arrival, the possibility of selecting a path from a given set, depending on some conditions. This in turn gives rise to two broad classes of routing algorithms. In the first class, the set is ordered, forming a *sequence* of potential choices. The rule is to pick the first path in the sequence that can carry the call. This process, known as *alternate routing*, comes in many flavors, depending on how the sequences are chosen.

The second class consists of choosing the path according to a value placed on each path in the set. These values can be fixed, but usually are computed from observations of some of the network components. For this reason, they are called *adaptive* methods.

The somewhat artificial distinction between alternate routing and adaptive techniques is a good example of the difficulty of classifying routing in rigidly defined categories. Alternate routing can be viewed as a special case of adaptive routing, where the path values are given by the following rule: The value of the paths is the negative of the order number in the sequence, and paths that are not available are given a value of $-\infty$. In this way, selecting the path with the largest value replicates the operation of alternate routing.

In the same way, alternate routing is in a sense adaptive since the actual path chosen for a call depends on the state of the network as reflected in the availability of the paths. In other words, alternate routing also adapts to changing conditions, and thus it could equally well be viewed as an adaptive method.

Because these methods are used in very different networks, however, we maintain the difference in their traditional meanings. Finally, as we shall see later, it is possible to mix the two classes to obtain a large variety of hybrid methods.

General Fixed Alternate Routing

Fixed alternate routing is one of the oldest and simplest routing techniques. Using this method, the first reduction in complexity over the Markov model is achieved by specifying in advance, for each origin-destination pair, a sequence of paths that are candidates for connecting the call. This set is generally much smaller than the full set of network paths allowed by the network topology. The second reduction is obtained by severely limiting the possible number of transitions: The set of alternate routes is scanned in some predetermined order, and the call is connected on the first free path that is found. (A path is said to be free if each of its links has at least one free trunk.) If a given path is not free, either the call can be lost or the next path may be tried. In this case, we say that the call *overflows* on the next path in the sequence. Which event happens depends on the type of routing control used and the particular link that was unavailable.

In the example in Fig. 2.5, the paths available for connecting (o, d) calls are, in order, (o, d), (o, a, d), (o, a, c, d), (o, a, e, f, d), and finally (o, b, e, f, d). Suppose now that links (o, d) and (a, d) are blocked and that links (o, a), (a, c) are available. It is possible to establish a partial connection from o to e through node a; we say that the call has progressed to node c. If link (c, d) is blocked, the

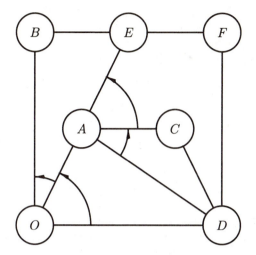

Figure 2.5   Alternate Routing and Overflow

call may be lost or may attempt the next path in the list, that is, (o, a, e, f, d). Which event occurs determines a particular variation of the alternate routing scheme.

Alternate routing schemes may be static or dynamic, depending on whether the sequence of paths is static or time-dependent. If the sequences are chosen as a function of the network state, they can also be adaptive. For now, suffice to say that fixed alternate routing is an alternate routing scheme where the path sequences are constant over long time periods, as measured with respect to the average call-holding time. We now describe in some detail two special cases of fixed alternate routing: hierarchical and two-link.

Fixed Hierarchical Routing

Fixed hierarchical routing is the oldest and most extensively used routing method for telecommunication networks. It originated with the old wired-logic switches, which had a severely limited capability for alternate routing, and thus in effect dictated the method that could be used. Although this limitation was soon overcome with the advent of stored-program control switches, by that time fixed hierarchical routing had become entrenched. It is used in most telephone networks to this day.

As its name indicates, fixed hierarchical routing is of the fixed alternate route type, with additional restrictions imposed on the nature of the paths that can be used for a call. The hierarchical character of the method arises from a partition of the offices into classes, five altogether in the North American network, and somewhat less in other countries (See Fig. 2.6 for the five-level network. Not all possible groups are indicated.) The class-five offices, the so-called *end offices*, are those to which subscriber lines are directly connected. Going up in the hierarchy, the toll, primary, sectional, and regional centers are encountered. Each office has and one and only one homing office of higher level to which it is connected by a so-called *final trunk* group (the reason for this name will become obvious soon). Of course, the office can be connected to other offices in the network by *high-usage* groups. Thus, given any pair of offices, there is a unique path, made up exclusively of final trunk groups, that connects them. We call such a path the hierarchical path, or sometimes the normal path. The hierarchical distance between two offices is defined as the number of groups needed to go from one to the other on the hierarchical path. For instance, in a full five-level hierarchy, the hierarchical distance between two end offices is 9, and the hierarchical distance between a regional office and an end office is 5.

Standard hierarchical routing operates within such a hierarchy of offices, with a few simple rules that can easily be implemented with limited hardware — the reason why this method was used in the first place. Although these rules are not uniform for all networks, in general they are simple variations on the following *fan rule*:

1. For a call arriving in an office, only the destination office is available to make the routing decision. The origin of the call is immaterial.

2. For a call arriving in an office, route it over the first available group in a sequence of alternate routes.

3. The sequence of alternate routes is defined by the end office of the group. The rule is to attempt the group whose extremity is the closest, in the sense of the hierarchical distance, to the destination office of the call — provided, of course, that the group exists.

4. The last choice in this list is always the hierarchical group of the office. If the call is blocked on this group, it is lost; this is why it is called a *final trunk* group.

The hierarchy induces a partition on the links into two classes: high-usage groups and final groups. The fact that a group is a final is independent of the particular traffic stream considered, and is a topological property of the network. This is in marked distinction to more general nonhierarchical routing methods, where a group may be a final for a given traffic stream, and a high-usage for another stream. This fact is important for the network performance evaluation and dimensioning methods discussed later in this book.

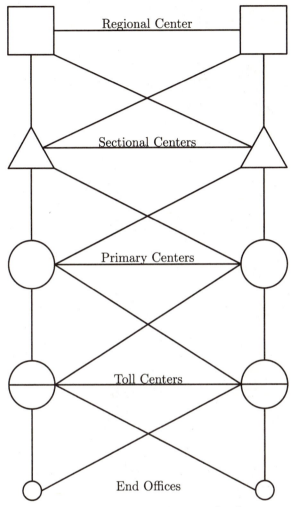

Figure 2.6 Five-Level Hierarchical Network. Some connections
left out.

Among the advantages of such a routing procedure is that there is no possibility
of introducing cycles in the routing of a call. Also, the procedure can be implemented on very simple hardware, with limited information and control. There
can be a number of variations on the fan rule, for instance by omitting some
groups from the list of an office or by modifying the loss condition 4 to allow the
selection of other routes (see Section 2.5).

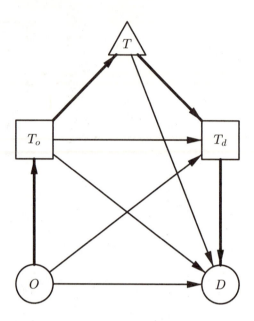

Figure 2.7   Hierarchical Alternate Routing

Dynamic Nonhierarchical Routing

Until the mid 1980s, hierarchical alternate routing, depicted in Fig. 2.7, was the universal routing method in telephone networks throughout the world. At that time, a major change was introduced in the routing of the long distance AT&T network in the United States, which represents a radical departure from the classical hierarchical method. This method is called *dynamic nonhierarchical routing* (DNHR) [4].

The most important element of DNHR is that there is no longer any hierarchical relation between offices. All switches in a DNHR network are of the same type, and can equally well receive calls from customers or serve as a tandem switch for alternate routing. As a consequence, there is no longer a hierarchical backbone, and the distinction between high-usage and finals does not hold networkwide. In other words, a group can be high-usage for a given traffic relation and the last choice for another.

The routing is still of the alternate type, but with the provision that alternate paths are limited to two links at most (see Fig. 2.8 for an example). This restriction was introduced because it is known that nonhierarchical routing methods that allow long paths for call completion can be highly sensitive to overloads, even though there may be a slight gain in efficiency at nominal loads.

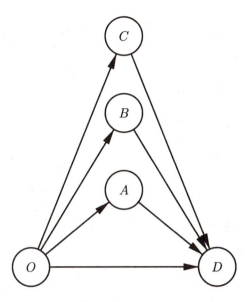

Figure 2.8   Two-Link Alternate Routing for DNHR

The routing is also dynamic, in the following sense. During the engineering phase of the network, the traffic demand is represented by a number of traffic matrices, each corresponding to a period of the day. Typically, about 10 periods are retained as significant for the design. One result of this design process, called the Unified Algorithm, is the production of a near-optimal alternate routing sequence for each of these periods, and of course for each traffic stream. After the design is complete, these routing tables are stored in the switches. As each time period arrives, the appropriate table is selected, and is used for the whole duration of the period, irrespective of the state of the network.

In addition to the nonhierarchical nature of the routing, *call crankback* is used throughout the network. In crankback mode, the control of overflow is such that a call blocked at an intermediate point on a path can still be offered to other paths in the sequence, and is not immediately lost.

DNHR is a good example of the arbitrariness in the use of terms like *dynamic* or *adaptive*. According to our definitions, DNHR is dynamic because it is changed at fixed time intervals, but is not adaptive since it uses no network feedback except the link-occupancy information. Routes are calculated off-line from the traffic forecast, and the results are used without change. Note, however, that if we look at the network operation for a period of time that is small with respect to a period, but long with respect to a call-holding time, then the routing looks like fixed alternate routing, and we may very well say that it is static. Conversely, looking at the operation of a switch on a call-by-call basis, we notice that for a given traffic stream from i to j, the actual path selected is different from one call to the next. We might also notice that the actual path depends on the occupancy of the trunk groups, in other words on the network state. On that basis, we could equally well declare that DNHR is an adaptive algorithm. Let us repeat that none of these views is wrong. Each emphasizes different components of the routing method; in our view, any attempt to find a "right" way to describe a routing method like DNHR (or most other techniques, for that matter) can only end inconclusively.

The DNHR routes are computed off-line, based on traffic forecasts for different times of day. Because these forecasts are subject to errors, the routing calculated is generally not the best one for the traffic conditions encountered in the network. Also, failures and overloads can and do occur — another factor that, because of the nonadaptive nature of the DNHR method, may cause inefficiency. Thus the routing algorithm must be able to react to real-time conditions [5]. This capability is provided by the so-called *real-time paths*. When routes are calculated, the first k best routes are computed for ordinary routing by the DNHR method as just described. From these, say that $m < k$ are actually available for routing. The remaining $k - m$ routes are kept in reserve, to be used whenever network performance seems to degrade. This procedure must be performed with some care, however, because using the real-time paths should not cause an increased loss of the traffic these paths were originally designed to carry. This precaution takes the form of a reservation level set on the real-time paths such that these paths will not be used unless the occupancy at the time they are needed is below the level.

Because it is necessary to change the routing tables relatively often, the use of DNHR is obviously limited to switches with stored program control. Also, the extensive use of crankback can be implemented more easily with out-of-band signaling, which is normally used in digital transmission networks. For these reasons, DNHR is generally limited to all-digital networks, although it could probably be used in networks with analog SPC switches as well. Another feature of DNHR is that, following the conversion of old switches to digital technology, it can be introduced smoothly in an existing network: The DNHR network coexists with the old hierarchical switches; it is used as a switching layer above the standard hierarchy and appears as a large network of regional centers.

The introduction of DNHR profoundly influenced network management and applicable engineering methods. Network operation and management has become more centralized, providing facilities to collect the networkwide statistics needed for the design stage. Design methods have also undergone a dramatic change; they are now quite different from classical design techniques even though they retain some basic principles. Perhaps the more significant change

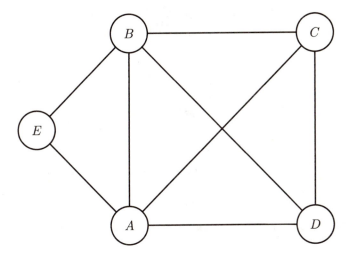

Figure 2.9   Example for Augmented Route Trees

is the need to optimize the routing, a problem that did not arise in the context of hierarchical networks. These questions are the subject of detailed discussions in Chapters 7 and 9.

2.5   Graphic Representations of Fixed Alternate Routing

Although routings can be represented directly on the network graph, their complexity grows so quickly that it is necessary to use a more detailed graphic description. This representation should be flexible enough to represent a wide class of routings, and accurate enough to define the routing uniquely. By this we mean that inspection of the representation should indicate precisely how the call can be connected or lost, as the case may be, for a given state of the network. We first describe a particularly useful representation, the so-called *augmented route tree*. Originally proposed by Lin et al. [6], it can be used for a very general class of alternate routing methods. Then we review a less general representation known as the *influence graph*, which is used mostly for hierarchical networks in the context of the notion of an ordered network.

Augmented Route Trees

To describe routing in terms of route trees [6], consider the origin-destination pair (E, D) of the network shown on Fig. 2.9, where all links are two-way.

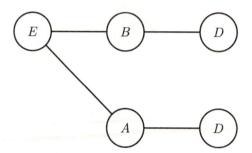

Figure 2.10   Route Tree for (E, D) Calls

We construct a graph that contains all the paths available to (E, D) calls, all starting at node E and terminating at node D. When read from top to bottom, these paths are put in the graph in the same order as the overflow. Thus suppose that there are only two paths available to (E, D) calls, that is, (E, A, D) and (E, B, D). Assume that calls that do not find the first path free overflow onto the second one. The corresponding route tree is shown in Fig. 2.10. Note that overflow can occur only on paths that originate at E. We say that overflow control is at node E. Since this is also the node at which calls originate, we speak of *originating-office control*, or OOC.

Because originating-office control has relatively few possibilities, we need to introduce more complex routings by allowing control to *spill forward* in the route tree, provided that the call can be connected to these nodes. For instance, we could have originating office control with spill at node B, as described by the route tree shown in Fig. 2.11. The interpretation is that overflow initially occurs on all paths originating at node E. If the (E, B) link is available, however, the control of overflow is transferred at node B. From then on, overflow can occur only on paths originating at node B. If no such path is available, the call is lost. In other words, once the control is transferred to B, it cannot return to E when all paths originating at B are blocked.

As noted earlier, the mode in which movement of overflow control can occur in the opposite direction is called *crankback*. The distinction between spill with crankback and without crankback lies in the conditions under which a call overflows on the (E, A, D) path. If there is no crankback, overflow to (E, A, D) happens only if the (E, B) link is blocked. In the case of crankback, overflow to (E, A, D) happens only if all the paths originating at node B are blocked. In other words, if (B, C) is blocked, call control returns to E and the next path on the list is attempted.

Finally, a frequently used method of control, *sequential-office control* (SOC), also called *progressive control* or *sequential control*, is simply OOC with spill

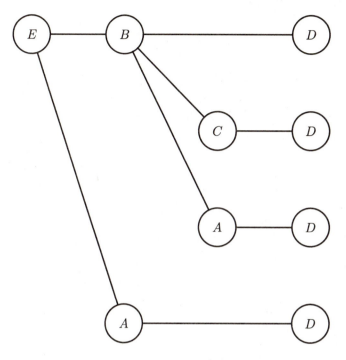

Figure 2.11   OOC with Spill at Node B

at all the nodes and no crankback. An example for (E, D) calls can be found in Fig. 2.12.

The route-tree representation is insufficient to distinguish between control with and without crankback. In some cases, it is not even possible to distinguish between OOC and SOC control even though the two methods behave quite differently. Consider, for instance, the route tree for (D, A) traffic shown in Fig. 2.13. This tree could represent equally well a routing with SOC, or OOC with spill at node C. Note, however, that the situation is quite different in the two cases. Suppose that links (D, A) and (B, A) are blocked but that links (D, B), (D, C), and (C, A) are free. Then, under SOC without crankback, a call will overflow to (B, D), then will be connected to B because the link (D, B) is available. At this point, the call is blocked because link (B, A) is not available. Because of the lack of crankback, it is impossible to return the overflow control to node D, and the call is lost. Under OOC with spill and crankback, however, the call will be connected because the possibility exists of transferring the overflow control back to node D. In practice, this means that the *originating* office D can detect that the (D, B, A) path is blocked before

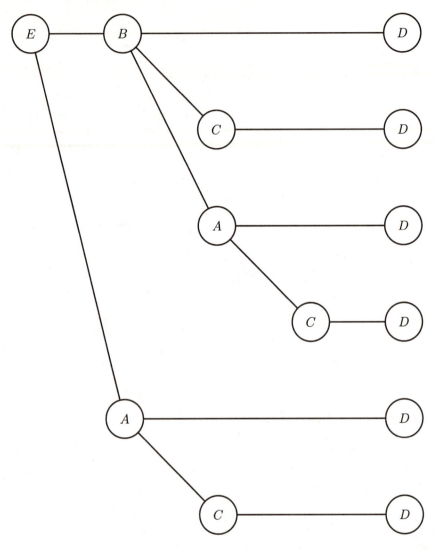

Figure 2.12   Route Tree with Progressive Control

attempting any connection on this path and instead can use the (D, C, A) path, which is free.

The graphic representation of routing should make the distinction between various forms of overflow control immediately obvious. The solution is to augment the route tree with so-called *loss nodes* — additional nodes similar to

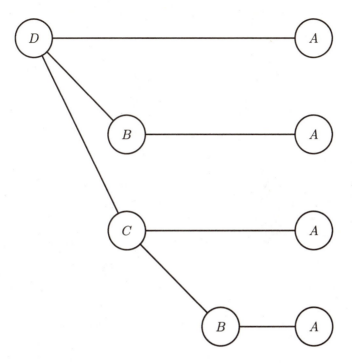

Figure 2.13 Route Tree for (D, A) Traffic

destination nodes, such that a call that reaches one of them is lost. By convention, the probability of blocking on a link leading to a loss node is zero. In our example, we obtain the *augmented tree* in Fig. 2.14 for SOC and in Fig. 2.15 for OOC with spill at C.

As we see in these two examples, although the original route tree is identical for the two types of commands, the augmented trees are different because the conditions under which blocking can occur are different. Overflow control is defined by the number and position of the loss nodes in the augmented trees.

The augmented-tree technique is a very powerful way to represent routing. Let us now use it to *define* what is meant by fixed alternate routing: A routing technique is a fixed alternate routing technique if and only if it can be represented by an augmented route tree. In fact, augmented route trees can be used in more general situations if they are made to depend either on time or on the network state. In the first case, they are used to represent dynamic routings; in the second, they are used for adaptive routings.

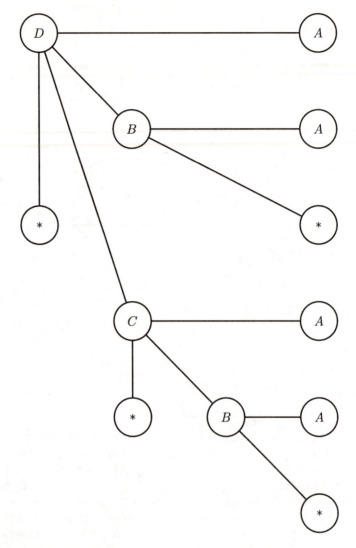

Figure 2.14 Augmented Tree for SOC Control

Influence Graph

The construction of a nonhierarchical routing must ensure that the routing does not lead to cyclic situations in which a call finding a link, say s, busy, overflows onto a link t, and finding this link also busy, overflows onto link s

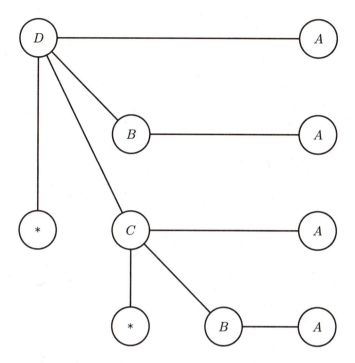

Figure 2.15   Augmented Tree for OOC with Spill

again. Two-link and hierarchical routing methods automatically ensure that this situation cannot occur. In more general cases, this overflow condition is a distinct possibility, and a systematic way to check for it must be used. Thus we introduce influence graphs, which can serve to check for cycles in routings in certain conditions. These graphs are also a basis for discussing the notion of order in a network, as well as for considering numerical algorithms for certain types of networks.

As we have seen, under SOC control routing decisions are based exclusively on the state of the links adjacent to the node that the call has reached. In this sense, SOC is shortsighted since no account is taken of the rest of the alternate paths to the destination. Thus, for general SOC route trees, there exists the possibility that the routing will eventually enter a cycle — the *ring-around-the-rosy* problem. Consider once more the network of Fig. 2.9 and its associated augmented route tree, Fig. 2.14. Suppose now that the routing is modified to look like the tree shown in Fig. 2.16. The presence of the (D, A) link as the last choice in the tree means that there is no unique action to be taken if a call is blocked on link (B, A). If the call is new, it should overflow onto

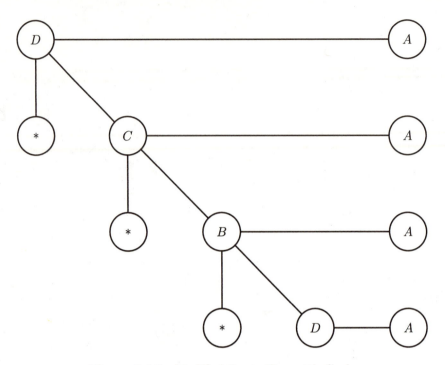

Figure 2.16   Modified Route Tree with Cycle

(B, D); it should be lost if it was already carried on (C, B). In practice, the routing algorithm will enter a cycle unless some signaling information is sent along with the call to indicate that it was already carried on link (C, B) and that it should be lost if blocked. Although most modern networks allow such transfer of information, this is not the case in older networks. Also, this kind of transfer may not be desirable in newer networks because it might increase unduly the amount of signaling information that must be transmitted. Thus it is desirable to have some systematic way to detect cyclic situations and to remove them when they occur.

The influence graph simplifies this task considerably. It is constructed as follows: For each link in the route tree, define a node of the influence graph. If the links in the real network are one-way, then there will be two corresponding nodes in the influence graph, one for (i, j) and one for (j, i). At a given node of the influence graph, define two arcs. One, the overflow arc, leads to the node representing the link to which a blocked call will overflow in the network. The other, the carry arc, represents the link on which a call that is carried will be offered. Note that the graph does not specify on which link a call will go; this

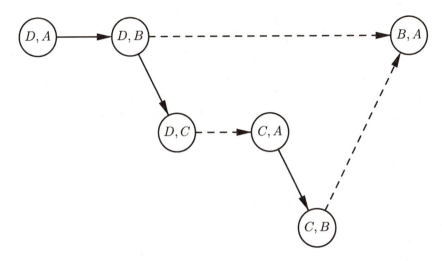

Figure 2.17   Influence Graph for SOC Route Tree without Cycle

depends on the blocking probabilities of the links, which are traffic dependent. The only purpose of the influence graph is to indicate the *possible* ways a call can go when it is offered to a link. For notational simplicity, we define two functions:

$\sigma(i,j)$ = For trunk group i, and calls destined for j, σ indicates the number of the trunk group to which blocked calls will overflow.

$\rho(i,j)$ = For trunk group i, and calls destined for j, ρ indicates the number of the trunk group to which calls that are carried on i will be offered.

The influence graph is a graphic representation of the ρ and σ arrays. With this definition, we can construct the influence graphs of the route trees corresponding to Figs. 2.17 and 2.18, shown on Figs 2.17 and 2.18, respectively, where overflow is indicated by a solid arrow and carried traffic by a dashed arrow.

The difference between the two graphs is immediately obvious. Corresponding to the routing with cycling is an influence graph containing a circuit. In fact, the presence or absence of circuits in the influence graph is equivalent to the presence or absence of cycling in the routing. Because there are standard methods of graph theory to detect the presence of cycles in directed graphs, it is possible to construct algorithms that check automatically for the presence of cycles in route trees. Furthermore, routings without cycling are characterized

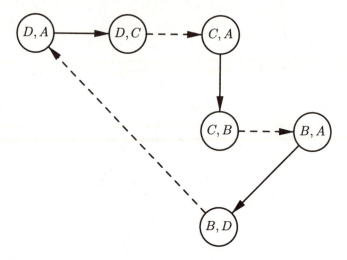

Figure 2.18   Influence Graph for Route Tree with Cycle

by a partial ordering of the links of the route tree since nodes of a directed graph without a circuit can be given such a partial ordering.

Mutual Overflow and Ordered Networks

The influence graph provides an easy way to detect circuits in a given route tree. In addition to such circuits, another type of circular situation can happen that is not as obviously undesirable as the ring-around-the-rosy problem. In this situation, called *mutual overflow*, one link i receives calls from another link j, which in turn receives calls from link i, generally from another traffic stream.

Consider for instance, the route tree for (C, A) calls shown in Fig. 2.19 and its influence graph, shown in Fig. 2.20. Viewed separately, neither this influence graph nor the one in Fig. 2.17 for the (D, A) traffic contains any circuits. If the two graphs are merged, however, we obtain an influence graph that *does* contain circuits. This means that, for any two nodes in this circuit, the corresponding links both receive calls from and send calls to the other node. This situation is not necessarily to be avoided — it may lead to more economical networks. Certainly, however, it makes the computation of the network performance more difficult (see Chapter 4).

In one special, particularly important class of routings, the combined influence graph *for all streams* contains no circuit. In this case, we can define a partial order μ on the nodes of the influence graph and consequently on the

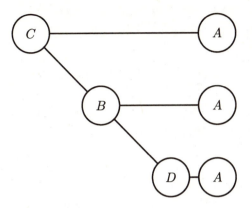

Figure 2.19   Route Tree for (C, A) Calls

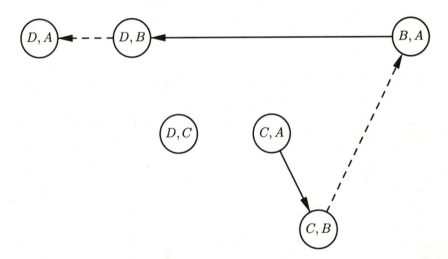

Figure 2.20   Influence Graph for (C, A) Calls

network links. Let $\mu(i)$ be the order number of node i. We say that node i is a descendant of node j if $\mu(i) > \mu(j)$. Define also

$$\mathcal{D}(j) \stackrel{\triangle}{=} \{i \mid \mu(i) > \mu(j)\}$$

$$\mathcal{A}(j) \stackrel{\triangle}{=} \{i \mid \mu(i) < \mu(j)\},$$

which are called, respectively, the descendants and the ancestors of j.   For ordered networks, we know that the calls offered to node i depend exclusively on the nodes $j \mid j \in \mathcal{A}(j)$. Ordered networks draw their importance from the fact that fixed hierarchical routing networks can be considered to be ordered under assumptions discussed in Chapter 4. As discussed there, this is an important property that simplifies the calculation of traffic flows considerably.

Combined Load Sharing and Alternate Routing

Although we have presented load-sharing and alternate-routing policies as distinct methods, they can be combined in a single, more general algorithm. To do this, we must introduce the notion of a *route*, that is, the set of alternate paths available to a given type of call. In this case, the sharing coefficients have the same meaning as in the simple case, with the understanding that the sharing is between routes, instead of simple paths. The actual operation and analysis of the routing are more complex, however, because of the presence of alternate routing. A general graph representation is a mixture of load-sharing graphs and augmented route trees (see Fig. 2.21).

2.6   Adaptive Routing

Alternate routing was designed to take into account the constraints imposed by the electromechanical switches, as well as the limited amount of information available about the state of the network. The widespread introduction of stored-program switches, digital transmission, and signaling have removed these constraints by increasing enormously the amount of information available for control. These advances in turn have made possible the introduction of more sophisticated routing methods, known under the generic name of *adaptive routing*.

While alternate routing operates on ordered sequences of paths, adaptive techniques operate from a fixed *set* of potential connection paths for each stream, with no predetermined order. Instead, a value is given to the paths in the set, and the path with the highest value at the time the call arrives is selected. Variations on this theme are possible, depending on the definition of the path value, the value-update mechanism, the use of probabilities for path selection, and potentially a number of other factors. Some variations are being implemented in public telephone networks, while others have only been proposed.

Residual-Capacity Routing

Of all the routing methods currently in use or proposed for use, *residual-capacity adaptive routing* (RCAR) has the largest information set with which to

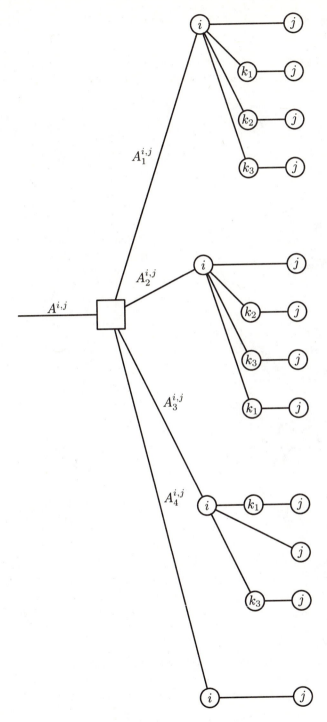

Figure 2.21 Route Formulation for Nonhierarchical Routing

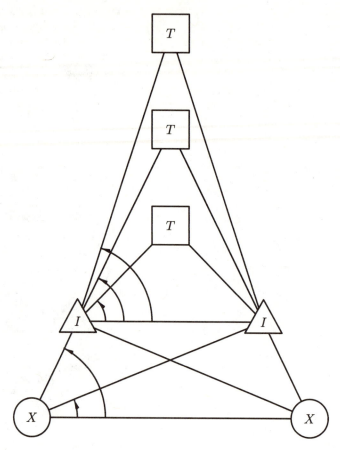

Figure 2.22   Two-level Network for Adaptive Routing

make its routing decisions: It uses occupancy information on *all* network trunk groups, information periodically updated via actual measurements made by the switches. From this point of view, RCAR is probably the most advanced routing technique now in existence, and for this reason deserves a thorough discussion.

Because of the need to alter the routing tables dynamically, residual-capacity adaptive routing can be implemented only in networks with stored-program control switches and advanced signaling capabilities. This method can, however, be made part of a two-level network, where a lower-level network of non-SPC switches, called X-nodes, overflows onto a higher-level network of SPC switches, called I- or T-nodes, where calls are routed according to the adaptive policy (see Fig. 2.22). T-nodes have a purely tandem function, while I-nodes have some originating traffic. Otherwise, both sets of nodes operate in exactly the same way and can act as tandem for any traffic flow. Needless to say, nodes without alternate routing capability, such as step-by-step switches, cannot become part of an RCAR network.

Because of the adaptive nature of the routing, some form of networkwide information collection is required, possibly a CCITT No. 7 signaling channel or a dedicated measurement network. Rather that discussing the implementation issues related to this system, we assume that it is given and that it can furnish the algorithm with whatever information is needed.

The first proposal for implementing an adaptive routing technique of the residual-capacity type in a public telephone network originated with [7,8]. Originally called *high-performance routing* (HPR) and now known as *dynamic call routing* (DCR), this method operates by sending calls on paths with the largest expected number of free trunks. DCR, the implementation of RCAR discussed in [9], operates with a single overflow path computed periodically for each origin-destination pair. Calls blocked on the direct link are offered to this path, where they are lost if blocked again. Path are selected at random, with selection probabilities proportional to the estimated residual capacity of all potential paths.

DCR Algorithm Definition.   Define the following:

N_s =   Number of circuits on link s.

$R_s(t)$ = Expected number of free trunks on trunk group s at time t.

$n_s(t)$ = Number of busy trunks on trunk group s at time t.

$A_s(t)$ = Estimated call-arrival rate to trunk group s at time t.

μ_s = Average call-holding time on trunk group s. In practice, this is independent of s.

$m_s(t)$ = State protection at time t on trunk group s. This is the level of occupancy at which overflow calls will be blocked.

$M_s(\tau)$ = Number of calls actually offered to trunk group s during a time interval τ.

$\alpha_k^{i,j}$ = Probability of selecting tandem k for a call between i and j.

Δ = Update interval. At every Δ seconds, the network control center queries the switches about the occupancy of their outgoing links. The information is processed, and new routing tables are sent to the switches that will be used for the next Δ seconds.

State protection is a control technique that protects fresh traffic against blocking by calls that overflow from other routes. It is implemented by setting a threshold, perhaps a distinct one for each link, such that when the number of busy circuits on the link exceeds this value, calls that are alternate routed will not be connected on the link. If the threshold is set at a value lower than the group capacity, this amounts to reserving the difference $N - m$ for first-offered traffic, which is known to be a good policy in case of traffic overload.

The estimated residual capacity on group s at time $t + \tau$ is given by a simple linear extrapolation:

$$R_s(t + \tau) = N_s - n_s(t) - \tau \left[A_s(t) - n_s(t)/\mu_s \right] - m_s(t). \qquad (2.11)$$

At time t, the estimated call-arrival rate is updated by

$$A_s(t) = \theta A_s(t - \Delta) + (1 - \theta) \frac{M_s(\Delta)}{\Delta}.$$

For intelligent nodes, the selection of a tandem is made at random, with probabilities

$$\alpha_k^{i,j} = \frac{\overline{\alpha}_k^{i,j}}{\sum_k \overline{\alpha}_k^{i,j}}, \qquad (2.12)$$

where

$$\overline{\alpha}_k^{i,j} = \max \left[0, \min \left\{ R_{i,k}, R_{k,j} \right\} \right]. \qquad (2.13)$$

For X-nodes, the tandems are selected on the basis of the residual capacities of the outgoing links only. A number of parameters can influence the performance of the algorithm:

τ The extrapolation interval.

Δ The update interval.

θ The weight of the updated arrival rate.

m_s The protection level. This can be made fixed or variable. If it is fixed, one must select its value; if variable, an algorithm to compute it is needed.

The proper selection can be made only through simulation and possibly experience, since we do not have analytic models to compute the performance as a function of these parameters. The reservation level can be made adaptive [10] by the formula

$$m_s(t) = g \times a'_s, \qquad (2.14)$$

where

$a'_s =$ Current amount of *first offered* traffic overflowing link s.

$g =$ A scale factor, usually chosen equal to one.

Field Trial. DCR has actually been implemented in a real telephone network under normal operating conditions. In 1979, a field trial was carried out in which a nine-node subnetwork of the Toronto metropolitan network was temporarily converted to DCR operation for part of the day. The standard hierarchical routing was kept as a backup, and a dedicated measurement network was implemented (at that time the Toronto network did not have a distinct control network). The actual parameter values selected for the trial were $\tau = \Delta = 16$ secs, $\theta = 0.9$, and $m_s = 2$. The results of the experiment are fully described in [9]. The main conclusions derived from the exercise were as follows:

1. DCR is a feasible routing technique, at least for small networks.

2. DCR offers substantial improvements in terms of traffic-carrying capacity over the standard hierarchical routing.

3. Δ is the most important parameter. Its value should be chosen as small as possible, consistent with technological constraints. The value of the other parameters is not very important and can lie in relatively large intervals without affecting the performance of the algorithm significantly.

4. In addition to these results on the routing algorithm itself, the field trial provided the opportunity to make numerous traffic measurements and to validate the network simulation used to study the algorithm.

As a result of the field test, it was decided to implement DCR in the long distance Telecom Canada network.

Trunk Status Map Routing

The original proposal for dynamic nonhierarchical routing was of the fixed nonhierarchical type (see Section 2.4). The only provision for adaptation to the network conditions was through the actual status of the alternate paths (which determined the path that was going to be used), as well as through the use of the real-time paths. The order of choices and the set of paths in a route were not subject to modification, except at fixed time periods determined by the original network routing and dimensioning. Routes for each period are selected on the basis of forecasted loads, which can take into account some systematic variations in demand but are nevertheless inherently subject to errors. Also, because the routing tables and network dimensioning are recalculated infrequently (typically, once a week for routing and twice a year for dimensioning), these computations cannot take into account short-term variations in load, say of the order of minutes. For this reason, some form of adaptation to these variations seemed desirable, and a second version of DNHR, called *trunk status map routing* (TSMR), has been proposed, incorporating some of the features of the RCAR method [11].

The algorithm operates on the set of paths as calculated for the original DNHR, but the actual selection of a path for a call to be routed is not strictly sequential. It can depend on the occupancy of the paths. The following rules were envisaged:

1. Route the current call on the least-loaded path from the set of available paths.

2. Route the call first on the direct path, if it exists, and then on the least-loaded path.

3. Route the call on the first path computed for nonadaptive DNHR. If this routing is not possible, select the least-loaded path.

4. Recompute a new set of alternate paths such that the total carried traffic will be maximized, at least for a short duration, starting from the current state of the network.

Obviously, Rule 4 is not practical, and was considered only as a lower bound on the efficiency of the other rules. As the result of simulation studies, it was found that Rule 3 generally performed better than Rules 1 and 2, and was only marginally inferior to Rule 4 — that is, it was nearly optimal. Rules 1 and 2 did not perform well because the least-loaded path or the direct path, as the case may be, are not necessarily the best choices as computed by the dimensioning and routing optimization algorithm. In this case, Rules 1 and 2 have a tendency to allocate traffic to expensive paths or to increase the amount of two-link routing in such a way that the crankback traffic becomes too large, reducing the efficiency of the routing.

The actual implementation of TSMR uses a centralized trunk status map (TSM), which coordinates the routing changes between all switches. Every T seconds, each switch sends to the TSM an update on the number of free trunks on each trunk group, provided this number has changed. The TSM then recomputes a new set of routes for each switch, which are sent back and used during the next T seconds to perform the alternate routing of calls. The route sequence stored in the switch consists of two parts: (1) the first path computed by the routing optimization based on forecasts and (2) the remaining paths, which are the recommendations sent by the TSM. In practice, it is not necessary to recompute all the paths in the second list, but changing the second choice according to the least-loaded rule is sufficient to achieve an adequate performance.

A threshold is used to determine whether an update is needed for each stream where the direct link exists. The use of a threshold is based on the reasonable assumption that, if the load on the direct and first alternate paths is sufficiently light, then all the calls that will arrive in the next T seconds can be carried on these two paths. In this case, there is no reason to change the second choice, and no update is sent. A practical value of $N/8$ has been suggested for this threshold, where N is the number of circuits on the direct link.

Whenever an update is needed, the TSM first retrieves the list of candidates for least-loaded path from a centralized database. The least-loaded path is then selected; if a routing change is implied, the update is sent to the switches. This must be done carefully because large groups are likely to have many free circuits for short periods of time. A straightforward selection rule based exclusively on the current residual capacity could mean that these groups would be selected very often, but thus would immediately fill up and become unavailable for some time. For this reason, the number of idle trunks on large trunk groups is discounted by some factor, with the suggested value of $N/36$, where N is the number of circuits in the group.

After it is determined that a routing change is in order, the new path sequence is sent to the switch. The first two paths in the second class, that is, those affected by the TSM, are replaced by the new values, and the third choice in this class is left unchanged.

The effects of this routing technique were simulated, with the finding that the number of crankback information is relatively small, and that the additional load on the switch processor is not significant. The value of the update interval T was estimated from the trade-off between a higher processing load caused by a small value of T and the increase in crankback traffic, and hence of processing load, caused by a large T. It turns out that a value between 2 and 10 seconds is nearly optimal, assuming that the crankback load is not a strong function of the update interval.

Other Pricing Functions

Both DCR and TSMR operate with path values that are essentially defined by the residual capacity of the path. Using other cost functions, adaptive routing can be formulated more generally. This can be done either in the context of the Markov decision process model [12] or in the selection of load-sharing coefficients [13].

The general algorithm in both cases is based on the following argument. Suppose that each call belongs to a type j that in general is related to the origin-destination pair of the call and perhaps to other parameters. Each call type has a revenue r_j that is obtained if the call is connected on some path. The decision to connect on a particular path j will then produce r_j. The decision will also have a detrimental effect since, by using one trunk on all the links in the path, it can cause calls of other classes to be lost, with a corresponding loss of revenue. This lost revenue, the sum of the individual link losses q_s on the path, is written $\sum_{s \in l} q_s$. The net gain g_l^j for routing a call of class j on path k

is simply the difference $g_l^j = r_j - \sum_{s \in l} q_s$. The call is then routed on the path with the largest net gain if it is positive; the call is lost if there is no positive gain.

This rule has the immediate advantage that flow control is already embedded — all the gains may turn out to be negative even though one or more free paths may be available for the call. The rule makes it possible to modulate the traffic in the network to effect network-management functions systematically, based on call classes — another advantage over current methods, many of which are based on manual or semiautomated intervention.

There are two major problems: (1) calculating the net gain of a decision, whether in the Markov or load-sharing context, and (2) evaluating the network performance (as with any other routing technique). Most results obtained to date apply to the first question; they are discussed in Chapter 4. The value of revenue-based adaptive routing in terms of network performance is currently the subject of investigation.

2.7   Learning Automata

As can be seen from the extensive bibliography of [14], *learning automata* have found many uses in control engineering. They are particularly useful when little is known about the response of the environment to actions of the system. In the automaton approach, knowledge about the environment is gained only through the responses received by the automaton after each of its actions. In fact, the only knowledge gained is that "this action is better than that one because a good response is received more frequently in the first case than in the second." That is, the action-reaction channel is the only way of learning about the world. This approach has some obvious advantages, the most important of which is simplicity. It suffers, however, from the corresponding inconvenience that learning may be quite slow since the information available is so severely limited.

It should be clear by now that routing is a rather complex process. Furthermore, networks are seldom stationary, because of either unexpected variations in demand or component failures (fortunately much less frequent) of the network itself. Add the real-time requirements of routing, which limits the amount of computation that can be done before a decision is taken, and all the requirements for a learning scheme for routing are present.

First we give a short outline of formal automata theory. Then we relate the general model to routing, describing the special cases of automata that have been studied in detail. Finally, a short discussion of the pros and cons of the automaton approach is given.

Formally, an automaton is defined by the quintuple $\{X, \Phi, \alpha, T, G\}$, where

$X =$ The sets of inputs to the automaton.

$\Phi =$ The set of internal states.

$\alpha =$ The set of actions $\{\alpha_1, \alpha_2, \ldots \alpha_r\}$.

$T =$ The state-transition map at stage n:

$$\Phi(n+1) = T\left[\Phi(n), \alpha(n), X(n)\right].$$

$G =$ The action-selection function:

$$G : \Phi \to \alpha.$$

The automaton is deterministic or stochastic depending whether T and G are deterministic or stochastic. The class of automata considered for routing, called *variable structure automata*, are of the form

$$\Phi = p_1, p_2, \ldots p_r$$
$$\sum p_j = 1, \quad p_i \geq 0$$
$$G(\Phi) = \alpha_i \text{ with probability } p_i$$

The states are defined by a probability vector, and the action map is the selection of an action i with probability p_i.

The environment in which the automaton operates is characterized by a set of inputs $\alpha(n)$ and random outputs $x_i(n) \in X$. Of special interest is the case where the environment output is binary, that is, a reward ($x = 0$) or a penalty ($x = 1$). In this case, the environment is characterized by a set of penalty probabilities $c_1, c_2, \ldots c_r$, where

$$c_i = Pr\left\{x(n) = 1 \mid \alpha(n) = \alpha_i\right\}.$$

The choice of symbols for the environment inputs and outputs is not coincidental. In the usual situation, the automaton outputs are fed into the environment, which reacts to these outputs by providing a reward or penalty. This response is then fed back as input to the automaton, which provides another action, and so on (see Fig. 2.23). A learning behavior is made possible by this feedback organization: The automaton is provided with some performance function that, it is hoped, will eventually be minimized. The behavior of the automaton is determined by the choice of the maps T and G, which in turn depend on the particular performance criterion that one is trying to minimize. Finally, note that the actual distributions for the response of the environment are *unknown*, and that the operation of the automaton in no way assumes any knowledge about these responses. In fact, one objective of the method is to determine the responses, and hence to choose the appropriate actions in view of the performance measure and what has been learned so far about the environment responses.

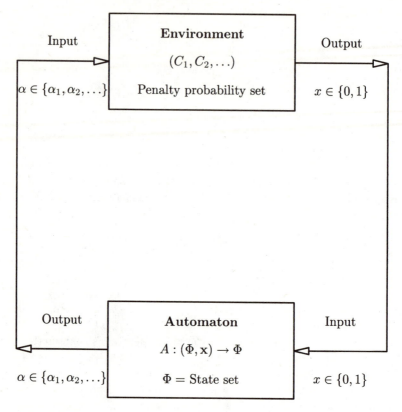

Figure 2.23 Input-Output Relationship of Learning Automaton

This general automaton formalism can be applied to the routing of calls in circuit-switched networks in the following way. Assume that in each node k there is an automaton, denoted $\mathcal{A}_k^{i,j}$, for each traffic stream i, j going through the node. If the origin of the call is not available, the automaton is denoted $\mathcal{A}_k^j$. Two sets of actions are possible for the automaton: (1) the set of all links out of the node and (2) the set of all *sequences* of links. The environment is the network beyond node k, and the responses are of the reward-penalty type, corresponding to a connected or a lost call, respectively. The objective, of course, is to minimize the number of lost calls. Three probability-update algorithms have been proposed.

The M-automaton [15] (M for mean) uses the choice of outgoing links as the action set. Define $g_i(n)$ as the estimated probability of loss if action i is used at stage n, where action i is to route the call via group i. These state variables are updated by

$$g_i(n+1) = g_i(n) + w[x(n+1) - g_i(n)],$$

where w is a constant and $x(n)$ is the network response at stage n and is given by

$$x(n) = \begin{cases} 0 & \text{if the call is completed} \\ 1 & \text{if the call is blocked} \end{cases}$$

The action at each stage is to compute the current value of g_i, rank the groups in decreasing order of g, and attempt to route the call in this order.

The linear reward-inaction (L_{R-I}) method [16] is more closely related to the general formalism just described. This method takes its name from the fact that the probability-update function is linear, and that an update is performed only when a reward (i.e., a call connection) is received. No change is made in the case of a penalty (a blocked call). Here, the actions are the sequences of groups available at the node, and the states are given by the probability p_i of choosing sequence i. The update formula, when action i has been chosen and the call has been completed, is

$$p_i(n+1) = p_i(n) + \sum_{j \neq i} (1 - \beta)p_j(n)$$

$$p_j(n+1) = \beta p_j(n)$$

$$0 \leq \beta \leq 1$$

No update is made when the call is blocked.

A natural generalization of the L_{R-I} scheme is to do something when either a reward or a penalty is incurred. In this case, we have a L_{R-P} scheme [17], where again the actions are sequences of groups to be used, and the update formula after action i has been chosen, is given by

$$p_j(n+1) = p_j(n) + \begin{cases} -ap_j(n) & \text{if } x = 0 \text{ (connected)} \\ \dfrac{b}{r-1} - bp_j(n) & \text{if } x = 1 \text{ (blocked)} \end{cases} \qquad j \neq i$$

$$p_i(n+1) = p_i(n) + \begin{cases} a[1 - p_i(n)] & \text{if } x = 0 \\ -bp_i(n) & \text{if } x = 1 \end{cases}$$

where r denotes the number of choices available to the automaton. The true L_{R-P} scheme is given for the values $a = b$. A variant is the $L_{R-\epsilon P}$ scheme, where $b \ll a$.

The use of learning automata for routing has many advantages. Perhaps the most obvious is simplicity, both computationally and in terms of measurements. Learning automata assume nothing about the network or the traffic flows, and in particular do not assume that the arrival process of new calls is stationary. Thus they should be particularly well-suited for networks in which there are large variations in traffic, or in which network reliability in not high. On the negative side are such questions as the stability of the algorithm, the rate of convergence, and the global optimality, in addition to the usual question about performance evaluation in a network. Because of the difficulties associated with these questions, the state of our knowledge about learning automata is not as advanced as for the other methods, and research continues.

Dynamic Alternate Routing

Although the full automaton approach has not yet been implemented — or even proposed for implementation — in a real network, a current proposal for implementing a routing algorithm in the United Kingdom trunk network has some of the features of an automaton routing. Called *dynamic alternate routing* (DAR), it is based on a very simple form of learning scheme. The main elements of the methods are the following:

1   Alternate routing is limited to two-link paths.

2   State protection is implemented.

3   A new call is offered first to the direct link.

4   If the call is blocked, it is offered to a single alternate route through tandem k, whose value is currently stored in the switch.

5   If the call is blocked on the alternate path, a new value is selected for tandem k. Currently, this selection is made randomly. If the call is connected, the value of k is left unchanged.

The DAR method is loosely related to learning schemes since no state measurement is ever made, and feedback is only via the success or failure of the connection on the current alternate path. The exact relation with learning automata is left as an exercise. This scheme can be extended in various ways, some suggested in [18]:

1   Use a cyclic order for selecting tandem nodes.

2   Use a nonuniform distribution for selecting the tandem node.

3   Introduce a second parameter such that if the traffic exceeds this value, and a call must be alternate routed, then a new tandem is selected. In other words, tandem reselection occurs before a call is blocked on the path, which would presumably give a better performance.

4   Use paths longer than two links, or use dummy first-choice paths in case the network is not fully connected.

Problems

2.1.   The state space for the Markov model of circuit-switched networks is quite large. It is suggested that all this information is not really needed, and that one could have a well-defined Markov model by using a state space where only the total number of busy circuits on each link is used. Explain clearly why such a description is not sufficient. (Try to explain how you could compute the transition matrix in this case.)

2.2.   Network states for the Markov model have been defined in terms of the number of calls on all paths in the network. We want to define a state description that involves only the number of calls of each type on all the links. Let f_s^k be the number of calls of commodity k on link s.

   1. Write down the three groups of constraints that the f must satisfy.

   2. Write the matrix of state transitions. Check carefully that these can be computed from the information available from the state description only.

   3. Show that, given the state in one representation, it is always possible to find the state in the other representation.

   You may assume that the network arc-path incidence matrix is known.

2.3.   For the three-node network 1 of Fig. 2.3,

   1. Construct the state-transition diagram for the routing policy where a connection is attempted on the direct link only, and the call is lost if the link is busy.

   2. Do the same thing for the policy where the direct link is attempted first, and then the alternate path if the direct link is blocked.

   3. Do the same thing for the policy where the alternate path is attempted first, and then the direct link.

2.4.   Calculate the number of states for the three-node network with one-way links of one circuit each.

2.5.   Give a continuous-time Markov model of the network such that the corresponding multicommodity flow representation is a true one, with equality constraints instead of Eq. (2.10).

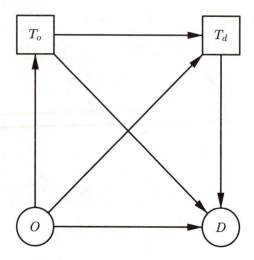

Figure 2.24   Double-Sector Tandem Network

2.6. Give a continuous-time Markov model with flow control. Construct the corresponding multicommodity representation.

2.7. Consider the network of Fig. 2.24 where the only traffic is between nodes O, D.

　　1. Define the state space.

　　2. Write down the general term of the transition matrix. Assume that the policy is the standard fan rule for hierarchical networks.

2.8. Consider the first three levels of the hierarchical network of Fig. 2.6. Assume that SOC control is used, and that the only links present are those indicated on the figure. Construct the augmented route tree corresponding to the full fan rule for a pair of end offices. Compare this with the description of overflow that would result if the network graph were used instead.

2.9. Construct the influence graph corresponding to Problem 2.8.

2.10. Show that the network of Problem 2.8 is ordered in the sense defined in Section 2.5.

2.11. Consider the three-node hierarchical network of Fig. 2.25. Assuming that the only flows are $A^{i,j}$ and $A^{j,i}$, show the influence graph in two

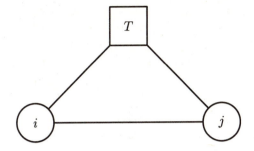

Figure 2.25 Three-Node Hierarchical Network

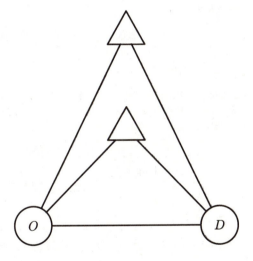

Figure 2.26 Adaptive Routing Network for State Space

versions:

1. When the circuits on the groups are one-way.

2. When the circuits are two-way.

2.12. Consider the network of Fig. 2.26, where there is a single flow from O to D, and $n_{i,j}$ circuits on group i,j. The network operates with

DCR with instantaneous information. That is, there is no estimation of residual capacity, but the correct values are available at all times. Give a state description for this network, and describe the state-transition probabilities.

2.13. Describe the DAR routing algorithms in terms of learning automata.

References

[1] Howard, R.A., *Dynamic programming and markov processes*, Wiley, 1960.

[2] Howard, R.A., *Dynamic probabilistic systems*, Wiley, 1971.

[3] Beneš, V.E., "Programming and control problems arising from optimal routing in telephone networks," *Bell System Technical Journal*, vol. 45, pp. 1373–1439, 1966.

[4] Ash, G.R., Cardwell, R.H., and Murray, R.P., "Design and optimization of networks with dynamic routing," *Bell System Technical Journal*, vol. 60, pp. 1787–1820, 1981.

[5] Ash, G.R., Kafker, A.H., and Krishnan, K.R., "Servicing and real-time control of networks with dynamic routing," *Bell System Technical Journal*, vol. 60, pp. 1821–1845, 1981.

[6] Lin, P.M., Leon, B.J., and Stewart, C.R., "Analysis of circuit switched networks employing originating office control with spill," *IEEE Transactions on Communications*, vol. COM–26, pp. 754–765, 1978.

[7] Szybicki, E., and Bean, A.E., "Advanced traffic routing in local telephone networks; performance of proposed call routing algorithms," *International Teletraffic Congress*, vol. 9, pp. SB1–SB8, 1979.

[8] Szybicki, E., and Lavigne, M.E., "The introduction of an advanced routing system into local digital networks and its impact on the network's economy, reliability and grade of service," *International Switching Symposium*, 1979.

[9] Cameron, H., Galloy, P., and Graham, W.J., "Report on the Toronto advanced routing concept trial," *Network Planning Symposium*, vol. 1, pp. 228–236, 1980.

[10] Cameron, H., "Simulation of dynamic routing: critical path selection features for service and economy," *International Conference on Communications*, vol. 81, pp. 55.5.1–55.5.6, 1986.

[11] Ash, G.R., "Use of a trunk status map for real-time DNHR," *International Teletraffic Congress*, vol. 11, pp. 4.4.A.4:1–4.4.A.4:7, 1985.

[12] Ott, T.J., and Krishnan, K.R., "State dependent routing of telephone traffic and the use of separable routing schemes," *International Teletraffic Congress*, vol. 11, pp. 5.1A.5.1–5.1A.5.6, 1985.

[13] Dziong, Z., Pióro, M., Körner, U., and Wickberg, T., "On adaptive call routing strategies in circuit-switched networks — maximum revenue approach," *International Teletraffic Congress*, vol. 12, pp. 3.1A5.1–3.1A5.8, 1988.

[14] Narendra, K.S., "Recent developments in learning automata: theory and applications," *Proceedings of the Third Yale Workshop on Applications of Adaptive Systems Theory*, vol. 3, pp. 90–99, 1983.

[15] Narendra, K.S., Wright, E.A., and Mason, L.G., "Application of learning automata to telephone traffic routing problems," *IEEE Transactions on Systems, Man and Cybernetics*, vol. SMC–7, pp. 785–792, 1977.

[16] Narendra, K.S., and McKenna, D.M., "Simulation study of telephone traffic routing using learning algorithms," Report No. 7806, Department of Engineering and Applied Science, Yale University, 1978.

[17] Srikantakumar, P.R., *Learning models and adaptive routing in communication networks*, Doctoral Dissertation, Yale University, 1980.

[18] Gibbens, R.J., Kelly, F.P., and Key, P.B., "Dynamic alternative routing — modelling and behaviour," *International Teletraffic Congress*, vol. 12, pp. 3.4A3.1–3.4A3.7, 1988.

CHAPTER 3

Traffic Models

As verified by numerous measurements, the holding times of ordinary telephone calls are exponentially distributed random variables, with a mean of a few minutes. Service requests from outside the network also have exponentially distributed interarrival times and are represented by Poisson processes. From a theoretical point of view, these features simplify network analysis, which is reduced to a straightforward problem in the theory of Markov processes.

Unfortunately, as is clear from the discussion of Chapter 2, the standard techniques of Markov processes are totally inadequate for the practical analysis of any network of reasonable size operating under a usual routing technique; solutions to the analysis problem can only be heuristic. Nevertheless, the use of probabilistic methods is unavoidable because of the stochastic character of the demand for telecommunication services. In this chapter, we study some simple systems that are amenable to the methods of queuing theory and are of interest in their own right. More importantly for our purpose, these systems form the elements on which all methods of network analysis are based.

There is extensive literature on the subject of traffic models for circuit-switching networks, most contained in the proceedings of the International Teletraffic Congress (ITC). Although the subject of this book is networks, some knowledge of traffic is required, if only because of the influence of traffic on the methods used to analyze and synthesize networks. Thus a short overview of the more widely used traffic models is in order, sufficient to give enough background for the rest of the material. (Excellent sources for the mathematical foundation of teletraffic are [1,2].) A knowledge of elementary stochastic processes and elementary queuing theory is assumed; a standard textbook on the subject, such as [3], should be consulted if this is not the case.

Teletraffic models are queues of the general type $G/M/N/\infty/N$, that is, with a general arrival process, exponential service times, N servers, an infinite source population and no waiting room. The cases of interest are thus determined by the form of G, the arrival process. Because the theory for general arrival is too complex to use in networks, the class of G is limited to special cases. In the first such case, the queue is analyzed as a birth-and-death (BD) process with a given state-dependent arrival rate and exponential service. Another, more recent approach studies arrival processes of the renewal type; this approach is characterized by the distribution function of the interarrival times, which is sufficient to define the process.

Standard methods of queuing theory can then be used to compute the distribution of busy servers in the group — in particular, the blocking probability. Because of the presence of alternate routing, this analysis is generally not sufficient, and other quantities are needed to analyze circuit-switched networks.

In the simplest case, the so-called *responsive system* case, the number of servers is infinite. Even if the analysis for finite N turns out to be too difficult or cumbersome to use, the results available for the infinite case often can be used instead. This is related to the notion of *offered traffic*, another way to characterize the arrival process that is often used in studying of circuit switching. For a $G/M/N/\infty/N$ queue, the offered traffic is defined as follows. First, imagine a parallel system of infinite capacity associated with the real system of size N. Whenever a call arrives at the real system, another call is set up in the parallel system. The actual holding time for the parallel call is drawn from an exponential distribution with the same mean as for the real calls, but independently of the actual holding time of the real calls. The offered-traffic process is the process whose state variable is the number of calls in progress on the parallel group at time t; the offered traffic is defined as the mean of this process. The calculation of the moments of the offered-traffic distribution plays an important role in network analysis, the reason why so much attention is given to the responsive system in forthcoming sections.

Because of the routing algorithms generally used in circuit-switched networks, customers blocked on one system are frequently routed to another system, where they attempt to be served. This process, called *overflow*, is a feature of virtually all circuit-switched networks. Because these blocked calls are being sent to some other part of the network, they also contribute to the arrival process of some other groups. Thus, in addition to the analysis of the $G/M/N/\infty/N$ queue, a great deal of attention must be paid to the *overflow* process, that is, the process generated by calls that cannot be accepted on the system.

Similarly, customers that can be served on a group often must attempt to obtain service in additional groups before their service period begins — for instance, whenever a call must traverse two or more links in tandem in order to reach its destination. This situation also contributes to the arrival process of other links, posing some additional difficulties that are discussed shortly. Unfortunately, the theory for carried calls in tandem is not nearly as developed as for the corresponding case of overflow.

The chapter is organized as follows. First, we examine the simplest case for $G = M$, that is, the Poisson arrival. The behavior of this system is well known and can be derived from elementary queuing theory. A detailed discussion of the overflow process is also presented, since overflow is better known and is the basis for many heuristics.

Then, because of the alternate routing of blocked calls and the multilink routing of accepted calls, we consider the case of non-Poisson arrivals. Needless to say, this theory is much more difficult, and the analytic results much more complex. Two classes of queues are considered, depending on the nature of their arrival processes. For state-dependent arrival rates, we use the methods of birth-and-death processes, while, for an arrival process of the general renewal type, we can rely on the known results of the $GI/M/N/\infty/N$ queue. In some cases, these processes can be characterized exactly in terms of the moments of the offered traffic. We compute the congestion probability, and in some cases the parameters of the overflow and carried processes. Finally, we introduce the notion of conserved flows, discussing in depth their relation to the queuing models presented previously and their possible use in network analysis.

This leads to the second part of the chapter, where we explain how the models based on queuing theory are used in actual problems for non-Poisson arrivals. Particular emphasis is placed on the characterization of processes by the offered traffic and on moment-matching techniques, which are the most frequently used network analysis methods. We see under what conditions the queuing models can be used to represent a traffic characterized by a small number of moments. We then consider the possibility of inverting nonlinear systems and the computational efficiency of these techniques.

Finally, we look at the traffic problems arising from the fact that the traffic offered to a link is a superposition of various streams, each having its own history. Models for the calculation of individual stream blocking are reviewed, with an emphasis on the simplifying assumptions required to make these models work. In addition, practical methods usable in large networks are described.

The following symbols are introduced in this chapter:

N = The number of servers in the group.

p_n = The stationary probability of being in state n.

$\overline{n}$ = The average value of n. When the group is finite, this is called the *carried* traffic and is denoted by $\overline{M}$. When the calls are offered to an infinite group, this is called the *offered traffic* and is denoted by M. M can also be defined as the expected number of arrivals during an average holding time.

E = The time congestion, simply $P(N)$. This is the fraction of the time when all the servers are busy. We say that the system is in the *blocked* state, and calls finding the system in that state are said to be blocked. From the point of view of traffic theory, calls that are blocked are lost and do not return. In practice, in a network, blocked calls may be sent to other groups, where they appear as requests for service.

B = The call congestion. This is the probability that an arriving call will find the system in state N. Note that, for a general arrival process, $E \neq B$.

M, V, Z = Mean, variance, and peakedness of distributions, respectively. The peakedness is defined as $Z = V/M$. Processes are said to be *peaked* or *smooth* according to whether $Z > 1$ or $Z < 1$, respectively. The M, V notation is used to emphasize the non-Poisson character of the traffic. Unless otherwise noted, a Poisson traffic is denoted by the symbol A.

$\alpha_q, \mu_q, M_q, \beta_q$ = The qth moment, central moment, factorial moment, and binomial moment of a distribution p, respectively.

Several other conventions are also used when representing traffic. Quantities dealing with overflow are of the form $\hat{x}$, while the corresponding quantities for carried traffic are of the form $\overline{x}$. It is sometimes necessary to distinguish a distribution at an arbitrary time from the corresponding distribution seen by a call arriving in the system. Variables have an asterisk in the first case, and none in the second. For instance, β_q^* denotes the qth binomial moment of the busy-circuit distribution at an arbitrary instant of time, and $\overline{M}_1$ denotes the first factorial moment of the distribution of busy circuits at the time of a call arrival.

3.1 Poisson Arrivals

The first system we analyze consists of a group of N servers offered calls according to a Poisson process. Many of the results discussed here are well known, although some are limited to the area of teletraffic. Our main purpose is to illustrate how the standard questions concerning traffic models have been answered in the simplest case, also showing the limitation of these techniques. First, we characterize the process, in terms of both its arrival rate and the interarrival time distribution, and introduce the notion of Poisson traffic. Next, we compute the congestion functions, characterizing the overflow and carried processes in terms of the distribution of busy circuits in a group of infinite size.

Characterization of the Poisson System

The Poisson system is a system where service requests arrive according to a Poisson process and where the service times have a negative exponential distribution. The Poisson process has some interesting properties, some of which we now recall.

This process is a pure birth process with an arrival rate λ independent of the system state, an initial state labeled 0 and a final, absorbing state labeled

N which may be at infinity. We compute the probability of having k customers in the system at time t when there is no finite absorbing state by the standard equation (A.14); we get

$$\frac{dp_k(t)}{dt} = -\lambda p_k(t) + \lambda p_{k-1}(t), \quad k \geq 1$$
$$\frac{dp_0(t)}{dt} = \lambda p_0(t)$$

These equations can be solved recursively, yielding

$$p_j(t) = e^{-\lambda t} \frac{(\lambda t)^j}{j!}. \tag{3.1}$$

We can readily compute the generating function

$$G(z) = \sum_{k=0}^{\infty} p_k(t) z^k$$
$$= e^{\lambda t(z-1)}.$$

If we let $N(t)$ represent the number of customers in the system at time t, we can compute the mean $\overline{N}(t)$ and the variance $\sigma^2(t)$ of $N(t)$ from $G(z)$ as

$$\overline{N}(t) = \lambda t$$
$$\sigma^2(t) = \lambda t$$

which is an important property of Poisson processes.

The Poisson process has other interesting properties; one is the fact that the interval between arrivals has a negative exponential distribution. Let τ be the random variable that represents the time between arrivals, and $A(t)$ and $a(t)$ its distribution and density functions. Since $A(t)$ is the distribution of interarrival times, we have

$$A(t) = 1 - Pr(\tau > t).$$

$Pr(\tau > t)$ is the probability that there is no arrival before t, and is given by

$$Pr(\tau > t) = 1 - p_0(t).$$

Replacing in Eq. (3.1) for $j = 0$, we have

$$A(t) = 1 - e^{-\lambda t}, \quad t \geq 0$$

and the density

$$a(t) = \lambda e^{-\lambda t}.$$

Thus we see that the specification of an arrival rate fixes the interarrival time distribution of the Poisson process — in the present case, the negative exponential.

Let us now return to the Poisson system, which we have defined as a birth-and-death process with Poisson arrivals and independent negative exponential holding times. It is defined mathematically by taking $\lambda_k = \lambda$ — that is, as a state-independent arrival rate — and a linear departure process with $\mu_k = k\mu$. In terms of queuing theory, the system is described by a $M/M/\infty/\infty$ queue. We can solve Eq. (A.14) for this case and obtain the stationary probability of having j customers in the system:

$$p_j = e^{-A} \frac{A^j}{j!}$$

$$A \triangleq \frac{\lambda}{\mu}.$$

From this, we get the first two moments of the busy-circuit distribution:

$$M = V = A$$

Recall that the offered traffic corresponding to an arrival process is character-ized by the moments of the busy-server distribution in an infinite system. We say that an offered traffic is a *Poisson traffic* whenever its mean is equal to its variance. We see from the preceding results that a Poisson traffic is pro-duced when the arrival process is a Poisson process (and of course when the holding times are exponentially distributed). The peakedness $Z = 1$ is an im-portant feature of the Poisson traffic that severely limits the use of this traffic as a model for call arrivals, since this feature applies only to an arrival process whose mean is equal to its variance.

Congestion Functions

A group of size $N < \infty$ is modeled as an $M/M/N/N$ queue. The distribution of busy servers can be found by noting that the BD equation has the same form as in the infinite case, but with the added condition that $p_k = 0$ whenever $k > N$. The state probabilities still have the form $p_k = p_0 A^k / k!$, but the normalization condition is different since it is only a partial sum from 0 to N. Thus the state probability distribution is given by the truncated Poisson distribution

$$p_k = \frac{A^k/k!}{\sum_{i=0}^{N} A^i/i!} \qquad (3.2)$$
$$= \frac{A^k/k!}{e_N(A)},$$

where the function $e_N(A) = \sum_{j=0}^{N} A^j/j!$ is called the *incomplete exponential function*. The probability that all the servers are busy, given by the well-known Erlang B function,

$$E(A, N) = \frac{A^N/N!}{e_N(A)}, \qquad (3.3)$$

is the time congestion of the system. In the present case, this probability is also the call congestion because of the exponential distribution of arrivals, which is memoryless. A useful relation is

$$\frac{1}{E(A, N)} = 1 + \left(\frac{N}{A}\right)\frac{1}{E(A, N-1)}, \tag{3.4}$$

which can be used for the evaluation of $E(A, N)$ over integers, and which is numerically stable. Although the recursive formula (3.4) is quite sufficient for small integer values, it becomes too time consuming when a large group must be evaluated; it probably should not be used as is within network-design algorithms if numerical efficiency is important. The question of efficient algorithms for the numerical evaluation of the Erlang B function is somewhat complex, and considering it would lead us far outside the scope of this discussion. We therefore refer the interested reader to the methods described in [4].

As we see later, it is often necessary to generalize the Erlang B function to fractional values, especially when dimensioning networks. The function can be extended to the complex half-plane by

$$E(A, N)^{-1} = A \int_0^\infty e^{-Ay}(1+y)^N dy, \quad \text{Re } A > 0 \tag{3.5}$$

The mathematical properties of this function and its derivatives have been studied extensively by Jagerman [5].

Overflow Process

We have characterized the Poisson process and computed its congestion functions. Remember, however, that blocked calls generally appear as requests for service somewhere else in the network. For this reason, we must characterize this overflow process. We do this via the distribution of busy circuits in the infinite group, which corresponds to the definition of offered traffic.

Following Kosten [6], we use the BD approach. The calls that are blocked in the primary group are offered to a secondary group of infinite size; we are interested in the nature of this arrival process. Although we wish to consider the distribution in the secondary group, the number of customers in this system alone is not sufficient to define a state of the Markov chain. Such a state can be defined only if we consider *both* the primary and secondary groups at the same time, which leads us to the study of a two-dimensional process — a fundamental limitation of the BD approach in the study of overflow. Nevertheless, because of the relative simplicity of the system, it is possible to solve the Kolmogorov equations exactly for the combined primary and secondary group, from which various quantities of interest can be derived. Because of their fundamental importance in practical situations, these equations are derived following a method proposed by Riordan as described in [6].

The joint probability distribution $p_{n,m}$ of having n busy servers in a primary group of size N, and m in a secondary group of infinite size is found by writing the equilibrium equations with $A = \lambda/\mu$:

$$(A + n + m)p_{n,m} - (n+1)p_{n+1,m}$$
$$- (m+1)p_{n,m+1} - Ap_{n-1,m} = 0 \qquad (3.6)$$
$$(A + N + m)p_{N,m} - Ap_{N,m-1}$$
$$- (m+1)p_{N,m+1} - Ap_{N-1,m} = 0 \qquad (3.7)$$

Once again, these equations can be written by inspecting the state-transition diagram to and from state (n, m). Because we are interested in the distribution of customers in the secondary system, we concentrate on the calculation of the factorial moments of this distribution, given that there are n customers in the primary group. For these moments, and for fixed n, we define the generating function

$$M(n, z) = \sum_{k=0}^{\infty} M_k(n) \frac{z^k}{k!}$$
$$= \sum_{k=0}^{\infty} (1 + z)^k p_{n,k}$$

This last relation is replaced in Eqs. (3.6) and (3.7), which then become differential equations for $M(n, z)$:

$$(A + n + \frac{d}{dz})M(n, z) - (n+1)M(n+1, z) - AM(n-1, z) = 0$$
$$(N - Az + z\frac{d}{dz})M(N, z) - AM(N-1, z) = 0$$

Replacing with the definition of the generating function, and equating equal powers of z, we obtain a recurrence relation for the factorial moments:

$$(A + n + k)M_k(n) - (n+1)M_k(n+1) - AM_k(n-1) = 0 \qquad (3.8)$$
$$(N + k)M_k(N) - AkM_{k-1}(N) - AM_k(N-1) = 0 \qquad (3.9)$$

Equations (3.8) and (3.9) form a recurrence on n and can be solved by introducing another generating function:

$$F_j(y) \triangleq \sum_{n=0}^{\infty} M_j(n)y^n.$$

Using Eq. (3.8), we once again obtain a differential equation for F,

$$\left[A + k - Ay + (y - 1)\frac{d}{dy}\right] F_k(y) = 0,$$

which can be integrated to yield

$$F_k(y) = Ce^{Ay}(1-y)^{-k},$$ (3.10)

where C is an integration constant given by the condition

$$C = M_k(0).$$

Having the expression for $F_k(y)$, we can expand the right-hand side of Eq. (3.10) to get the moments directly:

$$M_k(n) = M_k(0)S(n,k),$$ (3.11)

where $S(n,k)$ is the Brockmeyer polynomial (see [7]). The moments are uniquely determined from Eq. (3.11) up to the values $M_k(0)$; they can be calculated from Eq. (3.9) and the normalizing condition $\sum_{k=0}^{N} M_k(0) = 1$. We have

$$[(N+k)S(N,k) - AS(N-1,k)] M_k(0) = AkS(N,k-1)M_{k-1}(0),$$

and using the recurrence relations

$$(N+k)S(N,k) - AS(N-1,k) = (N+k-A)S(N,k) + A\,[S(N,k) - S(N-1,k)]$$
$$= (N+k-A)S(N,k) + AS(N,k-1)$$
$$= kS(N,k+1)$$

we obtain finally

$$M_k(0) = A\frac{S(N,k-1)}{S(N,k+1)}M_{k-1}(0)$$
$$= A^k\frac{S(N,1)S(N,0)}{S(N,k+1)S(N,k)}M_0(0)$$

After using the normalization condition, we obtain

$$M_k(n) = A^k\frac{S(N,0)S(n,k)}{S(N,k+1)S(N,k)}$$

and the moments of the distribution in the secondary group:

$$M_k = A^k\frac{S(N,0)}{S(N,k)}.$$

From the moments, we immediately obtain the joint state probability

$$p_{n,m} = \sum_{j=m}^{\infty}(-1)^{j-m}\binom{j}{m}\frac{A^j}{j!}\frac{R(N,0)R(n,j)}{R(N,j+1)R(N,j)}.$$

The marginal distribution in the primary group is the Erlang B distribution, while the marginal distribution in the secondary group is given by

$$p_m = \sum_{j=m}^{\infty}(-1)^{j-m}\binom{j}{m}\frac{A^j}{j!}\frac{R(N,0)}{R(N,j)}.$$ (3.12)

From this distribution, all the moments of the traffic can be computed. Of particular interest are the mean M and the variance V of the traffic carried in the secondary group, which are the required characterization of the overflow process and are of fundamental importance in many applications. They are given by

$$M = AE(A, N) \tag{3.13}$$

$$V = M \left(1 - M + \frac{A}{(N + 1 - A + M)} \right) \tag{3.14}$$

Although not obvious from Eq. (3.14), the peakedness of the overflow traffic is always greater than one — an important point for the study of overflow systems with peaked offered traffic. From this follows the conclusion that the overflow process is not Poisson.

Carried Processes for Poisson Arrivals

A complete study of Poisson arrivals requires knowledge of the carried process, of which we have a complete description by the probability distribution (3.2). From this, we obtain the generating function and the first two moments of the carried traffic:

$$G(z) = \frac{e_N(Az)}{e_N(A)}$$

$$\overline{M} = A(1 - E(A, N)) \tag{3.15}$$

$$\overline{V} = \overline{M} - A(N - \overline{M})E_N \tag{3.16}$$

The derivation is left as an exercise (Problem 3.1). Note that, for the carried traffic, we always have $\overline{Z} < 1$, another indication that this process is not Poisson either.

3.2   Other State-Dependent Arrival Processes

Since traffic flows inside a network are not Poisson in general, let us now consider other arrival processes. First, we review some frequently used models that can be analyzed with the two-dimensional BD methods that have state-dependent arrival rates. We characterize the arrival process and congestion functions, but in most cases do not characterize the overflow and the carried process explicitly.

Overflow Arrivals

As we have emphasized, traffic that overflows from a link is not lost, but is often offered to some other link in a network. It seems reasonable, then, to examine in the first place a link where the arrival process is precisely the overflow from a group of size N being offered Poisson traffic. As we already saw, analysis of the Kosten system gives the moments of the distribution of blocked calls in a group of infinite size, that is, characterizes the offered traffic when it is produced by overflow. We wish to analyze *this* traffic when it is offered to a group of size L, that is, its congestion function and the characterization of *its* overflow.

This amounts to a Kosten-like system where the secondary group is now of finite size L. In this case, we are interested in the busy-circuit distribution in the secondary group, as well as the distribution of the traffic that overflows from it onto a group of infinite size.

This system was analyzed by Brockmeyer [6,7], who gives a complete solution for the joint state probability in the primary and secondary groups. The solution technique is virtually identical to the one for the Kosten system, with some minor modifications of the state equation to take into account the finite size of the secondary group. For this reason, we do not go into a detailed derivation here, only quoting the main results. The actual derivation is left as an exercise (see Problem 3.5). The joint probability of having n busy servers in the primary and l in the secondary group is given by

$$p_{n,l} = \sum_{j=0}^{L-l}(-1)^j \binom{l+j}{l} S(n-j, l+j) p_{0,l+j} \tag{3.17}$$

$$p_{0,l} = \frac{1}{S(N+L,1)} \sum_{k=l}^{L}(-1)^{k-l} \binom{k-1}{l-1} \frac{1}{S(N,k)} \sum_{l=k}^{L} \binom{l-1}{k-1} S(N+l,0)$$

$$p_{0,0} = \frac{1}{S(N+L,1)}$$

The marginal state distribution for the secondary system is given by

$$p_l = \sum_{j=0}^{L-l}(-1)^j \binom{l+j}{l} S(N-j, l+1+j) p_{0,l+j}, \tag{3.18}$$

from which the mean and variance of the traffic carried in a finite group offered calls produced by an overflow source are given by

$$\overline{M} = A(E_N - E_{N+L}) \tag{3.19}$$

$$\overline{V} = A\left[\frac{A(E_N - E_{N+L})}{N+1-A(1-E_N)} - LE_{N+L}\right] + \overline{M}(\overline{M}-1) \tag{3.20}$$

Note that these formulas reduce to Eqs. (3.13) and (3.14) of the Kosten system whenever $L \to \infty$. In this case, it is not obvious whether the traffic carried in the secondary group is smooth or peaked. The time and call congestions for the secondary group are given by

$$E = E_{N+L} \frac{S(N, L+1)}{S(N, L)} \tag{3.21}$$

$$B = \frac{E_{N+L}}{E_N} \tag{3.22}$$

As for the characterization of the traffic blocked on the secondary system, note that the distribution of the overflow is nothing but the distribution of overflow from a Kosten system of size $N + L$, and as such poses no difficulty. One gets

$$\hat{M} = AE(A, N + L) \tag{3.23}$$

$$\hat{V} = \hat{M} \left(1 - \hat{M} + \frac{A}{N + L + 1 - A(1 - E(A, N + L))} \right) \tag{3.24}$$

As expected, the second overflow from the primary group is also peaked, and cannot be represented by a Poisson process. This is about as far as we can go in the sequence of overflows. Calculating the overflow of this traffic would require a three-dimensional BD process, which would probably be of little practical use because of its complexity. Instead, let us now analyze other arrival processes, the usefulness of which will become apparent when we consider approximate methods in Section 3.4.

Linear Arrival Rates

Consider an arrival process defined by a linear arrival rate:

$$\lambda_k = [\alpha + (k - \alpha)\beta]$$
$$\mu_k = k\mu$$

The usefulness of this process was pointed out first by Wilkinson [6], who noted that the distribution of busy circuits in a lightly loaded group receiving overflow traffic was closely approximated by a Pascal distribution, also known as a *negative binomial distribution*. We now show that the linear arrival rate does yield such a distribution and, as such, might be used to model the arrival process corresponding to overflow traffic. Replacing in Eq. (A.16), we get, after some simple algebraic manipulations,

$$p_k = p_0 \left(\frac{\beta}{\mu} \right)^k \frac{1}{k!} a(a+1) \dots (a + k - 1), \tag{3.25}$$

where

$$a \triangleq \frac{\alpha}{\beta}(1 - \beta).$$

The value of the normalization constant is easily obtained by the use of Eq. (A.3), yielding

$$p_k = \frac{1}{\left(1 - \frac{\beta}{\mu}\right)^{-a}} \left(\frac{\beta}{\mu}\right)^k \frac{a(a+1)\ldots(a+k-1)}{k!}. \tag{3.26}$$

This distribution can be identified as the Pascal distribution by noting that

$$\frac{x(x+1)\ldots(x+k-1)}{k!} = \binom{x+k-1}{k}.$$

The Pascal distribution can be obtained for integer x as the probability distribution for the waiting time in a sequence of Bernouilli trials with success probability p. It is written as

$$p_k = \binom{n+k-1}{k}p^n q^k, \quad p+q = 1, \quad 0 < p < 1$$

and has the first two moments

$$E(x) = \frac{nq}{p}, \quad var(x) = \frac{nq}{p^2}$$

If we identify $q = \beta/\mu$, $a = n$, and $p = 1 - \beta/\mu$, and set $\mu = 1$, the first two moments are expressed simply as

$$M = \alpha \tag{3.27}$$

$$V = \frac{\alpha}{1 - \beta} \tag{3.28}$$

As seen from these expressions, we must have $\alpha \geq 0$ and $0 < \beta < 1$ when $\mu = 1$ to ensure that the parameters do not become negative. We also see that the Pascal distribution can be used to represent peaked traffic only, but that the value of peakedness can be arbitrary as long as it is larger than one. A final advantage of the Pascal distribution is that it is very simple to compute the distribution parameters from the moments, that is, to invert Eqs. (3.27) and (3.28). This fact is of considerable importance for the use of the Pascal model in approximate methods.

Given that the negative binomial distribution can model an arbitrary peaked process (at least up to the first two moments), we might ask whether a similar process could be used to represent a smooth traffic, that is, one having $z \leq 1$. Since the negative binomial distribution is related to peaked arrivals, we might suspect that the ordinary binomial distribution is what we need for smooth processes. The answer to this question is left as an exercise (Problem 3.4), where it is shown that the standard binomial distribution can indeed be used for smooth traffic, but with some restrictions. Within these restrictions, the binomial distributions, both negative and standard, provide a unified framework with which to model non-Poisson traffic, the main reason these distributions have been so popular in network analysis.

In principle, the overflow process could be calculated in the same way as for the Kosten system. The only difference would be to replace the original Poisson arrival rate by the linear rate and to solve the Kolmogorov equations. This seems not to have been done, however; the Pascal distribution has been used mostly in the area of approximations.

Balking Systems

An implicit assumption in the BD analysis of queues is that a customer arriving in the queue and finding a free server will immediately enter service. These systems are called *full availability* for obvious reasons. In some cases, however, this assumption is not really justified: A customer may find a free server but not enter service, and is lost. In this case, we say that the system has *limited availability*, and that there is a nonzero probability of *balking*. Such systems occur quite frequently in networks; the simplest example is the case of two links in series where a call must find a free server on both links in order to begin service. If there is a free server on the first link and none on the second, an analysis of the first link taken in isolation would describe this link as a limited-availability system in order to take into account the presence of the second link.

In general, the balking probability is state dependent, and analyzing it is quite complex since the probability depends on the particular form of this dependence. One simple case, however, offers some insight into the operation of limited availability systems: where the balking probability β is independent of the state of the system. Assuming a Poisson arrival of rate λ, the BD model can be used with an arrival rate

$$\lambda_k = \begin{cases} \lambda(1-\beta) & \text{if } k \leq N \\ 0 & \text{otherwise} \end{cases}$$
$$\mu_k = \begin{cases} k\mu & \text{if } k \leq N \\ 0 & \text{otherwise} \end{cases}$$

The analysis proceeds exactly as for the Poisson case. The state probability is

$$p_k = p_0 \frac{[A(1-\beta)]^k}{k!},$$

where as usual $A = \lambda/\mu$. In other words, we find the truncated Poisson distribution, but with a reduced arrival rate $A(1-\beta)$, that is, with an offered traffic that is reduced by the balking probability. Returning to the simple case of two links in series, we can assume that $\beta = B_2$, where B_2 is the blocking probability on the second link. This is only an approximation, of course, since the balking probability is state dependent because of the correlation induced between the links by the common traffic. Nevertheless, if we make the independence assumption, then B_1, the blocking probability of the first link, becomes

$$B_1 = E[A(1 - B_2), N_1],$$

which is the apparently paradoxical result that the blocking probability and the traffic offered to the first link depend on the blocking probability on the second link. If we also note that the traffic offered to the second link depends on the blocking on the first link, we are faced with our first encounter with a recurrent problem in the analysis of networks. The two-link system, even with the independence assumption, is described in terms of a set of two nonlinear equations, and knowledge of the blocking probability requires this system to be solved. This topic is discussed in depth in Chapter 4, where numerous methods for the analysis of complex systems are proposed.

The apparent paradox resides in the picture of the offered traffic as a flow that is thinned sequentially as it passes from one link to the next. This situation is only a result of the decomposition of the path into two presumably independent components and of the attempt to take into account the presence of the second component when analyzing the first one. The real analysis should be done on the complete path using a three-dimensional birth-and-death process, which leads us outside the scope of this chapter. We consider the question in Chapter 4, where we look at decomposition methods for network analysis.

Throttled Arrivals

We now present *throttled arrivals*, another important BD process that is being increasingly used in networks [8]. In this system, two independent streams of Poisson traffic, say type 1 and type 2, are offered to a single group of size N. The first stream, say stream 1, can use any free server, while stream 2 can use a server only when the total number of busy servers is less than some fixed number $m \leq N$. The threshold m is called the *protection level*. The arrival rate is given by

$$\lambda_k = \begin{cases} \lambda_1 + \lambda_2 & \text{if } k < m \\ \lambda_1 & \text{otherwise} \end{cases}$$

$$\mu_k = k\mu.$$

The state probabilities, found by Eq. (A.15), are given by

$$p_k = \begin{cases} p_0 \left(\dfrac{\lambda_1 + \lambda_2}{\mu} \right)^k \dfrac{1}{k!} & \text{if } k < m \\[3ex] p_0 \dfrac{1}{n!} \dfrac{1}{(n+1)(n+2)\ldots(k)} \left(\dfrac{\lambda_1 + \lambda_2}{\mu} \right)^n \left(\dfrac{\lambda_1}{\mu} \right)^{k-n} & \text{otherwise} \end{cases}$$

In this system, p_0 is given by the ordinary normalization condition. Given the state probabilities, it is possible to compute all the moments of the traffic, in particular of the variance. Because the end result is quite complex, we do not pursue the computation of moments.

Note also that the throttled-arrivals model has two blocking probabilities of interest:

B = The probability that all of the n trunks are occupied.

B' = The probability that more than $m - 1$ trunks are busy.

These probabilities, which determine how much of the two streams will be blocked, are used in many network analysis algorithms. We have, for integer m and N [8],

$$B = p_0 \frac{a^N}{N!} (1 - r)^{N-m} \tag{3.29}$$

$$1 - B' = p_0 \sum_{j=0}^{m-1} \frac{a^j}{j!} \tag{3.30}$$

$$p_0^{-1} = \sum_{k=0}^{m} \frac{a^k}{k!} + \sum_{k=m+1}^{N} \frac{a^k}{k!} (1 - r)^{k-m} \tag{3.31}$$

where

a = Mean of total traffic offered to the group, $a = (\lambda_1 + \lambda_2)/\mu$.

r = Ratio of type two to total traffic, $r = \lambda_2/a\mu$.

m = Protection level.

This model can be used whenever we want to offer better service to one type of call, here type 1, by restricting the availability of servers to the other type of calls. This is particularly important as a way to stabilize networks operating with nonhierarchical routing.

The Interrupted Poisson Process

The interrupted Poisson process (IPP) has been used to generate non-Poisson traffic in simulations and also to evaluate network models. The calls are produced by a Poisson source of intensity λ independent of the system state. This source, however, is randomly interrupted for an interval with negative exponential distribution, and then turned on for an interval also exponentially distributed. Let

λ = The intensity of the Poisson source.

$1/\mu$ = The mean service time of the customers.

$1/\gamma$ = The mean on-time of the source.

$1/\omega$ = The mean off-time of the source.

k = The number of customers in the system.

m = The state of the switch; $m = 1$ indicates that the switch is on, while $m = 0$ indicates that it is off.

$p_{k,m}$ = The stationary probability of being in state (k, m).

We are interested in the distribution of busy servers in systems of infinite capacity, that is, in characterizing the offered traffic that can be produced by such a system.

The generating function of the occupancy distribution has been computed in [9] based on a two-dimensional Markov chain. The equilibrium equations can be written by examining the transition rates from and to state (k, m). They are written separately for the two possible values of m:

$$(k\mu + \omega)p_{k,0} = \gamma p_{k,1} + (k + 1)\mu p_{k+1,0}, \quad k \geq 0 \tag{3.32}$$

$$(k\mu + \gamma + \lambda)p_{k,1} = \omega p_{k,0} + (k + 1)\mu p_{k+1,1} + \lambda p_{k-1,1}, \quad k \geq 1 \tag{3.33}$$

$$(\gamma + \lambda)p_{0,1} = \omega p_{0,0} + \mu p_{1,1} \tag{3.34}$$

Equation (3.32) is obtained by noting that, if the switch is off ($m = 0$), the state $(k, 0)$ can be entered in only one of two ways: Either a call terminates from state $(k + 1, 0)$ (term $(k + 1)\mu p_{k+1,0}$) or the switch goes from the on to the off state with no change in the number of customers (term $\gamma p_{k,1}$). Similarly, from the state $(k, 0)$, only two other states can be entered: A call terminates from state $(k, 0)$ (term $k\mu p_{k,0}$) or the switch goes from the off to the on state with no change in the number of customer (term $\omega p_{k,0}$). The equilibrium between these flow rates out of and into state $(k, 0)$ yields Eq. (3.32). A similar argument permits the other equations to be constructed straightforwardly. The precise construction of the transition diagrams is left as an exercise (Problem 3.6).

The distribution of busy circuits is calculated by the generating function method. Let

$$G(z) = \sum_{k=0}^{\infty} p_k z^k$$
$$= G_1(z) + G_2(z),$$

where

$$G_i(z) \triangleq \sum_k p_{k,i} z^k, \quad i = 0, 1$$

and

$$p_k \triangleq p_{k,0} + p_{k,1}.$$

From this, it is obvious that $G_1(1) = \sum_k p_{k,1}$ is the probability that the switch is on, and is simply $\omega/(\gamma + \omega)$. Similarly, $G_0(1)$ is the probability that the switch is off, and is given by $\gamma/(\gamma + \omega)$. The solution technique consists of writing a differential equation for the generating function, from which one can obtain the factorial moments of the steady state distribution, as well as the probabilities themselves. Using the well-known properties of generating functions, $kp_k \longleftrightarrow zG'(z)$ and $p_{k-j} \longleftrightarrow z^j G(z)$, where the symbol $\longleftrightarrow$ means "is the transform of," we get from Eqs. (3.32) and (3.33) the coupled differential equations

$$\mu(z - 1)G_0'(z) + \omega G_0(z) - \gamma G_1(z) = 0 \qquad (3.35)$$

$$\mu(z - 1)G_1'(z) + (\gamma + \lambda - \lambda z)G_1(z) - \omega G_0(z) = 0 \qquad (3.36)$$

These equations can be uncoupled by a second derivation and substitution, yielding

$$\mu(z - 1)G_0''(z) + [\mu + \gamma + \omega - \lambda(z - 1)]\,G_0'(z) - \frac{\lambda}{\mu}\omega G_0(z) = 0 \quad (3.37)$$

$$\mu(z - 1)G_1''(z) + [\mu + \gamma + \omega - \lambda(z - 1)]\,G_1'(z)\frac{\lambda}{\mu}(\gamma + \omega)G_1(z) = 0 \quad (3.38)$$

Changing variables $x = (z - 1)(\lambda/\mu)$, we get

$$xF_0''(x) + (a - x)F_0'(x) - bF_0(x) = 0$$
$$xF_1''(x) + (a - x)F_1'(x) - (1 - b)F_1(x) = 0$$

where

$$a = 1 + \frac{\gamma + \omega}{\mu}, \quad b = \frac{\omega}{\mu}.$$

The solution to these equations is given in terms of the confluent hypergeometric function. We get

$$G(z) = \frac{\gamma}{\gamma + \omega}\,_1F_1\left[b; a; \frac{\lambda}{\mu}(z - 1)\right] + \frac{\omega}{\gamma + \omega}\,_1F_1\left[1 + b; a; \frac{\lambda}{\mu}(z - 1)\right],$$

where

$$_1F_1(x; y; z) \triangleq \sum_{k=0}^{\infty} \frac{x(x + 1)\dots(x + k - 1)z^k}{y(y + 1)\dots(y + k - 1)k!}, \qquad (3.39)$$

where the integration constants are found from the two conditions $G_1(1) = \omega/(\omega + \gamma)$ and $G_0(1) = \gamma/(\gamma + \gamma)$. Once we have the generating function, we can derive all quantities of interest from it. In particular, the factorial moments and the probabilities can be read directly from the definition of the hypergeometric functions (3.39); after setting $\mu = 1$, we get

$$M_q = \lambda^q \frac{\omega(\omega - 1)\dots(\omega + q - 1)}{(\gamma + \omega)(\gamma + \omega + 1)\dots(\gamma + \omega + q - 1)},$$

which satisfies the useful recurrence relation

$$M_{q+1} = \lambda \frac{\omega + q}{(\gamma + \omega. + q)} M_q,$$

from which we can write the distribution

$$p_m = \frac{\lambda^m}{m!} \sum_{j=m}^{\infty} \frac{(-\lambda)^{j-m}}{(j-m)!} \frac{\omega(\omega+1)\dots(\omega+j-1)}{\gamma + \omega(\gamma+\omega+1)\dots(\gamma+\omega+j-1)}.$$

The mean and the variance of this distribution are given by

$$M = A \frac{\omega}{\omega + \gamma} \tag{3.40}$$

$$V = M \left[\frac{A(\omega+1)}{(\omega+\gamma+1)} - M + 1 \right] \tag{3.41}$$

which characterize the traffic produced by an IPP generator. It is not hard to show that this traffic is always peaked if $\gamma > 0$.

Following the usual approach, we would investigate the character of the overflow and the carried traffic in a system of finite size. No formulas specifically designed for the IPP case, however, seem to exist. Instead, the parameters of such traffic are computed using the general $GI/M/N$ theory (see Section 3.3).

Most of the results obtained so far utilize techniques based on BD processes and state-dependent arrival rates. Before ending this discussion, we should mention some remarkable results due to Wallström [2], who gives a complete characterization of the offered traffic for an arrival process with an *arbitrary* state-dependent coefficient in terms of all the binomial moments of the distribution. Two classes of traffic have been examined: those where the dependence is on the total number of calls in the system, and those where the dependence is on the number of calls in the primary group only. Although these results constitute a *tour de force*, their application to network problems is somewhat limited because of the very heavy computational requirements implied by the technique. Also, the results cannot be used recursively to compute the overflow cascade since the dimension of the BD process increases with the number of overflow stages. For this reason, we believe that a full demonstration of these results, which is quite involved, would be of limited use in the present context; we refer the interested reader to reference [2].

3.3   Renewal Arrival Process

The solution of the single-overflow system with Poisson offered traffic by the BD methods, given by Kosten [10] and Brockmeyer [7], requires the use of a two-dimensional BD process. This is because the secondary group cannot be characterized only by the coefficients of the arrival process, but also depend on the state of the primary group. This fundamental factor limits the use of the BD approach in traffic models in the presence of overflow. Recall that many routing techniques allow *many* overflows for a blocked call. The exact analysis of a system of k groups operating in such a cascade requires a k-dimensional BD process, which is unmanageable for values as small as $k = 3$. The solution to this problem of cascade overflow, which has received a great deal of attention over the years, requires a new approach to teletraffic, one based on the theory of renewal stochastic processes. The results obtained this way are theoretically important because they give a complete solution to an arbitrary cascade of overflows, provided the first arrival process is a renewal process. These results, although not easily used in network calculations as such, provide a new collection of traffic models that are used in approximate methods such as those discussed in Section 3.4.

For these reasons, we now present results for the case when the traffic offered to a group of N servers is described by an arbitrary renewal process, with an exponential service time of mean $1/\mu$. A short derivation of the basic results from renewal theory can be found in Section A.3.

Congestion Functions and Carried Traffic

First, let us consider the distribution of busy servers in the group. Because of the independence of interarrival times, some time instants play an important role in the analysis of the $GI/M/N/N$ queue. These time instants occur when a new call arrives, since the evolution of the system after that time is independent of the previous history of the process. These points, called *regeneration points*, are labeled t_r.

The process of interest, denoted N_r, is the number of busy circuits when the rth call arrives. If t_0 is a regeneration point, the renewal property means that $Pr\{N(t_r) \mid N(t_0)\} = Pr\{N(t) \mid N(\tau) \ \forall \ \tau \leq t_0\}$. That is, there is an embedded Markov chain defined by the process N_r corresponding to the arrivals. A great deal of information can be learned from this Markov chain, in particular, the value of p_j, the stationary probability of being in state j at the time a call arrives in the system.

The calculation of the probabilities is straightforward if we have the transition matrix $Q_{i,j}$, the transition probability from i to j. We have

$$Q_{i,j} = Pr\{N_{r+1} = j \mid N_r = i\}$$

$Q_{i,j}$ is the conditional probability that an arriving call sees j busy circuits, given that the preceding call saw i busy circuits when it arrived. This expression can be evaluated using standard results for the age of an interval under renewal input. Immediately after the rth arrival, the state was $i + 1$. Just before the $r + 1^{\text{th}}$ arrival, the state was j. There must have been $i + 1 - j$ terminations during this interval. The conditional distribution of states during this interval is given by

$$Q_{i,j} = \binom{i+1}{j} \int_0^\infty e^{-\mu t j}(1 - e^{-\mu t})^{i+1-j} dF(t), \quad j - 1 \le i \le N - 1 \quad (3.42)$$

and

$$Q_{i,j} = 0, \quad i < j - 1$$
$$Q_{N,j} = Q_{N-1,j}.$$

The derivation of this equation is given in Section A.3.

We are now interested in the stationary probability of being in state j when a call arrives, which we denote p_j. This can be computed by the standard methods of Markov chains by solving the equation $\sum_{i=0}^N p_i Q_{i,j} = p_j$, with the normalization $\sum_{j=0}^N p_j = 1$ [1]. If we call $\psi(z) = \sum_{j=0}^\infty p_j z^j$ the z transform of p_j, and $\Phi(s)$ the Laplace-Stieltjes transform of $F(t)$, we have

$$\psi(z) = \sum_{j=0}^N \sum_{i=j-1}^{N-1} p_i z^j Q_{i,j} + p_N \sum_{j=0}^N z^j Q_{N,j}$$

$$= \sum_{i=0}^{N-1} p_i \sum_{j=0}^{i+1} z^j Q_{i,j} + p_N \sum_{j=0}^N z^j Q_{N,j}$$

$$= \sum_{i=0}^{N-1} p_i \int_0^\infty (1 - a + az)^{i+1} dF(t)$$

$$+ p_N \int_0^\infty (1 - a + az)^N dF(t), \quad (3.43)$$

where

$$a = e^{-\mu t}$$

We now compute the binomial moments of the distribution. We know from the properties of z transforms that

$$\beta_q \triangleq \sum_{j=q}^N \binom{j}{q} p_j$$

$$= \frac{1}{n!} \left(\frac{d^q \psi(z)}{dz^q} \right)_{z=0}$$

We differentiate Eq. (3.43) n times. For the binomial moments, we get

$$\beta_q = \Phi(q\mu) \left[\sum_{i=0}^{N-1} p_i \binom{i+1}{q} + p_N \binom{N}{q} \right]. \quad (3.44)$$

The recurrence for the coefficients is

$$[1 - \Phi(q\mu)]\beta_q = \Phi(q\mu)\beta_{q-1} - p_N \binom{N}{q-1} \Phi(q\mu), \qquad (3.45)$$

which is left as an exercise (Problem 3.11). The solution for the moments can be obtained in closed form starting the recurrence at 0. We obtain the binomial moments of the busy-circuit distribution at the time of a call arrival:

$$\overline{\beta}_i = h_i \frac{\displaystyle\sum_{j=i}^{N} \binom{N}{j}\frac{1}{h_j}}{\displaystyle\sum_{j=0}^{N} \binom{N}{j}\frac{1}{h_j}},$$

where

$$h_n = \prod_{j=1}^{n} \frac{\Phi(j\mu)}{1 - \Phi(j\mu)} \quad n \geq 1, \quad h_0 = 1$$

Given these expressions for the moments, we can get the state probabilities from Eq. (A.13), and in particular the call congestion, which is given by

$$B = p_N = \frac{1}{\displaystyle\sum_{j=0}^{N} \binom{N}{j}\frac{1}{h_j}}. \qquad (3.46)$$

The first two moments of this distribution, which is not to be confused with the carried traffic, are given by

$$\overline{\alpha}_1 = (1 - B)\frac{\Phi(\mu)}{1 - \Phi(\mu)}$$

$$\overline{\alpha}_2 = \frac{(\overline{\alpha}_1 + 1)\Phi(\mu) + \overline{\alpha}_1\Phi(2\mu) - B[\Phi(\mu) + 2N\Phi(2\mu)]}{1 - \Phi(2\mu)}.$$

Having solved the distribution of the embedded Markov chain, we can now obtain the distribution at an arbitrary instant in time and, from this, the time congestion and the distribution of carried traffic. Here, we use the asterisk superscript to emphasize that the quantities of interest refer to the distribution at an arbitrary instant in time. Let q_j be the stationary distribution of busy circuits at an arbitrary time t, Let $Q_{i,j}^*$ be the conditional probability that there are j busy circuits at time t, given that there were i busy circuits when the interval between these events began. This is the transition matrix, which can be expressed in terms of the transition matrix of the embedded Markov chain. By a similar argument, we have

$$Q_{i,j}^* = \binom{i+1}{j} \int_0^\infty (1-a)^{i+1-j} a^j \, dF^*(t), \quad j-1 \leq i \leq N-1$$

$$Q_{N,j}^* = Q_{N,j}^*$$

$$Q_{i,j}^* = 0, \quad i < j-1$$

The only difference from the Markov chain is in the expression of $F^*(t)$, the age of the interval since the last arrival. Because we are now looking at the interval at an arbitrary point in time, the value of this distribution is given by Eq. (A.24), as discussed in Section A.3.

$$F^*(t) = \lambda \int_0^t [1 - F(\tau)]d\tau$$

From this, we get

$$q_j = \sum_{i=j-1}^{N} p_i Q_{i,j}^*.$$

This is the required distribution, but it can be put in a more convenient form through the binomial moments. The calculation is the same as for the embedded Markov chain; we get

$$\overline{\beta}_i^* = \frac{A}{i}\left[\overline{\beta}_{i-1} - \binom{N}{i-1}B\right]. \tag{3.47}$$

From this, we immediately get the time congestion $E = q_N$ and the first two parameters of the carried traffic:

$$E = B\left(\frac{A}{N}\right)\frac{1 - \Phi(N\mu)}{\Phi(N\mu)}. \tag{3.48}$$

This equation establishes a general relation between the call and time congestion for arbitrary renewal input. It is not hard to show that, for Poisson arrivals, these are equal. The converse is somewhat more difficult, and is left as an exercise (Problem 3.12). The first two moments of the carried traffic are given by

$$\overline{\alpha}_1^* = \overline{M} = A(1 - B) \tag{3.49}$$

as one would expect, and

$$\overline{\alpha}_2^* = \overline{M}\left[1 - \overline{M} + h_1 - N\frac{B}{1 - B}\right]. \tag{3.50}$$

These results can be used to derive the characterization of a renewal process in terms of the first moment of the traffic carried in a group of infinite size, in other words, the parameters of the offered traffic generated by the renewal process. This is done by taking $N \to \infty$ in Eqs. (3.45) and (3.47); we get, respectively,

$$\beta_n = h_n \tag{3.51}$$

$$\beta_n^* = A\frac{h_{n-1}}{n} \tag{3.52}$$

From these values, we can compute the mean and variance of the offered traffic corresponding to F (i.e., the parameters of the traffic carried in the infinite group):

$$M = M_1^* = -\frac{1}{\mu \Phi'(0)} = A \tag{3.53}$$

$$V = M_2^* - (M_1^*)^2 = M \left(\frac{1}{1 - \Phi(\mu)} - M \right) \tag{3.54}$$

Note that Eq. (3.53) is in fact a theorem. It states that the expected number of busy circuits in the infinite group is precisely the intensity of the input stream. This point is generally taken for granted, since circuit occupancy is commonly used to measure input traffic, but nevertheless can be demonstrated mathematically.

As we said before, some calls accepted for service on the link may require service from other links in order to establish a connection to their destination. In this sense, the carried process can be viewed as the arrival process to some other link, just as was the case for overflow. Let us therefore end this discussion of the carried traffic by computing the interarrival time distribution of the carried calls. We follow the method described in [11]. As usual, let $F(t)$ be the distribution of interarrival times and $F_c(t)$ the distribution of the interval τ_n between a call accepted at t_n and the next accepted call. Let $N(t)$ be the number of calls in progress at time t. Then,

$$F_c(t) = Pr \left\{ \tau_n \leq t \mid N(t_n^-) < N \right\}.$$

We must consider separately two cases immediately after t_n. After the call is accepted, the group may be full or some free circuit may still be available. Corresponding to these two cases, we define

$$F_c[t \mid N(t_n^+) < N] = Pr \left\{ \tau_n \leq t \mid N(t_n^+) < N \right\}$$
$$\overline{F}_c(t) = Pr \left\{ \tau_n \leq t \mid N(t_n^+) = N \right\}$$

Now, if the group is not full after the call is accepted, the interarrival distribution is just given by

$$F_c[t \mid N(t_n^+) < N] = F(t),$$

so that

$$F_c(t) = F(t) \left[1 - \frac{p_{N-1}}{1 - p_N} \right] + \overline{F}_c(t) \left[\frac{p_{N-1}}{1 - p_N} \right],$$

where p_j is the probability that an arriving call will see j busy circuits. In particular, p_N is the call congestion as defined in Eq. (3.46). We can now take the Laplace-Stieltjes transform of the equation, and get

$$\Phi_c(s) = \Phi(s) \left[1 - \frac{p_{N-1}}{1 - p_N} \right] + \overline{\Phi}_c(t) \left[\frac{p_{N-1}}{1 - p_N} \right]. \tag{3.55}$$

The only element missing from this equation is the value of $\overline{\Phi}(s)$, the transform of the interarrival distribution to the next accepted call when the currently accepted call saturates the group. The derivation of this expression can be found in [12]; it is reproduced here without derivation. We have

$$\overline{\Phi}_c(s) = [1 - \Phi(s)] \int_0^\infty e^{-st} H(t) dM(t),$$

where $H(t) = 1 - e^{-Nt}$ and $M(t)$ is the expected number of arrivals in the interval $(0, t)$. Note the dependence of the distribution on the terms p_N and p_{N-1}. This dependence means that the interarrival times depend on the state of the system, and that the process is not a renewal process. As a consequence, we cannot use this distribution to characterize completely the traffic offered to the second link in a path. We see later that this is an important difference between the carried and overflow processes.

Let us now pause to consider what has been achieved. We assumed that the arrival process to a group of size $N \le \infty$ is an arbitrary renewal process. From this, we gave a complete description of the busy-circuit distribution in the group, in terms of both probabilities and moments. The case of the infinite group was handled as a special case; its importance will become clearer when we discuss moment-matching methods in Section 3.4.

Overflow Traffic

The next step in the study of the $GI/M/N/N$ queue is to characterize the overflow process. A very important result from the renewal approach is a complete solution to the overflow cascade. In this system, a first group of finite size is offered Poisson traffic or, more generally, an arbitrary renewal stream. Blocked calls are then offered to a second group of finite size, the overflow of which is offered to a third, and so on. While the analysis of such a system by BD methods becomes intractable very rapidly as the amount of overflow increases, the renewal method gives a recursive approach that allows a complete solution for an arbitrary number of overflows. The main advantage of the renewal method over the BD technique is that the same formulas can be used at any stage, although the actual expressions can become quite complex. Even though they generally cannot be written analytically, it is possible to have a numerical evaluation procedure that is the *same* at all stages, which is not possible with the BD approach.

To do this, we simply realize that if the input to the primary group is renewal, then the input to the secondary group is also renewal, and so on for all the groups in the cascade. This is why we want to compute the distribution function of the interarrival times of the overflow process from the knowledge of the distribution of the input interarrival times. Let us now proceed to do this, following Pearce and Potter [13]. We also give a complete characterization of the overflow distribution.

Define $F_n(t)$, the distribution function for the time interval T separating the following two events — first, at the time when a call arrives and finds n busy circuits and, second, at the time of the next overflow. We write a set of integral equations for this distribution. Consider the system immediately after the call is accepted: There are $n + 1$ calls in the system. Let Y be the interval of time starting immediately after the call is accepted during which there is no arrival. This random variable has a distribution $F(y)$, the interarrival distribution. During Y, there can be between 0 and $n+1$ call terminations. Because the calls in progress are independent, the probability of j terminations has a Bernouilli distribution with parameter $a = \exp(-\mu y)$. At the end of the interval, we are in state j, and calls start arriving. From this point on, the distribution of the interval to the next overflow is by definition $F_j(t - y)$. The event that the interval T is no greater than t is then the convolution of two events: The Y interval is no larger than y, and the state after Y is j. This is written

$$F_n(t) = \sum_{j=0}^{n+1} \int_0^t \binom{n+1}{j}(1-a)^{n+1-j}a^j F_j(t-y)dF(y), \ 0 \le n \le N \quad (3.56)$$

which is the set of required integral equations. We are interested in the interarrival time distribution of blocked calls. The interval between two overflows has a distribution that is the distribution between two consecutive arrivals that find N busy servers. If we call this distribution $G(t)$, we have

$$G(t) = \sum_{j=0}^{N} \int_0^t \binom{N}{j}(1-a)^{N-j}a^j F_j(t-y)dF(y),$$

which requires the calculation of the $F_j(t)$s.

We must compute this distribution or, more simply, its Laplace-Stieltjes transform. Let $\Psi_n(s)$ be the Laplace-Stieltjes transform of $F_n(t)$. Using the fact that the transform of a convolution is the product of the transforms of the individual distributions, Eq. (3.56) becomes, for $0 \le n \le N$ and Re $s \ge 0$,

$$\Psi_n(s) = \sum_{j=0}^{n+1} \Psi_j(s) \int_0^\infty e^{-st}\binom{n+1}{j}(1-a)^{n+1-j}a^j dF(t) \quad (3.57)$$

Note the condition $n \le N$ imposed on Eq. (3.57). To simplify, we remark that the solutions are the same if we lift this restriction on n but replace it with the condition that $\Psi_N(s) = 1$. Introducing the generating function,

$$\Psi(z) \stackrel{\triangle}{=} \sum_{n=0}^{\infty} \frac{\Psi_n(s)z^n}{n!}, \quad (3.58)$$

we multiply Eq. (3.57) by $z^n/n!$. Summing, we obtain

$$\Psi(z) = \sum_{j=1}^{\infty} \Psi_j(s) z^j \sum_{k=0}^{\infty} \int_0^{\infty} e^{-st} z^{k-1} \binom{k+j}{k} (1-a)^k a^j \, dF(t)$$

$$+ \Psi_0(s) \int_0^{\infty} e^{-st} (1-a) e^{z(1-a)} \, dF(t)$$

$$= \int_0^{\infty} e^{-st} \frac{d}{dz} \left\{ \Psi(az) e^{z(1-a)} \right\} dF(t)$$

$$= \int_0^{\infty} e^{-st} \frac{d}{dz} \left\{ e^z \Psi(az) e^{-az} \right\} dF(t)$$

$$= e^z \int_0^{\infty} e^{-st} \left[1 + \frac{d}{dz} \right] \left\{ \Psi(az) e^{-az} \right\} dF(t). \qquad (3.59)$$

Define

$$k(z) \overset{\triangle}{=} \Psi(z) e^{-z} \qquad (3.60)$$

Using Eq. (3.58), we get

$$k(z) = \int_0^{\infty} e^{-st} \left(1 + \frac{d}{dz} \right) k(za) dF(t),$$

which is an integral equation for $k(z)$. We can solve this by introducing yet another transform with the coefficients $k_j(s)$:

$$k(z) = \sum_{j=0}^{\infty} \frac{k_j z^n}{n!},$$

where it should be remembered that the coefficients k_j are in fact functions of s, the transform variable for t. Now replacing the value of $k(z)$ in Eq. (3.59) and setting equal the coefficients of identical powers of z, we get the recurrence relation

$$k_{n+1}(s) = k_n(s) \frac{[1 + \Phi(s + n\mu)]}{\Phi(s + (n+1)\mu)}$$

whose solution is

$$k_n(s) = k_0(s) \prod_{j=1}^{n} \frac{[1 - \Phi(s + (j-1))\mu]}{\Phi(s + j\mu)}, \qquad (3.61)$$

from which we can recover the transform

$$\Psi_n(s) = \sum_{j=0}^{n} \binom{n}{j} k_j(s). \qquad (3.62)$$

We know that $\Psi_n(s)$ is the Laplace-Stieltjes transform of $F_n(t)$. From the definition of the Laplace-Stieltjes transform, we see that $\Psi_n(0) = 1$; from Eq. (3.58), it follows that $\Psi(z) = e^z$ when $s = 0$. From Eq. (3.60), we can then conclude that $k_n(0) = \delta_{n,0}$. It can be verified that the solution where the normalization constant $k_0(s) = 1$ satisfies the original equation. The knowledge of Ψ_{N-1} is all that is needed for the distribution of intervals between overflows. Recall that Ψ_{N-1} is the transform of the distribution of the interval between the time a call arrives and finds $N - 1$ busy servers, and the time of the next overflow. After this call is accepted, however, the interval to the next overflow is statistically the same as the inter-overflow interval, whose distribution is defined as $G(t)$. We then have

$$\hat{\Phi}(s) = \frac{\displaystyle\sum_{j=0}^{N-1} \binom{N-1}{j} k_j(s)}{\displaystyle\sum_{j=0}^{N} \binom{N}{j} k_j(s)}. \tag{3.63}$$

The knowledge of the distribution of interarrival times for the overflow process is all that is needed to characterize the overflow traffic. In theory, all the moments could be computed by replacing the $\hat{\Phi}(s)$ of Eq. (3.63) in Eqs. (3.52) and (3.51), and the blocking probability could be obtained by substitution in Eqs. (3.46–3.48). The Laplace-Stieltjes transform of the overflow of *this* traffic can again be computed by Eq. (3.63), and so on recursively any number of times.

Recursive Formulation of Overflow Moments

In practice, the expressions for the moments of the overflow traffic in terms of the arrival process can become so complex that they cannot easily be used. Consider simply the calculation of the mean of the overflow traffic. To get this quantity, we need $\hat{\Phi}'(s)$. Taking the derivative at the origin of Eq. (3.63), and using the fact that $k_r(0) = \delta_{r,0}$, we get

$$\hat{\Phi}'(0) = \sum_{r=0}^{N-1} \binom{N-1}{r} k_r'(0) - \sum_{r=0}^{N} \binom{N}{r} k_r'(0)$$

$$= \sum_{r=1}^{N} \binom{N-1}{r-1} k_r'(0)$$

and, from the definition of the k_rs,

$$k_r'(0) = -\frac{\Phi'(0)}{\Phi(\mu)} \prod_{l=2}^{r} \frac{1 - \Phi[(l-1)\mu]}{\Phi(l\mu)}$$

$$= -k_{r-1}(\mu)\frac{\Phi'(0)}{\Phi(\mu)},$$

which gives

$$\hat{\Phi}'(0) = \frac{\Phi'(0)}{\Phi(\mu)}\sum_{r=0}^{N-1}\binom{N-1}{r}k_r(\mu), \qquad (3.64)$$

from which we get the mean of the overflow traffic from Eq. (3.53). In the same manner, we could compute the variance of the overflow by Eq. (3.54) with Φ replaced by $\hat{\Phi}$, but there is no simple expression in terms of the transform of the arrival process.

More useful expressions are given in [14] for the moments of the overflow traffic, and in particular for the mean and variance, directly in terms of the interarrival distribution for the traffic offered to the primary group. The recursion, given in terms of the order of the factorial moments and of the size N of the primary group, can be transformed readily into a numerical procedure. We must extend the notation for the moments to $M_q(N)$, which is the qth factorial moment of the overflow distribution when there are N circuits in the primary group. In the same way, transforms are indexed by N whenever necessary. First, we give some useful relations between the transforms of the arrival and overflow processes. The intensity of the renewal stream — none other than the mean offered traffic — is defined as $I = -1/\mu\Phi'(0)$; its inverse is called the *weakness* by Potter [14]. This inverse is denoted by w for an infinite group, in which case it represents the weakness of the offered traffic, or by W_N when we want to consider the overflow stream from a primary group of size N.

Because the weakness of the stream plays a central role in calculating the overflow moments, we first give a relation between weaknesses of input and overflow streams. From Eq. (3.64), we get the relation for the weakness:

$$W_N = -\mu\frac{\Phi'(0)}{\Phi(\mu)}\sum_{r=0}^{N-1}\binom{N-1}{r}k_r(\mu). \qquad (3.65)$$

We now use the fact that the call congestion is the ratio of the overflow mean to the offered mean, which we write as

$$B = \frac{\Phi'(0)}{\hat{\Phi}'(0)},$$

or equivalently, from Eq. (3.65),

$$B = \frac{\Phi(\mu)}{\displaystyle\sum_{r=0}^{N-1}\binom{N-1}{r}k_r(\mu)}. \qquad (3.66)$$

The call-congestion probability can also be written from Eq. (3.46) as

$$B = \frac{1}{\displaystyle\sum_{r=0}^{N} \binom{N}{r} \frac{1}{h_r(\mu)}}. \tag{3.67}$$

Combining Eqs. (3.66) and (3.67), we obtain

$$\frac{1}{\Phi(\mu)} \sum_{r=0}^{N-1} \binom{N-1}{r} k_r(\mu) = \sum_{r=0}^{N} \binom{N}{r} \frac{1}{h_r(\mu)}.$$

From this equation, the weakness of the overflow can be expressed as a function of the weakness w of the arrival process by replacing the left-hand side in Eq. (3.65), yielding

$$W_N = w \sum_{r=0}^{N} \binom{N}{r} \frac{1}{h_r(\mu)}, \tag{3.68}$$

which can be written as a recurrence for the weakness

$$\Delta^n W_N = w \sum_{r=0}^{N} \binom{N}{r} \frac{1}{h_{n+r}(\mu)}, \tag{3.69}$$

which can be proved by induction. In this equation, the operator Δ is defined as the forward difference operator. It is defined formally by the following equations:

$$\Delta^n f(n) = (E - 1)^n f(n)$$
$$E^k f(n) = f(n + k)$$
$$(E - 1)^k f(n) = \sum_{j=0}^{k} \binom{k}{j} E^k f(n)$$

Expression (3.69) provides an easy way to calculate the mean of the overflow given the transform of the arrival process by means of a recursion over the group size. In a sense, this is the generalization of the well-known recurrence of Eq. (3.4) for the Erlang B function.

We now continue the derivation of some results that will be needed in calculating all the moments of the overflow by a recurrence of the same type. From the definition of $\hat{\Phi}(s)$, and using the identity

$$\binom{n}{r-1} + \binom{n}{r} = \binom{n+1}{r},$$

we get

$$\frac{\hat{\Phi}_N(s)}{1-\hat{\Phi}_N(s)} = \frac{\sum_{r=0}^{N-1}\binom{N-1}{r}k_r(s)}{\sum_{r=0}^{N-1}\binom{N-1}{r}k_{r+1}(s)}.$$

We now use the relation

$$k_r(s+\mu) = k_{r+1}(s)\frac{\Phi(s+\mu)}{1-\Phi(s)},$$

which can be obtained directly from the definition of $k_r(s)$, to obtain

$$\hat{\Phi}_N(s+\mu) = \hat{\Phi}_N(s)\left(\frac{1-\dfrac{1}{\hat{\Phi}_N(s)}}{1-\dfrac{1}{\hat{\Phi}_{N+1}(s)}}\right). \tag{3.70}$$

Given these preliminary results, we can derive the promised recurrence equation for the moments of the overflow traffic. Setting $s = (n-1)\mu$, we have

$$\frac{1}{\hat{\Phi}_N(n\mu)} = \frac{1}{\hat{\Phi}_N((n-1)\mu)}\left[\frac{1}{\hat{\Phi}_{N+1}((n-1)\mu)}-1\right]$$

$$\times\left[\frac{1}{\hat{\Phi}_N((n-1)\mu)}-1\right]^{-1}. \tag{3.71}$$

We introduce the factorial moments in this expression by replacing $\hat{\Phi}$ in terms of the moments. Using Eq. (3.52), we get

$$\frac{1}{\hat{\Phi}_N(n\mu)} = 1 + n\frac{M_n(N)}{M_{n+1}(N)}.$$

Replacing in Eq. (3.71), we get

$$1 + n\frac{M_n(N)}{M_{n+1}(N)} = \left[1 + (n+1)\frac{M_{n+1}(N)}{M_n(N)}\right]$$

$$\times\frac{M_n(N+1)}{M_{n-1}(N)}\frac{M_n(N)}{M_n(N+1)}. \tag{3.72}$$

The general theory of renewal arrivals gives a complete characterization of an arbitrary arrival stream of the renewal type. In practice, this is used for simple arrival processes, where the computation of the carried and overflow parameters is much easier in the renewal framework. We now give two examples in which the general theory is used to describe well-known processes.

The IPP Process as a Renewal Process. As we have seen above, the description of the interrupted Poisson process as a two-dimensional Markov chain is somewhat involved, and it would be difficult to describe the overflow parameters. We now show that an arbitrary IPP process is of the renewal type; we compute its interarrival time distribution. From this, using the general theory, we immediately can find the moments of the overflow and carried traffic. We follow the method outlined in [9].

First recall some definitions:

$F(t)$ = The interarrival time distribution.

W_n = The waiting time from 0 to the nth arrival.

$H_n(t)$ = The distribution of W.

$N(t)$ = The number of arrivals from 0 to t.

$p_k(t) = P[N(t) = k]$.

$p_{km}(t)$ = The probability that there are k arrivals from 0 to t, given that there was an arrival at 0, when the switch is in state m. Recall that $m = 1$ (respectively 0) indicates that the switch is on (respectively off).

We have

$$H_n(t) = 1 - \sum_{k=0}^{n-1} p_k(t). \tag{3.73}$$

Taking the Laplace-Stieltjes transform of this equation, we get

$$h_n(s) = 1 - s \sum_{k=0}^{n-1} \pi_k(s) \tag{3.74}$$

$$h_n(s) \stackrel{\triangle}{=} \int_0^\infty e^{-st} dH_n(t),$$

$$\pi_k(s) \stackrel{\triangle}{=} \int_0^\infty e^{-st} p_k(t) dt$$

We can write a differential equation for $p_{km}(t)$ by the same techniques used to derive the stationary equations of Markov chains. We know that, in a small interval dt, the probability that the switch will go from the off state to the on state is given by ωdt. Similarly, the probability that a new customer will arrive is given by λdt. Using these arguments, we can write

$$p_{01}(t + dt) = \omega p_{00}(t) + (1 - (\lambda + \gamma)) p_{01}(t)$$

$$\frac{p_{01}(t + dt) - p_{01}(t)}{dt} = \omega p_{00}(t) - (\lambda + \gamma) p_{01}(t).$$

Letting $dt \to 0$,

$$\frac{d}{dt}p_{01}(t) = \omega p_{00}(t) - (\lambda + \gamma)p_{01}(t).$$

By a similar argument,

$$\frac{d}{dt}p_{k1}(t) = \omega p_{k0}(t) - (\lambda + \gamma)p_{k1}(t) + \lambda p_{k-1,1}(t), \quad k = 1,\dots$$

$$\frac{d}{dt}p_{k0}(t) = -\omega p_{k0}(t) + \gamma p_{k1}(t)$$

$$p_{01}(0) = 1$$

As usual, we take the Laplace transform of this set of equations:

$$s\pi_{01}(s) = \omega \pi_{00}(s) - (\lambda + \gamma)\pi_{01}(s) + 1 \tag{3.75}$$

$$s\pi_{k1}(s) = \omega \pi_{k0}(s) - (\lambda + \gamma)\pi_{k1}(s) + \lambda \pi_{k-1,1}(s), \quad k = 1,\dots \tag{3.76}$$

$$s\pi_{k0}(s) = -\omega \pi_{k0}(s) + \gamma \pi_{k1}(s) \tag{3.77}$$

where

$$\pi_{kj}(s) \triangleq \int_0^\infty e^{-st}p_{kj}(t)dt.$$

This set of difference equations can be solved readily, yielding

$$\pi_k(s) = \frac{s + \omega + \gamma}{g(s)}\left[\frac{\lambda(s+\omega)}{g(s)}\right]^k, \quad k = 1,\dots \tag{3.78}$$

$$g(s) \triangleq s^2 + (\lambda + \gamma + \omega)s + \lambda\omega$$

Replacing in Eq. (3.74), we have

$$h_n(s) = \left[\frac{\lambda(s+\omega)}{g(s)}\right]^n, \quad n = 1,\dots$$

and taking the inverse transform, we get the required distribution

$$F(t) = k_1(1 - e^{-r_1 t}) + k_2(1 - e^{-r_2 t}), \tag{3.79}$$

where

$$r_1 = \frac{1}{2}\left[\lambda + \omega + \gamma + \sqrt{(\lambda + \omega + \gamma)^2 - 4\lambda\omega}\right]$$

$$r_2 = \frac{1}{2}\left[\lambda + \omega + \gamma - \sqrt{(\lambda + \omega + \gamma)^2 - 4\lambda\omega}\right]$$

$$k_1 = \frac{\lambda - r_2}{r_1 - r_2}$$

$$k_2 = 1 - k_1$$

It is left as an exercise (Problem 3.14) to show that these parameters are nonnegative for an arbitrary IPP. Given the interarrival distribution, all the parameters of interest concerning the carried and overflow processes can be computed from the general model.

Multistage Systems

The IPP generator produces an arrival process with interarrival times given by the sum of two exponentials with different weights. This method of producing arrival processes can be extended to produce almost any type of arrival to any given accuracy.

   The simplest such system, the k-stage exponential process, is composed of k single-server queues in series with identical servers. A customer arrives at the entry of the system, passes through all the servers one after the other, and exits to produce the event that marks the arrival of a new call in the group. At each stage, the service time is drawn from the same negative exponential distribution with parameter $k\mu$. Immediately after the call arrives, another customer enters the first stage, and the process is repeated. It is evident that the total time spent by a customer in the system is the sum of k independent negative exponential variables. Thus the Laplace transform of the transit time, which is also the distribution of the interarrival time of calls in the group, is simply the convolution of the individual transit times. It is given by

$$\Phi(s) = \left(\frac{k\mu}{s + k\mu} \right)^k .$$

The interarrival time density is the Erlang$_k$ distribution, as can be seen in any table of Laplace transforms. It is given by

$$f(t) = \frac{k\mu(k\mu t)^{k-1} e^{-k\mu t}}{(k-1)!} .$$

This distribution has a straightforward interpretation as the distribution of the time required to collect k arrivals from a Poisson process of parameter μ.

   It is now quite easy to compute the first two moments of the traffic generated by this process. From Eqs. (3.53) and (3.54), we get

$$M = \mu$$

$$Z = 1 - \mu + \frac{(k\mu)^k}{(1 + k\mu)^k - (k\mu)^k}$$

It is not difficult to see that the traffic generated by this process is smooth, although computing the smallest peakedness available appears quite difficult.

   This technique can be extended in various ways to yield increasingly complex arrival distributions. One obvious choice is to draw the individual service times at each stage from negative exponential distributions with different means. Another possibility is illustrated by the two-stage Cox model [15]. Consider the system of Fig. 3.1, where the two stations are exponential servers with distinct rates α and β, respectively. Here, however, a customer entering the generator need not go through all stages. Instead, a customer arriving at A

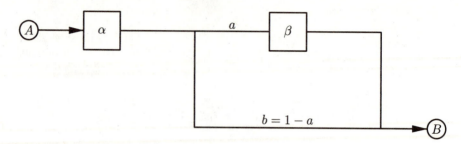

Figure 3.1   Equivalent System for Cox Model

immediately enters service at station 1. After its service is completed, the customer exits at B with probability $b = 1 - a$, or enters server 2 with probability a, Customers leaving server 2 then exit, generating a new call arrival, and a new customer immediately arrives at A. The time spent by a customer in the system is a weighted sum of exponential distributions with different holding times; its Laplace transform is given by

$$\Phi(s) = \frac{\alpha}{\alpha + s}\left[b + a\frac{\beta}{\beta + s}\right].$$ (3.80)

The moments of the traffic generated by the process can be computed by Eq. (3.52); the mean and peakedness are given by

$$M = \frac{\alpha\beta}{(a\alpha + \beta)}$$ (3.81)

$$Z = \frac{1 + \alpha + \beta}{1 + \alpha a + \beta} - \frac{\alpha\beta}{(1 + \alpha a + \beta)(\alpha a + \beta)}$$ (3.82)

Note that, in this case, the value of peakedness produced by this process depends on *three* parameters, making the analysis quite complex.

Let us now compute the carried and overflow distributions. Of course, we could do this using the general formulas (3.47) and (3.63). Instead, we show how to compute the interarrival distribution of the carried traffic directly from the description of the system, demonstrating that it is often possible to get representations that are simpler than for the general case by exploiting the structure of a given arrival process.

Suppose that a call is offered to a group of finite size N whenever a customer leaves the generator. We want the Laplace transform of the interarrival time distribution for calls accepted in the group. When a call is accepted, the generator can be in either one of two states: in state 1, where the customer is being served in stage 1, or in state 2, where it is in the second server. Thus we are led to define $X(i,j)$, the interval from an arbitrary instant to the next arrival when there are i customers in service in the group and the generator is in state j, where $j = 1, 2$. The corresponding transforms are denoted $\Phi_i^j(s)$.

Consider now the situation where the generator is in state 1. Two independent exponential service processes are running concurrently: the first server of the generator, at rate α, and the customers in service, at rate $i\mu$. The interval to the next event has a Laplace transform given by the combination of the two processes, that is, $(\alpha + i\mu)/(\alpha + i\mu + s)$. The next event can be one of three possibilities:

1. The customer leaves the server and leaves the generator, in which case a call arrival is produced. This has probability $\alpha b/(\alpha + i\mu)$. The Laplace transform of the subsequent interval is 1, since the waiting time for the next customer arrival to the first server is zero.

2. The customer leaves the server, and enters the second stage of the generator, with no consequent new-call arrival. This has probability $\alpha a/(\alpha + i\mu)$. The subsequent interval has a Laplace transform given by $\Phi_i^2(s)$.

3. The event is a call termination in the group, with probability $i\mu/(\alpha + i\mu)$. The subsequent interval has a Laplace transform given by $\Phi_{i-1}^1(s)$.

The Laplace transform of the interval distribution is then given by

$$\Phi_i^1(s) = \frac{\alpha + i\mu}{\alpha + i\mu + s} \left[\frac{\alpha b}{\alpha + i\mu} + \frac{\alpha a}{\alpha + i\mu} \Phi_i^2(s) \right.$$
$$\left. + \frac{i\mu}{\alpha + i\mu} \Phi_{i-1}^1(s) \right], \quad i = 0, \dots N \tag{3.83}$$

and by a similar argument for the other state:

$$\Phi_i^2(s) = \frac{\beta + i\mu}{\beta + i\mu + s} \left[\frac{\beta}{\beta + i\mu} + \frac{i\mu}{\beta + i\mu} \Phi_{i-1}^2(s) \right], \quad i = 0, \dots N \tag{3.84}$$

$$\Phi_k^j(s) = 0 \text{ if } k < 0$$

We end up with a system of $2(N+1)$ equations in as many unknowns. Because of the particular structure of the recurrence, using the fact that $\Phi_0^1(s) = \Phi(s)$, we can get a solution in closed form:

$$\Phi_N^1(s) = \frac{\alpha N\mu \left[\alpha\beta(\alpha + s) + (\beta + N\mu + s)(\beta + bs) \right]}{(\alpha + s)(N\mu + s)\left[\alpha a + \beta + N\mu + s \right](\beta + s)}. \tag{3.85}$$

Let p_n be the probability that the state of the group is n just after an arrival. We can compute the transform of the carried-call distribution by noting that

$$\overline{\Phi}(s) = (1 - p_N)\Phi(s) + p_N \Phi_N^1(s). \tag{3.86}$$

This equation simply states that if the group is not full immediately after a call is accepted, then the distribution until the next accepted call is just the interarrival distribution. If, on the other hand, the group is full after the last call accepted, then the interval is determined by $\Phi_N^1(s)$. Note that $\Phi_N^2(s)$ is not used since we know that, immediately after a call is accepted, the generator is in state 1. The probability of having a full group immediately after a call is accepted is given by

$$
\begin{aligned}
p_N &= E\frac{N\mu(\beta + \alpha a)}{\alpha\beta(1 - B)} \\
&= \frac{B}{1 - B}\frac{N\mu(\alpha a + \beta + N\mu)}{\alpha(\beta + bN\mu)},
\end{aligned}
$$

where the call congestion B can be computed from Eq. (3.46). From Eq. (3.86), the various moments of the carried traffic can be computed by standard methods, although an analytic formulation would probably be quite complex.

The final point in studying the Cox generator is to compute the transform $\hat{\Phi}(s)$ of the interarrival distribution of the overflow process. This can always be done using the general technique of Eq. (3.63). Although we can state the equations using a technique similar to the one by which we arrived at the transform of the carried traffic, there does not seem to be a closed-form solution such as in Eq. (3.85).

Let $\hat{\Phi}_i^1(s)$ be the transform of the interval between the current instant and the next overflow, given that i calls are present and that the generator is in state 1, and let $\hat{\Phi}_i^2(s)$ be the same transform for state 2. We can write the following general equation relating these transforms, using an argument along the same lines as for the carried traffic. We get

$$
(\alpha + i\mu + s)\hat{\Phi}_i^1(s) = \alpha b\hat{\Phi}_{i+1}^1(s) + \alpha a\hat{\Phi}_i^2(s) + i\mu\hat{\Phi}_{i-1}^1(s)
$$
$$
(\beta + i\mu + s)\hat{\Phi}_i^2(s) = \beta\hat{\Phi}_{i+1}^1(s) + i\mu\hat{\Phi}_{i-1}^2(s)
$$

This is a linear system in the unknown $\hat{\Phi}_i^1(s)$ and $\hat{\Phi}_i^2(s)$. Although there is no easy analytic solution for the system, it can be solved numerically by noting that the moments are obtained from the derivatives of the transform taken at the origin. Write the system as

$$
A(s)\mathbf{x}(s) = \mathbf{b}(s),
$$

where $\mathbf{b}(s)$ is the vector of $\hat{\Phi}_i^1(s)$ and $\hat{\Phi}_i^2(s)$, and $A(s)$ is the matrix of coefficients. It is possible to verify that $dA(s)/ds = I$, the identity matrix. Thus, taking the nth derivative of the linear system with respect to s and evaluating it at zero, we obtain

$$
A(0)\mathbf{b}^{(n)}(0) + \mathbf{b}^{(n-1)}(0) = 0,
$$

which we can then solve numerically for the value of the coefficient matrix, obtaining all the moments of the overflow distribution. These expressions are not particularly simple, for which reason we now end our discussion of the two-stage Cox model.

This model is a simple case of a more general class studied by Cox [16,3]. The n-stage Cox system is a straightforward extension of Fig. 3.1, where the n stages are placed in tandem, each having its own service time rate and probability of exit. Such a system can produce an arrival process having an arbitrary rational Laplace transform, subject to some mild constraints on the parameters. This generality in producing traffic streams is not particularly useful if the model has a large number of stages, in which case a large amount of information is required to specify the traffic streams present in a network. This can be a serious handicap (see Section 3.4).

Stochastic Models and Flow Conservation. As shown in the preceding discussion, analyzing the $GI/M/N/N$ queue is quite complex, especially when considering the description of the secondary system even when the input is Poisson (Eqs. 3.12 and 3.18). We would like a simplified view that somehow captures the essence of overflow and that can lead to simple numerical procedures. Such a view is provided by the notion of network flows as found in other areas of engineering, such as transportation or electrical flows. The most important feature of these models is that some form of conservation equation must be satisfied at the nodes of the network. The "thing" that is conserved at the nodes, and that thus flows in the network, is the mean of the arrival, carried, and overflow processes. This concept can be seen by considering the Kosten system, where some input enters the primary group, part of it accepted and part of it diverted to the secondary group. If we identify the mean of the three stochastic process in question — offered, carried, and overflow — with the magnitude of the flow, then it is not hard to see from Eqs. (3.49) and (3.53) that the standard conservation equation $A = \hat{A} + \overline{A}$ is verified. The notion of offered traffic is crucial for this model since offered traffic represents the magnitude of the entering flow, though it has no significance in terms of actual calls in the network.

This flow representation of the means of stochastic processes works well for the Kosten system, and can be extended to the Brockmeyer system. Consider, for simplicity, the case of Poisson input. Here the input flow is A, which splits into two parts in the ratio $E(A, N)$. The flow $A[1 - E(A, N)]$ goes into the primary group, and the part $A[E(A, N)]$ becomes the input to the secondary group. There is now a slight difference between the Brockmeyer system and the ordinary flow model. In the flow model, we would say that this flow splits into two parts, the part $AE(A, N)[1 - E(AE(A, N), L)]$ flowing onto the secondary group, and the part $AE(A, N)[E(AE(A, N), L)]$ being rejected. This approach, however, does not coincide with the results (3.19) and (3.23) for the Brockmeyer system. A better fit with the flow model is to suppose that the separation coefficients for two systems with overflow, such as for the Brockmeyer system, obey a combination law of the form $E_{N \otimes L} = E(A, N + L)$, where the notation $N \otimes L$ indicates a system where calls blocked on the primary group of size N are offered to the secondary group of size L. The flow carried on the secondary group is obtained as the difference between the offered and blocked flows. With this composition law, the Brockmeyer equations for the mean reduce to the conservation equations between offered, carried, and overflow traffic at both stages of overflow.

The analogy must not be carried too far; there are some difficulties with the flow model. Only the means of the stochastic processes can be approximated as conserved flows. Such a conservation rule does not apply to the second moment of the first overflow of the Kosten system, even in the case of Poisson input, since we have

$$V = A$$
$$\overline{V} = \overline{M} - A(N - \overline{M})E_N \tag{3.16}$$

$$\hat{V} = \hat{M}\left(1 - \hat{M} + \frac{A}{(N + 1 - A + \hat{M})}\right), \tag{3.14}$$

where it is obvious that there is no conservation of variance. Nevertheless, this conservation assumption is frequently made, if only to be able to use the conserved flow model. In these cases, one should always remember that using the flow model provides only an approximation, and that accuracy depends on the actual values of the parameters.

From a theoretical point of view, the passage from the stochastic description of the system to a flow model must be done very carefully. For another example of possible difficulties in setting up the appropriate definitions, consider the case of two links in series. We want to define the mean and variance of the traffic offered to the second link from the parameters of the process that represents the carried traffic on the first link. The usual procedure is to use the moments of the busy-circuit distribution on the first group as the moments of the offered traffic to the second group. This, however, is inconsistent with our definition of the offered traffic as the busy-server process on the infinite group, but with holding times that are chosen *independently* of the holding times of the calls in service in the finite group. This means that there are *two distinct* processes associated with carried traffic: (1) the busy-server process (BSP), whose state is the number of calls in service in the finite group, and (2) the carried-arrival process (CAP), whose state is the number of calls in progress in the infinite group. These processes are different: At a given time, the number of calls present in the two systems need not be identical since the durations of individual calls are different.

The peakedness of the BSP can be computed from Eqs. (3.15) and (3.16). As A becomes large, this peakedness understandably tends to 0 because the number of busy servers in the group cannot exceed N; as the arrival rate increases, the number of busy servers will tend to N while the variations in the number of busy servers will tend to zero, since most servers are busy all the time.

We can define a peakedness for the CAP if we construct an infinite group in which a call is set up every time an event occurs in the CAP — that is, whenever a call is accepted — but where the holding time is generated from a negative exponential distribution with the same mean, but independently from the holding time of the real call. As the arrival rate increases, whenever a call terminates, a new call is accepted almost immediately. Intervals between call terminations are exponentially distributed, however, and the distribution of time intervals of the accepted calls tends to a negative exponential; the peakedness will go to 1. For this reason, CAP is not equivalent to BSP; the two processes cannot be used interchangeably. Since we have defined offered traffic in terms of the infinite group, we normally should use the moments of the CAP as the moments of the offered traffic. In practice, calculating these moments is quite difficult both theoretically and numerically, and great care must be taken to ensure stability. For these reasons, the CAP is not used in network-analysis algorithms. We refer the interested reader to [11].

We must make a final remark concerning these flow representations. In other areas of engineering, network flows entering a node can emerge in arbitrary proportions, the only condition being that the conservation equation must be satisfied. An example is transportation networks, where the flow pattern can be selected arbitrarily subject to the capacity constraints of the arcs. In the case of stochastic flows in the Kosten and Brockmeyer systems, this is not possible. The amount of carried traffic is determined by a number of factors, none of which is directly under the user's control. The first factor, of course, is the size of the two groups. The second is the stochastic description of the entering flow: If the arrival process is a renewal process, we need the full knowledge of $F(t)$; if it is not, the situation is even more complex since we need the transition matrix of a semi-Markov process. The fact that the links are selected in a precise order is another element that constrains the separation of the offered traffic into carried and overflow parts. This element is related to the routing technique used in the network; we will return to it in other chapters.

For all these reasons, a direct application of flow models to obtain an arbitrary separation of flows at the nodes is generally not very accurate as a model of alternate routing. Nevertheless, flow representation of stochastic processes is such a useful simplifying device that it is used in many situations, modified to take into account the particular nature of alternate routing. Now we see why traffic moments play such a crucial role in network analysis. The moments are the quantities that allow the transformation from a completely stochastic description of traffic, with all its complexity, to a more manageable, but less accurate, representation in terms of deterministic vector flows, where this description is exact for the first moment, but only approximate for the others.

3.4   Moment-Matching Techniques for Overflow

Representing traffic by a small set of moments, although simpler than the full stochastic description, raises another problem. If we know only the first two moments of the traffic offered to a link, how can we compute the carried and overflow moments? One method, dating back to the introduction of alternate routing in telephone networks in the mid-1950s, is called the *moment-matching technique*. Let us now describe this class of methods and the particular problems raised by its use in network analysis.

A long-standing, much-studied problem in circuit switching is calculating traffic parameters subject to multiple overflows. This problem arises when a traffic stream, generally Poisson, is offered to some trunk group. The blocked calls are then offered to a second group, the calls blocked on this second choice are offered to a third one, and so on. The object is to compute the probability of not being able to make a connection on any of these groups, and to estimate the traffic carried on each one.

In principle, this problem is readily solved by repeated application of the techniques of Section 3.3, since the overflow process is also of the renewal type. In practice, this is not done for two reasons. Historically, the problem was studied, and partly solved, long before modern renewal theory was commonly used in teletraffic theory. Thus adequate methods already existed, making recourse to the exact renewal method somewhat redundant. Also, the renewal method is generally quite difficult to apply in practical cases because of numerical stability problems, long computation times, or both. For this reason, a discussion of the classical moment-matching systems is in order since these systems are the basis of all the techniques currently used in network analysis or synthesis.

Moment-matching techniques work as follows. The arrival process is represented by a small number of parameters, generally two or at most three. A process, called the *equivalent process*, is then selected to represent the actual arrival process. The parameters of the equivalent process are chosen in such a way that the moments of the traffic it generates are equal to the moments of the real offered traffic — hence the generic name moment-matching techniques. This equivalent process is then used to compute all the quantities of interest pertaining to the group: time and call congestion, moments of overflow and carried traffics, and so forth (see Fig. 3.2). The usefulness of this technique depends strongly on the possibility of choosing an equivalent process that yields accurate parameters for the overflow and carried traffics with reasonable computation times. Also, if the method is to be usable in network calculations, it must be reasonably easy to select the parameters of the equivalent process.

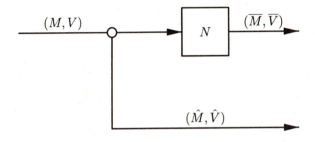

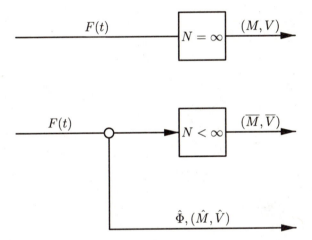

Figure 3.2 Moment-Matching Technique

Although not the only ones possible, renewal processes form an important class of equivalent processes. The general theory of renewal processes is well known, encompassing most of the equivalent methods currently used in network algorithms. For this reason, we review some of the more important processes of this type, only briefly indicating other types at the end of the discussion.

Equivalent Random Theory

Equivalent random theory (ERT) is the first application of the moment-matching

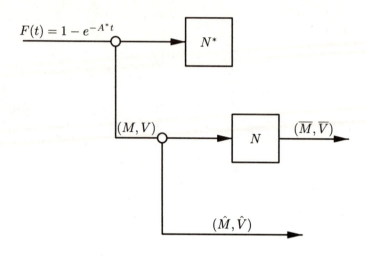

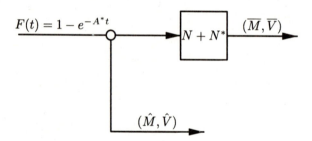

Figure 3.3   Equivalent Random Theory System

method to the analysis of overflow systems. As we have seen, the traffic overflowing a group offered Poisson traffic is always peaked. Thus it is reasonable to use the overflow model, where a primary group of N^* equivalent circuits offered some equivalent Poisson traffic A^*, as a generator of the (M,V) traffic whenever $V > M$. A^* and N^*, is chosen such that the parameters of its overflow are precisely M and V (see Fig. 3.3). From the Kosten model, we know that A^* and N^* must satisfy

$$M = A^* E(A^*, N^*) \tag{3.87}$$

$$V = M\left(1 - M + \frac{A^*}{N^* + 1 + M - A^*}\right) \tag{3.88}$$

Note that, in general, N^* is not an integer, which requires the use of a generalized Erlang B function. A fundamental question about the system defined by Eqs. (3.87) and (3.88) is whether there exist solutions $A^*, N^* \geq 0$ for an arbitrary pair M, V, with $V \geq M$. Although no formal proof seems to exist, this seems to be the case and the solution seems to be unique. Approximate values have been given by Rapp [2], which can either be used as such or as good starting values in the numerical solution:

$$A^* \approx V + 3Z(Z - 1) \tag{3.89}$$

$$N^* \approx \frac{A^*(M + Z)}{M + Z - 1} - M - 1. \tag{3.90}$$

Having computed the parameters of the equivalent system, we can compute the mean and variance of the overflow traffic using the Brockmeyer model; these values are given by

$$\hat{M} = A^* E(A^*, N + N^*) \tag{3.91}$$

$$\hat{V} = \hat{M} \left(1 - \hat{M} + \frac{A^*}{N + N^* + 1 - A^* + \hat{M}} \right). \tag{3.92}$$

The ERT method is iterative since it can be used to compute the blocking of the overflow traffic $(\hat{M}, \hat{V})$, which can also be peaked. Note, however, that the method is not iterative for the carried traffic, which can be smooth, and that it works only for peaked offered traffic. Thus the ERT method must be extended in order to be used for computing the overflow and carried parameters of carried traffic.

ERT for Smooth Traffic

In the case where $Z < 1$, the equations that define the equivalent system (3.87) and (3.88) generally have a negative solution for N^*. Possible extensions to standard ERT can be made along three directions by relaxing various parameters of the model: (1) use an equivalent traffic source that is smoother than Poisson, and match the moments of its overflow with the real parameters, (2) extend the Erlang B formula to the full domain of real N, or (3) generate the real smooth traffic by a mechanism other than overflow.

The first technique, although not widely used, falls within the framework of equivalent renewal processes and is dealt with below. The other methods have been proposed and used for network algorithms, and thus are described briefly here.

The second technique — the possibility of using an extended Erlang B function to construct an equivalent system for smooth traffic — was proposed first by Bretschneider [17]. The idea was extended by Nightingale [18] under the name of ERT-N, based on the analytic continuation of the Erlang B function in the complete (A, N) plane, as shown in [5]. For this case, only the extension to negative N is used; the extension to negative A has not been used in any practical case. The application of the method is straightforward. Given the parameters of the real traffic, the equivalent system is computed by solving the standard ERT equations (3.87) and (3.88); the parameters of the overflow are computed via Eqs. (3.91) and (3.92), where now N^* is negative if the traffic is smooth. Note that the equivalent system must still have nonnegative A. This, however, is not always possible. The derivation of the conditions in which the equivalent traffic is positive is left as an exercise (Problem 3.18).

The third way to extend ERT to smooth traffic is to assume that the mechanism producing the real traffic is something other than overflow. Such a model has been proposed by Katz [19] in which the real offered traffic is produced by the portion of the equivalent traffic that is *carried* in the equivalent group. The Laplace transform of the distribution of the interarrival time is given by Eq. (3.55). We know, however, that this process is not renewal and that its parameters cannot be computed using the general renewal method. The parameters of the equivalent system are given implicitly by the system:

$$M = A^* [1 - E(A^*, N^*)] \tag{3.93}$$
$$V = M - AB(N^* - M) \tag{3.94}$$

Having determined the value of the equivalent system, the parameters of the traffic overflowing the real group are computed as follows:

1. If $N^* \leq N$, then all calls carried in the equivalent system are also carried in the real group. Thus, we get $\hat{M} = \hat{V} = 0$; that is, there is no overflow from the real group.

2. If $N^* > N$, then some of the calls carried in the equivalent group are blocked in the real group. Assuming that the traffic offered to the real group is effectively A^*, we have for the parameters of the traffic carried in the real system

$$\overline{M} = A^* [1 - E(A^*, N)]$$
$$\overline{V} = \overline{M} + (\overline{M} - A^*)(N - \overline{M})$$

The parameters of the overflow traffic are computed by

$$\hat{M} = A^* - \overline{M}$$
$$\hat{V} = V - \overline{V}$$

Note that computing the variance in this way neglects the correlation that exists between the carried and overflow traffic on the real system.

It is claimed that in practice the accuracy of the method is comparable to the accuracy of the equivalent random method for peaked traffic and thus is adequate to evaluate network performance.

Generalized ERT

As mentioned in the preceding section, ERT (now standing for equivalent *renewal* theory) can be generalized to an arbitrary renewal input process by replacing the Poisson input by some arbitrary renewal stream. The moment matching is done between the traffic parameters available, on the one hand, and the moments of the renewal stream and the size of the equivalent group N^*, on the other. The blocking probabilities and overflow and carried traffic parameters are then computed for the equivalent renewal stream offered to a group of size $N + N^*$.

Such a generalized ERT was proposed by Potter [20], who suggested using input streams with various Erlang$_k$ interarrival distributions as input to the primary group for modeling smooth traffic. The equivalent streams have an interarrival time distribution of the E_n type, where $n = 1, 2, 3, 6, 10, \infty$. These streams have some interesting properties. As k increases, the peakedness of the overflow traffic decreases, with its smallest value attained for the deterministic stream. In fact, it has been shown [13] that $\hat{Z} \geq 0.5$ for any k. Thus these input processes cannot be used to model traffic whose peakedness is below 0.5. For a given phase k, the equivalent system has only two parameters: (1) the intensity of the Erlang stream and (2) the size of the equivalent group. Thus the model can be used directly for a two-moment representation of the traffic. Tables have been produced that relate the parameters of the overflow traffic of the equivalent group to these two parameters, allowing the equivalent system to be sized. No practical use of the technique, however, seems to exist in real network applications.

Equivalent IPP Model for Peaked Traffic

Consider again a peaked traffic (M, V). Such a traffic could be generated by an interrupted Poisson process [9,21], suitably chosen as to reproduce the values of M and V. Note, however, that the IPP is a three-parameter model, which means that the traffic should be characterized by a third parameter in addition to the mean and variance.

Let us first consider a somewhat simpler problem. Assume for the moment that the IPP is in fact produced by the overflow of some Poisson traffic A^* from a finite group of size N^*. In this case, the parameters of the IPP can be expressed as a function of the parameters of the equivalent system as

$$\lambda = A^* \frac{\delta_2(\delta_1 - \delta_0) - \delta_0(\delta_2 - \delta_1)}{(\delta_1 - \delta_0) - (\delta_2 - \delta_1)} \tag{3.95}$$

$$\omega = \frac{\delta_0}{\lambda} \left(\frac{\lambda - A^* \delta_1}{\delta_1 - \delta_0} \right) \tag{3.96}$$

$$\gamma = \frac{\omega}{A^*} \left(\frac{\lambda - A^* \delta_0}{\delta_0} \right) \tag{3.97}$$

where

$$\delta_n = \frac{1}{A^*} \frac{M_{n+1}}{M_n},$$ (3.98)

where the factorial moments M_n can be computed by the Kosten model of Section 3.1. Given an arbitrary value for A^* and N^*, there is no proof that the corresponding λ, ω, γ are not negative (although this seems to be the case in practice). The same question can be posed for an arbitrary set of three moments with $Z \geq 1$.

This relation between the moments of the IPP process and the overflow of a Poisson stream is useful when the real traffic is described by its first two moments only. The difficulty is that the IPP is a three-parameter process, and that there are only two quantities with which to match it. In this case, the IPP model can be used by making the following approximations. First, given M and V, compute A^* and N^* by the standard ERT. Then use these values to obtain the parameters of the IPP system by Eqs. (3.95–3.97), and use Eq. (3.72) to obtain the mean and variance of the overflow. Another possibility is to use the equivalent Poisson traffic computed from ERT as the value for λ. In this case, only two parameters are left to compute, given by

$$\omega = \frac{M}{A^*} \left(\frac{A^* - M}{Z - 1} - 1 \right)$$ (3.99)

$$\gamma = \omega \left(\frac{A^*}{M} - 1 \right)$$

In general, when a two-moment match is desired, one parameter of the IPP must be chosen arbitrarily. In practice, this choice is constrained by the requirement that the parameters of the equivalent IPP system should be non-negative, which imposes the requirement that $\lambda > M$. Finally, the method is recursive, since overflow traffic is always peaked, and the IPP method can be used again on this traffic. This is not the case for the carried traffic, which is generally smooth; some other method must be used to calculate its overflow.

The Two-Stage Cox Model

The Cox model of Section 3.3 can be used to represent a stream of traffic whose first three moments are known, provided the system of Eqs. (3.81) and (3.82) can be inverted. This question is discussed in detail by Guérineau and Labetoulle in [22], in which the following conditions are given. Let $P = \alpha\beta$ and $S = \alpha + \beta$. These can be written in terms of the coefficients δ_0, δ_1 and δ_2 as

$$P = \frac{2\mu^2 \delta_0 (\delta_2 - \delta_1)}{2\delta_1 - \delta_0 - \delta_2}$$

$$S = \frac{\mu\left[2(\delta_1 - \delta_0 + 1)(\delta_2 - \delta_1) + \delta_1(2\delta_1 - \delta_0 - \delta_2)\right]}{2\delta_1 - \delta_0 - \delta_2}$$

and of course we have

$$\alpha = \frac{S + \sqrt{S^2 - 4P}}{2}$$

$$\beta = \frac{S - \sqrt{S^2 - 4P}}{2}$$

$$b = \frac{P}{\mu\delta_0\alpha}$$

Obviously, there exist solutions if and only if

$$P > 0, \ S > 0, \ S^2 - 4P > 0, \ a > 0.$$

For peaky traffic, a necessary and sufficient condition is that $\delta_0 < \delta_1 < \delta_2 < 2\delta_1 - \delta_0$. In the case of smooth traffic, the condition $2\delta_1 - \delta_0 < \delta_2 < \delta_1 < \delta_0$ is necessary but not sufficient.

Because the parameters of the real offered traffic are computed from the superposition of various overflow and carried traffic streams, quite possibly the set of three moments does not meet the required conditions. In such a case, some further approximation is required. If the traffic is peaky, the first two moments can always be matched. Since the equivalent system is a three-parameter model, one parameter is arbitrary. Guérineau and Labetoulle suggest choosing $\mu\delta_1 < S < \infty$, with a recommended value of $S = 2\mu\delta_1$. Having chosen S, the parameters for the equivalent Cox generator are given by

$$\alpha = \frac{S + \sqrt{S^2 - 4P}}{2}$$

$$\beta = \frac{S - \sqrt{S^2 - 4P}}{2}$$

$$b = \frac{1}{\alpha}(S - P/\mu\delta_0)$$

where

$$P = \frac{\mu\delta_0}{\delta_1 - \delta_0 + 1}(S - \mu\delta_1).$$

In the case of smooth traffic, one first tries the same values as for peaky traffic. If the parameters of the generator are positive, then a solution has been obtained. If not, only the first two moments are matched. In order to do this, α and β are kept arbitrary, and a is fixed to 1. The parameters are then

$$\alpha = \frac{S + \sqrt{S^2 - 4P}}{2}$$

$$\beta = \frac{S - \sqrt{S^2 - 4P}}{2}$$

which is valid if and only if

$$\delta_1 \geq \frac{4\delta_0^2}{1 + 4\delta_0}.$$

This means that smooth traffic can be modeled by the Cox system if it is no smoother than Erlang$_2$. When this is not so, the authors suggest replacing it with an Erlang$_2$ traffic and using the Cox model. In this case, we have $\alpha = \beta = 2\mu\delta_0$.

After constructing the equivalent system, we must calculate the parameters of the carried and overflow traffics. This can be done by means of the transform of the overflow process from the primary group, using either the method proposed in [22] or the formulas derived in Section 3.3. It is not clear which of these two methods is preferable from the point of view of numerical stability and computation time.

The Bernouilli-Poisson-Pascal Process

As is well known [6], the overflow traffic offered to a large group has a busy-circuit distribution that is very close to a Pascal distribution. Given the mean and variance of a peaked traffic, the parameters of the corresponding Pascal distribution can be computed analytically from Eqs. (3.27) and (3.28). From the values of the parameters, the overflow could be analyzed just as for the Kosten system, with the arrival rate corresponding to a Pascal process instead of the constant rate of the Poisson process. Note, however, that the analysis would become quite complex — probably the reason why it has not been carried out.

Instead, the Bernouilli-Poisson-Pascal (BPP) method can be used to approximate the overflow system by making a second assumption [23]. Given an offered traffic with arbitrary mean and variance, *the busy-circuit distribution in a group of size N is given by the same distribution used to describe the offered traffic*, that is, the Pascal distribution (or Bernouilli distribution for smooth traffic). For a group of finite size N, the distribution (3.25) must be truncated; with $\mu = 1$, we have the truncated Pascal distribution, denoted by q_j:

$$q_j = \frac{p_j}{\sum_{i=0}^{N} p_i}, \quad j = 0, \ldots N$$

The time congestion for a group of size N is given by

$$E_N \triangleq q_N = \frac{\binom{-r}{N}(-\beta)^N}{\sum_{j=0}^{N} \binom{-r}{j}(-\beta)^j} \tag{3.100}$$

and the call congestion by

$$B = E\left[1 + \frac{N}{M}(Z - 1)\right]. \tag{3.101}$$

Equation (3.101) should be compared with the general relation (3.48) between time and call congestion in the case of a general renewal input. The time congestion obeys the interesting recurrence

$$E_k = \frac{q_{r+k-1} E_{k-1}}{k + q_{r+k-1} E_{k-1}} \quad k = 1, \ldots \quad (3.102)$$

$$E_0 = 1$$

which is a generalization of the well-known recurrence for the Erlang B function. Similarly, under this approximation, the mean and variance of the traffic carried in the group are given by

$$\overline{M} = \frac{nq - (n + N)qE}{1 - q} \quad (3.103)$$

$$\overline{V} = \frac{nq + \overline{M}(n + 1)q - (N + 1)(n + N)qE}{1 - q} - \overline{M}^2 \quad (3.104)$$

From these values, we can get $\hat{M} = M - \overline{M}$ and, neglecting the correlation, $\hat{V} = V - \overline{V}$. It is easy to show that these quantities reduce to the values already calculated for the Kosten system, that is, when $q \to 0$ and $n \to \infty$ while maintaining $Z = 1$.

As indicated in Problem 3.4, the BPP distribution is inadequate to describe smooth offered traffic because the probabilities given by the binomial distribution could become negative. The situation is better in the case of a finite group since a sufficient condition exists to guarantee that the probabilities do not become negative in the range of interest. That is, for $j \leq N$, $N \leq M/(1 - Z)$, a condition generally met in practical situations unless Z is very low. Although the method cannot represent all potential situations, the advantages of simplicity and uniformity in representing both peaked and smooth traffics make it attractive for modeling traffic in network studies.

Finally, let us comment on the accuracy of the method. The accuracy was checked in [23] by comparing the parameters of the carried traffic for a hyperexponential and a gamma distribution of the interarrival times. It was shown numerically that the values were similar for the two cases and were quite good. A strong assumption is needed for the BPP model, stating that the busy-circuit distribution is BPP for any arbitrary arrival process. In fact, the situation is even worse from a theoretical point of view, since it can be shown that there is *no* renewal input process such that its overflow has the Pascal distribution [13]. These two facts would seem to make the BPP model a very poor candidate indeed for the analysis of overflow. The accuracy of this model, however, is at least as good as that of the other models. Let us explain this apparent anomaly in the more general context of renewal arrival processes and moment-matching methods.

General Renewal Input

In general, when a traffic is represented by a renewal process, specifying a number of moments of the real traffic constrains the input process and to some degree determines the blocking experienced by this process. Moment-matching methods would be expected to work well if specifying the moments of the real traffic limits the equivalent renewal process to a small range. In this case, we would expect the moment-matching technique to be "forced" to choose the right equivalent process, which would explain the good accuracy obtained by moment matching.

From Eqs. (3.53) and (3.54), the values of M and V uniquely determine $\Phi'(0)$ and $\Phi(\mu)$ for *any* renewal input. In fact, these values constrain all of the $\Phi(\mu)$ since they must satisfy Eq. (3.52), where $\Phi(\mu)$ appears in all the terms through h_n. Bounds have been computed in [24] for $\Phi(x), x \geq 1$ as

$$[\Phi(\mu)]^x \leq \Phi(x) \leq \Phi_m(x) \stackrel{\triangle}{=} p_1 + p_2 e^{-bx},$$

where b is defined implicitly by the equation

$$b = \frac{A(1 - e^{-b})}{1 - \Phi(\mu)}$$

and

$$p_2 = \frac{A}{b}$$
$$p_1 = 1 - p_2$$

Furthermore, from Eq. (3.46), we see that $\Phi(\mu)$ is the leading term in the expression for the call congestion B although B also depends on all the $\Phi(\mu)$s. Using the bounds for Φ, it is possible to write bounds for the blocking experienced by an arbitrary renewal stream $B_{min} \leq B \leq B_{max}$ where

$$B_{min} = \left\{ 1 + \binom{N}{1} \frac{1 - \Phi(\mu)}{\Phi(\mu)} + \ldots + \binom{N}{N} \frac{[1 - \Phi(\mu)] \ldots [1 - \Phi^N(\mu)]}{[\Phi(\mu)]^{N(N+1)/2}} \right\}^{-1}$$

$$B_{max} = \left\{ 1 + \binom{N}{1} \frac{1 - \Phi_m(\mu)}{\Phi_m(\mu)} + \ldots + \binom{N}{N} \frac{[1 - \Phi_m(\mu)] \ldots [1 - \Phi_m(N\mu)]}{\Phi_m(\mu) \ldots \Phi_m(N\mu)} \right\}^{-1}$$

The point is that these bounds are sharp, and it is possible to identify renewal processes that reach them. The lower bound is given by a renewal input with constant interarrival times m', given by $\exp\{-m'\} = \Phi(\mu)$. Similarly, a renewal process with a step at time $t \to 0$ and another at $t \to \infty$ has a blocking probability arbitrarily close to 1. The upper bound can be viewed as such a process, but constrained by V to have the second step at finite t. The point is that the two bounds can be widely separated, as shown in [24]. This means that the blind selection of a renewal process to represent a traffic specified by only two moments cannot be expected to yield an accurate value for the blocking.

The excellent accuracy of moment matching has been explained in the case of the BPP method [23]. Assume that the system is divided into K subsystems of infinite size, and let p_i be the probability that an incoming call is served by the ith subsystem. Let X_i be the number of calls in subsystem i, and M_i and V_i its mean and variance. We then have

$$X = \sum_i X_i, \ M_i = Mp_i$$

$$V = M_i p_i (1 + p_i (Z - 1))$$

$$\text{cov}(X_i, X - X_i) = Mp_i(1 - p_i)(Z - 1)$$

If A_i is the interarrival time distribution at subsystem i, its Laplace-Stieltjes transform is given by

$$a_i(s) = \frac{a(s)\left(1 - (1 - p_i)\right)}{1 - (1 - p_i)a(s)}.$$

Choosing $p_i = 1/K$, we can choose K such that M_i/V_i is as close to 1 as desired. We also note that $a_i(s)$ tends to a negative exponential distribution as $p_i \to 0$. The mean carried traffic can then be viewed as the sum of a large number of infinitesimal quasi-regular traffics; this property is independent of the precise nature of the arrival renewal process. Because this microscopic structure of the stream is the important factor in the particular value of the mean, we can expect the BPP model to adequately describe the carried traffic in an infinite group, irrespective of the particular nature of the arrival renewal process. This is indeed the case.

More generally, equivalent methods are found to work well when used to evaluate overflow systems. The reason for this success is found not in the constraints imposed on the equivalent process by the prescribed values for the mean and variance, but in the additional information used in selecting the equivalent process. In other words, equivalent theory works because, when it is applied to overflow systems, the fact that the M, V traffic is produced by an overflow mechanism is used to select the equivalent renewal process. This is obvious when considering that the most successful equivalent systems for peaked traffic are the Poisson overflow and the IPP. Similarly, the success of the BPP method is also due to the choice of the correct distribution to represent carried traffic; it would probably be not as successful if an arbitrary renewal input stream with the correct M, V parameters were used. This is only a conjecture, however, and for now we only note that, for the problems arising in circuit-switched studies, the renewal equivalent method is generally sufficient.

Summary

Moment-matching techniques are widely used in analyzing networks. In fact, it is fair to say that these techniques are the only tools available that are rapid enough to be used in this context. Even so, the situation is not completely satisfactory, at least for certain problems. Network analysis really requires a technique that can represent *any* kind of traffic, smooth or peaked, within the same model, and for *arbitrary* values of the parameters. None of the methods we have discussed here meets these requirements; all are designed for a particular type of traffic, smooth or peaked — or, if they apply to both, do so by using different models for different ranges of peakedness.

As a case in point, consider the BPP model. Although probably the most attractive from the point of view of generality, it suffers from some defects. It cannot represents arbitrarily smooth traffic, and it represents smooth and peaky traffics by two separate models. Suppose that we want to use this model for network analysis or synthesis within a computer program. It is true that, in a real network, traffic will not be so smooth that the model cannot apply. This, however, is not the case in the design process, during which a search algorithm may produce some extreme traffic patterns when it is far from its optimal solution. Some care must be taken that these values do not cause a fatal error in the program. Similarly, the nature of the traffic offered to a given link may change, say from peaky to smooth, during this search procedure. Because the BPP model uses two different distributions for these two cases, the parameters of the overflow and carried traffic may not change continuously when this transition occurs — or, more likely, their derivatives may not be smooth. If the search algorithm uses gradients, these discontinuities in the derivative may cause the procedure to fail.

To avoid these difficulties, given that there exists no unified model that is guaranteed to be smooth and robust in terms of the parameters of the offered traffic, caution should be exercised when using moment-matching models in optimization procedures.

3.5   Heterogeneous Blocking

The traffic models described in Sections 3.1 to 3.4 apply to a single stream of offered traffic. Unfortunately, real networks are somewhat more complex since the traffic offered to a group is generally a mixture of streams, each with its own set of moments, and is not of the renewal type. Because of their different statistical characteristics, the streams effectively experience different blocking probabilities.

The heterogeneous blocking problem can thus be formulated as follows. Given n distinct streams of traffic offered to a group of size N, each with a known set of moments, compute the blocking probability (*parcel* blocking), as well as the carried and overflow traffic moments, for each stream. In this general form, the problem has no known solution, even under the assumption that the input streams are independent; only approximate methods are available. The problem with two streams has been solved exactly when one of the streams is Poisson and the other is renewal. The case of two renewal streams has also been analyzed, but simplifications are required to obtain a solution. For this reason, we concentrate here on practical methods that can yield sufficiently accurate results with relatively little computation.

First, we discuss the aggregation of the input streams and the assumption of independence. Then, we describe one case where an exact solution is known, mostly to illustrate the difficulty of the problem. Finally, heuristics usable in network problems are examined, starting with empirical formulas and moving to progressively more complex models based on those of Section 3.4.

Aggregation of Input Streams

The heterogeneous blocking problem arises because calls offered to a group in a network have been either blocked or accepted for service on some other group, but still must be connected through some intermediate group in order to establish a connection to their destination. Depending on the structure of the network and the routing method used, these processes cannot be expected to be independent. The dependence between various streams of traffic offered to a single group was investigated in [25] for simple arrangements of overflowing groups. Such dependence effects are quite difficult to compute; in practice, it is assumed that the streams to be merged are independent. This is a good approximation in large networks, where many different streams overflow on a given link (see Chapter 2).

Assuming this independence, and also assuming that stream i has k^{th} moment α_k^i, the kth moment of the aggregate stream is given by

$$\alpha_k = \sum_{k_1+k_2+\ldots k_m=1} \frac{k!}{k_1!k_2!\ldots k_m!} \alpha_{k_1}^1 \alpha_{k_2}^2 \ldots \alpha_{k_m}^m. \tag{3.105}$$

In the case of $m = 2$, we have

$$\alpha_1 = \alpha_1^1 + \alpha_1^2$$
$$\alpha_2 = \alpha_2^1 + 2\alpha_1^1\alpha_1^2 + \alpha_2^2$$
$$\alpha_3 = \alpha_3^1 + 3\alpha_2^1\alpha_1^2 + 3\alpha_1^1\alpha_2^2 + \alpha_3^2$$

Given the moments of the aggregate stream, its blocking probability and the parameters of the carried and overflow traffic can be computed by the methods of Section 3.4. The difficult part is determining how much of this blocking is actually experienced by each stream.

Heterogeneous Blocking for Poisson Inputs

The heterogeneous blocking problem has been solved in the case where all the input streams are Poisson. In this case, all streams experience the same blocking, and it is possible to characterize the individual streams overflowing in a common infinite group as follows. Let a^i, $i = 1, \ldots n$ be the parameters of each Poisson stream offered to a common group of size $N < \infty$, and let p_i be the probability that a given overflow call originates from stream i. Because all streams experience the same blocking probability, $p_i = a^i/a$, where a is the mean of the aggregate stream and is given by $a = \sum_i a^i$. Assume that, at a given instant, there are m calls in progress in the overflow group. The joint conditional probability of having $k_1, \ldots k_n$ calls of stream $1, \ldots n$, given that there are m calls in progress, is given by

$$p(k_1, \ldots k_n \mid m) = \frac{m!}{k_1! \ldots k_n!} p_1^{k_1} \ldots p_n^{k_n}, \tag{3.106}$$

where

$$m = k_1 + k_2 + \ldots k_n.$$

The jth conditional moment of the ith overflow stream α_j^i is given by

$$\alpha_j^i = \sum_{k_1, \ldots k_m, m} k_i^j p(k_1, \ldots k_n \mid m) p_m,$$

where of course $p(m)$ is the probability of having m calls in progress. This completely characterizes the overflow traffic. The first few moments are given by

$$\alpha_1^i = p_i \alpha_1 \tag{3.107}$$
$$\alpha_2^i = p_i^2 \alpha_2 + p_i(1 - p_i)\alpha_1 \tag{3.108}$$
$$\alpha_3^i = p_i^3 \alpha_3 + 3p_i^2(1 - p_i)\alpha_2 + (1 - 2p_i)p_i(1 - p_i)\alpha_1 \tag{3.109}$$

Note that these overflow traffics are not Poisson, as expected. Thus *their* blocking cannot be computed with this method; a more general technique is required.

Heterogeneous Blocking for Two Streams

Unfortunately, the traffic that overflows a primary group is not Poisson; since it becomes mixed with other streams, the real situation requires a more detailed analysis. In the simplest case, one overflow stream is combined with a number of background streams, all of which are Poisson. All the background streams can be aggregated into a single, equivalent Poisson stream, reducing the problem to a two-stream problem with one overflow stream and one Poisson stream. This problem dates back to the work of Wilkinson [6], where the magnitude of the heterogeneous blocking is estimated for the Brockmeyer system, that is, when the renewal stream is a Poisson overflow process. Assuming that the secondary group of the system is offered a Poisson traffic of given magnitude in addition to the overflow traffic, we can compute the blocking experienced by this Poisson stream B_1 and compare it with B_2, the overall blocking experienced by the aggregate traffic. B_1 can be computed from Eq. (3.21) since the call congestion for a Poisson traffic is just the marginal time congestion of the secondary group. B_2, on the other hand, is just the overall blocking probability of the system. Depending on the system parameters, the ratio between these two probabilities can be quite high, sometimes more than 10. This effect seems to be more pronounced for small groups, typically five circuits, but is still not negligible at large traffic values. For instance, for a traffic of 30 Erlangs in 15 circuits, the ratio is still almost 2.5, which should not be neglected.

An exact solution to the heterogeneous blocking problem was given by Kuczura [26] for the case of one Poisson and one general renewal streams offered to the same group. For the renewal stream, the call congestion is given by the busy-server distribution of the embedded Markov chain, which we shall now compute. The state probabilities of the system are obtained by solving the Kolmogorov equations, using the arrival times of the renewal calls as regeneration points. The Kolmogorov equations for the transition function $P_{i,j}(t)$ are

$$P'_{i,0}(t) = -\lambda P_{i,0}(t) + \mu P_{i,1}(t)$$
$$P'_{i,j}(t) = -\lambda P_{i,j-1}(t) - (\lambda + j\mu)P_{i,j}(t) + (j+1)\mu P_{i,j+1}(t) \quad (3.110)$$
$$P'_{i,N}(t) = -\lambda P_{i,N-1}(t) - N\mu P_{i,N}(t)$$

$$P_{i,j}(0) = \begin{cases} 1 & \text{if } i = j \\ 0 & \text{otherwise} \end{cases}$$

The system of equations has the unique solution [27]

$$P_{i,j}(t) = a_j + \sum_{k=1}^{N} a_k(i,j)e^{\lambda_k \mu t},$$

where

$$\rho = \frac{\lambda}{\mu}$$

$$a_j = \frac{\rho^j}{j!} \frac{1}{\sum_{k=0}^{N} \frac{\rho^k}{k!}}$$

$$a_k(i,j) = \frac{N!}{j!} \frac{\rho^{N-i} D_i(\lambda_k) D_j(\lambda_k)}{\lambda_k D_N(\lambda_k) D'_N(\lambda_k + 1)}$$

$$D_i(x) = \sum_{k=0}^{i} \binom{i}{k} \rho^{i-k}(x)^k$$

$$xD'_N(x+1) = \sum_{k=0}^{N} \rho^N(N)_k \frac{D^2_{N-k}(x)}{D_N(x)}$$

$$D_0(x) = 1$$

and where λ_k are the N roots of the polynomial $D_N(x)$. Of course, the knowledge of $P_{i,j}$ determines the embedded Markov process completely. More important, however, is knowledge of the stationary distribution of calls in the group and the congestion probabilities. As usual, let p_j be the stationary distribution just before an arrival. The one-step transition probability $r_{i,j}$ is then

$$r_{i,j} = \int_0^\infty P_{i+1,j}(t)dF(t), \quad 0 \le i < N, \quad 0 \le j < N$$

$$r_{N,j} = \int_0^\infty P_{N,j}(t)dF(t), \quad 0 \le j < N$$

Replacing the value of $P_{i,j}$ from Eq. (3.110), we obtain

$$r_{i,j} = a_j + \sum_{k=1}^N a_k(i+1,j)\phi(-\lambda_k\mu) \quad 0 \le i < N, \quad 0 \le j < N$$

$$r_{N,j} = a_j + \sum_{k=1}^N a_k(N,j)\phi(-\lambda_k\mu), \quad 0 \le j < N$$

The stationary distribution can be found as usual by solving the linear system

$$p_j = \sum_{i=0}^N p_i r_{i,j}$$

$$\sum_j p_j = 1$$

The call blocking seen by the renewal stream is given by P_N since the busy-circuit distribution as seen by this stream is the one for the Markov chain.

The call blocking for the Poisson stream can be obtained by using the memoryless property of the Poisson process. In this case, the busy-circuit distribution as seen by this process is the distribution at an arbitrary point in time q_j. It can be obtained by writing the equilibrium equation for the rates in and out of the state, and is expressed as usual in terms of the stationary probabilities for the embedded chain

$$(j+1)\mu q_{j+1} = \nu p_j + \lambda q_j,$$

which can be solved as

$$q_j = q_0 \frac{\rho^j}{j!} + \sigma \sum_{i=0}^{j-1} \left(\frac{i!}{j!}\right) \rho^{j-i-1} p_i,$$

where

$$\sigma = \frac{\nu}{\mu}$$

and

$$q_0 = \left[1 - \left(\frac{\sigma}{\rho}\right) \sum_{j=1}^{N} \left(\frac{\rho^j}{j!}\right) \sum_{i=0}^{j-1} \left(\frac{i!}{\rho^i}\right) p_i\right] \Bigg/ \sum_{j=0}^{N} \left(\frac{\rho^j}{j!}\right).$$

The time congestion is then given by q_N, which is also the call congestion for the Poisson stream.

At this point, let us consider the calculation of the overflow and carried-traffic parameters. From a practical point of view, that is, for use in network applications, this calculation is probably not very useful, considering the computations required by the technique just to evaluate blocking. All the roots of a Nth degree polynomial must be calculated in order to arrive at the transition matrix of the embedded Markov chain. After the transition matrix is computed, the stationary probabilities are computed by solving the linear system of order N. Care must be exercised in determining the roots of the polynomial in order to avoid numerical instability, as discussed in [26] in some depth. Similarly, the numerical solution of Markov chains is not always easy, especially for large systems, where great care must be taken to avoid propagating numerical errors while solving the linear system. For this reason, the calculation of the mean and variance of the carried and overflow traffics would probably be too difficult to use in a network context.

The heterogeneous blocking problem has been solved by Manfield and Downs, albeit approximately, in the case of two arbitrary renewal input streams [28]. Formulas are proposed for the moments of the overflow and carried streams, but these formulas are even more complex than in the case where one stream is Poisson; this complexity seems to preclude the use of these formulas in network algorithms. The formulas have been used to suggest approximate formulas based on the analysis of the two-stream case.

Let $F_1(t)$ and $F_2(t)$ be the interarrival time distribution of the two streams, let $\phi_i(s)$, $i = 1, 2$ be the respective Laplace-Stieltjes transforms of the corresponding density functions, and let λ_i equal the corresponding intensity. Also let $p_i = \lambda_i/(\lambda_1 + \lambda_2)$. The expected number of blocked calls during a period of congestion is given by

$$E^1 = \frac{p_1 \phi_1(N\mu)}{1 - \phi_1(N\mu)} + \frac{p_2 \lambda_1}{N\mu} \tag{3.111}$$

$$E^2 = \frac{p_2 \phi_2(N\mu)}{1 - \phi_2(N\mu)} + \frac{p_1 \lambda_2}{N\mu} \tag{3.112}$$

The distribution of congestion periods is quite complex, and Manfield and Downs make the simplification that the probability that a congestion period starts with an arrival of type i is given by p_i. They also assume that the interarrival time distribution is produced by an IPP process. Thus we have

$$F(t) = k_1(1 - e^{-r_1 t}) + k_2(1 - e^{-r_2 t}) \tag{3.79}$$

and the corresponding transforms,

$$\phi_i(s) = \frac{k_i^1 r_i}{s + r_i} + \frac{k_i^2 r_i^2}{s + r_i}, \quad i = 1, 2.$$

From this, we get the congestion probability for the two streams by replacing in Eqs. (3.111) and (3.112). This can be extended to more than two streams by taking

$$E^i = \frac{p_i \phi_i(N\mu)}{1 - \phi_i(N\mu)} + \frac{(1 - p_i)\lambda_i}{N\mu}, \qquad (3.113)$$

where

$$p_i = \frac{\lambda_i}{\sum_j \lambda_j}, \qquad (3.114)$$

which is an approximation for the individual stream-congestion functions.

Approximate Methods

The work on two-stream blocking clearly indicates the need to partition the blocking probability between the various streams in a reasonable manner, especially when designing and analyzing networks. Although the Brockmeyer system can be used for Poisson stream blocking, in general, one would like to partition the blocking among an arbitrary number of non-Poisson streams, either peaked or smooth. Furthermore, as shown by the work of Kuczura and of Manfield and Downs, exact methods based on the solution of the Kolmogorov equations call for too much computation to be usable for network problems. For these reasons, approximate methods are required.

The simplest approximations are based on a partition of the blocking derived from the values of the first two moments of the traffic streams. First we examine some simple empirical formulas based on numerical studies. Then we describe some partitioning models based on the techniques described in Section 3.4, with special emphasis on the generalization of the BPP and Cox models to the heterogeneous case.

Empirical Formulas.   These techniques assume that the aggregate blocking for all the streams has been computed, for instance, by one of the methods of Section 3.4. This probability is then partitioned between the streams using some reasonable formula, with the condition that the sum of the parcel overflows is equal to the aggregated overflow.

Let B be the aggregate blocking probability and B^k be the blocking for stream k. An early method to estimate the stream blocking was proposed by Katz [19] in the case of peaked traffic:

$$B^k = B \left[1 + K \left(\frac{V^k}{M^k} - \frac{V}{M} \right) \right]. \qquad (3.115)$$

Although this method is adequate for a given link, the constant K is traffic dependent and must be adjusted for each link. The actual form of K is given by

$$K \approx \frac{M}{V} \left[4.1 \times 10^{-4} \left(\frac{M}{V} \right) \left(\frac{1}{B} \right)^2 - 0.156 \left(\frac{M}{V} \right) \left(\frac{1}{B} \right)^{1/2} \right.$$
$$\left. - 0.0747 \left(\frac{1}{B} \right) + 0.69 \left(\frac{1}{B} \right)^{1/2} \right] - 0.183, \qquad (3.116)$$

where the coefficients were found by regression over simulation results of trunk groups in networks. The method was somewhat improved by Butto, Colombo, and Tonietti [29], and apparently independently by Deschamps [30], who gave an analytic approximation for the constant K when one of the streams is Poisson. The estimate of K is made by using Eq. (3.115) for the Poisson stream, for which we know that the variance is equal to the mean. For this parcel, B is given by the group time congestion of the corresponding Brockmeyer system as given by Eq. (3.21). The only remaining unknown in Eq. (3.115) is K, which can easily be computed. In cases where the resulting parcel blocking is not in the interval $(0, 1)$, the value is set at either 0 or 1, depending on whether the result was larger than 1 or smaller than 0.

Another empirical formula based on numerical experiments was proposed by Kuczura [21], who suggested

$$B^k = B \frac{M^k Z^k}{\sum_j M^j Z^j}, \qquad (3.117)$$

where M^k is the mean of the kth input stream. This formula partitions the flow in proportion to the variances instead of the means. The author claims that it is more accurate than Katz's formula, based again on numerical results.

Finally, we should also mention yet another formula proposed by Olsson as described in [13], where

$$B^i = B \left(\frac{M}{M^i} \right) \frac{V^i + \dfrac{M^{i2}}{V^i}}{\displaystyle\sum_j V^j + \dfrac{M^{j2}}{V^j}}. \qquad (3.118)$$

Clearly, it is possible to produce a rather large number of similar formulas, based on both intuition and numerical studies. Needed instead, however, is a more systematic way to generate such formulas, ideally in relation to the single-stream models of Section 3.4. Recent work on heterogeneous blocking takes this direction, suggesting models based on the BPP technique, the IPP model, and the Cox generator.

The BPP Approximation.   A systematic procedure for computing the stream-carried traffic, based on an application of the BPP technique to the individual streams, has been proposed by Delbrouck [23]. From the joint distribution of busy circuits, a convolution operation is performed over $n-1$ streams to get the marginal distribution for a given stream, from which the moments of the carried traffic can be computed. Let X_i be the number of calls of stream i present in the group. The basic assumption of the method is that this distribution is represented approximately by the truncated BPP distribution that satisfies the recurrence

$$p_i(x_i+1) = \frac{\alpha_i + \beta_i x_i}{x_i} p_i(x_i), \qquad (3.119)$$

which is obtained from Eq. (3.25) when applied to stream i, and where α_i and β_i are computed from the stream mean and peakedness by Eqs. (3.27) and (3.28). Next we assume that the joint occupation probability has the product form

$$p(x_1, x_2 \ldots x_n) = K \prod_{i=1}^{N} p_i(x_i), \qquad (3.120)$$

where K is the appropriate normalization constant

$$K^{-1} = \sum_{x_1+x_2\ldots x_n \leq N} p_1(x_1)p_2(x_2)\ldots p_n(x_n).$$

Given this joint distribution, we want to compute the moments of the carried traffic for each stream. This can be done in several ways consistent with Eqs. (3.119) and (3.120), which in turn determine which overflow parameters are available, as well as the computational requirements.

Convolution Method.   This method uses the marginal distribution of each stream, obtained by taking the convolution of the joint distribution over all but the ith stream. The marginal distribution is given by

$$\theta_i(x) = \sum p(x_1, \ldots x, \ldots x_n), \qquad (3.121)$$

from which we can get the carried traffic and variance

$$\overline{M}^i = \sum_{x=1}^{N} x\theta_i(x) \qquad (3.122)$$

$$\overline{V}^i = \sum_{x=1}^{N} x^2\theta_i(x_i)$$

where the sum is carried over $x_1 + \ldots x_{i-1} + x_{i+1} + \ldots x_n \leq N - x$, that is, over all streams but stream i. The call congestion is computed directly from the difference between offered and carried traffics:

$$B^i = \frac{M^i - \overline{M}^i}{M^i}. \qquad (3.123)$$

From the marginal distribution (3.121), we can get all the moments of the carried traffic of each stream. Note, however, that the technique implies a large amount of computation since each distribution is the result of a convolution over all the other streams in the group.

A simpler way to arrive at the individual congestion is to apply the call-congestion formula of Eq. (3.101) to each stream, replacing Z and M by Z^i and M^i. This would give

$$B^i = E\left(1 + \frac{N}{M}(Z^i - 1)\right). \tag{3.124}$$

This partition formula, proposed by Delbrouck [31], is called the *BPP2 formula*. This formulation has a number of advantages over the convolution method. The sum of the individual blocked traffic is identical to the value of the overall blocked traffic as computed from Eq. (3.101). This method is also much faster than the convolutions, but does not give the second moments of either the carried or the overflow traffic. Also, the formula overestimates the blocking for parcels having an individual peakedness greater than the total peakedness ($Z^i \geq Z$), and underestimates the blocking for the other parcels.

Another formula proposed to correct this, called the *BPP3 formula*, is written

$$C_i \propto E\left[1 + \frac{N}{M}\left(\left(\frac{V^i}{M^i}\right)^\gamma - 1\right)\right], \tag{3.125}$$

where γ is a constant that must be determined. The equation is only a proportionality since the sum of the parcel losses on the right-hand side does not add up to the total loss computed from the total blocking probability. The formula can be renormalized, so that the partition formula becomes

$$B^i = CE\left[1 + \frac{N}{M}\left(\left(\frac{V^i}{M^i}\right)^\gamma - 1\right)\right], \tag{3.126}$$

where

$$C^{-1} = \sum_i C_i,$$

which now satisfies

$$BM = \sum_i B_i M_i.$$

In practice, the value of the parameter γ is not important, and values in the range $0.4 \leq \gamma \leq 0.5$ appear to give satisfactory accuracy.

Recursive Method. The defects of the convolution method have been corrected in [31], where a recursive procedure is proposed for computing the time congestion of each stream and the first two moments of the carried traffic. The recursion is over N, the number of circuits in the group. Let

$m_i^j(N)$ = The ith moment of the distribution of calls from stream j that are present in the group. This is the carried traffic if $N < \infty$, and the offered traffic if $N = \infty$.

$m_1^{j*}(N)$ = The product of the time congestion with the average of X_j given that all N trunks are busy. In a sense, this measures the amount of traffic that could have been carried during the time when the group was busy. This is another measure of blocked traffic, but from the point of view of time congestion.

We also define

$$M^j = m_1^j(\infty)$$
$$v^j(N) = m_2^j(N) - (m_1^j(N))^2$$
$$V^j = v^j(\infty)$$

M^j and V^j have the usual interpretation of the mean and variance of the offered traffic of stream j, while m_1 and v have the same meaning for the carried traffic. E_N is the time congestion in the group of size N. The moments can be calculated recursively for groups of increasing size n:

$$E_n = \frac{\sum_{i=1}^k Z_i^{-1} \hat{a}^i(n-1)}{n + \sum_{k=1}^k Z_i^{-1} \hat{a}^i(n-1)}$$

$$m_1^j(n) = (1 - E_n)\left[\alpha_j + \beta_j m_1^j(n-1)\right]$$

$$m_1^{j*}(n) = (1 - E_n)\left[\alpha_j E_{n-1} + \beta_j m_1^{j*}(n-1)\right]$$

$$m_2^j(n) = (1 - E_n)\left[(\alpha_j + \beta_j)m_1^j(n-1) + \beta_j m_2^j(n-1) + \alpha_j\right]$$

$$\hat{a}^j(n) = M^j - m_1^j(n-1)$$

with the initial values

$$E_0 = 1, \quad m_i^j(0) = m_1^j(0) = 0, \quad \hat{a}^j(0) = M_j$$

The recurrence, solved from $n = 1$ to N, gives the time congestion and the first two moments of the carried traffic for stream i.

Overflow Parameters.   In addition to the mean of the overflow traffic $\hat{a}^j(N)$, we need the call congestion for each offered stream and the variance of the overflow streams. Although not directly available from the recurrence, these parameters can be estimated using the standard ERT method for each stream (see Fig. 3.4). Assume that there exists a fictitious primary group of size N^* to which a Poisson stream of intensity A^j is offered. Calls blocked on the primary group are then offered to the real group, which we will call the secondary group. Because we know that the traffic offered to this secondary

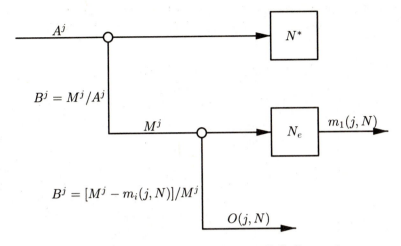

Figure 3.4   ERT Model for Stream Call Congestion

group has parameters M^j and V^j, the value of the equivalent Poisson traffic can be computed by Rapp's approximation,

$$A^j = M^j Z^j + 3Z^j (Z^j - 1),$$

and the call congestion in the primary group is given by M^j / A^j. Suppose now that this traffic is offered to a fictitious secondary group of size N_e that *carries exclusively calls from stream* j. N_e is chosen such that the traffic it carries is precisely $m_1^j(N)$. Obviously, $N_e \neq N$. Calls offered to this fictitious secondary group are blocked with a probability $\hat{a}^j(N)/M^j$. Hence the call congestion for stream j on the real group is approximated by

$$B^j = \frac{M^j - m_1^j(N)}{M^j}.$$

The overflow variance $\hat{v}^j$ for stream j can be computed with this equivalent system by noting that $\hat{a}^j(N)$ is the overflow of a Poisson traffic A^j in a group of size $N_e + N^*$. These sizes need not be computed since the overflow traffic is already known. The value of the offered and overflow traffics being known, Rapp's approximation prescribes the value of the peakedness of the overflow $\hat{Z}^j$ through the equation

$$A^j = \hat{a}^j(N)\hat{Z}^j + 3\hat{Z}^j(\hat{Z}^j - 1),$$

which in turn yields the variance

$$\hat{v}^j = \hat{Z}^j \hat{a}^j(N),$$

which is the required expression for the variance of the overflow. It has also been noted by Delbrouck [31] that the individual stream call congestion can be rewritten

$$B^j = E_N \left(1 + \frac{m_1^{j^*}(N)E_n^{-1}}{M^j}(Z^j - 1) \right).$$

Compare with Eq. (3.124). This in turn suggests the approximation

$$\frac{E_N M^j}{\sum_l M_l} = \frac{m_1^{j^*}(N)}{N}, \tag{3.127}$$

which has a straightforward interpretation. As pointed out by Delbrouck, this equation can easily be incorrect for particular values of traffic. Thus, although it has a strong intuitive appeal and seems well verified in most cases, it is not clear under what conditions Eq. (3.127) should be considered correct.

Akimaru's Approximation

Another partition formula, proposed by Akimaru and Takahashi [32], is based on the moment match of the overflow traffic to the IPP model. First consider Eq. (3.48), which links the time and call congestion for a renewal input stream offered to a group of finite size. Assume that this renewal stream is made up of the superposition of a Poisson stream and an IPP stream, and also that the parameters of the IPP stream are matched to the parameters of some overflow traffic. In this case, Eq. (3.48) becomes

$$\frac{B}{E} = 1 + (Z - 1)\frac{N}{M}\frac{M + 3Z}{N - 1 + M + 3Z}, \tag{3.128}$$

where M and Z are the mean and peakedness of the aggregate stream. Let B^1 and B^2 be the call congestion of the Poisson and IPP streams, respectively. Because the Poisson stream is memoryless, its call congestion is identical to the overall call congestion B, as noted by Wilkinson [6]. Using this fact, we can rewrite Eq. (3.128) as

$$B^1 = \left[1 + (Z - 1)\frac{N}{M}\frac{M + 3Z}{N - 1 + M + 3Z} \right]^{-1} B. \tag{3.129}$$

We can eliminate B from this equation by using the conservation equation $a^2 B^2 + a^1 B^1 = aB$, obtaining

$$\frac{B^2}{B^1} = 1 + (Z^2 - 1)\left(\frac{N}{M}\right)\frac{M + 3Z}{N - 1 + M + 3Z}. \tag{3.130}$$

We generalize to an arbitrary number of streams by

$$B_k = \frac{1 + (Z_k - 1)f(N, A, Z)}{1 + (Z - 1)f(N, A, Z)}B, \tag{3.131}$$

where

$$f(N, A, Z) = \frac{N(3Z + A)}{A(N - 1 + A + 3Z)}.$$

The total call congestion is computed by any one of the methods of Section 3.4, and then partitioned according to Eq. (3.128). Note that this method does not yield information on the second moment of the carried or overflow traffic.

The Cox Model for Heterogeneous Blocking

Finally, we briefly discuss the Cox model as a method for computing parcel blocking [15]. First consider the case where two renewal streams are offered to a common trunk group. To be able to use the Cox generator we represent the input streams by their first three moments, from which the parameters of the two generators are computed. Define a busy period as an interval during which all the circuits of the group are busy. Parcel blocking is calculated on the system where the sources are the equivalent Cox generator.

Let E_i, $i = 1, 2$ be the expected number of calls from stream i that are blocked during a busy period, and p_i the probability that a blocked call belongs to stream i. Obviously we have $p_i = E_i/(E_1 + E_2)$. We can calculate the parcel-blocking probabilities as follows. First we distinguish busy periods as being of type 1 or type 2, depending on whether the call that has caused the saturation belongs to stream 1 or stream 2. Let $E_{i,j}$ be the expected number of blocked calls of stream i, given that stream i is in state j. Recall that the state of the stream is given by the state of the associated Cox generator since we have replaced the actual renewal process by the generator via the appropriate moment match.

Then, for $i = 1$, we have

$$E_{1.1} = \frac{\alpha_1 b_1}{\alpha_1 + N\mu}(1 + E_{1.1}) + \frac{\alpha_1 a_1}{\alpha_1 + N\mu}E_{1.2}$$

$$E_{1.2} = \frac{\beta_1}{\beta_1 + N\mu}(1 + E_{1.1})$$

and similar equations for stream 2. These equations are derived by considering the possible states of the generator and the probabilities of being in these states. Suppose that the generator is in the first stage. In this case, the system has $N + 1$ exponential servers, one of rate α_1 (the customer in the first stage), and N servers at rate μ. The Cox server may end service first, with probability $\alpha_1/(\alpha_1 + N\mu)$; a new call is then generated with probability b_1, or the generator stays in state 1, which produces the term $(1 + E_{1.1})$. Or the generator may enter state 2, with probability $a_1\alpha_1/(\alpha_1 + N\mu)$, which gives the term $E_{1.2}$, or the busy period may end, with probability $N\mu/(\alpha_1 + N\mu)$. The combination of these events yields the expression for $E_{1.1}$, and a similar argument yields the corresponding equation for $E_{1.2}$. The solution to the system of equations is

$$E_{1.1} = \frac{\alpha_1(\beta_1 + b_1 N\mu)}{N\mu(\alpha_1 a_1 + \beta_1 + N\mu)}$$

$$E_{1.2} = \frac{\beta_1(\alpha_1 + N\mu)}{N\mu(\alpha_1 a_1 + \beta_1 + N\mu)}$$

We must now consider whether the current busy period is of type i, that is, whether it is caused by a call of stream i. Let r_i be the probability that it is of type i. We can assume that this probability is proportional to the arrival rate of the two streams; we get

$$r_1 = \frac{\alpha_1\beta_1}{\beta_1 + a_1\alpha_1} \bigg/ \left[\frac{\alpha_1\beta_1}{\beta_1 + a_1\alpha_1} + \frac{\alpha_2\beta_2}{\beta_2 + a_2\alpha_2}\right]$$

$$r_2 = \frac{\alpha_2\beta_2}{\beta_2 + a_2\alpha_2} \bigg/ \left[\frac{\alpha_1\beta_1}{\beta_1 + a_1\alpha_1} + \frac{\alpha_2\beta_2}{\beta_2 + a_2\alpha_2}\right]$$

Also assume that the system is in a stationary state when a busy period begins, and let q_1 be the probability that stream 1 is in state 1 when a busy period of type 2 starts. Then,

$$q_1 = \frac{\beta_1}{\beta_1 + a_1\alpha_1}.$$

From this,

$$E_1 = r_1 E_{1,1} + r_2 \left[q_1 E_{1,1} + (1 - q_1)E_{1,2}\right].$$

The corresponding equation for E_2 can be obtained in the same manner.

The solution of an arbitrary number of streams m is computed by solving m two-stream problems. One stream is singled out for calculation, and the remaining $m - 1$ streams are aggregated into a single stream. The assumption here is that this aggregated stream is also of the renewal type. We calculate the overflow traffic for the stream of interest by the methods just described, repeating the process m times to get the mean of the overflow traffic for all the input streams.

It is also possible to calculate the transform of the individual overflow processes by generalizing the results of Section 3.3, although the results cannot be used to evaluate network performance because of the computational requirements. Thus we give only a brief outline of the procedure, which is not fundamentally different from the one used in calculating the overflow and carried parameters for a single stream.

First we must define the transforms for four types of intervals. Assume that the group is in state i at the current time. We are interested in the interval until the next overflow from stream 1. There are four conditions under which this can happen, coming from the product of the current state, denoted by $k = 1, 2$

of generator $m = 1, 2$. We then have four transforms $\hat{\Phi}_i^{(k,m)}(s)$ to compute. We write the Kolmogorov equations for these functions, using an argument similar to that of Section 3.3, obtaining a system of order $4(N + 1)$. Here, too, taking the rth derivative and evaluating it at zero gives the moments of all the distributions of the overflow. Because we are concentrating on stream 1, we are interested in the overflow distribution $\hat{\phi}(s)$ caused by this stream. Letting P_2 be the probability that the generator for stream 2 is in state 1 immediately after an overflow from stream 1, we have

$$\hat{\Phi}(s) = \hat{\Phi}^{(1,1)}P_2 + \hat{\Phi}^{(1,2)}(1 - P_2),$$

where

$$P_2 = \frac{\alpha_1 b_1 p_N(1, 1) + \beta_1 p_N(2, 1)}{\alpha_1 b_1 p_N(1, 1) + \beta_1 p_N(2, 1) + \alpha_1 b_1 p_N(1, 2) + \beta_1 p_N(2, 2)},$$

where $p_k(i, j)$ is the probability distribution corresponding to $\hat{\Phi}^{(i,j)}(s)$. Clearly the amount of computation can become quite large for a given link, and the total computation time required for the analysis of a network precludes the use of this method except in the simplest cases. Nevertheless, such a model can be useful to check the accuracy of the approximations that must be used in network analysis.

3.6   Computational Considerations and Accuracy

The traffic models discussed in the previous sections are those mentioned most frequently in the literature on circuit-switched networks. These models represent only a small part of the work on the subject; the number of actual and potential models that can be generated from the birth-and-death and renewal techniques is quite large. A natural question is which of these models should be used in network problems. This is a complex question to which there is no definite answer. It is possible, however, to state some considerations in selecting a traffic model to implement on a computer and use in the automated design and analysis of networks. Computation time, robustness, regularity, and accuracy are the more important factors, in that order, and a few words of advice are offered to the unwary on each of these topics. (Manual design using charts is a different matter, and is not discussed here, since traffic models suitable for one method may or may not be suitable for the other.)

Computation Time

The time required to evaluate the blocking and the parameters of the traffic streams is of primary importance in network problems. Unfortunately, this topic is not discussed often in the teletraffic literature. This omission is understandable when the sole purpose of the exercise is to compute the performance of a single isolated system, perhaps to study the effect of one parameter, or to evaluate the accuracy of an approximate method on a small system.

The picture changes dramatically if we envisage using computer implementations of these methods for network study. In such a case, we must evaluate blocking probabilities hundreds, if not thousands of times for a single network evaluation. Any method, however accurate, that requires long computation times, must be rejected, since the total computation time would quickly become prohibitive for a network of any significant size. Similar remarks hold for the amount of storage required by a model. It may be useful to evaluate a group using a five-moment match, as has been proposed, but the amount of data required in the case of a moderately large network certainly makes the method impractical.

Robustness

Robustness, also an important aspect, especially for computer implementation, is related to the finite size of numbers that can be represented on computers and to the consequently limited accuracy in their representation. A robust implementation must meet at least three requirements: (1) It should yield meaningful results even when its input takes extreme values, (2) the computation algorithm must not be subject to fatal errors in evaluating intermediate results, and (3) no significant errors must be introduced by the calculation process.

Input may take on extreme values when the traffic algorithms are used within other design or evaluation procedures that may be searching for solutions well outside the expected range of parameter values. For instance, an Erlang B program, when asked to compute $E(A = 1, N = 200)$, should return a value of zero, not some cryptic message about overflow or underflow. Although any human designer would immediately know the correct answer, the computer implementation must be carefully designed to avoid meaningless error messages or fatal errors at execution time. This same remark holds for moment-matching methods, where two methods that are equally fast may turn out to be quite different from the point of view of robustness. A good example is the calculation of equivalent systems for smooth traffic, which may not exist for certain values of the parameters. A robust implementation should be able to recognize this fact and arrive at a sensible solution, instead of blindly going into a loop and terminating with an answer of dubious value. For this reason, equivalent systems that are known to exist for all values of the parameters are superior to those that are known not to exist in some ranges (e.g., ERT-N) — or worse, to those where it is not known under what conditions the equivalent system exists.

The second aspect of robustness concerns the actual steps to compute a value. This is better explained by way of a trivial example. Suppose we want to compute $p_j = e^{-A}A^j/j!$ for the Poisson model. To make this more precise, let us take $A = 100$ and $j = 100$. Note that the numerical value of this probability is quite reasonable, about 0.513296. A naive implementation would compute each term separately and then take the product. This, of course, would not work, since the evaluation of 100! would probably exceed the largest number that can be represented on the computer, causing an overflow error. A more astute implementation would recognize the fact that p_j can be computed recursively, since

$$p_j = p_{j-1}A/j \qquad (3.132)$$

The proper normalization would be done at the end by summing all terms and dividing the *p*s by this sum. Of course, in the present case, we know what the normalization constant should be. In general, we do not have such an expression; we can only guess what the value of p_0 could be and then renormalize after the calculation is completed. This approach would be somewhat better but would not meet the requirement for robustness. This is because of the form $A^k/k!$; for large-enough A, the numerator will grow initially much faster than the factorial, and the iteration term may become too large before the denominator has time to catch up.

Nevertheless, it is possible to get a very robust implementation in one of two ways. For the particular case of the Poisson formula, we first compute the $\log p_j = j \log A - \log \Gamma(j + 1)$, using a specialized algorithm to evaluate the logarithm of the Gamma function directly without the computation of the factorial itself. If the logarithm is larger than the logarithm of the smallest number available, the value of p_j is given by $p_j = e^{\log p_j}$. Otherwise, a value of zero is returned. Another robust implementation, which can be applied in other contexts, is based on the fact that the sequence p_j typically increases as j increases, goes by a maximum when j is nearest A, and then decreases monotonically to zero. The recurrence (3.132) is then computed in two directions. Choose the starting value $m = [A]$, the integer that is closest to A. The general step is

$$p_m = 1$$

$$p_k = p_{k-1}\frac{A}{k} \qquad k \geq m$$

$$p_{k-1} = p_k\frac{k}{A} \qquad k < m$$

In other words, solve the recurrence in two separate loops — for increasing and decreasing values of the index, respectively — in such a way that the terms are monotone decreasing on each side of the initial point. In this way, all the significant terms are included, and no underflow error can occur if each recurrence is stopped when the term becomes sufficiently small. The correct values are then obtained by normalization as usual.

This small example shows how the numerical calculation of traffic models can be very different from their analytic formulation. In other cases, an even more drastic reformulation must be made in order to prevent round-off errors and ensure the stability of the computation, which is the third aspect of robustness mentioned previously.

Consider again the traffic model with throttled arrivals, which is defined for integer values of N and m. This model is used in network-optimization algorithms, which are often evaluated over the reals. For this reason, we want to extend the model to fractional values for both N and m, much in the same way that the Erlang B function can be extended to fractional values. A simple extension is first presented and shown to be numerically unstable over some values of the parameters. A recursive approach is then explained that is both robust and efficient for an integer number of reserved trunks and arbitrary parameters [33]. The model is finally extended to arbitrary trunk numbers, and an efficient and robust algorithm is proposed.

Recall the equations for the model:

$$B = p_0 \frac{a^N}{N!}(1-r)^{N-m} \tag{3.29}$$

$$1 - B' = Q' = p_0 \sum_{j=0}^{m-1} \frac{a^j}{j!} \tag{3.30}$$

$$p_0^{-1} = \sum_{k=0}^{m} \frac{a^k}{k!} + \sum_{k=m+1}^{N} \frac{a^k}{k!}(1-r)^{k-m} \tag{3.31}$$

We want to extend Eqs.(3.29–3.31) to real m and N. Recall the definition of the incomplete exponential function,

$$e_m(x) = \sum_{j=0}^{m} \frac{x^j}{j!}, \tag{3.133}$$

which is used to express Eqs. (3.31) and (3.30):

$$p_0^{-1} = e_m(a) + (1-r)^{-m}\left[e_N(\bar{a}) - e_m(\bar{a})\right] \tag{3.134}$$

$$B = p_0 \frac{a^N}{N!}(1-r)^{N-m} \tag{3.135}$$

$$Q' = p_0 e_{m-1}(a) \tag{3.136}$$

We obtain the required generalization by noting that

$$E(a,m) = \frac{a^m/m!}{e_m(a)}, \tag{3.137}$$

where $E(\cdot,\cdot)$ is the Erlang B function, for which we have a generalization to nonnegative reals, and $N!$ is extended to the reals by the Gamma function. In what follows, $N!$ should be understood to mean $\Gamma(N+1)$ whenever N is not integer. We can express Eqs. (3.134–3.136) for fractional values as

$$p_0^{-1} = \frac{a^m/m!}{E(a,m)} + (1-r)^{-m}\left[\frac{\bar{a}^N/N!}{E(\bar{a},N)} - \frac{\bar{a}^m/m!}{E(\bar{a},m)}\right] \tag{3.138}$$

$$B = p_0\frac{a^N}{N!}(1-r)^{N-m} \tag{3.139}$$

$$Q' = p_0\frac{a^{m-1}/(m-1)!}{E(a,m-1)} \tag{3.140}$$

For $0 < m < 1$, Eq. (3.140) is written as

$$Q' = p_0\frac{a^m}{m!}\left(\frac{1}{E(a,m)} - 1\right).$$

Eqs. (3.138–3.140) are the required generalizations for arbitrary nonnegative m and N. Mathematically, they give the correct value of the probabilities for any argument. In practice, however, the form of the equations is such that severe numerical difficulties can arise if we want to carry out the calculation as indicated. This is best understood by looking at Eq. (3.138). This quantity requires the computation of

$$\left[\frac{\bar{a}^N/N!}{E(\bar{a},N)} - \frac{\bar{a}^m/m!}{E(\bar{a},m)}\right], \tag{3.141}$$

where both terms may be large but close to each other; since we must compute their differences, large round-off errors may occur that would make the final answer virtually useless.

A general solution could be to use a program for computing the Erlang B function with very high accuracy. This would have the effect of slowing down the computation in all cases, even those where it is not required. As we shall now show, we can rearrange the calculation to avoid numerical instabilities in all cases of interest. From a mathematical point of view, Eqs. (3.138–3.140) are perfectly adequate. The massive reformulation described below is required only because computers can do arithmetic only to a limited accuracy.

Recursive Formulation. First we give an expression for the blocking probabilities for integer $N-m$ but real N and m. In itself, this expression can be used when the number of reserved trunks is a fixed integer. The algorithm proposed is a recursion on the number of reserved trunks. We can write

$$\frac{1}{B(a,r,m,N+1)} = \frac{\displaystyle\sum_{k=0}^{m}\frac{a^k}{k!} + \sum_{k=m+1}^{N}\frac{a^k(1-r)^{k-m}}{k!} + \frac{a^{N+1}(1-r)^{N+1-m}}{(N+1)!}}{\dfrac{a(1-r)}{(N+1)}\dfrac{a^N(1-r)^{N-m}}{N!}}$$

$$= \frac{(N+1)}{\bar{a}}\frac{1}{B(a,r,m,N)} + 1, \tag{3.142}$$

and also for Q',

$$\frac{1}{Q'(a,r,m,N+1)} = \frac{\displaystyle\sum_{k=0}^{m}\frac{a^k}{k!} + \sum_{k=m+1}^{N}\frac{a^k(1-r)^{k-m}}{k!} + \frac{a^{N+1}(1-r)^{N+1-m}}{(N+1)!}}{\displaystyle\sum_{j=0}^{m-1}\frac{a^j}{j!}}$$

$$= \frac{1}{Q'(a,r,m,N)} + \frac{a^{N+1}}{(N+1)!}\frac{(1-r)^{N+1-m}}{\displaystyle\sum_{j=0}^{m-1}\frac{a^j}{j!}}. \tag{3.143}$$

Using the well-known recursion for the Erlang function,

$$\frac{1}{E(a,N)} = 1 + \frac{N}{a}\frac{1}{E(a,N-1)}, \tag{3.4}$$

we obtain the following expression for the last term:

$$\frac{a^{N+1}}{(N+1)!}\frac{(1-r)^{N+1-m}}{\displaystyle\sum_{j=0}^{m-1}\frac{a^j}{j!}} = \frac{a^{N+1-m}(1-r)^{N+1-m}}{(N+1)N\ldots(m+1)}\frac{E(a,m)}{1-E(a,m)}.$$

Replacing in Eq. (3.143), we get

$$\frac{1}{Q'(a,r,m,N+1)} = \frac{1}{Q'(a,r,m,N)} + \frac{a^{N+1-m}(1-r)^{N+1-m}}{(N+1)N\ldots(m+1)}\frac{E(a,m)}{1-E(a,m)}, \tag{3.144}$$

which is the required recursion. The initial values are given by

$$B(a,r,m,m) = E(a,m) \tag{3.145}$$
$$Q'(a,r,m,m) = 1 - E(a,m) \tag{3.146}$$

This technique is particularly efficient when the number of reserved trunks is small, as is often the case. The total amount of work required is then approximately equal to that required to compute the Erlang B function for Eqs. (3.145) and (3.146), with a few additional iterations.

Fractional Number of Reserved Trunks. The recursion with integer $N - m$ is not adequate for network optimization, where both N and m may vary. Thus an extension is also required for noninteger $N - m$.

A robust method has been proposed in [33] for this case, based on the model developed for integer $N - m$. We extend recursions (3.142) and (3.144) to a fraction $0 < \delta < 1$ above N. Using Eqs. (3.138–3.140) and (3.137), we have

$$
\frac{1}{B(a,r,m,N+\delta)} = \frac{e_m(a) + (1-r)^{-m}\left[e_{N+\delta}(\bar{a}) - e_m(\bar{a})\right]}{\frac{\bar{a}^{N+\delta}}{(N+\delta)!}(1-r)^{-m}}
$$

$$
= \frac{(N+\delta)!}{N!}\frac{1}{\bar{a}^{\delta}}\frac{1}{B(a,r,m,N)}
$$

$$
+ \frac{(N+\delta)!}{\bar{a}^{N+\delta}}\left[e_{N+\delta}(\bar{a}) - e_N(\bar{a})\right] \tag{3.147}
$$

and also

$$
\frac{1}{Q'(a,r,m,N+\delta)} = \frac{e_m(a)}{e_{m-1}(a)} + \frac{(1-r)^{-m}}{e_{m-1}(a)}\left[e_{N+\delta}(\bar{a}) - e_m(\bar{a})\right]
$$

$$
= \frac{e_m(a)}{e_{m-1}(a)} + \frac{(1-r)^{-m}}{e_{m-1}(a)}\left[e_{N+\delta}(\bar{a}) - e_N(\bar{a}) + e_N(\bar{a}) - e_m(\bar{a})\right]
$$

$$
= \frac{1}{Q'(a,r,m,N)} + \frac{(1-r)^{-m}}{e_{m-1}(a)}\left[e_{N+\delta}(\bar{a}) - e_N(\bar{a})\right]. \tag{3.148}
$$

Let

$$
S_N(\bar{a}) = \frac{(N+\delta)!}{\bar{a}^{N+\delta}}\left[e_{N+\delta}(\bar{a}) - e_N(\bar{a})\right]. \tag{3.149}
$$

As we see, we can compute Eqs. (3.147) and (3.148) by Eqs. (3.142) and (3.144) to the nearest $N - m$ integer, expressing the correction term of Eqs. (3.147) and (3.148) in terms of Eq. (3.149). It remains only to obtain Eq. (3.149) for arbitrary values of a, r, m, and N. Incidentally, we can easily check that, if $0 < \delta < 1$, then $0 < S_N < 1$. In particular, if $\delta = 1$, we get back Eqs. (3.142) and (3.144) for an integer number of reserved trunks, as we should.

Computation of the Correction Term. We now give an expression for Eq. (3.149) that is robust for all values of traffic and trunk numbers. Using Eq. (3.137), we get

$$
S_N(a) = \frac{1}{E(a,N+\delta)} - \frac{(N+\delta)!}{N!}\frac{1}{a^{\delta}}\frac{1}{E(a,N)}. \tag{3.150}
$$

We encounter the same difficulty as with Eq. (3.141). If a/N is small, we must compute the difference of two large quantities that differ by a small amount, causing large numerical errors.

Thus we must use a technique less sensitive to these errors. First we consider the case $a \leq N$, since in the other case we can compute Eq. (3.150) directly with good accuracy. From Jagerman [5], we know that

$$
E(a,N)^{-1} = \psi(a,N)^{-1} - \sum_{j=1}^{\infty} \frac{a^j}{(N+1)(N+2)\ldots(N+j)} \tag{3.151}
$$

where

$$\psi(a, N) = e^{-a} \frac{a^N}{\Gamma(N+1)}$$

We use Eq. (3.151) to compute both terms of Eq. (3.150) simultaneously. We get

$$S_N(a) = \sum_{j=1}^{\infty} \frac{a^j}{(N+\delta+1)(N+\delta+2)\ldots(N+\delta+j)}$$

$$\times \left[\frac{1}{a^\delta} \frac{(N+\delta+j)!}{(N+j)!} - 1 \right], \qquad (3.152)$$

a convergent series with positive terms, which can be computed with excellent accuracy whenever $a \le N$, and also when $a \le 1$.

Summary.   The point of this discussion is that although we may have a mathematically sufficient formulation of a traffic model, in the present case, expressed by Eqs. (3.139) and (3.140), the numerical evaluation may require some rather profound transformations to be numerically robust. We can summarize the computation as follows. Define

$$N_r = N - m$$
$$K = \lceil N_r \rceil$$
$$\delta = N_r - K$$

1. Compute $B(a, r, m, N - \delta)$ and $q(a, r, m, N - \delta)$ by Eqs. (3.142) and (3.144). If $\delta = 0$ we have an integer number of reserved trunks, and we stop.

2. If $\delta > 0$, compute $S_{N-\delta}(\bar{a})$

   a. If $\bar{a} \le N$ or $\bar{a} \le 1$, use Eq. (3.152).

   b. Otherwise use Eq. (3.150).

3. Correct the values obtained in (1) by Eqs. (3.147–3.149).

Unfortunately, the numerical problems that can be encountered depend to a large extent on the particular model being calculated; for this reason, it is not possible to give general rules that would guarantee a robust implementation. Most of the difficulties come from the evaluation of the normalization constant, but, as we have seen here, other problems can be associated with the numerical calculation. Each case must be analyzed separately, and ad hoc transformations must be made that depend on the structure of the model.

Continuity

Finally, an equally important requirement is continuity in the numerical implementation of an algorithm. In many cases, we must compute the derivative of a probability with respect to the parameters of the system. Typical examples that occur quite frequently are $\partial B/\partial N$ and $\partial B/\partial a$. These derivations are often computed by finite differences, with the resulting necessity of computing the blocking probability of a link at two slightly different values of traffic. A potential problem can occur if the traffic model crosses a significant boundary between these two points. For instance, the traffic may be smooth for the initial value and peaked for the incremented value, or N may be an integer for the initial value and a fraction for the incremented one. If the traffic model used is not smooth at this boundary, very inaccurate values can ensue for the derivative, with potentially disastrous results for the algorithm that requires them.

Smoothness of the model has two very distinct meanings. The first is the smoothness of the analytic representation when two models are used to represent the same function on different parts of its domain. An example is the ERT method extended to smooth traffic by Katz's method. In this case, there are two potential points of trouble: $Z = 1$ and the value of Z where the overflow is set to zero. At these points, the first derivative is not necessarily continuous — which may or may not be important, depending on the application. The potential discontinuity comes from the fact that the models for peaked and smooth traffics are different, with no guarantee of continuity.

The second meaning of smoothness is related to the algorithmic implementation when a smooth function is evaluated by different numerical techniques over different parts of its domain — for example, the computation of the Erlang B function by the method proposed in [4], where different formulas are used for N integer and N real. The point is that, unless suitable precautions are taken, the numerical values computed by the algorithm may show a discontinuity at these points in spite of the fact that the function is continuous in the first sense.

Accuracy

Finally, the methods should be accurate, in the sense that the values computed for blocking and traffic should closely approximate the values measured in a real system. This requirement, however, is the least important, at least within reasonable limits. The reason is that network design and evaluation methods have simplifying assumptions of their own, generally unavoidable, which limit the accuracy of the results. In other words, it does not make much sense to compute link-blocking probabilities with five-digit accuracy if the network-blocking algorithm that uses these procedures is accurate only to two digits.

In practice, one should use the simplest model that gives sufficient accuracy in the network parameters being evaluated. Standard ERT has a long history in the analysis of hierarchical networks, and IPP and BPP have been used successfully for some types of nonhierarchical ones. The latter models may not be required for certain types of networks where traffic is nearly Poisson, or where high accuracy in the blocking is not required — for example, in some dimensioning problems, a straightforward single-moment model may be sufficient. In any case, experimentation is nearly always required, and a network-simulation program is always needed to check the accuracy of the traffic model.

Problems

3.1. Derive the value of the mean and variance of the carried traffic for the Poisson arrival process in a group of size N Eqs. (3.15) and (3.16).

3.2. Demonstrate the recursion relation (3.4) for the Erlang B function.

3.3. Show that the integral representation of the Erlang B function satisfies Eq. (3.4).

3.4. This problem is related to the use of the binomial distribution as a means of representing smooth traffic with arbitrary parameters M, $V < M$. First, show that a finite-population model yields an ordinary binomial distribution. More precisely, let n be the finite number of sources of traffic, each arriving into a group of servers of infinite size. The BD coefficients are given by $\lambda_k = \lambda(n-k)$ and $\mu_k = k\mu$. Show that

$$ p_k = \binom{n}{k} \left(\frac{\lambda}{\lambda + \mu} \right)^k \left(\frac{\mu}{\lambda + \mu} \right)^{n-k}. $$

Discuss the use of this model for representing smooth traffic.

3.5. Write the Kolmogorov equations for the Brockmeyer system. From these, derive the joint state probability distribution Eq. (3.17).

3.6. Draw the transition diagram that corresponds to Eqs. (3.32–3.34) for the IPP.

3.7. Using Eqs. (3.81) and (3.82), show that the traffic generated by the two-stage Cox process can have arbitrary peakedness.

3.8. Derive Eq. (A.20) for the residual life of a renewal process.

3.9. Consider a renewal process where the distribution of lifetimes for the intervals is given by $F(t)$. Show that the probability that the interval lasts up to time s given that it has already lasted up to $t-s$ is given by $(1 - F(s))/(1 - F(s - t))$.

3.10. Consider a renewal arrival process with negative exponential distribution for the intervals between the arrivals with mean $1/\lambda$. The renewal paradox is as follows. We can argue that if we start observing the arrivals at a random point in time, the average time before the next arrival should be $1/2\lambda$, that is, half the average duration between arrivals. Using Eq. (A.24), show that in fact this average value is given by $1/\lambda$. Explain the apparent contradiction.

3.11. Derive Eq. (3.44) for the binomial moments of the renewal traffic at an arbitrary point in time.

3.12. Show that the time and call congestion for a renewal arrival process are equal if and only if the arrival stream is Poisson. The "only if" part can be proved by considering a fixed interarrival distribution $U(t)$. If the ratio E/B is equal to 1, then $\Phi(N)$ must satisfy a particular relation. The proof is by showing that this relation does not hold except when $U(t)$ corresponds to the Poisson process.

3.13. Derive Eq. (3.78) for the IPP process.

3.14. For an arbitrary IPP, verify that $r_1, r_2 > 0$.

3.15. Consider an arrival process produced by the k-stage Erlang generator. Show that the traffic thus produced is always smooth.

3.16. Starting from Eqs. (3.53) and (3.54) for the renewal arrival process, show that the first two parameters of the overflow traffic are indeed those found by the Kosten model when the input is Poisson.

3.17. Demonstrate Eq. (3.59) for the overflow traffic of a renewal input stream.

3.18. Suppose that we want to use the extended ERT method to represent smooth traffic. Compute the condition under which the equivalent system exists.

3.19. Consider the equivalent carried model of Eqs. (3.93) and (3.94) for generating smooth traffic. Show that the equivalent system always exists if $Z < 1$.

3.20. Consider an offered traffic represented by a negative binomial distribution. Show that no renewal input can have this distribution. As a consequence, the representation of overflow traffic by a Pascal distribution is incorrect, at least theoretically. This is done by considering the ratio of β_{n+1}^*/β_n^* in the limit $n \to \infty$, both for the general renewal input and for the Pascal distribution, and showing that the limits are different.

3.21. Derive Eqs. (3.107–3.109).

3.22. Consider the use of the BPP approximation in the computation of stream blocking. A requirement is that the partitioning formulas for the stream blocking must be such that the sum of the overflow traffics are identical to the aggregate overflow. Verify that this is indeed the case for Eq. (3.124). Is it also the case for Eq. (3.123)?

3.23. Consider the calculation of stream blocking using the BPP model. Using the recursive formulation, show that

$$\frac{m_1^j(N)}{M^j} = \frac{m_1^i(N)}{M^i} \quad \text{if } Z^i = Z^j$$

$$\frac{M^j - m_1^j(N)}{M^j} = E_N \quad \text{if } Z^j = 1$$

Interpret these equalities.

3.24. Interpret Eq. (3.127).

References

[1] Syski, R., *Introduction to congestion theory in telephone systems*, North-Holland, 1986.

[2] Wallström, B., "Congestion studies in telephone systems with overflow facilities," *Ericsson Technics*, vol. 22, pp. 187–345, 1966.

[3] Kleinrock, L., *Queuing Systems* , Wiley, 1975.

[4] Farmer, R.F., and Kaufman, L., "On the numerical evaluation of some basic traffic formulae," *Networks*, vol. 8, pp. 153–186, 1978.

[5] Jagerman, D.L., "Some properties of the Erlang loss function," *Bell System Technical Journal*, vol. 53, pp. 525–551, 1974.

[6] Wilkinson, R.I., "Theories for toll traffic engineering in the USA," *Bell System Technical Journal*, vol. 35, pp. 421–514, 1956.

[7] Brockmeyer, E., "The simple overflow problem in the theory of tele phone traffic," (in Danish), *Teleteknik*, vol. 5, pp. 361–374, 1954.

[8] Akinpelu, J.M., "The overload performance of engineered networks with nonhierarchical and hierarchical routing," *International Teletraffic Congress*, vol. 10, pp. 3.2.4.1–3.2.4.7, June 8–15, 1983.

[9] Kuczura, A., "The interrupted poisson process as an overflow process," *Bell System Technical Journal*, vol. 52, pp. 437–448, 1973.

[10] Kosten, L., "On the blocking probability of graded multiples," (in German), *Elektr. Nachr.-Techn.*, vol. 14, pp. 5–12, 1937.

[11] Heffes, H., and Holtzman, J.M., "Peakedness of traffic carried by a finite trunk group with renewal input," *Bell System Technical Journal*, vol. 52, pp. 1617–1642, 1973.

[12] Takács, L., *Introduction to the Theory of Queues*, Oxford University Press, 1962.

[13] Pearce, C.E.M., and Potter, R.M., "Some formulae old and new for overflow traffic in telephony," *International Teletraffic Congress*, vol. 8, 1976.

[14] Potter, R.M., "Explicit formulae for all overflow traffic moments of the Kosten and Brockmeyer systems with renewal input," *Australian Telecommunication Research*, vol. 13, pp. 39–49, 1980.

[15] Guérineau, J.P., Labetoulle, J., and Lebourges, M., "A three moment method for traffic in a network based on a coxian input process," *International Teletraffic Congress*, vol. 10, pp. 4.4b.1–4.4b.7, 1983.

[16] Cox, D.R., "A use of complex probabilities in the theory of stochastic processes," *Proc. Cambridge Phil. Soc.*, vol. 51, pp. 313–319, 1955.

[17] Bretschneider, G., "Extension of the equivalent random method to smooth traffics," *International Teletraffic Congress*, vol. 7, pp. 411/1–411/9, 1973.

[18] Nightingale, D.T., "Computation with smooth traffics and the Wormald chart," *International Teletraffic Congress*, vol. 8, pp. 145.1–145.7, 1977.

[19] Katz, S., "Statistical performance analysis of a switched communication network," *International Teletraffic Congress*, vol. 5, 1967.

[20] Potter, R.M., "The equivalent non random method and restrictions imposed on renewal overflow systems by the specification of a finite number of overflow traffic moments," *International Teletraffic Congress*, vol. 9, pp. potter-1–potter-6, 1979.

[21] Kuczura, A., and Bajaj, D., "A method of moments for the analysis of a switched communication network's performance," *IEEE Transactions on Communications*, vol. COM–27, pp. 185–193, 1977.

[22] Guérineau, J.P., and Labetoulle, J., "End to end blocking in telephone networks: a new algorithm," *International Teletraffic Congress*, vol. 11, pp. 2.4.A.1:1–1.4.A.1:7, 1985.

[23] Delbrouck, L.E.N., "A unified approximate evaluation of congestion functions for smooth and peaky traffics," *IEEE Transactions on Communications*, vol. COM–29, pp. 85–91, 1981.

[24] Holtzman, J.M., "The accuracy of the equivalent random method with renewal inputs," *Bell System Technical Journal*, vol. 52, pp. 1673–1679, 1973.

[25] Wallström, B., and Reneby, L., "On individual losses in overflow systems," *International Teletraffic Congress*, vol. 9, pp. wallstrom-1–wallstrom-8, 1979.

[26] Kuczura, A., "Loss systems with mixed renewal and Poisson inputs," *Operations Research*, vol. 21, pp. 787–795, 1972.

[27] Riordan, J., *Stochastic Service Systems*, Wiley, New York, 1962.

[28] Manfield, D.R., and Downs, T., "Decomposition of traffic in loss systems with renewal input," *IEEE Transactions on Communications*, vol. COM–25, pp. 44–58, 1977.

[29] Butto, M., Colombo, G., and Tonietti, A., "On point to point losses in communication networks," *International Teletraffic Congress*, vol. 8, 1976.

[30] Deschamps, P.J., "Analytic approximation of blocking probabilities in circuit switched communication networks," *IEEE Transactions on Communications*, vol. COM–27, pp. 603–606, 1979.

[31] Delbrouck, L.E.N., "Use of Kosten's system in the provisioning of alternate trunk groups carrying heterogeneous traffic," *IEEE Transactions on Communications*, vol. COM–31, pp. 741–749, 1983.

[32] Akimaru, H., and Takahashi, H., "An approximate formula for individual call losses in overflow systems," *IEEE Transactions on Communications*, vol. COM–31, pp. 808–811, 1983.

[33] Girard, A., "Blocking probability of noninteger groups with trunk reservation," *IEEE Transactions on Communications*, vol. COM–33, pp. 113–120, 1985.

CHAPTER 4

Link-Decomposition Method

Performance measures for circuit-switched networks can take many forms, depending on the time scales considered and the ultimate objective of the planner. The most common — and probably most important — measure of the quality of a network is its ability to carry calls under normal circumstances. This qualitative measure is captured by the notion of total or average (over all origin-destination pairs) loss probability of the network. This global performance index, used to compare networks or routing algorithms, is also the main constraint in dimensioning.

Because it averages all the customers, the average blocking index gives no indication of the individual grade of services actually seen by customers. These grades of service are represented by $L^{i,j}$, the probability that a first-offered call presenting itself at node i, with node j as its destination, cannot be carried by the network. The grade of service can be expressed by the $L^{i,j}$s themselves or by the average

$$\overline{L} = \frac{\sum L^{i,j} A^{i,j}}{\sum A^{i,j}}. \tag{4.1}$$

These objectives are adequate for long-term planning, where decisions are made on an annual basis or longer, and where we can assume that the network parameters, such as the offered traffic, are stationary. In the shorter term, however, networks are not stationary. Traffic demands exhibit seasonal, daily, even hourly variations. This kind of consideration leads to other measures of the grade of service, such as the robustness of the network under traffic fluctuations — in particular, under generalized and focused overload. Similarly, network components are subject to failure. In this context, another measure of quality is the robustness of the network under failures, measured as the fraction of the nominal traffic that can be carried under specified failures. These questions are not specific to circuit-switched networks, but arise for all kinds of communication networks and indeed in other contexts. Because these problems are generally dealt with in the circuit-routing stage of network planning, they will not be discussed here any further.

We limit ourselves to network performance viewed in the context of dimensioning and routing optimization. In this case, the following assumptions generally hold:

1. External calls are represented by independent stationary Poisson processes.

2. Call-holding times are exponentially distributed.

3. Blocked calls have zero holding times.

4. Calls that cannot be routed in the network are cleared and do not return.

5. There is no blocking in switches.

6. The network topology is stable, and does not change during the calculation.

There are a number of known parameters from which to compute the loss probability. The matrix of the rates of the Poisson processes that describe the arrival of new calls to the network, called the *traffic matrix*, is denoted $A^{i,j}$. We also know the vector N_s, the number of circuits on all the links of the network. Finally, the routing policy used in the network is given, denoted by the symbolic value α whenever it is necessary to express some dependence on this parameter.

The full state-space model is far too complex to allow performance evaluation except in the case of very small networks. The difficulty lies in the fact that decisions taken at one point affect components located far away in the network, and that these interactions must somehow be accounted for. On the other hand, we generally have quite accurate models for the individual links, provided that the link parameters, especially the link-offered traffic, are known. The link-decomposition method is an approximation technique whereby the overall network problem is decomposed into a set of independent link-evaluation problems. The performance of each link is easily computed; under suitable assumptions, the overall network performance can be recovered from the individual link-performance measures. The only difficulty with the method arises from the fact that the exact values of the coupling coefficients — the link-offered traffic — are generally unknown. In practice, these values are approximated by a relaxation method, leading in most cases to an iterative procedure for the blocking evaluation.

Conceptually, the method contains two distinct stages:

1. Given the link-blocking probabilities, a computation of the end-to-end blocking for all traffic flows. The emphasis is on the combinatorial aspect of the network operation, relying heavily on the route-tree representation

for the routing. Computational methods are similar to those used to compute the reliability of a network whose links are subject to random failures.

2. An evaluation of the correct link-offered traffic, which in turn yields, via the link-blocking model, the correct values for the link-blocking probability. These values are the coupling coefficients of the system just mentioned. Here, the emphasis is on representing the traffic in terms of flows in the influence graph.

We first discuss how to calculate the end-to-end blocking for load sharing. This routing, though simple, exhibits some of the difficulties of all the other routing methods. We introduce the notion of the Erlang map and of its fixed points, proving some simple results of these equations. Then we extend the discussion to the case of fixed alternate routing. We discuss the combinatorial aspect of the blocking calculation in a route tree, showing how the Erlang fixed point also appears in the context of nonhierarchical routing. After a short discussion of the special case of hierarchical routing, we show that the Erlang map does not necessarily have a unique solution. We give a plausible explanation for this surprising result and indicate how to avoid this difficulty using state protection.

4.1 Load Sharing

After the trivial case of routing only on a direct link, load sharing is the simplest routing method. Load sharing makes a good starting point in discussing performance evaluation; we use it to introduce some basic concepts that will reappear in the remainder of this chapter and others, also providing some interesting theoretical results. Most of the discussion here is taken from [1], but is somewhat simplified; the notation has been made consistent with our conventions.

Load sharing normally operates by separating a given traffic stream corresponding to an origin-destination pair (o, d) into a number of substreams, each offered to a single path between o and d. To simplify notation, we assume that this separation has already been made and that the input parameters are the substreams obtained after the separation process instead of the original traffic matrix $A^{i,j}$. In this way, we can consider a set of streams A^l, each offered to a single path l. The calculation is simplified in the case of load sharing since the event that corresponds to a call loss is identical to the event that the path to which this call is offered is blocked. As we shall see when considering complex methods with alternate routing, this feature of load sharing greatly simplifies the calculation.

We denote the arc-path incidence matrix of the network by $\mathcal{I}_{s,l}$, where a matrix element $a_{s,l}$ is 1 or 0, depending whether link s is in path l or not. Also, let $\mathcal{P}_l$ denote the probability that path l is blocked. The problem is then to compute the value of $\mathcal{P}_l(A, N)$ for all values of l; from these values, the total loss probability is easily obtained by

$$\overline{L} = \frac{\sum_l \mathcal{P}_l A^l}{\sum_l A^l}. \tag{4.2}$$

Because we have good probabilistic models for the individual links, we would like to relate the calculation of the path blocking to the value of the link-blocking probabilities. There are two difficulties with this decomposition. The first is due to the fact that a path may have many links in tandem; the second, to the fact that different paths may intersect and therefore cannot be considered independent.

Since the loss probability cannot be calculated with the Markov model, we must consider what available models might be used to evaluate the path blocking. One model that comes to mind is the Erlang B function since it is so easily computed. Note, however, that the Erlang B function applies to a link in isolation: How can it be related to the calculation of $\mathcal{P}_l$? Now, the Erlang B function has two parameters: (1) the traffic offered to the link and (2) the number of circuits. The second parameter, which has a direct correspondence in the network, is simply the number of circuits in the group. The first parameter, however, appears nowhere in the list of parameters used to define the problem. It must therefore be computed from these values — a computation that constitutes the major difficulty encountered in evaluating $\mathcal{P}_l$.

Assuming that we can find a reasonable definition for a_s, the traffic offered to link s, we could compute a link parameter B_s, called the *link-blocking probability*, from the expression $B_s = E(a_s, N_s)$. The question is then how to relate this link-blocking probability to the path-blocking probability. This is where we start to make simplifying assumptions. We assume that, for a given path l, the events "link $s \in l$ is blocked" are all independent. Under this assumption, we then have the simple expression

$$\mathcal{P}_l = 1 - \prod_{s \in l}(1 - B_s). \tag{4.3}$$

The interpretation of this formula is quite simple. A call can be connected through the path if *all* links on the path are simultaneously free. The probability that a given link s is free is simply $(1 - B_s)$; because of the independence assumption, the probability of the combined event is the product of the individual probabilities. The path-blocking probability is then simply the complement of the probability of connecting the call.

The Erlang Fixed-Point Equation

In the preceding discussion, we reduced the problem of evaluating $\mathcal{P}_l$ to the definition and computation of the traffic offered to each link in the network. The correct definition of the offered traffic can be obtained from the results of Chapter 3. For each call request on the link, we set up a fictitious call in an infinite group. The offered traffic is the process that represents the number of busy servers in the fictitious group. Although theoretically correct, this definition is not very useful since it requires the arrival process at each link to be calculated. We would prefer to use some flow model to represent traffic, even though some ambiguity can arise in defining the flow representation.

For the sake of this discussion, let us consider a path l, numbering the links on the path sequentially in the direction from the origin to the destination. Thus link 1 is the first link encountered by the call, and so on until the last link, say z. One way to represent the flow is to assume that A^l is a flow that becomes thinned by a factor $(1 - B_s)$ as it proceeds on the path. Using this model, the traffic offered to the ith link on path l is given by

$$a_i^l = A^l \prod_{s=1}^{i-1}(1 - B_s), \tag{4.4}$$

and the traffic that finally comes out of the path is given by

$$\overline{A}^l = A^l \prod_{s=1}^{z}(1 - B_s).$$

Although quite intuitive, this model suffers from a serious defect. Because of the thinning process at each link, the traffic of type l carried on each link is given by $\overline{a}_s^l = a_s^l(1 - B_s)$; it is *different* for each link. This, however, is inconsistent with the operation of circuit switching, where the number of calls of a given type carried on all the links of a path must be equal at all times — not the case for our flow model.

We can obtain a different definition of the traffic offered to a link by starting from the condition that the traffic of a given type carried on a path should be carried on all links of that path. Under the independence assumption, the path blocking is given by Eq. (4.3). We now impose the conditions that, first, $\overline{A}^l = (1 - \mathcal{P}_l)A^l$, and that, second, for each link i in the path, we must have $\overline{a}_i^l = \overline{A}^l$. Using the relation between offered and carried traffic on a link $\overline{a}_i^l = (1 - B_i)a_i^l$, we get the so-called reduced-load model:

$$a_s^l = A^l \prod_{i=1}^{z}(1 - B_i)/(1 - B_s). \tag{4.5}$$

Note the crucial difference between the definitions (4.4) and (4.5). In Eq. (4.4), the product runs from 1 to $i - 1$. In other words, the traffic offered to link i

depends on the blocking probability of the links that *precede* i in the path. This is no longer the case with definition (4.5), where the product runs from 1 to z: The traffic offered to link i depends on the blocking probability of links that precede and *follow* it on the path.

This result is often viewed as an indication that the definition of the offered traffic given by Eq. (4.5) should be rejected, since it does not coincide with our intuition of how a flow model should behave. In fact, Eq. (4.5) represents the real behavior of the path better than does Eq. (4.4). To see why the traffic offered to a link should depend on the blocking on links that appear after it on a path, consider once again the Erlang B function. The derivation of this function rests on two assumptions: (1) that the arrival process is Poisson and (2) that the holding times are exponentially distributed. There is, however, another hidden assumption in the model: A call that arrives and finds a free server always enters service immediately. This assumption is no longer true when we examine a link in a path. A call request that arrives at a link and finds a free server does not immediately produce a new call in service. There is a nonzero probability that this call request will not begin service even though there is a free server on the link; this probability is precisely the probability that the rest of the path after link i is blocked. In other words, the correct model to analyze a link in a path is not the $M/M/N$ queue, but the $M/M/N$ queue with balking. Now, if we assume that the balking probability β is independent of the state of link i, it is not hard to show that β is just the product of the blocking probabilities on the remaining path after link i, and that the correct expression for blocking on link i is given by the Erlang B function, but with the value of traffic given by Eq. (4.5), not by Eq. (4.4). This in turn explains why Eq. (4.5) is generally more accurate than Eq. (4.4).

Given Eq. (4.5) for the calculation of the traffic of type l offered to link s, we can compute the total traffic offered to this link simply by adding up the carried traffic of all paths that go through link s. Using the arc-path incidence matrix $\mathcal{I}$, this is simply expressed by

$$\bar{a}_s = \sum_l \mathcal{I}_{s,l} \bar{A}^l$$

$$= \sum_l \mathcal{I}_{s,l} A^l \prod_t (1 - B_t)^{\mathcal{I}_{t,l}},$$

and the offered traffic by

$$a_s = \sum_l \mathcal{I}_{s,l} A^l \prod_t (1 - B_t)^{\mathcal{I}_{t,l}} / (1 - B_s). \tag{4.6}$$

We now begin to see how the traffic flows are tightly coupled by the routing. The traffic offered to a link in the network depends directly on the blocking probability of all links on all paths that use this link. This means that there can be some long-range effects such that a change in one part of the network may affect components located far away.

This dependence is quite pronounced. Now that we have an expression of the traffic offered to link s in terms of the link-blocking probabilities, we must recall that the blocking probabilities are themselves given as functions of the traffic offered to the link, in the present case by the Erlang relation $B = E(a, N)$. Because a depends on the Bs of other links, as seen by Eq. (4.6), we are led to the unavoidable conclusion that the correct values for the link-blocking probabilities can be given only implicitly, as the solution of the set of coupled nonlinear equations:

$$B_s = E\left(\frac{\sum_l \mathcal{I}_{s,l} A^l \prod_t (1 - B_t)^{\mathcal{I}_{t,l}}}{(1 - B_s)}, N_s \right). \tag{4.7}$$

This set of equations is the first manifestation of a phenomenon that will reappear throughout our discussion of performance analysis of circuit-switched networks. In fact, this type of nonlinear behavior is probably the rule, and only under very exceptional conditions can the situation be avoided.

The set of equations in (4.7) is called the Erlang map and its solution the Erlang fixed point; its study is fundamentally important in analyzing circuit switching. Two aspects particularly merit attention, the first of which concerns the number of solutions of the system. While a linear system can only have zero, one, or an infinite number of solutions, a nonlinear system can have any number of solutions, depending on the parameters of the equations. We will show that, in the case of load sharing, the solution is fortunately unique. The second aspect, of course, is the choice of a numerical method to solve the system.

Unicity of the Erlang Fixed-Point Solution

An interesting theoretical result concerning load sharing is the proof that the Erlang fixed-point equation has a unique solution [1]. This proof is carried out by showing that a solution of the fixed-point equations also satisfies the Kuhn-Tucker conditions of a convex minimization problem, and consequently must be unique. First, we introduce the transformation $B_s = 1 - e^{-y_s}$ for link s. Note that this mapping is one-to-one and maps the interval $[0, 1]$ of probabilities onto the interval $[0, \infty]$. In other words, we can equally well refer to B_s or y_s since they can be converted uniquely into each other. We also define for a link the function $\bar{a}_s(y_s, N_s)$, which is the traffic carried on the link for the value y_s. Note that, for a fixed N_s, this function is monotone increasing in y; it can be computed as follows. Given y, compute $B = 1 - e^{-y}$. From this, solve the equation $B = E(a, N)$ to obtain the offered traffic a. From the value of a, compute $\bar{a} = a(1 - B)$.

Consider now the optimization problem:

$$\min_{y} \sum_{l} A^l e^{-\sum_m y_m \mathcal{I}_{m,l}} + \sum_{s} \int_{0}^{y_s} \bar{a}(z, N_s) dz \qquad (4.8)$$

$$y \geq 0$$

The first term is a sum of convex functions. The integrand of the second function is monotone increasing in z, which means that the function defined by the integral has an increasing derivative: It is thus also convex. As a consequence, if the problem has a minimum, this minimum is unique. We can write the Kuhn-Tucker necessary conditions — and in this case they are also sufficient — for optimality; we get

$$\sum_{l} \mathcal{I}_{s,l} A^l e^{-\sum_t y_t \mathcal{I}_{t,l}} = \bar{a}_s(y_s, N_s). \qquad (4.9)$$

We now show that a solution to the fixed-point equation (4.7) is also a solution to Eq. (4.9). Rewriting Eq.(4.7) in terms of $\mathbf{y}$, we get

$$1 - e^{-y_s} = E\left(e^{y_s} \sum_{l} A^l \mathcal{I}_{s,l} e^{-\sum_t y_t \mathcal{I}_{t,l}}, N_s \right).$$

We know that the traffic offered to link s is given by

$$a_s = e^{y_s} \sum_{l} A^l \mathcal{I}_{s,l} e^{-\sum -t y_t \mathcal{I}_{t,l}}.$$

Replacing, we obtain

$$1 - E(a_s, N_s) = e^{-y_s}.$$

Multiplying both sides by a_s, we get

$$a_s \left[1 - E(a_s, N_s) \right] = a_s e^{-y_s}$$

or

$$\bar{a}_s(y_s, N_s) = \sum_{l} A^l \mathcal{I}_{s,l} e^{\sum_t y_t \mathcal{I}_{t,l}},$$

which shows that the solution of the fixed-point equation is also a global optimum of the minimization problem defined by Eq. (4.8). Because this optimum is unique, there can be no other solution to the fixed-point equation.

Numerical Solutions

Like most sets of nonlinear equations, Eq. (4.7) cannot be solved analytically, which means that numerical calculations are the only way to obtain solutions. Also, because these solutions will be used as part of other algorithms, such as routing optimization and dimensioning, the efficiency of the selected technique is of paramount importance.

Solving nonlinear equations numerically is generally quite difficult. Rather than going into depth on this vast subject, we briefly review some of the more popular methods [2] for solving systems of nonlinear equations $F_i(\mathbf{x}) = 0$, indicating how they apply to the problem of finding a solution of the Erlang fixed-point equations.

Newton's Method. The first method that comes to mind to compute a solution of nonlinear equations is that of Newton [2]. This technique uses the first-order development of the vector $\mathbf{F}(\mathbf{x})$ near the current point $\mathbf{x}_0$ to compute a new estimate of the solution. Developing each component of the vector into a power series, we get

$$F_i(\mathbf{x}) = F_i(\mathbf{x}_0) + <(\mathbf{x} - \mathbf{x}_0), \nabla F_i(\mathbf{x}_0)>,$$

which can be written in matrix form as

$$\mathbf{F}(\mathbf{x}) = \mathbf{F}(\mathbf{x}_0) + (\mathbf{x} - \mathbf{x}_0)\mathbf{J}, \tag{4.10}$$

where $\mathbf{J}$, called the *Jacobian matrix* of the system, is given by $J_{i,j} = \partial F_i / \partial x_j$. Since we are looking for the solution of $F_i(\mathbf{x}) = 0$, we choose $\mathbf{x}$ as the next approximation for Eq. (4.10) when $F_i(\mathbf{x}) = 0$. We obtain

$$0 = \mathbf{F}(\mathbf{x}_0) + (\mathbf{x} - \mathbf{x}_0)\mathbf{J}$$

and

$$\mathbf{x} = -\mathbf{F}(\mathbf{x}_0)\mathbf{J}^{-1} + \mathbf{x}_0, \tag{4.11}$$

which becomes the new approximation of $\mathbf{x}_0$. The procedure is repeated; this time $\mathbf{x}$ becomes the new value $\mathbf{x}_0$. The main advantage of Newton's method is that it is known that, if $\mathbf{x}_0$ is close enough to the solution, the method has a quadratic convergence rate. This fast convergence has a price, however, since it requires the Jacobian matrix to be computed and inverted at each iteration, which can impose a heavy computational load.

In the present case, the system to be solved is

$$E_s(a_s(\mathbf{B}), N_s) = B_s.$$

The F functions are

$$F_s = E_s(a_s(\mathbf{B}), N_s) - B_s,$$

and the Jacobian matrix is given by

$$J_{s,t} = \frac{\partial E_s}{\partial a_s} \frac{\partial a_s}{\partial B_t} - \delta_{s,t}.$$

The first partial derivative, computed at fixed B_s, is a diagonal matrix. The coupling between the links comes from the second term, generally a full matrix, which can be evaluated as follows. Rewrite Eq. (4.6) as

$$a_s = \sum_{l|s\in l} A^l \prod_{\substack{t\in l \\ t\neq s}} (1 - B_t)$$

and, taking the derivative with respect to B_r,

$$\frac{\partial a_s}{\partial B_r} = -\sum_{l|s\in l} A^l \prod_{\substack{t\in l \\ t\neq s \\ t\neq r}} (1 - B_t). \qquad (4.12)$$

We have pointed out two elements of Newton's method that can lead to excessive computation. One is the requirement to invert the Jacobian matrix at each iteration. In fact, there exist algorithms in which this inversion is never done and that operate with successively more accurate representations of the inverse of the Jacobian matrix itself, rather than the matrix J. These methods, called *quasi-Newton*, are described in any standard textbook on numerical analysis or optimization, such as [3].

Even with these methods, derivatives must be calculated. For some idea of the amount of calculation required, let us assume that we are calculating the full Jacobian matrix. We see from Eq. (4.12) that, for a given component, it is necessary to go through all the paths, computing partial products of probabilities along these paths. Although we could probably organize the calculation to avoid duplication, this is still a heavy computational burden, tending to limit the use of Newton's method to small networks.

Also, we must point out that Newton's method, at least in its original form, suffers from another defect that prevents its use for the solution of the Erlang fixed point: We must have $0 \leq B_s \leq 1$ at all times during the calculation. We say that a solution that meets these requirements is *feasible*. Newton's method, however, has no built-in mechanism to allow such restrictions to be placed on the solution set. In other words, Newton's method is unconstrained, while the fixed-point equation requires a constrained solution. We could guarantee that the algorithm remain in the domain by a change of variable of the form $\sin^2 x_{s,t} = B_{s,t}$ and solve for x with an unconstrained method. In this case, we must be careful to avoid the artificial solutions introduced by the transformation, which generally requires looking at second-order information at the solution point. We could also arbitrarily prevent the solution from going out of the domain by setting any variable at the nearest bound if it goes outside the range $[0, 1]$. This, however, may have a detrimental effect on the convergence of the method, and is probably not a good way to proceed.

Minimization.   A more natural way to obtain a feasible solution is by means of nonlinear minimization techniques. If we compute $\min z = \sum_i F_i(\mathbf{x})^2$, then the solution, if one exists, is found when $F_i(\mathbf{x}) = 0$. The advantage of this method arises from the existence of very efficient minimization techniques [4] when the only constraints are bounds on the variables, which computationally are no more complex than unconstrained problems. Note that the computational requirements of these methods are largely determined by the calculation of the gradient of the objective function

$$\frac{\partial z}{\partial B_r} = \sum_i \frac{\partial F_i}{\partial B_r},$$

which is precisely the computation required for the Jacobian matrix in Newton's method. Thus, although the question of feasibility is handled more naturally in the context of minimization, the numerical efficiency is still too low to permit large-scale applications.

Relaxation.   The method used most frequently, and the one with the smallest computational requirement, is the *relaxation method*, also known as *repeated substitution*. Using the fact that the system equations have the form $\mathbf{x} = \mathbf{F}(\mathbf{x})$, we replace the current value of $\mathbf{x}$ in F to obtain the new value. The advantage is that the gradients of F need not be computed, which is the reason this method is so efficient numerically. The relaxation method also ensures that the variables remain in the domain $0 \le \mathbf{x} \le 1$, which is not the case for the other unconstrained methods. On the negative side, however, is the fact that convergence is not guaranteed unless the eigenvalues of J are all less than 1 at the solution or unless we can show that F is a contraction mapping. In fact, it is not difficult to construct simple examples where the solution is known analytically but where the substitution method fails to find it (see Problem 4.12). These conditions cannot be verified unless we happen to know the solution, and the relaxation method could fail to converge even though there is a unique solution to the system. It would then be necessary to resort to another method, with a corresponding increase in computation time.

4.2   Computation of L^k as a Function of B_s for Alternate Routing

In the case of load sharing, the relationship between end-to-end loss probability and link-blocking probability is given by $L^k = \mathcal{P}^k$, since a blocking event on a path corresponds to a call loss. This is not the case in alternate routing, the first truly practical method we analyze. In alternate routing, the event that a path is blocked at the time a call attempts to use it *does not* imply a call loss. This relation is much more complex, depending on the structure of the route tree that describes the routing. In the first part of our work on alternate routing, therefore, we explore this relationship, as well as efficient numerical methods to calculate it.

The notion of calculating end-to-end probability from the given values of the link-blocking probabilities is fairly recent. The method is adapted from the techniques used in network reliability — in particular, from the work of Lee [5] on linear probability graphs. These techniques were originally developed to compute of the internal blocking of switches; its application to switched communication networks originated with Butto, Colombo, and Tonietti [6] in 1976. The problem of computing blocking for a given set of Bs is purely combinatorial since it depends only on the route trees and is independent of $A^{i,j}$ and $N_{s,t}$.

The algorithms proposed in the literature fall into three categories. The first method [6,7] consists of writing the exact formulas for the blocking, given the particular structure of the route trees considered. This, of course, severely limits the flexibility of the method since a new set of formulas must be derived whenever a new routing is considered. An important breakthrough occurred when Chan [8] pointed out that the calculation is recursive for a wide class of routings. This insight has led to a variety of algorithms, both for the general case and for important special cases. Independently of the work of Chan, another technique was proposed [9] based on tree-enumeration techniques. These last two methods are closely related; it is known that any recursive procedure can be given a tree-enumeration form. We now present examples of the three types of algorithms for a variety of special routing methods and for the most general case.

Two-Link Paths

We first study the simplest case, where overflow paths have a single tandem. Although there can be many overflow paths for any given origin-destination pair, the structure of the route trees permits a simple evaluation algorithm. This is because all the paths in the route of a given origin-destination pair are disjoint (see Fig. 4.1).

Because of the simple form of the trees, we can write analytic formulas giving the value of the loss probabilities $L^{i,j}$ as a function of the blocking on the links. In fact, the loss probability is simply given by $L = \prod_k \mathcal{P}^k$, where $\mathcal{P}^k$ is the blocking probability of the kth path in the route tree. This can also be presented as a recursive procedure, which is easier to implement for numerical calculations. To simplify our presentation, we assume that the direct link (i, j) is always found in the first position in each route tree, although the more general case of an arbitrary first path poses no difficulty. We define P_k as the probability of an overflow to tandem k. P_k is also the probability that a call cannot be routed on any of the paths preceding the path through k.

For an OOC command, $L^{i,j}$ can be computed using the recursion formula and assuming that the link-blocking probabilities are independent. We define

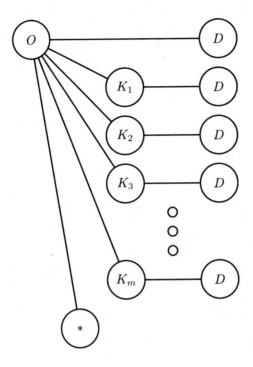

Figure 4.1   Two-Link Alternate Routing with OOC

P_1 as equal to B_{ij}, the probability of having to overflow on the first alternate path. For general k, we have

$$P_k = P_{k-1}\left[1 - (1 - B_{i,k-1})(1 - B_{k-1,j})\right] \qquad (4.13)$$

In the case of m overflow paths, we find

$$L^{i,j} = P_{m+1}. \qquad (4.14)$$

Similar formulas can be easily found for SOC control (see Problem 4.1).

Trees without Multiple Arcs

The two-link case is probably the most important practical case of nonhierarchical alternate routing; it is used almost exclusively in all currently proposed techniques. To gain some understanding of the inherent complexity of the blocking calculation when more than two links are permitted for some alternate paths, we now turn to more complex route trees. We consider three approaches to the calculation. First we express the procedure in terms of scanning the nodes of the route tree. Then we exhibit, in a more general context, the enumerative aspect of the calculation, demonstrating its intrinsic exponential complexity. Finally we reformulate the procedure in recursive terms.

The first case is for route trees in which paths are no longer disjoint but can share some links. We can take advantage of a simple structure when the trees are such that a link appears no more than once in a given tree. This condition simplifies the calculation for the following reason. Suppose we are considering the probability that a call will be routed on a particular path. This involves the probabilities that the path is free and that the call overflows to the path. If some links on the path appear on some other path before the one considered, these two probabilities are not independent, even assuming that the individual link-blocking probabilities are independent. Thus conditional probabilities must be computed, with a worst-case complexity that grows very fast with the network size. One way to ensure that this does not occur is to assume that no arc appears more than once in a given route tree, in which case unconditional probabilities can be used.

Another reason to describe this model in detail is that it constitutes a good example of the use of tree-enumeration techniques in the blocking calculation. First we give a set of recursive equations that implicitly define the value of L^k. Although these equations could be solved directly by a recursive program, they are expressed in such a way that a straightforward tree-enumeration method can be used to compute a solution.

We distinguish two types of nodes in the tree: (1) *overflow control nodes* or, more simply, *control nodes*, of degree higher than 2, and (2) the others, called *ordinary nodes*. Control nodes are important because they represent the choices between overflow or loss at different points in the tree. The sequence of possible choices, given that previous choices have led to a control node, is contained in the subtree originating at the control node in question.

Define o and d as the origin and destination nodes, respectively, for the tree under consideration. Control nodes are labeled according to their depth in the tree. The depth of control node k is defined as the number of control nodes between k and o plus one. The origin has depth 0. If node i is a control node, and l the lth subtree originating at i, we define

$D_{i,l}$ = The probability of overflow on l, given that one has reached i.

$D_{i,0} = 1$, $i = o, \ldots$ We arbitrarily define the probability of overflow on the first path on the subtree to be 1.

$C_{i,l}$ = The probability that the next control node will be reached on the lth alternate path, given that node i has been reached.

Suppose we now choose a leaf in the tree, for example, node m; define P_m as the probability of reaching node m. This node m can be either the

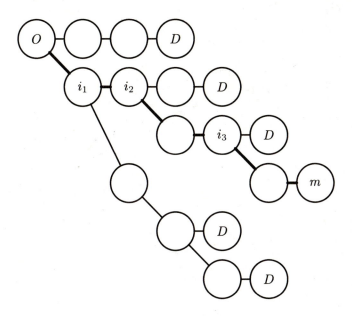

Figure 4.2   Route Tree with No Repeated Arc

destination node D or a loss node. We are interested in P_m because it represents the occurrence of a completed call or a lost call, depending on the nature of m; Either quantity is of interest. If the event of using path m represents a call completion, we can use its probability to compute link-offered traffic, as described in Section 4.3. If the event is a lost call, its probability is used in evaluating the end-to-end loss probability for the traffic stream corresponding to the tree being considered.

The selection of m defines a set of control nodes i_1, i_2,... from o to m and, at each control node, a corresponding overflow on levels l_1, l_2, ... (see Fig. 4.2). Since the probabilities of blocking on the network links are independent, we can write

$$P_m = D_{o,l_0} C_{o,l_0} D_{i_1,l_1} C_{i_1,l_1} \ldots C_{i_m,l_m}. \tag{4.15}$$

Because of the independence assumption, calculating the Cs poses no difficulty. Since the paths are disjoint, no link appears more than once in the tree at level k, and we can write

$$C_{i,l} = \prod_s (1 - B_s), \tag{4.16}$$

where s denotes all the links between the two consecutive control nodes i and $i+1$ on path l. Because arcs are not repeated, sequences of links between control

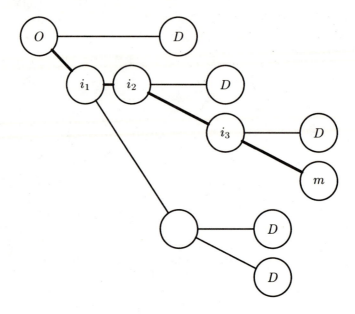

Figure 4.3   Equivalent Route Tree

nodes can be replaced by a single equivalent link, with blocking probability $C_{i,l}$. The equivalent route tree then takes the form shown in Fig. 4.3. From now on, we assume for simplicity that such a reduction has been made whenever possible.

The difficult part of the calculation is in the Ds. For this, we require additional variables:

$Q_{i,l}^{(k)}$ = The probability that we will reach any leaf by following path l out of node i, assuming that we have reached node i at level k.

$Q_i^{(k)}$ = The probability that we will reach any leaf, assuming that we have reached node i at level k.

$Q_i^{(k)}$, the connection probability from node i, summarizes all the events that may lead to a connection after having reached the node. It is obvious that

$$Q_i^{(k)} = \sum_{j=0}^{r} D_{i,j} Q_{i,j}^{(k)}, \qquad (4.17)$$

where r is the number of subtrees at node i. A recursion formula can also be given for the Qs:

$$Q_{i,l}^{(k)} = C_{i,l} Q_l^{(k+1)}, \tag{4.18}$$

where the node corresponding to $Q_l^{(k+1)}$ is the first control node encountered when we follow path l out of i and at level $k+1$.

Finally, we can express the Ds as functions of Qs by

$$D_{i,l} = \left(1 - Q_{i,l-1}^{(k)}\right) D_{i,l-1}. \tag{4.19}$$

The set of formulas (4.16–4.19) defines exactly the Cs and Ds, and thus the probabilities of reaching a leaf. Note that the recursion formula (4.19) uses only $Q_{i,l-1}^{(k)}$ and $D_{i,l-1}$ for the computation of $D_{i,l}$. It follows the sequence of overflows and can be computed in that order if the Qs from the lower level are known.

The recursions (4.18) and (4.17) proceed in the opposite direction from the sequence of overflows. Note, however, that only the $D_{i,l}$ from the preceding subtree are required to calculate Eq. (4.17); the Q_is from the immediate lower level are required for Eq. (4.18). Thus the complete computation can be done by enumerating the tree nodes once in each direction. This algorithm is efficient because one need go through each of the $N(N-1)$ route trees *only once*; all the required quantities can be computed in this single passage. This property is derived from the fact that any given link never appears more than once in a tree. As we shall see, the more general route trees require several iterations in each tree — or essentially the same thing, the storage of a quantity of information that increases exponentially with the size of the problem.

General Route Trees with OOC

The next most complex case is for originating office control, with the possibility that an arc may appear more than once in a given route tree. A complete analysis of the problem is given by Butto, Colombo, and Tonietti [6] in the form of equations clearly showing the exponential nature of the calculation. For this discussion, assume that we are considering a particular route tree k. To simplify the notation, the tree index is not used in the exposition. Under the independence assumption, the probability $\mathcal{P}_j$ that a path j in the tree is blocked is given by

$$\mathcal{P}_j = 1 - \prod_{s \in j} (1 - B_s).$$

Assume there are m paths altogether in the tree. For a tree with an arbitrary structure, but with OOC control, an event corresponding to the blocking on one path is not independent of an event corresponding to the blocking of another path. The solution of [6] is to consider all possible combination of states (blocked or not blocked) on all the links that are shared between paths. These links are called *repeated* links since they would show up more than once in an enumeration of all the paths represented by the tree. The blocking probabilities on the paths can be expressed as conditional probabilities as follows.

Let $l = \{l_1, l_2, \ldots l_t\}$ denote the list of repeated links. To each repeated link i associate a state variable δ_i, which is 0 or 1 according to whether the link is free or busy. Let $\mathbf{\Delta} = \delta_i, i = 1 \ldots t$ be the state vector for the repeated links. Consider now the 2^t functions $L(\delta_1, \delta_2, \ldots \delta_t)$, defined as the conditional probability that the call cannot be routed through the tree, given the state vector $\mathbf{\Delta}$. The loss probability for the tree k can be written as

$$
\begin{aligned}
L^k = {} & (1 - B_{l_1}) \ldots (1 - B_{l_t}) L(0, 0, \ldots 0) \\
& + B_{l_1} (1 - B_{l_2}) \ldots (1 - B_{l_t}) L(1, 0, \ldots 0) \\
& + \ldots \\
& + B_{l_1} B_{l_2} \ldots B_{l_t} L(1, 1, \ldots 1).
\end{aligned}
\tag{4.20}
$$

As is clear from this expression, the number of terms to be considered is of the order 2^t, which has exponential worst-case growth. Having removed the repeated links from the tree, the conditional blocking probabilities are independent and are the product of individual path-blocking probabilities, with the repeated arcs removed. We get

$$
L(\delta_1, \delta_2, \ldots \delta_t) = \prod_{j=1}^{m} \mathcal{P}_j(\mathbf{\Delta}),
\tag{4.21}
$$

where the blocking probability on path j is given by

$$
\mathcal{P}_j(\mathbf{\Delta}) = [1 - \prod_{s \in j} (1 - B'_s)]
\tag{4.22}
$$

and

$$
B'_s = \begin{cases} B_s & \text{if } s \notin l_i \\ 0 & \text{if } s \in l_i \text{ and } \delta_i = 0 \\ 1 & \text{if } s \in l_i \text{ and } \delta_i = 1 \end{cases}
$$

and $s \in j$ indicates that link s is in path j. We also define for further reference the probability that all paths between and including paths i and j are blocked for a given tree and a given state vector $\mathbf{\Delta}$ as

$$
\begin{aligned}
C(i, j, \mathbf{\Delta}) &= \prod_{k=i}^{j} \mathcal{P}_k(\mathbf{\Delta}) \quad j \geq i, \\
&= 1 \quad i > j.
\end{aligned}
\tag{4.23}
$$

We get

$$
L(\mathbf{\Delta}) = C(1, m, \mathbf{\Delta})
\tag{4.24}
$$

$$
L^k = \sum_{\mathbf{\Delta}} L(\mathbf{\Delta})
$$

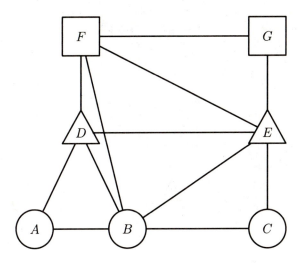

Figure 4.4   Seven-Node Hierarchical Network

where the last sum is to be understood in the sense of Eq. (4.20) over all state vectors Δ. This formulation does not take into account the recursive nature of the calculation, but clearly shows its exponential growth, since a complete enumeration of all the state vectors Δ is required.

Manual calculations are reasonably easy to use as long as the route trees are not too complex, as can be seen from the seven-node network of Fig. 4.4. Considering the route tree for stream (A, C) shown on Fig. 4.5, we see that three links — 1, 3, and 4 — are shared among multiple paths. The state vector Δ has three components, and there are eight terms to consider in the calculation (see Table 4.1).

Summing the eight terms, we obtain

$$L = B_2 B_5 \left[1 - (1 - B_6)(1 - B_7) \right]$$
$$(1 - B_1)(1 - B_3)(1 - B_4) + B_2(1 - B_1)(1 - B_3)B_4 + 1 - B_1)B_3 + B_1$$

General Route Trees with SOC

Another simplification that occurs for networks with SOC control was first noted by Butto, Colombo, and Tonietti [6]. They also perceived the recursive nature of the calculation, using a somewhat more complex notation than given here. In this case, although there may be arcs in common on many paths, it is unnecessary to compute conditional probabilities when calculating the

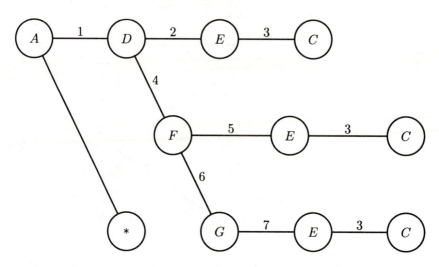

Figure 4.5   Route Tree for Stream (A, C) for Seven-Node Network

Link Number			P	Factor
1	3	4		
0	0	0	$B_2 B_5 \left[1 - (1 - B_6)(1 - B_7) \right]$	$(1 - B_1)(1 - B_3)(1 - B_4)$
0	0	1	B_2	$(1 - B_1)(1 - B_3)B_4$
0	1	0	1	$(1 - B_1)B_3(1 - B_4)$
0	1	1	1	$(1 - B_1)B_3 B_4$
1	0	0	1	$B_1(1 - B_3)(1 - B_4)$
1	0	1	1	$B_1(1 - B_3)B_4$
1	1	0	1	$B_1 B_3(1 - B_4)$
1	1	1	1	$B_1 B_3 B_4$

Table 4.1   Calculation of End-to-End Blocking for the Seven-Node Network Using the Method of Butto, Colombo, and Tonietti [6]

probability of using path i: The probability of using a path is independent of the state of the arcs on this path that appear elsewhere in the route tree. To

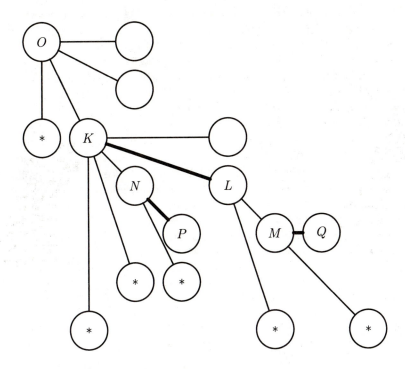

Figure 4.6   Route Tree for SOC Control. Link s Indicated by Thicker Line.

see this, consider the fragment of a route tree indicated in Fig. 4.6. Let path i be (O, K, N, P). Suppose that link s, indicated by a thicker line, appears elsewhere in the tree before path i. Note that the two ends of link s, which in reality correspond to the same nodes of the network, are labeled differently in the route tree in order to clarify the discussion.

Let (O, K) be the arc leading to path i from O, and (K, N) the arc leading from node K to path i. If s occurs somewhere in the tree before path i, this can happen in one of two ways. Either s is adjacent to one of the nodes on path i, such as the arc (K, L), or it is not adjacent to one of these path nodes, such as the arc (M, Q). In the first case, there is zero probability that we will use path i. In the second case, the probability of using path i is independent of the state of s before path i; this is so because if a call reaches node M, it will never be carried on path i. It either will be carried on the remainder of the path from M or will be lost because of the presence of the loss node adjacent to node M.

As an aside, route trees such as the one in Fig. 4.6, although perfectly correct from a theoretical point of view, are almost never found in practice (see Section 2.5). The reason is that the routing of a call that reaches s depends on the previous history of that call, that is, whether it came as an overflow from a link originating at i or whether it was partly carried on the route tree. Normally this kind of information for making routing decisions is not available to switches, and route trees of this kind are only of theoretical interest. This simplifying feature of full SOC networks is exploited in the algorithms proposed by Butto, Colombo, and Tonietti [6] in the form of equations, and, in a recursive form, by Gaudreau [10], who emphasizes its use for hierarchical networks.

The recursive nature of the calculation can be seen from the following argument. First note that, in a SOC network, all nodes are control nodes. Thus the level of a node is simply its distance from the origin, measured by the number of links encountered to reach the node. A calculation similar to that of Section 4.2 can be used to compute the end-to-end blocking probability. Equations (4.16–4.19) become

$$D_{i,l} = \prod_{j=1}^{l-1} B_{i,j} \tag{4.25}$$

$$C_{i,l} = (1 - B_{i,l}) \tag{4.26}$$

$$Q_i^{(k)} = \sum_{l=1}^{m} (1 - B_l) Q_l^{(k+1)} \prod_{s=1}^{l-1} B_s \tag{4.27}$$

which can be solved by a single passage over the route tree, by decreasing level.

Arbitrary Route Trees

Let us now consider the case of a completely general route tree for traffic k. Following the notation of [8], we introduce the notion of a *link set*. For a given route tree, link sets are subsets of links that are present in the tree. The actual composition of a link set is determined by the structure of the tree — in particular, by the relative position of links that appear more than once in the tree. The precise composition of link sets is given recursively in the algorithm; for now, let us think of them as fragments of paths in the tree.

Let U_i be defined as the ith link set in some list. The link sets may be either complete paths or portions of paths. The link sets are ordered in the list according to the order of paths in the route tree. We want to compute $Pr(U_i)$, the probability that U_i is used. We consider two distinct cases, according to whether U_i is the first link set in the tree or not. If the link set is the first one in the list, we have

$$Pr\,(U_1) = \prod_{s \in U_i} (1 - B_s)\,.$$

If the link set is one to which there is some overflow, we have

$$Pr\{U_i \text{ is used}\} = Pr\{U_i \text{ is available}\} \times \qquad (4.28)$$
$$Pr\{\text{None of } U_1 U_2 \ldots U_{i-1} \text{ has been used } | U_i \text{ is available}\}$$

where the condition "U_i is available" means that all the links on link set i are free. The complexity of the problem stems from the fact that the "U_i is available" condition *must* be taken into account in evaluating Eq. (4.28), since the fact that link set U_i is free may affect the probability of overflow to i. If the links of U_i do not appear in $U_1 U_2 \ldots U_{i-1}$, then the condition is no longer required, and we find the equations described in Section 4.2.

Define the link set

$$U_{k(i)} = U_k - U_i,$$

where U_k belongs to a path preceding U_i. $Pr\{U_{k(i)}\}$ is then the probability that all the links in the link set $U_{k(i)}$ are free. Eq. (4.28) is thus written as

$$Pr\{U_i \text{ is used}\} = Pr\{U_i \text{ free}\} Pr\{U_{1(i)} U_{2(i)} \ldots U_{i-1(i)} \text{ all busy}\}$$
$$= Pr\{U_i \text{ free}\} \left[1 - Pr\{\text{at least one of } U_{1(i)} U_{2(i)} \ldots U_{i-1(i)} \text{ free}\}\right]$$

Define, for arbitrary link sets $U_1, U_2, \ldots U_i$,

$$Q(U_1 \ldots U_i) \triangleq Pr\{U_i \text{ is used}\}. \qquad (4.29)$$

This probability depends on the link sets preceding U_i. We can then define recursively

$$Q(U_1) = \prod_{s \in U_1} (1 - B_s) \qquad (4.30)$$

$$Q(U_1 \ldots U_i) = \prod_{s \in U_i} (1 - B_s) \times \left[1 - \sum_{k=1}^{i-1} Q(U_{1(i)} U_{2(i)} \ldots U_{k(i)})\right] \qquad (4.31)$$

We thus have a recurrent formation for the Qs that can be evaluated as the tree is enumerated. This calculation proceeds as follows for the route tree of Fig. 4.5:

$$Q(U_1) = (1 - B_1)(1 - B_2)(1 - B_3)$$

$$Q(U_1 U_2) = (1 - B_1)(1 - B_4)(1 - B_5)(1 - B_3) \left[1 - \sum_{k=1}^{1} Q(U_{1(2)})\right]$$

Since $U_{1(2)}$ is simply link 2, the corresponding $Q(U_{1(2)}) = (1 - B_2)$; replacing, we have

$$Q(U_1 U_2) = (1 - B_1)(1 - B_4)(1 - B_5)(1 - B_3) B_2.$$

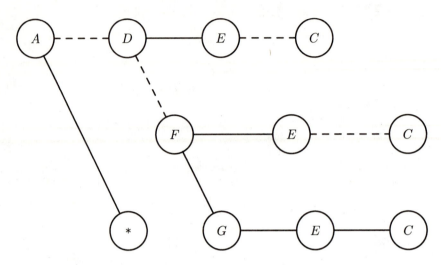

Figure 4.7   Partial Route Tree for Calculating the Probability of Connection on Link Set

The probability of connection on the third path is given by

$$Q(U_1 U_2 U_3) = (1 - B_1)(1 - B_4)(1 - B_6)(1 - B_7)(1 - B_3)$$
$$\times \left[1 - Q(U_{1(3)}) - Q(U_{1(3)} U_{2(3)})\right].$$

Here, too, the partial link sets take a simple form since $U_{1(3)}$ is link 2 and $U_{2(3)}$ is link 5. Under these conditions, we get

$$Q(U_{1(3)}) = 1 - B_2.$$

The second probability of connection on the link set can be calculated from the partial route tree shown in Fig. 4.7. In this tree, the links that do not contribute to the probability are shown with a dotted line; the others are solid. The probability of using link set $U_{1(3)} U_{2(3)}$ can be computed from this tree as usual, simply by dropping the dotted arcs from the calculation. We then get

$$Q(U_{1(3)} U_{2(3)}) = B_2(1 - B_5),$$

and replacing, we get

$$Q(U_1 U_2 U_3) = (1 - B_1)(1 - B_4)(1 - B_6)(1 - B_7)(1 - B_3)$$
$$\times \left[1 - (1 - B_2) - B_2(1 - B_5)\right],$$

which is the remaining term in the calculation. Because we are considering OOC control, the only loss node is in the last position in the route tree; the loss probability is given by

$$L = 1 - \sum_{k=1}^{3} Q(U_1 U_2 \ldots U_k).$$

This recurrence can be used to compute the probability of loss as well as the probability of connection, since loss nodes are treated like ordinary destination nodes in the route tree. The complexity cannot be polynomially bounded, however, because the number of conditional clauses on the probabilities can grow arbitrarily large for an arbitrary network and routing plan. Finally, note that this formulation covers all the static routing cases with alternate routing and therefore can be used to calculate the probability of end-to-end blocking for hierarchical routes such as those found in most telephone networks [10].

4.3 The Erlang Fixed-Point Equation for Alternate Routing

Section 4.2 describes how the $L^{i,j}$ can be computed, given the $B_{s,t}$. This purely combinatorial problem does not depend on the traffic matrix or the link capacities, but only on the structure of the route trees. Here we present the second part of the evaluation method: computation of the correct link-blocking probabilities. A general discussion of the problem, using a simple one-moment model, leads us back to the Erlang fixed-point equation; we investigate its properties. We show that the solution need not be unique, indicating how such undesirable behavior can be prevented through the use of state protection.

Ordered Networks

Before presenting the general case of alternate routing, let us discuss an important special case that shows that every alternate routing policy does not necessarily lead to a fixed-point system. First we introduce the notion of an *ordered network*, basing our discussion on the concept of an ordered routing (see Section 2.5). For such a routing, the sequence of overflow and carried calls occurs so that it is possible to find a partial ordering $\mu(i)$ between all the network links that is identical for all traffic streams. This notion is useful for calculating traffic in cases where this partial ordering is also valid for the link-offered traffic.

More specifically, we say that a network is ordered if the links can be ranked in such a way that the traffic offered to link s of rank $\mu(s)$ depends only on the traffic offered to links $t \in \mathcal{A}(s)$. This notion is similar to the notion of order for routing but is now applied to the traffic. A network is ordered only if certain conditions are met on the overflow of blocked calls, as well as on trunks in tandem. First, the overflow must proceed according to the partial order determined by the routing, which is itself ordered. This condition is not sufficient, however, because the traffic offered to the first link of a path composed of many links in tandem depends on the blocking on the downstream links. In addition to the condition on overflow, the network is ordered if either the downstream links precede the link in the routing — which is a contradiction — or the blocking on these downstream links is small enough that it can safely be neglected when calculating the traffic offered to the link. This distinction is important because the order assumption is commonly made for hierarchical networks, but without reference to links in tandem. Fortunately, for hierarchical networks operating at their design grade of service, the blocking probability is always small on the hierarchical route leading from any given node to the destination. Hence it is valid to assume that the balking effect can be neglected; we can safely assume that these networks are ordered. This assumption, however, is *not* valid if the network is operated at high blocking on the finals. It is also not valid for nonhierarchical networks, where there is not necessarily a low-blocking path from a given node to the destination. In these cases, although it is possible to have an ordered routing, as in the case of the hierarchical network, the network itself is not ordered.

Calculation of Offered Traffic for Ordered Networks

In cases where the network *is* ordered, the solution procedure is not iterative. To see this, consider the influence graph corresponding to a given ordered network. Link blocking is calculated in a single iteration over all nodes of the influence graph, in increasing node order. Let k be the current value of the order:

1. For node i of order k, the value a_i^m of all parcels offered to it is known by the order assumption. Using the appropriate blocking model (e.g., the Erlang B function if the Poisson model is used for internal traffic), compute

$$a_i = \sum_m a_i^m$$
$$B_i = E(a_i, N_i) \qquad (4.32)$$

and from this, $\hat{a}$, $\bar{a}$, and, if necessary, the other moments.

2. Update the traffic offered to the two nodes out of i:

$$a_{\rho(i,m)} \leftarrow a_{\rho(i,m)} + \bar{a}_i^m$$
$$a_{\sigma(i,m)} \leftarrow a_{\sigma(i,m)} + \hat{a}_i^m$$

A call is lost when $\sigma(i, m) = 0$.

3. Repeat for all parcels of node i.

4. Repeat for all nodes at level k.

This method is widely used for dimensioning networks in almost all telephone administrations. Let us mention some of its more important features.

First note that the method consists of finding a multicommodity flow in the influence graph, using some peculiar routing rules. Consider for simplicity the case where all traffics are Poisson. Each node has a parameter N_s that determines how the flow entering the node will be split between the overflow and the carried arcs. We emphasize again that, because of the nature of alternate routing, this separation cannot be assigned arbitrarily, but is a function of the entering traffic and N_s. In this simple model, no other information is used to effect this separation, although we will see other cases where this is not so.

Second, consider Eq. (4.32). It is very similar to Eq. (4.7) and also to Eq. (4.39). Eq. (4.32), however, has a simplifying feature that is not present in the other two equations: The total offered traffic a_i depends only on the traffic offered to the links $j \mid \mu(j) < \mu(i)$. The consequences of this fact are explored in more depth in Problem 4.13.

Finally, the end-to-end blocking and the link-blocking probabilities are computed "on the fly." No use is made of route trees, and the lost traffic is simply the sum of traffic parcels that have nowhere to go at a given stage of the calculation. This technique is often sufficient for hierarchical networks, particularly in the context of dimensioning, where only the link-blocking probabilities are of interest (see Chapter 8 for a discussion of dimensioning hierarchical networks).

This method of progressively moving through the influence graph in increasing order of level is closely related to the SOC mode of overflow control used in telephone networks. Other overflow control rules cannot easily be modeled using the influence graph, usually requiring the use of the route tree.

Calculation of Offered Traffic for Two-Link Routing

First note that given the route trees and the B_ss, the link-offered traffics a_s can be computed — an operation called *link loading*. In general, these traffics are functions of *all* the B_ss and can be written $a_s(\mathbf{B})$ to emphasize this dependence. The calculation of the link-offered traffic depends on the structure of the route trees for each traffic stream. We show how this can be done in the case of two-link alternate paths with OOC control, following the technique of Lin, Leon, and Stewart [7] in presenting the traffic calculation. We define

$A_l^k =$ Traffic offered to the lth path in the route tree for traffic k. This is the amount of new traffic that has been blocked on all paths preceding l in the tree.

$\overline{A}_l^k$ = Traffic carried on the lth path in the route tree for traffic k.

$\mathcal{P}_l^k$ = Blocking probability of the lth alternate path in the route tree for traffic k.

P_l^k = The probability that a call arriving at the origin node of stream k will overflow to level l.

The index l will also be called the *level* of the path in a particular tree.

The route trees are scanned in some arbitrary order. For route tree k, scan the tree in increasing order of l, the index of overflow paths. At each level l in the tree, assume that the two links are, respectively, s and t:

1. Using the independence assumption, compute the path blocking:

$$\mathcal{P}_l^k = 1 - (1 - B_s)(1 - B_t). \tag{4.33}$$

   Note that the link-loading procedure described here would also be valid if we used a different path model.

2. Compute the traffic carried on the path. The underlying assumption behind the path model is that this traffic is also carried on the two links in the path. Thus we have

$$\overline{A}_l^k = A_l^k(1 - \mathcal{P}_l^k)$$
$$\overline{a}_x^k = \overline{A}_l^k, \quad x = s, t \tag{4.34}$$

3. The contribution of this route tree to the traffics offered to links s and t is given by

$$a_x^k = \frac{\overline{a}_x^k}{(1 - B_x)}, \quad x = s, t \tag{4.35}$$

   Calculating the offered traffic in this way takes into account the possibility that the call may be blocked downstream.

4. Compute the cumulative probability of overflow and the traffic offered to the next alternate path:

$$P_{l+1}^k = \mathcal{P}_l^k P_l^k \tag{4.36}$$
$$A_{l+1}^k = A_l^k P_l^k \tag{4.37}$$

This last step yields the current estimate for L^k when the last path of the route tree is processed. When all the route trees have been processed, we know all the traffic parcels being offered to all the links; the total traffic offered to a link is given by

$$a_s = \sum_k a_s^k. \qquad (4.38)$$

To summarize, we see that the traffic offered to a given link s is a function of the link-blocking probabilities B_t through Eqs. (4.33–4.35). To be consistent with the assumptions already made about the traffic — that is, that it is described by a Poisson process — we must also impose the condition that

$$B_s = E(a_s(\mathbf{B}), N_s), \qquad (4.39)$$

where we emphasize the dependence of a_s on all the blocking probabilities by writing it as $a_s(\mathbf{B})$. The correct values of a_s (and, by the same token, of B_s) are given by the solution of the system (4.39). This, of course, is another manifestation of the Erlang fixed point; we must examine the two standard questions about this system: (1) the number of solutions and (2) how to solve the system efficiently. Note that the relation $a_s(\mathbf{B})$ is different from the equivalent relation obtained in the case of load sharing and thus that the answers obtained for that case will not necessarily apply here.

Solution Methods

The solution techniques are identical to those described in Section 4.1, with one addition: the calculation of the Jacobian matrix of the system for use with either Newton's method or one of the optimization techniques.

In this case, the system to be solved is

$$E_s(a_s(\mathbf{B}), N_s) = B_s.$$

Consequently, the functions are

$$F_s = E_s(a_s(\mathbf{B}), N_s) - B_s$$

and the Jacobian matrix is given by

$$J_{s,t} = \frac{\partial E_s}{\partial a_s} \frac{\partial a_s}{\partial B_t} - \delta_{s,t}.$$

The first partial derivative $\partial E / \partial a_s$, computed at fixed B_s, is a diagonal matrix. The coupling between the links comes from the second term, which generally is a full matrix. It can be evaluated as follows. Consider a particular route tree corresponding to a commodity k, and let m be the level of link s in the tree, j the level of some link t, and l a running index referring to levels in this tree. We adopt the convention that the other link in addition to s, in a path is denoted by s', and that all quantities indexed by s' take the expected value if s happens to be the direct link. For instance, if s is the direct link, the quantity

$(1 - B_{s'})$ is the probability of completing the call on the second link, which in this case does not exist. The convention means that in this case $(1 - B_{s'}) = 1$. With this notation, we get

$$\frac{\partial a_s}{\partial B_t} = \sum_{k|s\in k} A^k \frac{\partial}{\partial B_t} \prod_{l=1}^{m-1} \mathcal{P}_l^k(\mathbf{B})(1 - B_{s'}).$$

This last derivative is given by

$$\frac{\partial}{\partial B_t} \prod_{l=1}^{m-1} \mathcal{P}_l^k(\mathbf{B})(1 - B_{s'}) = \begin{cases} \displaystyle\prod_{l=1}^{m-1} \mathcal{P}_l^k(\mathbf{B}) & \text{if } t = s' \\ \displaystyle\prod_{\substack{l=1 \\ l\neq j}}^{m-1} \mathcal{P}_l^k(1 - B_{t'})(1 - B_{s'}) & \text{if } j < \text{level of } t \\ 0 & \text{otherwise} \end{cases} \quad (4.40)$$

Although not iterative, the calculation can be made by scanning the route trees that contain the link with respect to which the derivative is being computed. Nevertheless, there can be a large amount of computation, as was the case for load sharing, and for precisely the same reasons.

In addition to evaluating the performance of a given network, these gradients play a central role in many areas of routing optimization and dimensioning of circuit-switched networks. Algorithms are needed that permit the efficient calculation of these gradients for large networks. This subject has not received the attention it deserves and requires more research.

The relaxation method can also be used to solve the equations. In practice, this method is favored because it has the lowest computational requirements of the three techniques. The usual word of caution is in order here: There is no guarantee that the relaxation method will find a solution, even if one exists. Because the theoretical conditions for convergence cannot be tested until a solution is reached, the algorithm may fail to converge (although this possibility seems rare for the Poisson model used here).

4.4   Stability and State Protection

We have seen that computing the link-blocking probabilities involves the solution of a system of nonlinear equations (4.39). The existence of a solution to the nonlinear system (4.39) is generally not in doubt. Until recently, the question of uniqueness had not received a great deal of attention. All practical computation methods implicitly assume that there is only one solution to the model, not examining the possibility that others may exist. Let us now turn to the question of uniqueness, leading into the study of stability and state protection.

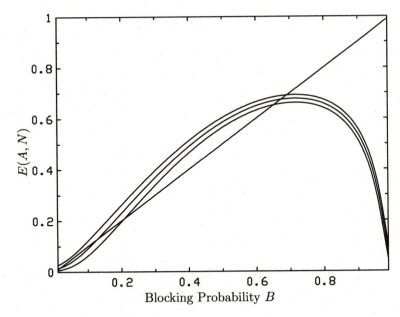

Figure 4.8 Multiple Solutions of the Erlang Fixed-Point Equation for Symmetric Networks; Traffic = 40, 42 and 44 Erlangs, 100 Trunks, 9 Alternate Routes

Nonlinear systems need not have a unique solution; as we will see, the flow equations for two-link nonhierarchical alternate routing do indeed have multiple solutions. These solutions, a consequence of mutual overflow and multiple alternate routing, can be viewed as a form of classical hysteresis. We will describe a state-protection technique that seems to prevent this behavior.

Multiple Solutions

First, let us exhibit networks in which the Erlang fixed-point equation has more than one solution. To do this, we simplify the general system of equations by introducing the notion of a symmetric network, defined by selecting $A_{i,j} = A$ and $N_{i,j} = N$. In addition, the route trees are such that the offered traffic is identical for all links. (Incidentally, the production of a truly symmetric alternate routing is not trivial, and requires some thought; here we say only that this can be done in general [11].)

Because of the symmetry, we can say that $B_s = B$, and similarly that $a_s = a$. Under these conditions, the system (4.39) reduces to a single nonlinear equation in B, which is much easier to study, and which can be plotted. We give

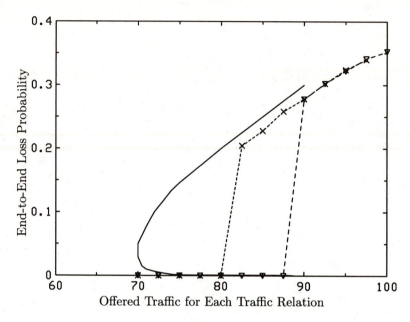

Figure 4.9   Multiple Values for End-to-End Blocking

an example in Fig. 4.8, where each side of Eq. (4.39) is traced as a function of a single variable B, the link-blocking probability, for a number of values of the offered traffic A. Solutions are given by the intersection of one of the curves with the diagonal; as the traffic changes, multiple solutions appear to the system, then disappearing. This phenomenon has also been reported in [12,13]. The net effect is that, for some values of the parameters, there can be three values of the end-to-end blocking probability, as shown on the solid curve of Fig. 4.9 (only two branches are visible on the plot because of the vertical scale).

This behavior is somewhat surprising since it contradicts the conclusion obtained from our analysis of the network as a Markov chain, which guarantees that there exists a unique set of stationary state probabilities and hence a unique end-to-end loss probability. The question is then how to reconcile this apparent contradiction.

The first possible explanation is that the apparent contradiction is a by-product of the rather severe assumptions that were made in the model — either the assumption of Poisson traffic used for calculating link-blocking probabilities or the independence assumption used for calculating the path-blocking probabilities. Unfortunately, as recent work [14] indicates, these multiple solutions arise in connection with real instabilities in networks operating with nonhierar-

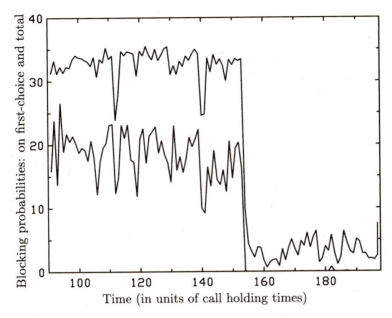

Figure 4.10 Simulation of Metastable Network

chical routing. The results show that a network that has reached a stationary regime at a relatively high blocking value can stay in this state for a very long time, up to 14 holding times, after the input traffic has been reduced to a value where the blocking should be quite low.

This phenomenon is also present in the network represented in Fig. 4.10. In this network, the total input traffic is reduced by 3% at time $t = 152$. The total end-to-end loss probability (the lower curve in the figure) and the probability of overflow (the upper curve) both undergo dramatic drops, from about 20% to virtually zero in the first case. The point is that this abrupt change in blocking probability is completely out of proportion to the change in the input value — an indication that something is not quite right in the network.

An even more troublesome phenomenon occurs in Fig. 4.11, where the traffic is dropped by 2% at time $t = 65$. Once again, we note a very large drop in loss probability; the network enters a low blocking state for approximately 10 holding times. Most disturbing, however, is that the network then undergoes a spontaneous transition to the high blocking state again, where it remains for a very long period. Note also the spontaneous transition to the low blocking state that occurs at $t = 55$ but that does not last very long.

Another way to view this phenomenon is as a classical hysteresis. This is shown in Fig. 4.9, where the network blocking is measured for different values

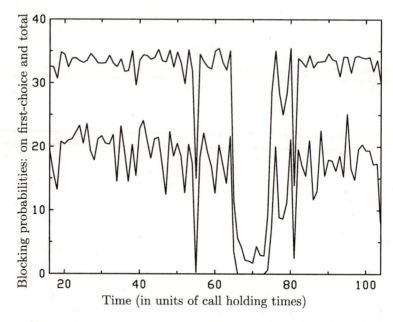

Figure 4.11   Spontaneous Transitions in Unstable Network

of the total offered traffic. The upper portion of the curve was produced by gradually decreasing traffic, while the lower portion corresponds to measurements made while increasing traffic. Each point was obtained after the network had reached a quasi-stable mode of operation after 200 holding times. As we see, the upper branch drops suddenly to a low value following the trajectory at the left, while the lower branch jumps to a high blocking value following the trajectory at the right, at a point higher than for the trajectory followed by the upper branch. This is the classical behavior of systems with hysteresis.

These results clearly show that the phenomenon is real, not a by-product of the simplifications used to compute a solution. Two questions remain: (1) What is the cause of this phenomenon? (2) How can it arise in an ergodic system in a stationary state?

We can obtain some indication concerning the first question by noting that load sharing does not exhibit such a behavior since the Erlang fixed point is unique. Also, we know that the fixed-point system for hierarchical routing (and for all ordered routings) is triangular, and can be solved in a single iteration over the links. It therefore seems that this hysteresis phenomenon is due not only to alternate routing, but also to the presence of mutual overflow in a network. Unfortunately, this is about as far as we can go in this direction; there is no definite proof that these statements are indeed true in general.

As for the second perplexing question, the answer, of course, is that the simulation results are not the true stationary results. What really happens is that the state space is divided into two groups of states, which we could call *macrostates*. In one macrostate, most calls are alternate routed with a correspondingly high loss while, in the other, most calls are direct routed with a much lower loss probability. It is plausible that once the network has entered the high-blocking regime, it will remain there for a long time: Once this regime is established, the probability that a new call can be routed directly is small, and most new traffic will continue to be alternate routed. The situation will endure until enough calls terminate in such a way that the probability of direct routing once again becomes large, at which time the network will drop into the low-blocking regime. This happens because of the statistical nature of the input processes; eventually there will be a time period during which few new calls arrive, permitting the transition. Depending on the load, the probability that the system will leave a macrostate can be small; when considered over time periods that are short with respect to the mean interval between transitions between the macrostates, the network appears to be in a nonstationary regime.

Note that stationarity is defined as a limit as $t \to \infty$. Even though the system may oscillate periodically between two macrostates with very different blocking, taking measurements for long periods gives a stationary measure of loss probability, which will lie somewhere between the two values. The point is that this value is not a very meaningful description of a network's performance. In other words, although the network has a precise mean performance, we would not want to operate it under conditions where there are large deviations from this mean for long time periods — precisely what happens in the cases we have seen. Such undesirable behavior must be prevented.

Theoretical Results

In certain simple cases, sufficient conditions can be imposed that guarantee a unique solution of the Erlang fixed point for alternate routing — for symmetric networks, for example, if it is assumed that the network is of infinite size. A straightforward calculation of this kind can be found in [15]. Consider once again the model with state protection given by Eqs. (3.29–3.31). With the assumption that, for each stream, there is an infinite number of overflow paths of S links each, we can compute the link-offered traffic as

$$a = A \left[1 + \frac{2B}{1 - B'} \right], \tag{4.41}$$

where A is the total first-offered traffic for each link. Replacing in the traffic model, we obtain the following equation for the link-offered traffic:

$$\sum_{i=0}^{m-1} \frac{a^i}{i!} \left(\frac{a}{A} - 1 \right) = S a^m \frac{A^{N-m}}{N!}. \tag{4.42}$$

The problem is to determine under what conditions — and in particular, for what value of m, the state protection level — this equation has a unique solution. The problem can be solved if we consider Eq. (4.42) as a polynomial equation of degree m in a with coefficients b_k, $k = 0, \ldots m$. Expanding in powers of a, we get

$$0 = \left(\frac{1}{(m-1)!A} - S\frac{A^{N-m}}{N!} \right) a^m + \left(\frac{1}{(m-2)!A} - \frac{1}{(m-1)!} \right) a^{m-1}$$
$$+ \ldots + \left(\frac{1}{A} - 1 \right) a - 1.$$

We can use Descarte's rule to determine the maximum number of solutions to this equation. We consider two cases, $k < m$, and $k = m$. In the first case, we see that $b_k < 0$ whenever $A > k$. In particular, we can ensure that all these coefficients have the same sign (all negative) if $A > m-1$. For the second case, we have $b_m < 0$ if

$$A > \left(\frac{N!}{S(m-1)!} \right)^{\frac{1}{N-m+1}} \triangleq A^*.$$

We can express the condition on b_m as

$$b_m \begin{cases} < 0 & \text{if } A > A^* \\ > 0 & \text{if } A < A^* \end{cases}$$

Suppose now that we select a protection level m^* such that

$$m^* - 1 = A^*$$
$$= \left\lfloor \left(\frac{N!}{S(m^*-1)!} \right)^{\frac{1}{N-m^*+1}} \right\rfloor.$$

Whenever $A < m^* - 1$, there is a single change in sign in the coefficients, and hence there is a unique solution. When A exceeds this threshold, all the coefficients of the polynomial have the same sign, and there is no solution. If the protection threshold is different from m^*, then there can be more than a single sign change in the coefficients for $A^*(m) < m^* - 1$, indicating that there can be more than one solution to the polynomial equation. Also, we can see that, unless state protection is used, all asymptotic networks are unstable if $N > 2$.

A similar analysis is due to Marbukh [16], who considered the state equations for the symmetric network in the asymptotic case. Given an (o, d) call, define the set of available paths $R(o, d, s, m)$ as all paths between o and d with exactly s intermediate nodes and no more than m circuits busy on each link of the path. Two classes of routing were considered. Type 1 routings randomly select a path in $R(o, d, s, m)$, while type 2 routings randomly select a path from the subset of $R(o, d, s, m)$ made of the least-loaded paths. Let $p_i(t)$ be the probability of having i busy circuits at time t on a given trunk. We can write the Kolmogorov equations for these probabilities as follows:

$$\frac{dp_i}{dt} = -p_i\left(i + A[1 - \delta_{i,N}]\right) - Aq_i(\mathbf{p}) + p_{i-1}A\left(1 - \delta_{i,0}\right)$$

$$+ Aq_{i-1}(\mathbf{p}) + p_{i+1}\left(i + 1\right)\left(1 - \delta_{i,N}\right). \tag{4.43}$$

The arrival rate at the link in question is composed of first-offered Poisson traffic A and some unknown amount of overflow traffic. The fraction of the first-offered traffic that arrives at the link, represented by q_i, is given by

$$q_i = \begin{cases} sp_i p_N \Big/ \sum_{j=0}^{m-1} p_j & \text{if } i < m \\ 0 & \text{otherwise} \end{cases} \quad \text{when } r = 1$$

$$= \begin{cases} sp_N & \text{if } i < m, \ j < i, \ p_j = 0 \\ 0 & \text{otherwise} \end{cases} \quad \text{when } r = 2$$

The system has two asymptotically stable solutions depending on the value of A. The asymptotically stable solutions for routing $r = 1, 2$ are

$$p_i = \begin{cases} (p_1^*, p_2^*, \ldots p_n^*) & \text{if } A < A_r^*(s, n) \\ (0, 0, \ldots 1) & \text{if } A > N/s \end{cases}$$

For $r = 1$, A_1^* is the smallest value of A such that

$$E(A(x), N) = x \tag{4.44}$$

has a solution $x \in [0, 1]$, and where

$$A(x) = A\frac{1 + (s - 1)x}{1 - x}$$

and the p_i^*s are given by

$$p_i^* = x^* \frac{N!}{i!} \left[\frac{1 - x^*}{A(1 + (s - 1)x^*)}\right]^{N-i},$$

where x^* is the smallest solution of Eq. (4.44). Note that $A(0) = A$ and $A(1) = \infty$. Thus the system always has a solution at $x = 1$, and the left-hand side is $E(A, N)$ at $x = 0$. Given the shape of the Erlang B function, the system either has a single solution or has three solutions. Two of these are stable; the implication (although there is no formal proof) is that the third one is unstable.

For $r = 2$,

$$A_2^* = \max_{i=0,1,\ldots N-1} \left(\frac{1}{s}\frac{N!}{i!}\right)^{\frac{1}{N-i}}.$$

The stationary probabilities are given by

$$p_i^* = \begin{cases} 0 & \text{if } i \le l-1 \\ p_N^* \dfrac{(N! - sl!A^{N-i})}{(A-l)l!A^{N-l-1}} & \text{if } i = l \\ p_N^* \dfrac{N!}{i!A^{N-i}} & \text{otherwise} \end{cases}$$

where l is determined by the inequality

$$\left(\frac{lN!}{sl!}\right)^{\frac{1}{N-l+1}} < A < \left(\frac{N!}{sl!}\right)^{\frac{1}{N-l}}$$

and p_n^* is given by the normalizing condition on the P_is.

This phenomenon is intimately related to alternate routing with mutual overflow. Ordered networks have no mutual overflow, and the nonlinear system of equations (4.39) is triangular. Given that the Erlang B function is uniquely invertible, the system has a unique solution. In any event, the reality of the phenomenon is no longer in doubt. Furthermore, it is conceivable that a network operating on the lower portion of the curve may suddenly jump on the upper part because of a temporary surge in traffic. The implication is that the network would then stay in that high blocking state for very long periods, long after the original perturbation disappeared. This behavior is clearly undesirable, and ways of preventing it must be found.

State Protection

As is clear from the previous discussion, networks with mutual overflow are inherently unstable, at least to the extent that they can operate in the hysteresis mode that we just described. As is also clear, a mode of operation such as the one described by Fig. 4.11 is absolutely unacceptable in a real network, and some means must be provided to prevent it. One such technique, originally suggested by Grandjean in a different context [17], was proposed by Akinpelu [14] under the name *trunk reservation*. The technique has also been proposed for adaptive routing methods based on residual capacity under the name *state protection* [18]. Because of the potential for confusion with physical trunk reservation, we shall use the second term here, with the understanding that it has precisely the same meaning as in [14].

The current practice in telephone networks is to connect a call whenever there is a free trunk on a group. A call is blocked only when all trunks are busy. State protection operates by distinguishing among various types of calls offered to a group, blocking some of them *before* all trunks are busy. Specifically, first-offered calls are blocked only in the all-trunk-busy condition, where calls overflowing from some other group are blocked whenever $m < N$ trunks are busy.

The term *trunk reservation* naturally arises because part of the group's capacity $N - m$ is reserved for first-offered traffic. This, however, is very different from *physical* trunk reservation, where some specific trunks are marked inaccessible for some calls. Here, any call can occupy any trunk, and the restriction is only on the *number*, not the *identity*, of the trunks that cannot be occupied by overflow calls. For this reason, we use the term *state protection*, which does not have the connotation of physical reservation.

Given that such a state-protection scheme is to be used, one must be able to compute the link-blocking probabilities in order to compute the network performance. Thus the traffic model must be modified to take into account the state protection. The link-loading phase is the computation of a and $\hat{a}$ given B and B'. In this case, stream 1 is identified with first-offered traffic, and stream 2 with overflow traffic. The actual computation of the link-offered traffic, a straightforward modification of the equivalent formulas for alternate routing without protection, is left as an exercise (Problem 4.21). The link-blocking stage is given by Akinpelu's model (see Section 3.6).

For this discussion, we assume that there are two functions of the trunk sizes, traffic parameters and reservation level, such that, for each link,

$$p = f(a, \hat{a}, m, N) \tag{4.45}$$

$$\hat{p} = g(a, \hat{a}, m, N) \tag{4.46}$$

and where, of course, a and $\hat{a}$ are functions of p and $\hat{p}$. As usual with the two-phase method, the correct values of p and $\hat{p}$ are given by the solution of this system of equations.

Effect of State Protection

We can estimate the effect of state protection both on the theoretical solution of the flow equations and on the behavior of the network. In the first case, we must express the analog of Fig. 4.8 for the case of state protection. The single-moment model had a single unknown variable for the symmetric network case, and the model with state protection now has two, that is, p and $\hat{p}$, whose value determines the network blocking probability. In order to have a graphic representation, it is necessary to rewrite the system (4.45) and (4.46) as

$$F(a, \hat{a}, m, N) \triangleq p - f(a, \hat{a}, m, N) = 0 \tag{4.47}$$

$$G(a, \hat{a}, m, N) \triangleq \hat{p} - g(a, \hat{a}, m, N) = 0 \tag{4.48}$$

The system can be represented graphically by plotting the isocontours of F and G at the value 0 in the p and $\hat{p}$ plane. The intersection(s) of these contours defines the solution(s) of the system. An example of multiple solutions is shown in Fig. 4.12, and the effect of increasing the protection level is shown in Figs. 4.13 and 4.12.

It is obvious that no level of protection ensures that multiple solutions do not occur. Mason, DeSerres, and Meubus [19] have given sufficient conditions

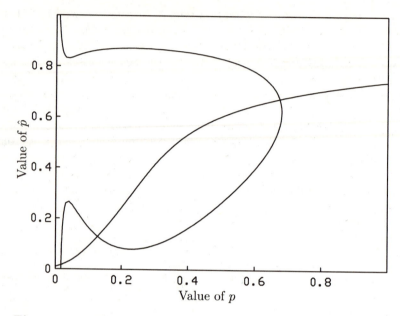

Figure 4.12 Contours of F and G Functions for No State Protection; Traffic = 42 Erlangs, 100 Trunks, 9 Alternate Routes

under which this cannot occur, again for symmetric and asymptotic networks. The actual effect of the reservation on the behavior of realistic asymmetric finite networks remains to be determined.

Finally, as shown in Fig. 4.15, state protection, in this case at a level of one, indeed eliminates the sudden changes of states, and the network operates in a much more satisfactory mode.

4.5   Summary

What have we learned so far? The most important fact to come out of this discussion is the presence of a lurking fixed-point system of equation in most cases of alternate routing and load sharing. This system determines to a large extent the difficulty of evaluating the performance of a network and, to an even larger extent, the difficulties in other areas of network optimization. We have also encountered one consequence of this system, the possibility of hysteresis, and indicated how it can be prevented by state protection.

Because of the simplifying assumptions made in the discussion, these results are mostly of theoretical significance. Our assumptions include the use

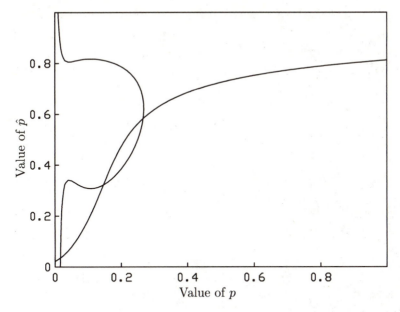

Figure 4.13 Contours of F and G; $N - m = 1$, Traffic = 42 Erlangs, 100 Trunks, 9 Alternate Routes

of the Poisson model for the internal traffic and the reduced-load path model of Eq. (4.5). In practice, analysis methods do not always use these assumptions, and one objective of the next chapter is to see how the two-phase method described here can be extended to cover other cases.

We will also describe other generalizations of the link-decomposition method — in particular, the cluster- and path-decomposition techniques. Although these techniques have not yet been used, they may turn out to be useful for analyzing circuit-switched networks with more complex types of traffic than voice.

Problems

4.1. Compute the end-to-end blocking probability as a function of link blocking probability for SOC control in the case of two-link nonhierarchical routing.

4.2. Consider the double-sector tandem network of Fig. 4.16. Assuming that the link-blocking probabilities are known for all the links, compute

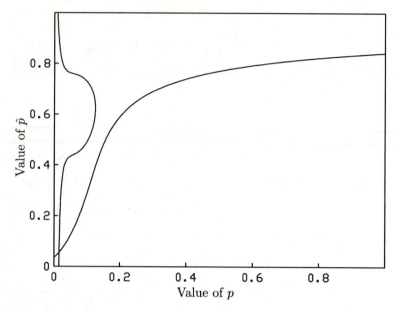

Figure 4.14   Contours of F and G; $N - m = 2$, Traffic $= 42$ Erlangs, 100 Trunks, 9 Alternate Routes

the end-to-end blocking probability for the (O, D) traffic under OOC control, using the method of Chan [8], in two ways:

1. Using the correct expression for conditional occupancy as described by Eq. (4.28).

2. Neglecting the conditional probability.

4.3.   Compute the end-to-end blocking probability for the hierarchical network of Fig. 4.16, using the method of Butto, Colombo, and Tonietti [6]. Show that the result is identical to the one obtained in Problem 4.2.

4.4.   For the route tree of Fig. 4.17, compute the probability of using each of the paths leading to the destination, and the paths leading to a loss node, as a function of the link-blocking probabilities.

4.5.   Using a suitable form of pseudo-code, write a complete program specification for computing the end-to-end blocking probability as a function of the link-blocking probabilities for nonhierarchical routing, when there are no repeated arcs in any route trees.

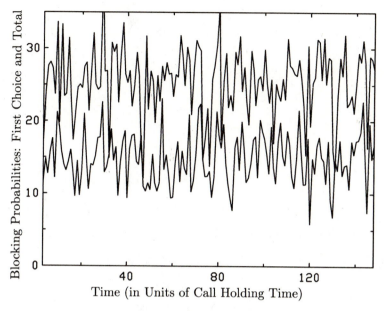

Figure 4.15   Dynamic Behavior of Network with State Protection

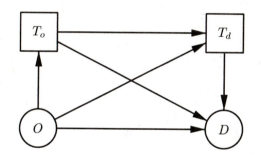

Figure 4.16   Double-Sector Tandem Network

4.6. Code the specification of Problem 4.5 in some suitable language and check that it gives the correct answer for two-link alternate routing.

4.7. Compute the end-to-end blocking probability for two link alternate routing with OOC control using the method of Chan [8] — that is, using Eqs. (4.30) and (4.31). Express the result in closed form.

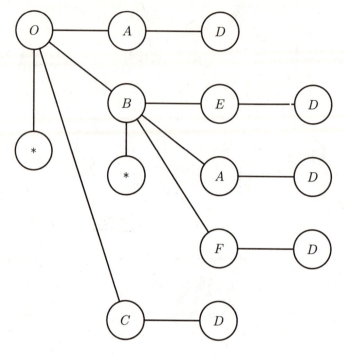

Figure 4.17   Augmented Route Tree

4.8.   Write Eq. (4.24) for the stream $B - C$ in the network of Fig. 4.4 and for a standard hierarchical routing with the fan rule and OOC.

4.9.   Repeat the procedure of Problem 4.8, but for the case of SOC.

4.10.   Derive Eq. (4.27) for the case of SOC.

4.11.   Derive the expression for the Jacobian matrix of the Erlang fixed-point equation (4.40) for the case of two-link alternate routing.

4.12.   Consider the solution of the equation $rx^2 + (1 - r)x = 0$. Rewrite the equation in such a way that the relaxation algorithm can be used to solve it. Examine the solution process when r changes values, depending on the starting point.

4.13.   Verify that the system of Eq. (4.39) is triangular for the double-sector tandem network.

4.14.   Consider the network of Fig. 4.18. There is a flow $A^{i,j} = 10$ between

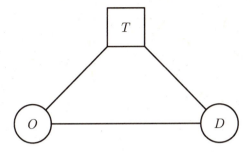

Figure 4.18   Three-Node Network

all pairs of nodes. Compute the end-to-end blocking probability of the (i, j) traffic with fixed hierarchical routing, where node T is the tandem:

1. When there are 10 one-way circuits between each pair of nodes.

2. When there are 20 two-way circuits between each pair of nodes.

    You may use a one-moment model for all traffic flows.

4.15.   Compute the end-to-end blocking probability for the network of Problem 4.14 with two-way circuits and fixed nonhierarchical routing with overflow and OOC control.

4.16.   Generate a symmetric two-link alternate routing for a complete four-node network. Try the same thing for the five-node case (this is somewhat harder).

4.17.   Compute the traffic offered to a link as a function of the link-blocking probability in a symmetric network operating with OOC control and two-way links.

4.18.   Repeat the procedure of Problem 4.17, but for SOC control.

4.19.   Consider a hierarchical network with SOC control. Compute the link-offered traffic using the influence graph only and compare with the result obtained using a more accurate method such as that of Butto, Colombo, and Tonietti [6].

4.20.   Consider a symmetric network of N nodes operating with nonhierarchical alternate routing with two-link alternate paths. The first choice is the direct link, links are two-way, all possible overflows are used, and OOC control is used. Let A be the total external traffic offered to a link.

We want to derive conditions of stability for the infinite network when $N \to \infty$.

1. Compute a, the total traffic offered to a link as a function of the link-blocking probability.

2. Assuming that all traffics are Poisson, show that the fixed-point equation for this model is

$$E(a,n) = \frac{a-A}{a+A}. \tag{4.49}$$

3. Discuss qualitatively the number of solutions that one can expect to obtain.

4. Using Descarte's rule, indicate values of A for which one can determine the number of solutions of the system.

4.21.   Give an expression for the link-offered traffic as a function of the link-blocking probabilities in the case of a symmetric network with state protection.

References

[1] Kelly, F.P., "Blocking probabilities in large circuit switched networks," *Advances in Applied Probability*, vol. 18, pp. 473–505, 1986.

[2] Ortega, J.M., and Rheinbolt, W.C., *Iterative Solutions of Nonlinear Equations in Several Variables*, Academic Press, 1970.

[3] Luenberger, D.G., *Linear and Nonlinear Programming*, Addison-Wesley, 1984.

[4] Polak, E., *Computational Methods in Optimization*, Academic Press, 1971.

[5] Lee, C.Y., "Analysis of switching networks," *Bell System Technical Journal*, vol. 34, pp. 1287–1315, 1955.

[6] Butto, M., Colombo, G., and Tonietti, A., "On point to point losses in communication networks," *International Teletraffic Congress*, vol. 8, 1976.

[7] Lin, P.M., Leon, B.J., and Stewart, C.R., "Analysis of circuit switched networks employing originating office control with spill," *IEEE Transactions on Communications*, vol. COM–26, pp. 754–765, 1978.

[8] Chan, W.S., "Recursive algorithms for computing end to end blocking in a network with arbitrary routing plan," *IEEE Transactions on Communications*, vol. COM–28, pp. 153–164, 1980.

[9] Girard, A., and Ouimet, Y., "End-to-end blocking in circuit-switched networks: polynomial algorithms for some special cases," *IEEE Transactions on Communications*, vol. COM–31, pp. 1269–1273, 1983.

[10] Gaudreau, M., "Recursive formulas for the calculation of point to point congestion," *IEEE Transactions on Communications*, vol. COM–28, pp. 313–316, 1980.

[11] Körner, U., and Wallström, B., "On symmetric two-link routing in circuit switched networks," *International Teletraffic Congress*, vol. 11, pp. 5.1.A.3:1–5.1.A.3:6, 1985.

[12] Nakagome, Y., and Mori, H., "Flexible routing in the global communication network," *International Teletraffic Congress*, vol. 7, pp. 426.1–426.8, 1973.

[13] Krupp, R.S., "Stabilization of alternate routing networks," *International Conference on Communications*, pp. 31.2.1–31.2.5, 1982.

[14] Akinpelu, J.M., "The overload performance of engineered networks with nonhierarchical and hierarchical routing," *International Teletraffic Congress*, vol. 10, pp. 3.2.4.1–3.2.4.7, 8–15 June 1983.

[15] Mason, L., "On the stability of circuit switched networks with nonhierarchical routing," *Conference on Decision and Control*, vol. 25, pp. 1345–1347, 1986.

[16] Marbukh, V.V., "Asymptotic investigation of a complete communications network with a large number of points and bypass routes," *Problemy Peredachi Informatsii*, translated in *Problems of Information Transmission*, vol. 16, pp. 212–216, 1981.

[17] Grandjean, C., "Call routing strategies in telecommunication networks," *International Teletraffic Congress*, vol. 5, 1967.

[18] Cameron, H., Galloy, P., and Graham, W.J., "Report on the Toronto advanced routing concept trial," *Network Planning Symposium*, vol. 1, pp. 228–236, 1980.

[19] Mason, L., Deserres, Y., and Meubus, C., "Circuit-switched multipoint service performance models," *International Teletraffic Congress*, vol. 11, pp. 2.1A-5-1–2.1A-5-6, September 1985.

CHAPTER 5

Other Decomposition Methods

In this chapter, we extend the results of Chapter 4 on the link-decomposition method for evaluating the loss probability of a given network. In that chapter, we simplified the exposition for clarity; the method described there would not be used in practice, but would require modifications. We therefore introduce more complex — and hence more realistic — link-decomposition methods by removing some of these simplifications. These methods lead to a great variety of practical algorithms that seem to give relatively similar results — a conclusion supported by a few numerical studies.

The second part of this chapter deals with other decomposition methods for the network-evaluation problem with alternate routing. Although the link-decomposition methods appear satisfactory when used for networks that carry voice traffic exclusively, there is no guarantee that this will also be true for networks that carry a variety of traffic types. The discussion, therefore, merely introduces the possibility of other evaluation techniques, as well as the form they take for single-traffic networks. It is not yet clear whether these methods will be needed, and, if so, their eventual form in a multiservice environment.

5.1   Two-Phase Methods

Let us review briefly some of the algorithms proposed for network-performance evaluation. The general assumptions stated at the beginning of Chapter 4 are quite accurate, especially for a digital network; all the methods described here share these assumptions. They differ from the methods of Chapter 4, however, in a number of ways, the most important of which follow:

1. The description of internal traffic flows by single, double, or three-moment models.

2. The calculation of individual parcel-blocking probabilities on links, which may be more or less detailed, and sometimes ignored completely.

3. Various ways to approximate the correlations between traffic streams in a given link.

4. The path model used and the algorithm used to evaluate downstream blocking.

5. The actual calculation of end-to-end blocking. More recent methods use the route tree method, either in its recursive form, or write the actual analytic expression for the blocking. Earlier methods evaluate the end-to-end blocking iteratively; the end-to-end blocking is the sum of the blocked traffic on links that has no overflow. This latter case is more restrictive since it generally does not allow crankback of blocked calls.

Conceptually, the link-decomposition method was described with two very distinct parts: (1) the evaluation of end-to-end blocking given the link blocking probabilities and (2) the calculation of the correct values of the link blocking probabilities. In practice, these two steps are often combined in a numerical algorithm, also made up of two parts: (1) link-loading, where, given the link-blocking probability vector, the total traffic offered to each link is computed and (2) link blocking, where, given the total traffic offered to each link, the link-blocking probability vector is computed. The end-to-end blocking, generally obtained within this procedure by calculating the traffic lost at each stage in the calculation, does not appear as a separate step.

In the link-loading step, the external demands represented by the traffic matrix, are mapped onto a set of link-offered traffics. This is done under the assumption that a set of blocking variables is known, either from the previous iteration or from the initialization. These blocking variables determine the value of the overflow and carried parameters. The links are processed in some arbitrary order, and the carried and overflow traffics apportioned according to the routing plan.

The link-blocking step, the converse of the link-loading step, maps the link-offered traffics onto a new set of blocking variables, which are used in the link-loading step at the next iteration.

All the methods considered here follow the general pattern just described. They differ considerably, however, in the way they represent internal traffic. Also, they handle path-blocking calculations differently. We review the most representative methods, outlining for each how each phase differs from the analogous phase in the other methods.

The Method of Schneider and Minoli

A simple method of evaluating the average blocking (over all origin-destination pairs) has been proposed by Schneider and Minoli [1]. The method is two-phase and single-moment, but the link-loading and link-blocking phases are merged.

Furthermore, the link-loading procedure is somewhat different from the one considered in Section 4.3. We describe the method using route tree terminology, although this concept is not employed in the original paper. Recall that, in Section 4.3, the outer iteration is on route trees, and all links appearing in a tree are loaded before the next tree is processed. In the present case, the outer loop is in terms of path levels, and links are loaded sequentially on a given path level for all trees. This procedure, of course, is embedded in an overall iteration loop, which is the relaxation over link-offered traffics.

The following calculations are made in the link-loading phase. Assume that this is iteration m of the relaxation, that we are currently processing paths that are level l in all route trees, and that we are looking at link s in route tree k. Let a_s^k be the current estimate of the traffic parcel k offered to the link. The link loading is done by evaluating

$$\bar{a}_s^k = a_s^k(1 - E(a_s, N_s)) \tag{5.1}$$
$$\hat{a}_s^k = a_s^k E(a_s, N_s) \tag{5.2}$$

where a_s is the current estimate of the total traffic offered to link s. Note that there is no link-blocking variable as such. Blocking estimates are computed as needed during the calculation, and carried and overflow traffics added to the appropriate link according to the routing plan. If there is no possibility of overflow at the current node, the traffic is lost; a running sum is incremented to obtain an estimate of the total lost traffic.

The problem with Eqs. (5.1) and (5.2) is in the calculation of a_s: Link s may appear in route trees k' other that k, and at levels l' other than l. Although all these trees contribute equally to the total link-offered traffic, the contribution depends on the value of l'. If $l' < l$, then the *new* value of the parcel $a_s^{k'}$ is used; otherwise, the value computed at the previous iteration is used. If $m = 1$, the value of the first-offered traffic is used to estimate the offered traffic for each parcel. The method requires two major simplifications:

1. There is no attempt to take into account downstream blocking when computing the link-offered traffic. According to Schneider and Minoli, this results in an overestimate of the average blocking.

2. The method can handle arbitrary sequential routing (in fact, Schneider and Minoli claim that they originated this term), with SOC or OOC control possible, but no crankback. This is mainly due to the fact that the route description used has no notion of a loss node. The routing is essentially described by the original route trees without augmentation, which does not permit the handling of crankback.

Katz's Two-Phase Method

Katz [2] was the first to propose a two-phase method for calculating blocking in nonhierarchical networks. This method, similar to that of Section 4.3, places particular emphasis on computing internal traffic flows accurately. It is characterized by the following features:

1. Internal traffic flows are modeled by the first two moments of their distribution.

2. The network can have an arbitrary fixed alternate routing, but must operate with SOC control.

3. Link-offered traffics are reduced to take into account the blocking on links downstream from the current link.

4. Traffic parcels on a link experience distinct blocking probabilities.

5. No attempt is made to take into account correlations on a link.

Traffic streams on a link are characterized by their destination only; thus the origin of a call that has reached a node is immaterial. Traffic on a link is described by two vectors a_s^k and v_s^k corresponding to the mean and variance, respectively, of traffic offered to link s, with k for their destination. A particular component of the vectors is called a *traffic parcel*. Variables without a superscript refer to the total value, over all parcels, of the quantity. We also define B_s^k as the blocking probability on link s of traffic parcel k.

Link Loading.   The blocking variables for Katz's model are the link-blocking probabilities B_s^k and B_s. Also introduced is another blocking quantity, denoted $\hat{L}_j^k$, the probability that an overflow call, having reached node j, and destined for node k, will be blocked. This partial end-to-end blocking probability is *not* the end-to-end blocking probability for external traffic originating at node j for destination k. Instead, it is used to compensate for the downstream blocking of traffic parcels k that are in transit at node j. At the beginning of the current iteration, these quantities are known, from either the initialization or the previous iteration. The superscript (m) is used whenever the iteration index is required. From these values and the external loads, a new estimate of the link-offered traffic parameters is computed.

The link-loading step consists of processing all the network links in some predetermined order. Assume that the current link s has end nodes i and j, and that parcel k has destination t. This link currently has an estimate of the offered traffic, which may be only the external traffic; it may also have transit traffic from some other links. The first step in the calculation is to reduce the link-offered traffic to take into account the downstream blocking of each traffic parcel:

$$a_s^{k'} = a_s^k \left[1 - (1 - B_s^k)\hat{L}^{j,t} \right] \qquad (5.3)$$

$$v_s^{k'} = v_s^k \left[1 - (1 - B_s^k)\hat{L}^{j,t} \right] \qquad (5.4)$$

These values are added to the current estimate of the total link-offered traffic, which is used in the link-blocking phase to evaluate the total blocking probability. Next the overflow parameters for each parcel offered to the link are evaluated:

$$\hat{a}_s^k = a_s^k B_s^k \qquad (5.5)$$

$$\hat{v}_s^{k\,(m)} = \frac{\hat{a}_s^k}{a_s^{(m-1)} B_s^{(m-1)}} v_s^{(m-1)} \qquad (5.6)$$

Having apportioned the overflow for each traffic parcel, the parameters of the carried traffic are computed:

$$\bar{a}_s^k = a_s^k - \hat{a}_s^k \qquad (5.7)$$

$$\bar{v}_s^k = v_s^k - \hat{v}_s^k \qquad (5.8)$$

Computing the variances in this way neglects a possible correlation effect between various traffic parcels on a given link. According to Katz, including such correlation effects does not seem to increase the accuracy of the model significantly. The overflow and the carried traffics are then added to the parameters of the appropriate links, as specified by the routing plan:

$$a_{\rho(s,k)}^k \leftarrow a_{\rho(s,k)}^k + \bar{a}_s^k \qquad (5.9)$$

$$a_{\sigma(s,k)}^k \leftarrow a_{\rho(s,k)}^k + \hat{a}_s^k \qquad (5.10)$$

$$v_{\rho(s,k)}^k \leftarrow v_{\rho(s,k)}^k + \bar{v}_s^k \qquad (5.11)$$

$$v_{\sigma(s,k)}^k \leftarrow v_{\rho(s,k)}^k + \hat{v}_s^k \qquad (5.12)$$

A call is assumed to be lost if $\sigma(s, k) = 0$. In this case, a running sum is updated that contains the current estimate of the total traffic lost, and hence of the average end-to-end blocking probability. Thus the model applies only to the SOC case, since a more general routing control with crankback could allow additional routes for a call blocked on a last link out of a node. After all links are processed, a new estimate of the link-offered traffic is known, allowing the link-blocking phase to start.

   Link Blocking.   In the second phase of Katz's method, new estimates of the link blocking are computed, given the parameters of the link-offered traffic. This is generally done in two steps. First the total blocking is evaluated; from this value, parcel blocking probabilities are computed. In the present case, a new estimate of the $\hat{L}^{j,t}$ also must be computed.

The total blocking is computed from the current estimate of the total link-offered traffic, obtained from Eqs. (5.3) and (5.4). Three cases must be considered, according to whether the total traffic is Poisson, peaked, or smooth. In the first case, the Erlang B function is used; in the second, the standard equivalent random theory (ERT) method is applicable; in the third, an equivalent carried method is used. The equivalent carried method was described in Chapter 3; here we need only say that it is an extension of the ERT technique for smooth traffic, where the equivalent traffic is now considered to be carried on the equivalent trunk group instead of being offered, as in standard ERT.

Having computed the overall link-blocking probability B_s, one must evaluate the parcel blocking probabilities. The total parcel offered to the link is known from Eqs. (5.9) and (5.10). This step is carried out as follows:

$$B_s^k = B_s \left[1 + K \left(\frac{v_s^k}{a_s^k} - \frac{v_s}{a_\varepsilon} \right) \right]. \tag{5.13}$$

This computation is adequate for a given link. It has been found, however, that the constant K is in fact traffic dependent, and thus must be adjusted for each link. The actual form of K is given by

$$K \approx \frac{a_s}{v_s} \left[4.1 \times 10^{-4} \left(\frac{a_s}{v_s} \right) \left(\frac{1}{B_s} \right)^2 - 0.156 \left(\frac{a_s}{v_s} \right) \left(\frac{1}{B_s} \right)^{1/2} - \right.$$

$$\left. 0.0747 \left(\frac{1}{B_s} \right) + 0.69 \left(\frac{1}{B_s} \right)^{1/2} \right] - 0.183, \tag{5.14}$$

where the coefficients are estimated by regression over simulation results. Finally, a new value of the partial end-to-end blocking probabilities must be computed. This is done by

$$\hat{L}^{j,t} = 1 - \prod_m (1 - B_m)$$

if there is only one path from j to t, and by

$$= \hat{L}^{j,t^{(m-1)}} \left\{ 1 + \left[\frac{v_s^k}{a_s^k} - 1 \right] \left[K_1 + K_2 \left(\frac{1}{\hat{L}^{j,t^{(m-1)}}} \right)^{1/2} \right] \right\} \tag{5.15}$$

otherwise. Here again, the values for the constants were selected by regression over simulation results, which gave $K_1 = 0.3$ and $K_2 = 0.08$. The procedure iterates between the link-loading and link-blocking phases, and the convergence rule is the difference between two successive values of the overall network-loss probability. This method has been used to assess the blocking of large networks and also to dimension networks of as many as 70 nodes [3].

Partition Coefficients and Correlation.   Katz's method was improved somewhat by Butto, Colombo, and Tonietti [4] and, apparently independently, by Deschamps [5], who gives an analytic approximation to the K

factors used in computing the parcel blocking probabilities (Eq. 5.13). The estimate of K is made by using Eq. (5.13) for the first-offered traffic, which is Poisson and in which the variance thus is equal to the mean. For this parcel, B_s is given by the group time congestion

$$\beta(n, m, A) = E(A, n + m) \frac{\sigma_{m+1}(n)}{\sigma_m(n)} \qquad (5.16)$$

$$\sigma_m(n) = \sum_{j=0}^{n} \binom{m - 1 + j}{j} \frac{A^{n-j}}{(n - j)!} \qquad (5.17)$$

The only unknown in Eq. (5.13) is K, which can easily be computed. In cases when the result is not in the interval $(0, 1)$, the value is set at either 0 or 1, depending whether the result was larger than one or smaller than 0.

Deschamps [5] has estimated the correlation between parcels on a link, based on the following model. Suppose that a link is offered K Poisson streams of mean a^1, a^2, ..., a^K. Let $a = \sum_k a^k$ be the total offered traffic. We are interested in the probability that n_1, n_2, ..., n_K calls of stream 1, 2, ..., K, respectively, are carried on the link *given that* a total of $N = \sum_k n_k$ calls are carried. The first two moments and the covariance of the individual parcels are then given by

$$E_k = \frac{a^k}{a} M \qquad (5.18)$$

$$V_k = V \left(\frac{a^k}{a}\right)^2 + M \left(\frac{a^k}{a}\right)\left(1 - \frac{a^k}{a}\right) \qquad (5.19)$$

$$\mathrm{cov}\,(n_k, n_j) = (V - M) \left(\frac{a^k}{a}\right)\left(\frac{a^j}{a}\right) \qquad (5.20)$$

where M and V are the mean and variance, respectively, of the total number of busy circuits. E_k and V_k are the parameters of the carried traffic, and in our standard notation denoted $\bar{a}$ and $\bar{v}$, respectively. These expressions of Eqs. (5.18–5.20) are used to compute the variance of the traffic offered to a link from the parameters of the traffic from a preceding link, be it overflowing or carrying traffic on s.

Consider, for instance, link s. Assume that some of the parcels carried on link t are offered to s. The problem is to compute the total variance of this offered traffic v_s. The means $\bar{a}_t^k$ of the traffic carried on t are known, as are the total mean $\bar{a}_t = \sum_k \bar{a}_t^k$ and the total carried variance $\bar{v}_t$. We want to partition the total variance v_t into the variances of the individual traffic parcels, more accurately computing the variance of those parcels offered to s. To do this, we use Eqs. (5.18) and (5.19), assuming that the $\bar{a}_t^k$ represent independent Poisson processes. At the same time, the correlation coefficients are computed using Eq. (5.20). Having the values of the $\bar{v}_t^k$, one wants to use them to compute the value of v_t, the total variance of the traffic offered to t. Let $I(s,t)$ be the set of parcels carried on t that are actually offered to s. The contribution of t to v_s, denoted by $V_s(t)$, is computed as follows:

$$V_t(s) = \sum_{k \in I(s,t)} \overline{v}_t(s)^k + 2 \sum_{\substack{k \in I(s,t) \\ l \in I(s,t)}} \text{cov}\,(\overline{a}_t^k, \overline{a}_t^l).$$

The total variance of the traffic is then computed by summing over all links t that send some of their carried traffic to s:

$$V(s) = \sum_t V_t(s).$$

Although the correlations between parcels on a given link are taken into account, the correlations between various links are not. The same technique is used for overflow traffic.

The Method of Manfield and Downs

Manfield and Downs [6] have proposed a link-blocking model that takes into account the downstream blocking effect on the calculation of the link-offered traffic. The presence of downstream links means that, although a call may find a free server on the first link of a path, it may nevertheless fail to be carried on that link because of blocking on other links. Thus the first link operates as a system with N servers, but with a given *balking* probability — that is, a probability that although a server is free, the call will be blocked. As a consequence, all links except the last one on a path are subject to the balking effect. An important assumption is that traffic that has been carried on a link is effectively Poisson. All links on a path except the first one are offered Poisson traffic, simplifying considerably the computation of traffic on a path since it is sufficient to know the traffic means to carry out the calculation. Finally, overflow traffic is characterized by three moments and thus requires a more complex link-blocking model for the first links in each path that can overflow.

    Link Loading. Consider the link-loading phase for traffic that is carried on a path; by hypothesis, it is Poisson and is completely described by its mean. In this case, the balking technique yields the same result for link-offered traffic as the standard method of Lin, Leon, and Stewart [7]. The link loading is done as in that method (see Section 4.3), using augmented route trees. For each link on a path, however, the balking probability β_s is calculated by

$$\beta_s = 1 - \prod_{\substack{t \in j \\ t > s}} (1 - B_t) \tag{5.21}$$

For some path j in route tree k, we have, for the mean of the traffic carried on j,

$$\overline{A}_j^k = A^k P\{U_1, U_2, \ldots U_{j-1} \text{ blocked} \mid U_j \text{ free}\}\, P\{U_j \text{ free}\}. \tag{5.22}$$

The probability is calculated by any algorithm suitable for the route tree under consideration (see Section 4.2). Having the path-carried traffic, the contribution of this traffic to the traffic offered to some link in the path is given by

$$\overline{a}_s^k(j) = \overline{A}_j^k \beta_s, \tag{5.23}$$

and the carried and offered traffics on link s are related by

$$\overline{a}_s^k = a_s^k(1 - B_s)(1 - \beta_s), \tag{5.24}$$

which yields the same value as with the method of Lin, Leon, and Stewart.

Link Blocking.   Link-blocking evaluation is somewhat more complex because it uses a three-moment description with balking. As usual, the global blocking parameters are computed first, and then the individual parcel parameters. We know from the link-loading phase the values of the first three moments of each parcel offered to the link. The overall offered moments are computed as the sum over all parcels for each one. Note, however, that each traffic stream k offered to the link has its own β^k; this is because the balking depends on the position of link s in tree k, which in general is different for different k. The overall balking probability is given by

$$\beta = \frac{\sum_k \overline{a}^k \beta^k/(1 - \beta^k)}{\sum_k \overline{a}^k/(1 - \beta^k)}. \tag{5.25}$$

In the case of two streams, the first three factorial moments of the overflow process can be computed by generalizing the method of Section 3.5. For a stream of multiple parcels, the model is used iteratively. A particular parcel is singled out, and the remaining parcels are lumped into an equivalent stream. The moments of the singled-out parcel are computed, and the process is repeated for all parcels. A thorough discussion of this model is given in [8], to which the interested reader is referred.

The Method of Butto

As shown in Section 4.2, Butto, Colombo, and Tonietti [4] were the first to dissociate the calculation of the end-to-end blocking from the traffic calculation, and to use reliability-type methods to do so. They have also proposed methods for evaluating the correct link-blocking probabilities, for both general OOC and SOC route trees. Their method is two-phase and of the standard type.

Link Loading.   The main point of interest in the link-loading phase is the way in which Butto, Colombo, and Tonietti handle downstream blocking. Two methods are proposed, corresponding to two different principles. Let s and t be two links in tandem, s before t, and A the traffic offered to the path. The problem is how to define a_s, the traffic offered to s. The first principle is that a_s should be the sum of the traffic carried on the path and the traffic overflowing because of blocking on the links. The second principle is to assume that the traffic carried on the path should be carried on *both* links in the path. Thus, assuming link-blocking independence, we get for the two cases

$$a_s = A\left[B_s + (1 - B_s)(1 - B_t)\right]$$
$$a_s = A(1 - B_t)$$

which can be summarized by

$$a_s = A\left[(1 - B_t) + \beta B_s B_t\right], \tag{5.26}$$

where $\beta = 1$ corresponds to the first principle and $\beta = 0$ to the second. For a multilink path, this generalizes as

$$a_s = A\left[(1 - Q) + \beta \delta_s Q\right], \tag{5.27}$$

where Q is the path-blocking probability, *excluding* link s; A is the total traffic offered to the path; and $\delta = 0$ or 1 if link s is free or blocked, respectively. These traffic models facilitate a comparison, at least numerically, between the two principles used for defining the offered traffic in the presence of downstream blocking.

Link-Loading for General OOC. The link-loading phase for the general case of OOC is similar to the end-to-end blocking calculation of Section 4.2. All configurations for the blocking state of repeated arcs in a particular route tree are enumerated, and a contribution to the offered traffic is computed for each case. The total offered traffic is the sum of these components, properly weighted by the probability that such a configuration occurs.

First consider the calculation of the mean for a particular route tree k and some link s in that tree. We have, for the mean of the traffic parcel offered to that link,

$$\begin{aligned}
a_s^k = {} & (1 - B_{l_1}) \dots (1 - B_{l_t}) a_s^k(0, 0, \dots 0) \\
& + B_{l_1}(1 - B_{l_2}) \dots (1 - B_{l_t}) a_s^k(1, 0, \dots 0) \\
& + \dots \\
& + B_{l_1} B_{l_2} \dots B_{l_t} a_s^k(1, 1, \dots 1),
\end{aligned} \tag{5.28}$$

where $a_s^k(\mathbf{\Delta})$ is the traffic offered to link s for the state of repeated arcs defined by $\mathbf{\Delta}$. Note again that the total traffic is the sum over all state vectors, just as in the case of the end-to-end evaluation by Eq. (4.20). Also, because link s may appear at more than one place in the route tree, the total parcel mean is the sum of all these components, which are evaluated as follows. Let $k_1, k_2, \dots k_n$ be the paths, in the order of overflow, where link s appears in route tree k. We can write

$$a_s^k(\mathbf{\Delta}) = \sum_{j=1}^{n} a_s^k(\mathbf{\Delta}, j), \tag{5.29}$$

where $a_s^k(\mathbf{\Delta}, j)$ is the contribution to the offered traffic arising from the jth path where link s occurs in tree k for state $\mathbf{\Delta}$. The contribution arising from the first path is

$$a_s^k(\mathbf{\Delta}, 1) = A^k C(1, k_1 - 1)\left[(1 - Q_{k_1}) + \beta \delta_{k_1} Q_{k_1}\right]. \tag{5.30}$$

The overflow from this path that reaches path k_2 is given by

$$A^k C(1, k_1 - 1)Q_{k_1}\left[(1 - \delta_{k_1})(1 - \beta)\delta_{k_1}\right] C(k_1, k_2 - 1),$$

where $C(k, l)$ is given by Eq. (4.23) and the contribution from the second path is

$$
\begin{aligned}
a_s^k(\mathbf{\Delta}, 2) &= A^k C(1, k_1 - 1)Q_{k_1}\left[(1 - \delta_{k_1}) + (1 - \beta)\delta_{k_1}\right] C(k_1, k_2 - 1) \\
&\quad \times \left[(1 - Q_{k_2}) + \beta \delta_{k_2} Q_{k_2}\right] \\
&= a_s^k(\mathbf{\Delta}, 1)\frac{\left[(1 - \delta_{k_1}) + (1 - \beta)\delta_{k_1}\right]}{\left[(1 - Q_{k_1}) + \beta \delta_{k_1} Q_{k_1}\right]} C(k_1, k_2 - 1) \\
&\quad \times \left[(1 - Q_{k_2}) + \beta \delta_{k_2} Q_{k_2}\right],
\end{aligned}
\tag{5.31}
$$

which is clearly recursive. Note how Eqs. (5.30) and (5.31) relate the traffic offered to the path to the traffic mean offered to link s.

The variance of each parcel of traffic offered to link s is also computed, according to the two different philosophies expressed by Eq. (5.26). The total parcel variance offered to the link is computed by an equation identical to Eq. (5.28):

$$
\begin{aligned}
v_s^k &= (1 - B_{l_1}) \ldots (1 - B_{l_t})v_s^k(0, 0, \ldots 0) \\
&\quad + B_{l_1}(1 - B_{l_2}) \ldots (1 - B_{l_t})v_s^k(1, 0, \ldots 0) \\
&\quad + \ldots \\
&\quad + B_{l_1} B_{l_2} \ldots B_{l_t} v_s^k(1, 1, \ldots 1),
\end{aligned}
\tag{5.32}
$$

and the contribution corresponding to each state vector $\mathbf{\Delta}$ is computed by an equation similar to (5.29):

$$v_s^k(\mathbf{\Delta}) = \sum_{j=1}^{n} v_s^k(\mathbf{\Delta}, j) \tag{5.33}$$

The individual contribution of each occurrence of link s in tree k is computed somewhat differently than for the mean. Rather than using Eqs. (5.30) and (5.31) to calculate the path-offered variance and its contribution to the link, we calculate the variance offered to the mth path of route tree k, V_m^k, by an equivalent random method. The probability of reaching level m in tree k, $C(1, m - 1)$, is known from the link-blocking phase. Assuming that the traffic offered to the tree is Poisson, we can compute an equivalent system N^* such that $E(A^k, N^*) = C(1, m-1)$. Using the value of N^*, we then compute the mean M_m^k and variance V_m^k of the overflow traffic by standard formulas. M_m^k and V_m^k are used as the required mean and variances offered to the path. From these values, the variance offered to link s can be computed using the correction equation (5.27). Depending on the particular values chosen for δ, we get

$$v_s^k(\boldsymbol{\Delta}, m) = V_m^k(1 - Q_m) \tag{5.34}$$

$$v_s^k(\boldsymbol{\Delta}, m) = \begin{cases} V_m^k(1 - Q_m) & \text{if } \delta = 0 \\ \begin{cases} V_m^k & \text{if } s = 1 \text{ in the path} \\ 0 & \text{otherwise} \end{cases} & \text{if } \delta_s = 1 \end{cases} \tag{5.35}$$

$$v_s^k(\boldsymbol{\Delta}, m) = \begin{cases} \overline{V} & \text{if } \delta = 0 \\ \begin{cases} V_m^k & \text{if } s = 1 \text{ in the path} \\ 0 & \text{otherwise} \end{cases} & \text{if } \delta_s = 1 \end{cases} \tag{5.36}$$

where the variance of the traffic carried on the path $\overline{V}$ is computed from an equivalent system derived as follows. The mean M_m^k and variance V_m^k of the traffic offered to the path are known from the equivalent system for the paths preceding m, and the path blocking D_m^k is also known from the link-blocking phase. Using the standard two-moment model of ERT, we can compute an equivalent system of size N^* offered a two-moment traffic characterized by M_m^k and V_m^k such that the blocking is precisely D_m^k. Having this equivalent system, the carried variance is given by (neglecting the m and k indices for simplicity)

$$\overline{V} = (1 - D)\left[V + DM^2\right] - M - DN^*. \tag{5.37}$$

Which technique for computing the variance is best can be determined only by comparing the values they provide with simulation results.

Link-Loading for General SOC.   The link-loading phase is much simpler in the case of SOC, for the same reasons that the computation of the L^k's was simpler than for the OOC case with repetition. For a particular tree k, let the extremities of link s be i and l. With the usual notation, we have

$$a_s^k = \sum_j a_s^k(j),$$

where the sum is over all paths in the route tree where link s is present, and $a_s^k(j)$, the parcel offered to the link on path j, is given by

$$a_s^k(j) = A^k G_i F_i,$$

where G_i is the probability of reaching node i and F_i is a correction factor to take into account the blocking downstream from link s. Label the nodes $i - 1$, $i - 2$, $\ldots$ from i to the origin o. Also, let l_1, l_2, $\ldots$ be the number of overflows at each of these nodes to reach the path leading to the current arc s. We have

$$G_i = G_{i-1}(1 - B_{i-1,i}) \prod_{j=1}^{l_i - 1} B_{i-1,j} \tag{5.38}$$

$$F_i = (1 - D_i) + \beta B_s D_i \tag{5.39}$$

where

$$D_i = 1 - \prod_{k=s+1}^{m} (1 - B_k), \tag{5.40}$$

where the product is taken over all links after s in the path. Note that D_i is the probability that a call will be blocked downstream from node i on the currently examined path. Because of the form of Eq. (5.38), the calculation is recursive, and can be done in one pass over each route tree.

The calculation of the total link variance follows the same lines. The downstream blocking effect for the variance is modeled exactly as for the mean, using the same factor F_i.

Link Blocking.   The problem is how to evaluate the parameters of the carried and overflow traffic parcels once the parameters of the offered parcels are known. The mean and variance of the total offered traffic, represented by a_s and v_s, are given by the sum of the individual parcels. From these values, the overall blocking for a trunk group is calculated by standard ERT for peaked traffic. For smooth traffic, an approximation is proposed, which is claimed by Butto, Colombo, and Tonietti to be sufficiently accurate and faster than others.

Butto, Colombo, and Tonietti also discuss a number of techniques for the computation of the parcel blocking probabilities. One technique is that of Katz [2], as described by Eqs. (5.3–5.8), with an analytic value for the K factors as given by Eq. (5.14). A simpler way to compute the variances is to equalize the stream peakednesses to the stream values:

$$\hat{v}_s^k = \hat{v}_s \frac{\hat{a}_s^k}{\hat{a}_s} \qquad \overline{v}_s^k = \overline{v}_s \frac{\overline{a}_s^k}{\overline{a}_s} \tag{5.41}$$

Another, somewhat more complex formula for apportioning the variances is as follows:

$$\hat{v}_s^k = \hat{v}_s \frac{\hat{a}_s^k v_s^k / a_s^k}{\sum_m \hat{v}_s^m \hat{a}_s^m / \hat{a}_s} \qquad \overline{v}_s^k = \overline{v}_s \frac{\overline{a}_s^k v_s^k / a_s^k}{\sum_m \overline{v}_s^m \overline{a}_s^m / \overline{a}_s} \tag{5.42}$$

There is no theoretical reason for choosing one method over the other. Their respective merits can be assessed only by using simulation to compare the values they provide.

Comparison of Methods

As noted earlier, we consider only some of the models used to compute network performance. A summary of the various assumptions used in the methods we have covered is found in Table 5.1. Other models can be found in the proceedings of the International Teletraffic Congress. See, for example, Guérineau

	Routing	L	Moments	Downstream Blocking	Parcel Blocking
Katz	SOC	No overflow	2	Traffic Reduction	Simulation K
Butto, Colombo, and Tonietti	OOC, SOC, no crankback	Reliability equations	2	Two Methods β	Analytic K
Lin, Leon, and Stewart	Fixed Alternate	Augmented trees Equations	1	$a = \frac{\bar{a}}{(1-B)}$	No
Schneider and Minoli	SOC, OOC no crankback	No overflow	1	No	No
Kuczura	Fixed	Linear graph	IPP 3	$a = \frac{\bar{a}}{(1-B)}$	Yes
Manfield and Downs	Fixed	Augmented trees	Renewal 3	Balking	Yes
Guérineau and Labetoulle	Ordered Hierarchical	No overflow	2 Overflow 1 Carried	Augmented group size	Yes
Deschamps	SOC	No overflow	2	No	Analytic K
Vo-Dai	SOC	Augmented trees	1	$a = \frac{\bar{a}}{(1-B)}$	Multiple streams

Table 5.1 Summary of Traffic Calculation Methods

and Labetoulle [9], who modeled the downstream blocking effect by reducing the group size to a smaller number of circuits, in the context of hierarchical networks with high blocking on the finals. In another case [10], two distinct traffic streams are present in the network, and a closed queuing model is used for the link-blocking evaluation phase. Analytic formulas for end-to-end blocking have been given by Vestmar [11] for lattice networks; bounding techniques have been proposed by Dotson and Gobien [12] for probabilistic networks. In probabilistic networks, a probability of existence is assigned to each arc, which is analogous to the probability that a link is free in a circuit-switched network.

Instead of going into the details of each method, one may ask which should be used for network evaluation. The answer, of course, depends on what one wants to do with the answer. A relative error of 20% may be quite acceptable for use within a dimensioning algorithm, where other sources of error are of this order of magnitude, while 20% may be much too high if trying to choose between two routing methods that differ by small amounts of carried traffic.

The authors of all the algorithms described here have compared their results with those produced by simulation, and all have declared that their techniques are satisfactory. Given the wide differences in assumptions, this conclusion is surprising. In fact, there have been few systematic studies of the relative merits of these algorithms. Results have been presented for different networks, with different routing methods, and with different objectives in view. Thus it is not surprising that Katz would conclude, "It is evident, therefore, that the average blocking probability $(B_{i,j})$ computed for each trunk group, although correctly estimating the total mean overflow from the total offered load, cannot accurately be applied to each traffic parcel comprising the aggregate load." On the other hand, Schneider and Minoli [1], using a single-moment model and completely neglecting the downstream blocking effect, conclude that their model "provides an estimate of $\overline{L}$ which is reasonably close to the actual value." Compare this with the remark of Manfield and Downs [13] that "a great deal of emphasis is placed on the distinguishing of the separate blocking probabilities for streams of traffic offered to a common link. However, it is felt that this particular problem is not critical to the overall accuracy."

The reason for these discrepancies is probably the particular context in which each model was used. Katz was modeling hierarchical networks, where, as is well known, a large fraction of the traffic offered to final groups has overflowed from high-usage groups and is highly peaked. In this case, a two-moment model is necessary, and it is important to take parcel blocking into account. Schneider and Minoli, however, seem to emphasize the generality of the routings that can be handled by their model. Thus, although no data is presented in their paper to substantiate this guess, the routings were probably nonhierarchical. In such a case, traffic offered to groups is not strongly peaked, and may even be smooth [14,15]. This in turn explains why a single-moment model is sufficiently accurate.

The Butto-Colombo-Tonietti Study.   Butto, Colombo, and Tonietti made a systematic comparison between some of the link-blocking models, for SOC and OOC general control on a seven-node hierarchical network. In the case of SOC, six models were considered, called P_1 to P_6. Model P_1 is a single-moment model with $\beta = 1$. Model P_2 neglects the influence of downstream blocking, computing the variances of carried and overflow traffics by Eq. (5.41). Model P_3 takes into account downstream blocking via Eq (5.40) and with $\beta = 1$, while model P_4 is identical to P_3 but with $\beta = 0$. Model P_5 uses $\beta = 1$ and Eq. (5.42) for the variance of overflow and carried traffics, while model P_6 uses the same equations but with $\beta = 0$. The results are presented in Fig. 5.1, showing the average end-to-end blocking as a function of the uniformly scaled total load; an expanded version is shown in Fig. 5.2.

The case of OOC control was similarly evaluated for four models, called C_1 to C_4. Model C_1 is a single-moment model; the others are two-moment models. Model C_2 uses $\beta = 1$ for both the mean and variance, computing the variance offered to a group by Eq. (5.36). Model C_3 uses $\beta = 0$ and Eq. (5.35), while Model C_4 uses Eq. (5.28) for the mean and Eq. (5.37) for the variance. The

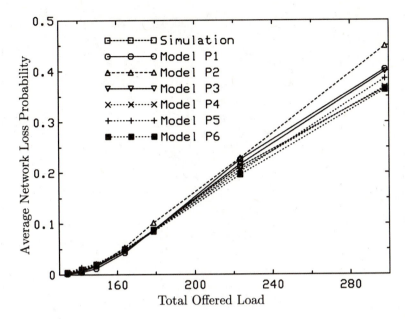

Figure 5.1 Traffic-Model Comparison for SOC

results of the comparison appear in Fig. 5.2. The conclusion is that model C_3 is the most accurate overall for OOC, with an average error of approximately 20% relative to the simulation results. For SOC, models P_5 and P_6 are the best, with relative errors in the same range. Butto, Colombo, and Tonietti give no indication of computation times, and it is not known whether these results hold for other types of routing — in particular, for nonhierarchical routing.

The Pióro Study. Pióro [18] compared some networks for which results had already been published. He considered the average network blocking obtained by three methods: (1) the single-moment method of Lin, Leon, and Stewart, (2) the two-moment method of Butto, Colombo, and Tonietti, and (3) a variant of the latter in which the time congestion of the links is used as the relaxation variables instead of the call congestion. The results are given for the average end-to-end grade of service, as well as for some of the origin-destination pairs. Pióro's results for the average blocking are shown in Table 5.2.

5.2 Cluster Decomposition

Because of its complexity, the network blocking-evaluation problem must be solved by decomposition into smaller, presumably easier subproblems, from

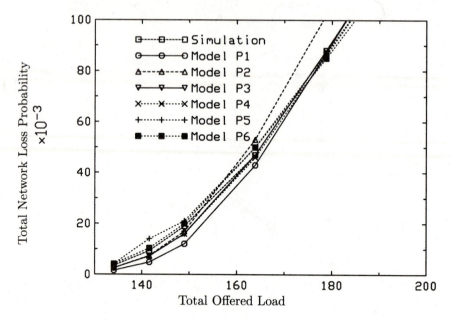

Figure 5.2 Traffic-Model Comparison for SOC: Low Blocking Values

which the global solution can be recovered. Most frequently, the subproblems are independent link-blocking evaluations. The resultant gain in efficiency entails a loss of accuracy, which may or may not be acceptable, depending on the application. These inaccuracies can be related to the simplifying assumptions that are essential to the link decomposition method: independence of the link blocking probabilities, handling of the downstream blocking, and approximate representation of the internal traffic flows. The last two assumptions can be modeled to various degrees of accuracy (see Section 4.3).

If greater accuracy is desired, then the independence assumption must be weakened. This means that the subproblems arising from the decomposition procedure deal with network components more complex that simple links. There are two obvious candidate methods of decomposition. In the first, *decomposition by cluster*, the subproblems are related to the blocking probability of a whole cluster, without assuming the independence of blocking probabilities for links in the same cluster. In this section, the term *cluster* means the set of links originating at a particular node. These links represent the set of exit routes out of a node, and an accurate model for the cluster blocking should provide a better overall value for network blocking. In the other candidate method, *path decomposition*, the network-blocking evaluation is decomposed into a set

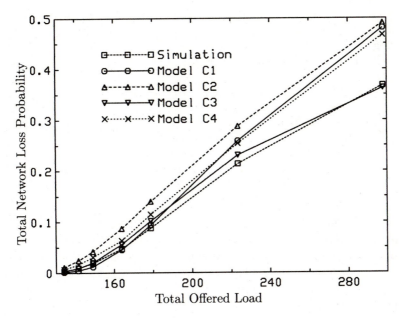

Figure 5.3   Traffic-Model Comparison for OOC

	Simulation	Published	Lin	Butto	Time Congestion
8 Nodes Symmetrical	.034 − .037	.028 [7]	.028	.034	.031
8 Nodes Nonhierarchical	.056 − .063	.045 [13]	.038	.063	.049
8 Nodes Nonhierarchical	.151 − .172	.157 [13]	.147	.170	.170
29 Nodes Hierarchical	.025 − .028	.02 [16]	.005	.028	.015
29 Nodes Hierarchical	.0021 − .0025	.02 [16]	.00002	.0019	.0006
Adelaide Network		.02 [17]	.014	.027	.021

Table 5.2   Comparison by Pióro. The results in the column labeled "Published" are the ones found by the authors.

of independent path-blocking evaluation subproblems, which are then handled without the assumption of blocking independence on a path. Recently, cluster decomposition has been proposed as a means of evaluating the network blocking probability [19,20]. This method is based on a single-moment model for traffic, but without the use of the independence assumption for the cluster-blocking evaluation. Although the original formulation is in terms of a nonstationary blocking model, we give only the stationary version of the algorithm. More information about the time-dependent model appears in [19].

Two Links with Mutual Overflow

First consider two links with N_1 and N_2 circuits, offered A_1 and A_2 erlangs of Poisson traffic. Calls blocked on a link overflow onto the other, where they are lost if blocked a second time. Let B_{12} be the probability that both links are busy when a call arrives. The first assumption of the model is that

$$B_{12} = E(A_1 + A_2, N_1 + N_2). \tag{5.43}$$

This explains the name we have chosen for the method: *cluster decomposition*. Not only do we have traffic and probabilities for the individual links composing the cluster, but we also define traffic and blocking corresponding to *both* links simultaneously, that is, for the cluster considered as a whole. The ensuing nonlinear model determines the value of the parameters for the individual components, as well as the cluster components, subject to the condition that they are coherent. In addition to the overall blocking probability, it is necessary to compute the amount of traffic carried on each link or, equivalently, the link-offered traffics a_1 and a_2. Let B_1 and B_2 be the blocking probabilities on links 1 and 2, respectively. Define

$$B_i \triangleq E(a_i, N_i) \quad i = 1, 2 \tag{5.44}$$

$$\overline{a}_i \triangleq a_i(1 - B_i) \quad i = 1, 2 \tag{5.45}$$

where $\overline{a}_i$ is the traffic carried on link i. The offered traffics are then defined implicitly by the equations

$$\overline{a}_1 = A_1(1 - B_1) + A_2(B_2 - B_{12}) \tag{5.46}$$

$$\overline{a}_2 = A_2(1 - B_2) + A_1(B_1 - B_{12}) \tag{5.47}$$

The first term represents the portion of the first-offered traffic carried on the link; the second, the overflow from the other link that is not lost. This method of computing the overflow traffic carried on a link is central to the method. Whenever there is overflow, a joint blocking probability such as B_{12} is defined, and a corresponding joint traffic is introduced. This extra variable is defined implicitly by an extra equation forming a set of nonlinear equations that globally define the internal traffic streams. The correct values for the link-offered traffic are given as the solution of the nonlinear system (Eqs. 5.44–5.47). As might be expected, the accuracy of the model is much better than that obtained with the model of Lin, Leon, and Stewart (see Table 5.3).

	B_1	B_2	B_{12}	$\bar{a}_1$	$\bar{a}_2$
Markov model	.3325	.2346	.1250	8.488	5.927
Cluster decomposition	.3240	.2081	.1252	8.485	5.948
Link decomposition	.350	.273	.0955	9.04	4.07

Table 5.3 Blocking Values for Two-Link Mutual Overflow. $N_1 = 10$, $N_2 = 8$, $A_1 = 12$, and $A_2 = 4.5$

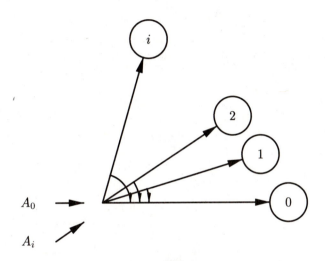

Figure 5.4 Multiple Overflow on a Single Link

The technique just described provides substantially improved accuracy at really no expense in terms of computation time, since a nonlinear system of order two must be solved just as for the link-decomposition technique. To see how the complexity of the model grows, consider the following situation.

Multiple Overflow on a Single Link

There are now K groups of size N_i, each offered Poisson traffic A_i. Calls blocked on each of these trunk groups overflow onto group 0, of size N_0 and offered Poisson traffic A_0. Calls blocked on link 0 are lost (see Fig 5.4). Here again, we are interested in the overall blocking probability for each traffic stream, as well as the amount of each stream carried on the links. We know that

$$B_i = E(A_i, N_i) \quad i = 1 \ldots K$$
$$\bar{a}_i = A_i(1 - B_i) \quad i = 1 \ldots K$$
$$B_0 = E(a_0, N_0) \tag{5.48}$$
$$\bar{a}_0 = a_0(1 - B_0) \tag{5.49}$$

where a_0 is the total traffic offered to link 0 that must be determined. Link 0 receives a number of overflow traffic streams, which we denote by a_{0i} for the stream coming from link i. The individual blocking probabilities of these streams are represented by B_{0i}. The global blocking of stream i, by analogy with Eq. (5.43), is

$$B_{0i} = E(a_{0i}, N_0 + N_i).$$

Note the introduction of one extra fictitious traffic a_{0i} for *each* pair of links having some overflow traffic in common. The $K + 1$ unknown traffics a_0 and a_{0i} are determined implicitly by the following equations:

$$\bar{a}_0 = A_0(1 - B_0) + \sum_{i=1}^{K} A_i(B_i - B_{0i}) \tag{5.50}$$

$$\bar{a}_0 + \bar{a}_i = a_{0i}(1 - B_{0i}) \quad i = 1 \ldots K \tag{5.51}$$

	B_0	B_{02}	B_{01}	$\bar{a}_0$
Markov model	.4283	.1885	.1753	2.121
Cluster decomposition	.3965	.1985	.1920	2.080
Usual single moment	.463	.165	.160	2.22
Usual two moment	.495	.177	.171	2.09

Table 5.4   Results for Overflow onto a Single Group. $K = 2$, $N_0 = 3$, $N_1 = 3$, $N_2 = 4$, $A_0 = 1.5$, $A_1 = 3$, and $A_2 = 4.5$

Table 5.4 compares the results obtained by this model with the results obtained by a link-decomposition method with one- and two-moment models for the traffic offered to link 0. It is evident that the cluster-decomposition method gives somewhat better results: The values of link-blocking probabilities are more accurate, although the carried traffic is slightly less accurate than the value obtained by the two-moment model. Note, however, that the price is high. The link-decomposition technique is not iterative. The overflow traffics are computed directly, and the blocking is evaluated on group 0 to yield the lost traffic. In the cluster method, on the other hand, a set of $K + 1$ nonlinear equations (5.48–5.51) must be solved, which in general takes considerably longer than the link-decomposition method.

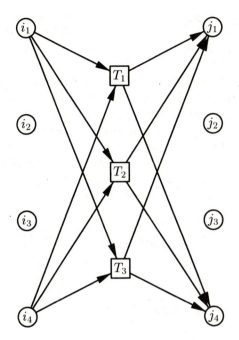

Figure 5.5   Two-Level Network Used for Comparison

Network Analysis by Cluster Decomposition

The cluster method with equivalent traffic gives accurate results when analyzing isolated clusters. It can also be used for network analysis, provided the blocking of carried traffic is properly handled. The simplest way to do this is to assume independence of blocking probabilities for links in tandem. The procedure is described in [19], where an example is provided for a small network. The independence assumption for carried traffic is somewhat inconsistent, however, since it means that the independence assumption is not used for overflow but is assumed to hold for calls carried on a path. There is no reason to believe that this assumption is more justified in one case than the other. A similar technique for avoiding it for links in tandem is desirable, as done in [20].

For now, we give the analysis and results for a small network of the type shown in Fig. 5.5. The original discussion was in terms of load sharing, omitted here for simplicity. There is a set of origin nodes, denoted collectively by the subscript $i = 1 \ldots I$; a set of destination nodes, denoted by $j = 1 \ldots J$; and a set of tandem nodes, denoted by k or $l = 1 \ldots K$. There are no direct links between origin and destination nodes. Calls are offered to a two-link first path and, if blocked, overflow onto a second path; hence there is the possibility of mutual overflow, as well as of having many links overflow onto a given link. No further alternate routing is permitted, and overflow calls that are blocked are lost. Let $A_k^{i,j}$ be the amount of i, j traffic that uses tandem k for its first choice path.

In order to use these techniques, the usual link-blocking probabilities, offered traffic, and carried traffic are defined by B_s, a_s, and $\bar{a}_s$, respectively. In addition, for each possibility of overflow as described by the routing plan, equivalent blocking probabilities and traffics are defined. More specifically, if the routing plan allows link (i, k) to overflow onto link (i, l), then we define $B_{ik,il}$ as the joint probability that both link (i, k) and link (i, l) are blocked. Corresponding to these values, we also define an offered traffic $a_{ik,il}$ and a carried traffic $\bar{a}_{ik,il}$, which are also related by

$$B_s = E(a_s, N_s)$$
$$\bar{a}_s = a_s(1 - B_s)$$
$$B_{ik,il} = E(a_{ik,il}, N_{ik} + N_{il})$$
$$\bar{a}_{ik} + \bar{a}_{il} = a_{ik,il}(1 - B_{ik,il})$$

Finally, the carried traffic must satisfy the equations

$$\bar{a}_{ik} = \sum_j \left[A_k^{i,j}(1 - B_{ik})(1 - B_{kj}) \right.$$

$$\left. + \sum_l A_l^{i,j}(B_{il} - B_{ik,il})(1 - B_{kj}) \right] \quad \forall i = 1 \dots I \quad \forall k = 1 \dots K \quad (5.52)$$

The sum over j is carried over all destinations that use link (i, k) in their first path, and the sum over l over all traffics that use tandem $l \neq k$ as their first choice, and then overflow onto path (i, k, j). An equation similar to Eq. (5.52) can easily be derived for the second leg of path (i, l, j). Note that calls blocked on the second leg of path (i, l, j) do not overflow onto path (i, k, j): The model derived here is thus for progressive overflow control without crankback, that is, SOC control.

We can compare the complexity of the cluster-decomposition method with that of the link decomposition method in terms of the size of the nonlinear system that must be solved in each case. For link decomposition, the system is of order N_a, the number of links in the network. For cluster decomposition, the order of the system depends on the particular routing employed. For each overflow pattern — that is, for each link that overflows onto some other link — we must define a cluster, with its corresponding traffic and blocking probability. Let K be the number of tandem nodes and I the number of origins. In the worst case, the order of the nonlinear system will grow like $O(IK^2)$ — much faster than for link decomposition.

	1	2	3	4
1		.126	.113	.128
		.129	.131	.154
		.121	.126	.145
2	.084		.160	.086
	.117		.190	.109
	.115		.191	.110
3	.181	.048		.118
	.201	.069		.163
	.192	.059		.145
4	.185	.174	.063	
	.232	.213	.077	
	.210	.196	.062	

Table 5.5   Comparison of End-to-End Blocking for Four Stream in a Two-Level Network. Simulation, Cluster-Decomposition and Link-Decomposition Methods.

The question, then, is whether this increase in complexity is worth it. There is no absolute answer since the level of acceptable error depends on the use to be made of the results. Simulation results for the end-to-end blocking probabilities are compared in Table 5.5 with results obtained by the cluster-decomposition method and Lin, Leon, and Stewart's link-decomposition method. The end-to-end probabilities are given for the streams between four nodes, labeled from 1 to 4. In each cell of the array, the simulation results, the values obtained by the cluster-decomposition method, and the values obtained by the link-decomposition method are given.

Clearly, the difference between the two models is much smaller than was the case for the simple system of mutual overflow. This is as expected: The presence of many independent streams on a given link should decrease the correlation of overflow traffics, making the independence assumption more accurate as network size increases.

Finally, note the basic inconsistency in the approach just described. Great care is taken to model accurately the correlation of traffics that overflow onto each other, while the traffics carried on links in tandem are treated as if they were completely independent. There is no a priori reason be believe that correlations are more important in one case than in the other. If a method more accurate than link decomposition is desired, it should logically take into account both types of correlations, at least as long as it has not been demonstrated that one type clearly dominates the other. Such considerations form the subject of the next section, which takes up the matter of path-decomposition methods.

5.3   Path Decomposition

Path-decomposition techniques assume that, without using the independence assumption of link-blocking probabilities on a path, the network-blocking computation can be replaced by a set of path-blocking calculations. The basic entity to which the traffic model applies is a complete path; the end-to-end blocking must be expressed in terms of these path blocking probabilities. We present the method in two parts. First we describe two path-blocking models, relating the path-blocking probability to some traffic parameters. (This will take the place of the usual traffic model based on the Erlang B function that is used in the simple link-decomposition method.) Next we show how to compute the traffic parameters that serve as input to the path-blocking model, taking into account the particular routing method implemented in the network.

Two-Link Path Model

Let us first examine the simple case of a two-link path on which some common traffic uses both links, while each link carries other background traffic. Let E_1 and E_2 be the events that a common call is blocked because links 1 and 2, respectively, are blocked. The blocking probability for the common calls is given by

$$Pr\{E_1 \cup E_2\} = Pr\{E_1\} + Pr\{E_2\} - Pr\{E_1 \cap E_2\}$$
$$= Pr\{E_1\} + Pr\{E_2\} - Pr\{E_1 \mid E_2\}Pr\{E_2\},$$

which is sometimes approximated by

$$= Pr\{E_1\} + Pr\{E_2\} - Pr\{E_1\}Pr\{E_2\}.$$

An accurate calculation of the true probability is therefore based on a calculation of the conditional probability $Pr\{E_1 \mid E_2\}$. This probability can be analyzed if we assume that the three traffics are independent Poisson processes, with parameters λ_{12}, λ_1, and λ_2 for the common, first, and second traffic streams, respectively. In this case, there is a closed-form solution given by

$$Pr\{E_1 \cup E_2\} = \frac{\displaystyle\sum_{k=0}^{N_2} \frac{\lambda_{12}^k}{k!} \sum_{i=0}^{N_1-k} \frac{\lambda_1^i}{i!} \sum_{j=0}^{N_2-k} \frac{\lambda_2^j}{j!}}{\displaystyle\sum_{\substack{i+k \le N_1 \\ j+k \le N_2}} \frac{\lambda_1^i}{i!} \frac{\lambda_2^j}{j!} \frac{\lambda_{12}^k}{k!}}.$$

This formula, although exact, is too complex for use in network calculations; Holtzman [21] suggests the following approximation. First let $N_1 \geq N_2$. Suppose the link-blocking probabilities are known, from some unspecified method. One possibility is to use the approximation

$$B_1 = E\left(\lambda_1 + \lambda_{12}(1 - B_2)\right)$$
$$B_2 = E\left(\lambda_2 + \lambda_{12}(1 - B_1)\right)$$

which can be solved by relaxation to get B_1 and B_2. Given the Bs, we can compute the conditional probability as

$$Pr\{E_1 \mid E_2\} = \frac{\displaystyle\sum_{k=0}^{N_2} \frac{\lambda_{12}^k}{k!} \frac{\lambda_2^{N_2-k}}{(N_2-k)!} \frac{\lambda_1^{N_1-k}}{(N_1-k)!}}{\displaystyle\sum_{k=0}^{N_2} \frac{\lambda_{12}^k}{k!} \frac{\lambda_2^{N_2-k}}{(N_2-k)!} \sum_{i=0}^{N_1-k} \frac{\lambda_1^i}{i!}}$$

$$= \frac{\displaystyle\sum_{i=0}^{N_2} \binom{N_2}{i} p^i q^{N_2-i} \frac{\lambda_1^{N_1-i}}{(N_1-i)!}}{\displaystyle\sum_{i=0}^{N_2} \binom{N_2}{i} p^i q^{N_2-i} \sum_{j=0}^{N_1-i} \frac{\lambda_1^i}{i!}},$$

where

$$p = \frac{\lambda_{12}}{\lambda_{12} + \lambda_2}$$
$$q = 1 - p$$

These formulas can be used as they stand to compute the blocking probability of the common calls on the path. A number of approximations are discussed in [20].

Equivalent-Path Model

We now describe the equivalent-path model (EPM) proposed by Dziong [22], as well as its use in a network-blocking algorithm [23]. This model applies to a more general case than that of Holtzman since it can handle non-Poisson background streams and multilink paths. In order to establish a connection between the origin of the first link and the extremity of the last one of a path made up of a number of links, calls are attempting to seize a circuit on all links of the path. Each link is carrying a different kind of traffic, with a different origin and/or destination. The problem is to compute the probability that one of the calls attempting the path connection will be blocked. The equivalent-path technique consists of replacing the path by an equivalent system such that the blocking of Poisson traffic in this system will approximate the blocking on the path.

Consider a network operating with fixed alternate routing. Let A_l^k denote the traffic offered to the lth alternate path of traffic stream k. The overflow is denoted $\hat{A}_l^k$ and the traffic carried on the path is denoted $\overline{A}_l^k$. Note that, depending on the particular overflow control used, one may or may not have $A_{l+1}^k = \hat{A}_l^k$. Path l is composed of a number of links in tandem, of sizes N_1, N_2, ..., collectively represented by $\mathbf{N}$. Each of these links i is offered a background traffic a_i (vector $\mathbf{a}$), composed of calls *not* of type k. The background traffic is either overflowing from other paths or carried on other paths that have sections in common with path l of stream k. Assume now that k and l are fixed. We can drop these indices, denoting the traffic offered to the path by A and the set of background traffics by $\mathbf{a}$. The problem is then to compute the blocking probability for calls of stream A given $\mathbf{N}$ and $\mathbf{a}$, or, equivalently, to compute the carried and overflow traffics.

Consider now a k-call arriving at the path. This call sees a system with $N_0 = \min_i N_i$ servers, some already occupied by background calls and some occupied by other k-calls. Let X be the number of k-calls present on the path at that time, X_i the number of background calls present on link i, and X_b the number of background calls *visible* to the arriving k-call at that time. A call is visible on a link if $X_i > N_0$; visible traffic represents the number of calls in excess of $N_i - N_0$ carried on the link. We must distinguish between visible and invisible background calls since the links on the path do not have the same capacity. As a consequence, some background calls can be carried on portions of the path on circuits that are not available to the k-call, not entering directly into the blocking calculation. Their effect is felt, however, by the fact that we have

$$X_b = \max_i \left\{ X_i - N_i + N_0 \right\}.$$

The equivalent-path method consists of replacing the path by an equivalent system of N_0 servers, offered two independent streams of traffic, of value A' and A_e. A_e, called the *equivalent traffic*, represents the effect of the background streams. Let the random variables X' and X_e denote, respectively, the number of origin-destination and background calls present in the equivalent system at a given instant. The value of the equivalent traffic is determined by the following conditions:

$$Pr\left\{X = x\right\} = Pr\left\{X' = x'\right\} \quad \text{when } x = x' \tag{5.53}$$

$$Pr\left\{X_b = x_b\right\} = Pr\left\{X_e = x_e\right\} \quad \text{when } x_b = x_e \tag{5.54}$$

Because these conditions tend to be quite difficult to satisfy, an additional simplification is made. Eqs. (5.53) and (5.54) are said to hold under the assumption that blocked calls are nevertheless carried in the system. This amounts to neglecting the finite size of the trunk groups; under this assumption, we have

$$Pr\{X_e = m\} = Pr\left\{\max_i \{X_i - N_i + N_0\} = m\right\}.$$

In this case, the distribution of X_i and X_e, which are really carried traffics, amounts to the distribution of offered traffic, since by definition offered traffic is traffic carried in a system with an infinite number of servers. Thus knowing the distribution of X_e is equivalent to knowing A_e, which is what is required to compute the blocking.

We now calculate the distribution of X_e for the following case. Assume that the background streams do not overlap and that they are adequately represented by Poisson processes. Background streams do not overlap if any portion of the path carries a single background stream. This condition is not restrictive in the case of two-link alternate routing, where it is always verified. The total background traffic offered to link i, represented by a_i, is the sum of the components. Letting l = the number of links in the path, the equivalent distribution is then

$$Pr\{X_e = m\} = \sum_{i=1}^{l}\left[Pr\{X_i = m + N_i - N_0\}\prod_{n=1}^{i-1}Pr\{X_n \leq m + N_n - N_0 - 1\}\right.$$

$$\left.\times \prod_{n=i+1}^{l}Pr\{X_n \leq m + N_n - N_0\}\right] \tag{5.55}$$

For Poisson processes, the distribution is

$$Pr\{X_n = j\} = \frac{a_i^j}{j!}e^{-a_i} \tag{5.56}$$

$$Pr\{X_n \leq j\} = \sum_{i=0}^{j}Pr\{X_n = i\} \tag{5.57}$$

where

$$\prod_{i=j}^{k}(\ldots) = 1 \quad \text{if } j > k.$$

Knowing the distribution of X_e, it is possible to compute all its moments, especially the mean and variance A_e and V_e, and then to use them in computing the blocking of the equivalent system. This evaluation can be carried out in a number of ways, depending on the number of parameters used to represent the traffic. For the single-moment model, this is just the Erlang B function. For the two-moment models, Dziong [23] suggests adding the parameters of the two traffics and then computing the blocking using Hayward's approximation [24] for traffic with peakedness $Z = V/A$:

$$B = E\left(\frac{A + A_e}{Z}, \frac{N_0}{Z}\right). \tag{5.58}$$

The method can be extended to the case where background streams overlap [22], although then it is not possible to obtain a simple closed-form formula like Eqs. (5.53) and (5.54); an approximate method is required. The results are summarized by two functions f and g that give the carried and overflow traffics for an isolated path as a function of the offered traffic A^k, the background traffic vector $\mathbf{a}$ and the link capacity vector $\mathbf{N}$.

$$\overline{A}_m^k = f(A_m^k, \mathbf{a}, \mathbf{N}) \tag{5.59}$$
$$\hat{A}_m^k = g(A_m^k, \mathbf{a}, \mathbf{N}) \tag{5.60}$$

The accuracy of the method has been evaluated by comparisons either with an exact solution whenever one was available, or with simulation results. Katz's method of traffic reduction and Manfield and Downs's technique based on balking were evaluated for the same systems. In all cases tested, the equivalent-path method proved most accurate; the other methods sometimes were in error by more than 50% relative to the blocking probability. These results were obtained for isolated paths. As in the case of cluster decomposition, it remains to be seen whether these large differences still show up in a network context.

Other path-blocking models have been proposed in [20] and [25], the latter mostly in the context of dimensioning.

Network Blocking with Equivalent-Path Model

We now explain how the equivalent-path model can be used to compute the network end-to-end blocking probability. The end-to-end blocking probability for traffic stream k is given by

$$L^k = 1 - \frac{\sum_m \overline{A}_m^k}{A^k}. \tag{5.61}$$

The traffic carried on path m for stream k (represented by (k, m)) is given by $f(A_m^k, a_i)$, and depends on the portion of stream k offered to path m (A_m^k) as well as on all the background traffics on that path (a_i). Since all these quantities depend in turn on the blocking of other paths in the network, the correct value of the blocking must be computed iteratively, just as for the link-decomposition method.

Evaluation of Background Streams.   The background streams on path (k, m) are made up of traffic carried on other paths in the network, say (l, n), which have some part in common with path (k, m). To compute the background traffic, we separate path (k, m) into two parts: (1) those links that are common with (l, n) and (2) those that are separate from it. Denote the first subpath π' and the second π'', and a' and a'' their respective offered traffic (see Fig. 5.6). It is reasonable to assume that the traffic offered to the common part π' is indeed the background offered traffic; we have

$$a_i = a'.$$

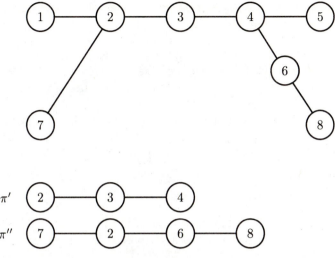

Figure 5.6   Path Structure for Background Stream Evaluation

The problem of computing the background traffic on the common portion is then reduced to computing the offered traffic arising from path (l, n) on the common portion. We can assume that the traffic *carried* on (l, n) is the same as the traffic carried on both the common part π' and the disjoint part π''; we have

$$\bar{a}' = \bar{a}'' = \overline{A}^l_n.$$

Assuming now that we know $\overline{A}^l_n$ (for which we have only the current estimate), we can evaluate the traffic offered to that segment by inverting the equation that links the offered and carried on that portion, that is, solving for a' the equation

$$a' = \overline{A}^l_n = f(a', a'_j), \qquad (5.62)$$

where a'_j are the background traffics on π', which are assumed to be known.

   Evaluation of Path-Offered and Path-Carried Traffics.   In the second part of the calculation, we compute the traffic that is offered to and carried on path (k, m). Given the current estimate of the background streams from Eq. (5.62), the calculation of the carried traffics is straightforward (Eq. 5.59). The overflow traffic depends on the path level in the route trees, the overflow control used, and the presence or absence of crankback. For $m = 1$, this is only A^k. For other levels $m > 1$, and for conditional selection, we get

$$A^k_m = \hat{A}^k_{m-1} \quad m \geq 2, \qquad (5.63)$$

which can be computed using the equivalent-path model for path $m - 1$, again assuming that the path parameters are known.

Solution of the Traffic Equations. Just as in the case of link decomposition, the correct values of the path-offered and background traffics are determined implicitly by a set of nonlinear equations (5.59–5.63) since the traffic streams depend on the background streams, which in turn depend on the path-carried and overflow traffics. These could be solved in a number of ways, but a straightforward relaxation method is adequate. The procedure is as follows. All route trees are scanned in some predetermined order. For a given route tree, the following operations are performed:

1. Assuming that the path-carried traffics are known for this tree, compute the background streams using Eq. (5.62).

2. Keeping the background streams fixed, compute for each path in the tree the carried and overflow traffics, in the order of overflow, using Eq. (5.63).

3. Add the overflow traffic to the appropriate path according to the route plan.

This iteration is performed until the path-offered traffics reach a stationary value. The method can have a number of variants, depending on the particular technique used for updating background streams (after each tree, after each path, or after all the trees are processed). Little has been published on the conditions of convergence of the method, by Dziong or anyone else.

	Low Blocking	High Blocking
Simulation	.0132 − .0176	.086 − 0.099
EPM	.0137	.093
Pióro	.01	.116
Lin, Leon, and Stewart	.0054	.099

Table 5.6 Results for Three-Node Symmetric Network: Average End-to-End Loss Probability

Numerical Results

Only the originator of path decomposition has published results so far — in [22] for the case of isolated paths, and in [23] for the use of this method in networks. In both cases, Dziong compared the results obtained by the equivalent-path method with the results obtained using the methods of [7,26,13, and 18]. Of the four networks considered, the first three operated with nonhierarchical alternate routing. The first two are symmetric networks, of three and five nodes, respectively, under low and high blocking conditions. The comparison is given in Tables 5.6 and 5.7 for the network average loss probability.

	Low Blocking	High Blocking
Simulation	.0025 – .0069	.073 – .108
EPM	.003	.093
Pióro	.0022	.135
Lin, Leon, and Stewart	.0001	.123

Table 5.7 Results for Five-Node Symmetric Network: Average End-to-End Loss Probability

The third network was a five-node asymmetrical network with nodes labeled A–E and one-way trunks, operating under OOC and SOC. The results are shown in Tables 5.8 and 5.9, which show the end-to-end loss probability for some traffic streams, identified by the origin and destination nodes (e.g., A–C).

	A-B	C-B	D-B	E-B
Simulation	.043 – .049	.087 – .101	.068 – .078	.050 – .058
EPM	.041	.098	.105	.054
Pióro	.027	.105	.071	.039
Lin, Leon, and Stewart	.022	.094	.052	.025
Manfield and Downs	.028	.080	.055	.046

Table 5.8 Nonhierarchical Network with OOC: End-to-End Loss Probability Between Pairs of Nodes

The last case was for a hierarchical network with one-way trunks, four class-five offices, and a single tandem office. The results for the network loss probability appear in Table 5.10.

5.4 Summary

We have seen how the results of Chapter 4 can be extended in two directions. First, the elementary link-decomposition method has been generalized to more

	A-B	C-B	D-B	E-B
Simulation	.046 − .052	.081 − .093	.062 − .068	.048 − .056
EPM	.052	.091	.086	.049
Pióro	.042	.101	.064	.038
Lin, Leon, and Stewart	.035	.089	.047	.023
Manfield and Downs	.037	.077	.051	.045

Table 5.9   Nonhierarchical Network with SOC: End-To-End Loss Probability Between Pairs of Nodes

	Low Blocking	High Blocking
Simulation	.009 − .013	.056 − .067
Katz	.0125 − .0127	.065 − .070
EPM	.0113	.063
Pióro	.0121	.064

Table 5.10   Hierarchical Network: Average End-To-End Loss Probability

realistic cases, taking into account the peakedness of the traffic, the parcel blocking, and different path-blocking models. Each of these refinements has been used at one time or another in some practical procedure, but, as we have seen, no systematic comparison has been made of the benefits and costs of each method. Only two studies are currently available on this subject. The different models give similar results for the average network-blocking probability, at least for the network used in these comparisons.

Next two other approaches to the network-analysis problem were presented, where the decomposition is no longer done in terms of link blocking, but rather more complex network elements. These elements are the trunk-group clusters originating out of a node and the individual paths for a given stream. In each case, a simple analysis was given of the blocking probability of the component (cluster or path), with some indication of the relation between the component and network blocking. Although these models have not been used to analyze circuit-switched networks with homogeneous voice traffic, they may turn out to be useful for analyzing networks that carry more complex, heterogeneous traffic.

We now end the discussion on the analysis of networks operating with fixed alternate routing. The following chapter deals with the corresponding problem for networks using various types of adaptive routing methods.

Problems

5.1. Starting with Eq. (5.31), compute the link-offered traffic for two-link alternate routing. Show that the result is identical to the one obtained using the method of Lin, Leon, and Stewart [7].

5.2. Explain the derivation of Eq. (5.55) and, in particular, explain *clearly* why there is a -1 term in the first product and not in the second.

5.3. For the equivalent-path method, compute the path-offered traffic for SOC control. (That is, compute the equivalent of Eq. (5.63) for SOC.)

5.4. We have derived the equivalent-path model under the assumption that blocked calls were carried, which has led to the use of the Poisson formula for the state probabilities for background traffic. It is suggested that this simplification could be partially removed by using the Erlang B formula instead, which takes into account the finite size of the trunk group. Discuss whether this formula gives an exact solution or not — that is, whether its use is an exact representation of the system. Also compare numerically for a two-link path the distribution of busy circuits in the equivalent system obtained from the Poisson distribution to the Erlang distribution for background traffic on the two links.

References

[1] Schneider, K.S., and Minoli, D., "An algorithm for computing average loss probability in a circuit switched communication network," *IEEE Transactions on Communications*, vol. COM–28, pp. 566–575, 1980.

[2] Katz, S., "Trunk engineering of non hierarchical networks," *International Teletraffic Congress*, vol. 6, pp. 142.1–142.8, 1971.

[3] Fischer, M.J., Garbin, D.A., Harris, T.C., and Knepley, J.E., "Large scale communication networks — design and analysis," *The International Journal of Management Science*, vol. 6, pp. 331–340, 1978.

[4] Butto, M., Colombo, G., and Tonietti, A., "On point to point losses in communication networks," *International Teletraffic Congress*, vol. 8, 1976.

[5] Deschamps, P.J., "Analytic approximation of blocking probabilities in circuit switched communication networks," *IEEE Transactions on Communications*, vol. COM–27, pp. 603–606, 1979.

[6] Manfield, D.R., and Downs, R., "A moment method for the analysis of telephone traffic networks by decomposition," *International Teletraffic Congress*, vol. 9, 1979.

[7] Lin, P.M., Leon, B.J., and Stewart, C.R., "Analysis of circuit switched networks employing originating office control with spill," *IEEE Transactions on Communications*, vol. COM–26, pp. 754–765, 1978.

[8] Manfield, D., and Downs, T., "On the one-moment analysis of telephone traffic networks," *IEEE Transactions on Communications*, vol. COM–27, pp. 1169–1174, 1979.

[9] Guérineau, J.P., and Labetoulle, J., "End to end blocking in telephone networks: a new algorithm," *International Teletraffic Congress*, vol. 11, pp. 2.4.A.1:1–1.4.A.1:7, 1985.

[10] Vo-Dai, T., "Some contributions to the theory of traffic engineering in circuit switched communication networks," *International Conference on Communications*, pp. 67.3.1–67.3.5, 1981.

[11] Vestmar, B.J.A., "Probability of blocking in honhierarchical networks," *International Teletraffic Congress*, vol. 8, pp. 332.1–332.8, 1976.

[12] Dotson, W.P., and Gobien, J.O., "A new analysis technique for probabilistic communication networks," *National Telecommunication Conference*, pp. 48.5.1–48.5.10, 1977.

[13] Manfield, D.R., and Downs, T., "Decomposition of traffic in loss systems with renewal input," *IEEE Transactions on Communications*, vol. COM–25, pp. 44–58, 1977.

[14] Cameron, H., Galloy, P., and Graham, W.J., "Report on the Toronto advanced routing concept trial," *Network Planning Symposium*, vol. 1, pp. 228–236, 1980.

[15] Girard, A., and Bell, M.A., "Blocking evaluation for networks with residual capacity adaptive routing," Report No. 86–12, INRS-Télécommunications, 1986.

[16] Berry, L.T.M., and Harris, R.J., "A simulation study of the accuracy of a telephone network dimensioning model," *Australian Telecommunication Research*, vol. 9, pp. 50–59, 1975.

[17] Berry, L.T.M., *A mathematical model for optimizing telephone networks*, Ph.D. Thesis, University of Adelaide, 1971.

[18] Pióro, M.P., "A uniform approach to the analysis and optimization of circuit switched communication networks," *International Teletraffic Congress*, vol. 10, pp. 4.3A:1–4.3A:7 1983.

[19] Legall, F., and Bernussou, J., "An analytical formulation for grade of service determination in telephone networks," *IEEE Transactions on Communications*, vol. 31, pp. 420–424, 1983.

[20] Legall, F., Bernussou, J., and Garcia, J.M., "A state dependent one-moment model for grade of service and traffic evaluation in circuit switched networks," *International Teletraffic Congress*, vol. 11, pp. 5.2.b. 2:1–5.2.b.2:6, 1985.

[21] Holtzman, J.M., "Analysis of dependence effects in telephone trunking networks," *Bell System Technical Journal*, vol. 50, pp. 2647–2662 1971.

[22] Dziong, Z., "A method for calculation of traffic carried on network paths," *International Teletraffic Congress*, vol. 10, pp. 4.3b.1–4.3b.7, 1983.

[23] Dziong, Z., "Equivalent path approach for circuit switched networks analysis," *International Teletraffic Congress*, vol. 11, pp. 4.2.b.5.1–4.2.b. 5.7, 1985.

[24] Fredericks, A.A., "Congestion in blocking systems: a simple approximation technique," *Bell System Technical Journal*, vol. 59, pp. 805–827 1980.

[25] Berry, L.T.M., "An application of mathematical programming to alternate routing," *Australian Telecommunication Research*, vol. 4, pp. 20–27, 1970.

[26] Katz, S., "Statistical performance analysis of a switched communication network," *International Teletraffic Congress*, vol. 5, 1967.

CHAPTER 6

Performance Evaluation of Adaptive Routing

Adaptive routing has three characteristics that differ from alternate routing: (1) the set of available paths is not ordered, (2) paths are selected on the basis of some form of "cost," and (3) a form of measurement of the network state is used to construct these costs. For example, in residual-capacity adaptive routing, the cost is based on the residual capacity of the network paths, which in turn are computed from the link residual capacities. The state measurement is the periodic evaluation of the traffic offered and carried on each network link, and paths are selected based on the estimated maximum cost, suitably randomized to avoid instabilities.

Even under stationary inputs, the traffic pattern produced by adaptive routing is quite different from the corresponding pattern produced by fixed alternate routing. As a consequence, we can expect the stationary end-to-end loss probabilities also to be different. The question, then, is how to compute these probabilities, at least in a stationary regime. In this chapter we consider the few instances for which such computation methods have been proposed.

Let us emphasize that these methods are purely static, in the sense that they take into account only the first two characteristics of the adaptive routing methods. They do not take into account the truly adaptive aspect of these routing techniques: the change in the algorithm's parameter values as a function either of time or of the time-varying components of the input parameters, such as traffic. To take these aspects into account, we would need a specific time-dependent model of the network behavior. No such model has been developed.

We know that adaptive routing relies on measurements of network parameters as inputs to the path-selection algorithm. Because of technical constraints, these measurements are necessarily out of date by the time they are used. Simulation results tell us that this update interval has a critical influence on the network performance, and should be chosen as small as possible. Because of the static nature of the evaluation algorithms, the update delay is never taken into account by the computation algorithms, which always operate on the assumption that there is no delay and hence that the state information is exact

236

at the time a decision is taken. As we have also seen, one of the main advantages of the adaptive methods is their ability to track slowly varying changes in network parameters, especially traffic demands. This dynamic aspect of the routing methods also cannot be taken into account, unless we can assume that the changes occur at such a slow rate that the network can be viewed as in an essentially stationary mode at all times. To summarize, then, in this chapter we assume that the network is characterized by a single set of parameters: one traffic matrix, one set of trunk group sizes, and a single set of costs, for instance, the tandem-selection probabilities for the residual-capacity algorithm.

Currently, there are published evaluation algorithms for only two adaptive methods seriously considered for use in networks. The first method is residual-capacity adaptive routing as implemented in the dynamic call routing (DCR) method of Bell-Northern Research (BNR). We start with a description of two evaluation algorithms for this routing. The first algorithm relies heavily on the fact that the network is in a stationary regime, assuming that the selection probabilities can be viewed as constant. Hence, if these probabilities can be computed, the problem more or less reduces to fixed alternate routing, which can be solved by a straightforward adaptation of the link-decomposition method described in Chapter 4. The second evaluation method is a form of cluster decomposition (somewhat different from the one of Section 6.2).

The other adaptive method, known as state-dependent routing, is based on a Markov decision process formulation of the routing problem. In this chapter, we describe the method only briefly, postponing the full derivation of the algorithm to Chapter 7 because of its intimate relation to routing optimization. We then review a stationary evaluation algorithm, recently proposed, that uses some of the same techniques suggested for the residual-capacity case.

6.1   Link-Decomposition Method for Residual-Capacity Routing

First we describe a simple method for evaluating the loss probability of a network operating under the RCAR routing considered in chapter 2 [1]. The parameters defined in Section 2.6 are time-varying quantities that depend on either the instantaneous network state or on some future estimate of that state. A basic assumption underlying the following derivations is that, given stationary inputs, these quantities have well-defined average values. The link-decomposition method follows from the assumption that the long-term behavior of the adaptive algorithm can be accurately represented by a nonadaptive routing with suitably chosen parameters. This routing is defined by separating each traffic stream a^k into $n - 2$ streams, where each stream has a single overflow path through a particular tandem (see Fig. 6.1 for a graphical representation).

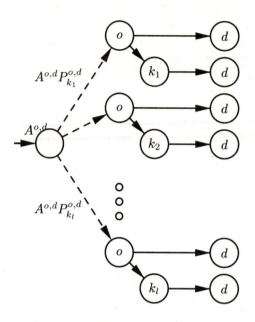

Figure 6.1   Traffic Separation for Adaptive Routing

The parameters are the separation coefficients, which play the role of load-sharing coefficients. Their value is computed from approximating the average values of the tandem selection probabilities in such a way that the operation of the static routing is the stationary image of the adaptive routing. Because the static routing is composed of two parts, load sharing and alternate routing, we call it *load-sharing alternate routing* (LSAR). The advantage of the LSAR approach is that it allows overall network performance to be analyzed using known techniques for fixed nonhierarchical routing. If the LSAR routing approximates the stationary behavior of the adaptive algorithm well enough, we have a fast evaluation algorithm in a stationary mode for the adaptive version.

Let us now describe the performance-evaluation algorithm for the LSAR method, a classical two-phase method. In the sequel, we assume that the update interval $\Delta = 0$, and that either fixed or adaptive state protection is used. We also use the variables defined for the link-decomposition technique of Lin, Leon, and Stewart [2] (see Section 4.2).

Link Loading

Assuming independence for both path blocking and selection probabilities, the end-to-end blocking for commodity m is given by

$$L^m = B_{i,j} \sum_k \alpha_k^m \mathcal{P}_k^m, \qquad (6.1)$$

where $o(m) = i$ and $d(m) = j$ in the following, α_k^m is the probability of selecting the kth path for a call of type m, and $\mathcal{P}_k^m$ is the probability that this path will be blocked. The terms of (6.1) depend on the external traffic and the trunk group sizes in a complex way, described next.

Tandem-Selection Probabilities.   The assumption of zero update time means that the exact values for the trunk group occupancy are known whenever a call must be routed. Thus there is no need for extrapolation, and the link residual capacity is calculated by Eqs. (2.12) and (2.13) with $\tau = 0$. The max operation is now superfluous, and, taking averages, we get for the link's residual capacity

$$R_s = N_s - \bar{a}_s. \qquad (6.2)$$

The path residual capacity, given by the numerator of Eq. (2.12), involves a min operator. Computing the expectation of the minimum of two random variables is somewhat complex; considering the objective of speed that we have set at the beginning, we commute the min and expectation operations, writing for the expected residual capacity of the path

$$\overline{R}_k^m = \min\{R_{i,k}, R_{k,j}\}. \qquad (6.3)$$

Thus, by a similar argument, the tandem-selection probability is

$$R_k^m = \frac{\overline{R}_k^m}{\sum_k \overline{R}_k^m}. \qquad (6.4)$$

Adaptive State Protection Level.   The residual-capacity adaptive routing method was originally designed with a fixed level of state protection. Because we have no way to estimate the amount of protection required in a particular network, this parameter has been made adaptive. The link-decomposition method can operate in both modes, provided we can estimate the average state protection level for link s. Taking the expectation of Eq. (2.14), we have

$$\bar{r}_s = \frac{\Delta}{\mu} \min\{N_s, A^m B_s\}$$

after permuting the expectation operation inside the other operators, where $1/\mu$ is the average holding time for a call. In what follows, we have chosen $\Delta/\mu = 1$, which normally overestimates the amount of protection in the network — in practice, the time intervals over which the blocked calls are counted are much smaller than an average holding time. In fact, for the networks currently in use, the average reservation is so small that the choice of this particular factor is not significant, not having much effect on the numerical results presented later.

Traffic Calculation.   A procedure similar to that of Lin, Leon, and Stewart (see Section 4.2) can be carried out for the various traffic flows in the network. Using the same definitions, we get, for the traffic carried on the path through tandem k,

$$\overline{A}_k^{i,j} = A^{i,j} B_{i,j} \alpha_k^{i,j} (1 - \mathcal{P}_k^{i,j}). \tag{6.5}$$

The overflow traffic carried on each link is

$$\overline{a}_{i,k} = \sum_j \overline{A}_k^{i,j} + \overline{A}_i^{j,k} \tag{6.6}$$

$$\overline{a}_{k,j} = \sum_i \overline{A}_k^{i,j} + \overline{A}_j^{k,i} \tag{6.7}$$

The overflow traffic offered to the links are expressed in terms of the carried traffic by

$$\hat{a}_{i,k} = \frac{\overline{a}_{i,k}}{(1 - B'_{i,k})} \tag{6.8}$$

$$\hat{a}_{k,j} = \frac{\overline{a}_{k,j}}{(1 - B'_{k,j})} \tag{6.9}$$

Path Blocking.   Equations (6.1–6.9) are independent of the particular model used for path blocking. We now make the assumption that

$$\mathcal{P}_k^{i,j} = 1 - (1 - B'_{i,k})(1 - B'_{k,j}), \tag{6.10}$$

where the B's must be used because overflow calls will attempt to use the path. This is equivalent to saying that the two-link system that makes up the path can be analyzed as two independent single-link systems, each with its own link-blocking probability. This assumption is obviously false, but has the advantage of making the path-blocking calculation as simple as possible.

Link Blocking

We have expressed the elements of Eq. (6.1) in terms of the link-blocking probabilities B_s and B'_s, using the link-offered traffics as intermediate variables Eqs. (4.45) and (4.46). Unfortunately, these probabilities are unknown, and depend on the link traffics via the link-blocking model. Since we are using the Poisson model for all traffic streams, this model is given by Eqs. (4.45) and (4.46). Note that, because these equations relate *all* link-offered traffics to *all* blocking probabilities, they therefore constitute a *system* of nonlinear equations that must be solved in order to know the end-to end blocking (6.1). As discussed in Section 4.2, these calculations are generally done by a relaxation procedure, here on the variables B_s and B'_s.

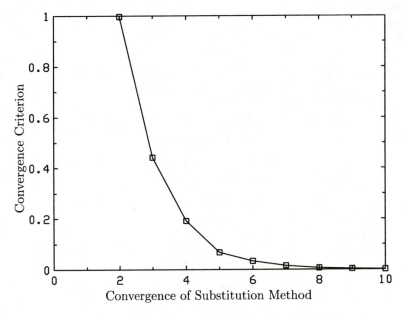

Figure 6.2   Convergence of Relaxation Method

Numerical Results

The performance of this model has been reported in [1]; a summary of the results is presented here. First we examine the computation speed of the evaluation algorithm, in terms of both CPU time and the convergence rate of the method. Then we look at the accuracy of the approximation, first with respect to the LSAR routing, and then as an approximation of the RCAR routing.

Convergence

The link-decomposition method, of the same type as for the fixed alternate routing case, is subject to the same theoretical difficulties. There still exists the possibility that there are multiple solutions to the system of equations, although this is unlikely because of the presence of state protection, as well as the small amount of alternate routing allowed for each traffic stream. Also, since the solution is computed by relaxation, there is no theoretical proof of convergence. In practice, for the cases tested, the algorithm always seems to converge to a unique value. As an example of the speed of the process by relaxation, the convergence rate for a 10-node asymmetric network is shown in Fig. 6.2.

Computation Times of the Relaxation Algorithms for the LSAR Model

The main reason for proposing the link-decomposition method for adaptive routing is that we expect the computation times to be small compared with other methods. Table 6.1 displays some values of the computation times reported for this algorithm as a function of ϵ, the stopping tolerance. The significance of these results will become clear in Section 6.2, when we compare them with the other evaluation technique based on the cluster model.

	$\epsilon = 10^{-5}$		$\epsilon = 10^{-4}$		$\epsilon = 10^{-3}$		$\epsilon = 10^{-2}$	
	CPU (sec)	Number of iterations	CPU (sec)	Number of iterations	CPU (sec)	Number of iterations	CPU (sec)	Number of iterations
400	2.24	19	2.08	17	1.75	14	1.40	11
425	2.19	17	1.97	15	1.65	12	1.25	9
450	2.37	17	1.96	14	1.72	12	1.28	9
475	1.63	11	1.44	10	1.15	8	1.05	7
500	1.92	14	1.70	12	1.40	10	1.17	8
38	997.2	64	828.0	54	704.3	44	510.5	33

Table 6.1   Computation Times of the Relaxation Algorithm for the LSAR Method

Accuracy

The accuracy of the algorithm can be understood in two ways. First, we can ask whether the evaluation algorithm gives an accurate value for the loss probability of a network operating with LSAR. Then we can ask whether the performance of the LSAR algorithm is a good approximation of the stationary performance of the adaptive routing.

The accuracy of the algorithm can be compared only with results from the real system — in the present case, a computer simulation of the network operating with the proposed algorithm. We reproduce the results of [1] in the case of the nine-node network that was used for the field trial of the DCR algorithm, described in [3]. There are five variations of the network, labeled "400" to "500." The difference is that the 400 network is taken from [4], while the 500 network is redimensioned with the heuristic described in [5]. The three other networks are intermediate cases, computed by linear interpolation of the trunk group sizes between the 400 and the 500 networks. Finally, network 38

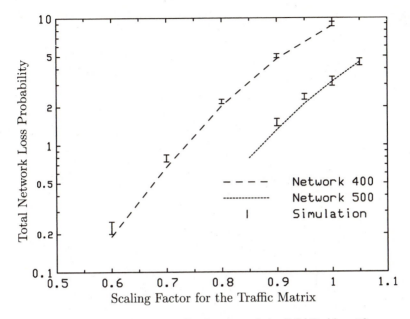

Figure 6.3   Performance Evaluation of the LSAR Algorithm

is a 38-node network representing the long distance telephone network of the Trans-Canada telephone system.

Figure 6.3 compares the accuracy of the algorithm with the actual performance of the 400 and 500 networks operating with the LSAR method. As is clear from the figure, this method gives an accurate evaluation of the average network-blocking probability over a wide range of blocking values.

The second aspect of accuracy concerns the representation of the stationary behavior of the adaptive method by the LSAR algorithm. In Table 6.2, the total computed end-to-end blocking is compared with simulation results for six networks operating with the adaptive residual capacity algorithm. Although the calculated values may be acceptable for high blocking, the relative accuracy degrades at lower values, and may be unacceptable in some circumstances. Note that the absolute error seems to remain constant, independent of the network, at 2%.

The reason for the discrepancy is found in Table 6.3, which gives, for the six cases, the amount of direct and overflow traffics carried in the network. The amount of overflow traffic is systematically underestimated by the algorithm. This underestimation allows slightly more traffic to be carried on the direct link, but not enough to compensate for the error in carried overflow.

Network	Simulation	Calculation
400	.068	.085
425	.047	.068
450	.014	.038
475	.007	.03
500	.005	.027
38-node	.0056	.031

Table 6.2 Calculation of End-to-End Blocking of Adaptive-Routing Networks by the LSAR Method: Simulation versus Computation

Network	Simulation	Calculation
400	184/32	199/13
425	188/33	203/13
450	199/29	210/13
475	203/27	212/13
500	207/24	214/12
38	10236/1302	10500/733

Table 6.3 Direct/Overflow Carried Traffic in the LSAR Method: Simulation versus Computation

The link-decomposition model has many simplifications that could explain this lack of accuracy. Most obvious are the use of Poisson model for traffic flows, the assumption of independent link-blocking probabilities, and the various simplifications in computing the expected values of residual capacities and tandem-selection probabilities. The influence of these various approximations was investigated in [1], where it was found that relaxing these simplifying assumptions either has very little influence on the accuracy or causes large and unpredictable changes. Thus the difference in performance between the LSAR method and truly adaptive routing lies in the adaptation of the latter. Hence it is postulated that an evaluation algorithm based on a stationary model will perform much better than the LSAR method, irrespective of the traffic model or other simplifying assumptions, as long as the underlying system is nonadaptive. Only further experiments, however, will tell whether it is possible to approximate adaptive routing by a nonadaptive method of the link-decomposition type.

6.2 Cluster Decomposition

Another method, proposed by Régnier, Blondeau, and Cameron [3], is roughly similar to the cluster-decomposition method of Section 5.2. The similarity lies in the fact that blocking probabilities are computed for the cluster as a whole, then partitioned among parcels according to the tandem-selection probabilities. The main difference, discussed in [3], is that a complete cluster model calculates the conditions under which a call will be blocked more accurately. The blocking is decomposed into individual stream blocking only after the overall blocking probability is evaluated for the cluster, therefore avoiding the inaccuracies introduced by the LSAR method, where the partitioning is done *before* the blocking is computed.

Recall from Chapter 2 that the nodes that do not participate in the adaptive scheme are called *X-nodes*; the other nodes are called *I-nodes* if they do not carry tandem traffic, or *T-nodes* if they do. Calls originating at X-nodes can overflow only onto T-nodes — the reason we speak of a lower-level network, composed of X-nodes only, and a higher-level network, made up of I- and T-nodes, where the adaptive algorithm is used. Simplifications of the DCR algorithms are required here also, such as the following:

1. No state protection is considered.

2. The effect of the delay in updating residual capacities is neglected.

3. Traffic originating at X-nodes and carried to the high-level network are treated as external calls at the T-node where they arrive.

Because of the different routing for calls originating from X-nodes as compared with calls originating from I- or T-nodes, it would be desirable to decouple the calculation into a separate part for each type of call. This is not entirely possible, however, since the X-calls carried in the high-level network modify the link-blocking probabilities of this network, which in turn change the tandem-selection probabilities for X-calls. Thus an iterative procedure is required, of the following form:

1. Assuming that the end-to-end blocking probabilities of the high-level network are known, compute the end-to-end blocking for X-calls. At the same time, compute the fraction of X-calls offered to the high-level network.

2. Given the offered traffic to the high-level network, either first-offered or originating from the lower-level network, compute the end-to-end blocking probabilities in the high-level network.

Corresponding to these two phases are two algorithms, the first for traffic originating at X-nodes (X-traffic or X-calls), the second for calls originating at I-nodes or T-nodes (I-calls).

Blocking for Calls Originating at an X-Node

The first part of the algorithm computes the end-to-end blocking probability for calls originating at an X-node. The calculation is simplified because the tandem-selection probabilities for these nodes are based exclusively on the residual capacity of adjacent links. This is distinct from nodes in the upper-level network, where these probabilities are computed from the residual capacities of all the links in that level. The end-to-end blocking is composed of two parts, depending at which point the call may be blocked in the network. The first part deals with the probability of reaching a tandem node. Calls that arrive at the high-level network still may be blocked in this network; this is the second part of the total blocking. Assuming that these two components are independent, we have

$$L^{o,d} = \frac{\hat{M}^{o,d}}{A^{o,d}} \left[1 - (1 - B_1)(1 - B_2) \right], \qquad (6.11)$$

where

$B_1 =$ The probability that an o, d call blocked on the direct link will not be able to reach *any* of the tandems. $1 - B_1$ is thus the probability that a specific o, d call will reach any of the tandems.

$B_2 =$ The probability that an o, d call that has reached *any* tandem will be blocked in the high-level network.

$\hat{M}^{o,d} =$ The amount of $A^{o,d}$ traffic that has been blocked on the (o, d) link and must take an alternate path through the high-level network.

When we can assume that the blocking is low in the high-level network ($B_2 \approx 0$), Eq. (6.11) reduces to

$$L^{o,d} = \frac{\hat{M}^{o,d}}{A^{o,d}} B_1,$$

and the end-to-end blocking of the X-calls can be computed directly without iterations. If, however, the blocking in the high-level network cannot be neglected, then the value of B_2 must be calculated. This can be written

$$B_2 = \sum_j \alpha_j^{o,d} B_{T_j,d} \qquad (6.12)$$

and depends both on the tandem-selection probabilities $\alpha_j^{o,d}$ and the blocking probabilities for calls originating at tandem T_j. Because these latter quantities depend on the link blocking in the high-level network, iterations between the two levels are required to evaluate the $L^{o,d}$, even for the X-nodes.

The general algorithm for X-nodes is divided into three parts:

1. For each direct o, d link, compute the parameters of the overflow traffic.

2. For each traffic stream o, d out of node o, compute the probability of reaching *any* tandem. This is actually done in two parts.

   a. Compute the probability of reaching any tandem node for the aggregate stream composed of all the o, d streams, that is, the cluster-blocking probability.

   b. Compute the parcel blocking probabilities in the cluster of node o. This uses the global probabilities computed in step a, with a partition rule for the individual parcels.

3. Compute the tandem-selection probabilities and the traffic parcels carried on the various links to the tandems.

Let us examine how each of these three steps is actually carried out.

Parameters of the Overflow Traffic from Direct Groups.   Here, we have first-offered Poisson traffic to a group of $N_{o,d}$ trunks. We must compute the first moments of the overflow distribution, which can be obtained from the Kosten equations (3.91) and (3.92), after dropping the superscripts for clarity:

$$\hat{M} = AE(A, N_s)$$
$$\hat{V} = \hat{M}\left[1 + \frac{A}{N + 1 - A + \hat{M}} - \hat{M}\right] \tag{6.13}$$

Loss Probability in the Cluster.   The calls blocked on the direct link overflow onto the high-level network via one of the tandem nodes. This traffic then shows up in the high-level network, where it contributes to the offered load that must be carried in that level. For this reason, we must know how much of the low-level overflow traffic gets through to any one of the tandem nodes, as well as where this traffic enters the high-level network. These calculations lead to two additional, interrelated problems: (1) the calculation of the cluster blocking and (2) the calculation of the individual stream-carried traffic.

First a blocking probability is computed for the cluster as a whole, yielding the aggregate loss probability for all calls out of the node. Then individual parcel blocking probabilities are computed using the aggregate loss probability and some heuristic rules for the proportions of the carried traffic.

Cluster Blocking.   In the first step of the calculation, we combine all the trunk groups out of node o into a single system of servers, called a *cluster*, for which we compute the blocking probability. The probability of reaching any tandem node for the aggregate traffic stream composed of all blocked calls out of node o is called the *cluster blocking*. We assume that X calls blocked on the direct link are offered to a facility made up of a number of trunks N_b, which is simply the sum of all the trunks from o to all tandems:

$$N_b = \sum_j N_{o,T_j}.$$

The implicit assumption of this model — and its fundamental difference from the link-decomposition method — is that a call that overflows from the direct link has access to *all* the groups in the cluster, and that it is blocked only if all the groups are blocked. Assuming no update delay, a call is lost only if all the cluster groups are blocked, as is the case in the actual operation of the algorithm. The link-decomposition method based on LSAR routing does not behave this way: There was already a load-sharing stage before a call reached the cluster, and the call may be blocked even though some other group may be free.

Let us now compute $Q(N_b)$, the time congestion when a non-Poisson traffic of known mean and variance is offered to a system of N_b trunks. A number of techniques exist for computing this blocking. It is usually approximated using moment-matching techniques, the more important of which are the standard equivalent random theory (ERT), the Bernouilli-Pascal-Poisson distribution (BPP), and the interrupted Poisson process technique (IPP), all described in Chapter 3. The result of this calculation gives the cluster blocking, which is the probability that a call blocked on the direct link will not reach any tandem node. From this, we compute the parcel probabilities and the tandem-selection probabilities.

Parcel Blocking.   The blocking of each parcel, and consequently the amount of traffic carried to each tandem node, can be computed by a number of techniques, all of which rely on the partition of the blocking for the aggregate stream into individual blocking probabilities for each parcel. Numerous partitioning formulas have been proposed in the literature [3,6,7,8,9], (see Chapter 3). A comparison of their accuracy for adaptive routing can be found in [3]. The main result is that the partition formulas roughly divide into two classes, good and bad. Using the better ones, most of the errors (as compared with simulation) are below 30%; the methods of Olssen [8], BPP3 [10], and Manfield and Downs [9] fall into this category. For the poorer approximations — the proportional, BPP2 [10], Kuczura [6], and Katz [11] methods — a significant proportion of error is above this value, sometimes as high as 100%.

Tandem-Selection Probabilities.   Calls blocked on the o, d direct link are offered to the group leading to tandem j according to some probability $\alpha_j^{o,d}$. So far, we have considered the set of all trunks originating at node o as a single facility, computing blocking probabilities without taking into account the actual repartition of overflow traffic between tandem trunks. This effect must now be estimated. There are two reasons:

1. The tandem-selection probabilities are required for the computation of the end-to-end blocking of o, d calls when $B_2 \not\equiv 0$.

2. Overflow calls from the lower-level network that are not blocked in the cluster are treated as external calls arriving at the tandem node. Because they appear at distinct nodes, the overflow o, d calls carried to *each individual tandem* are required when computing the blocking in the high-level network.

Thus the third part of the calculation for X-nodes is the evaluation of tandem-selection probabilities $\alpha_j^{o,d}$. An iterative procedure is again required: These selection probabilities depend on the residual capacities on the links, which in turn depend on the traffic effectively offered to the links. Since this traffic in turn depend on the tandem-selection probabilities, the following type of iterative procedure is needed. To simplify notation we omit the superscript o, d.

0. Initialize the selection probabilities α_j to some value.

1. Knowing the parameters of the overflow from each direct link, compute the parameters of the aggregate traffic offered to each tandem link i:

$$\hat{M}_i = \hat{M}\alpha_i$$
$$\hat{V}_i = \hat{M}_i \left[1 + \alpha_i \left(\frac{\hat{M}}{\hat{V}} - 1 \right) \right]$$

This composition of the traffics is valid under the assumption that a particular tandem is selected independently of the others.

2. Compute the *average* number of free trunks on each tandem link R_{o,T_i}.

3. Compute new estimates of the selection probabilities

$$\alpha_i^{o,d} = \frac{R_{o,T_i}}{\sum_l R_{o,T_l}}. \tag{6.14}$$

4. Iterate from step 1 until the selection probabilities stabilize to some value.

End-to-End Blocking for X-calls. We now have an estimate of the link blocking on the low-level network and of the overflow traffic offered to each

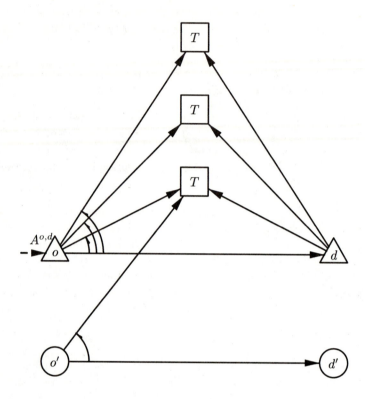

Figure 6.4 Traffic for Upper-Level Nodes

of the tandem nodes. Given the end-to-end blocking probabilities in the high-level network, we can compute the end-to-end blocking for calls originating from the X-nodes by Eq. (6.11). It now remains to compute the blocking and traffic patterns for the high-level network.

Blocking for Calls Originating at an I-Node

The blocking for trunk groups originating at nodes that operate with the adaptive algorithm is calculated by the same method as for the nonadaptive nodes. After the cluster-blocking probability is computed, the individual stream-blocking probabilities are computed by one of the standard formulas already described for parcel blocking. For two reasons, however, the calculation of blocking in the SPC network is more complex than for the X-nodes (see Fig. 6.4):

1. Traffic offered to an arbitrary T-T group is of three kinds:

   a. First-offered Poisson traffic $A^{o,d}$,

   b. Overflow traffic from the X-X groups $\hat{M}_{o',d'}$, and

   c. Overflow traffic from I-I groups.

2. The tandem selection probabilities and the end-to-end blocking probabilities depend on the *complete* two-link path — specifically, on the blocking of the T_j, d groups.

The second item constitutes the main difference from the non-SPC network, where selection probabilities were computed from the blocking on the first link only. The three traffic streams just described are reduced to two types by assuming that the overflow from the X-nodes is Poisson and is therefore handled as if it were made up of external calls. Although incorrect, this assumption is only a second-order effect and does not affect the accuracy of the computation significantly. Traffic offered to any group in the higher-level network is thus a mixture of first-offered Poisson traffic and non-Poisson overflow from other high-level groups.

We have already seen how to calculate the blocking for nodes in the low-level network, where the cluster blocking was calculated from the residual capacities of the links adjacent to the node. The method proposed here attempts to use the techniques already developed for the low-level nodes, even though the tandem selection is based not only on the residual capacity of the links adjacent to the node, but on the residual capacity of the complete paths linking the node to the destination. The two-link alternate path is replaced by a single equivalent system, allowing us to use the same methods. After this system is calculated, evaluating the blocking of overflow traffic is similar to the case of the low-level network. For this reason, we begin with a discussion of path-equivalent systems.

Equivalent System for a Single Overflow Path. First we consider the replacement of a single alternate path by an equivalent trunk group. Consider the simple network of Fig. 6.5, which we wish to replace by a simpler system of $N_e = \min(N_s, N_t)$ trunks offered some equivalent traffic A_e to be determined. The following condition defines this traffic: Its distribution should be such that the distribution of free circuits in the equivalent system approximates the distribution of free circuits in the alternate path, *neglecting the presence of the overflow traffic.*

The calculation proceeds in two parts. Assume that the busy-circuit distributions $Q_j(x)$ are known for the individual links making the alternate path. First compute the distribution of free circuits in the path. Then find the equivalent traffic having a busy-circuit distribution identical to that in the

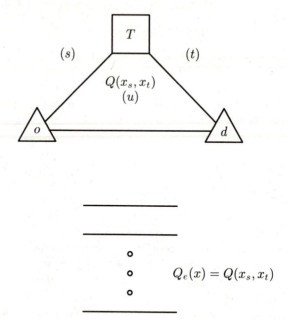

Figure 6.5   Analysis of Single-Path Overflow System by the Equivalent-Path Method

path. To simplify the notation, label the links (o, d), (o, T), and (T, d) as u, s, and t, respectively. Also define the following:

$P(f)$ = Probability of having f free paths on (s, t). Here a free path is composed of two free circuits, one on each link.

$Q_j(x)$ = Probability of having x busy circuits on link $j = s, t$ *neglecting the presence of the overflow traffic from* u.

$Q_e(x)$ = Probability of having x circuits simultaneously busy in the equivalent system.

Neglecting the presence of overflow traffic implies that the state distributions on s and t are independent. We then get

$$P(f) = Q_s(N_s - f) \sum_{l=0}^{N_t - f} Q_t(l) + Q_t(N_t - f) \sum_{l=0}^{N_s - f - 1} Q_s(l) \qquad (6.15)$$

and

$$Q_e(x) = Q_s(N_s - N^* + x) \sum_{i=0}^{N-N^*+x} Q_t(i) + Q_t(N_t - N^* + x)$$

$$\times \sum_{i=0}^{N-N^*+x-1} Q_s(i). \tag{6.16}$$

The problem is now to construct the distribution of some offered traffic such that it creates a busy-circuit distribution identical to Eq. (6.16) when offered to N^* circuits. This problem is of course underdetermined, since an infinite number of distributions will do the trick. Also, it is not necessary to represent the equivalent offered traffic very accurately, since other approximations will be made in the rest of the method. A possibility [3] is to use an equivalent distribution, defined as follows. Assume that the mean and the variance of the equivalent offered traffic are given, M^* and V^*. As usual, let $Z = V^*/M^*$. Then the distribution of busy circuits in the equivalent system is defined by the recurrence

$$Q_e(x) = \frac{1}{x} \left[\frac{M^*}{Z} + (x-1) \right] \frac{Z-1}{Z} Q_e(x-1). \tag{6.17}$$

This choice defines a Pascal distribution whenever $Z \geq 1$. When $Z < 1$, Q_e may become negative, in which case it is set equal to zero. The Pascal approximation is useful because there is a simple relation between the mean and variance of the offered and carried traffics, given by

$$M^* = \left[\frac{\overline{m}^*}{N^* Q_e(N^*)} - 1 + \frac{\overline{v}^* + \overline{m}^{*2} - N^* \overline{m}^*}{\overline{m}^*} \right]$$

$$\times \left[\frac{1 - Q_e(N^*)}{N^* Q_e(N^*)} + \frac{\overline{m}^* - N^*}{\overline{m}^*} \right]^{-1} \tag{6.18}$$

$$V^* = \left[\frac{\overline{v}^* + \overline{m}^{*2} - N^* \overline{m}^*}{\overline{m}^*} - M^* \left(\frac{\overline{m}^* - N^*}{\overline{m}^*} \right) \right] \times M^{*-1} \tag{6.19}$$

The mean and variance of the carried traffics $\overline{m}^*$ and $\overline{v}^*$ can be computed from Eq. (6.16). These values can then be replaced in Eqs. (6.18) and (6.19), which in turn yield the parameters of the equivalent offered traffic. Note that this procedure is only approximate because it relies on the assumption that the offered traffic is Pascal, which may or may not be the case.

Equivalent System for the Cluster. Consider now two I-nodes and the set of alternate routes as shown in Fig. 6.6. Using the equivalent group technique, we want to compute the loss probability for this stream. We could replace each alternate path by an equivalent group and then use the techniques already developed for calls originating at an X-node to compute

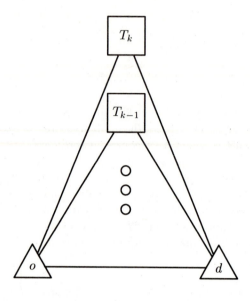

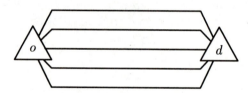

Figure 6.6   Equivalent System for Alternate Routes

the blocking, where the various equivalent traffics are offered to a system of $N_e = \sum_i \min(N_{o,T_i}, N_{T_i,d})$. Note, however, that the operation of the cluster differs from the cluster originating at an X-node in a significant way. In the case of X-nodes, we assume that blocked calls have access to *all* the trunks in the cluster, opening the possibility of replacing the cluster by a single group. In the case of a cluster originating at an I-node, as is the case here, it does not make much sense to assume that a call offered to the cluster has access to all equivalent systems in the cluster, simply because of the way the real routing algorithm operates. This difficulty is solved by making the equivalent system from the *whole* cluster, with size N_e, but this time with an equivalent traffic that reproduces the busy-circuit distribution of the complete cluster — that is,

$$P_e(l) = \sum_{l_1 + \ldots + l_k = l} P_1(l_1) P_2(l_2) \ldots P_k(l_k),$$

where the distribution of busy circuits in the equivalent system is given by

$$Q^*(x) = P_e(N^* - x)$$

and the $P_i(l_i)$ are given by Eq. (6.16). We have replaced the set of trunks out of node o *and* the set of trunks into node d by a simple system of N_f servers offered non-Poisson traffic, with parameters M_f and V_f computed by Eqs. (6.18) and (6.19). This model allows us to use all the same techniques that we used for calls originating at an X-node to compute the blocking in this group — a good approximation of the end-to-end blocking for the o, d traffic.

Link-Offered Traffic.   The apparent simplicity of this calculation is somewhat deceptive, however, since Eq. (6.16) in fact contains unknown quantities, the Q_s and Q_t terms. These quantities are the busy-circuit distributions on the links, which in effect depend on the link-blocking probabilities through the tandem-selection probabilities. We must therefore express the Qs in terms of the selection probabilities, again using some iterative procedure to find a coherent set of Q and α.

In the first part of the algorithm, we evaluate the link-offered traffic as a function of the tandem-selection probabilities and provide an expression for the latter. We do this in three stages; two of them, fairly simple, assume that the busy-circuit distribution on the links is known. The third, more difficult stage is the evaluation of this distribution:

1. For each link, determine the parameters of the overflow traffic. Although calls offered to the link can be either first-offered or overflow calls, only the parameters of the blocked first-offered calls need be computed. Overflow calls that are blocked on a link are lost, and their parameters are of no interest.

2. For each link, determine the tandem-selection probabilities and route the blocked calls to the appropriate tandem.

3. Update the busy-circuit distribution, given the parameters of the overflow traffic computed in the previous step.

4. If the iterative procedure has not converged, go back to step 1.

Overflow-Traffic Parameters.   In the first step, we assume that we know the busy-circuit distribution and hence the time congestion $Q(N)$ on the link, either from the initialization or from step 3 of the previous iteration. We want to compute the parameters of the first-offered calls that overflow from the link. The calculation of the overflow parameters for the alternate calls blocked on the link is of no interest, since these calls are lost and do not reappear as traffic anywhere else in the network. The link is then replaced by an equivalent system of N_e trunks such that the time congestion is the same as the congestion postulated for the link, that is,

$$E(A, N_e) = Q(N).$$

From our knowledge of the equivalent system, the overflow parameters can be computed in the same way as for the X-nodes (Eq. 6.13). Note that the traffic offered to the equivalent system is made up only of first-offered traffic; the effect of the overflow streams is taken into account by the value of N_e. Overflow calls that are blocked will be lost, and their distribution is of no interest.

Tandem-Selection Probabilities.   The second step, calculating the tandem-selection probabilities, is done exactly as for the low-level network (Eqs. 6.14 and 6.15), again assuming that the distributions of busy circuits are known for all links. These distributions are used to allocate overflow traffic among the various paths to the tandem nodes, a step that is needed to update of the busy-circuit distribution, as described next.

Busy-Circuit Distribution on the Links.   The third step, computing the link distributions and parameters of the total offered traffic, is the most difficult and most important step, since it is required for the other two. We want to compute the parameters of the link-offered traffic, based on the state distribution of the trunk group. Such state distributions, however, themselves depend on the link-offered traffic. Once again, an iterative procedure is required to arrive at a consistent set of traffics and distributions.

At each iteration in the procedure, assume that there is an approximation for the distribution $Q^i(x)$, and that a modification $Q(x)$ is computed taking into account another parcel of traffic. Because these parcels can be of three types, there are three different update procedures, two of them very similar. In the first case, the correction is made for first-offered Poisson traffic; we have for the joint distribution of the first-offered calls and the initial distribution [7]

$$Q(x) = K \sum_{j=0}^{x} \frac{A^j}{j!} Q^i(x-j)$$

$$K = \left[\sum_{x=0}^{N} \sum_{j=0}^{x} \frac{A^j}{j!} Q^i(x-j) \right]^{-1} \qquad (6.20)$$

where

$Q^i(x)$ = Busy-circuit distribution without considering the presence of first-offered calls.

$Q(x)$ = Busy-circuit distribution including the effect of first-offered calls.

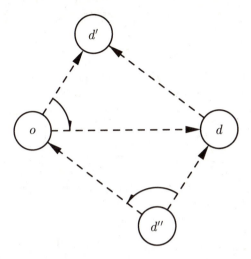

Figure 6.7   Overflow Traffic Offered to an SPC Link

The two other update procedures are for calls that have already overflowed from some direct link; such calls can be of two types (see Fig. 6.7). Consider some o, d' traffic that has been blocked on the direct link and is being offered to the path (o, d, d'). Let

$Q^i(x)$ = The current estimate of the busy circuit distribution on link (o, d).

$Q_{d,d'}$ = The current distribution on link (d, d').

$Q(x)$ = The new estimate of the distribution on (o, d), taking into account the overflow parcel from (o, d') to be computed.

$O_s(x)$ = The distribution for the overflow traffic from a given link s. In the present case, we assume that the offered traffic is peaked; we use the Pascal distribution.

Furthermore, assume that the overflow process from link (o, d') is described by a Pascal distribution and that the tandem-selection probability $\alpha_d^{o,d'}$ is known from the previous step of the algorithm. From this, and the current values of the mean and variance of the overflow, we can compute the $O_s(x)$ distribution. The new value of Q is then

$$Q(x) = C \sum_{m=0}^{\bar{r}} Q^i(x-m)O(m) \sum_{l=m}^{N_{d,d'}} O_{d,d'}(l) \qquad (6.21)$$

$$C^{-1} = \sum_{x=0}^{N_{o,d}} \sum_{v=0}^{\bar{r}} Q^i(x-v)O_{o,d}(v) \sum_{s=v}^{N_{d,d'}} O_{d,d'}(s)$$
$$\bar{r} = \min(x, N_{d,d'}) \tag{6.22}$$

Since both the o,k and the k,d links are important in this calculation, the value of the previous iteration is used for one of these links when computing the other. The case for the overflow from (d'',d) is handled in the same way.

Numerical Results

Results given in [3] indicate that the cluster-decomposition method described in Section 6.2 is quite accurate when compared with simulation on small networks. Computation times, however, are another matter. On an IBM 3033, it takes approximately 3 minutes to evaluate a 44-node network, and 20 minutes to evaluate a 178-node network.

Compare this with the computation times reported in [1] for the link-decomposition method, where the results for the 38-node network are particularly significant. A direct comparison of the two methods is virtually impossible, given that the adaptive algorithm was coded in PL/I and ran on an IBM, while the results for the LSAR method were programmed in Fortran and ran on a VAX 8600. Since the ratio of computation times between the two machines is approximately 20–30/1, we can speculate that substantial gains in computation times appear to be possible with the LSAR method over the more exact technique of [3]. A more definitive statement would require careful control of the elements that can affect computation times, such as type of computer, language of implementation, and code optimization.

Although its results are acceptable when computing the performance of a network, the cluster-decomposition algorithm is totally unsuitable to use for *optimization*, where the blocking must be computed a very large number of times in the course of an optimization. In this case, a feasible procedure is to use the faster but less accurate link-decomposition methods, if necessary switching to the more accurate cluster-decomposition model at the end.

Clearly a fast and accurate blocking-evaluation algorithm for residual-capacity adaptive routing has not yet been developed.

6.3   State-Dependent Routing

There is currently only one other adaptive-routing method for which an evaluation algorithm has been proposed. This method, the state-dependent routing technique [12], is based on a approximation of the Markov decision process for optimal routing. Because this model is related to routing optimization, its derivation appears in Chapter 7. Here we give only a short description of the method, sufficient to understand the evaluation algorithm.

State-dependent routing is a minimum-cost routing, where the cost of a two-link path l for a given stream k is given by

$$
\begin{aligned}
C_l &= C_1(X_1) + C_2(X_2) \\
&= \frac{E(a_1, N_1)}{E(a_1, X_1)} + \frac{E(a_2, N_2)}{E(a_2, X_2)},
\end{aligned}
\tag{6.23}
$$

where a_1, a_2 are some suitably chosen offered traffics and X_1, X_2 represent the number of calls in progress on each link at the time the call arrives. For each link, the cost is the expected number of calls that will be lost during a call-holding time if we add one more call to the link. The path cost is simply the sum of the link costs on the path. The call is rejected if the expected loss on all paths is larger than one; otherwise, the call is routed on the least-cost path.

The basic assumption of the algorithm is that we can model the traffic pattern by assuming that there exists, for each stream k, a set of load-sharing coefficients α_l^k that determine the fraction of the traffic that will go on path l. The method is a classical two-phase evaluation algorithm:

1. Compute the blocking probability on all links.

2. Compute the load-sharing coefficients.

3. Allocate the traffic on alternate paths.

4. Check for convergence.

The main differences from the corresponding algorithm for residual-capacity routing lies in the calculation of the load-sharing coefficients and in the link model employed.

Computation of Load-Sharing Coefficients

The load-sharing coefficient for path l of stream k is a selection probability that is proportional to α_l^*, the cost of path l averaged over some suitable interval:

$$
\alpha_l = \frac{\alpha_l^*}{\sum_m \alpha_m^*}.
$$

The problem is thus to compute these averages, based on the available network parameters. This can be done if we interpret each of the link costs in Eq. (6.23) as the expected number of lost calls on the link during an interval that is the expected lifetime in a state. This is the mean passage time from state j to state $j + 1$ (term $E(a_s, X_s)^{-1}$), which can be computed from the distribution of the offered traffic. With this interpretation, we can write for each link

$$\alpha^* = f(\overline{T}_{0,1}, \overline{T}_{1,2}, \ldots \overline{T}_{N-1,N}),$$

where $\overline{T}_{i,i+1}$ is the average of the first passage time from state i to state $i + 1$ on the link.

In the next step, we assume that this function is a linear combination of the expectations of the individual first passage times, and that we can write

$$\alpha^* = \sum_{i=1}^{N-1} \beta_i \overline{T}_{i-1,i}.$$

The coefficients can be defined from the following argument. The cost (first-passage time) of a transition is composed of two elements: (1) the time it takes to reach i and (2) the time it takes to go from i to $i + 1$, given that we are in i. Because we want to model the link cost as a sum of transition costs, we must somehow remove the effect of the time to reach state i from the expression of the transition cost. Let us do this by taking β_i as the inverse of the average first-passage time into state i from the initial state 0,

$$\beta_i = 1/\overline{T}_{0,i},$$

where

$$T_{0,i} = \sum_{k=0}^{i-1} T_{k,k+1},$$

finally yielding

$$\alpha^* = \sum_{i=0}^{N-1} \frac{\overline{T}_{i,i+1}}{\overline{T}_{0,i+1}}.$$

Link Model

The second element of a link-decomposition method is the link model that relates the offered traffic to the blocking probability. The model used in this case is based on the assumption that the arrival process to the link is composed of two Poisson sources, representing the direct and overflow traffics, respectively. The direct source is always on, while the alternate source is turned on and off based on whether or not it is being used as an alternate path. We immediately recognize in this description the operation of the interrupted Poisson process, which we know how to evaluate from the discussion of Chapter 3. One additional quantity is necessary to use this model: the ratio of on-to-off times of the source. The natural assumption is that this ratio is the same as that for the direct *versus* alternate traffics, which are known from the link-loading phase.

Implementation

Although the evaluation algorithm is described by Koussoulas, no numerical results are presented. The author recognizes that the system is in fact an algorithm for computing one of the solutions of the Erlang fixed point, and that there may not be a unique solution. Koussoulas also suggests that it may be possible to implement the algorithm in a decentralized way, but again gives no information on the numerical performance of the method. Finally, there is no indication of the accuracy of the evaluation method as compared with the actual operation of the network. These omissions are quite understandable, given the early stages of development of the adaptive techniques, which should be the subject of interesting developments in the near future.

6.4   Link-System Model

Another approach to the end-to-end blocking computation has been proposed by Szybicki [13]. In this approach, the trunk groups going out from a node are considered together, as a cluster. Calls arriving at this cluster are either first-offered calls, which enter the group by attempting to seize the direct group, or overflow calls, which have entered the cluster at some other trunk group and are trying to seize a trunk in the group under consideration. In either case, the cluster can be viewed as a single entity to which first-offered calls are offered, trying to seize a circuit first in some well-known set (the direct trunk group), and then attempting to find a circuit *at random* in other groups.

Four assumptions must be made in order to apply the well-known theory of blocking calculation in link systems:

1. The probabilities of selecting various groups in the cluster are identical.

2. The blocking probabilities of the outgoing clusters are independent of the blocking on the incoming ones.

3. All trunk groups are of the same size.

4. Blocking on the trunk groups is given by truncated binomial distributions.

An internal switch blocking is also provided for in the model, with the additional assumption that these blocking probabilities are mutually independent. Define

$R_{r,t}$ = Blocking probability between intelligent nodes r and t.

m = Number of tandem offices available to r, t traffic.

n_r = Number of first-choice trunks out of node r.

$G_1(n_r, \mu)$ = Probability that the n_r direct trunks are busy, and that precisely μ trunks of the outgoing cluster are busy.

$F_1(s, \mu)$ = Probability of internal congestion of exactly s out of $m - 2 - \mu$ offices.

$H(m - 2 - \mu - s)$ = Probability that $m - 2 - \mu - s$ trunk groups originating from a specific set of $m - 2 - \mu - s$ offices (the ones with no internal blocking) and terminating in the destination node t are busy. This is the blocking probability on the second leg of the path out of nonblocked nodes.

With these definitions, the end-to-end blocking probability is given by

$$E_{r,t} = e_t + (1 - e_t) \sum_{\mu=0}^{m-2} G_1(n_r, \mu) \sum_{s=0}^{m-2-\mu} (1 - F_1(s, \mu)) H_1(m - 2 - \mu - s). \quad (6.24)$$

Jacobaeus's theory can be used to compute the elements of this double sum:

$$G_1(n_r, \mu) = \binom{m-2}{\mu} \sum_{\nu=0}^{m-2-\mu} (-1)^\nu \binom{m-2-\mu}{\nu} \times$$

$$\frac{E(N_r, b_r, c_r)}{E(N_r - x_r, b_r + x_r, c_r)} \quad (6.25)$$

$$F_1(s, \mu) = \binom{m-2-\mu}{s} e_t^s (1 - e_t)^{m-2-\mu-s} \quad (6.26)$$

$$H_1(m - 2 - \mu - s) = \left[\frac{E(N_r, b_r, c_r)}{E(N_r - n_r, b_r + n_r, c_r)} \right]^{m-2-\mu-s} \quad (6.27)$$

$$N_r = (m - 1)n_r$$

$$x_r = (\nu + \mu + 1)n_r$$

$$E(N, b, c) = \frac{\binom{-b}{N}(-c)^N}{\sum_{k=0}^{N} \binom{-b}{k}(-c)^k}$$

Szybicki compares these formulas with simulations in which there is no internal switch blocking, as well as with symmetrical networks. The accuracy seems moderately good; a factor of 2 is the largest departure from the simulated values. No comparisons with nonsymmetrical networks seem to have been made.

Although the author gives no computation times, it is probable that these may become quite large, in view of the double sum involved in equation (6.24), which involves yet another summation in the normalizing constants of the $E(.)$

functions. This approach may suffer from the same defect as the iterative method, and it could be difficult to use in optimization routines because of the long computation times.

6.5 Conclusion

In at least two respects, the question of performance evaluation is still far from complete. The link-decomposition model, although fast enough to use in network-dimensioning procedures, is not very accurate, especially at low blocking values; more work is needed along these lines. The cluster-decomposition method, although much more accurate, has correspondingly longer computation times. Also, the latter method does not take into account state protection, an essential feature of any implementation. The model is probably too slow for use in iterative procedures, although it has been used as a network-evaluation tool. The accuracy and speed of the link-decomposition method for state-dependent routing remain to be demonstrated.

Problems

6.1. Derive Eq. (6.15) for the distribution of free paths on the set of links s, t for the cluster-decomposition method for the residual-capacity adaptive routing.

6.2. Derive Eq. (6.16) for the equivalent distribution in the same case.

6.3. Show that Eq. (6.17) does indeed yield the Pascal distribution.

6.4. Show that Eq. (6.16) is a special case of the path model described by Eq. (5.55).

References

[1] Girard A., Bell M.A., "Blocking Evaluation for Networks with Residual Capacity Adaptive Routing," *IEEE Transactions on Communications*, vol. COM–37, pp. 1372–1380, 1989.

[2] Lin, P.M., Leon, B.J., and Stewart, C.R., "Analysis of circuit switched networks employing originating office control with spill," *IEEE Transactions on Communications*, vol. COM–26, pp. 754–765, 1978.

[3] Régnier, J., Blondeau, P., and Cameron, W.H., "Grade of service of a dynamic call-routing system," *International Teletraffic Congress*, vol. 10, pp. 3.2.6.1–3.2.6.9, 1983.

[4] Cameron, H., Galloy, P., and Graham, W.J., "Report on the Toronto advanced routing concept trial," *Network Planning Symposium*, vol. 1, pp. 228–236, 1980.

[5] Huberman, R., Hurtubise, S., Le Nir, S.A., and Drwiega, T., "Multihour dimensioning for a dynamically routed network," *International Teletraffic Congress*, vol. 11, pp. 4.3A-5-1–4.3A-5-7 , September 1985.

[6] Kuczura, A., and Bajaj, D., "A method of moments for the analysis of a switched communication network's performance," *IEEE Transactions on Communications*, vol. TCOM–27, pp. 185–193, 1977.

[7] Delbrouck, L.E.N., "A unified approximate evaluation of congestion functions for smooth and peaky traffics," *IEEE Transactions on Communications*, vol. TCOM–29, pp. 85–91, 1981.

[8] Pearce, C.E.M., and Potter, R.M., "Some formulae old and new for overflow traffic in telephony," *International Teletraffic Congress*, vol. 8, 1976.

[9] Manfield, D.R., and Downs, T., "Decomposition of traffic in loss systems with renewal input," *IEEE Transactions on Communications*, vol. COM–25, pp. 44–58, 1977.

[10] Delbrouck, L.E.N., "Use of Kosten's system in the provisioning of alternate trunk groups carrying heterogeneous traffic," *IEEE Transactions on Communications*, vol. COM-31, pp. 741–749, 1983.

[11] Katz, S., "Statistical performance analysis of a switched communication network," *International Teletraffic Congress*, vol. 5, 1967.

[12] Koussoulas, N.T., "Performance analysis of state-dependent routing in circuit-switched networks," *International Teletraffic Congress*, vol. 12, pp. 3.4A1.1–3.4A1.7 1988.

[13] Szybicki, E., "Calculation of congestion in trunk networks provided with adaptive traffic routing and automatic network management systems," *International Conference on Communications*, pp. 55.6.1–55.6.6, 1981.

CHAPTER 7

Routing Optimization

The notion of routing optimization was almost never raised in the planning of classical telephone networks operating with a fixed hierarchical rule. The hierarchy was generally selected more for administrative reasons than for considerations of traffic efficiency or grade of service; once the hierarchy was chosen, the routing was almost completely specified. The only remaining choice was whether or not to use high-usage trunk groups, a question handled within the dimensioning algorithms.

Because of new signaling techniques, it is now possible to obtain more information on the state of the network. Also, the gradual replacement of wired-logic switches by switches with stored program control means that this information can be used to route calls very flexibly. Thus let us examine the issue of the optimal selection of a routing algorithm in the context of network synthesis, where the network performance is to be optimized for a given stationary input. Also important are questions such as the impact of routing on the reliability and survivability of networks, but the answers often depend on the dynamic behavior of the network, which is much more difficult to analyze.

First we examine the routing-optimization problem for two specific classes of routing. We present a short discussion on multicommodity flow models, the most widely used techniques for studying routing in other areas of engineering. We then try to use this model to analyze the simplest routing method — load sharing. We discover the limitations of the flow models, making some generalizations about the flow-deviation technique that can lead to an adaptive load-sharing routing scheme. We then consider the optimization of alternate routing, describing two approaches, based on flow models and combinatorial optimization, respectively. We also discuss the synthesis problem that arises from the flow model. Finally, we extend the scope of the discussion to cover the choice of a particular routing method based on more fundamental principles, leading to the theory of Markov decision processes (MDP). We briefly introduce some elementary concepts of MDP theory, noting why the exact solution methods are not feasible in practice. We end the chapter with an example of an approximate solution of the MDP model that can be implemented in a network of realistic size; the example also covers some routing techniques already implemented as special cases.

7.1 Multicommodity-Flow Models

The successful use of multicommodity-flow models in the study of optimal routing for transportation and packet-switched telecommunication networks has been a strong incentive to adapt these models to circuit switching. Such adaptation is possible because the average number of calls present in the network has the structure of a multicommodity path-flow, although with a more complex structure because the loss function is present. The structure is there, however, and the many well-known methods of multicommodity flows can be applied to obtain information on optimal routing.

Our interest in multicommodity-flow models comes from two important features of the optimal solutions and algorithms: (1) the optimal choice of flows must be such that, for each commodity, the marginal cost of the flows is equal on all paths available to that flow and (2) these solutions can be computed by specialized algorithms that reduce to a series of shortest-path calculations, allowing relatively large networks to be solved. We review how these two properties arise in the standard multicommodity model, showing how it must be modified to represent some classes of routing policies.

Nonlinear Multicommodity Flows

Consider the following uncapacitated nonlinear-cost multicommodity problem:

$$\min_x \; z = g(\mathbf{x}) \tag{7.1}$$

$$\sum_l x_l^k = r^k \quad (v^k)$$

$$\mathbf{x} \geq 0 \quad (u_l^k)$$

where r^k is the demand for commodity k. The vector $\mathbf{x}$, a path-flow vector in the network, represents the amount of flow of type k carried on path l; there is a nonlinear cost function to be minimized that depends on these flows. We examine the properties of the optimal solution to Problem 7.1, then describe a simple solution algorithm that exploits the multicommodity structure of the problem. The first-order optimality conditions are written

$$u_l^k = \frac{\partial g}{\partial x_l^k} - v^k, \quad \forall k, \; \forall l$$

$$v^k \left(\sum_l x_l^k - r^k \right) = 0$$

$$x_l^k u_l^k = 0$$
$$u_l^k \geq 0$$

At the optimal solution, the commodity r^k is carried on some of the paths connecting $o(k)$ to $d(k)$, for which we have $x_l^k > 0$. In this case, the complementarity conditions imply that the corresponding multipliers vanish, and the optimality equation for these flows becomes

$$v^k = \frac{\partial g}{\partial x_l^k} \quad \forall x_l^k > 0$$

Note that v^k does not depend on the path index l, and, for a given commodity k, is effectively a constant. This means that the optimal flows of a given commodity must *equalize* the marginal cost on all the paths where they appear. This fundamental notion appears frequently in work on optimal routing.

The great attraction of this model is that it makes available a particularly elegant and efficient solution technique. The technique is a specialization of the Frank-Wolfe method for nonlinear programming with linear constraints [1], which is based on successive linearization of the objective function. Consider the general nonlinear problem, subject to linear constraints:

$$\min \ z = f(\mathbf{x}) \tag{7.2}$$
$$A\mathbf{x} = \mathbf{b}, \quad \mathbf{x} \geq 0$$

At each iteration i, a linearized version of (7.2) is constructed for the current solution $\mathbf{x}^i$:

$$\min \ z_i = <\nabla f(\mathbf{x}^i), \mathbf{y}> \tag{7.3}$$
$$A\mathbf{y} = \mathbf{b}, \quad \mathbf{y} \geq 0$$

The solution $\mathbf{y}^i$, constituting the subproblem at the current iteration, is then computed. This solution is used to search for a minimum of f on the segment $[\mathbf{x}^i, \mathbf{y}^i]$ by

$$\min_{0 \leq \alpha \leq 1} \ f(\alpha \mathbf{x}^i + (1 - \alpha)\mathbf{y}^i)$$
$$\alpha \mathbf{x}^i + (1 - \alpha)\mathbf{y}^i \geq 0$$

The method is guaranteed to converge to at least a local optimal solution of the nonlinear problem [1]. In practice, the objective function has a fast rate of decrease at the beginning of the procedure, but this rate slows as the algorithm proceeds toward the solution; at the end the rate can be quite slow. Thus the method is best used when the accuracy of the solutions need not be high, as is often the case in practice.

The method is interesting because its specialization to the multicommodity problem yields extremely simple subproblems when the objective function is separable — that is, when $g(\mathbf{x}) = \sum_s g(f_s)$, where f_s is the total flow on arc s. In this case, the domain $A\mathbf{x} = \mathbf{b}$ of Problem 7.3 becomes the standard multicommodity flow domain. The solution to the problem is then to compute a *linear* minimum-cost multicommodity flow — easy to do by calculating, for each commodity *independently*, the minimum-cost path from the origin to the destination, and routing all of the flow on this path. Numerous extremely efficient algorithms for doing shortest-path calculation exist that make the flow-deviation method attractive [2, 3]. This concept of solving the routing problem by a sequence of shortest-path calculations, the second important notion produced by this model, is also found time and again in work on routing optimization.

The subproblems of the Frank-Wolfe method become shortest-path problems only when the original multicommodity flow is unconstrained. If capacity constraints are present, of the form $\sum \mathcal{I}_{s,l} x^l \leq C_s$, the subproblems are not so simple, and it is not always advantageous to use the Frank-Wolfe algorithm. There is, however, an important practical case in which the capacity constraints can be disregarded — when the objective function contains a natural penalty term, which bounds the solution away from the capacity constraints. A well-known example is the expected delay of an $M/M/1$ queue as a function of traffic carried in the queue, which has the form $f/(C - f)$, where C is the link capacity and f is the total traffic offered to the link. In this case, this term becomes very large as the flow becomes close to the capacity. Thus, provided the algorithm can be started inside the feasible region, we can ignore the capacity constraints, using shortest-path methods to arrive at a solution.

The solution algorithm for the multicommodity flow problem is sometimes called *flow deviation* [4] because it can be implemented according to the following rule. First, at the current iteration, compute the shortest path for each commodity, using the marginal costs as link lengths. If it turns out that these costs are not all equal on the paths that carry traffic, the traffic patterns must be rearranged by removing some of the flow currently carried on the paths and sending it to the shortest path. In other words, the flow deviates from its current route toward a currently more economical route. This deviation continues as long as the objective function decreases and remains feasible, at which point a new iteration begins. The precise specification of the flow-deviation method is left as an exercise (Problem 7.1).

System and User Optimality

Consideration of optimal routing leads to a discussion of various types of optimality for networks. The two important concepts related to this field are *system* optimality and *user* optimality. A flow pattern is said to be system optimal if it solves the nonlinear multicommodity flow defined in Eq. (7.1). The Kuhn-Tucker optimality conditions can be rephrased as follows. Suppose that each user of the network is represented by a small amount of flow Δx. Each user selects its path in such a way that the total cost of using this path is as small as possible; in the flow pattern employed, no user can be reallocated to another path where the path cost would decrease. As we have seen, this policy is optimal if the cost charged to the user is in fact the marginal cost of using the link at the current load.

This way of charging for use of a facility is used infrequently. Instead, the total cost of using an arc is divided equally among all users of the link; each individual user ends up paying the same amount. It is reasonable to assume that, in this situation, users select their paths in such a way that their total cost is as small as possible and that there is no cheaper alternative than the current one. Mathematically, this can be formulated as follows. Let $\bar{c}_s(f_s)$ be the average cost of link s for a total traffic f_s on the link. Then, each user pays

$$\bar{c}_s(f_s) = \frac{c_s(f_s)}{f_s},$$

and the path cost for a unit flow (a user) is

$$\overline{C}_l = \sum_s \mathcal{I}_{s,l}\bar{c}_s.$$

An *equilibrium flow* is a flow that has the following property. Choose a path l with the corresponding flow $x_l > 0$, and a number $0 < \Delta x < x_l$. Consider also some other path k between $o(l)$ and $d(l)$, and a modified flow x' defined as

$$x'_l = x_l - \Delta x$$
$$x'_k = x_k + \Delta x$$

All other path flows are unchanged. In other words, the flow x' is obtained from the flow x by the deviation of a small amount Δx from path l to path k. We say that x is an equilibrium flow if the cost of changing from l to k is not negative for all pairs (l, k) and all small Δx — in other words, that

$$\overline{C}(x')\Delta x \geq \overline{C}(x)\Delta x.$$

As should be obvious, the operation of the system-optimal network is essentially the same as for the user-optimal network. In a user-optimal network, all paths that carry some flow have an equal *average* cost, which is no greater than the average cost for the unused paths. The only difference is that the system-optimal network uses marginal costs to route traffic, while the user-optimal network uses average costs.

The notion of user optimality is important from two points of view. First, it corresponds to the actual pricing mechanisms used for facilities. Second, a user-optimal solution requires less computation since the link costs are averages; the calculation of a system-optimal solution, however, requires the evaluation of derivatives, which are more difficult to obtain.

It should also be clear from the previous discussion that a user-optimal solution cannot be better than a system-optimal one, since the former does not satisfy the Kuhn-Tucker optimality conditions. This leads to two questions: What are the conditions such that both solutions are equivalent? If the solutions are not equivalent, what is the amount of the nonoptimality of the user-optimal solution?

The first question can be answered nicely [5]. Suppose that we have a user-optimal flow $\bar{\mathbf{x}}$ corresponding to some cost function $\bar{c}_s$. Then, we can find a set of cost functions $c_s(f_s)$ such that the system-optimal flow $\mathbf{x} = \bar{\mathbf{x}}$. It is quite easy to see that the choice of

$$c_s(f_s) = \int_0^{f_s} \bar{c}_s(h_s)dh_s \qquad (7.4)$$

gives the required flow. Conversely, given a system-optimal flow $\mathbf{x}$ corresponding to the cost functions $c_s(f_s)$, we can find cost functions $\bar{c}_s(f_s)$ such that the solution $\bar{\mathbf{x}}$ of the user optimal flow is precisely $\mathbf{x}$. The required cost functions are

$$\bar{c}_s(f_s) = f_s \frac{dc_s}{df_s}. \qquad (7.5)$$

Here too, the demonstration that this cost yields the required flow is straightforward, and is left as an exercise (Problem 7.2).

From these results, we can derive a condition under which the user- and system-optimal flows are equivalent. We must have

$$c_s(f_s) = \eta \int_0^{f_s} \bar{c}_s(h)dh.$$

This equation has the solution

$$c_s(f_s) = c_0 f_s^n$$

where c_0 is an arbitrary constant. This type of power-law cost function is the only one for which we can guarantee that the system- and user-optimal solutions are identical for an arbitrary network. Note, however, that other cost functions can lead to identical solutions if the network has some special properties. This can be determined only by analyzing the particular case.

When the cost functions do not guarantee equivalent user- and system-optimal solutions, the magnitude of the difference between the two solutions cannot be determined a priori except by computing each type of solution for the case of interest. Because there are cases where this difference can be large, user-optimal solutions should be used with care.

Generalized Networks

The structure of the domain for the multicommodity model rests on the assumption that flow is conserved at all nodes in the network such that all the traffic offered to a link is eventually carried on that link. This is clearly not true for networks operating with a blocked-calls-lost policy, where we know that not all the calls offered to the network are connected.

Nonconservation of traffic in the network can be modeled more accurately by generalized networks. Here we introduce the subject briefly, showing how link losses can be taken into account and pointing out the lack of results applicable to circuit-switched networks.

Generalized networks are defined for single-commodity flows by a simple modification of the conservation constraints. The underlying model is that of a flow that is expanded by a constant factor $k_{i,j}$ as it passes in an arc (i,j). The node-arc incidence matrix is modified to reflect this change, where the -1 elements of the matrix are replaced by the gain factors $-k_{i,j}$. The conservation equations then become

$$\sum_j f_{i,j} - \sum_j f_{j,i}k_{j,i} = d_i.$$

The other equations remain the same. This is a linear program with a special constraint structure; specialized versions of the simplex algorithm can produce solutions much faster than a general-purpose method (see [6] for a bibliography of relevant references). Although these gains in computational efficiency are significant, they are not nearly as good as those realized with the specialized simplex methods for the ordinary minimum-cost flow problem. Thus the size of generalized networks that can be solved is generally smaller than for ordinary network flows.

From this point, the model can be extended in two directions. In the first, we consider nonlinear gain *functions*, examining how specialized solution methods apply to this case. This was done in [6], where it was found that the maximum-flow version has a global optimum at a point that satisfies the Kuhn-Tucker conditions if and only if $k(\cdot)$ is differentiable and convex, in addition to satisfying the usual constraint-qualification condition. The minimum-cost flow is somewhat more difficult, since these conditions are not sufficient to guarantee a global optimum. A solution algorithm based on successive linearization is proposed; the specialized simplex method with constant gains is used to solve the subproblems.

The other generalization is for multicommodity flows, where each component of the flow changes as it traverses an arc. The case of linear gains has been discussed in [7], but the completely general case of the multicommodity flow with nonlinear gain functions does not appear in the literature. This, however, is precisely the model required to represent independent arc losses if the nonconservation of traffic on links is to be taken into account. It could take the form

$$\min_{f,s} z(\mathbf{f},\mathbf{s}) \tag{7.6}$$

$$\sum_j f_{i,j}^k - \sum_j f_{j,i}^k h_{j,i}^k(f_{j,i}) = \begin{cases} d^k & \text{if } i = o(k) \\ -s^k & \text{if } i = d(k) \\ 0 & \text{otherwise} \end{cases}$$

where $f_{i,j}$ is given by

$$f_{i,j} = \sum_k f_{i,j}^k$$

$$s^k,\ f_{i,j}^k \geq 0$$

and $h_{i,j}^k(f_{i,j})$ is the gain function for commodity k on link (i,j). We have indicated a dependence on the total flow on the link $f_{i,j}$, but this could be made more complicated if required by the particular situation. The problem domain is more complex than in the case of ordinary multicommodity flows because the conservation equations apply only at the source node of each commodity. Once the flow has entered the network, the amount that reaches the destination depends on the routing — that is, on the values of $\mathbf{f}$. In this case, s^k is the amount of flow k that reaches its destination and is also a variable of the problem. The objective function can take many forms. If there is a routing cost, we may have $z = \sum_s C_s(f_s)$. We may also wish to maximize the traffic carried in the network, in which case we would choose $z = -\sum_k s^k$. Similarly, the constraint set could be modified to guarantee that at least a certain fraction of each stream reaches its destination, in which case we would have the constraints $s^k \geq \alpha^k d^k$. Obviously, many such combinations are possible, depending on the situation. The model could be generalized even further by making the function depend on the particular commodity in question, but this does not seem necessary for the kinds of problems considered here.

Equation 7.6 is a nonlinear optimization problem with nonlinear constraints. It can be solved by a general-purpose nonlinear programming algorithm, although the current efficiency of these methods probably precludes the solution of large networks. Obviously, research in this area is needed to construct optimization techniques based on the special structure of the constraints.

Note that the generalized network equations assume that the flow on a link is reduced by some gain function $h(\cdot)$ that depends only on the total flow on that link. Although this is an improvement over the pure conservation of flow, it still does not describe accurately the operation of circuit-switched networks: For many types of routing, the blocking probability on a given link in a path depends not only on the link flow, but also on the state of all the other links in the path. Thus only when this effect can be neglected can the generalized model be used for routing calculations.

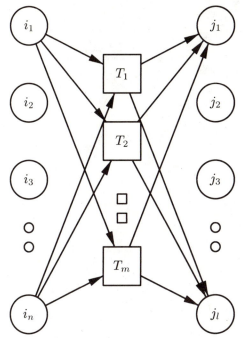

Figure 7.1 Hierarchical Network

7.2 Load Sharing

As shown in the previous section, optimal multicommodity flows are well understood and can be computed easily. Such flows, however, do not apply directly
to the routing of calls in circuit-switched networks; it would be interesting to
see the extent to which the results of the multicommodity theory apply in a
network operating with a commonly used routing method.

Because of their simplicity, load-sharing policies are often selected as potential candidates for optimization in routing studies — probably more because
of the relative ease with which these policies can be optimized than because of
their intrinsic efficiency. The study of load sharing is nevertheless instructive
because it shows how the simple multicommodity-flow models can represent
real routing in circuit-switched networks, as well as to what extent the flow-
deviation method can be used to compute solutions.

We examine two different cases of load sharing. In the first case, two-link
paths are studied in the context of a hierarchical network; in the second, the
model is generalized to paths with an arbitrary length.

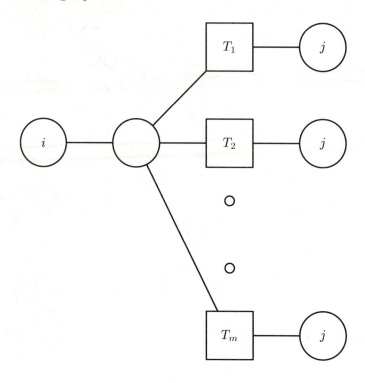

Figure 7.2   Generalized Route Tree for Hierarchical Routing Optimization

Two-Link Paths

First consider the case of a two-level hierarchical network where it is found that the strict hierarchical rule is no longer adequate, and where we would like to make the routing more flexible. Under the hierarchical rule, calls with different homing offices for their origin and destination nodes can use at most one three-link path and only two two-link paths. It has been suggested that the routing could be enlarged by permitting the use of more than the two two-link paths available in the hierarchical routing, but also eliminating the three-link path. This model could arise in the study of a hierarchical network similar to that of Fig. 7.1, where the squares represent tandem nodes, and circles are lower-level nodes [8]. The corresponding route tree is shown in Fig. 7.2. Also, the routing method is no longer alternate routing with overflow, but rather load sharing. Because the offices retain their character of being either local or tandem, the network can still be said to be hierarchical even though the routing is no longer of this type.

If we assume that the traffic offered to the direct links and the direct trunk-group sizes are given, we can compute the amount of overflow traffic offered to the tandem links for each destination. We can then ignore the direct links and the first-offered traffic, using the overflow traffic as decision variables for the routing optimization. For simplicity, we assume that this traffic is Poisson, although a more realistic traffic model taking into account the higher moments could also be used. Define

$A_k^{i,j}$ = The amount of $A^{i,j}$ offered to tandem k. These are the routing variables and are the subject of the optimization.

If no monetary cost is associated with the routing, the objective is to minimize the total traffic lost in the network. This should be given by $z = \sum_{i,j} L^{i,j} A^{i,j}$. In the case of hierarchical networks with low blocking on the final groups, however, we can simplify this measure of network performance as

$$\min_{A_k^{i,j}} z = \sum_{i,k} \hat{a}_{i,k} + \sum_{k,j} \hat{a}_{k,j},$$

with the constraints

$$\sum_k A_k^{i,j} = A^{i,j} \quad (v^{i,j})$$

$$A_k^{i,j} \geq 0 \quad (u_k^{i,j})$$

Let us now examine the first-order optimality conditions, describing the nature of the optimal solution to this load-sharing problem. The Lagrange function is given by

$$\mathcal{L}(A, \mathbf{u}, \mathbf{v}) = \sum_{i,k} \hat{a}_{i,k} + \sum_{k,j} \hat{a}_{k,j} - \sum_{i,j} v^{i,j} \left(\sum_k A_k^{i,j} - A^{i,j} \right) - \sum_{i,j,k} u_k^{i,j} A_k^{i,j}.$$

The first-order conditions are given by $\partial \mathcal{L} / \partial A_k^{i,j} = 0$, which can be expressed as

$$u_k^{i,j} = -v^{i,j} + \sum_{l,n} \gamma_{l,n} \frac{\partial a_{l,n}}{\partial A_k^{i,j}} + \sum_{n,m} \gamma_{n,m} \frac{\partial a_{n,m}}{\partial A_k^{i,j}}, \qquad (7.7)$$

where

$$\gamma_{i,k} = \frac{\partial \hat{a}_{i,k}}{\partial a_{i,k}}$$

This last expression is called the marginal overflow of link (i, k). Indices l, m, and n denote an origin, destination, and tandem node, respectively. We can use expression (7.7) to study the characteristics of the optimal routing — in particular, the conditions under which a multicommodity solution is possible.

This optimal flow pattern depends strongly on the model used to define the link-offered traffic.

The first model considered assumes that traffic is conserved in the network — that is, that the blocking probabilities on the links is so small that it can be neglected. For a call from origin i to destination j through tandem k, we have

$$a_{i,k} = \sum_j A_k^{i,j} \tag{7.8}$$

$$a_{k,j} = \sum_i A_k^{i,j} \tag{7.9}$$

It is not hard to show that the optimality equation (7.7) reduces to

$$u_k^{i,j} = -v^{i,j} + \gamma_{i,k} + \gamma_{k,j}. \tag{7.10}$$

This equation has the following interpretation. Consider a particular flow (i,j). The sum $\gamma_{i,k} + \gamma_{k,j}$ is the total marginal overflow on the path through tandem k for this traffic stream. Because $v^{i,j}$ is independent of k, the optimal load sharing is as follows. If the right-hand side of Eq. (7.10) is positive, we have found a $u_k^{i,j} > 0$ and, by the complementarity conditions, $x_k^{i,j} = 0$ — that is, we should not use the path through k. Conversely, for all paths where there is some flow $x_l^k > 0$, share the load to equalize the marginal overflow on all paths. This is obvious from the form of the optimality equation, which becomes $v^{i,j} = \gamma_{i,k} + \gamma_{k,j}$. Because $v^{i,j}$ is independent of k, for a given commodity, the marginal blocking probabilities must be the same on all paths and must be equal to $v^{i,j}$.

The appearance of an equal marginal overflow solution is not surprising: The domain of the variables has become a multicommodity flow by the conservation assumption, as well as by the form of the objective function. This suggests that, if the link costs are defined as the marginal overflow at the current solution, the flow-deviation algorithm is a realistic solution method under the stated assumptions.

Compare this result with [9], where load-sharing policies are examined under some rather artificial assumptions. In addition to the assumptions already mentioned, the link-blocking model must be a power function of the traffic offered to the link, and path-blocking probabilities must be independent of traffic. In this case, it is shown that the optimal load sharing equalizes blocking *probabilities* on all paths. Because of the strong assumptions required, an equal-blocking sharing is usually not optimal in a real case.

The conservation condition used to derive Eq. (7.10) may not be satisfied — for instance, when the network is operating in an overload condition. In this case, we must take into account the blocking on the paths and the fact that traffic is lost on the link. Here again, the particular optimal flows obtained depend on the path model used. More precisely, as discussed in Chapter 4, we can have two principles to model links in tandem. The principle used in [8] is based on the representation

$$a_{i,k} = \sum_j A_k^{i,j} \tag{7.11}$$

$$a_{k,j} = \sum_i A_k^{i,j} \left[1 - B_{i,k}\right] \tag{7.12}$$

Here, we assume that the traffic offered to the first link in a path is independent of the blocking on the second link, but that the converse is not true, and that the traffic offered to the second link has been thinned by an amount proportional to the blocking probability of the first link. Note that the set of variables produced is *not* a multicommodity flow; one can expect neither an optimal solution with equal marginal cost nor a solution algorithm of the flow-deviation type. In fact, it is not difficult to show that the set of variables corresponds to a generalized network model. In this case, the optimality equation becomes

$$u_k^{i,j} = -v^{i,j} + \gamma_{i,k} + (1 - B_{i,k})\gamma_{k,j} - \frac{\partial B_{i,k}}{\partial a_{i,k}} \sum_m A_k^{i,m}\gamma_{k,m}. \tag{7.13}$$

For those paths where there is some positive flow $x_l^k > 0$, we have, from the complementary conditions,

$$v^{i,j} = \gamma_{i,k} + (1 - B_{i,k})\gamma_{k,j} - \frac{\partial B_{i,k}}{\partial a_{i,k}} \sum_m A_k^{i,m}\gamma_{k,m}, \tag{7.14}$$

where the sum is taken over all destination nodes m. Note that these equations can no longer be separated by commodity since an interference is produced on the (i, k) link by traffic originating at i, destined for all nodes other than j and going through tandem k. Also, as expected, a load sharing based on equal marginal overflow on all paths is not necessarily optimal, even when weighted by the linking probability on the first link in the path — unless the coupling term is small, which is often the case in hierarchical networks operating at a low blocking value on the finals.

The more complex case, where downstream blocking is also taken into account, is left as an exercise. In this example, generalized networks do not apply since the gain functions depend on the complete path flows, as opposed to the individual links. In this case the optimal load-sharing policy cannot be expressed explicitly, but only as the solution of a linear system of equations. Similarly, this technique can be extended to the case where the intertandem links are taken into account. Approximate techniques for load-sharing optimization are described in [10].

Multilink Paths

Let us now consider the more general case of load sharing on paths with an arbitrary number of links. Just as in the previous section, we simplify the notation by assuming that the calls that belong to a given stream are split between a number of substreams, and that calls in each substream are offered to a *single* path. Calls blocked on the path are lost and do not return. This model has been studied extensively by Kelly [11,12] in the context of revenue-maximization methods. Let $A_k^{i,j}$ be the traffic offered to the kth path between i and j and $L_k^{i,j}$ be the probability that an (i,j) call offered to the kth path is blocked. We assume that paths can be labeled by a single index m whenever it is not necessary to specify the triplet (i,j,k), and that path-blocking probabilities and offered traffic can be written in the notation L^m and A^m whenever there is no ambiguity as to the path in question. We have

$$\min_{A_k^{i,j}} z = \sum_{i,j,k} L_k^{i,j} A_k^{i,j} \tag{7.15}$$

$$\sum_k A_k^{i,j} = A^{i,j}$$

$$A_k^{i,j} \geq 0$$

where

$$L_k^{i,j} = 1 - \prod_{s \in (i,j,k)} (1 - B_s) \tag{7.16}$$

Throughout this section, we use the reduced-traffic method to compute the traffic offered to a link, where

$$\bar{a}_s = \sum_{m \mid s \in m} \bar{A}^m$$

$$\bar{A}^m = A^m (1 - L^m) \tag{7.17}$$

$$a_s = \frac{\bar{a}_s}{(1 - B_s)}$$

$$= \frac{1}{(1 - B_s)} \sum_{m \mid s \in m} A^m (1 - L^m)$$

$$= \sum_{m \mid s \in m} A^m \prod_{\substack{t \in m \\ t \neq s}} (1 - B_t) \tag{7.18}$$

As we know from Eq. (7.18), a network operating with load sharing is not ordered, even though there is no overflow. This is because the traffic offered to a link on a given path depends on the blocking probability of all the other links of the path, both preceding and following the link in question. The blocking probabilities are not known explicitly but instead are given as the solution of the nonlinear system (4.10). The presence of this fixed-point system to characterize the correct values of the link-blocking probability makes it more difficult to derive the Kuhn-Tucker conditions since we must compute derivatives with respect to quantities that are linked through a system of nonlinear equations. This can be avoided by reformulating the optimization problem (7.15) in a manner that is equivalent but easier to analyze. Note that this transformation, although it simplifies the analysis, is not necessarily advantageous for numerical calculations. The transformation removes the requirement that the fixed-point system be computed at each iteration, but at the expense of increasing the number of variables — and worse, the number of constraints. Considering that the computation time of nonlinear programming algorithms increases rapidly with the number of constraints, it is not clear that the transformation will yield smaller overall times. Nevertheless, the transformation is useful for theoretical reasons, which is how the development is presented.

We reformulate the optimal routing as a function of three sets of *independent* variables, $A_k^{i,j}$, B_s, and a_s. The first set represents the true decision variables, while the others are linked to the traffic and trunk-group sizes by the traffic model. To ensure that the B_s and a_s variables conform to the traffic model, we add *constraints* to the optimization problem that force the correct relation between these variables. From Eq. (7.16), we see that L^m is a function of the B_s only; from Eq. (7.17), that $\overline{A}^m$ is a function of A^m and L^m only. The optimal load sharing is given by the solution of

$$\min \ z = \sum_{i,j,k} L_k^{i,j} A_k^{i,j}, \tag{7.19}$$

subject to the constraints

$$B_t = E(a_t, N_t) \quad (w_t) \tag{7.20}$$

$$a_t = \sum_{m|t\in m} \frac{\overline{A}^m}{(1 - B_t)} \quad (z_t) \tag{7.21}$$

$$\sum_k A_k^{i,j} = A^{i,j} \quad (v^{i,j})$$

$$A_k^{i,j} \geq 0 \quad (u_k^{i,j})$$

Constraints (7.20) and (7.21) force the correct traffic model on the offered traffic and link-blocking variables, while the other two sets represent real constraints on the decision variables. We can construct the Lagrange function by the standard method, obtaining

$$\mathcal{L} = \sum_m L^m(B)A^m + \sum_s w_s \left[B_s - E(a_s, N_s) \right] + \tag{7.22}$$

$$\sum_s z_s \left[a_s - \sum_{m|s\in m} A^m \prod_{\substack{q\neq s \\ q\in m}} (1 - B_q) \right] -$$

$$\sum_{i,j} v^{i,j} \left[\sum_k A_k^{i,j} - A^{i,j} \right] - \sum_{i,j,k} u_k^{i,j} A_k^{i,j}$$

We now set the derivative with respect to the independent variables a_s, B_s, and $A_k^{i,j}$ equal to zero, obtaining

$$z_s = w_s \frac{\partial E_s}{\partial a_s} \tag{7.23}$$

$$w_s (1 - B_s) = - \sum_{m|s\in m} \overline{A}^m - \sum_{t\neq s} w_t \eta_t \sum_{\substack{m|t\in m \\ m|s\in m}} \overline{A}^m \tag{7.24}$$

$$u_k^{i,j} = v^{i,j} + L^{i,j} - (1 - L^{i,j}) \sum_{t\in(ijk)} z_t \frac{1 - L_k^{i,j}}{1 - B_t} \tag{7.25}$$

where

$$\begin{aligned} \eta_s &\triangleq \frac{\partial E_s}{\partial a_s} \frac{1}{1 - B_s} \\ &= E(a_s, N_s - 1) - E(a_s, N_s) \\ &= (\overline{a}_s(N) - \overline{a}_s(N - 1))/a_s \end{aligned} \tag{7.26}$$

We now rewrite Eq. (7.24) in a simpler form. First we multiply Eq. (7.24) by η_s. We then change the sign of w_w to simplify the interpretation — we can do this because w_s is the multiplier of an equality constraint and is not constrained in sign. Note that $\sum_{m|s\in m} \overline{A}^m$ is the total traffic carried on link s and that $\sum_{m|s\in m} \overline{A}^m/(1 - B_s)$ is then a_s, the total traffic offered to s. Denote $a_s \eta_s \triangleq \Delta \overline{a}_s(N)$. This is the amount of traffic carried on the last circuit *assuming that the offered traffic a_s is constant*. We call this quantity the *gross marginal capacity* of trunk group s. Similarly, $\sum_{\substack{m|t\in m \\ m|s\in m}} \overline{A}^m$ is the traffic carried on s that was also carried on t; in other words, this is the amount of carried traffic that does not belong to the $(o(s), d(s))$ stream. When divided by $(1 - B_s)$, this is the offered traffic that does not belong to the $(o(s), d(s))$ stream, which we denote by $\Delta \overline{a}_s^t$. Eq. (7.24) can then be written

$$w_s \eta_s = \Delta \overline{a}_s - \sum_{t\neq s} w_t \eta_t \Delta \overline{a}_s^t \tag{7.27}$$

From this equation, we see that $w_s \eta_s$ can be interpreted as the *net* marginal capacity of group s. We have seen that $\Delta \overline{a}_s$ is the gross marginal capacity: It is the amount of traffic that can be carried on the last trunk on s at fixed offered traffic. The effect on the traffic carried on group s of increasing the group size from $N - 1$ to N is more complex if link s is in a network than the simple expression for $\Delta \bar{a}_s$. Adding an extra circuit has two effects: (1) the carried traffic increases by the amount $\Delta \bar{a}_s$, but (2) the offered traffic a_s changes to reflect the change in the solution of the fixed-point system. Eq. (7.27) means that the marginal capacity has to be corrected to take into account this effect and that the correction term is the sum of the net marginal capacities on the other links in the network that belong to all the paths that use link s.

Equation (7.25) also has an interesting interpretation. For a given stream (i,j), and for those paths that carry some traffic, the multipliers $u_k^{i,j} = 0$ because of the complementary conditions. Eq. (7.25) then becomes:

$$v^{i,j} = L_k^{i,j} - (1 - L_k^{i,j}) \sum_{t \in (i,j,k)} w_t \eta_t \tag{7.28}$$

Since $v^{i,j}$ does not depend on k, the optimal routing is given by the condition that for this stream, we should have

$$L_k^{i,j} = (1 - L_k^{i,j}) \sum_{t \in (i,j,k)} w_t \eta_t$$

The optimal policy is not to equalize the blocking, as might be guessed. Rather, the parameters to be equalized are more complex, depending on the interrelation of the traffic on all the links represented by the ws. Note, however, that there exist link weights w_t *independent of the commodity*, such that the optimal sharing equalizes the right-hand side of Eq. (7.28). The actual derivation of Eqs. (7.23–7.25) presents no difficulty and is left as an exercise (Problem 7.8).

Revenue Optimization

Similarly, we can analyze the optimal routing using some revenue-maximization principle. We rephrase the derivation of [12], but using the expanded model to obtain simpler optimality conditions. The model also serves to introduce the notion of the net revenue of a call on a path — the basis for many proposed new routing methods. First we assume that a call connected on path r brings a revenue w^r. As usual, we avoid the difficulty of the fixed-point system by expanding the number of variables, adding constraints to reflect the traffic model selected. In the present case, the extra variables are B_s, and the link-offered traffic is only an intermediate variable used in the calculations. The optimization problem is defined as

$$\min_{A,B} - \sum_r \overline{A}^r w^r \tag{7.29}$$

$$A^r \geq 0 \quad (u^r) \tag{7.30}$$

$$B_s = E(a_s, N_s) \quad (v_s) \tag{7.31}$$

We know that, at the solution, we must have $B_s < 1$ since the blocking probability on a link can never attain the upper limit. This condition means that we can set the multiplier corresponding to this constraint equal to zero and that the multiplier will not appear in the expression of the Lagrange function. We make the further simplification that, at the optimal value, we will have $B_s > 0$. With this assumption, we can also set the other multiplier to zero, and thus we need not include it in the Lagrange function. Although there is no guarantee that a solution has a blocking probability of zero, this simplification does not invalidate the conclusions that follow. The same conclusions could be drawn without the simplification, but at the cost of a more complex notation, obscuring the important features of the method.

We define the auxiliary quantities a_s, the total traffic offered to link s, and Q^r, the connection probability on path r,

$$a_s = \frac{\bar{a}_s}{(1 - B_s)}$$

$$= \frac{1}{(1 - B_s)} \sum_{j|s \in j} \bar{A}^j$$

$$= \frac{1}{(1 - B_s)} \sum_{j|s \in j} A^j (1 - L^j).$$

$$Q^r = \prod_{s \in r} 1 - B_s$$

where once again we use the reduced-traffic method in calculating the traffic offered to a link in a multilink path. The Lagrange function can be written

$$\mathcal{L} = -\sum_r w^r A^r (1 - L^r) - \sum_r u^r A^r + \sum_s v_s [B_s - E(a_s, N_s)], \quad (7.32)$$

and the complementary conditions,

$$v_s (B_s - E(a_s, N_s)) = 0,$$

$$u^r A^r = 0, \quad u^r \geq 0$$

The optimality conditions are written in two groups, corresponding to the A and B variables, respectively. In the first case, we obtain the optimality equation for path j:

$$u^j = -w^j (1 - L^j) - (1 - L^j) \sum_{s \in j} v_s \frac{\partial E}{\partial a_s} \frac{1}{1 - B_s}.$$

This equation can be interpreted from the complementarity conditions to yield a useful routing rule. Suppose that $A^j > 0$ on some path j. Then, we must have $u^j = 0$, and the optimality condition is just that

$$w^j = \sum_{s \in j} v_s \eta_s.$$

If, on the other hand, $u^j > 0$, then $A^j = 0$, and the path should not be used. In this case, we must have

$$\sum_{s \in j} v_s \eta_s > w^j. \tag{7.33}$$

Recall that w^j is the revenue generated by the call carried on path j. The equation states that a path should not be used if this revenue is less than the left-hand side. To understand why a call should not be connected on a path that is not blocked, consider the following economic explanation. The call connection will change the loss probability on the other network paths, inducing a loss of revenue on these paths. From an economic point of view, it is reasonable not to use a path if this loss of revenue is larger (in absolute value) than the revenue expected from the call — precisely what Eq. (7.33) says if we interpret the left-hand side as this loss of revenue on the path. In this case, each term of the sum is the lost revenue on each link in the path; we can interpret $v_s \eta_s$ as the lost revenue for each additional call carried on link s. This interpretation is, of course, supported by Eq. (7.26).

Note that the existence of a set of multipliers v_s is guaranteed by the existence of an optimal solution — somewhat unexpected, since there are many more paths than links in the network. It is not at all obvious that it is possible to find a set of link multipliers, independent of the commodity, that determine the optimal-path costs such that all optimality conditions are met for all paths simultaneously. Nevertheless, the existence of the Kuhn-Tucker multipliers precisely implies the existence of link parameters that take exactly the right value at the optimum solution to ensure the correct selection of paths. This solution suggests a practical routing rule based on the flow-deviation principle, which routes calls on the least-cost path, where the path cost is computed from the link costs $v_s \eta_s$.

Although the preceding result has a reasonable economic interpretation, we still do not have a value for the multipliers v_s. We can obtain this value by considering the other set of necessary conditions, obtained by taking the gradient with respect to B_s. We get

$$v_t \eta_t = -\frac{\Delta \bar{a}_t}{\bar{a}_t} \left(\sum_{s \neq t} v_s \eta_s \sum_{j \mid \substack{s \in j \\ t \in j}} \overline{A}^j + \sum_{j \mid t \in j} w^j \overline{A}^j \right). \tag{7.34}$$

In other words, v_s is the solution of a linear system, where the coefficients are given by traffic parameters on the links through the quantities η_s and B_s. The expression $\Delta \bar{a}_t / \bar{a}_t$ is the fraction of the total carried traffic that is carried on the last trunk of group t. The expression $\left(\sum_{s \neq t} v_s \eta_s \sum_{j \mid \substack{s \in j \\ t \in j}} \overline{A}^j + \sum_{j \mid t \in j} w^j \overline{A}^j \right)$ is the net value of all the traffic carried on the group: The first part is the cost induced on groups other than t by the traffic carried on t while the second term is the value of this traffic on t. This is another manifestation of the strong coupling that occurs in networks operating with nonhierarchical routing, where the state of one link may affect the rest of the network in a very complicated way.

Calculating a solution of the optimal load-sharing coefficients is still quite difficult: The optimality equations form a set of coupled nonlinear equations, whose solution is not particularly easy. The theory discussed here can lead to a practical rule if we make the following assumptions [13]. Suppose that the network has some capability for computation and traffic measurement. Note that the coefficients of the linear system that determines the multipliers depend on link-traffic parameters and on the traffic carried on each path. If measurements are taken for traffic values, then these coefficients can be computed on-line. From these values, it is possible to compute the current best value for the v_s and then to use Eq. (7.34) to select the least-cost path for routing. The solution of the linear system may be done in either a centralized or a decentralized manner, provided the nodes can exchange sufficient information during the solution process. In this way, an adaptive decentralized algorithm can be implemented to track the optimality conditions of the revenue-maximization problem in the presence of slow variations of the input parameters — the essence of adaptive routing.

A number of comparisons have been made among the various adaptive methods [14,15,16]; all indicate that adaptive load sharing is a potentially useful routing policy. Because of the small number of studies, however, we cannot yet determine how adaptive load sharing competes with other methods such as DCR, or what adaptation rule is best under realistic conditions. For these reasons, we now turn to alternate routing, a class of routing policies more frequently used in today's networks, as well as to the corresponding optimization problems.

7.3   Alternate Routing

We have seen how to achieve routing optimization over the set of load-sharing policies. While load sharing has many interesting theoretical properties, it is inefficient and has a poorer performance than the other routing techniques — the reason it is not often used in real networks, where most current methods are of the alternate routing type. Even when limited to two-link alternate routes, these policies are considerably more difficult to optimize than load-sharing policies, since the optimum route must be searched over the finite set of tandem nodes available to each stream and over the permutations of these nodes. This requires nonlinear combinatorial optimization methods, which are difficult to solve numerically. Most integer programming methods, such as branch and bound, rely on some relaxation of the problem to the reals in order to compute a bound for the optimal solution and to prune the tree of possible solutions.

Purely combinatorial problems cannot easily be extended to some real domain. As an example, if the optimization is done over all permutations of some set of N variables, this amounts to searching for the optimal solution over the set of all $N \times N$ permutation matrices. A relaxation of the problem could then be defined by replacing the search over the permutation matrices by a search over the set of doubly stochastic matrices, which is a closed subset of the reals; standard mathematical programming methods could be used for this search. The difficulty is that it is unclear how to compute the objective function in terms of these matrices. In the case of routing, it is unclear even how to *express* the notion of alternate routing in terms of these stochastic matrices, making the *calculation* of any quantity such as the network blocking from these variables even less clear. Thus most of the standard techniques of integer programming are useless for optimizing alternate routing directly. Considering the nonlinear character of the functions, implicit enumeration is generally unfeasible — which leaves heuristics as the only feasible method for networks of realistic sizes.

The optimization of alternate routing has been studied from two practical points of view. In the first, load-sharing methods are extended to what has been called the *route formulation* of routing optimization. In the second, greedy heuristics operating directly in the problem domain are used in a direct attack on the problem.

Alternate Routing Optimization by Load Sharing

Load sharing can be used to optimize alternate routing by assuming that the objective function is very flat around the optimal solutions or, conversely, that there exist a large number of routes having potentially very different structures, but all producing essentially the same value for the objective function. One selects a small sample of routes, using load sharing to determine which route is most attractive. If the load-sharing coefficients are all nearly equal, this indicates that the selected routes are nearly equivalent and that any of them could be used with good results. (This conclusion, of course, would have to be checked by evaluating the objective function for this case.) On the other hand, if one of the selected routes is not good, its load-sharing coefficient will be small in the solution; it can be excluded from consideration.

Note that the actual alternate path sequences are *not* the subject of optimization, but are given a priori; the only decision variables are the sharing coefficients. The optimization method is conceptually the same as that used for ordinary load sharing, but the objective function is more difficult to evaluate since it is derived from a complex set of route trees.

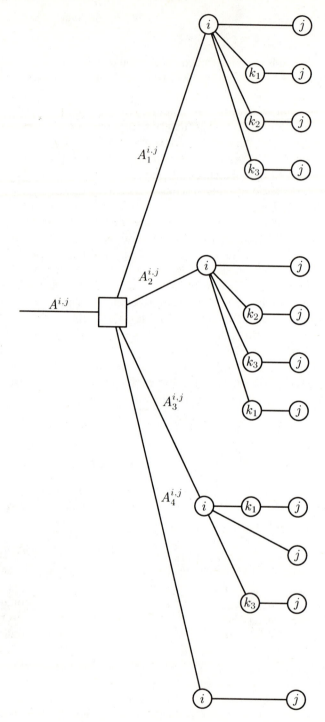

Figure 7.3 Route Formulation for Nonhierarchical Routing

The method can be represented graphically as in Fig.7.3, where the original flow is split among the various routings, then merged to obtain the carried traffic. The routing optimization problem is given by

$$\min_{A} \ z = \sum_{i,j} A_k^{i,j} L_k^{i,j}(A),$$ (7.35)

subject to

$$\sum_k A_k^{i,j} = A^{i,j} \quad (v^{i,j})$$

$$A_k^{i,j} \geq 0 \quad (u_k^{i,j})$$

Computing $L_k^{i,j}(A)$ is a straightforward extension of the methods of Chapter 4 for the evaluation of end-to-end blocking in nonhierarchical networks, where each offered traffic $A^{i,j}$ is offered to a single route. In this case, this single route is replaced by a set of $M^{i,j}$ routes, each offered a traffic $A_k^{i,j}$. Because the original traffic is split at random, the input streams to the various i, j routes are independent, and each such stream can be considered as a new traffic flow with its own routing. Thus the evaluation of $L_k^{i,j}(A)$ with $N(N-1)$ route trees, and the same number of traffic flows, is replaced by the calculation of the end-to-end blocking with $\sum_{i,j} M^{i,j}$ traffic flows, and the same number of routes, which can be solved by standard methods.

The optimal solution of this optimization problem has been characterized in [17] by writing the first-order Kuhn-Tucker conditions

$$\frac{\partial z}{\partial A_l^k} - v^k - u_l^k = 0$$

and, for those routes having positive traffic,

$$\frac{\partial z}{\partial A_l^k} = v^k.$$

Hence we find the same equal-sharing rule for the optimal strategy: Share the load in such a way that the marginal loss is equalized *on each route*. A flow-deviation-like algorithm can be defined [17] to compute a solution as follows. At a given point A_k^l, compute a search direction **d** for each stream l given by (we drop the stream index for simplicity)

$$c_l = \frac{\partial z}{\partial A_l} - \frac{\partial z}{\partial A_j} \quad \forall j$$

$$d_l = \min_j \{A_k, \epsilon c_j\}$$

where ϵ is a constant chosen to ensure convergence of the algorithm. This direction is then used to search for a minimum, which serves as the current point for the next iteration. Although there is no proof, it is claimed that the algorithm has converged in practice.

The optimality equations are expressed in terms of route blocking. In the spirit of multicommodity-flow methods, it would be interesting to have a condition in terms of paths, as described for the load-sharing case. Although accomplished somewhat, it is not obvious whether this leads to a practical implementation for routing optimization.

We can write a set of Kuhn-Tucker equations similar to Eqs. (7.23–7.25) by expanding the problem to include the fixed-point equations as constraints. We assume that the link-blocking probabilities B_s and the link-offered traffic a_s are independent variables, in addition to the flow values offered to each route. We add constraints to the optimization problem to ensure that the proper relation between these quantities corresponding to the solution of the fixed-point equations is met at the optimal solution. The traffic model has the same form as in Eqs. (7.16–7.18), with one important difference: In Eq. (7.17), the traffic offered to path m is the variable A^m and is independent of the link-blocking probabilities. It can be considered as a constant when deriving the optimality equation (7.23–7.25). This is not so in the present case because the traffic offered to a path is the overflow from other paths in the route tree to which m belongs; this traffic *does* depend on the blocking probabilities in that tree. Calculating the optimality equations thus becomes somewhat more complex, as we proceed to show.

For simplicity, we assume that the alternate routing is via two-link paths with originating office control. This is not necessary; the technique used here could be used with other control methods and more complex paths. The assumption, however, simplifies the notation and is justified by the fact that two-link alternate routing is the rule for all nonhierarchical routing methods currently implemented in or proposed for real networks. Under this assumption, we can express $\overline{A}^m$, the traffic carried on this path, as a function of the link-blocking probabilities B_s. First we must define some auxiliary quantities. Consider a route tree r. Suppose that path m appears on the lth position in the tree and denote the two links on this path l_1 and l_2. In some cases, when the index of one link is given by s, we label the other link by s'. Let the probability that this path is blocked $\mathcal{P}_l^r = [1 - (1 - B_{l_1})(1 - B_{l_2})]$, and the probability that a call is blocked on all paths preceding level l by $P_l^r = \prod_{j=1}^{l-1} \mathcal{P}_j^r$, which is the probability that a call will overflow beyond level $l - 1$. We also use the convention that $B_{l_2} = 0$ if the path is the single-link path. The traffic carried on the path is given by the reduced-load method

$$
\begin{aligned}
\overline{A}^m &= A^r P_l^r (1 - B_{l_1})(1 - B_{l_2}) \\
&= A^r P_l^r (1 - \mathcal{P}_l^r),
\end{aligned}
\tag{7.36}
$$

where A^r is the traffic offered to route tree r. The total traffic offered to link

s is given by

$$a_s = \sum_{m|s\in m} \frac{\overline{A}^m}{(1 - B_s)},$$

where the sum is carried over all paths m. This sum can be replaced by a sum over all route trees by using the fact that link s appears at most once in a given route tree. We get

$$a_s = \sum_{l|s\in l} \frac{\overline{A}^l}{(1 - B_s)}$$

$$= \sum_r \sum_{l|\substack{s\in l \\ l\in r}} \frac{A^r}{(1 - B_s)} P_m^r (1 - B_s)(1 - B_{s'})$$

$$= \sum_{r|s\in r} A^r P_m^r (1 - B_{s'}).$$

It should be emphasized that A^r is the traffic offered to route r and is independent of the link-blocking probabilities. The Lagrange function is exactly as in Eq. (7.22). Taking the derivative with respect to the variables, we obtain the same first-order optimality conditions as for the load-sharing case (7.23–7.25). The derivation of the equation for the w_s multipliers is more complex, however, since A^m is not independent of the B_ss. We get

$$w_t = \sum_{s\neq t} z_s \sum_{m|s\in m} A^m \prod_{\substack{q\in m \\ q\neq s \\ q\neq t}} (1 - B_q) + \sum_s z_s \sum_{m|t\in m} \prod_{\substack{q\in m \\ q\neq s}} (1 - B_q) \frac{\partial A^m}{\partial B_t}$$

The second term appears because the variation of blocking probabilities of other links may affect A^m, the traffic offered to path m. This effect is summarized in the computation of $\partial A^m / \partial B_t$:

$$\frac{\partial A^m}{\partial B_t} = \sum_{r|s\in r} A^r \frac{\partial P_l^r}{\partial B_t}.$$

This derivative can be computed by considering the following cases:

1. The blocking probability of the traffic offered to some path l in a tree r does not depend on the blocking probability of links that do not appear in r or do not precede l in r. This is the case because of the assumption that the link-offered traffics are independent variables, and that the path-blocking probabilities are functions of the B_t variables only. For these cases,

$$\frac{\partial A^m}{\partial B_t} = 0.$$

2. Assume now that link t does appear in tree r at level $k < l$. The variable B_t occurs only in the term $(1 - \mathcal{P}_k^r) = (1 - B_t)(1 - B_{t'})$. Taking the derivative, we get

$$\frac{\partial A^m}{\partial B_t} = \prod_{\substack{j=1 \\ j \neq k}}^{l-1} \mathcal{P}_j^r (1 - B_{t'})$$

$$= A^r P_l^r \frac{(1 - B_{t'})}{\mathcal{P}_m^r}.$$

This calculation can be made relatively efficiently, and the results used to compute search directions in optimizing the load-sharing coefficients. Note, however, that the optimal-routing rule is to equalize the marginal routing cost on *routes*, which does not translate easily in a condition on the the marginal cost of *paths*. As a consequence, the use of the flow-deviation method, although still possible in theory, can no longer be based on calculating shortest paths for resolving the subproblems.

Production of Candidate Routes

The route-formulation method relies on a predetermined set of candidate routes that remain unchanged throughout the optimization procedure. Little work has been done on methods for generating candidate routes. For nonhierarchical two-link alternate routing, limited statistical sampling [18] indicates that there is a large number of very different routings with approximately the same blocking. Thus, provided some simple conditions are fulfilled, the actual choice of routes may not be very important for the final result [19]. This area remains to be studied in more detail.

Combinatorial Methods

Routing optimization by load-sharing techniques uses a predefined set of alternate routes whose structure is given in advance. The final result depends on the initial choice of candidate routes — a rather small number because of the computational requirements of the optimization method To avoid the possibility that a good routing has been left out of the initial set, the routes can be optimized over all possible configurations. This problem is considerably more difficult to solve because of the discrete domain of the problem (that is, the set of permutations of tandems in each route), as well as the decision to include each particular node in each route tree. Needless to say, an exact solution is unthinkable for any network of reasonable size, and only heuristics have been proposed to optimize routing in this way.

We now present such a combinatorial method, using it to compute the optimal routing directly by a search in the space of route trees. Despite the fact that only heuristics are available, we shall see that the results are quite close to those obtained by some path models and thus may be close to optimal. We seek to minimize Eq. (7.35) over all the routing trees and therefore must solve the optimization problem

$$\min \ z = \sum_{(i,j)} L^{i,j} A^{i,j},$$

where the minimization is to be carried over the set of all route trees that describe two-link alternate routing. We limit the case to two-link alternate routes since we wish to avoid alternate routing over long paths because it produces very high blocking under overload. Obviously, more complex route trees could be handled by the method, at the expense of longer computation times and more complex approximations.

The heuristic is defined by analogy with descent methods in compact domains. The notion of an infinitesimal displacement is replaced by elementary transformations of route trees, and neighborhoods by sets of route trees that can be reached from the current point by a single elementary transformation. The transformations retained are of three types. In a given tree, we can

a. Add a tandem in the last position,

b. Remove the last tandem, or

c. Permute two adjacent tandems.

This set is complete in the sense that we can span the routing space by repeated applications of a, b and c, as we can span $\Re^n$ by a series of displacements in the neighborhood of the current point. We must also define descent directions, as in the optimization in $\Re^n$. Let

$$\delta_l^{i,j} = z^0 - z^l \qquad i = a, b, c$$

where

z^l = Performance of the network after elementary transformation l.

z^0 = Performance of the network at the current point.

$\delta_l^{i,j}$ represents the improvement in performance when transformation l is applied to the route tree of commodity (i,j). A simplified descent algorithm can be defined as follows:

1. Initialize the routing. For example, we can take the routing without overflow. Evaluate z^0.

2. For each origin-destination pair (i, j), evaluate

$$\delta_a^{i,j}, \delta_b^{i,j}, \delta_c^{i,j}.$$

3. Compute

$$\min_{i,j} \min_{k \in \{a,b,c\}} \delta_k^{i,j}.$$

We retain the transformation that gives the greatest reduction. Let δ^* be the maximum blocking variation.

4. If $\delta^* < \xi$, stop. If not,

    a. Modify the routing tables according to the transformation corresponding to δ^*.

    b. Update $z_0 \leftarrow z_l$.

    c. Go to 2.

This method requires considerable computation time and thus cannot be used on networks of more than a few nodes. It can be made more efficient by using an approximate algorithm to evaluate the δs, and by retaining more than one elementary transformation at each iteration.

Estimation of δ.   In principle, one must completely recompute the value of z for each elementary transformation, requiring the computation of all the $L^{i,j}$s and consequently the solution of the fixed-point equations (4.39). We can, however, speed the procedure by noting that one elementary transformation creates a very small change in the link flows to define an approximation of δ for a given tree. Take, for example, the case where we add a tandem node k in the last position in tree (i, j). To simplify the notation, we assume that there are $k - 1$ tandem nodes in the tree before the addition of the new node. Thus the index k denotes the number of the tandem in the list of nodes, as well as its position in the i, j tree. The addition of a tandem to the (i, j) tree produces two opposite effects:

1. The blocking probability $L^{i,j}$ decreases since an additional path is available to route the (i, j) calls.

2. Some of the $L^{k,l}$ increase since the probabilities of blocking on (i, k) and (k, j) will increase because of the added traffic offered to path (i, j, k).

We must evaluate these two effects under the following simplifying hypotheses:

h_1: The probabilities of blocking on all the network links remain unchanged, except for links (i, k) and (k, j).

h_2: The blocking variation introduced by a transformation affects only the (i, j) traffic, and we must make a computation for the (i, j) tree only.

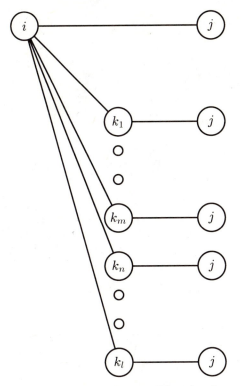

Figure 7.4 i, j Route Tree before Transformation

These assumptions are required in order to avoid solving the Erlang fixed-point system after each elementary transformation.

The traffic normally lost before the addition of k was $A^{i,j} P_k^{i,j}$ and, with the new tandem, we get

$$A^{i,j} P_k^{i,j} \left[1 - (1 - B_{i,k})(1 - B_{k,j}) \right].$$

The difference is therefore

$$A^{i,j} P_k^{i,j} \left[1 - (1 - (1 - B_{i,k})(1 - B_{k,j})) \right]$$

and

$$\delta_1 = A^{i,j} P_k^{i,j} (1 - B_{i,k})(1 - B_{k,j}).$$

Hypotheses h_1 and h_2 permit us to compute this expression by using the B_{ik} and B_{kj} *before* the elementary transformation, making it unnecessary to solve the flow equations again.

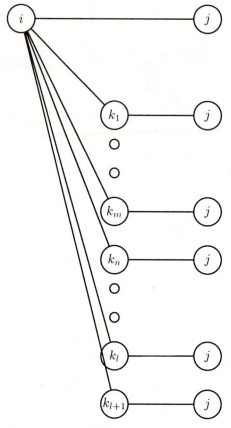

Figure 7.5   Route Tree after Elementary Transformations

The traffic offered to link (i, k) increases by a quantity $\delta a_{ik} \simeq \delta_1$. The variation of the blocking probability thus produced can be expressed by

$$\delta B_{i_k} \approx \frac{\partial E}{\partial a_{i_k}} \delta a_{i_k},$$

and we can estimate the corresponding variation in traffic:

$$\delta T_{i,k} \simeq -\delta B_{ik}(a_{ik} + \delta a_{ik}).$$

The net estimate of the variation in traffic carried for this elementary transformation is given by

$$\delta_a^{i,j} = \delta_1 + \delta T_{ik} + \delta T_{kj}. \tag{7.37}$$

We proceed in the same way for δ_b and δ_c. Calculating the approximation in performance variation for these two cases is left as an exercise (see Problem 7.9).

Number of Transformations per Iteration. By using the approximations described in the previous section, we need not recompute a solution of the fixed-point equations at each tentative transformation. This still must be done after a transformation has been chosen, placing a heavy computational load on the method. Another way to shorten the computation times is to use the fact that introducing a single change in the routing is unlikely to change the solution of the fixed point very much. Assuming this is true, we could implement not one, but say the k best transformations before recalculating a solution of the fixed point. If we make many changes in a given iteration, however, the estimates of the gains in the objective function δ^* are less accurate since the changes in the link-blocking probabilities are larger. A balance must be found between the two improvements. In practice, it seems best to undertake 50 to 100 changes per iteration for average-size networks.

Method	Optimal Blocking (%)	CPU Time (secs.)
Shortest path (one moment)	.00317	18.9
Shortest path (two moments)	.00331	89.6
Combinatorial	.00324	38.7

Table 7.1 Comparison of Two Routing-Optimization Methods

Performance Comparison. Few direct comparisons have been made between routing-optimization algorithms. We present here the results of [20], where the path algorithm for iterative route construction is compared with the route-generation method of Section 7.3 in terms of both the speed of the calculation and the cost of the final solution. The methods were compared for the nine-node network of [21]. In practice, the two methods both achieved reasonable computing times and equivalent performances. The values of the actual computation times and total network blocking are shown in Table 7.1.

The main advantage of routing optimization through load sharing is that it is easy to control the size of the optimization problem to be solved by adjusting the number of candidate routings. The size of the problem, as measured by the number of variables, is given by $N(N-1)K$, where K is the number of choices (often identical for all commodities) permitted for each traffic stream. In both cases, we end up with optimization problems with a nonlinear differentiable objective, and linear constraints with a particularly simple structure. Very efficient methods [22] exist for solving problems of this type when the size is not overly large, providing yet another advantage for the route formulation.

The major disadvantage is that the candidate routes are chosen a priori, and because the number of possible routes is extremely large, they may not include the optimal route, or even a good solution. Also, the optimization problems tend to be large if enough routes are included that there is a significant chance of a good one in the original set. This means that quasi-Newton optimization methods cannot be used because of their large memory requirement. Also, the family of load-sharing policies may not be the most efficient possible, as indicated by some partial results obtained by simulation.

The combinatorial optimization method operates from the policies used in practice but is considerably harder to compute. It seems that good heuristics are possible, but relatively little work has been done on the subject; there is obviously room for more.

7.4   Route-Realization Techniques

A multicommodity model is defined by its congestion and objective functions. The congestion functions are defined for the link flows, corresponding either to a measure of transmission cost or to blocking. Based on these functions, an objective function is constructed representing a network grade-of-service measure. The traffic streams are then allocated to the various paths to minimize the objective function, generally the average blocking or some measure of marginal cost. The net result of the optimization is a set of *carried* flows on all the paths of the network that is optimal for the multicommodity problem. This method obviates the need to propose a fixed set of paths a priori, since paths appear as the *result* of the optimization process. There is also the advantage of using efficient optimization methods such as the flow-deviation algorithm.

The flows produced by the solution of the multicommodity model represent the expected values of the state variables of the Markov decision process. This is the only information produced by the model, which does not prescribe an actual implementation of a routing policy. As a consequence, an extra step must be performed after the multicommodity optimization — to synthesize a policy, subject to the constraints imposed by the values computed from the model.

In general, simply sharing the load between the paths in the same proportion as those given by the flows will not work: The relation between the traffic offered to a path and the traffic it carries is a complex function of the statistical character of the arrival and service processes that cannot be controlled by the use of load sharing. This is best explained by a simple example. Consider a two-node network with two distinct links of sizes N_1 and N_2, respectively, connecting the nodes. Assume that there is some traffic A offered at node i for node j and that we want to optimize the routing. The problem consists of finding the amount of flow that will go on each path subject to some constraints. The particular type of constraints determines the optimization model used to compute the solution. Let f_1 and f_2 denote the amount of flow carried on links

1 and 2, respectively. If we choose to solve the routing-optimization problem by a multicommodity flow algorithm, then the feasible domain is given by the equation $f_1 + f_2 = A$ and the usual nonnegativity conditions. If, on the other hand, we choose to use the load-sharing model, then the domain constraint is

$$f_1 = \alpha A[1 - E(\alpha A, N_1)]$$
$$f_2 = (1 - \alpha)A[1 - E(A(1 - \alpha), N_2)]$$
$$0 \le \alpha \le 1$$

Similarly, the domain of alternate routing of the overflow of link one on link 2 is given by

$$f_1 = AE[1 - E(A, N)]$$
$$f_2 = (A - f_1)[1 - E(A - f_1, N)]$$

and reduces to a single point as shown in Fig. 7.6. It is not difficult to see that the domain defined by the load-sharing equations is different from the multicommodity domain. This is clearly shown in the figure. The point is that if we compute a solution in the multicommodity domain, then there does not exist any load-sharing solution that can realize these flows, since the two domains are disjoint. Also note that, in the present case, alternate routing is not a solution either. The dilemma, then, is whether to use a fast multicommodity algorithm, attempting to implement the resulting flows with a sufficiently accurate routing algorithm, or to work directly with the chosen routing technique, but at the expense of solving a much more difficult problem.

In practice, some set of flows is often realized by selecting a class of routing policies (the most frequent being a combination of alternate routing and load sharing), and fitting some suitably chosen set of parameters of the routing. In all cases, there is a question of the feasibility of the prescribed flows from within the chosen class, as well as selecting the appropriate parameters to meet the prescribed flows. This synthesis procedure can be repeated after each flow computation, or can be performed only once, at the end of the flow optimization.

Iterative Route Construction

Consider the situation where a multicommodity flow model has been used to produce a set of path flows that minimizes some objective function. As noted before, this solution does not specify how to route the individual calls in order to produce these flows. One possibility is to construct these routes iteratively *while doing the flow optimization*. The routes are modified in discrete steps, which means that ordinary flow-deviation algorithms cannot be used. Nevertheless, some measure of flow optimization can be retained, as shown by the following method [20].

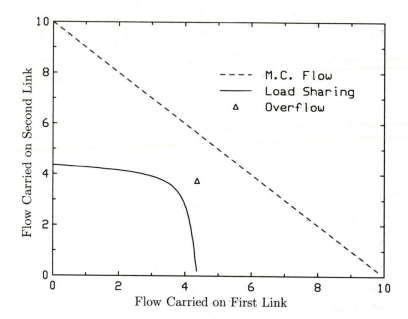

Figure 7.6 A Comparison of the Multicommodity and Load-Sharing Domains for a Two-Link Network: $A = 10$, $N_1 = N_2 = 10$

The policy selected is fixed nonhierarchical alternate routing. In this case, the link costs are based on marginal blocking, although any other function could be used. The important difference with ordinary flow deviation is that the routing tables are constructed as the flow optimization is done. The algorithm has the following form:

1. Set $n = 1$. Here n denotes the number of tandems in the route trees; $n = 1$ means we use only the direct path.

2. Compute, for the current n, the end-to-end blocking probability and the traffic flows in the network.

3. From the current values of the traffic in the network, compute $\partial E/\partial A$ for each link, where A is the total traffic to the link. This function was chosen in [20] by analogy with ordinary flow deviation, although, as we have seen, marginal overflow might be a better choice.

4. Sort all the paths in increasing order of length, where this length is defined by $\sum \partial E/\partial A$ on the path. This constitutes the routing table for the current iteration.

5. Compute the network performance for the current tables. If there is an improvement, go to 3. If not, stop. The optimum routing corresponds to the current value of n.

6. Repeat steps 2 to 5 for n until $N - 1$.

At the end of the procedure, we have a set of routing tables and the corresponding network flows. Thus, no synthesis phase is required — the main advantage of the method.

Another possibility is to carry out the flow optimization to optimality, constructing the corresponding alternate routing tables after this procedure is completed. Although usually examined in the context of the Unified Algorithm for DNHR [23], this possibility is discussed here because it is really a routing-optimization problem. Three methods have been proposed for realizing a set of path flows. In decreasing order of accuracy, they are

1. The Chung-Graham-Hwang algorithm [24].

2. The skip-one-path algorithm.

3. The sequential path algorithm.

We briefly review each algorithm, outlining the main results and pointing out the computational requirements for both network planning and real-time implementation.

The Chung-Graham-Hwang Algorithm

The routing algorithm proposed in [24] to realize a given flow pattern is a mixture of load sharing and alternate routing. In its most general form, all routes that can be constructed from a given set of paths can be used. The problem is to compute a set of load-sharing coefficients, one for each route, such that the flows carried on each path will match the prescribed value. In practice, this is too difficult since the number of potential routes for k paths is $k!$; a number of simplifications are used to achieve a more manageable algorithm. The example discussed here applies to OOC, but the method could presumably be extended to other controls.

Consider the following situation. It has been determined by some unspecified mean, typically a flow-deviation algorithm, that the traffic for a given origin-destination pair, should be carried on paths numbered from 1 to n, and that each path k should carry a traffic of $\overline{A}_k$. Also, each path has a known blocking probability $\mathcal{P}_k$. The $\overline{\mathbf{A}}$ and $\mathcal{P}$ vectors are given; we would like to construct a sequence of alternate routes out of the given paths that generates carried flows as close as possible to the $\overline{\mathbf{A}}$ vector. A particular route R is defined by a permutation π of the original set of paths, where the paths are attempted

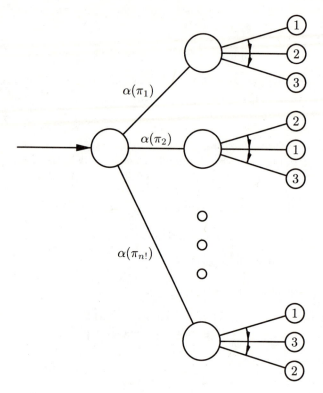

Figure 7.7   The Algorithm of Chung, Graham, and Hwang

in the order $(\pi(1), \pi(2) \ldots \pi(k))$, allowing us to speak equivalently of a route or of the permutation that characterizes it. Because it is quite unlikely that a single permutation will have the prescribed carried flows, we assume that all the $k!$ permutations can be used to carry traffic, with load sharing between each route with coefficient $\alpha(\pi)$ (see Fig. 7.7). Thus $\alpha(\pi)$ is the fraction of the offered traffic offered to the route $R(\pi)$ defined by permutation π.

For a given route π, we can compute the proportion of the traffic offered to the route that is carried on each path, denoted by the vector $\mathbf{F}(\pi)$, as

$$\mathbf{F}(\pi) = [Q_1, P_1 Q_2, P_1 P_2 Q_3, \ldots P_1 P_2 \ldots P_{k-1} Q_k],$$

where Q_l denotes the probability of connection on the lth path. Note that the overall blocking probability $L = P_1 P_2 \ldots P_n$ is independent of π. The route-synthesis problem is then to find a set of load-sharing coefficients $\alpha(\pi)$ such that

$$\overline{\mathbf{A}} = \sum_\pi \alpha(\pi)\mathbf{F}(\pi) \tag{7.38}$$

$$\sum_\pi \alpha(\pi) = 1$$

$$\alpha(\pi) \geq 0$$

where the sums run over all the permutations of the original set of paths. In other words, we want to express the path flows as a convex linear combination of $\mathbf{F}(\pi)$. This means that the $\mathbf{F}$ vectors are the extreme points of the domain of the flows that are accessible to this particular reconstruction method. As an example, Table 7.2 lists permutations and extreme points for the case of three paths.

π	$\mathbf{F}(\pi)$
123	$Q_1,\ P_1Q_2,\ P_1P_2Q_3$
132	$Q_1,\ P_1Q_2P_3,\ P_1Q_3$
213	$Q_1P_2,\ Q_2,\ P_1P_2Q_3$
231	$Q_1P_2P_3,\ Q_2,\ P_2Q_3$
312	$Q_1P_3,\ P_1Q_2P_3,\ Q_3$
321	$Q_1P_2P_3,\ Q_2P_3,\ Q_3$

Table 7.2   Permuations and Extreme Points for the Three-Path Case

The set of all permutations is quite large even for a moderate number of paths, and the computation time required for the solution of the linear system (7.38) grows exponentially as the number of paths increases. Because of this, it has been suggested [24] that using only a subset of the permutations should be sufficient to reproduce a given set of path flows. This subset should span a sufficiently large number of path flows while being simple enough that the load-sharing coefficients can be computed rapidly. Chung, Graham, and Hwang have suggested that the cyclic permutations of the original set of paths would probably meet these conditions; they provide a numerical method for solving the realization problem in this particular subset of routes.

It turns out that the solution of the linear system (7.38) is particularly simple if the routes are limited to those that can be constructed by *cyclic* permutation of the original set of paths. To see this, consider the three-path example already mentioned. The original linear system had six equations in six unknowns, while the system corresponding to the cyclic permutations has only three equations and three coefficients. We can write the equations from the values given in Table 7.2:

$$\alpha_1 Q_1 + \alpha_2 Q_1 P_2 P_3 + \alpha_3 Q_1 P_3 = \overline{A}_1$$
$$\alpha_1 P_1 Q_2 + \alpha_2 Q_2 + \alpha_3 P_1 Q_2 P_3 = \overline{A}_2$$
$$\alpha_1 P_1 P_2 Q_3 + \alpha_2 Q_3 P_2 + \alpha_3 Q_3 = \overline{A}_3$$

The solution of the system is given by

$$\alpha_1 = \frac{1}{1-L} \left[\frac{\overline{A}_1}{Q_1} - \frac{P_3 \overline{A}_3}{Q_3} \right]$$

$$\alpha_2 = \frac{1}{1-L} \left[\frac{\overline{A}_2}{Q_2} - \frac{P_1 \overline{A}_1}{Q_1} \right]$$

$$\alpha_3 = \frac{1}{1-L} \left[\frac{\overline{A}_3}{Q_3} - \frac{P_2 \overline{A}_2}{Q_2} \right]$$

In fact, it is not difficult to see that, for a system of n paths, the general solution is given by

$$\alpha_{k+1} = \frac{(\sigma_{k+1} - \delta_k)}{(1-L)}, \quad k = 1 \ldots n, \tag{7.39}$$

where

$\sigma_i = \overline{A}_i / Q_i$, the amount of traffic that should be offered to path i to be consistent with the prescribed carried flows and connection probability,

$\delta_i = \sigma_i P_i$, the overflow from path i that is consistent with the choice of σ_i as the offered traffic to path i,

and where the addition of indices is to be made modulo n. Here, α_k is the fraction of the original traffic offered to the route made by the kth cyclic permutation from the original set of paths. The condition that the load-sharing coefficients should not be negative becomes a condition on the flows via the set of inequalities

$$\sigma_{k+1} \geq \delta_k, \tag{7.40}$$

which can be interpreted by saying that the traffic offered to the $k + 1^{\text{st}}$ path should not be smaller than the traffic overflowing from the preceding path in the route. In other words, the set of prescribed path flows can be realized by a set of cyclic permutations of the paths if it is possible to find an ordering of the original set of paths such that Eq. (7.40) is satisfied.

This problem has been given an interesting interpretation in terms of circuits in graphs. First construct a graph whose nodes are the paths that have an arc (i, j) whenever $\sigma_j \geq \delta_i$. It is possible to rearrange the original set of paths by cyclic permutation to meet the requirement given by Eq. (7.40) if and only if there exists a Hamiltonian circuit in the graph. To see that the existence of a Hamiltonian circuit is both necessary and sufficient, first note that the condition (7.40) is independent of the numbering of the paths. Hence, in order to reconstruct the path sequence, we can start at any point in the circuit. Second, we need a Hamiltonian circuit to ensure that all the paths are used once and only once. Although the problem of constructing a Hamiltonian circuit in an arbitrary graph is NP-complete, and no efficient method is known to solve it [25], it is possible to find an algorithm of complexity $O(n \log n)$ that solves the Hamiltonian circuit problem *for this class of graphs only* — because the graph in question has a special structure.

The existence of a polynomial algorithm for this special case of Hamiltonian circuits rests on the following properties. First, it is simple to show that a necessary condition for the existence of a Hamiltonian circuit in the graph is that

$$|\{i \mid \sigma_k \geq \delta_i\}| \geq n - k + 2, \qquad (7.41)$$

where the symbol $|\cdot|$ denotes the cardinality of the set in question. To prove the necessity, consider a graph having a Hamiltonian circuit, and some node k. Partition the nodes into two sets $\{k, k+1, \ldots n\}$ and its complement $\{1, 2, \ldots k-1\}$. Also, let t' be some node after k ($t' \geq k$) and t'' be some node before k ($t'' < k$). We must then have

$$\sigma_k \geq \sigma_{t'} \geq \delta_{t''}.$$

From this, we must have

$$\{i \mid \sigma_k \geq \delta_i\} \supseteq \{i \mid i \geq k\} \cup \{t''\},$$

from which we conclude that

$$|\{i \mid \sigma_k \geq \delta_i\}| \geq n - k + 2.$$

This condition is necessary, but it is also sufficient for the existence of the Hamiltonian circuit. This is proved by induction on the number of nodes n as follows. First, it is obvious that the statement is true for $n = 2$. Assume that it is also true for $n - 1$. We show that it holds for all graphs of this type with n nodes. Assume that there are n nodes that satisfy Eq. (7.41). Let G' be the induced subgraph on the nodes $\{1, 2, \ldots n-1\}$, where we have assumed as usual that $\sigma_1 \geq \sigma_2 \geq \ldots \sigma_{n-1}$. By the induction hypothesis, G' has a Hamiltonian circuit, say $\{j_1, j_2, \ldots j_{n-1}\}$. Because G satisfies Eq. (7.41), we know that

$$\sigma_n \geq \delta_{j_l} \quad \text{for some } i, \ 1 \leq i \leq n$$

and also that

$$\sigma_k \geq \sigma_n \geq \delta_n \quad \forall k, \ 1 \leq k \leq n-1.$$

As a consequence, the set $\{j_1, j_2 \ldots j_l, n, j_{l+1}, \ldots j_{n-1}\}$ is also a Hamiltonian circuit in G, which proves the sufficient part of the theorem.

The algorithm proposed in [24] for finding a cyclic route to realize a given set of flows is based on this sufficient property. It operates as follows:

1. Sort the σ_i in decreasing order and start the construction process with the first node in the list, that is, with the one having the largest σ.

2. Initialize the variables $\pi = (1)$, $i = 2$, $y = \delta_1$ and $z = 1$.

3. If at the current iteration $\sigma_i < y$, then there does not exist a Hamiltonian circuit. Go to step 6. Otherwise, insert i after z in π.

4. If $y > \delta_i$, update $y = \delta_i$, $z = i$. If $y \leq \delta_i$, then y and z are left unchanged. If $i < n$, then update $i = i+1$ and go back to step 3.

5. The Hamiltonian circuit is constructed by following the nodes in π.

6. Stop. The procedure ends with either a circuit or the indication that it is impossible to construct one.

The procedure ends when either all nodes have been included in the circuit, or the rule can no longer be applied, in which case the paths cannot be permuted cyclically to satisfy Eq. (7.40) and there does not exist an Hamiltonian circuit in the graph.

In practice, it is generally not known whether a given set of path flows can be realized with a cyclic permutation, and most likely this will not be possible. The reason is that the path flows have been generated by some algorithm with little relation to alternate routing. Examples are the straightforward use of flow deviation, or flows created from the marginal link costs produced by a dimensioning algorithm (see Chapter 9). In such a case, it may not be possible to synthesize the flows from a cyclic permutation, although the technique can still be used, even if in an approximate way.

In the approximation, the routing is synthesized from a combination of disjoint circuits, some of which may be degenerate and represent single paths. This means that the flows are not synthesized from a set of cyclic permutations over all paths, but rather are divided into disjoint blocks, to each of which the cyclic permutations are applied independently. When the process cannot continue because these conditions can no longer be met, the set of paths included in the Hamiltonian circuit so far is retained, and the route for these paths is constructed from cyclic permutations of these paths. The procedure is then restarted at the current node, and another block is constructed until the algorithm breaks down again or all paths are included in the current block. The algorithm is as follows [23]:

1. Sort the σ_i in decreasing order.

2. At the current iteration, where we are forming a new cyclic block, the first path used is the one with the largest σ that has not been used yet.

3. Insert a path i after a path j already in the block if i has not been used yet, and if it has the largest σ among the remaining paths, provided that $\sigma_i > \delta_j$. This insertion operation is repeated until it can no longer be carried out.

4. The current cyclic block ends when step 3 terminates.

5. The process of block construction is repeated until all paths have been used. Note that some of these blocks may consist of a single path.

The routes are constructed from cyclic permutations of the paths in the blocks according to the following procedure. Assume that there are s disjoint blocks $S_1, S_2, \ldots S_s$, each composed of paths P_i^k. Here, P_i^k denotes the ith path in the kth block; $k = 1, \ldots n_i$; and n_i is the number of paths in block i. The first route is constructed from $P_1^1, P_2^1, \ldots P_{n_1}^1, P_1^2, P_2^2, \ldots P_{n_2}^2, \ldots P_1^s, P_2^s, \ldots P_{n_s}^s$. The second route is constructed by selecting the blocks in the same sequence, but with a cyclic permutation applied once to each block. Thus the second route is $P_2^1, P_3^1, \ldots P_{n_1}^1, P_1^1, \ldots P_2^s, P_3^s, \ldots P_{n_s}^s, P_1^s$. The other routes are constructed in the same manner, with an additional application of a cyclic permutation in each block for each new route. The process stops when all cyclic permutations have been exhausted for all blocks. The traffic is split between the routes according to coefficients given by $\alpha_1^1, \alpha_2^1, \ldots \alpha_{n_s}^s$ where the α are given by

$$\alpha_i^k = \frac{\beta_i^k}{\sum_{i=1}^L \beta_i^k}$$

$$\beta_i^k = \sigma_{m(i)} - \delta_j$$

$$m(i) = i^{\text{th}} \text{ position in the } k^{\text{th}} \text{ block}$$

$$j = \text{ path preceding } m(i) \text{ in the block}$$

In this calculation, β_i^k is the fraction of the traffic offered to block k that is offered, through load sharing, to path i, and the αs are the corresponding load-sharing coefficients. The accuracy of the method as tested on some realistic networks is quite good, since it can realize the flows with an error of a few percent [24]. In practice, it is rather complex, imposing some computational requirements on the switch that may be unacceptable in some cases. For this reason, other, simpler methods have been proposed that may be sufficiently accurate and less complex.

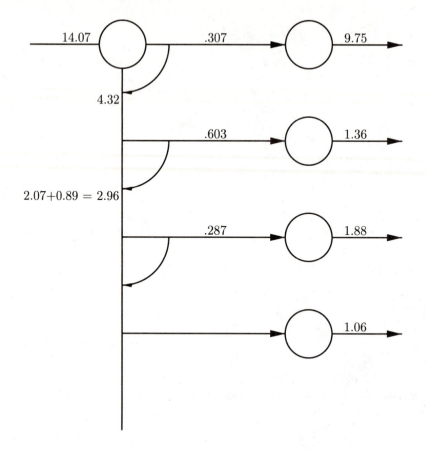

Figure 7.8   Example of Skip-One-Path Algorithm

The Skip-One-Path Method

The skip-one-path method attempts to realize the flow by a modified form of alternate routing. Because the path-blocking probabilities and carried traffic are prescribed by the routing-optimization algorithm, we can compute a required offered traffic σ_i for each path i. The idea is to construct the route by ordering paths in decreasing order of σ_i and to let the calls overflow according to this sequence. A difficulty can arise if the amount of overflow traffic is larger than the required offered traffic consistent with the path-blocking probability and carried traffic. In this case, a fraction of the calls are not offered to the next path in the sequence, but to the following one. These calls skip a path in the overflow sequence — hence the name of the algorithm.

As an example, consider the case of Fig.7.8, where a route is to be constructed for four paths; the path-blocking probabilities and carried traffic are indicated in the figure. From the blocking and traffic values of the first path, we compute a required traffic of 14.07, which is also the required value for the traffic offered to the route. Because the overflow from the first path is 4.32 and the required offered traffic on the second path is only 3.43 (a value prescribed by the blocking and carried traffic on the second path), 0.89 Erlangs will be directly offered to the third path. This in turn will be added to the overflow of path 2 when computing the traffic offered to path 3. This method is obviously simpler than the CGH method. Although less accurate, it is sufficient for design purposes. Nevertheless, it still imposes additional work on the switch because the skipping of paths must be implemented by pseudo-random numbers drawn each time a call overflows. For this reason, an even simpler method has been proposed that does not impose any additional computational requirement above that normally needed for alternate routing.

The Sequential-Path-Selection Method

From the measure of link length provided by the path-flow calculation, we can compute the path length for each origin-destination pair of the network. Routing tables are then constructed by sorting paths in decreasing length, up to some predetermined value. Although this technique is rather ad hoc, the results given in [23] indicate that the accuracy, as measured by the link flows realized in this way, may be sufficient for the purpose of network design. This method is simpler than the CGH and skip-one-path methods, but its accuracy is still lower than that of the skip-one-path method. Nevertheless, it is still sufficient for design purposes, and since its real-time computational requirements are minimal, it is the method of choice for network implementation.

Implementation

The choice of a particular flow-realization method depends on its accuracy and on the computational load it imposes on switches. As can be expected, the more accurate CGH method is also more complex computationally. Proportions of traffic allocation must be stored, along with markers to indicate where the cyclic blocks begin. Also, random numbers must be generated for each call to determine the route actually selected for that call.

Skip-one-path does not require cyclic blocks to be stored, but still requires random numbers whenever the overflow of one path is larger than the required traffic on the next one; this is an additional processing load for the switch that is not present in the sequential realization. Considering the simplicity of this implementation, and given the small difference in network cost produced by the three methods (about 1%), the sequential-path method seems the most likely to be chosen, as was the case for the DNHR of AT&T.

7.5   Markov Decision Processes

We have seen how to optimize the parameters of some of the more frequently used routing methods. The algorithms that we described yield a routing with a performance that is probably quite close to the optimal value *for this class of routing*. This gives no indication, however, whether the routing class selected, admittedly on an ad hoc basis, is really the one best suited for the network and the traffic pattern under consideration. In other words, although we know how to optimize within a given class, we would also like to optimize among routing classes. To do this, we must return to basics, reformulating the whole question in terms that are amenable to a general analysis — that is, use the network Markov model. We know that a complete and exact analysis cannot lead to implementable results because of the size of the state space. We still use the Markov process because we hope it will lead to approximate policies that are not subject to a priori selection of a method, but instead are derived from a clearly stated optimization model.

A Review of Elementary Markov Decision Theory

First, we briefly review some of the elements of the theory of Markov processes with rewards. A number of solution techniques are available for this well-known problem [26,27,28]. Consider a continuous-time Markov process with a finite state space $\{\mathbf{x}\}$ and a transition-rate matrix $Q_{i,j}$. The system earns a reward $r_{i,j}$ for each transition $i \rightarrow j$ and earns a reward at the *rate* $r_{i,i}$ as long as it remains in state i. We are interested in $v_i(t)$, the expected value of the process at time t given that the initial state was i. We know that it is given by the differential equation

$$\frac{dv_i(t)}{dt} = q_i + \sum_j Q_{i,j} v_j(t),$$

where

$$q_i \overset{\triangle}{=} r_{i,i} + \sum_{j \neq i} Q_{i,j} r_j.$$

Although this equation would yield the value at a finite time t, we are often more interested in the asymptotic behavior of the process. It is known that, as $t \rightarrow \infty$, the equation has the solution

$$v_i(t) = t g_i + v_i, \tag{7.42}$$

where

$$0 = \sum_j Q_{i,j} g_j \tag{7.43}$$

$$g_i = q_i + \sum_j Q_{i,j} v_j \tag{7.44}$$

and g_i is the process *gain* for the initial state i. If the chain is ergodic, then all the gains are identical, and the subscript i disappears from the equations. Note also that the system that determines the value vector is not of full rank. Thus values are significant only up to an additive constant, and it is customary to select a state to have the value zero. Viewed another way, only differences in values are significant for the optimal decision. Suppose now that there is a finite set of transition-rate matrices $Q^k, k = 1, \dots K$ from which to choose. Clearly, all the variables such as the gain and the values will depend on the matrix selected. The Markov decision process problem is to select that matrix Q that will maximize some performance measure. If we are interested in a system operating in a finite time interval $[0, t]$, this would be $v_i(t)$. More often, however, we can assume that the system will keep on operating for an unlimited amount of time. In this case, the value of $v_i(t)$ is unbounded, and the appropriate performance measure is the gain of the process, which is the asymptotic earning rate far off into the future. This is the view we take here, where we consider the infinite horizon case, maximizing the process gain. This amounts to solving

$$\max_k g_i^k = \max_k q_i^k + \sum_j Q_{i,j}^k v_j^k, \qquad (7.45)$$

where the dependence on the matrix index k has been explicitly included. A standard solution procedure is by relaxation over the values, known as *policy iteration*. The algorithm is straightforward:

0. Initialize the vs at some value.

1. For the current vs, compute the best transition-rate matrix by solving Eq. (7.45). Note that, although it requires a maximization operation over all matrices, it can be done independently for each state i. Let k^* be the index where the maximum occurs.

2. Compute a new set of values and gains by solving the linear system (7.43) and (7.44) for k^*.

The procedure is iterated until the values and gains stabilize. A well-known theorem of Markovian decision theory ensures that the relaxation procedure converges to the globally optimal solution to problem (7.45).

   The routing-optimization problem has been stated in terms of the optimal selection of a transition-rate matrix Q^k from a given finite set. There are equivalent ways of stating the problem that may turn out to be more convenient in some circumstances. From Eq. (7.45) we have an equivalence, at the optimal solution, between the transition matrix, on the one hand, and the value vector and gains, on the other. If we are given the set of optimal values v_i, g_i, we can compute the optimal policy from this equation. Conversely, if we have the optimal transition-rate matrix, we can compute the optimal $\mathbf{v}$ and g_i by solving the system (7.43) and (7.44). The specification of an optimal policy can therefore be stated in terms of either the transition matrix or the value vector.

Another, perhaps more convenient way to do the same thing is via the notion of actions and policies. *Actions* are what can be done at each event time in the system, and *action sets* are the sets of all possible actions available to the controller of the system. A *policy* is a mapping from the state set to the action set and is denoted by π. A policy is generally presented in the form of a rule that gives, for every possible state, what action to take for each event type. Policies can be static or dynamic, depending whether they are time dependent or not. They can be deterministic or stochastic, depending on whether they prescribe a unique action for each state and event, or a probability of selecting an action. Note that a deterministic policy does not make the decision process deterministic. Although such a policy prescribes a unique action for every state, the generation of events is still a stochastic process, and the transition matrix still prescribes probabilistic transition rates.

These three methods of representing the routing are equivalent. Given a rule, we can construct the transition-rate matrix (see, for instance, Chapter 2). Conversely, given the matrix, we can deduce the rule by inspection since, for each state, we know which transitions can occur.

MDP Formulation of Circuit-Switched Routing

We now formulate routing optimization in the framework of the theory of continuous-time Markov decision processes, and show how some of the classical results apply to this problem. To do this, we must describe the events, the action space, and the policies considered, as well as an appropriate objective function. Recall that the Markov chain describing the network under any policy has a finite number of states. If we eliminate the transient states, then the chain is ergodic, because all states communicate through the empty state. As a consequence, there is a unique set of state probabilities and a unique gain independent of the initial state.

The events in a circuit-switched network are of two kinds: (1) arrival of a new call from outside the network and (2) termination of a call in progress. As usual, we assume that nothing of interest happens between events and that the probability of having more than one event in an interval Δt goes to zero as $\Delta t \to 0$. There is some flexibility in choosing the set of actions available, and the selection of one set over another determines a broad class of network routing algorithms. This choice depends to a large degree on technical and administrative constraints.

For instance, the possibility of using call rearrangement, or *call repacking*, in order to increase network utilization and stability has been examined in [29].

By *call repacking* we mean that a call currently in progress on some path can be disconnected and reconnected on a different, presumably better path (generally the direct link for the call) because another call has ended in the network. Such an operation must be done fairly rapidly in order to pass unnoticed to the network users. Although call repacking seems to improve network performance in almost any conceivable situation, it cannot be implemented with current switching and signaling technology, although the next generation of switches may be fast enough to permit it. Because of this technical constraint, we limit the action space and assume there is no possibility of rearranging calls in progress. As a consequence, no action need be taken when a call terminates, and the action set must be specified only on call arrival.

Another example of limitation on the action set is the question of flow control. Flow control is the possibility of rejecting a call even though a path is available to connect it. The decision of whether to have flow control in a network is traditionally made outside the planning process, based on administrative and technical constraints. This decision, however, changes the action set available to the decision process. When there is no flow control, a call is always connected if a path is available to do so. The only actions available are either to route the call on some path or to reject it because all paths are blocked. The action set is then the set of columns of the arc-path incidence matrix **a**. If flow control is allowed, then this action set must be augmented with one more action — that is, to reject the call even though a path is available to connect it. Note that one advantage of the Markov formulation is that flow control can be integrated into the routing-optimization problem by adding a dummy path of infinite capacity for each traffic stream, including an extra column in the arc-path incidence matrix for each such stream. These paths carry the rejected calls, making the rejection just another routing decision.

Finally, some further constraints on the action set are imposed by the structure of the problem itself. The connection on a path is possible only if it does not violate the capacity constraints on all its links. These capacity constraints can be viewed either as conditions on the states or as restrictions imposed on the transitions or the action set. In the following discussion, we implicitly assume that these conditions are always satisfied.

The routing-optimization problem is then to find a policy π that maximizes some suitably defined performance function. Because we are interested in infinite-horizon systems, we know that the appropriate objective is the process gain. The particular form of this gain, however, depends on the choice of the reward coefficients $r_{i,j}$. Each choice of rewards defines a different model, with the emphasis placed on a different aspect of the network process. We can define positive $r_{i,i}$ to represent the actual revenue generated by a call carried in the network, in which case we would maximize the expected rate of revenue for the network. Or we may put a negative revenue of lost calls, in which case we would attempt to maximize traffic carried by the network. The choice of an objective function depends to a large degree on the context in which the network is operated, whether in a regulated or nonregulated environment, as well as on other administrative considerations. The important point is that the Markov model is sufficiently flexible to accommodate most reasonable objective functions within a unified framework.

An interesting result from the theory of MDP is that, for systems with finite state and action spaces, there exists an optimal *deterministic* policy [30]. Although some of the currently proposed adaptive schemes use a randomized strategy, the theorem states that if complete information was available, it would be possible to do as well with a deterministic policy. It is not clear whether this is still true when the information is incomplete, as is always the case in networks of practical sizes. This is a difficult question, but the existence of optimal deterministic policies shows that it must be faced eventually.

The exact Markov model described here is not very useful in practice because of its memory requirements. The state space of any typical network is very large. In addition, the action space is the set of all paths, and the set of policies is the set of all maps from states to actions, which is even larger. Finally, even if it were possible to compute a policy, the amount of information required to implement it would still be so large that the collection of data would make the scheme unfeasible. For these reasons, it is necessary to examine approximate methods that may eventually lead to applications.

Separable Policies

One such routing method, proposed in [19] under the name of *separable routing*, is based on the Markov model and could be implemented. As we saw in the section on load sharing, the optimal routing could be implemented via a shortest-path algorithm and the flow-deviation method, where the link costs were given by the solution of a linear system. Because they can be implemented easily shortest-path routing methods seem quite attractive. Separable routing belongs to the class of shortest-path methods, but here the link costs are derived from a Markov formulation of the routing problem and depend on the instantaneous state of the network at the time a call must be routed. It is hoped that the routing will be more flexible than is straight adaptive load sharing, and that the costs will represent the optimal paths more accurately.

To arrive at routing that can be implemented in a network of reasonable size, both the state and policy spaces of the MDP model must be simplified. This function, which maps the states onto the actions, must be simple to compute, and its arguments readily available. This last requirement implies that the state space must be reduced to something that can easily be measured in a network of reasonable size. A policy that satisfies these requirements is said to be implementable.

The state space is reduced by assuming that, once a call is connected on a path of m links, it behaves as m independent calls. In other words, call terminations on a path occur *independently* on all the links in this path. Under this assumption, it is unnecessary to have complete path information in order to describe the state; it is sufficient to know the number of calls in progress on each link, independently of their origin or destination. Thus the state space is given by the set of vectors $\mathbf{y} = y_1, y_2, \dots y_l$, where y_i denotes the number of calls in progress on link i.

Let us now derive the precise model for routing optimization. First we define a suitable objective function by the appropriate choice of $r_{i,j}$. In the present case, we choose

$$r_{i,j} = \begin{cases} -1 & \text{if the transition } i \to j \text{ is a call loss} \\ 0 & \text{in all other cases} \end{cases}$$

This choice of a reward function means that we are trying to minimize the total number of calls lost by the network in an interval $[0, t]$, or, in the case of an infinite horizon, the total rate at which calls are lost. From now on, we state the problem in terms of minimization, assuming that the coefficients $r_{i,j}$ corresponding to call losses are positive. We can also interpret the various quantities used in defining the Markov decision process. Recall that the state reward rate is given by

$$q_i = r_{i,i} + \sum_{j \neq i} Q_{i,j} r_{i,j},$$

which reduces, in the present case, to

$$= \sum_{j \neq i} Q_{i,j} \quad \text{such that } i \to j \text{ is a loss}$$

We see that q_i is the loss rate when in state i. We also know that the gain is given by $g = <\mathbf{p}, \mathbf{q}>$, where $\mathbf{p}$ is the vector of stationary probabilities. Hence g is the total rate of call loss in the network. Similarly, from the equation

$$v_i(t) = gt + v_i,$$

the value can also be interpreted as the number of calls lost in the interval $[0, t]$. Since we are minimizing v, the choice of rewards amounts to the minimization of the total number of lost calls in $[0, t]$, or, for an infinite horizon, to the minimization of g, the loss rate of the network. For notational simplicity, we give the following definitions:

$N_A(t) =$ The number of arrivals during the interval $[0, t]$ for the whole network.

$N_B(t) =$ The number of blocked calls during the same interval.

λ = The arrival rate, defined as

$$\lambda = \lim_{t \to \infty} \frac{N_A(t)}{t},$$

assuming that the limit exists.

g = The blocking rate of the network, also defined as the limit:

$$g = \lim_{t \to \infty} \frac{N_B(t)}{t}.$$

These definitions, given in terms of the overall network rates, could be expressed in terms of individual rates for each stream, or be extended to include some form of revenue. The basic model would not be much different, but for simplicity we develop the theory in terms of the model just defined. In the following, we denote a value by the form v_i or $v(\mathbf{y})$, with the understanding that the state i is in fact represented by the vector $\mathbf{y}$. We choose the notation that is more convenient, depending on whether we must express explicitly the dependence on the link occupancy. We can now write the basic equation of dynamic programming for the policy k as $t \to \infty$ as

$$v_i^k(t) = E\{N_B(t) \mid \mathbf{y}(0) = i, k\} = tg^k + v_i^k, \qquad (7.46)$$

where v, the value of the the process at time t if the initial state is $\mathbf{y}$, is the number of lost calls in the interval. We now calculate an expression for g using the fundamental idea of infinite-horizon dynamic programming. Equation (7.46) is an asymptotic equation that determines the process gain from 0 to some time t. The same equation also governs the asymptotic behavior of the process if we assume that it has started immediately after the first event that has occurred after $t = 0$. This is because of the ergodic nature of the system, where the initial state has no effect on the asymptotic behavior of the process far enough in the future. We can get a recurrence equation for g by writing Eq. (7.46) for a starting time $t = 0$ and $t = $ first event after $t = 0$.

Suppose now that there are K Poisson traffic streams arriving at the network from the outside. Let λ_j be the rate of stream j. To simplify the notation, we also assume that the network is fully connected. If we are in state $\mathbf{y}$, then we know that there are y_s calls currently in progress on link s. Because we are assuming that a call in progress on a path of r links behaves as if there were r independent single-link calls, we know that the rate at which calls will terminate on link s is given simply by y_s. Because of the independence between links, the rate at which calls terminate throughout the network is given simply by $\sum_s y_s$ when in state $\mathbf{y}$. Finally, we can calculate γ, the rate at which events, both arrivals and terminations, occur throughout the network, as

$$\gamma = \sum_j \lambda_j + y_j,$$

where once again we assume that there is a link j for each and every stream of traffic. Note that this restriction is made only for convenience. At the expense of a more complex notation, the case of a network that would not be completely connected could be handled in exactly the same way.

From the knowledge of γ, we can say that the average time between two events is $1/\gamma$ and in particular, because of the memoryless property of the network, that the average time until the first event after $t = 0$ is precisely $1/\gamma$. We still do not know what this first event is going to be. Because of the independence, however, we know that the probability that it is a call termination on link j is given by y_j/γ, and the probability that it is a call arrival from stream j is similarly given by λ_j/γ.

Suppose now that we have solved the problem, say by the method of policy iteration. Given the optimal values v_i, we have computed the optimal policy by solving Eq. (7.45). For a call arriving at stream k, the actions available are the $\mathbf{a}_l^k$, $l = 1, \ldots M_k$, the columns of the arc-path incidence matrix that describe the M_k paths available to this stream, including the loss path at $l = 0$. The optimal policy is then to select the l such that

$$\min_{0 \leq l \leq M_k} \left(\delta_{0,l} + v(\mathbf{y} + \mathbf{a}_l^k) \right), \tag{7.47}$$

in other words, to select the path that has the smallest value (recall that we are minimizing lost calls). If it is more profitable, lose the call by choosing $l = 0$ as the solution. From this discussion, we can express the optimal value for the gain as

$$gt + v(\mathbf{y}) = g \left[t - \frac{1}{\gamma} \right] + \frac{1}{\gamma} \sum_k y_k v(\mathbf{y} - \mathbf{e}_k) +$$
$$\frac{1}{\gamma} \sum_k \lambda_k \min_{0 \leq l \leq M_k} \left(\delta_{0,l} + v(\mathbf{y} + \mathbf{a}_l^k) \right), \tag{7.48}$$

which is simply Eq. (7.46) written twice, the left-hand side for an infinite horizon starting at $t = 0$, and the right-hand side for an interval starting after the first event after $t = 0$. This can be rewritten as

$$g = \sum_k y_k \left[v(\mathbf{y} - \mathbf{e}_k) - v(\mathbf{y}) \right] + \sum_k \lambda_k \min_{0 \leq l \leq L_k} \left[\delta_{0,l} + v(\mathbf{y} + \mathbf{a}_l^k) - v(\mathbf{y}) \right]$$
$$v(\mathbf{y} + \mathbf{e}_k) - v(\mathbf{y}) \geq 1 \text{ if } y_k \geq N_k.$$

This equation gives the optimal value of the process gain at $t \to \infty$. It is not particularly simple, however, and the solution by policy iteration is not possible in practice. Even if it were, there is some doubt that the result could be used in a network. The reason is that the vector $\mathbf{v}(\mathbf{y})$, which determines the optimal policy, depends on $\mathbf{y}$, the complete state vector. In other words, the decision to route a given call on some path depends on the state of *all* the groups in the network, even those in a part of the network that has little interaction with the traffic stream to which the call belongs. This means that in practice, even if we had an optimal, state-dependent policy, we would require far too much information to implement it.

This difficulty is removed by restricting the values, and hence the policies, to a subset of all policies. This subset is defined by the assumption that the value functions are *separable*, that is, are of the form

$$v(\mathbf{y}) = \sum_s v_s(y_s). \tag{7.49}$$

Obviously this is only a small subset of all state-dependent policies. Whether it is large enough to encompass nearly optimal policies is a question that cannot easily be answered. Before considering the accuracy of this assumption, however, we must be able to compute an optimal separable policy. Suppose that we were to do this by value iteration. We would start with an initial guess for a policy, compute its values, then recalculate another, better policy, and so on until convergence. In practice this cannot be done, even with separable policies, because of the size of the state and action spaces.

The separable-policy method is based on the first iteration of this process, where the initial policy is the direct-link-only policy. In this policy, there is no alternate routing of calls, and a call that cannot be routed on the direct link is lost. To carry out one iteration of the value-iteration method, we must compute the value vector and the gain of this initial policy. This calculation can be made independently for each link because the arrival processes are independent. Also, because only one path is available, the decision is either to connect or to reject the call. This depends on the state of the system k, the number of calls in progress in the group at the time a call arrives. The optimality equation for the MDP for a single link of N trunks offered a Poisson traffic λ is given by Eq. (7.48), which can be rewritten for a single group:

$$tg + v(k) = \left[t - \frac{1}{k+\lambda}\right]g + \frac{k}{k+\lambda}v(k-1) + \frac{\lambda}{\lambda+k}v(k+1), \quad k < N$$

$$tg + v(N) = \left[t - \frac{1}{N+\lambda}\right]g + \frac{N}{N+\lambda}v(N-1) + \frac{\lambda}{\lambda+N}(1+v(N)), \quad k = N$$

These equations, much simpler than the general ones for the whole network, can be solved exactly. Using induction for $k = N$ first and decreasing, it is not difficult to show that

$$v(k+1) - v(k) = \frac{E(\lambda, N)}{E(\lambda, k)}, \tag{7.50}$$

which is the relative value needed to compute the new policy. Another interpretation of this equation, whose demonstration is left as an exercise (Problem 7.12), is that this is the expected number of lost calls on the link during an average holding time (Problem 7.13). Viewed this way, the routing rule has a very intuitive interpretation. We accept the call if we expect that, on the average, we will lose less than one call on the link because of the presence of the additional call. If this expectation is larger than one, then we reject the call because it would cause too many losses while it remains connected.

We now have the values for the first iteration of the policy-iteration method. The new policy is then to choose the path with the least cost, where the cost of a path is given by Eq. (7.50), which is given by solving Eq. (7.47). We now have a new policy, which is generally better than the initial, no-alternate-routing policy used at the start. We would now go on to recompute the values of this policy, and so on, until the optimal value is reached. In practice this is impossible, again because of the complexity of the calculation, as easily seen by considering once again Eq. (7.50). Note that the cost is given by a ratio of Erlang functions on each link, where the link-offered traffic is λ, the first-offered traffic coming from outside the network. This expression is correct in the case of the initial routing, which has no alternate routes, but the introduction of alternate routing caused by the first policy iteration changes the value of the traffic offered to all the links. Thus, to calculate a second set of values, we would have to compute the link-offered traffics. The problem is that these values depend on the routing in a complex way, which will generally appear as some form of nonlinear system. From what we know of these systems, it should be clear that a solution is not practical for any network of reasonable size.

Nevertheless, we can make the calculation of the first policy more accurate by anticipating the effect of the second iteration and replacing the value of the traffic offered to the links by a more accurate approximation. This is done by computing an optimal load sharing for the network, using the values of the offered traffic corresponding to the optimal solution as the link-offered traffic in Eq. (7.50). In this way, Ott and Krishnan [19] claimed that the new policy is more accurate than that computed with the original traffic streams.

Note that the weight functions are derived from some simple, obviously nonoptimal policies. We have made a number of simplifications to arrive at something that is both computable and implementable:

1. The state space has been reduced to the set $\{y\}$ by the assumption that calls that are connected on r-link paths terminate independently as r single-link calls.

2. The set of policies has been limited to separable policies.

3. The corresponding Markov decision process has been solved only approximately, by doing a single iteration of the policy-iteration process.

4. This evaluation has been done with an approximate value for the traffic offered to the links.

At this time, the worth of the resulting policies can be determined only by numerical comparisons with the exact solutions. Because the latter are extremely difficult to compute, the accuracy of the approximate policies can be tested only on small networks. These comparisons were made in [19]; the results indicate that they are indeed very close to the optimum over a wide range of traffic values. As a point of comparison, the load-sharing policies from which the values have been derived are also computed; it turns out that these are *not* very good. It is found that the direct-routing policy approaches optimality only at very high blocking values. This confirms a well-known fact: At high traffic values, routing should be limited to one link only because the use of alternate paths may block more calls than are actually routed through the path.

It is clear that the separable policy model can be extended in a number of ways — the most obvious one, to maximize revenues instead of minimizing lost calls [31]. It is also clear that some of the routing techniques described earlier are special cases of separable policies. For instance, residual-capacity adaptive routing is such a special case, corresponding to the choice of link costs:

$$C_s = \begin{cases} 1 & \text{if } y_s = N_s \\ 1 - \dfrac{N_s - y_s}{N_s - m_s} & \text{if } m_s \leq y_s \leq N_s \\ \dfrac{1}{2} - \epsilon \dfrac{1 - \epsilon^{m_s - y_s}}{1 - \epsilon} & \text{if } 0 \leq y_s < m_s \end{cases}$$

As a consequence, a well-chosen separable routing should perform better than the standard RCAR method. The magnitude of this difference is not yet known and can be determined only by empirical tests on significant networks.

7.6   Conclusion

Routing methods have evolved continually over the last 15 years, starting with standard hierarchical routing, going through nonhierarchical fixed alternate routing, residual-capacity adaptive routing, and gradually evolving toward a state-dependent method based on revenues. The advantages of these methods in networks operating with a single type of traffic and under stationary conditions have been documented through case studies on presumably representative networks. In these cases, most of the potential gains available from these methods appear to be obtained from the move away from fixed hierarchical routing toward a nonhierarchical scheme, either adaptive or nonadaptive. For a well-designed network operating under normal conditions, the differences in performance between these methods are not significant.

The situation is quite different when the assumptions of stationarity and homogeneity are no longer made. If the input is not stationary, as is generally the case, then it is quite clear that the adaptive methods of one type or another are superior to the nonadaptive ones. This is the main reason that the pure DNHR routing method has been improved by the addition of an adaptive second choice, yielding the TSMR method. The choice of a particular adaptive method is probably not all that critical since the few available results do not indicate significant differences in performance for truly adaptive schemes, whether of the residual-capacity type or based on some form of revenue maximization.

This situation is most likely to change when nonhomogeneous traffics are carried in the same network — for instance in a circuit-switched integrated services digital network (ISDN). In this case, if the calls have different bandwidths and holding times, it is not clear what is a useful objective function to maximize. For instance, minimizing the number of lost calls is clearly inadequate because a wide-band call of long duration, corresponding say to a video call, clearly affects network performance more significantly than an ordinary voice call. Seemingly the only common feature of these various types of traffic is the fact that they all generate revenues, based on the call characteristics. Thus, in the ISDN context, the revenue-maximization principle may be the only rational way to route calls in a network, in either a load-sharing or a state-dependent mode. Although there are some preliminary results in this area, this is a still unexplored subject of network planning that requires some further research.

Problems

7.1. Consider the Frank-Wolfe algorithm for nonlinear multicommodity flow. Show (1) that the direction-finding step reduces to a shortest-path calculation and (2) that the step-size calculation corresponds to a flow deviation.

7.2. Show that Eqs. (7.4) and (7.5) give the right cost functions for the equivalence between user- and system-optimal solutions to the routing problem.

7.3. Derive Eq. (7.13) for the optimal value of the load-sharing coefficients for two-link hierarchical routing.

7.4. Write a program in pseudo-code that expresses a flow-deviation algorithm for the load-sharing model with traffic conservation.

7.5. Show how the generalized network model of Section 7.1 can be specialized to yield the load-sharing model of Section 7.2 with the traffic model of Eqs. (7.11) and (7.12), where traffic losses on the first link of two-link paths are taken into account.

7.6. Consider the optimal load sharing with flow conservation when the traffic model is given by Eqs. (7.8) and (7.9). Show that the optimality equation (7.14) reduces to Eq. (7.10) when the link-blocking probabilities are small (especially the coupling term).

7.7. Starting from Eq. (7.7), derive the optimality equations for the load-sharing parameters in the case of two-link alternate routing for the pseudo-hierarchical routing described in Section 7.2. Take into account the downstream blocking effect — that is, the traffic offered to the links in a path is given by

$$a_{i,k} = \sum_j A_k^{i,j} \left[1 - B_{k,j}\right]$$

$$a_{k,j} = \sum_i A_k^{i,j} \left[1 - B_{i,k}\right]$$

Show that the values of the partial derivatives of the link-offered traffic with respect to the decision variables are given by a linear system. Use this to suggest a two-stage algorithm for resolving the Kuhn-Tucker equations.

7.8. Derive Eqs. (7.23–7.25) for the optimal load-sharing coefficients.

7.9. Give an approximation similar to Eq. (7.37) when the last tandem is removed and two adjacent tandem nodes in a given route tree are permuted.

7.10. Check whether the solution of Eq. (7.38) is indeed given by Eq. (7.39).

7.11. Make the algorithm used for constructing path flows by the CGH method precise enough to be coded in some computer language.

7.12. Derive Eq. (7.50) using the induction argument starting at N.

7.13. Prove that Eq. (7.50) can be interpreted as the number of lost calls expected during a call-holding time.

References

[1] Frank, M., and Wolfe, P., "An algorithm for quadratic programming," *Naval Research Logistics Quarterly*, vol. 3, pp. 95–110, 1956.

[2] Dial, R., Glover, F., Karney, D., and Klingman, D., "A computational analysis of alternative algorithms and labelling techniques for finding shortest path trees," *Networks*, vol. 9, pp. 215–248, 1979.

[3] Grigoriadis, M.D., and Hsu, T., "RNET: Rutgers Minimal Cost Network flow subroutines—user documentation," Report No. V 3.61, Department of Computer Science, Rutgers University, October 1979.

[4] Fratta, L., Gerla, M., and Kleinrock, L., "The flow deviation method: an approach to store-and-forward communication network design," *Networks*, vol. 3, pp. 97–133, 1973.

[5] Dafermos, S., and Sparrow, F.T., "The traffic assignment problem for a general network," *Journal of Research of the National Bureau of Standards—B. Mathematical Sciences*, vol. 73B, pp. 91–118, 1969.

[6] Truemper, K., "Optimal flows in nonlinear gain networks," *Networks*, vol. 8, pp. 17–36, 1978.

[7] Demmy, W.S., "Multicommodity flows in generalized networks," Wayne State University, 1969.

[8] Garcia, J.M., "Processus de décision markovien, application à l'acheminement d'appels téléphoniques," Report No. LAAS–83007, Laboratoire d'automatique et d'analyse des systèmes, Toulouse, France, January 1983.

[9] Srikanta Kumar, P.R., "On optimal flows in circuit-switched networks," *Globecom'84*, pp. 27.3.1–27.3.5, 1984.

[10] Girard, A., Lansard, P.D., Liau, B., and Thibault, J.L., "Optimization of out-of-chain routing," *Network Planning Symposium*, vol. 4, 1989.

[11] Kelly, F.P., "Blocking probabilities in large circuit switched networks," *Advances in Applied Probability*, vol. 18, pp. 473–505, 1986.

[12] Kelly, F.P., "Adaptive routing in circuit-switched networks," Statistical Laboratory, Cambridge University, Cambridge, England, 1986.

[13] Kelly, F.P., "Routing in circuit-switched networks: optimization, shadow prices and decentralization," *Advances in Applied Probability*, vol. 20, pp. 112–144, 1988.

[14] Chemouil, P., Filipiak, J., and Gauthier, P., "Analysis and control of traffic routing in circuit-switched networks," *Computer Networks and ISDN Systems*, vol. 11, pp. 203–219, 1986.

[15] Garcia, J.M., *Problèmes liés à la modélisation du trafic et à l'acheminement des appels dans un réseau téléphonique*, Ph.D. Thesis, Université Paul Sabatier, Toulouse, France, November 1980.

[16] Dziong, Z., Pióro, M., and Körner, U., "An adaptive call routing strategy for circuit switched networks," Department of Communication Systems, Lund Institute of Technology, Lund, Sweden, 1987.

[17] Krishnan, K.R., "Routing of telephone traffic to minimize network blocking," *IEEE Conference on Decision and Control*, vol. 21, pp. 375–377, 1982.

[18] Girard, A., Côté, Y., and Ouimet, Y., "A comparative study of non-hierarchical alternate routing in circuit-switched networks," *International Network Planning Symposium*, vol. 2, pp. 70–74, March 1983.

[19] Ott, T.J., and Krishnan, K.R., "State dependent routing of telephone traffic and the use of separable routing schemes," *International Teletraffic Congress*, vol. 11, pp. 5.1A.5.1–5.1A.5.6, 1985.

[20] Girard, A., and Côté, Y., "Sequential routing optimization for circuit switched networks," *IEEE Transactions on Communications*, vol. COM-32, pp. 1234–1243, 1984.

[21] Cameron, H., Galloy, P., and Graham, W.J., "Report on the Toronto advanced routing concept trial," *Network Planning Symposium*, vol. 1, pp. 228–236, 1980.

[22] Gill, P.E., Murray, W., and Wright, M., *Practical Optimization*, Academic Press, 1981.

[23] Ash, G.R., Cardwell, R.H., and Murray, R.P., "Design and optimization of networks with dynamic routing," *Bell System Technical Journal*, vol. 60, pp. 1787–1820, 1981.

[24] Chung, F.R.K., Graham, R.L., and Hwang, F.K., "Efficient realization techniques for network flow patterns," *Bell System Technical Journal*, vol. 60, pp. 1771–1786, 1981.

[25] Garey, M.R., and Johnson, D.S., *Computers and Intractability*, Freeman, 1979.

[26] Howard, R.A., *Dynamic Programming and Markov Processes*, Wiley, 1960.

[27] Howard, R.A., *Dynamic Probabilistic Systems*, vols. 1 and 2, Wiley, 1971.

[28] Derman, C., *Finite State Markovian Decision Processes*, Academic Press, 1970.

[29] Girard, A., and Hurtubise, S., "Dynamic routing and call repacking in circuit switched networks," *IEEE Transactions on Communications*, vol. COM–31, pp. 1290–1295, 1983.

[30] Beneš, V.E., "Programming and control problems arising from optimal routing in telephone networks," *Bell System Technical Journal*, vol. 45, pp. 1373–1439, 1966.

[31] Dziong, Z., Pióro, M., Körner, U., and Wickberg, T., "On adaptive call routing strategies in circuit-switched networks — maximum revenue approach," *International Teletraffic Congress*, vol. 12, pp. 3.1A5.1–3.1A5.8, 1988.

CHAPTER 8

Dimensioning
Hierarchical Networks

Much work has been carried out on the optimal dimensioning of hierarchical networks for a single demand matrix [1,2,3,4]. Efficient numerical methods allow the calculation to be made for large long distance and metropolitan networks comprising hundreds of nodes. Because each method currently in use was developed by a different organization, these techniques are often described in ways that hide their common structure; in fact, they are fundamentally similar.

Starting from the mathematical program corresponding to the optimal dimensioning problem, we derive the standard ECCS equations of Truitt [1] and those of Pratt [4]. By setting these equations in a more general context, we see how to extend them to the multihour case. We also discuss other formulations of the dimensioning problem with different grade-of-service constraints.

8.1 The ECCS Method for Single-Hour Dimensioning

Current dimensioning methods for telephone networks originated with Truitt [1] on the ECCS method. These results were later improved by Pratt [4], who extended Truitt's simple triangular network to the double-sector tandem case. At the same time, Rapp [3] gave a simple characterization of direct, high-usage, and final trunk groups that could be used in manually designing small- to medium-scale networks. All of this work led to the derivation of numerous computer implementations by virtually all postal administrations or telephone operating companies in the industrialized world for the design of their telephone networks. Most of these methods are still in use today, forming basic dimensioning tools for the new networks.

We now present a general nonlinear optimization model of hierarchical dimensioning. We derive, under suitable assumptions, the ECCS equations of Truitt and the double-sector tandem equations of Pratt, showing how these equations lead to a technique applicable to arbitrary networks. The presentation is based on a general nonlinear programming formulation, differing somewhat from the traditional method, where the only variables are the sizes of the high-usage groups. This approach not only helps us better understand the theoretical foundation of the method, but also helps justify the simplifying assumptions that make it so efficient. In addition, it provides a basis for studying multihour dimensioning of hierarchical networks, as well as generalizing dimensioning under end-to-end grade-of-service constraints.

Problem Definition

In this section, we consider the classical case where the grade-of-service constraints are expressed as blocking constraints on final groups. It is useful to define a special notation for trunk groups:

$\{J\}$ = The index set of final trunk groups.

$\{I\}$ = The index set of high-usage trunk groups.

B_j = The blocking probability on the jth final. This is a function $B(A, N)$ of the traffic offered to the link and the number of trunks. A simple case is the Erlang B function for Poisson traffic.

$C'_s = dC_s/dN_s \geq 0.$

$\overline{B}_j$ = The maximum blocking allowed on the jth final.

Unless otherwise specified, an index i or j refers to a high-usage or final trunk group, respectively. The optimal dimensioning problem is then

$$\min_{N} z(\mathbf{N}) = \sum_{s} C_s(N_s)$$
$$B_j(\mathbf{N}) \leq \overline{B}_j \quad j \in \{J\} \qquad (\mathbf{u}) \tag{8.1}$$
$$N_s \geq 0 \qquad (\mathbf{v})$$

where the minimization is carried over the reals, and $\mathbf{u}$ and $\mathbf{v}$ are the vectors of multipliers corresponding to the blocking and positivity constraints, respectively. The Lagrange function is given by

$$\mathcal{L}(\mathbf{N}, \mathbf{u}, \mathbf{v}) = \sum_{s} C_s(N_s) + \sum_{j} u_j(B_j - \overline{B}_j) - \sum_{s} v_s N_s,$$

and the first-order Kuhn-Tucker conditions are

$$C'_i + \sum_{j \in \{J\}} u_j \frac{\partial B_j}{\partial N_i} - v_i = 0 \quad i \in \{I\} \tag{8.2}$$

$$C'_j + \sum_{m \in \{J\}} u_m \frac{\partial B_m}{\partial N_j} - v_j = 0 \quad j \in \{J\} \tag{8.3}$$

$$u_j(B_j - \overline{B}_j) = 0 \quad j \in \{J\} \tag{8.4}$$

$$v_s N_s = 0 \quad \forall s \in \{I\} \cup \{J\} \tag{8.5}$$

The equations for the final trunk groups and the high-usage groups are written separately. These equations take a simple form under assumptions that generally hold for public telephone networks.

Optimality Equations for the Final Trunk Groups

Assume $N_j \neq 0$, $j \in \{J\}$, which is necessary if we have a hierarchical routing. If the optimal size of a final group turns out to be zero, the hierarchy has not been well chosen: Either it should be changed, or we should accept a nonoptimal solution, with the final of nonzero size. Then, at the optimal solution, $v_j = 0$ and Eqs. (8.3) and (8.4) become

$$C'_j + \sum_m u_m \frac{\partial B_m}{\partial N_j} = 0$$

$$u_j(B_j - \overline{B}_j) = 0$$

We also know that, at the optimal solution, the blocking constraints will be tight — a direct consequence of the facts that the costs are nondecreasing and that the optimization is done over the reals, as well as of the form of the constraints, where there is exactly one variable N_j for each constraint. Thus we need not worry about Eq. (8.4), which will be automatically satisfied. This fact is crucial for the efficiency of the method described here. We now make the second simplifying assumption,

$$\frac{\partial B_m}{\partial N_j} = \frac{\partial B_j}{\partial N_j} \delta_{m,j}, \tag{8.6}$$

which is reasonable if the blocking is low on the finals. Under these conditions, we can solve Eq. (8.3) explicitly, computing the value of the multipliers at optimality as follows:

$$u_j = -\frac{C'_j}{\partial B_j / \partial N_j}. \tag{8.7}$$

Thus the important conclusion follows that, under the assumptions of tight constraints at the optimal solution and of Eq. (8.6), the multipliers can be computed explicitly; they disappear from the problem.

Optimality Equations for High-Usage Groups

Using Eq. (8.7), Eq. (8.2) becomes

$$v_i = C'_i - \sum_{j \in \{J\}} \frac{C'_j}{\partial B_j / \partial N_j} \frac{\partial B_j}{\partial N_i}. \tag{8.8}$$

Equation (8.8) forms a set of simultaneous nonlinear equations, one for each high-usage group; each solution yields a stationary point of (8.1). Before

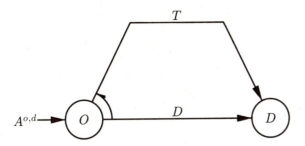

Figure 8.1 Two-Link Network

discussing general solution methods, we look at some simple cases, recovering the classical ECCS equations for the two-path and square networks. At first we will assume that $N_i > 0$, $i \in \{I\}$, which implies that $\mathbf{v} = \mathbf{0}$ and permits us to ignore Eq. (8.5). Although not a valid assumption for realistic networks, this simplifies the theory; we shall see later how to handle the cases where $N_i = 0$.

The ECCS Method for Simple Networks

Equation (8.1) is a nonlinear optimization with differentiable functions. A number of general-purpose algorithms and computer implementations are available to solve this problem [5]. These methods are not used here for a variety of reasons, most importantly because of the very large size of the problems that must be resolved, even for moderately large networks. Specialized, extremely efficient techniques have been developed to take advantage of the special features of the dimensioning problem.

While general-purpose nonlinear programming techniques rely on *descent* methods, these special techniques attempt to find a solution to the optimality conditions for the high-usage case (8.8) *directly*. The following equation uses the blocking constraints to size the finals:

$$B_j(N_j) = \overline{B}_j.$$

We show how the technique is carried out for some simple networks, deriving the standard equations proposed in the literature.

Two-Link Network. The first case is a two-node, two-link network with alternate routing; calls blocked on the direct D link are offered to the tandem T link [1] (see Fig. 8.1). Following the usual method, we assume that the cost functions are linear (although, with suitable modifications, all that follows could equally be stated for differentiable cost functions).

$$C(N_D) = C_D N_D$$
$$C(N_T) = C_T N_T$$

and

$$N_i > 0$$

Eq. (8.8) becomes

$$C_D = \frac{C_T}{\partial B_T / \partial N_T} \frac{\partial B_T}{\partial N_D}.$$

Let

A_D = The total traffic offered to the direct link. This is the first-offered traffic.

a_T = The total traffic offered to the tandem link. This is the sum of the first-offered traffic plus the overflow from the direct link.

$\hat{a}_D$ = The overflow traffic from the direct link.

$\overline{a}_D$ = The total traffic carried on the direct link.

Then

$$\frac{\partial B_T}{\partial N_D} = \frac{\partial B_T}{\partial a_T} \frac{\partial \hat{a}_D}{\partial N_D},$$

and Eq. (8.8) becomes

$$\frac{C_D}{C_T} = \frac{\partial B_T / \partial a_T}{\partial B_T / \partial N_T} \frac{\partial \hat{a}_D}{\partial N_D},$$

where $\partial B_T / \partial a_T$ means that the partial derivative of B_T is evaluated at a_T, the current value of the total link-offered traffic. Because a_T is the sum of the first-offered and overflow traffic, the partial derivative depends on the size of the direct group. We now use the fact that, at the optimal solution, the blocking constraint on the final is tight. For this group, there are three parameters B, a, and N that are linked through the traffic model, in this case the Erlang B function

$$B = E(a, N).$$

Any variation of one parameter will produce a variation of at least one of the other two parameters. We can write the following differential equation to express this relation:

$$dB = \frac{\partial E}{\partial a} da + \frac{\partial E}{\partial N} dN. \tag{8.9}$$

Because we know that, at the final solution, the blocking on the final is tight, we must compensate for any variation in the traffic offered to the link by a variation of the number of circuits such that $dB = 0$. Replacing this condition in Eq. (8.9), we get

$$\frac{\partial B_T / \partial a_T}{\partial B_T / \partial N_T} = -\left(\frac{dN_T}{da_T}\right)_{\overline{B}_T}.$$

The right-hand side denotes the variation in the number of trunks required to maintain the blocking at $\overline{B}_T$ for a small variation of total offered traffic. This yields the optimality equation

$$\frac{C_D}{C_T} = -\left(\frac{\partial \hat{a}_D}{\partial N_D}\right)\left(\frac{dN_T}{da_T}\right)_{\overline{B}_T}. \tag{8.10}$$

This is a nonlinear equation in which the right-hand side has two terms that depend on the single variable N_D. The solution yields the optimal value for the number of trunks on the direct route. We can reformulate Eq. (8.10) by defining the marginal capacity of the final β_T:

$$\frac{1}{\beta_T} \triangleq \left(\frac{dN_T}{da_T}\right)_{\overline{B}_T}. \tag{8.11}$$

We also define the marginal occupancy of the high-usage group:

$$H \triangleq -\left(\frac{\partial a_D}{\partial N_D}\right) = \left(\frac{\partial \overline{a}_D}{\partial N_D}\right), \tag{8.12}$$

which represents the rate of change of the traffic carried on the direct link with respect to the number of circuits on this link for a fixed value of the offered traffic. Finally, if we let $CR = C_T/C_D$, the equilibrium condition becomes

$$\frac{\beta}{CR} = H, \tag{8.13}$$

where CR is called the *cost ratio* for obvious reasons. In the North American literature, this equation is generally written

$$ECCS = \frac{\gamma}{CR}, \tag{8.14}$$

with

$$ECCS \triangleq H$$
$$\gamma \triangleq \beta$$

Hence the name of the method. The name can be understood from Eq. (8.14) as follows. Traffic was traditionally measured by counting the number of busy circuits on a group during periods of 100 seconds. Thus a convenient unit of traffic was the number of calls present during these 100 seconds, which became the number of CCS, each CCS representing 100 call seconds. The term ECCS means *economic* CCS. From Eq. (8.12), we see that it is the amount of traffic that can be carried on the direct route for a small increment in the capacity of this route. For integer sizes, ECCS can be defined as the amount of additional traffic that can be carried on the last trunk added to the route. Similarly, Eq. (8.11) defines the additional amount of traffic that can be carried on the final for a small increment of capacity, leaving the blocking unchanged (for

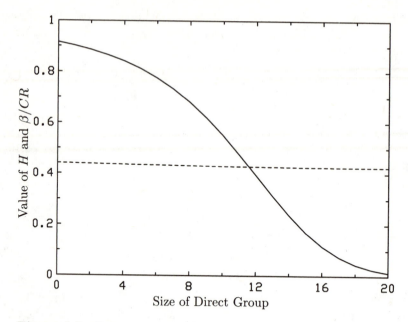

Figure 8.2 Representation of ECCS Equation. $A_T = 20$, $A_D = 10$, $CR = 2$, and $B = 0.01$

the final, we assume that carried $\approx$ offered). The equilibrium equation (8.13) defines the optimal size of the direct group as the number of circuits such that the traffic carried on the last circuit of the direct route (the *economical* CCS) is the same as the traffic carried on the last circuit of the alternate route, scaled by the ratio of provisioning costs on the two routes. Equation (8.10) can be rewritten

$$C_D \left(\frac{\partial N_D}{\partial \bar{a}_D} \right) = C_T \left(\frac{\partial N_T}{\partial a_T} \right)_{\overline{B}_T}.$$

That is, the optimal group size is the one where the cost of routing a small increment of traffic on the direct route is the same as the cost of routing over it the alternate route at the same blocking level. This characterization of the optimal group size is another manifestation of Wardrop equilibrium conditions for transportation networks and marginal-cost equilibrium condition for nonlinear multicommodity flows.

The optimal value for N_D is computed from Eq. (8.13), a nonlinear equation in the variable N_D. Although there are many numerical methods for solving nonlinear equations, in practice the following technique is used. Let β be constant, for example, $\beta = 28$ CCS/circuit. Given the value of CR, the

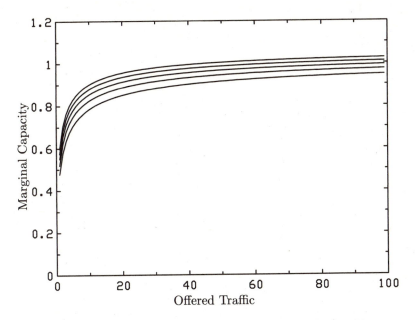

Figure 8.3 Value of Marginal Capacity. Blocking from 0.01 to 0.05

ratio of costs on the direct path to costs on the overflow path, the only term containing N_D is H. We can therefore solve the problem simply by examining a graph of $\partial \bar{a}_D / \partial N_D$ for A_D equal to the known value of the first-offered traffic. Figure 8.2 shows a plot of the two functions H and β as functions of N_D for typical values of traffic. It is clear that β is a very slowly varying function of N_D and that it can safely be taken as a constant while the optimality equations are solved. The particular value that must be chosen depends more on the traffic offered to the final than on N_D, as can be seen from Fig. 8.3. Nevertheless, the assumption of constant β is often sufficient to give satisfactory values for the direct group.

The ECCS equation has been derived under the assumption that $N_D > 0$. Such a solution will occur whenever $\beta/CR < 1$. If this is not so, Eq. 8.13 has no solution. In this case, we can see that the value $N_D = 0$ is a solution of the Kuhn-Tucker equation (8.13). We have, from Eq. (8.8),

$$v_D = C_D - C_T \frac{\partial B_T / \partial N_D}{\partial B_T / \partial N_T}$$

$$= C_D - C_T \frac{H}{\beta_t}. \tag{8.15}$$

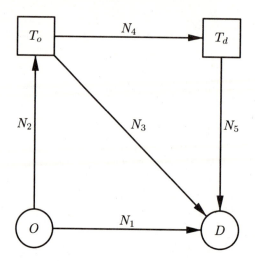

Figure 8.4 Double-Sector Tandem Network

It is not difficult to show that, if $N_D = 0$, then the right-hand side is non-negative, and that the value $N_D = 0$ satisfies the Kuhn-Tucker equation (see Problem 8.3).

Double-Sector Tandem Network. The second simple case is the familiar double-sector tandem network, with two tandem and two lower-level nodes [4] (see Fig. 8.4). Here too, we assume that $N_i > 0$ at the optimal solution. We write the first component of Eq. (8.8), the gradient in the direction N_1:

$$\frac{\partial B_j}{\partial N_1} = \frac{\partial B_j}{\partial a_j} \frac{\partial a_j}{\partial \hat{a}_1} \frac{\partial \hat{a}_1}{\partial N_1}.$$

A new term appears in the form of $\partial a_j/\partial \hat{a}_1$, the variation of traffic offered to the final with respect to a variation of overflow from the direct. Because intermediate group 3 stands between these two groups, we expect this derivative to depend somehow on the parameters of group 3. Using Eq. (8.7), Eq. (8.8) becomes

$$C_1' = \sum_j C_j' \frac{\partial B_j/\partial N_j}{\partial B_j/\partial a_j} \frac{\partial a_j}{\partial \hat{a}_1} \frac{\partial \hat{a}_1}{\partial N_1}. \qquad (8.16)$$

Using the fact that the constraints are tight at the optimum, we can write for each final

$$-\frac{\partial B_j/\partial a_j}{\partial B_j/\partial N_j} = \left(\frac{dN}{da}\right)_{\overline{B}}$$

$$= \frac{1}{\beta_j}.$$

Assuming low losses on the finals, we get

$$\frac{\partial a_j}{\partial \hat{a}_1} = \frac{\partial a_j}{\partial \hat{a}_3} \frac{\partial \hat{a}_3}{\partial \bar{a}_2} \frac{\partial \bar{a}_2}{\partial \hat{a}_1}, \quad j = 4,5$$

$$= \frac{\partial a_j}{\partial \hat{a}_3} \frac{\partial \hat{a}_3}{\partial a_3}$$

$$= \frac{\partial a_j}{\partial \hat{a}_3} \gamma_3,$$

where

$$\gamma_3 \overset{\triangle}{=} \frac{\partial \hat{a}_3}{\partial a_3}, \tag{8.17}$$

where γ_3 is called the marginal overflow and should not be confused with the quantity γ used in the traditional form of the ECCS equation (8.14). Similarly,

$$\frac{\partial a_2}{\partial \hat{a}_1} = 1.$$

Again we define the marginal occupancy of the high-usage group,

$$H_1 = -\frac{\partial \hat{a}_1}{\partial N_1}, \tag{8.18}$$

and Eq. (8.16) becomes

$$C_1' = H_1 \left\{ \left[\frac{C_5'}{\beta_5} + \frac{C_4'}{\beta_4} \right] \gamma_3 + \frac{C_2'}{\beta_2} \right\}, \tag{8.19}$$

which is the form in [4]. The equation for the other high-usage group N_3 can be derived in the same manner, yielding

$$C_3' = H_3 \left[\frac{C_4'}{\beta_4} + \frac{C_5'}{\beta_5} \right]. \tag{8.20}$$

(See Problem 8.1.) We have reduced the dimensioning problem to finding the solution of two *simultaneous* nonlinear equations (8.19) and (8.20) in two unknowns N_1 and N_3. Although we could solve the equations by any general-purpose method for nonlinear systems, we use instead a special relaxation technique that relies on their structure. Note that $H_1 = H_1(N_1)$ and, similarly, that $H_3 = H_3(N_3)$; that is, the marginal occupancies depend only on the parameters of the high-usage group being dimensioned if the traffic offered to the group is known. If we take all the βs and γs of Eqs. (8.19) and (8.20) to be constants, then the two equations *separate*, and the values of N_1 and N_3 can be computed by solving each equation independently. An iterative procedure can be used to adjust the coefficients after each sizing until convergence is achieved — which in turn suggests the general relaxation method discussed below.

These optimality equations are derived under the assumption that, at the optimal solution, we have $N_i > 0$. Clearly this need not be the case; we should examine how the equations change without this assumption. This point is closely related to the nature of the dimensioning equations for the high-usage group, as given by Eqs. (8.19) and (8.20). We know that the $H(N_i)$ function is a monotone-decreasing function of N_i and that $H(0) \leq 1$. For the particular choice of cost ratios, the equation may well turn out not to have any solution. The traditional procedure when this occurred was to take $N_i = 0$ as the solution of the equation, using the heuristic argument that the cost ratio is so low that it is not worth using the direct route, and that all the traffic should go on the final. In fact, this argument can be given a rigorous basis; it is left as an exercise (Problem 8.3) to show that, if the dimensioning equation has no solution, then the value $N_i = 0$ satisfies the optimality conditions for the problem reformulated without the assumption that $N_i > 0$ at the optimal solution.

One final remark is in order concerning solutions at zero. Because the group does not exist, it obviously cannot be used, indicating in turn the best routing to use in the network. In other words, although we may have assumed initially that the routing used the group in question, the group may be uneconomical to put in the network, in which case our assumption about the routing was clearly wrong. In this sense, we can say that the results of dimensioning can affect the routing decisions taken for the network. This is about as far as the matter goes, however, since the presence of a high-usage group may be economically justified for the assumed routing, but could equally well not be for some other routing. In other words, solving the dimensioning problem usually does not give much information concerning the routing, contrary to what is sometimes stated in the literature [6].

General ECCS Method

For a general hierarchical network, Eq. (8.8) represents a set of simultaneous nonlinear equations whose solution yields the optimal value of the high-usage trunk group sizes. The finals are dimensioned from the grade-of-service constraints, given that these constraints are tight at the optimal solution.

These equations must be solved for all high-usage groups. They are coupled because of the terms $\partial B_j / \partial N_i$, whose evaluation is also the most time-consuming part of the calculation. We give here a recursive procedure for this computation, using the fact that the groups are ordered, at least to the accuracy required for dimensioning. This, incidentally, yields a relaxation technique for solving the equations.

First note that the derivatives are computed for fixed group sizes. Group j and group i can therefore be coupled only through overflow or carried traffics. That is, a small perturbation of the size of group i will induce a variation of overflow and carried traffics that will propagate toward j via the groups actually used to go from i to j by all traffic components offered to i. As a consequence,

$$\frac{\partial B_j}{\partial N_i} = 0 \quad \forall j \mid \mu(j) \le \mu(i).$$

Consider now the case where j is after i. Let

$$B_j = E(a_j, N_j)$$

$$a_j = \sum_k a_j^k$$

where a_j^k is the traffic offered to link j that came along the kth path from link i; we call this a component of the traffic offered to the link. In what follows, we assume that all traffic streams offered to a group experience the same blocking. Thus B_j is a function of the *total* traffic offered to the link, not of the particular composition of this flow. We can write

$$\frac{\partial B_j}{\partial N_i} = \frac{\partial B_j}{\partial a_j}\frac{\partial a_j}{\partial N_i}$$

$$= \frac{\partial B_j}{\partial a_j}\sum_k \frac{\partial a_j^k}{\partial N_i}.$$

The computation is reduced to evaluating the derivative of each component of the traffic offered to j with respect to N_i. This computation can be done recursively, looking at all the paths from i to j in the influence graph. Let $i = m_0, m_1, m_2, \ldots, j = m_j$ be some such path for component k. We have

$$\frac{\partial a_{m_1}^k}{\partial N_i} = \begin{cases} a_i^k \dfrac{\partial B_i}{\partial N_i} & \text{if } i \text{ overflows on } m_1 \\[2mm] -a_i^k \dfrac{\partial B_i}{\partial N_i} & \text{if } i \text{ is carried on } m_1 \end{cases}$$

$$\frac{\partial a_{m_\ell}^k}{\partial N_i} = \begin{cases} \dfrac{\partial a_{m_{\ell-1}}^k}{\partial N_i}\left[B_{m_{\ell-1}} + a_{m_{l-1}}^k \dfrac{\partial B_{m_{\ell-1}}}{\partial a_{m_{\ell-1}}^k} \right] & \text{if } m_{\ell-1} \text{ overflows on } m_\ell \\[4mm] \dfrac{\partial a_{m_{\ell-1}}^k}{\partial N_i}\left[1 - B_{m_{\ell-1}} - a_{m_{l-1}}^k \dfrac{\partial B_{m_{\ell-1}}}{\partial a_{m_{\ell-1}}^k} \right] & \text{if } m_{\ell-1} \text{ is carried on } m_\ell \end{cases} \tag{8.21}$$

The calculation is clearly recursive, the order proceeding from i to j along all the paths between these two nodes of the influence graph. Let

$$G_{i,m_1}^k = \frac{\partial B_i}{\partial N_i}$$

$$G_{m_\ell}^k = \begin{cases} \left[B_{m_\ell} + a_{m_{l-1}}^k \dfrac{\partial B_{m_\ell}}{\partial a_{m_\ell}^k} \right] & \text{if } m_\ell \text{ overflows on } m_\ell \\[4mm] 1 - \left[B_{m_\ell} + a_{m_{l-1}}^k \dfrac{\partial B_{m_\ell}}{\partial a_{m_\ell}^k} \right] & \text{if } m_\ell \text{ is carried on } m_\ell \end{cases}$$

Note that G does not depend directly on the component, except that the arc of the influence graph is an overflow or a carry arc. This arc is a parameter only of the link since it involves the current total link-offered traffic, as well as derivatives of the blocking function with respect to this traffic. We can write

$$\frac{\partial a_j^k}{\partial N_i} = a_i^k \prod_{s=0}^{j} G_{m_s}^k$$

$$= a_i^k \frac{\partial B_i}{\partial N_i} \prod_{s=1}^{j} G_{m_s}^k.$$

The derivative of the blocking is then

$$\frac{\partial B_j}{\partial N_i} = \frac{\partial B_j}{\partial a_j} \sum_k a_i^k \frac{\partial B_i}{\partial N_i} \prod_{s=1}^{j} G_{m_s}^k$$

$$= \frac{\partial B_j}{\partial a_j} \frac{\partial B_i}{\partial N_i} a_i \sum_k \frac{a_i^k}{a_i} \prod_{s=1}^{j} G_{m_s}^k$$

$$= -\frac{\partial B_j}{\partial a_j} H_i(N_i) \sum_k \frac{a_i^k}{a_i} \prod_{s=1}^{j} G_{m_s}^k. \tag{8.22}$$

We can thus calculate the derivatives with respect to N_i recursively by scanning all the links from i that lead to j. Because the same components are used for all j downward from i, the information can be stored; only a single pass is required for calculating all the descendants.

The optimality equations (8.8) can be rewritten, assuming $N_i > 0$,

$$0 = C_i' - \sum_j C_j' \frac{\partial B_j/\partial a_i}{\partial B_j/\partial N_j} H_i(N_i)\Gamma_{i,j}(\mathbf{N})$$

$$= C_i' - H_i(N_i) \sum_j \frac{C_j'}{\beta_j} \Gamma_{i,j}(\mathbf{N}), \tag{8.23}$$

where

$$H_i(N_i) = -\left(\frac{\partial \hat{a}_i}{\partial N_i}\right)$$

$$= -a_i \frac{\partial B_i}{\partial N_i}$$

$$\Gamma_{i,j} = \sum_k \frac{a_i^k}{a_i} \prod_{s=1}^{j} G_{m_s}^k \tag{8.24}$$

Eq. (8.23) can be solved by a relaxation method similar to the one used for the simple two-path network. Assuming that the $\Gamma_{i,j}$ and β_j are constants independent of the value chosen for the N_is, Eq. (8.23) separates into independent nonlinear equations in a single variable. An iterative procedure is used to find the correct values for the $\Gamma_{i,j}$s and β_js. The relaxation algorithm is as follows:

1. The β_j and $\Gamma_{i,j}$ are known, either from the previous iteration or from some initial estimate. Making them fixed separates the system (8.8) into independent equations, one for each high-usage group.

2. Using Eq. (8.23), calculate the value of H_i for each direct link. Knowing these quantities as well as the first-offered traffic to these links allows us to calculate the number of circuits N_i that must be installed according to the current values of the $\Gamma_{i,j}$.

3. Knowing the values of N_i and the first-offered traffic, calculate the total traffic offered to each overflow link.

4. Knowing the value of traffic offered to the overflow links, calculate new values for the β_j and the $\Gamma_{i,j}$.

5. If the new values differ from the old ones by more than a preset limit, return to step 1, using these new values of the β_j and the $\Gamma_{i,j}$. Otherwise, a stationary point has been found.

We call an ECCS method any dimensioning method that attempts to solve the Kuhn-Tucker conditions directly by such a relaxation procedure. As we see later, similar techniques can be used in different contexts; the efficiency obtained on these problems should be comparable to that of the standard ECCS method explained here. In practice, the procedure can be modified in several ways:

1. Most important, the traffic must be updated frequently during an iteration, every time the size of a high-usage group is changed. Otherwise the relaxation procedure often will not converge.

2. The procedure can be speeded up by taking the βs and Γs constant, reducing the relaxation procedure to a single iteration. Even if these terms are not assumed to be constant, they converge very quickly to a stationary value, so that it is seldom necessary to iterate more than two or three times.

3. Because solutions must be in integers, trunk sizing is often done for integer N only. This may speed up the calculation of the trunk groups.

A word should be said about traffic models used in the dimensioning. Traffic flows within a hierarchical network can be broadly classified into two categories. The high-usage direct groups receive external flows only; for these links, the Poisson model is accurate. The finals, however, receive traffic that has been blocked somewhere else in the network. Thus the traffic offered to these groups is highly peaked; the Poisson model is *not* adequate to compute their blocking. The ECCS method can easily be modified to work with a two-moment model for traffic throughout the network. The simpler technique of using Poisson models for high-usage and intermediate groups, and a two-moment model for the finals, may be adequate in many situations, avoiding the larger storage requirements of the full two-moment model.

Summary

The relaxation procedure described here can be applied to the dimensioning of very large hierarchical networks, with hundreds of nodes. This impressive efficiency is the consequence of four features of the problem:

1. For a given value of the group sizes, traffic flows are not computed iteratively, but in a single pass over all the links. This is because the links can be ordered, which in turn is a consequence of *both* the routing and the assumption of low blocking on the finals.

2. The method works directly on the Kuhn-Tucker equations, and is more like a Newton method for solving nonlinear equations than a traditional descent method for nonlinear optimization.

3. The grade-of-service constraints are expressed on a link-by-link basis, facilitating the separation of the Kuhn-Tucker equations during the procedure.

4. The constraints are tight at the solution, which, in conjunction with the low blocking on finals, allows the multipliers to be eliminated from the Kuhn-Tucker equations.

As we shall see, these characteristics are not always present when more complex routings are used or when more than one traffic demand is considered. Nevertheless, the ECCS method can still be used in the latter case and large gains in efficiency can be expected over other methods proposed so far.

8.2   Multihour Dimensioning

The dimensioning methods described in Section 8.1 are based on the existence of a single matrix representing the traffic for between all the offices. It is known, however, that traffic demand is not a stationary process and that the average traffic flow between two offices can vary substantially. Within metropolitan networks, variations occur during the day because of the different periods of peak demand between the city core and the suburbs. A similar daily effect is present in international traffic or in long distance networks spanning different time zones, as in North America. Finally, multiple traffic demands may vary seasonally because of large population movements during holidays and vacation periods.

A simplistic solution consists of either (1) ignoring the effect, dimensioning the network based on a single, presumably representative, traffic matrix, or (2) taking the effect into account, dimensioning the network for a matrix made of the peak values of each individual matrix. The first method does not guarantee an adequate grade of service in all periods, while the second provides adequate service but at a much higher cost than necessary.

The technique of multihour dimensioning specifically takes into account these variations in the offered load. The basic idea is to utilize the fact that demand peaks do not occur at the same time between all pairs of offices, thus reducing the number of circuits that must be provided but still maintaining an adequate grade of service in all time periods. The potential economies depend on the existence of alternate routing to efficiently utilize network capacity during off hours; trunk savings might be greater than otherwise the case for fixed routing if the routing rules were modified as the demand varies over time. This topic is discussed elsewhere in the chapters dealing with dynamic and adaptive routings (Chapters 7 and 9). For now, we restrict ourselves to the case of fixed hierarchical alternate routing.

This section is divided as follows. First we give a precise mathematical programming formulation of the multihour-dimensioning problem. Then we review several types of solution methods, the first of which is so-called *equivalent methods*, where the multihour problem is reduced to a single problem, or perhaps a sequence of single-hour problems. Then we examine two methods that deal directly with the multihour problem: (1) a primal method that requires the techniques of nondifferentiable optimization and (2) a dual method that generalizes the multihour case of the single-hour ECCS method (see Section 8.1).

Problem Definition

The mathematical programming formulation of multihour dimensioning, quite similar to Eq. (8.1), can be written

$$\min_N \sum_i C_i(N_i)$$

$$B_j^t(\mathbf{N}) \leq \overline{B}_j^t, \quad j \in \{F\}, \quad t = 1, \ldots T \quad (\mathbf{u}^t) \qquad (8.25)$$

$$N_i \geq 0 \quad (\mathbf{v})$$

where

A_t = The traffic matrix for period t.

$\overline{B}_j^t$ = The grade of service constraint on the jth final in period t.

$B(\mathbf{N})^t$ = The blocking function on the finals in period t. This function depends implicitly on the traffic matrix A_t, a dependence made explicit when needed by writing the function as $B_j^t(A_t, \mathbf{N})$.

$\mathbf{u}, \mathbf{v}$ = The Kuhn-Tucker multipliers for the blocking and positivity constraints, respectively.

Note two points about this formulation. First, Eq. (8.25) differs from Eq. (8.1) by the *addition* of constraints. This means that the solution of the multihour problem *cannot* be less costly than the solution of a single-hour problem with any one of the A_t as the traffic matrix. Claims to the effect that multihour methods are lower cost than single-hour methods mean that the single-hour problem has a different matrix from that of any one of the matrices used for multihour dimensioning.

Second, the grade of service can be made period dependent — a very reasonable assumption if rates are period dependent, the usual case in telephone networks. After all, if one is paying $x\%$ less during weekends, it is quite reasonable that the grade of service during that period should be somewhat poorer that during weekdays, when the full rate is applied.

Equivalent Single-Hour Methods

Because the ECCS method is an extremely efficient way to dimension hierarchical networks for a single-traffic matrix, it is natural to try to use it in solving the multihour problem. This has been done is two different ways. The first, called the *sizing-up* method, solves a sequence of problems, each with the correct demand matrix, but with additional constraints on the group sizes [7]. Sizing up works as follows:

1. Rank the A_t in some predetermined order.

2. Solve a sequence of T single-hour problems, each of the form

$$\min_{N_s^{(t)}} \sum_s C_s(N_s^t)$$

$$B_j^t(A_t, N^{(t)}) \le \overline{B}_j^t$$

and with the additional constraints

$$N_s^{(t)} \ge N_s^{(t-1)} \ge 0.$$

The method yields a sequence of nondecreasing values N^t; the solution to (8.25) is given by N^T. The network thus produced meets the grade-of-service constraints in all periods and for the appropriate matrix. Furthermore, it is linear in T, probably as good as could be expected in terms of computational requirements. On the negative side, the final solution strongly depends on the ordering of the matrices, and it is not known how far the solution is from the true optimum of (8.25). Published results [7] indicate that the method may "overdimension" networks — the gains obtained by using it over the usual cluster busy-hour technique explained next are lower than those obtained by the more accurate methods of Elsner and of Girard, Lansard, and Liau. Beshai, Pound, and Horn claim that the sizing-up method gives comparable savings on other networks, but no such evidence has yet been presented.

Another kind of approximate method is based on computing a matrix A that is equivalent to the set of matrices A_t in that it somehow captures the important effects of noncoincidence, and then to use this matrix with the single-hour ECCS method. Two approaches of this type have been devised: (1) the so-called *cluster busy-hour method* and (2) the *equivalent-matrix method* of Rapp [8]. Both methods assume that the grade of service is the same in all periods, ensuring that the saturation period is the period when the largest traffic is offered to the final, which is not the case if the grades of service are different.

The cluster busy-hour method is a way of choosing a period t that will be used in a single-hour ECCS method to dimension the network [9]. Because the constraints are expressed in term of blocking on the finals, the significant period in which to do the dimensioning should be when the traffic offered to a final is greatest. This concept is captured by the notion of a cluster, which is, for an originating office i, the set of all (i, m) high-usage groups and the (i, T_i) final. The cluster busy-hour is defined as the period when the total cluster traffic is greatest, or, more precisely, the period when the total carried traffic on the high-usage groups plus the total traffic offered to the (i, T_i) final is greatest. If t_i is the busy hour for a cluster originating at i, the equivalent traffic matrix has row $\mathbf{a}^i = \mathbf{a}^i_{t_i}$. The equivalent matrix is then used in the single-hour ECCS method to dimension the network.

Because the method does not guarantee that the grade of service is met in all periods, a further sizing-up stage is sometimes required to increase the capacity of the finals to meet the actual demand in off-hours. Given that the sizes of the high-usage groups are left unchanged during this operation, this poses no difficulty. The method is currently used to dimension telephone networks for more than one traffic matrix. It can also be extended to take into account both legs of the alternate route, in which case it is called the *significant-hours* method [9].

Rapp's method [8] can be best understood by considering the dimensioning of a high-usage group i, j within a two-level network with tandem T. This

i, j group is sized according to the single-hour ECCS principle, but with the equivalent traffic demands given by

$$\overline{A}^{i,j} \triangleq \frac{1}{2} \left[\max_t \left(A_t^{i,T} + A_{0,t}^{i,T} \right) + \max_t \left(A_t^{T,j} + A_{0,t}^{T,j} \right) \right.$$
$$\left. - \left(\max_t A_{0,t}^{i,T} + \max_t A_{0,t}^{T,j} \right) \right], \tag{8.26}$$

where $A_{0,t}^{i,T}$ and $A_{0,t}^{T,j}$ represent the traffic offered to the tandem links i, T and T, j for all traffic relations except i, j. Note that the value obtained for the equivalent traffic depends on the maximum of the overflow traffic offered to the finals. Since these values in turn depend on the choice made for the corresponding high-usage groups, the method can only be iterative. Its accuracy for isolated triangles has been estimated in [8], where the results were within 1% of the exact solution computed by complete enumeration. No results on the efficiency or accuracy of the method have been published for more complex cases, and apparently the method has not been used in any realistic network.

Primal Method

The first attempt to solve (8.25) was made by Elsner and Eisenberg [9,10,11]. Their approach is best understood by again considering the single-hour problem (8.1). We know that, for any value of the $N_i, i \in \{H\}$, we can compute a value of the finals N_j such that all of the constraints are tight. Thus, although the objective function $z(\mathbf{N})$ has been written as a sum over all trunk groups, one might as well consider it as a function $F(N_i)$ of the high-usage sizes N_i only, the N_j being uniquely determined by the constraints. We denote this set of independent variables by the vector $\mathbf{N}$. This is the traditional solution to the dimensioning problem [4]; the results are identical to those presented in Section 8.1. The reason is that F is a continuous differentiable function of N_i, at least as long as the Jacobian matrix of the constraints is not singular. Thus the optimality equations (8.2) and (8.3) can be obtained by setting $\nabla F = 0$. The method is called *primal* because it operates on (8.25) directly, and the solution is feasible at each iteration since the finals are dimensioned to meet the constraints.

The primal method of Elsner, a generalization to the multihour case of this F function, is a solution technique for two-level networks. In what follows, we consider the simple network described in [11], showing that the function F is not differentiable everywhere. Moreover, it is likely that the minimum of the cost function occurs at one of the points at which the gradient does not exist; thus deriving optimality conditions by setting the gradient to zero is out of the question.

We see how the theory of nondifferentiable optimization can be used instead for this problem. After explaining an exact descent method, we briefly

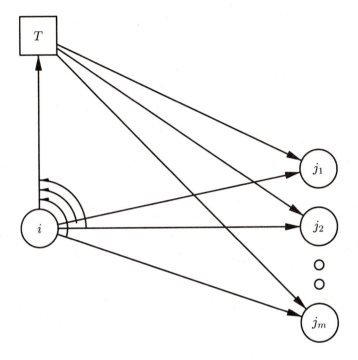

Figure 8.5   Two-Level Network

explain an approximate solution technique based on coordinate descent and present some computational results. We then relate the technique to a reduced-gradient formulation of the solution algorithm, shedding light on the nature of the multihour problem and its relation to the ECCS equations.

Two-Level Single-Tandem Network.   Consider the case of a single originating office i, its tandem T, and m terminating offices j located within the same sector (see Fig. 8.5). We derive the theory for the multihour dimensioning of such a network by nondifferentiable methods, slightly modifying the arguments found in [11] to take into account the possibility of having different grades of services during different periods. We assume a linear cost model, with unit costs $C_{i,j}$, $C_{i,T}$, and $C_{T,j}$ for the corresponding groups, and a switching cost C_s per Erlang of traffic switched through the tandem, denoted here by a_s. The primal algorithm can best be stated in terms of a number of auxiliary functions, the meaning of which should be clear. Define

$$a_s^t \triangleq \sum_j A_t^{i,j} E(A_t^{i,j}, N_{i,j})$$

$$n_{i,T}^t \stackrel{\triangle}{=} \arg\left\{E(a^t, n_{i,T}^t) = \overline{B}_{i,T}^t\right\}$$

$$n_{T,j}^t \stackrel{\triangle}{=} \arg\left\{E(a^t, n_{T,j}^t) = \overline{B}_{T,j}^t\right\}$$

where a^t is the total overflow traffic offered to the final in period t. Each of the $n_{i,T}^t$ and $n_{T,j}^t$ is a function of the $N_{i,j}$ through a^t, representing the number of trunks that would be required on the finals in each period to meet the grade-of-service constraint for that period. Because the finals must meet the constraints in *all* periods, this multihour-dimensioning problem can be stated as

$$\min F(N_{i,j}) = \min_{N_{i,j}} \sum_j C_{i,j} N_{i,j} + C_s \max_t a_s^t(N_{i,j})$$

$$+ C_{i,T} \max_t n_{i,T}^t(N_{i,j}) + \sum_j C_{T,j} \max_t n_{T,j}^t(N_{i,j}) \qquad (8.27)$$

$$= \min_{N_{i,j} \geq 0} \sum_j N_{i,j} C_{i,j} + \max_t C_t(N_{i,j})$$

where

$$C_t(N_{i,j}) \stackrel{\triangle}{=} C_s a_s^t(N_{i,j}) + C_{i,T} n_{i,T}^t(N_{i,j}) + \sum_j C_{T,j} n_{T,j}^t(N_{i,j}).$$

$C_t(N_{i,j})$ is the portion of the total cost incurred by provisioning the finals and the switch. It is also the nondifferentiable part of the objective function since it contains max operations.

Differentiability Conditions.   Although the function of (8.27) is not differentiable everywhere, it is possible to characterize the conditions under which its gradient exists. Let

t_i^{*k} = The kth period at which a maximum occurs for $n_{i,T}^t$.

t_s^{*k} = The kth period at which a maximum occurs for a_s^t.

t_j^{*k} = The kth period at which a maximum occurs for $n_{T,j}^t$.

Note that the t^* are functions of $N_{i,j}$. Define the saturation index for the C_t function for a given value of the $N_{i,j}$ as the set

$$\tau(\mathbf{N}) = \left\{t_i^{*k}, t_s^{*k}, t_j^{*k}\right\}.$$

We now partition the space $N_{i,j} \geq 0$ into disjoint regions characterized by the property that, *inside* a particular region, each of the t^* assumes a single value; that is, the individual cost functions reach their maximum value at a single period. Thus a region is characterized by an $m + 2$ vector of period values t_i^*, t_s^*, t_j^*. By construction, we have the strict inequalities

$$a_s^{t^*} > a_s^t, \quad t \neq t_s^* \qquad (8.28)$$

$$n_{i,T}^{t^*} > n_{i,T}^t, \quad t \neq t_i^*$$
$$n_{T,j}^{t^*} > n_{T,j}^t, \quad t \neq t_j^*$$

Thus there is a neighborhood $\Delta N_{i,j}$ of the current point where the function F is continuously differentiable for any displacement within $\Delta N_{i,j}$, and the gradient exists at this point. Consider now the case where, say, one of the a_s or $n(\cdot)$ functions has a maximum for more than a single value of t. For notational simplicity, take the case where this happens for a_s, which has, for a particular value of $N_{i,j}$, a minimum at period $t_s^{(1)}$ and $t_s^{(2)}$. The gradient does not exist because a small displacement in the variable N_{i,j_1} follows the $a_s^{t_1}$ surface, while a displacement in the $-N_{i,j_1}$ direction follows the $a_s^{t_2}$ surface, which in general is different.

The condition that $\tau(\mathbf{N})$ be a singleton effectively partitions the space of $\mathbf{N}$ into disjoint regions where the objective function is differentiable. Thus the optimal solution of a multihour-dimensioning problem can be of only two types. A multihour problem having its solution inside one of these regions is said to be solvable by the ECCS method — at least in principle — because the minimum-cost point can be characterized by the solution of the equation $\nabla F = 0$, which takes the form

$$\frac{\partial C_{i,j}}{\partial N_{i,j}} - \sum_{t \in \tau} \left[C_{i,T} \frac{H_s^{t_{i,T}^*}(N_s)}{\beta_{i,T}^{t_{i,T}^*}} + C_s H_s^{t_s^*}(N_s) + C_{T,j} \frac{H_s^{t_{T,j}^*}}{\beta_{T,j}^{t_{T,j}^*}} \right] = 0. \qquad (8.29)$$

This is the standard ECCS equation, except now that each term is calculated at that particular period where each component of the F function saturates. Although quite similar to Eq. (8.19), it is not very useful because it requires that the minimum indeed occurs inside a region, and that the τ vector for this particular region is known. Since the τ vectors are not known in advance, the equation cannot be used to compute a solution. Only when the solution is internal to a region, *and* all the elements of the set τ are identical, can the problem be solved by a standard ECCS equation.

The other case arises when the solution is at the boundary of two or more regions. At such a point, there is no gradient, the solution cannot be characterized in the usual way as a zero of ∇F, and other techniques must be used.

Nondifferentiable Optimization. Thus, for a true multihour problem, methods of nondifferentiable optimization must be used to compute a primal solution. An exposition of this theory is clearly outside the scope of this book. Excellent references can be found on the subject, for instance in [12]. Here we only outline a solution strategy, point out the computational requirements, and indicate approximate solution techniques.

At a given point $\mathbf{N}$, we say that a vector $\mathbf{y}$ is a feasible direction if there exists a $\lambda > 0$ such that $\mathbf{N} + \lambda \mathbf{y} \geq 0$. In the following, and unless otherwise stated, the symbol $\mathbf{y}$ should be understood to mean such a feasible direction.

We have seen that, at a boundary of the regions, ∇F does not exist: A small displacement in one direction follows one surface of the function F, while a small displacement in the opposite direction moves onto another surface. Thus the direction of movement at $\mathbf{N}$ is important. In fact, this notion of displacement is used in the definition of a generalization of the notion of gradient, that of directional derivative. The directional derivative is defined, at $\mathbf{N}$ and in z(feasible) direction $\mathbf{y}$, as

$$F(\mathbf{N};\mathbf{y}) = \lim_{\lambda \to 0+} \frac{F(\mathbf{N} + \lambda\mathbf{y}) - F(\mathbf{N})}{\lambda}.$$

In the case where ∇F exists at $\mathbf{N}$, we have

$$F(\mathbf{N};\mathbf{y}) = <\mathbf{y}, \nabla F>,$$

where the direction of ∇F is the $\mathbf{y}$ for which $F(\mathbf{N};\mathbf{y})$ is maximum. A direction of descent is a $\mathbf{y}$ such that $F(\mathbf{N};\mathbf{y}) < 0$. Nondifferentiable optimization methods use directions of descent in very much the same way that ordinary descent algorithms do for differentiable functions. Such algorithms take the following general form:

1. At the current point, compute a (feasible) direction of descent $\mathbf{y}$. A good choice is to use the steepest descent, in which case the direction is computed by solving

   $$\min_{y} F(\mathbf{N};\mathbf{y}).$$

2. If the value found in step 1 is 0, stop. The current point is a local minimum.

3. If not, $\mathbf{y}$ is a direction of descent. Compute the step size by solving

   $$\min_{\alpha>0} F(\mathbf{N} + \alpha\mathbf{y}).$$

4. The new point is $\mathbf{N} + \alpha\mathbf{y}$. Return to step 1.

We now look at this procedure in the case where F is given by (8.27) — in particular, the computation of the direction $\mathbf{y}$. Note that each of the C_t functions of (8.27) is differentiable. The steepest descent condition can be expressed as

$$\min_{y} F(\mathbf{N};\mathbf{y}) = \min_{y} \max_{t} <\mathbf{y}, \nabla C_t(\mathbf{N})>$$

$$\|\mathbf{y}\| \leq 1$$

$$\mathbf{y} \text{ feasible}$$

The difficulty is that this is a nonlinear minimax optimization problem, which is likely to be difficult to solve. Instead of an exact solution, approximations have been proposed.

Approximate Direction.   The first one [11] is to replace the minimax problem by a linear program of the form

$$\min \sigma$$
$$<\mathbf{y}, \nabla C_t(\mathbf{N})> \leq \sigma$$
$$|y_i| \leq 1$$
$$y_i \geq 0 \text{ whenever } N_{i,j} = 0$$

Although the solution of this linear program is no longer a direction of steepest descent, the general algorithm still converges.

Coordinate Search.   The other method, proposed by Eisenberg [10], is a standard coordinate-search technique, closely related to that of Rapp. It operates by sizing each high-usage group separately, keeping the others fixed at the current value:

1. At the current iteration k, the $N_{i,j}^k$ are known, either from initialization or from the previous iteration.

2. From the $N_{i,j}^k$, compute the overflow traffics in all periods. This yields the total traffic offered to the finals in each period. This is important since the optimal size of the high usage depends on these values.

3. Select a high-usage group not previously chosen at this cycle for dimensioning, say (i, m). Keeping all other $N_{i,j}$ fixed, optimally size $N_{i,m}$ with the currently available background and overflow traffics on the finals. This can be done easily, since the network cost function is a function of a single variable.

4. Having sized (i, m), recompute new values for the overflows in all periods.

5. Repeat the procedure for all high-usage groups.

6. At the end of the current cycle, check for stationarity of the group sizes

$$\|\mathbf{N}^{(k+1)} - \mathbf{N}^{(k)}\| \leq \epsilon.$$

If the stopping rule is not met, start another cycle. Otherwise, stop.

Such a search method is suboptimal whenever the minimum lies on a ridge of the objective function that is not oriented along one of the coordinate axes.

Reduced-Gradient Interpretation of Primal Algorithm.   The reduced-gradient method is a general-purpose nonlinear optimization technique that maintains the feasibility of the original problem throughout. For this reason, it is a primal method. Originally designed for linearly constrained problems, the technique was further generalized to the case of nonlinear constraints in [13,14,15]. Because of its generality, the notion of a reduced gradient can serve as a unifying model for both the single- and multihour dimensioning problems, although it does not lead to an algorithm suitable for large networks. We first give another derivation of the ECCS equations for the single-hour problem, based on the reduced-gradient method. We then see the form of the equations in the multihour case, as well as how the nondifferentiability of the function is reflected on the form of the reduced gradient.

Consider the classical double-sector tandem network of Fig. 8.4 for a single matrix. We want to solve (8.1) by the reduced-gradient method. We choose a priori a basis made up of the finals, the high-usage variables being the free variables. This choice is justified because we know that, at the optimal solution, all the constraints are tight. The Jacobian matrix is given by

$$
B = \begin{bmatrix}
\dfrac{\partial B_2}{\partial N_2} & \dfrac{\partial B_2}{\partial N_4} & \dfrac{\partial B_2}{\partial N_5} \\[2mm]
\dfrac{\partial B_4}{\partial N_2} & \dfrac{\partial B_4}{\partial N_4} & \dfrac{\partial B_4}{\partial N_5} \\[2mm]
\dfrac{\partial B_5}{\partial N_2} & \dfrac{\partial B_5}{\partial N_4} & \dfrac{\partial B_5}{\partial N_5}
\end{bmatrix}. \tag{8.30}
$$

Assuming as usual that $\partial B_j/\partial N_k = 0$, $j \in \{F\}$, $k \in \{F\}$, $j \neq k$, the Jacobian matrix takes the form

$$
B = \operatorname{diag}\left(\partial B_j/\partial N_j\right), \quad j \in \{F\}. \tag{8.31}
$$

The dual-variable approximation is given by

$$
\pi_j = C'_j \Big/ \frac{\partial B_j}{\partial N_j}, \quad j \in \{F\} \tag{8.32}
$$

and the reduced gradient corresponding to this basis is given by

$$
\nabla F = \begin{bmatrix}
C'_1 - \sum_j C'_j \dfrac{\partial B_j/\partial N_1}{\partial B_j/\partial N_j} \\[3mm]
C'_3 - \sum_j C'_j \dfrac{\partial B_j/\partial N_3}{\partial B_j/\partial N_j}
\end{bmatrix}. \tag{8.33}
$$

The choice of the symbol $F(\cdot)$ for this function is intentional. In fact, this function is precisely the same as the $F(\cdot)$ function used in Eq. (8.27). Consider now the component of the reduced gradient with respect to N_1. Using the same arguments as in Section 8.1, and replacing by the usual definitions of marginal occupancy, the first component of Eq. (8.33) becomes

$$
\nabla_1 F = C'_1 - H_1 \left\{ \left[\frac{C'_5}{\beta_5} + \frac{C'_4}{\beta_4} \right] \gamma_3 + \frac{C'_2}{\beta_2} \right\}. \tag{8.34}
$$

Thus we reach the important conclusion that *the ECCS equations are none other than the equation $\nabla F = 0$ for the basis made of the finals*. Because the notion of reduced gradient is valid for any nonlinear program, it can also be applied to the multihour case.

Consider again the double-sector tandem network, but this time with two matrices. The problem has five variables; there are six constraints. As a consequence, at the optimal solution, there can be between three and five active constraints. In general, it is impossible to satisfy six equations with five variables; we know that three of the equations can always be satisfied. Thus, for the multihour problem,

1. We do not know in advance what is the basis at the solution.

2. The bases may, and in general will, be larger than the number of variables corresponding to the size of the finals.

Consider now the case where the three constraints in period 1 and the blocking on final 2 in period 2 are the tight constraints. We must select a basis; we choose the three finals and N_1. The basis matrix now has the form

$$B = \begin{bmatrix} \dfrac{\partial B_2^2}{\partial N_1} & \dfrac{\partial B_2^2}{\partial N_2} & \dfrac{\partial B_2^2}{\partial N_4} & \dfrac{\partial B_2^2}{\partial N_5} \\[2ex] \dfrac{\partial B_2^1}{\partial N_1} & \dfrac{\partial B_2^1}{\partial N_2} & 0 & 0 \\[2ex] \dfrac{\partial B_4^1}{\partial N_1} & 0 & \dfrac{\partial B_4^1}{\partial N_4} & 0 \\[2ex] \dfrac{\partial B_5^1}{\partial N_1} & 0 & 0 & \dfrac{\partial B_5^1}{\partial N_5} \end{bmatrix} \tag{8.35}$$

under the usual assumptions. It is clear that the inverse does not have a simple form and that the reduced gradient is much more complex than for the single-hour problem. Furthermore, even if it were possible to invert the basis, the dimensioning equations could not be found by setting the reduced gradient to zero. This is so because the function F is not differentiable everywhere, as is well known from the theory of reduced gradient. To see this another way, consider under what conditions the basis is diagonal: whenever each constraint is tight in only one period. But this corresponds precisely to the condition defining the regions in Eq. (8.28). Moving from one region to the next, Eq. (8.29) changes abruptly at the boundary, and the reduced gradient is discontinuous at this point. Thus it is impossible to use a condition such as $\nabla F = 0$ to define a minimum point; more complex conditions related to nondifferentiable optimization must be used.

Summary of Primal Methods.   To summarize, we have seen that the primal method of Elsner operates by minimizing a function of the high-usage group sizes only, satisfying the constraints at all times. The objective function is not differentiable everywhere. We have characterized regions where it is differentiable and shown that nondifferentiability occurs at the boundaries between regions. Finally, we related this formulation to the more general theory of the reduced gradient, showing that the regions of differentiability of the function correspond to a diagonal basis for the reduced gradient. This also demonstrates why the reduced-gradient technique, although applicable in theory to any nonlinear optimization, cannot be simplified to take advantage of the particular structure of the multihour-dimensioning problem.

Dual Method

We have seen that the primal method of Elsner, although it works on the original problem, does not lead to a generalization of the standard ECCS method. The method requires nondifferentiable optimization techniques, which may not be suitable for large networks with more complex hierarchies than that of the simple network of Fig. 8.5. The main difficulty with Eq. (8.37) is that it does not yield the value for the multipliers — an essential feature of the multihour problem, since the difficulty resides precisely in the fact that it is not known a priori which constraints will be tight at the solution. Thus we are led to solution techniques that incorporate some way to estimate the multipliers.

Because we are interested in solving (8.25) in a way similar to the single-hour ECCS method, we want to solve the Kuhn-Tucker equations directly, instead of using a normal descent method. If it is to be efficient enough for large networks, this solution must also be of the relaxation type, without need for gradient calculations. We now see how these requirements can be met. Because we are dealing with dual variables, the solution technique is of the dual type, which means that feasibility is not maintained at all iterations. The exposition is in two steps. First we assume that the values of the multipliers are known, showing how the multihour-dimensioning equations can be solved by a generalization of the single-hour ECCS method. Then we give a method for estimating the multipliers.

Dimensioning for Given Multipliers.   Suppose now that the correct values for the u_j^ts are known; the dimensioning becomes much easier, although not quite as easy as in the single-hour case. We derive the Kuhn-Tucker equations first for the finals and then for the high-usage groups. Write the Lagrangian corresponding to Eq. (8.25):

$$\mathcal{L}(\mathbf{N}, \mathbf{u}) = \sum_i C_i(N_i) + \sum_{t=1}^{T} \sum_{j \in \{F\}} u_j^t (B_j^t - \overline{B}_j^t). \qquad (8.36)$$

Let $u_j^t \geq 0$ be the multiplier for the jth final in period t. Setting the components equal to zero, we get

$$0 = C_j' + \sum_{t=1}^{T} u_j^t \frac{\partial B_j^t}{\partial N_j} \quad j \in \{F\}. \qquad (8.37)$$

Similarly, we obtain, for the ith high usage,

$$0 = C_i' + \sum_{t=1}^{T} \sum_{j \in \{F\}} u_j^t \frac{\partial B_j^t}{\partial N_i}$$

$$= C_i' + \sum_{t=1}^{T} \Gamma_{i,j}^t(\mathbf{N}) H_i^t(N_i) \qquad (8.38)$$

Note that if $T = 1$, Eq. (8.37) becomes

$$C_j' = u_j \frac{\partial B_j}{\partial N_j},$$

as it should.

First consider Eq. (8.37) for the finals. Note that there is one independent equation for each link, as was the case for the single-hour problem. The right-hand side is now a sum of terms, all of the form $\partial B_t^t / \partial N_j$, and in general there is more than one of these for some finals. This is another essential feature of the multihour problem: A given final may saturate in more than one period. Suppose furthermore that the sizes of the high-usage groups are known. Then the traffic offered to each final in each period can be calculated; the right-hand side is a nonnegative combination of strictly decreasing functions of a single variable, and is therefore also a decreasing function. It has a unique solution N_j, which can easily be calculated by a bisection technique. Provided that the multipliers are given, and the high-usage groups properly sized, the dimensioning of the finals separates neatly into independent problems, which can be solved quickly.

The dimensioning of high-usage trunks is given similarly by the set of simultaneous nonlinear equations (8.38). The coupling coefficients are the $\Gamma_{i,j}^t$s, which in general depend on all the N_i. A relaxation method is possible by taking these coefficients as constants. In this case, the equations separate into $|\{I\}|$ independent equations, one for each high-usage group. Their structure is similar to that of the high-usage equations for the single-hour ECCS method, except for the following differences. First recall that the $H_i(N_i)$ are monotone-decreasing functions of their argument. Thus, in the single-hour case, the solution, if it exists, is unique. In the present case, however, the right-hand term of the equation is given by a linear combination of H_i functions, and not all the coefficients are necessarily nonnegative. It follows that the multihour case is intrinsically more complex because theoretically the high-usage dimensioning equation may have more than one solution. In practice, the coefficients are frequently of different sign, but one term is generally dominant; this seems to cause no difficulty.

To summarize, we have found a relaxation procedure for solving the Kuhn-Tucker equations of the multihour-dimensioning problem, assuming that the multipliers are known:

1. Initialize the high-usage groups to some value $N_i^{(0)}$ at iteration 0.

2. At iteration k, dimension the high-usage groups:

   a. Compute $\Gamma_{i,j}^t(\mathbf{N}^{(k-1)})$.

   b. Keeping these values fixed, dimension the high-usage groups individually from Eqs. (8.38).

3. Compute the traffic flows in the network from the current values of the high-usage groups.

4. Dimension the final groups using Eqs. (8.37).

5. Check some stopping rule, for example, $\sum_i \left(N_i^{(k)} - N_i^{(k-1)} \right)^2 \le \epsilon$. If the condition is not met, iterate once more. Otherwise, stop.

Computing the Multipliers.   The calculation of the previous section is the multihour analog of the traditional ECCS method. It relies on knowing the correct multipliers at the optimal solution, which of course are not known at the outset. Therefore some way must be found to compute these values, a process that necessarily involves duality, which we briefly review here. Further information can be found in textbooks such as [16]. We assume that $N_i > 0$, which is reasonable for the final groups. As for the high-usage groups, we make this assumption for simplicity of exposition. We indicate later how to handle the case when one of the high-usage groups has value 0. The dual function is then

$$w(\mathbf{u}) = \min_{N \ge 0} \mathcal{L}(\mathbf{N}, \mathbf{u}), \tag{8.39}$$

and the dual problem is

$$\max_{\mathbf{u} \ge 0} w(\mathbf{u}). \tag{8.40}$$

The solution of the dual problem yields the correct values for the Kuhn-Tucker multipliers of Eq. (8.25). Thus computing the multipliers involves solving the dual problem, where each evaluation of the dual function requires in turn the minimization of the Lagrangian.

Consider now this minimization:

$$w(\mathbf{u}) = \min_{N \ge 0} \mathcal{L}(\mathbf{N}, \mathbf{u}). \tag{8.41}$$

The first-order Kuhn-Tucker conditions are obviously given by Eqs. (8.37) and (8.38). In the previous section we saw how to solve these equations. Thus the multihour ECCS algorithm can be used to evaluate the dual function at a given point u_j^t.

It remains to maximize w. Nonlinear duality theory [16] states that $w(\mathbf{u})$ is continuous and concave for any primal, but in general nondifferentiable. Because nondifferentiable optimization is generally quite difficult to perform, a rather crude method, called the subgradient method [16], is used to maximize the dual function. The method relies on the property that, for a given $\mathbf{u}$, the quantity $B_j^t - \overline{B}_j^t$ at the solution $\mathbf{N}^*$ of Eq. (8.40) is a subgradient of $w(\mathbf{u})$. Thus this direction is a direction of ascent of w at $\mathbf{u}$ and can be used to search for a maximum. The subgradient method does not attempt to find such a maximum accurately. Instead, a single step is taken in the direction of the subgradient, in the hope that this will yield an improvement. The updating formulas of [16] can be used:

$$\mathbf{u}^{(k+1)} = P^+ \left[\mathbf{u}^{(k)} + \rho_k \mathbf{Q}^{(k)} \right], \tag{8.42}$$

where

P^+ = The projection on the positive orthant.

ρ_k = The step size at iteration k.

$\mathbf{Q}^{(k)}$ = Any subgradient of w at iteration k.

The method is known to converge for the choices

$$0 < \epsilon_1 \leq \lambda_k \leq 2 - \epsilon_2, \quad \epsilon_2 > 0$$
$$\rho_k = \frac{\lambda_k \left[w^* - w(\mathbf{u}^{(k)}) \right]}{\|\mathbf{Q}^{(k)}\|^2} \tag{8.43}$$
$$\mathbf{Q}^{(k)} = \mathbf{B} - \overline{\mathbf{B}}$$

and w^* is the optimal value of the dual solution. In practice, w^* is replaced by an overestimate (in the present case the current value of the primal feasible solution).

Computing a Primal Feasible Solution.   A dual method does not guarantee that the current solution is feasible, which in general does not occur until an optimal point is found. Because the optimization procedure may be stopped before optimality is reached, it is useful to be able to compute a feasible solution from the current dual solution. Such a quantity also can be used in computing the step size as in Eq. (8.43) to estimate the optimum. For hierarchical networks, this is straightforward. Given a dual solution, fix the N_is at their current value. Then compute the traffic flows in the network, following the order of trunk groups. Whenever a final group appears in that calculation, size it so that it satisfies the grade-of-service constraints in all periods. This is possible because of the partial ordering of the groups, which guarantees that, when a final group is reached during the traffic calculation, the total traffic offered to it is known in each period. The result is a network

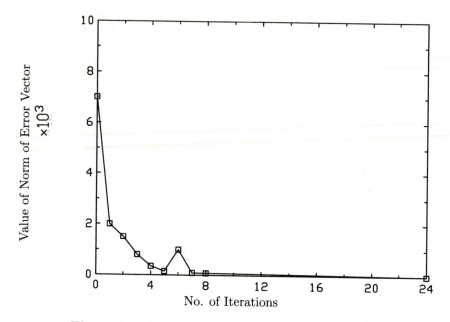

Figure 8.6   Norm of Subgradient for Primal Method

that meets the constraints, and thus is feasible in all periods, although not optimal.

Numerical Results.   Although it would be interesting to compare the primal and dual methods with regard to numerical efficiency, this is virtually impossible. The main reason is the scarcity of published data by the authors of the various methods, as well as the large effort required to develop computer codes in each case. We can, however, look at the behavior of each method individually, from the point of view of convergence rate and robustness.

Primal Method.   The only results known for the primal method have been presented in [10,11] for three subnetworks of the type described in Fig. 8.5. In this work, the groups from the tandem office to the local offices were not considered as terminating finals, but rather were sized according to an unspecified marginal-cost factor. This makes a direct comparison impossible with methods that size these groups for a specified blocking. For the former cases, the primal method converges rather slowly, at least in terms of the number of iterations required to reach the stopping rule (see Fig. 8.6). This rule may be too stringent, however, since the network cost ceases to decrease significantly after the first few iterations (see Fig. 8.7). Unfortunately, no data is given on the computation times required for these calculations, nor is there any indication of the suitability of the method for networks of realistic sizes.

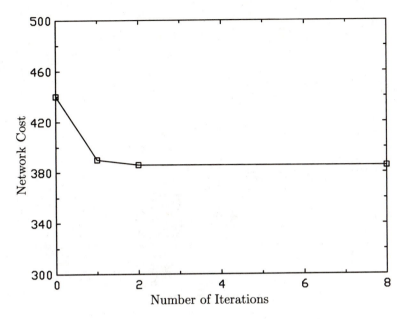

Figure 8.7   Network Cost for Primal Method

The results, shown in Table 8.1, demonstrate a clear saving in trunk and switching cost over a network designed by the cluster busy-hour method.

Component	CBH Method	Multihour
High-usage trunks	295	287
Final trunks	37	29
Switch cost	60	45
Total	437	403

Table 8.1   Cost Reductions over Cluster Busy-Hour Method

Dual Method.   The only published results for the dual method appear in [17]. The method was tested on small networks, where convergence was studied as a function of such parameters as the step size for the dual-ascent algorithm. Typical results are presented in Figs. 8.8 and 8.9 for a small five-node network, showing the effects of using small and large step sizes. The method was also used on larger networks — up to 15 nodes and 210 links — where the solution obtained with the dual algorithm was compared, whenever possible,

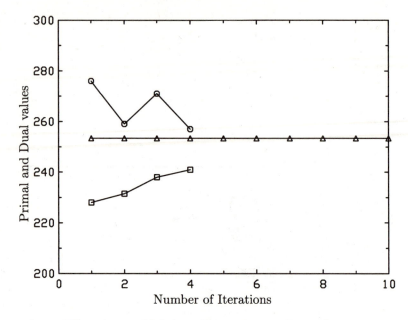

Figure 8.8 Multihour Dimensioning, Large Step

with the exact solution obtained by a general-purpose nonlinear programming program. The results are shown in Table 8.2.

Summary

There is no doubt that the approximate methods are fast enough to be used to dimension large networks. Because these methods do not rely on a precise mathematical model, however, they may not achieve the full benefits of multihour engineering. Exact methods, because they are based precisely on such a model, generally produce solutions that are more economical, while at the same time giving an adequate grade of service. Although the primal method can realize significant gains over the standard cluster busy-hour method, it does not seem obvious that this method can be used for large networks with many hierarchical levels. The computation times for the dual method, on the other hand, are encouraging. Also, because it can deal with arbitrary hierarchies, the dual method appears to be the most promising technique for dimensioning hierarchical networks for more than one demand matrix.

Finally, note that multihour engineering techniques can be used to construct networks that satisfy robustness constraints. For instance, if the network must be able to sustain a $x\%$ overload and still maintain a B' grade of service,

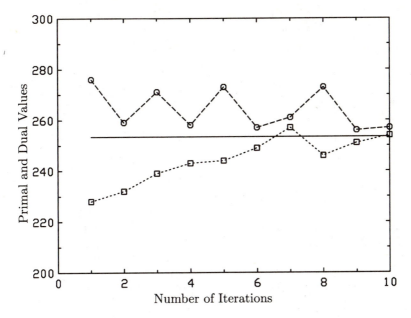

Figure 8.9   Multihour Dimensioning, Small Step

a multihour method can be used with two matrices, the second one scaled up by $x\%$, with B' as the grade of service for that matrix.

8.3   Dimensioning for End-to-End Grade of Service

The grade-of-service constraint for hierarchical telephone networks is traditionally expressed in terms of blocking probability on the final groups. While convenient both practically and theoretically, this is poorly related to the actual grade of service as perceived by the users. The reason is that the end-to-end blocking probability depends not only on the finals, but also on all the other groups present in the network. As a case in point, consider the following example, taken from [18]. There are two end offices in a five-level hierarchical network dimensioned for 1% on the finals. In the first case, all high-usage groups are present; in the second, only the finals are present (see Fig. 8.10). A straightforward application of one of the algorithms of Chapter 4 shows that, in the first case, end-to-end blocking is then 0.2%, while in the second it is as high as 8.6%. Since a real network would have some, but probably not all, high-usage groups present, we can expect the end-to-end grade of service to be different for different pairs of users, and in some cases to be much higher than the 1% provided on the finals.

Solution Method	Iteration	w	z	CPU secs
Subgradient	1	1842	1879	
	2	1838	1873	144
GRG2	1872			
Network 3, 1% ,1% ,4%				
Subgradient	1	1866	1893	
	2	1877	1893	117
GRG2	1894.2			
Network 3, 1% ,1% ,1%				
Subgradient	1	3436	3452	114
E04VAF	3452.1			
Network 4				
Subgradient	1	6922	7217	
	2	*	*	
	3	*	*	
	4	7053	7213	
E04VAF	Not done			
Network 5 (Multihour)				
Subgradient	1	7349	7554	
	2	7532	7557	
E04VAF	Not done			
Network 5 (Single hour)				

Table 8.2   Dimensioning for Networks 3, 4, and 5

   Although end-to-end blocking is generally not measured in telephone networks, the actual grade of service is quite good, considering the high degree of satisfaction with the telephone service, at least in most industrialized countries. A further indication of this high level of service can be found in Fig. 8.11, which indicates the actual distribution of blocking probabilities encountered in a portion of the Bell Canada network, a typical network in an industrialized country. The fact that 90% of all pairs experience less than 0.2% blocking is a sure indication of the high quality of service provided by the blocking-on-finals specification. Conversely, this indicates that some trunk savings may be possible by using a different dimensioning method based on the actual end-to-end

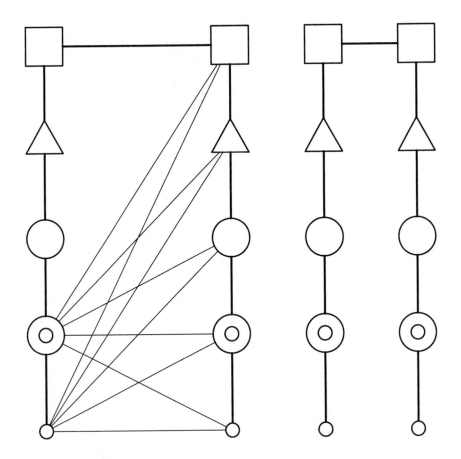

Figure 8.10 End-to-End Blocking for Hierarchical Network

constraints, which would presumably allocate capacity more efficiently.

All the methods designed for nonhierarchical routings operate on an end-to-end grade-of-service specification. Since some of these methods also apply to hierarchical routing networks, some of the results discussed in Chapter 4 apply here. These methods, however, may not be advantageous for hierarchical networks — by design, such methods cannot take advantage of the simplifying structure of the routing, in particular, of the fact that the groups are ordered. Thus a dimensioning method specifically designed for hierarchical networks with an end-to-end grade of service may be of interest. This is the subject of the next section.

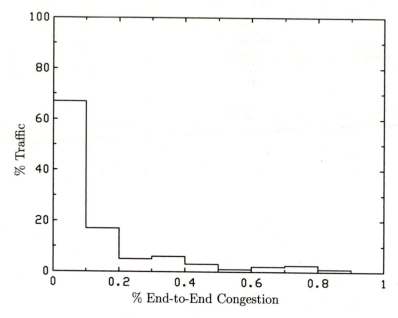

Figure 8.11   End-to-End Blocking for Hierarchical Network

End-to-End Dimensioning Model

First we state the exact mathematical programming formulation for the end-to-end dimensioning of hierarchical networks. After writing the optimality equations, we outline the required computations. The question of the existence and use of a generalization of the ECCS method is also discussed.

The optimization to be performed is, as usual,

$$\min \sum_s C_s(N_s) \qquad (8.44)$$

$$L^k(\mathbf{N}) \le \overline{B}^k \qquad \forall k \qquad (\mathbf{u})$$
$$N_s \ge 0 \qquad (\mathbf{v})$$

Writing the Kuhn-Tucker equations for each trunk group, we get

$$v_s = \frac{\partial C_s}{\partial N_s} + \sum_k u^k \frac{\partial L^k}{\partial N_s} \qquad \forall s \qquad (8.45)$$

where **u** and **v** are the two vectors of multipliers corresponding to the two sets of constraints. For a given value of **N**, we can use any of the methods of Chapter 4 to evaluate L^k. Thus any general-purpose nonlinear programming method can be used to solve (8.44), although perhaps not in the most efficient way.

An interesting question is whether there exists an ECCS method for solving (8.44). Remember that an ECCS method solves the Kuhn-Tucker equations directly by a relaxation procedure. First note that, contrary to the case of (8.1), there is no guarantee that all the constraints will be tight at the solution. In fact, is is unlikely that it will be so. Thus it is impossible to compute from the outset the optimal value of the multipliers, as in (8.7), and to eliminate them from the Kuhn-Tucker equations. Any ECCS method must incorporate some computational technique for evaluating **u** and **v** along with computing the solution. A potential candidate is the subgradient method described in Section 8.2, or any other technique for estimating the multipliers quickly.

Even assuming that the correct **u** and **v** are known, it is not easy to see how to split Eq. (8.45) to give it the standard ECCS form: The constraint functions L^k do not depend on a single group, but on a generally large number of variables, as can be seen from the algorithms described in Chapter 4. Let $I(k)$ be the set of groups j such that j appears in the calculation of L^k. We have, using Eq. 8.21,

$$\frac{\partial L^k}{\partial N_s} = \sum_j \frac{\partial L^k}{\partial B_j} \frac{\partial B_j}{\partial N_s} \quad \forall j \in I(k),$$

where

$$\frac{\partial B_j}{\partial N_s} = \begin{cases} -\dfrac{\partial B_j}{\partial A_j} H_s(N_s) \sum_k \dfrac{A_s^k}{A_s} \prod_{t=1}^{j} G_{m_t}^k & \text{if } j \in \mathcal{D}(s) \\ 0 & \text{otherwise} \end{cases}$$

The Kuhn-Tucker equations could then be split as in the standard ECCS method by taking all terms except $H_s(N_s)$ as constant, then dimensioning the groups individually for the current values of the coefficients. Thus, although an ECCS equation is conceivable for the end-to-end case, it is somewhat more complex since it involves computing the $\partial L^k/\partial B_j$ terms, which are not present when the constraints are expressed in terms of blocking on the final groups. This calculation depends on the blocking algorithm used. It can be done analytically, if analytic expressions are available for the end-to-end blocking as a function of the link blocking, or by finite differences, if a recursive algorithm is used.

Dimensioning over Link-Blocking Probabilities

We have seen that the ECCS method for the end-to-end dimensioning equation requires the introduction of additional terms to represent the coupling between the link blocking probabilities and the end-to-end blocking. This in turn suggests that the problem be transformed to explicitly reflect this fact. This form turns the link-blocking probabilities into the independent variables since, for a given value of these probabilities, the link costs can be computed by inverting the link-blocking model (assuming that the offered-traffic parameters are known). In this case, the mathematical programming model is

$$\min_B \sum C_s\,[N_s(\mathbf{B})]$$

$$L^k(\mathbf{B}) \le \overline{B}^k \qquad \forall k \qquad (\mathbf{u}) \tag{8.46}$$

$$0 \le B_s \le 1 \qquad (\mathbf{v}, \mathbf{w})$$

The Kuhn-Tucker equations are

$$v_j - w_j = \sum_s \frac{\partial C_s}{\partial B_j} + \sum_k u^k \frac{\partial L^k}{\partial B_j}. \tag{8.47}$$

It is left as an exercise (Problem 8.11) to derive an ECCS equation for this case and to show that the actual work is basically the same as for the case of Eq. (8.44).

The potential advantage of this formulation lies in the fact that, if general-purpose nonlinear programming methods are to be used, it may be faster to compute $L^k(B)$ than $L^k(N)$. This is because, given the Ns, evaluating the Bs requires the calculation of link-offered traffics, while the direct evaluation sidesteps this stage. The difference may not be large for hierarchical networks but can become so for other routings with mutual overflow; thus this formulation is worth considering in the context of hierarchical routings. Also, it forms the basis for the only published heuristic [19] specifically designed for the end-to-end dimensioning of hierarchical networks and using link blocking probabilities as the independent variables.

A Heuristic Dimensioning Method

The only known dimensioning algorithm for hierarchical networks under end-to-end blocking constraints is that of Beshai and Horn [19]. Although not an exact method, it is useful because it introduces techniques that are employed in other contexts. Also, the Beshai-Horn technique relies specifically on the fact that hierarchical networks are ordered. The discussion of [19] covers a two-moment model for traffic; we will simplify the discussion by using a Poisson model. This poses no difficulty since the necessary modifications for a two-moment model are obvious.

The procedure takes the link-blocking probabilities as the independent variables. There are two phases. In the first, a maximum value of the link blocking probabilities is computed such that all the end-to-end blocking constraints are satisfied. The second phase is iterative and attempts to increase the link-blocking probabilities, based on a variant of the ECCS method, while at the same time remaining in the domain. The model is the same as Eq. (8.46).

The first phase of the heuristic relies heavily on the ordering of groups in the network to assign an upper bound to the link blocking probabilities. Using the notation of Chapter 4, we let $\mu(j)$ be the level of group j, with $\mu(j) = 1$ if j is a direct group, and with $\mu(j) = m$ if j is a terminating final, where m depends on the number of levels in the hierarchy and the actual routing used. The algorithm for setting upper bounds to the link blocking probabilities works as follows. Assume for simplicity that all the end-to-end blocking constraints are at the same value, say $\overline{B}$.

1. $$B_j \le \overline{B} \quad \forall \{j \mid \mu(j) = m\}$$

2. Assume now that all groups of level m are at their bound $\overline{B}$. We want to compute the largest blocking value of groups of order $m - 1$. We know that these can overflow only on one level-m group with known probability $\overline{B}$. Using one of the models from Chapter 4, we can assign a value B_j, $\mu(j) = m - 1$. With Gaudreau's model [20], we get $B_j = 1/(2 - \overline{B})$ for all level $m - 1$ groups.

3. The remaining procedure is now obvious. The bounds for level $m - 2$ groups can be computed from the previously assigned values to groups at level m and $m - 1$, again using some model of Chapter 4. Using Gaudreau's model, we get for the general case, at level n, $B_j = (\overline{B} + (m - n)(1 - \overline{B}))/(1 + (m - n)(1 - \overline{B}))$.

In the case of uniform $\overline{B}$, it is not possible to have *all* end-to-end constraints at their bounds if some of the direct links are not present. This is another way of saying that it is generally impossible to satisfy $N(N - 1)$ nonlinear equality constraints with fewer than $N(N - 1)$ variables. Having computed these maximum link blocking probabilities, it is now straightforward to compute all the link-offered traffics, again using any technique described in Chapter 4. These values are used to initiate the second phase.

The second phase, iterative in nature, decreases the group sizes while remaining within the feasible domain of the problem. This phase also relies on the fact that the groups can be ordered to select a processing order for the reductions. At the beginning of the current iteration, the link-offered traffics are known, as are the link-blocking probabilities, which are feasible. The process attempts to compute a new set of blocking probabilities that will yield a presumably lower network cost:

1. Links at level m are left unchanged from the previous iteration and are at their maximum value. Their offered traffic, blocking probabilities, and βs are known.

2. Each link at level $m - 1$ is examined in turn, in an attempt to decrease its blocking. This is done as follows for link j at level $m - 1$:

   a. Fix the traffic offered to link j at its current value.

   b. Fix the blocking on the two level-m links k and i to which link j overflows at their current value.

   c. Find a new value of N_j such that

      i. It is no smaller than the current value (so that the link blocking will not increase and the solution will remain feasible).

      ii. And such that

      $$\frac{\partial C}{\partial N_j} = \frac{C'_i}{\beta_i} + \frac{C'_k}{\beta_k}.$$

      That is, dimension link j using the standard ECCS equation for the current marginal costs on the overflow route.

   The new blocking B_j is now given by

   $$B_j = E(A_j, N_j).$$

   d. At the same time, using A_j, compute β_j at the value B_j.

3. Here again, the procedure is fairly obvious. Having done all level-$m - 1$ links, one can proceed to size all level-$m - 2$ links, using the newly calculated values of the B_j and β_j at level $m - 1$ in the corresponding ECCS equation. The calculation proceeds in this manner until all groups have been processed.

4. After a new set of link blocking probabilities is computed, the link-offered traffics are recomputed, and a new cycle is started.

5. Convergence is either on a sufficient decrease of the network cost or on a stabilization of the link-offered traffics.

8.4   Results

Relatively few numerical results have been published on the value of dimensioning hierarchical networks for an end-to-end grade of service. The results of [19] indicate a decrease of network cost of approximately 1% from the value obtained from standard ECCS methods at 1% blocking on the finals. The end-to-end grade-of-service constraint actually used is not specified, making it difficult to evaluate the cost saving.

A more detailed comparison, made by Harris [6], used the Berry model for dimensioning nonhierarchical networks (see Section 9.3 for a detailed description of the Berry method). Although it can handle nonhierarchical networks, the Berry model also applies to networks with a standard hierarchical routing. Because the model works for nonhierarchical networks, it must operate on an end-to-end grade of service constraint, making it possible to compare the standard ECCS method and end-to-end methods. The comparison was carried out on the Adelaide metropolitan network, which has 43 level-five exchanges, and four tandem exchanges used exclusively to switch alternate routed traffic. The route plan had an intermediate high-usage group to the terminating tandem, but not from the originating tandem to the destination office. For a small number of small traffic values, only one overflow on the final was allowed. First the network was dimensioned by the standard ECCS method for a 1% grade of service on the finals. Gaudreau's algorithm was then used to compute, for this network, the end-to-end blocking probabilities for all node pairs, and the average weighted blocking for all pairs. These values were kept to be used as input to the second stage of the comparison. The main characteristics of the distribution of end-to-end blocking probabilities are summarized in Table 8.3.

Grade of Service	Value (%)
Average	0.64
Weighted average	0.24
Maximum	1.64
Minimum	0.08

Table 8.3 Loss Distribution

It was also found that the distribution of loss probabilities had two distinct peaks. The first peak was related to parcels having three paths available for connection, while the second, higher one corresponded to traffic parcels having only two paths. The network was redimensioned for an end-to-end grade-of-service constraint in three different ways. First, the actual end-to-end values computed by Gaudreau's algorithm were specified as equality constraints for the end-to-end blocking. The second comparison was made using the weighted-average blocking as an equality constraint for all pairs. A third dimensioning was done using the extended Berry model of [6], which allows inequality constraints for the grade-of-service specification. The actual network costs obtained in each case are presented in Table 8.4.

Savings of the order of 5% over the traditional ECCS technique were obtained by using an end-to-end dimensioning method. These savings are directly comparable: Both cases offered the *same* end-to-end grade of service (with the

Cost	ECCS	Same	Individual	Extended
Direct	2.557	1.999	2.000	1.981
Alternate	2.185	2.596	2.560	2.539
Total	4.742	4.595	4.560	4.521

Table 8.4   Dimensioning of the Adelaide Network

extended Berry model, some node pairs experienced a grade of service even better than the required value). Other studies performed on smaller networks indicate much larger relative savings by using an end-to-end grade of service — up to 23%.

Summary

The dimensioning of hierarchical networks for end-to-end grade-of-service constraints is a feasible option, although currently much more difficult than for a grade of service specified in terms of blocking on the final groups. The most promising method to date is that of Berry, although this model was designed for more general routing techniques. A heuristic has also been presented; although it seems efficient, its accuracy is unknown. An extension of the standard ECCS method to the end-to-end case appears possible. Virtually no work, however, has been done on the subject.

The main advantage of dimensioning for an end-to-end grade of service lies in the fact that network performance can be more closely matched to what the customer sees. Because current hierarchical networks sized on the basis of blocking constraints on the finals are apparently oversized from this point of view, redimensioning on an end-to-end grade of service may lead to savings in trunks. Finally, end-to-end dimensioning can guarantee a more uniform grade of service to all users, surely a desirable feature for any multiuser system.

On the negative side is the fact that end-to-end performance is generally not measured in hierarchical networks. Thus it would be difficult, if not impossible, to actually check that a network is operating within its design objectives. Also, there is no rational basis for selecting a particular value for the constraints. Although this is also true for current hierarchical networks, the full benefits of end-to-end dimensioning can be achieved only when the largest tolerable blocking is used in the network, in the same way that attenuation criteria are used in designing transmission systems.

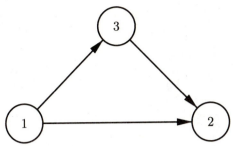

Figure 8.12   Three-Node Network

Problems

8.1. Show that the ECCS equation for the three-node network of Fig. 8.12 can be written as

$$\frac{C_1}{H_1} = \frac{C_2}{\beta_2} + \frac{C_3}{\beta_3}.$$ (8.48)

Discuss under what conditions we obtain the standard ECCS equation

$$\text{ECCS} = \frac{\gamma}{\text{CR}}.$$ (8.49)

8.2. Compute the optimal dimension of the trunk groups of the three-node network of Fig. 8.12 with the following data: $A^{1,2} = 10$, $A^{1,3} = A^{3,2} = 5$, $C_{1,2} = 1$, $C_{2,3}/C_{1,2} = C_{3,2}/C_{1,2} = 0.8$, for a grade of service of 1% on the finals. Start the iteration with $\beta = 0.5$, and iterate at least twice to see the rate of convergence of the method.

8.3. For the simple alternate path network of Fig. 8.1, show that the value $N_d = 0$ always satisfies the Kuhn-Tucker equations if

$$\frac{\beta(N_D = 0)}{CR} \geq H_d(0).$$

Show that $N_D > 0$ is always a solution otherwise.

8.4. Consider again Fig. 8.3. The curves plotted are for blocking values of 1% to 5%.

1. Identify which curves correspond to which blocking values.

2. Discuss the asymptotic value of the curves for large N. Note that this depends on the blocking value.

8.5. Derive explicitly Eq. (8.21). What assumptions are needed?

8.6. Check that Eq. (8.21) gives the correct answer when applied to the triangular network of Fig. 8.12.

8.7. Give a rigorous argument showing that the function F is differentiable inside a region defined by Eq. (8.28).

8.8. Prove Eq. (8.29).

8.9. For the three-node network, compute the change in the reduced gradient when crossing the boundary between two regions.

8.10. Construct a case of Eq. (8.38) in which not all the coefficients are positive. Try a four-node network with two periods.

8.11. Derive an ECCS equation for Eq. (8.47).

References

[1] Truitt, C.J., "Traffic engineering techniques for determining trunk requirements in alternate routing trunk networks," *Bell System Technical Journal*, vol. 33, pp. 277–302, 1954.

[2] Rapp, Y., "Planning of junction networks in a multi-exchange area. I: general principles," *Ericsson Technics*, vol. 20, pp. 77–130, 1964.

[3] Rapp, Y., "Planning of junction networks in a multi-exchange area. II: extensions of the principles and applications," *Ericsson Technics*, vol. 21, pp. 187–240, 1965.

[4] Pratt, C.W., "The concept of marginal overflow in alternate routing," *Australian Telecommunication Research*, vol. 1–2, pp. 76–82, 1967.

[5] Gill, P.E., Murray, W., and Wright, M., *Practical Optimization*, Academic Press, 1981.

[6] Harris, R.J., "Comparison of network dimensioning models," *Australian Telecommunication Research*, vol. 18, pp. 59–69, 1984.

[7] Beshai, M.E., Pound, L.A., and Horn, R.W., "Traffic data reduction for multiple-hour network dimensioning," *Network Planning Symposium*, vol. 2, pp. 112–118, 1983.

[8] Rapp, Y., "Planning of junction networks with non coincident busy hours," *Ericsson Technics*, vol. 27, pp. 3–23, 1971.

[9] Eisenberg, M., "Multi-hour engineering in alternate-route networks," *International Teletraffic Congress*, vol. 8, pp. 132.1–132.6, November 1976.

[10] Eisenberg, M., "Engineering traffic networks for more than one busy hour," *Bell System Technical Journal*, vol. 56, pp. 1–20, 1977.

[11] Elsner, W.B., "A descent algorithm for the multi hour sizing of traffic networks," *Bell System Technical Journal*, vol. 56, pp. 1405–1430, 1977.

[12] Rockafellar, R.T., *Convex Analysis*, Princeton University Press, 1970.

[13] Abadie, J. and Carpentier, J., "Generalization of the Wolfe reduced gradient method to the case of nonlinear constraints" in *Optimization*, ed. R. Fletcher, pp. 37–47, Academic Press, 1969.

[14] Abadie, J., and Guigou, J., "Numerical experiments with the GRG method" in *Integer and Nonlinear Programming*, ed. J. Abadie, North-Holland, 1970.

[15] Lasdon, L.S., Warren, A.D., Jain, A., and Ratner, M., "Design and testing of a generalized reduced gradient code for nonlinear programming," *ACM Transactions on Mathematical Software*, vol. 4, pp. 34-50, 1978.

[16] Shapiro, J.F., *Mathematical Programming: Structures and Algorithms*, Wiley, 1979.

[17] Girard, A., Lansard, P.D., and Liau, B., "A multi-hour ECCS theory and applications," *Network Planning Symposium*, vol. 3, pp. 78–84, June 1986.

[18] Horn, R., "End-to-end connection probability: the next major engineering issue?," *International Teletraffic Congress*, vol. 9, October 1979.

[19] Beshai, M.E., and Horn, R., "Toll network dimensioning under end-to-end grade of service constraints," *Network Planning Symposium*, vol. 1, pp. 101–108, 1980.

[20] Gaudreau, M., "Recursive formulas for the calculation of point to point congestion," *IEEE Transactions on Communications*, vol. COM-28, pp. 313–316, 1980.

CHAPTER 9

Dimensioning Nonhierarchical Networks

The dimensioning of networks operating with nonhierarchical routing has none of the simplifying features of hierarchical-network dimensioning. Traffic flows are calculated iteratively, grade-of-service constraints are not specified on arcs but are given in terms of end-to-end blocking, and there is no distinction between high-usage and final trunk groups. Thus the dimensioning problem is considerably more difficult than was the case for hierarchical networks.

Because of the difference in routing, the model used to formulate the dimensioning problem cannot be the same as for hierarchical networks; similarly, the solution techniques are different. As a consequence, we start with a discussion of various mathematical models for the dimensioning problem — in particular, the appropriate choice of an objective function and of constraints. We continue with a discussion of cost minimization with loss constraints, emphasizing various problem transformations that may be useful in calculating numerical solutions. Because these models are based on mathematical programming techniques, they cannot be used to optimize large networks, but instead give some insight on the structure of the problem. Finally, we discuss some heuristic methods used to dimension large nonhierarchical networks, focusing on the two most important nonhierarchical routings, dynamic call routing (DCR) and dynamic nonhierarchical routing (DNHR). Some of the presentation is not as detailed as desirable because many implementation details have not been made public. Nevertheless, this material gives an idea of the transformations required to go from a mathematically correct model to one that can be calculated fast enough for realistic networks.

9.1 Dimensioning Principles

The dimensioning of traditional hierarchical networks is modeled as a cost minimization, with grade-of-service constraints expressed in terms of the blocking probability on the final groups. For nonhierarchical routing methods, this characterization of grade of service is no longer possible since a given trunk group may be a final group for a particular stream and a high-usage group for some other stream. For this reason, we must decide upon suitable constraints for nonhierarchical networks. We also take this opportunity to describe other, potentially interesting choices of objective functions.

Unconstrained Methods: Moe's Principle

First we look at dimensioning models that impose no constraints on the performance of the network to be constructed. The dimensioning rule known as Moe's principle, first proposed in the late 1920s in Denmark, is described in detail in [1]. As one of the CCITT standards for dimensioning telephone networks, Moe's principle is worth a brief explanation. Its main feature is that it takes a purely economic view of the dimensioning problem, where the size of the various network components are determined solely from economic considerations, without the notion of grade of service. The network is viewed as a device for producing goods — in this case telephone calls — that can be sold on the open market at some price. The size of the network is determined by some profit-maximization rule or, in the case of monopolies, by some other economic function.

The full description of Moe's principle is given in [1] for a wide class of network components, for both lost-call and delayed-call systems. We present here a much simplified version of the method, highlighting its main features and relating to some of the dimensioning algorithms described in Chapter 8.

We assume for simplicity that we must dimension a network where there are only direct high-usage groups, and no alternate routing, in which case the network-dimensioning problem separates into independent link-dimensioning problems. We assume that the traffic offered to the link is a known Poisson process represented by A. The decision variables are $\overline{A}$ and N, the traffic carried on the link and the number of circuits on the link, respectively. Moe's principle relies on two economic functions:

$C(N)$ = The cost of providing N circuits on the group.

$D(\overline{A})$ = The revenue generated when $\overline{A}$ calls are carried on the link.

The design rule is that the group should be dimensioned so as to maximize profit, leading to the following formulation:

$$\max_{\overline{A}, N} \; z = P(\overline{A}, N) \stackrel{\triangle}{=} D(\overline{A}) - C(N) \qquad (9.1)$$

$$\overline{A} = A[1 - E(A, N)] \qquad (\lambda)$$
$$\overline{A} \geq 0 \qquad (\nu)$$
$$N \geq 0 \qquad (\mu)$$

Although the variables $\overline{A}$ and N are not independent, we assume that they are, and add the relation between them as an additional constraint on the maximization. This is the same transformation used many times in our discussion of routing. The first-order optimality conditions are given by

$$\mu = \frac{\partial C}{\partial N} + \lambda A \frac{\partial E}{\partial N} \tag{9.2}$$

$$\nu = \lambda - \frac{\partial D}{\partial \overline{A}} \tag{9.3}$$

where both multipliers must be nonnegative. Assuming that $N > 0$ and $\overline{A} > 0$, the corresponding multipliers vanish, and we get from Eq. (9.3)

$$\lambda = \frac{\partial D}{\partial \overline{A}}.$$

Substituting in Eq. (9.2),

$$\frac{\partial C}{\partial N} = \frac{\partial D}{\partial N},$$

which is the equilibrium equation for the optimal group size. This last equation has an interesting interpretation. It states that the group should be dimensioned in such a way that the cost of providing the last circuit is precisely equal to the revenue generated by this circuit.

Another, less attractive feature of the method, is that a solution with $N = 0$ is quite possible. Because λ is not constrained in sign, we can eliminate it from the system of Kuhn-Tucker equations by replacing λ in Eq. (9.2). We get

$$\mu = \frac{\partial C}{\partial N} - \frac{\partial D}{\partial N} + A\nu.$$

If the right-hand side is strictly positive, then, by the usual complementarity conditions, we have $N = 0$ — in other words, no capacity should be provided for this traffic stream. Depending on the cost and the revenue used for dimensioning, it is quite possible to get solutions of this kind, where no service at all is provided to some customers. In practice, these solutions are unacceptable, at least for services such as basic telephone access that are considered essential. The solution is obviously to add to the model some constraints that ensure that at least a minimum grade of service is provided to all customers. For this reason, we now concentrate on those models that specifically take such constraints into account.

Constraints

The unconstrained model is inadequate for a regulated environment, where minimal service must be provided to all potential users that wish to have it.

This is why we must now consider grade-of-service constraints and how they can be expressed. The most frequently used measure of grade of service, the end-to-end blocking probability, either can be specified on a networkwide basis or can be given for each traffic stream separately. This method corresponds closely to what is really seen by the user, but is difficult to use in a dimensioning algorithm because of the nonlinear relationship between end-to-end blocking probabilities and traffic (see Chapter 4).

It is also possible to define the grade of service without recourse to the end-to-end blocking probabilities. In a straightforward extension of the specification used for hierarchical networks, a link-blocking probability is imposed on all the network groups, and the groups are dimensioned to meet this blocking at the lowest cost. Although simpler to use, this method may lead to networks more costly than needed or with poor end-to-end blocking probabilities.

Note that the selection of the grade of service as the constraint on the dimensioning problem is not the only reasonable choice. Consider, for instance, a country where the telephone network is totally inadequate to meet the demand, and where the financial resources available do not even come close to meeting this demand [2]. In such a case, the constraint on the dimensioning problem could be stated as a budget constraint limiting the expenses that can be incurred in upgrading the network.

Objective Functions

The objective function can also be the subject of different choices, leading to different dimensioning philosophies. As we have seen, Moe's principle maximizes the net revenue generated by the network. In the case of developing countries, where the capital available is a constraint on the dimensioning, a reasonable choice of an objective function is the amount of traffic carried by the network [2]. Note that it is not clear how the ECCS method would apply in such a situation; this subject has not been examined. Nevertheless, the objective function most often chosen is some form of cost representing the value of the network, which is to be minimized subject to some constraints.

Even in this case, there is still some flexibility in the choice of an objective. An interesting discussion can be found in [3] in the context of a particular dimensioning technique. In this method, the network to be designed is a fully connected network, and end-to-end blocking probabilities are used as constraints. Each traffic stream is viewed as a user with a flow requirement given by the value of the traffic that must be carried in the network. The dimensioning problem consists of routing this multicommodity flow through the network, building up the group sizes in such a way that the groups can accommodate the carried flows. This procedure is described in detail in Section 9.3, but for the time being, we need only say that there is a computable function

$C\left[\mathbf{N}(\mathbf{x})\right]$ that yields the network cost for a given multicommodity vector $\mathbf{x}$ via the group size vector $\mathbf{N}$.

Within this framework, we can define at least three ways to view the network-dimensioning problem, each corresponding to a particular view of the objective. The first principle is that the network should be designed in such a way that the total cost is minimum; this is called a *system-optimal* network. As we saw in our study of routing, the optimal solution can be characterized easily. We have, for an optimal flow $\mathbf{x}$,

$$u^k = D_1^k = D_2^k \ldots = D_m^k \le D_{m+1}^k \ldots D_j^k, \tag{9.4}$$

where

$$x_1^k \ldots x_m^k > 0$$
$$x_{m+1}^k \ldots x_j^k = 0$$

and

$$D_i^k \triangleq \frac{\partial C(\mathbf{x})}{\partial x_i^k}.$$

In other words, the optimal solution is characterized by a set of flows that equalizes the marginal cost on all paths that are actually used in the solution, doing this for all commodities simultaneously.

A second principle that could be used to dimension the network is that no user (in this case, each commodity) has any incentive to change its routing from the routing computed. A network (or a routing) optimized from this principle is said to be *user-optimal*; the optimality condition is

$$v^k = \overline{C}_1^k = \overline{C}_2^k \ldots = \overline{C}_m^k \le \overline{C}_{m+1}^k \ldots \overline{C}_j^k, \tag{9.5}$$

where

$$x_1^k \ldots x_m^k > 0$$
$$x_{m+1}^k \ldots x_j^k = 0$$

The cost on path (k, i) is given by

$$\overline{C}_i^k = \sum_s \mathcal{I}_{s,i} \overline{c}_s,$$

where the cost on link s is

$$\overline{c}_s = \frac{C_s N_s}{f_s},$$

with f_s, the flow on link s, given by

$$f_s = \sum_j \mathcal{I}_{s,j} x_j.$$

A user-optimal solution is one that equalizes the *average* cost on each path that carries some flow.

A third principle, proposed in [3], has received less attention. In this case, that of free competition, each user tries to optimize its own routing cost, irrespective of the presence of the other users. In this game-theoretic formulation, each commodity plays against the others. The optimality condition for this case is that the marginal cost of each commodity is equal on the paths that carry some flow, independently of the others. We have

$$D_1^k = D_2^k \ldots = D_m^k \leq D_{m+1}^k \ldots D_j^k, \tag{9.6}$$

where

$$x_1^k \ldots x_m^k > 0$$
$$x_{m+1}^k \ldots x_j^k = 0$$

and

$$D_i^k \triangleq \frac{\partial C^k(\mathbf{x})}{\partial x_i^k}$$

$$C^k \triangleq \sum_i \mathcal{I}_{i,k} C_i N_i$$

C^k is the total cost on all paths available to commodity k. Note that, although Eq. (9.6) looks very much like Eq. (9.4), it should be interpreted as an optimality condition that is to hold for each commodity *independently* of the others. Here the marginal costs are equalized on all paths available to a given commodity, but marginal costs are not equalized across commodities. Each user operates independently, trying to get the least cost without regard to the presence of other customers.

Dimensioning the network based on the principle of user optimality, or on the game-theoretic formulation, cannot yield a lower cost than the system-optimal network. Nevertheless, the user-optimal method is of interest because it does not require the gradients of the objective function to be computed, the most time-consuming part of the algorithm. Thus a user-optimal solution should be easier to compute than a system-optimal one.

The same is true for the cost of the game-theoretic formulation. Because the method still requires marginal costs to be calculated, one would not expect it to be significantly faster than the system-optimal method. The game-theoretic formulation, however, can be used to model deregulated telecommunication environments, where each user of a network tries to optimize its own service, and where the company has no power to regulate these requirements, but can only offer the capacity as requested by the user.

In each case, an important question is the degree to which the user-optimal and game-theoretic solutions differ from the system-optimal solution. This question is addressed in [4], where it is found that, for small networks, the difference is relatively small, although it could become quite large as the networks get bigger. In these cases, the user-optimal network could still be used as a starting solution of a system-optimal algorithm, providing some savings in computation.

9.2 Dimensioning Models and Transformations

We now turn to mathematical models for dimensioning networks, with cost minimization as the objective and grade-of-service constraints expressed in terms of end-to-end blocking probabilities. These models are formulated in terms of cost minimization instead of revenue maximization, as in Moe's method, probably reflecting the traditional organization of telephone companies in state or regulated monopolies. The models turn out to be nonlinear optimization problems with a rather large number of variables and, in some formulations, many nonlinear constraints. For these reasons, a straightforward approach to the computation of a solution by ordinary mathematical programming methods is not feasible, except for very small networks. After discussing the models, we review some problem transformations that may lead to more efficient algorithms. In all that follows, the network operates with a given alternate routing with two-link paths.

Group Sizes as Variables

Optimal dimensioning is a nonlinear minimization of the form

$$\min_{N_s} \sum_s C_s(N_s), \tag{9.7}$$

subject to individual constraints,

$$L^k(N_s) \leq \overline{L}^k, \tag{9.8}$$

or an average end-to-end blocking constraint,

$$\frac{1}{\gamma} \sum_k A^k L^k(N_s) \leq \overline{L} \tag{9.9}$$

$$N_s \geq 0$$

Although the values of $\mathbf{N}$ should normally be chosen from a finite set, corresponding to the transmission-system capacities available, they are generally relaxed to the nonnegative reals, avoiding the use of integer-programming methods and making the solution tractable.

A straightforward solution method is to use one of the many general-purpose algorithms for nonlinear constrained minimization [5,6], since all the problem functions are differentiable functions of the variables $\mathbf{N}$. Most of the computation time of these algorithms is spent in calculating a direction in which to search for an optimal solution, which in turn requires evaluating the gradients of the constraint and objective functions at each iteration. Because of the importance of these quantities, we now describe some of the difficulties encountered in calculating the gradients of the constraint functions.

The simplest way to compute the gradients is to use finite differences with

$$\frac{\partial L^k}{\partial N_s} \approx \frac{L^k(N_s + \Delta N_s) - L^k(N_s)}{\Delta N_s}. \tag{9.10}$$

This can be extremely time consuming because each end-to-end blocking probability L^k must be computed for each *independent* variation of N_s, and the system of flow equations (4.39) must be solved each time. Furthermore, the flow equations must be solved to a high degree of accuracy because ΔN_s must be small in order to provide an accurate value for the derivative. In turn, this produces small variations in the values of the constraint vector $\mathbf{L}$, and L^k must be calculated to a high accuracy if the difference in Eq. (9.10) is to be meaningful. Although one can use the previous solution as the starting solution when solving the Erlang fixed point by relaxation, the time required to evaluate these derivatives dominates, by orders of magnitude, all other parts of the optimization.

It is possible to give analytic formulas for the gradients that avoid the need to solve the nonlinear system of flow equations repeatedly. To simplify the exposition, we assume that two-link alternate routing with OOC control is used. The technique can be extended to other routing methods, as in [7], where the same technique is used to dimension a network with trunk reservation. A variation in the size of a trunk group is reflected on the constraint functions via the (constrained) variation of the link-blocking probabilities $\mathbf{B}$, the constraint being that the link-blocking formulas must remain valid. We have, by the chain rule,

$$\frac{\partial L^k}{\partial N_t} = \sum_m \frac{\partial L^k}{\partial B_m} \frac{\partial B_m}{\partial N_t}. \tag{9.11}$$

Taking now the explicit form of L^k as a function of $\mathbf{B}$ in the case of two-link alternate routing, we have

$$\frac{\partial L^k}{\partial B_m} = \begin{cases} \prod_{j \neq r} P_j^k (1 - B_{m'}) & \text{if } m \text{ is in tree } k \\ 0 & \text{otherwise} \end{cases}$$

The other derivative must take into account the fact that the group-size variables $\mathbf{N}$ and the link-blocking variables $\mathbf{B}$ are not independent, but are linked by the flow equations $F_s[a_s(\mathbf{B}), N_s] - B_s = 0$. Expanding these equations near their current solution, we get

$$F_s(\mathbf{B} + d\mathbf{B}, \mathbf{N} + d\mathbf{N}) \approx F_s(\mathbf{B}, \mathbf{N}) + <\nabla_B F_s, d\mathbf{B}> + <\nabla_N F_s, d\mathbf{N}>.$$

Because we are at a stationary point, $F_s(\mathbf{B} + d\mathbf{B}, \mathbf{N} + d\mathbf{N}) = F_s(\mathbf{B}, \mathbf{N})$, and we can write

$$<\nabla_B F_s, d\mathbf{B}> = -<\nabla_N F_s, d\mathbf{N}>.$$

Let $\mathbf{F}'_B$ be the matrix $\nabla_B \mathbf{F}$, and $\mathbf{F}'_N$ the matrix $\nabla_N \mathbf{F}$. The relation between a variation in $\mathbf{N}$ and a variation in $\mathbf{B}$ is then

$$\mathbf{F}'_B d\mathbf{B} = -\mathbf{F}'_N d\mathbf{N}$$

or

$$d\mathbf{B} = -\mathbf{F}'_B{}^{-1} \mathbf{F}'_N d\mathbf{N}$$
$$= \mathbf{M} d\mathbf{N}. \tag{9.12}$$

The value of dB_j/dN_k is thus given by $M_{i,j}$, which is the derivative required for the second term of Eq. (9.11). Note that the calculation of this quantity requires the inversion of a matrix of order equal to the number of links in the network, which dominates in the evaluation of the gradients.

The method used to compute the gradients of the constraint functions can significantly influence the overall computation time for a network-dimensioning problem. Results presented in [7] compare the time required for network optimization, using Eq. (9.12), with that required to calculate the constraint gradients with finite differences. The traffic model must use state protection in order to avoid multiple solutions during the dimensioning process, which would prevent convergence of the algorithm. The introduction of state protection in a dimensioning problem is another source of conceptual difficulty. If the reservation level is fixed, say to m_s circuits on link s, then one must ensure that the corresponding group size has a lower bound of m_s. This may be undesirable because it could prevent the dimensioning algorithm from eliminating uneconomical groups. Although such groups could be eliminated a posteriori by examination of the final solution, this can be avoided by using a fractional reservation level $m_s = \alpha N_s$, which has the advantage of vanishing smoothly when a group is eliminated by the optimization algorithms. The results presented here were obtained in this way [7], with $\alpha = 0.01$ for all groups. In all cases, the problem is solved with Eqs. (9.9) under assumptions that $C_s(N_s) = N_s$ and that the average end-to-end grade-of-service constraint is $\overline{L} = 0.2\%$.

The networks used for testing had the properties shown in Table 9.1. All traffic matrices were randomly generated, except for networks 4 and 5, where the matrices were taken from [8]. Table 9.2 compares the total run time and the value of the final solution when the gradients are computed by Eq. (9.12) with the same values when the calculation is done by finite differences. We can see a substantial reduction in time when the analytic method is used. Accuracy also increases since the Kuhn-Tucker conditions are more closely verified by the solutions obtained from the analytic method than by the solutions computed

Network	Trunk Direction	No Nodes	No Arcs (No Variables)	No Traffic Relations
1	Two-way	6	15	30
2	One-way	6	30	26
3	Two-way	8	28	56
4	Two-way	9	36	64
5	One-way	9	72	64
6	Two-way	10	45	90
7	Two-way	12	66	132
8	Two-way	15	105	210

Table 9.1 Network Parameters for Numerical Results

by finite differences. In fact, in some cases, computing the gradients by forward differences is so inaccurate that the program misses a local minimum entirely (e.g., network 7). Only by using central differences, at the cost of a much higher computation time, is it possible to get the same answer as with the analytic method.

Cost of Uniform Average Blocking

Eq. (9.9) limits only the average blocking probability weighted over all traffic relations. As a consequence, the optimization procedure can give a relatively poor grade of service to a particular relation, if this turns out to reduce the total cost, as long as it does not increase the average blocking over the prescribed limit.

Strictly speaking, the constraints should be of the form (9.8), but this would introduce as many constraints as there are traffic relations. Considering that the computation time of optimization algorithms often depends heavily on the number of constraints, this approach seems undesirable. Nevertheless, the spread in the individual grades of service can be reduced by a single additional constraint of the form

$$\sum_k \left(\theta(L^k - B_0)\right)^2 \leq N_r \gamma,$$

where

θ = A scaling factor used to bring the probabilities $L^k - B_0$ close to 1. This is often useful to improve the stability of numerical solution methods.

N_r = The number of traffic relations.

Network	CPU (mins:secs) t_1/t_2	Network Costs C_1/C_2
1	2:30/5:02	212/224
2	4:10/8:15	226/223
3	3:57/13:32	498/507
4	14:01/47:21	325/334
5	39:14/38:54	511/513
6	9:49/19:28	656/660
7	14:46/17:10	1316/1275
8	42:55/153:03	3892/3886
Total	131/302	7635/7622

t_1 = Time using analytic method
t_2 = Time using finite differences
C_1 = Cost using analytic method
C_2 = Cost using finite differences

Table 9.2 Comparison of Analytic versus Finite Differences for Calculating Gradients

Thus, as γ becomes larger, this constraint becomes less stringent, and the spread in individual grade of service becomes larger, while the total cost decreases. The effect of this parameter is shown in Table 9.3, taken from [7], where the symbol Δ is used to indicate the largest and smallest individual blocking probabilities in the network under consideration. As expected, the constraint reduces the spread in blocking values, but the cost penalty can sometimes be quite high. It seems that the introduction of this second constraint is sufficient to keep the individual grade of service within reasonable bounds.

Relaxation of the Flow Equations

The nonlinear relationship between the constraints L^k and the decision variables $\mathbf{N}$ is the main source of computational difficulty in the dimensioning problem. The problem can be reformulated in ways that are mathematically equivalent, but may be easier to solve numerically.

One possibility is suggested by the remark that the flow model in itself need not be known very accurately. High accuracy is required only if the constraint gradients are computed by finite differences; in fact, high accuracy is a requirement of the optimization method more than of the problem itself.

Network	$C_{0.5}/C_\infty$	$\Delta_{0.5}$ (%)	Δ_∞ (%)
1	230/212	.40/.082	1./.04
2	230/226	.44/.082	.6/.05
3	537/498	.38/.083	.85/.01
4	465/324	.37/.080	5.9/.004
5	587/511	.35/.075	1./.03
6	666/656	.41/.070	.75/.02
7	1328/1316	.43/.1	.52/.01
8	3987/3892	.33/.07	.88/.001

C_γ = Cost for a particular value of γ

Δ_γ = Value of Δ for value of γ

Table 9.3   Cost of Reducing the Grade-of-Service Dispersion

Also, it can be argued that the model need not be solved accurately in early iterations of the optimization algorithm, when the solution is not very good anyway, and that high accuracy is needed only at the end, near the optimal solution.

This in turn suggests that the flow model should be solved at the same time that the optimization model is computed. The dimensioning problem can be reformulated by doubling the number of variables and adding N_a equality constraints, using a technique similar to that used to calculate optimal load sharing. In this model, the group sizes **N** and the link-blocking probabilities **B** are the *independent* variables. The link model is added to the dimensioning problem as additional constraints that the final solution must satisfy. We get

$$\min_{N,B} \sum_s C_s(N_s)$$

$$L^k(\mathbf{B}) \leq \overline{L}^k$$
$$E[a_s(\mathbf{B}), N_s] = B_s$$
$$N_s \geq 0$$
$$0 \leq B_s \leq 1$$

where we have explicitly noted that the L^ks and the offered traffic a_s depend only on **B**. The group sizes and the traffic are coupled via the link-traffic model — in the present case, the Erlang B function.

The gradients of the constraint functions take a simple form since, for two-link alternate routing with OOC, $L^k(\mathbf{B})$ is a polynomial in **B**, as seen by

Eqs. (4.13) and (4.14). We get

$$\frac{\partial L^k}{\partial N_s} = 0$$

$$\frac{\partial L^k}{\partial B_s} = \begin{cases} \prod_{t \neq s} [1 - (1 - B_t)(1 - B_{t'})] \, (1 - B_{s'}) & \text{if } s \text{ is in tree } k \\ 0 & \text{otherwise} \end{cases} \qquad (9.13)$$

and, letting $h_s = E(a_s, N_s) - B_s$,

$$\frac{\partial h_t}{\partial N_s} = \frac{\partial E_s}{\partial N_s} \delta_{s,t}$$

$$\frac{\partial h_t}{\partial B_s} = \frac{\partial E_t}{\partial a_t} \frac{\partial a_t}{\partial B_s} - \delta_{s,t}$$

The trade-off is between an increase in the number of variables and constraints, on the one hand, and the absence of a need to solve the flow equations or a linear system, on the other. An added advantage is that the link model need not be solved to a high accuracy for the optimization method to converge. This reduced accuracy can be taken into account in the optimization by setting the tolerance at which one considers the flow equations to be satisfied at a high value. This technique does not seem to have been actually used, and it remains to be seen whether it is more efficient than the other techniques discussed here. It would certainly require that the optimization algorithm be tailored to the particular structure of the constraint gradients — in particular, to the fact that part of this matrix has a very special structure (some blocks are full of zeros, while others are diagonal).

Blocking Probabilities as Variables

Another way to speed the calculation of the optimal size is to take into account the fact that the traffic model is a characteristic of the links, somehow decoupling the nonlinear system to obtain separate nonlinear equations for each group. This is possible because, given a vector of link-blocking probabilities $\mathbf{B}$, the end-to-end constraints can be evaluated directly without iteration, as can the link-offered traffics. Given a_s and B_s for a link, the group size is found by solving the link model, that is, computing the number of trunks required to make the link-blocking probability and the offered traffic consistent with each other and with the traffic model used for the link — but this time independently for each link. This procedure, called the *link-dimensioning model*, is an important feature of all the methods based on a change of variable, such as the one proposed here.

We now write this model, examining the computational requirements for a solution by standard mathematical programming methods. Although a two-link nonhierarchical alternate routing with OOC is discussed, the technique can be applied to a variety of routing methods with suitable modifications. We must compute

$$\min_{B} \; z = \sum_{s} C_s[N_s(\mathbf{B})] \tag{9.14}$$

$$L^k(\mathbf{B}) \leq \overline{L}^k$$

$$0 \leq \mathbf{B} \leq 1$$

where $N_s(\mathbf{B})$ is a function of the blocking probability vector through $a_s(\mathbf{B})$, the link-offered traffic. There is a single set of nonlinear constraints; their gradients are given by Eq. (9.13). The gradient of the objective function, more complex than was the case when the variables were the trunk group sizes, is given by

$$\frac{\partial C_s}{\partial B_t} = \frac{\partial C_s}{\partial N_s} \frac{\partial N_s}{\partial a_s} \frac{\partial a_s}{\partial B_t}$$

$$= \frac{\partial C_s}{\partial N_s} \frac{1}{\beta_s} \frac{\partial a_s}{\partial B_t}. \tag{9.15}$$

This requires the derivatives of the link-offered traffic to be calculated with respect to the link-blocking probabilities (see Eq. (4.12)). Note that the gradients can be computed by scanning the route trees once for each variable, but that the linear system need not be solved. Neither is it necessary to solve the flow equations repeatedly, as when calculating the derivatives by finite differences in the model with group sizes as variables.

This model, then, has the advantages both of the model with the trunk group-sizes as the variables, since it has only one set of constraints and variables, and the relaxation model, since the coupling between the links that occurs naturally via the flow equations has been separated into independent link-dimensioning models. This is indeed the case for the one-moment model, as described here. The situation is more complex if a two-moment model must be used, for instance, in hierarchical networks. In that case, the flow equations relate both the mean and the variance of the offered traffic on a link to the blocking probability. It is significantly more complex to evaluate the link dimensioning since this generally cannot be done exactly. Furthermore, the gradients of the objective function are not simple, and some of them must be computed iteratively, undoubtedly adding to the computational burden.

The only comparative result concerning the relative merit of these approaches known to this author is found in [9], where the accuracy of the one- and two-parameter models is compared for the performance evaluation on a few networks. The general conclusion is that the one-parameter model is accurate for nonhierarchical routing, while two parameters are required in the case of hierarchical routing. No comparison is made between the computation times required by the two dimensioning methods examined.

The ECCS Method for Nonhierarchical Networks

We have defined an ECCS method as one where the dimensioning algorithm consists of solving the Kuhn-Tucker equations directly, and where this solution is obtained by a relaxation procedure by which the coupled set of optimality equations is separated into individual dimensioning problems for each link. Originally developed for single-hour dimensioning of networks operating with hierarchical routing, the ECCS method is extended to the multihour case in Chapter 8. As we have seen, the multihour case is more complex, in terms of both the general formulation and the individual link-dimensioning equations. The first difficulty arises from the fact that, in the multihour case, it is not known in advance which of the constraint equations are tight at the solution. This forces us to embed the ECCS method within a dual procedure that is required to estimate the correct value of the Kuhn-Tucker multipliers at the solution. This feature is also present in the nonhierarchical problem, where in general there are many more equations than variables. Thus we can expect that some dual procedure will be required there also, and that the ECCS method, if it can be defined, will apply only in calculating the dual function, as was the case for the multihour problem for hierarchical networks. We can also expect a nonhierarchical ECCS technique to lead to more complex dimensioning equations, since the marginal cost of the overflow traffic is not computed only on the hierarchical path for the overflow, but in principle involves *all* the alternate paths in the network.

Each model proposed for the dimensioning problem has its own set of Kuhn-Tucker equations. Because we want to obtain a dimensioning equation for each trunk group, we investigate the possibility of having an ECCS equation for the model defined by Eqs. (9.7) and (9.9), where the group sizes are the optimization variables. The Kuhn-Tucker equations are given by

$$
\begin{aligned}
\mu_s &= \frac{\partial C_s}{\partial N_s} + \sum_k \lambda^k \frac{\partial L^k}{\partial N_s} \\
&= \frac{\partial C_s}{\partial N_s} + \sum_k \lambda^k \frac{\partial L^k}{\partial \hat{a}_s^k} \frac{\partial \hat{a}_s^k}{\partial N_s}
\end{aligned}
\tag{9.16}
$$

The sum over all commodities in this last equation is required because the variation of the group size can potentially affect all commodities, which are not restricted to certain groups, but can use any link permitted by the nonhierarchical routing. We have

$$
\frac{\partial \hat{a}_s^k}{\partial N_s} = -\frac{\partial \bar{a}_s^k}{\partial N_s}
$$

and, assuming equal blocking for all parcels,

$$
= -\frac{a_s^k}{a_s} H_s(N_s).
$$

Replacing in the Kuhn-Tucker equation (9.16), we get

$$\mu_s = \frac{\partial C_s}{\partial N_s} - \sum_k \Gamma_s H_s(N_s), \qquad (9.17)$$

where

$$\Gamma_s \triangleq \sum_k \lambda^k \sum_m \frac{\partial L^k}{\partial \hat{a}_s^m} \frac{a_s^m}{a_s}.$$

Note the formal similarity of Eq. (9.17) to the corresponding equation (8.23) for hierarchical networks. Γ_s represents the marginal cost of overflow from link s; the ECCS principle is as follows. If the right-hand side of Eq. (9.17) is positive, then we have found a solution $\mu_s > 0$, and $N_s = 0$ is a solution. This is reasonable since, in this case, the marginal cost of providing a small amount of capacity on link s is larger than the corresponding cost on all the available alternate routes, and the link should not be provisioned. If, on the other hand, this link is to be present, then we must have $\mu_s = 0$, which means that the groups should be sized such that

$$\frac{\partial C_s}{\partial N_s} = \Gamma_s H_s(N_s).$$

That is, the groups should be dimensioned such that the marginal cost on link s equals the marginal cost of overflow in the rest of the network. This is the formal generalization of the ECCS rule for fixed nonhierarchical routing.

It is also possible to solve the dimensioning equation by relaxation, as in the case of the multihour dimensioning case for hierarchical routing. To do this, we must assume that the value of λ^k is known. The value either can be provided by an outer procedure that is responsible for computing the correct values for the multipliers, or, more simply, these values can be estimated as the cost of lost traffic and kept as constants. In the first case, solving the ECCS equations amounts to computing a value of the dual of the original dimensioning problem. The relaxation is over the Γs, in which case a straightforward dimensioning equation results for each group individually. An iterative procedure is needed to adjust the values of the coefficients after a dimensioning step is carried out.

Although it seems conceptually simple, such an ECCS method is probably quite difficult to implement. First note that the coefficients require the evaluation of the marginal cost of alternate routing, given by $\partial L^k / \partial \hat{a}_s^m$, at each iteration. These derivatives must be calculated at a fixed point of the network-flow equations, eventually requiring the inversion of a matrix. Also, there is no guarantee that the relaxation will converge; relatively little is known about the Jacobian matrix of the system being solved. Nevertheless, this possibility should be investigated in more depth, considering the extraordinary efficiency of the ECCS method for hierarchical networks, both with single and with multihour structures.

Multihour Engineering and Problem Transformation

The multihour version of the dimensioning model of Eqs. (9.7–9.9) is straightforward. The grade-of-service constraint for each commodity is replaced by a set of similar constraints, one for each time period $L^k(A^t, N) \leq \overline{L}_t^k$, while the objective function is unchanged. The solution by general nonlinear programming methods is identical, except that many more constraints must be taken into account, in turn limiting the size of problems that can be handled by these methods.

Although there is a single $\mathbf{N}$ vector of group sizes, there are many $\mathbf{B}^t$ vectors, each corresponding to a set of blocking probabilities for a given period. This has an important effect on methods based on problem transformations such as Eq. (9.14), where the link-blocking probabilities are the independent variables. Under these conditions, the link-offered traffics a_s^t are determined completely in each period from the route trees, the traffic matrices, and the probability vector for the period $\mathbf{B}^t$; we can write $a_s^t = a_s^t(\mathbf{B}^t)$. We then dimension the links by inverting the link-traffic model — that is, solving

$$E(a_s^t, N_s) = B_s^t \quad s = 1 \dots N_a \quad t = 1 \dots T \tag{9.18}$$

Recall that the link dimensioning is required to compute the value of the cost function during the optimization procedure. During this procedure, the decision variables must not change, and we must assume that the $\mathbf{B}^t$ variables are fixed. Under these conditions, the system (9.18) is overdetermined since we have $N_a \times T$ equations to be satisfied and only N_a variable N_s available. It is generally not possible to find a single vector of group sizes $\mathbf{N}$ such that Eqs. (9.18) will be satisfied simultaneously in all periods. Thus the change of variables from the $\mathbf{N}$ to $\mathbf{B}^t$ does not apply to the multihour case. It does not help to ignore the conditions that the $\mathbf{B}^t$s must not change because we have $N_a \times (T+1)$ variables and only $N_a \times T$ equations, yielding an underdetermined system. Also, the effect of this on the optimization procedure is not clear — it would amount to evaluating the objective function at some point different from the one for which the search has been computed.

A heuristic procedure for link dimensioning is described in Section 9.4. For now, we describe a modification of the multihour dimensioning model that would allow the use of blocking probabilities as independent variables. We also give a technique for decomposing the multihour problem into a sequence of independent single-hour problems, based on a technique originally developed for optimal circuit routing with reliability constraints [10,11]. We know that the difficulty arises because only one variable is available for the link dimensioning, while the link model must be verified for many periods. This suggests the introduction of dummy variables $\mathbf{N}^t$, $t = 1, \dots T$, in addition to the normal link sizes $\mathbf{N}$. The network-dimensioning model becomes

$$\min \sum_s C_s(N_s) \tag{9.19}$$

$$L_t^k(A^t, \mathbf{N}^t) \leq \overline{L}_t^k$$
$$0 \leq N_s^t \leq N_s \qquad (9.20)$$

This is equivalent to the original model if the cost functions $C_s(N_s)$ are increasing since, in this case, the real variables N_s must equal one of the dummy variables in at least one period, just as was the case for the multihour dimensioning problem for hierarchical networks. The link-dimensioning problem separates into T independent link-dimensioning models, and the correct value N_s is used to compute the cost.

Another important advantage of this formulation is that it immediately provides a way to decompose the multihour engineering problem into a sequence of single-hour problems. This is seen when we relax constraints (9.20) by including them in the objective function. We get the problem

$$\min \ \sum_s C_s(N_s) + \sum_t \sum_s u_s^t(N_s^t - N_s)$$

$$= \sum_s \left[C_s(N_s) - N_s \sum_t u_s^t \right] + \sum_t \left[\sum_s u_s^t N_s^t \right] \qquad (9.21)$$

with the constraints

$$L_t^k(A^t, N_s^t) \leq \overline{L}_t^k$$
$$N_s^t \geq 0$$

The original problem separates into $T + 1$ independent single-hour problems. The first problem is unconstrained; the other T ones are standard single-hour dimensioning problems. This may be a practical solution method if a subgradient procedure is used to compute the multipliers, as was the case for the multihour dimensioning problem for the hierarchical case.

Summary

All the dimensioning models described here are based on a precise mathematical programming formulation. As we have seen, the presence of the fixed-point system of equations complicates the solution of the model based on trunk group sizes. We have also suggested some problem transformations that could lead to more efficient algorithms, although it is not clear to what extent the trade-offs involved would be more efficient. Given the state of the art of nonlinear programming methods, it is quite clear that these techniques will be inadequate for the dimensioning of realistic networks, where the number of variables may be in the thousands, and with many more constraints than variables. For this reason, we now turn to heuristic methods, which may not be formulated rigorously but are practical engineering solutions to the dimensioning of nonhierarchical networks.

9.3   Large-Scale Dimensioning Methods

The models of Section 9.2 are based on mathematical programming formulations and algorithms and have nonlinear objective and constraint functions. For these reasons, these models cannot solve very large networks. Because they address the exact dimensioning problem, however, they can be used to study small networks and to provide a measure of the accuracy of heuristic methods. Let us now examine some heuristics that are used to dimension networks of practical sizes — at the cost of drastic simplifications in the model and the solution algorithm.

Katz's Method

First we discuss a method originally proposed by Katz [12], probably the first attempt to dimension nonhierarchical networks. The method makes heavy use of this author's two-phase method for network evaluation (see Section 5.1). It does not attempt to minimize costs, but rather to find a set of feasible flows and to equalize the end-to-end blocking probabilities as much as possible — the implication being that a network with uniform grade of service is nearly cost optimal. Upper and lower bounds can be set on the group sizes, as well as on the link-blocking probabilities. The algorithm is specialized to alternate routing with sequential-office control (SOC), making heavy use of the progressive nature of the overflow control. For this reason, the extent to which the method could be applied to other types of control or routing is unclear.

Katz's method operates in two stages. First the flow equations are solved. An initial set of link-blocking probabilities is computed, then used for this stage. Given these blocking probabilities, a set of flows compatible with the traffic model is computed by a straightforward link-loading procedure, using Katz's network-evaluation algorithm (see Section 5.1). At the same time, the end-to-end blocking probabilities are computed from the traffic that reaches the loss nodes in the route tree.

The second stage consists of computing group sizes that are compatible with the flows and blocking values given by the first stage. Given the link-blocking probabilities, the link-loading procedure gives, for each link, the mean and variance of the total traffic offered to the link. Dropping the link index to simplify notation, we have M and V as the parameters of the traffic, and B as the required blocking probability; we want to determine N the group size. The description of the link-sizing algorithm is based on the assumption that the traffic is always peaked, which may not be accurate for nonhierarchical routing. Nevertheless, the method is based on the equivalent random theory (ERT) and, if required, can easily be extended to smooth traffics by any of the methods of Chapter 3. First an equivalent system A^*, N^* is calculated using

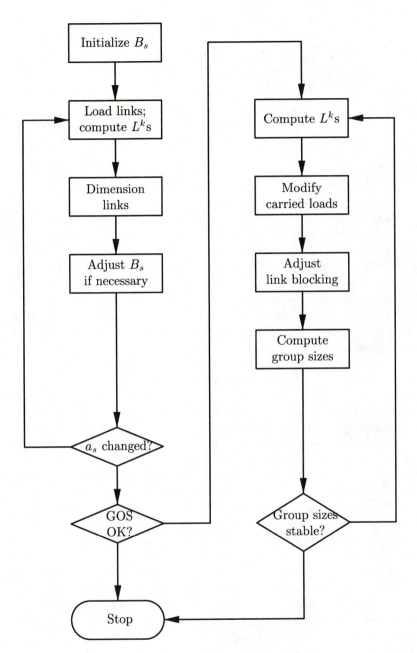

Figure 9.1   Katz's Dimensioning Algorithm

Rapp's approximation:

$$A^* \approx V + 3Z(Z - 1) \tag{3.89}$$

$$N^* \approx \frac{A^*(M + Z)}{M + Z - 1} - M - 1 \tag{3.90}$$

The trunk group N is then given by the solution of the equation

$$E(A^*, N^* + N) = B,$$

which can be solved for either fractional or integer values, depending on the requirements of the model. The solution of this equation need not lie between the bounds initially prescribed for the group sizes. At this stage in the process, these constraints can most easily be taken into account by setting the value of N to whichever bound is being exceeded. If this is done, however, the values of the offered traffic are no longer correct. In other words, the relation among traffic, group size, and blocking probability that is prescribed by the traffic model is no longer valid, and one or more parameters must be adjusted. Since the bounds cannot be changed and the size has just been readjusted, the blocking and the traffic must be changed, leading to an iterative adjustment procedure. This procedure is represented by the first loop in Fig. 9.1, a flow chart of Katz's method.

The second stage adjusts the blocking probability to meet the grade-of-service constraints, with the link-offered traffics fixed at their value at the end of the first stage. This is done by adjusting the traffic carried on the links on the routes where the grade-of-service constraints are not met. To satisfy the traffic model, the blocking probabilities are changed at the same time. Convergence occurs when the group sizes stabilize. The grade-of-service verification is intimately related to the progressive control of alternate routing. Recall that, for SOC control, calls are lost if all the groups adjacent to a node are busy when the call arrives. Given the route tree, the end-to-end blocking probability can be represented by combining individual blocking probabilities encountered at each node of the route tree, here represented by P_i. These probabilities are simply given by $P_i = \prod_s B_s$, where s runs over all the arcs from node i, and is valid only for progressive overflow control.

Suppose now that some grade-of-service constraint is not met for some route tree k. This can happen because either the lower or the upper bound is violated. When the upper bound is exceeded, the blocking constraint is met by adjusting the P_is to increase the traffic carried in the route tree k. The nodes of the route tree are then examined to identify those in which the blocking is too large. Letting $\hat{a}_i$ be the amount of traffic k lost at node i, we consider node i to be a candidate for modification if $P_i > \hat{a}_i / A^k L_{min}^k$, that is, if the fraction of the stream loss at node i is above the lower bound for the grade-of-service constraint.

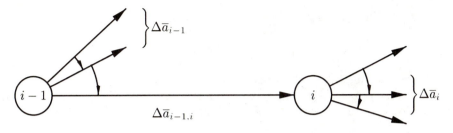

Figure 9.2 Katz's Method of Adjusting Carried Traffic

Having identified the nodes where there is some slack in the constraints, we must correct the traffic carried in the tree to decrease P_i. Let $i-1$ be the node preceding i in the route tree. This can be done three ways: (1) decrease the traffic carried on the link $(i-1, i)$, (2) increase the traffic carried on the links adjacent to node $i-1$, or (3) increase the traffic carried on the links adjacent to node i (see Fig. 9.2). Let $\Delta\bar{a}_{i-1,i}$, $\Delta\bar{a}_{i-1}$, and $\Delta\bar{a}_i$ be the corresponding variations in carried traffic. We use

$$\Delta\bar{a}_i = \hat{a}_i \frac{w_i}{W}\delta_i$$

$$\Delta\bar{a}_{i-1} = \hat{a}_i \frac{w_{i-1}}{W}\delta_n\delta_{i-1,i}$$

$$\Delta\bar{a}_{i-1,i} = \hat{a}_i \frac{w_{i-1,i}}{W}\delta_{i-1}$$

where

$$\delta_i = \begin{cases} 0 & \text{if } n_i = 0 \\ 1 & \text{otherwise} \end{cases}$$

$$\delta_{i-1} = \begin{cases} 0 & \text{if } i-1 = o(k) \\ 1 & \text{otherwise} \end{cases}$$

$$\delta_{i-1,i} = \begin{cases} 0 & \text{if } n_{i-1} = 0 \\ 1 & \text{otherwise} \end{cases}$$

and

$$W = w_i\delta_i + w_{i-1}\delta_{i-1}\delta_{i-1,i}\delta_{i-1} + w_{i-1,i}\delta_{i-1,i}.$$

Here the ws are the weights given to each correction term, and n_l is the total number of trunks adjacent to node l, which can be used by calls in stream k. Once the variation of carried traffic is determined at node i, it must be assigned to the groups adjacent to the node. In other words, a correction to the traffic carried on these links must be calculated that is consistent with the total variation of the carried traffic at the node. This is done in the same proportion as the blocking probabilities of the groups, in the order of overflow at node i. If we let P_j be the probability that a call overflows to group j, we have

$$P_j = \prod_{l=1}^{j-1} B_l,$$

where B_l is the link-blocking probability computed at the previous iteration. The increase in carried traffic at node i is distributed among the groups in proportion to these overflow probabilities by

$$\Delta \bar{a}_s = \frac{P_s}{\sum_{l=1}^{n_i} P_l} \Delta \bar{a}_i.$$

In practice, setting $\delta_{i-1,i} = 0$ is always a better choice than any other value. The particular values of w_i and w_{i-1} are not very important; both are generally set at 0.5.

When the grade of service is below its prescribed lower bound, the carried traffic is adjusted on the trunk groups that carry at least 5% of the load A^k. The carried-load reduction on group s is given by

$$\Delta \bar{a}_s^k = - \left(\frac{L_{min}^k + L_{max}^k}{2} - L^k \right) \bar{a}_s.$$

These changes in carried traffic, accumulated over all route trees, are used in adjusting the group-blocking probabilities:

$$\Delta B_s = - \frac{\Delta \bar{a}_s}{a_s}.$$

Finally, the groups are again dimensioned to take into account the new value of the blocking probabilities, once again taking into account the bounds that can be imposed on the trunk groups. This method has been used to design networks as large as 70 nodes with small computation times. The relative accuracy of the solution produced by the algorithm is unknown.

Network-Synthesis Model

The dimensioning techniques based on network-synthesis methods are closer to the theoretical model of Section 9.2 than Katz's method. Network-synthesis methods attempt to minimize a measure of the network cost under grade-of-service constraints described in terms of the end-to-end blocking probability. As is well known, other things being equal, optimization problems with linear constraints are much easier to solve than are those with nonlinear constraints. In network synthesis, the dimensioning problem is viewed as an optimal routing problem in an uncapacitated network, where the commodities are the elements of the traffic matrices. It is assumed that there exists a fully connected network for which a multicommodity flow must be found. In this way, the nonlinear blocking constraints are replaced by flow constraints, simplifying the solution process at the expense of solving a problem that is somewhat different from the true dimensioning problem.

The cost function is determined by the amount of capacity required to carry the flow on the links. This function depends on the assumptions made about the traffic, as well as on the actual routing method used for the calls. The total routing cost is thus a complex nonlinear function of the link capacities, but, since the carried traffics have the structure of a nonlinear multicommodity flow, the constraints are linear and have a structure that can be exploited.

A simplified version of such a method was devised by Knepley [13], making some drastic simplifications. First, the end-to-end blocking constraints are replaced by constraints on the link-blocking probabilities, which are given constants, chosen as $B_s = 2\overline{L}$ in the application considered. Even with this restriction, a second, apparently contradictory assumption is that there is no loss in the network and that the traffic offered to a link is identical to the traffic carried on it. These assumptions, however, are contradictory in appearance only — they are used for different purposes. The link-blocking probabilities are used in the link-loading phase, while the conservation of flow is required to use the standard multicommodity model for the optimization. Let x denote the multicommodity representing the traffic carried in the network. The dimensioning problem is then

$$\min_{x} \; \sum_{s} C_s(a_s)$$

$$a_s = \sum_{l} \mathcal{I}_{s,l} x_s$$

where $C_s(a_s)$ is the cost of carrying an amount a_s of traffic on link s. The synthesis problem is solved by a sequence of linearizations, where the tangent to the objective function is

$$\frac{\partial C_s(a_s)}{\partial a_s} = \frac{\partial C_s}{\partial N_s}\frac{\partial N_s}{\partial a_s}$$

$$= \frac{\partial C_s}{\partial a_s}\beta_s,$$

since $\partial N_s/\partial a_s$ is taken at a fixed value of the link-blocking probability. Given the linearized approximation at the current value of the flow, the routing is simply done over shortest paths, where the arc length is given by $l_s = \beta_s$. The traffic is then loaded on these paths, using the assumption that the traffic offered to a link is completely carried on it, that is, that there is no blocking on the link. The links are sized by inverting the traffic model, in this case by solving

$$E(a_s, N_s) = B_s$$

for N_s. Obviously, more complex traffic models could be used in this step of the algorithm. The stopping rule is given as the stationary values for the link costs.

After the algorithm has converged, a number of steps are required. The solution is expressed as a multicommodity flow representing the traffic carried on the network paths. An alternate routing plan must be synthesized from this flow; any one of the methods of Chapter 7 could be used. In the present case, the paths are sorted in increasing path length, where the length is given by the marginal capacity. The route is then constructed by assuming that overflow occurs from the first path toward the last path in the list, that is, from the path with smallest marginal capacity to the one with the largest value. The generation of alternate paths is not limited to a single tandem; there may be longer paths, and care must be taken that cycles are not formed in the process. A final verification of the blocking constraints is then performed since the use of alternate routing gives traffic flows different from those computed by the optimization step. If adjustments are required, Knepley suggests using a method similar to that of Katz. A simplified flow chart of the method is found in Fig. 9.3.

The Berry Model

A more accurate method based on multicommodity flows is proposed by Berry [14]. The method is closely related to the optimal routing of traffic with load sharing as discussed in Chapter 7 and to the circuit routing problem briefly described in Chapter 1, as well as to the optimal routing of traffic in transportation networks. The model of [13], however, uses a fixed alternate routing plan that is taken into account in the link-dimensioning process.

Berry's original model is defined for networks with nonhierarchical routing, but with a sharp distinction between first-offered and overflow traffics. The trunk groups belong to two mutually exclusive classes. One set receives only first-offered traffic; the calls blocked on these groups are offered to the second set, which receives only overflow traffic. In effect, there are two networks, one for fresh traffic and one for overflow. Although the distinction is not essential for discussing the method, we maintain it to relate the method more closely to the published numerical results.

The routing in the overflow network is of the nonhierarchical alternate routing type, with no limitation on the length or the number of alternate paths. It is further assumed that a fixed list of these alternate paths is given a priori for each origin-destination pair in the network. Let $\mathcal{D}$ be the set of links that correspond to the direct trunk groups, and $\mathcal{O}$ the set of trunk groups in the overflow network. The model is stated as

$$\min \ \sum_{s \in \mathcal{D}} C_s[N_s(\mathbf{x})] + \sum_{s \in \mathcal{O}} C_s[N_s(\mathbf{x})], \qquad (9.22)$$

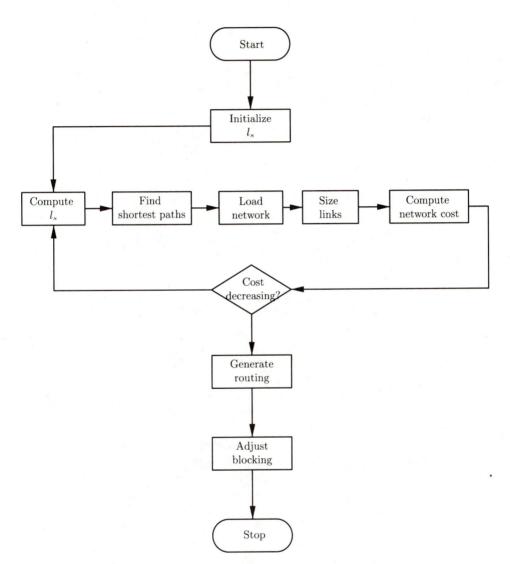

Figure 9.3   Dimensioning by Network Synthesis

subject to the constraints

$$\sum_l x_l^k = A^k(1 - \overline{L}^k) \tag{9.23}$$

$$x_l^k \geq 0$$

where $\mathbf{x}$ is a multicommodity flow representing the traffic carried on the network paths. The functions $N(\mathbf{x})$, which depend on the link-carried traffic, represent the number of circuits that must be installed on the link in order to have the given value of $\mathbf{x}$ with the prescribed routing plan. This cost function is called the *link-dimensioning model*; its definition is a central element of the method.

The original model is overly restrictive: It is defined with equality constraints, while inequality constraints would be sufficient. This is because the solution technique originally proposed, Rosen's gradient-projection method, operates best with problems with equality constraints. The technique could be used equally well with inequality constraints, provided an active set strategy is used, but again we keep the original model in order to compare results with those published on the accuracy and speed of the method.

The nonlinear blocking constraints of the original model are replaced by much simpler linear ones corresponding to an unconstrained multicommodity flow, since A^k and $\overline{L}^k$ are known parameters. This simplification of the constraint domain does not come cheap — the objective function is correspondingly more difficult to evaluate. It requires, for a given flow $\mathbf{x}$, that group sizes be calculated corresponding to the alternate routing plan given for the network such that $\mathbf{x}$ will represent the carried traffic. Called the *group-dimensioning problem*, this calls for a detailed discussion. First we examine the one-parameter model, and then the two-parameter model as used in [14]. Note the similarity to Knepley's model. The important difference is that in Knepley's model the routing was constructed *after* the multicommodity optimization, while in Berry's model alternate routing is intrinsically taken care of by the method.

One-Parameter Model.   The problem under consideration is as follows. Assume that, at some point in the iterative process, we are given a flow vector $\mathbf{x}$ representing the traffic carried on the network paths. We must compute a set of group sizes $\mathbf{N}$ such that the traffic carried on all paths is precisely $\mathbf{x}$ *when the given alternate routing plan is used*. We start by noting that, for given $\mathbf{x}$ and routing trees, it is possible to compute the total traffic carried on all the links as

$$\overline{a}_s = \sum_{k|s\in k} x_k.$$

If we impose the condition that the link model must be satisfied, we must verify

$$E[a_s(\mathbf{B}), N_s] = B_s. \tag{9.24}$$

Since neither the link-blocking probability nor the link size is known, the problem appears undetermined. Note, however, that the carried traffic is known and that it depends solely on the link-blocking probabilities via the route trees. Let $g_s(\mathbf{B})$ denote the function that maps the link-blocking probabilities and the traffic matrix onto the link-offered traffic. (An example of g_s can be found in Section 4.3 for two-link alternate routing.) We must have

$$a_s = g_s(\mathbf{B}), \tag{9.25}$$

which gives the set of equations to be satisfied by $\mathbf{B}$:

$$\bar{a}_s = (1 - B_s)g_s(\mathbf{B}). \tag{9.26}$$

The dimensioning problem then reduces to computing a set of link-blocking probabilities by solving the nonlinear system (9.26), then sizing the groups by solving the independent nonlinear equations (9.24). The usual questions about the solutions of nonlinear systems can be raised here also, and it is not known under what conditions they have one, more than one, or no solution. Also, a relaxation method could be defined using the a_s as the relaxation variables. Care should be taken, however, to ensure that the variables remain in the domain of feasibility (see Problem 9.6). In practice, the system is never solved explicitly; rather, approximate solutions are computed via heuristics, as described in the following section.

Two-Parameter Model.   Let us now describe Berry's original solution method for the dimensioning model [14], which utilizes a two-parameter model. We consider first the direct network and then the alternate routing network. In each case, we assume that a multicommodity flow $\mathbf{x}$ is given, corresponding to the mean traffic *carried* on each path of the network. The problem is to compute trunk-group sizes that produce this flow under the given alternate routing. Also note that the multicommodity flow is given for both networks at the same time, since overflow from the direct network is sent to the overflow network. We also assume that, given a flow, the traffic carried on a link is simply the sum of the flows on the paths using that link.

Direct Network.   The direct network is the easier part of the link-dimensioning process because the traffic offered to the links in this group is Poisson. Let s be some direct link for commodity k and let the component of the flow vector corresponding to this link be x_1^k. The traffic offered to the link is given by $a_s = A^k$ and the mean of the overflow $\hat{a}_s$ is computed from the given multicommodity flow $\mathbf{x}$ by $\hat{a}_s = A^k - \sum_{l>1} x_l^k$; it is the difference between the first-offered traffic and the amount of the commodity that has been carried on paths preceding s in the route tree. We can size the direct link by solving the blocking formula for N_s:

$$\hat{a}_s = a_s E(a_s, N_s).$$

Given the size of the direct group, the variance of the overflow can be obtained by Kosten's model:

$$\hat{v}_s = \hat{a}_s \left[1 - \hat{a}_s + \frac{A^k}{N_s - \bar{a}_s + 1} \right].$$

All the direct groups are sized first, and the mean and variance of the overflows are then used in the first stage of the iterative procedure that sizes the groups in the overflow network.

Overflow Network.   The corresponding problem in the overflow network is more difficult since the dimensioning of a group is determined by the mean and variance of its offered traffic as well as the mean and (possibly) the variance of the carried traffic. The calculation is done in two stages. First, from the alternate routing plan and the parameters of the traffic overflowing from the direct network, a set of parameters M_s^k, V_s^k is determined for the traffics offered to the various paths. From these parameters, the parameters of the link-offered traffics m_s and v_s are computed. A dimensioning procedure based on ERT can then be used to size the groups.

Consider again the situation where the mean of the traffic carried on all paths is given, represented by the multicommodity vector $\mathbf{x}$. The mean traffic $\hat{A}_l^k$ overflowing from a path (k,l) is given by

$$\hat{A}_l^k = A^k - \sum_{j=1}^{l} x_j^k, \tag{9.27}$$

where (k,l) denotes the lth path in the route tree for commodity k. $\hat{A}_l^k$ is whatever is left of the original traffic after it has attempted all the paths up to and including path l in the alternate path sequence. This traffic is the mean of the traffic offered to the next path, that is, A_{l+1}^k.

We now know the value of the overflow mean from path (k,l); it remains only to compute the value of the variance of the overflow from a path, which is the variance of the traffic offered to the next path on the route. This is done by applying ERT to path (k,l). Assume that the mean and variance of the traffic offered to path (k,l) are known and that they are represented by M_l^k and V_l^k. These quantities are known if the traffic is calculated for each tree in the same order as for the overflow. We can replace the (k,l) path by an equivalent system, with parameters A^* and N^* given by the standard ERT equations:

$$A^* = V_l^k + 3Z_l^k(Z_l^k - 1) \tag{9.28}$$

$$N^* = A^* \frac{M_l^k + Z_l^k}{M_l^k + Z_l^k - 1} - M_l^k - 1 \tag{9.29}$$

In effect, the equivalent system represents the operation of the paths preceding the path for which we want to compute the variance.

Having the parameters of the equivalent system, it is straightforward to compute the variance of the overflow from this system, which is the variance of the traffic overflowing from the path. Using Rapp's approximation, we get an implicit solution as

$$A^* = \hat{V}_l^k + 3\hat{Z}_k^k(\hat{Z}_l^k - 1), \tag{9.30}$$

which can be solved for $\hat{V}_l^k$, which is V_{l+1}^k. This solution is possible because, at this point, the mean overflow traffic from the path is known; it has been calculated from the multicommodity flow via Eq. (9.27). In this case, there is only one unknown in Eq. (9.30), which can be inverted numerically to yield $\hat{V}_l^k$. Note that this equation, although formally identical to Eq. (9.28), is solved for $\hat{V}_l^k$, where A^* and $\hat{M}_l^k = \hat{A}_l^k$ are known. This process is continued for all paths in each route tree, after which the parameters M and V of the traffic offered to each path are known. Having the parameters of the path-offered traffics, we must combine them to obtain the parameters of the traffic offered to each link in the overflow network. Given the arc-path incidence matrix corresponding to the routing, these are computed as

$$a_s = \sum_k \sum_l \mathcal{I}_{s,l}^k M_l^k$$

$$v_s = \sum_k \sum_l \mathcal{I}_{s,l}^k V_l^k$$

where the second sum is taken only up to the number of the *first* path that uses link s for commodity k. Although not really necessary, this limitation is intuitively justified because the parameters of each traffic stream offered to a link should be determined to a large extent by the parameters of the first path that uses that link, the others contributing only in the proportion of the overflow from this first link. This simplification can be justified only by comparison with real or simulated systems, as we shall see later.

Having computed the total mean m_s and variance v_s of the traffic offered to each link, it is now necessary to size them such that the mean of the carried traffic prescribed by the multicommodity flow is realized. Once again, this is done via the ERT method. Suppose that M_s and V_s are produced by the overflow of some group of size N^* offered a Poisson traffic A^*. The parameters of the equivalent system are computed as usual, then used to dimension group s as follows. Assume that the equivalent traffic is offered to a group of size $N_s + N^*$, where N_s is the quantity to be determined. The mean carried traffic $\bar{a}_s$ is known from the current multicommodity flow, so that the mean overflow from the group is $\hat{a}_s = M_s - \bar{a}_s$. The variance of the overflow traffic is given implicitly by

$$A^* = \hat{v}_s + 3\frac{\hat{v}_s}{(M_s - \bar{a}_s)}\left[\frac{\hat{v}_s}{(M_s - \bar{a}_s)} - 1\right],$$

and the group size by

$$N_s = A^* \left[\frac{(M_s - \overline{a}_s) + \dfrac{\hat{v}_s}{(M_s - \overline{a}_s)}}{(M_s - \overline{a}_s) - 1 + \dfrac{\hat{v}_s}{(M_s - \overline{a}_s)}} \right] - (M_s - \overline{a}_s) - N^* - 1,$$

which solves the link-dimensioning problem for a given flow vector $\mathbf{x}$. Comparisons with simulation show that this formula is not sufficiently accurate, especially at low blocking values. An improved link-dimensioning model, given in [15], seems sufficient for dimensioning purposes.

Optimization Methods. The link-dimensioning problem evaluates the objective function of the dimensioning problem. We now turn to the other part of the problem, that is, calculating the optimal solution. Berry's original solution technique was expressed in terms of Rosen's gradient-projection method. Because network-dimensioning problems can have a very large number of variables, for the method to be practical for realistic networks, it was necessary to devise very efficient ways to compute the projected gradient, without matrix inversions. Harris [16] proposed a subsequent model in terms of the reduced-gradient method, where again the general method was specialized to the multicommodity problem. Both Berry and Harris were able to derive the optimality equations, as well as a dimensioning technique identical to the flow-deviation method. Searching along the direction of either the projected gradient or the reduced gradient amounts to removing some flow from the paths that currently carry them, and to reallocating that flow to the path with the smallest total marginal cost, defined by the derivative of the cost function with respect to the flow variables. This is indeed the flow-deviation method as derived from the Frank-Wolfe formulation. Therefore, we need not present the derivation of the optimality conditions: The Frank-Wolfe method is much more intuitive and leads to the same results.

Note, however, that both methods require the derivative of the cost function to be computed with respect to the flow variables. Because of the complexity of these functions, it is not possible to have simple analytic forms for the gradients, which in most cases must be evaluated by finite differences or by other iterative methods. For this reason, evaluating the gradients is the most time-consuming part of the algorithm, and ways have been sought to improve this calculation. One possibility is to compute a user-optimal routing in the solution of the multicommodity flow. This is much simpler than calculating a system-optimal solution, since the optimality conditions given by Eqs. (9.5) require the equalization of the *average* cost per path, as opposed to the marginal cost, which must be equalized for a system-optimal solution. In practice, the difference between the user-optimal and system-optimal costs is too large to use only a user-optimal solution; several iterations of the system-optimal algorithm are still required.

Numerical Results

The technique, which has been refined continuously since first proposed, can now be used to dimension fairly large metropolitan and long distance networks — for instance, it was used to provision the Australian networks. A metropolitan network of up to 890 nodes with a hierarchical routing has been dimensioned; the required modifications to the original method and necessary interactions with the network description database are described in [17].

9.4   Unified Algorithm for DNHR

We now turn to a very important heuristic method for dimensioning nonhierarchical networks: the so-called Unified Algorithm, developed for planning the introduction of dynamic nonhierarchical routing (DNHR) in the AT&T network. Currently the most complete network-synthesis method for nonhierarchical networks, the Unified Algorithm integrates routing optimization and dimensioning in a single procedure — the only such algorithm to do so. At this writing, it is the only published method capable of calculating large networks of 100 nodes or more. The Unified Algorithm has the following features:

1. It is both a trunk-dimensioning *and* a routing-optimization method.

2. It is also a multihour engineering method.

3. It uses the link-blocking probabilities as independent variables.

4. It replaces a number of elements with heuristics in order to handle large networks.

   This method works equally well with a route or a path formulation. Most of the discussion will be on the route formulation, with some indications of the requirements of the path formulation. More details on the path formulation are found in an article by Ash, Cardwell, and Murray [18]. We shall summarize the description in that work [18], relating it to some of the topics already covered on routing optimization and dimensioning.

Problem Transformation

The network-synthesis problem is to choose trunk sizes N_s and routing variables α such that the network cost is minimized, subject to end-to-end grade-of-service constraints under multiple demands, represented by a set of traffic matrices A_t:

$$\min_{N_s,\alpha} \sum_s \hat{C}(N_s) \tag{9.31}$$

$$L_t^k(A^t, N, \alpha_t^k) \leq \overline{L}_t^k \quad t = 1,\ldots T, \ k = 1,\ldots K \tag{9.32}$$

Note that this formulation allows different grade-of-service constraints for different periods, which could take into account the change of rates at different times in the day.

In this formulation, the design variables are the trunk sizes N_s and the routing variables α_t^k. The precise meaning of α_t^k depends on the routing-optimization technique. In the *route* formulation, a set of candidate route trees is chosen initially for each period and each commodity. The routing is a load sharing between these trees; in this case, the α_t^k represent a vector of load-sharing coefficients. In the other formulation, called the *path* formulation, routing optimization is done via a multicommodity-flow model; the alternate routing is synthesized afterwards (see Section 7.4). Here the α variables represent a set of multicommodity flows.

As noted many times, this problem is too difficult to be solved by a straightforward mathematical programming technique, and thus a number of transformations and simplifications must be made. In the first modification, the N_s are replaced as independent variables by the B_s^t, the blocking probability on trunk s in period t. This removes the fixed-point system from the constraint equations. The cost function of (9.31) depends on the B_s^t and the α_t^k, instead of the N_s as before, and is denoted $C(\cdot)$. The relation between C and $\hat{C}$ is straightforward, given the link-blocking model. For a given value of the link-blocking probability and of the offered traffic, the required number of trunks can be obtained by inverting the blocking function. We get

$$N_s = \arg \left\{ E(A_s, N_s) = B_s^t \right\}$$
$$C(B_s, \alpha_t^k) = \hat{C}(N_s, \alpha_t^k)$$

In the second modification, we replace the grade-of-service constraints expressed in terms of the end-to-end loss probability for each stream by a set of constraints, one for each route available to the streams. The problem becomes

$$\min_{B,\alpha} \sum_s C(B_s)$$

$$L_{j,t}^k(B, \alpha) \leq \overline{L}_{j,t}^k \tag{9.33}$$

where $L_{j,t}^k$ is the blocking probability on the jth route of traffic k in period t.

Solution Technique

Even with these transformations, the model is still nonlinear and too difficult for an exact solution. This means that approximate solution methods are required. The Unified Algorithm is a heuristic that proceeds in two phases. The outer loop is a cost minimization over the B variables, and indirectly on the trunk sizes. Inside this loop, at each iteration, the routing is optimized in

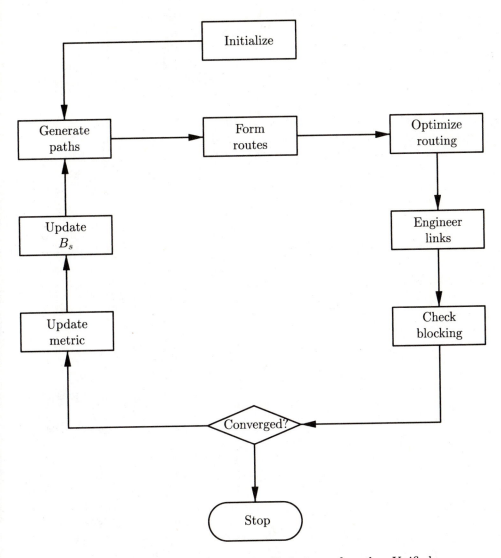

Figure 9.4 Heuristic Solution Technique for the Unified Algorithm

the space tangent to the current point in the B variables (see Fig. 9.4). The general outline is as follows. (We assume that, at the beginning of the current iteration, we have an estimate of the B_s^ts).

1. Generate a set of candidate routes for each origin-destination pair, based on the results of the previous iteration or on some other rule for an initial value. Given the link blocking probabilities in each period, compute for each route the amount of traffic carried in all links. This is expressed as the fraction of the total traffic offered to a relation that is carried in each path of the route.

2. With these traffic proportions, optimize the load-sharing coefficients in order to minimize the marginal cost of the network. This is done by linearizing the link costs at the current point, using techniques very similar to those discussed in previous chapters. The important feature is that this procedure leads to a linear program since the objective function has been linearized.

3. Calculate the trunk sizes. This procedure is iterative since a set of sizes must be found that will yield the prescribed trunk blocking probabilities for all periods.

4. Check the feasibility of the route constraints. Routes having a high blocking are modified by increasing the sizes of some groups according to a heuristic.

5. Compute a new set of link blocking probabilities B_s by a variant of the classical ECCS method.

Let us examine each of these steps, indicating where crucial assumptions are being made and where the main numerical difficulties may occur.

   Route Generation.   At the beginning of each iteration, a set of candidate route trees must be generated for each commodity. In general, there is more than a single tree per commodity per period. Although this selection could be made from the results of the preceding iteration, using some rule to try to obtain "good" routings, this seems unnecessary. Ash, Cardwell, and Murray suggest that using cyclic permutations of a basic routing may be sufficient, in the spirit of the CGH routing-synthesis method. The advantage is that, for a given value of the link-blocking probabilities, all route trees have the same loss probability, and only the carried traffics on the links differ from one tree to the next.

   Computing the Proportions.   In a route formulation, we have a given set of route trees for each origin-destination pair in the network. At this point in the algorithm, the link-blocking probabilities are also known because of the iterative nature of the method. From this information, the partition of the traffic offered to each tree is fixed, and is represented by $P_{s,t}^{j,k}$, the *proportion* of the offered traffic k carried on link s in the jth route during period t. The calculation of the proportions is a straightforward link loading, which we know how to solve from the discussion of Chapter 4. The calculation takes a particularly simple form in the case of two-link alternate routing, where the efficient methods of Section 4.3 can be applied.

Routing Optimization.   In the next step, the routing variables α are chosen. In a route formulation, the actual routes available to a commodity in a given period are fixed. The only choice available is the amount of flow k that will go on each of the routes available to this flow in each period. This is a routing optimization by load sharing and alternate routing, as described in Section 7.3 for the case of alternate routing. Because it is a nonlinear problem, solutions are quite difficult especially when the network becomes large. For this reason, the optimal load sharing is transformed into a linear program, although a large one. First the marginal cost of the network is used as the objective function — not the lost traffic, the objective we used in our description of routing optimization. This marginal cost — the cost of carrying a small increment of traffic on the link — is evaluated at the current value of the group sizes and defines the link metrics M_s. The constraint set can also be linearized, using the known link proportions and blocking probabilities. We must solve

$$\min_{\overline{A}^k_{j,t}, a_s} \sum_s \frac{\partial C}{\partial a_s} a_s$$

$$\sum_k \sum_j P^{j,k}_{s,t} \overline{A}^k_{j,t} \le a_s \quad s = 1, \ldots S, \quad t = 1, \ldots T \qquad (9.34)$$

$$\sum_j \frac{\overline{A}^k_{j,t}}{1 - L^k_{j,t}} = A^k_t \quad t = 1, \ldots T, \quad k = 1, \ldots K \qquad (9.35)$$

$$a_s \ge 0$$

$$\overline{A}^k_{j,t} \ge 0$$

where

$P^{j,k}_{s,t}$ = The fraction of the offered traffic k carried on link s in the jth route in period t.

a_s = The maximum amount of traffic carried on link s over all periods.

$\overline{A}^k_{j,t}$ = The amount of traffic carried on the jth route of traffic k in period t.

The linearized constraints have a straightforward interpretation. Equation (9.35) is a statement of the grade-of-service constraint, while Eq. (9.34) ensures that a_s truly represents the largest amount of traffic carried on the link over all periods. The algorithm tries to allocate traffic in the network such that the blocking constraints are satisfied in all periods, at the same time trying to minimize the incremental cost of carrying this traffic. Thus the nonlinear relation between trunk groups and traffics is removed from this step; a linear program remains.

Calculation of Trunk-Group Sizes.   Having computed the maximum amount of traffic carried on each link over all periods, we must find the appropriate number of trunks. Because the Unified Algorithm operates with the link-blocking probabilities as the independent variables, we are faced with the problem described in Section 9.2 in a multihour context. Either we keep the B_s^t fixed at their current value, in which case it is not possible to dimension the groups, or we allow them to vary, in which case we have an underdetermined system. Normally, the latter possibility is not realistic if the dimensioning algorithm is a standard nonlinear programming technique: These methods operate by successive searches in directions of descent, which are computed at the current point in the iterative process. This point must not change during the evaluation of the objective or constraint functions; this would completely invalidate the direction calculation and almost certainly prevent the convergence of the algorithm.

In the present case, since the Unified Algorithm is not a rigorous optimization algorithm but rather a set of heuristics, we could consider modifying the optimization variables — that is, the $\mathbf{B}^t$ — during the calculation of the objective function. But, as we have seen, if we allow this, the system of nonlinear equations that defines the link-dimensioning model becomes underdetermined. This difficulty is solved in the Unified Algorithm by imposing another set of equations, as follows. Let $\bar{t}_s = \arg\max_t a_s^t$, the period during which the offered traffic is the largest for link s. The additional condition imposed is that the group size satisfy the blocking model in period $\bar{t}_s$,

$$N_s = \arg\left\{B_s^{\bar{t}_s} = E(a_s^{\bar{t}_s}, N_s)\right\}.$$

With this set of N_a additional equations, the link-dimensioning model is in principle well defined, since there are as many equations as variables. Of course, the usual questions remain about the existence and number of solutions, but they do not cause problems in practice. The solution is computed by a relaxation procedure, as described in [18]. Let k be the current iteration index and assume that $a_s^{t,(k)}$ is known, either from the initial value or from the previous iteration (these are the relaxation variables). The procedure is as follows:

1. Compute the saturation period for each link:

$$\bar{t}_s = \arg\max_t a_s^t \quad s = 1\ldots N_a$$

2. Size each group for the blocking probability in this period:

$$N_s = \arg E(a_s^{\bar{t}_s}, N_s) = B_s^{\bar{t}_s} \quad s = 1\ldots N_a$$

3. Recompute the blocking probability of all links in all other periods:

$$B_s^t = E(a_s^t, N_s) \quad s = 1 \ldots N_a, \quad t = 1, \ldots T \quad t \neq \bar{t}_s$$

4. Perform a new link loading for all periods:

$$a_s^{t,(k+1)} \doteq a_s^{t,(k+1)}(\mathbf{B}^t) \quad s = 1, \ldots N_a \quad t = 1 \ldots T$$

After this, the saturation period may change, which means that the procedure is iterative. Convergence is achieved when the change in the link-blocking probabilities in two successive iterations is less than a prespecified threshold.

Feasibility. The network-engineering procedure changes the values of the link-blocking probabilities during the relaxation process to match the blocking to the group sizes in all hours. As a result, the end-to-end grade-of-service constraints may no longer be met. For this reason, a feasibility check is performed, where yet another adjustment is made to the blocking probabilities for those constraints that are violated. Recall that we have replaced the original set of end-to-end constraints (9.32) by route constraints (9.33). The latter are easier to handle since the constraints can be checked on each route separately. The procedure is as follows:

1. Order all routes in decreasing order of total blocking.

2. Perform the following iterations until all route blocking probabilities are within specified values:

    a. Correct the route with the highest blocking in the list by decreasing the blocking on the first path on the route.

    b. Recompute for all links in the network the new values of traffic and the new link blocking probabilities.

Because this procedure changes the blocking probabilities, it may invalidate the engineered solution computed in the previous step. For this reason, the two steps are interrelated, and iterations are performed between both steps until a stable solution is obtained that satisfies all the route-blocking constraints and that matches the link-blocking probabilities to the link-blocking model.

Calculating a New Metric. After the network is sized, we must recompute two quantities used as inputs for the next iteration: the link metric and the link-blocking probabilities. The metric for link s is defined as the marginal cost of carried traffic at constant blocking probability, given by

$$M_s = \frac{\partial N_s}{\partial \bar{a}_s}$$
$$= \frac{1}{\beta_s}.$$

This choice is reasonable in view of the objective of the routing optimization — to route over least cost routes. It is left as an exercise (Problem 9.8) to provide a model in which this particular choice of metric is derived from the optimality conditions for the routing variables.

Modification of Link Blocking probabilities.   The final step of an iteration is to recompute new link-blocking probabilities by modifying the classical ECCS theory for hierarchical networks, optimizing the trade-off between routing calls on a link s and routing the same call over some alternate path in the network. This calculation is made at fixed offered traffic, so that a group size corresponds to a unique link-blocking probability via the traffic model. For each link s, an equivalent alternate routing cost M_s is computed. The authors of [18] do not specify how the equivalent alternate routing cost is computed. From our discussion of the extension of the ECCS method to the nonhierarchical case, we know that the marginal cost of alternate routing involves complex calculations of the marginal blocking of the route trees, as well as of the multipliers. Since the latter are unknown and the former are difficult to compute, heuristics must be used. The cost function for the link is then

$$C_{tot} = C_s(N_s) + \hat{a}_s M_s$$
$$= C_s(N_s) + a_s E(a_s, N_s) M_s.$$

The size of link s, and consequently the link blocking B_s, are calculated by minimizing C_{tot} over N_s.

Path Formulation

As pointed out in Chapter 7, routing optimization by the route formulation has a potential problem: Routes must be selected a priori and, if good routes are left out of the original design, then the final result of the optimization may be poor. The path formulation of the Unified Algorithm (see Fig. 9.5) attempts to avoid this difficulty by using a multicommodity-flow approach. Instead of generating complete routes and then allocating the traffic to those selected routes, a set of paths is generated for each commodity and each time period. A linear multicommodity-flow model is then used to compute the optimal amount of traffic carried on each path; the routes are generated at the end of the optimization process. The optimization model is as follows:

$$\min \sum_s M_s \bar{a}_s \tag{9.36}$$

$$\mathcal{I}_t^{k,j} x_t^{k,j} \leq \bar{a}$$

$$\sum_j x_t^{k,j} = \overline{A}_t^{k,j} \tag{9.37}$$

$$x_t^{k,j} \leq \overline{x}_t^{k,j} \tag{9.38}$$

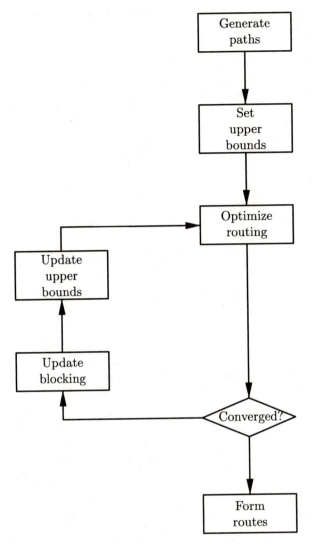

Figure 9.5   Path Formulation of the Unified Algorithm

The last set of equations represents upper bounds on the flows, which are required for reasons described shortly. Although the variables are similar to those used in the route formulation, their interpretation is quite different:

$$x_t^{k,j} = \text{The flow } \textit{carried} \text{ on the } j^{\text{th}} \text{ path for commodity } k \text{ in period } t.$$

$\mathcal{I}_t^{k,j}$ = The arc-path incidence matrix for commodity k in period t.

$\overline{A}_t^{k,j}$ = The *required* amount of commodity that must be carried on path (k,j) in period t; it is a known constant.

M_s = The link metric, given by $\partial C_s / \partial a_s$.

The required amount of each commodity can be computed as follows for each routing-optimization stage. The routing optimization is used within an optimization procedure where the link-blocking probabilities are the decision variables. This means that, when the problem is stated, these blocking probabilities are known and, in principle, invariant. Given the link-blocking probabilities, one can compute the path-blocking probabilities $\mathcal{P}_t^{k,j}$. Given these path-blocking probabilities, the smallest route-blocking probability possible is given by $L_t^{k,*} = \prod_j \mathcal{P}_t^{k,j}$ if all paths are used. The amount of traffic k to be carried is then prescribed by these probabilities, and is given by

$$\overline{A}_t^{k,j} = A_t^k \left(1 - \max \left\{ L_t^k, L_t^{k,*} \right\} \right),$$

which is used in Eq. (9.37) as the constraints in the routing optimization.

The other point to be clarified is the need for bounds on the flows given by Eq. (9.38), closely related to the realization of alternate routing from a multicommodity flow. Suppose that (9.36) is solved without the constraints (9.38). The solution is an uncapacitated multicommodity flow that may take any value compatible with the grade-of-service constraints (9.37). After the routing-optimization phase ends, these flows must somehow be used to construct the actual routes in the alternate routing network. An unconstrained set of flows of this kind, however, may turn out to be unfeasible for any arrangement of alternate routing between the available paths. A simple example, taken from [18], illustrates this point. Suppose that three paths are available for a commodity, with blocking probabilities 0.2, 0.1, and 0.2, respectively, and suppose further that the traffic offered to the route is 10 Erlangs. The grade-of-service constraint is set at 0.005. This solution is feasible since the blocking probability of the three paths is 0.004. With these values, not all carried flows can be realized by alternate routing. A case in point is when the values produced by the multicommodity problem turn out to be 8, 1.95, and 0 Erlangs, respectively, for the three paths. In such a case, no arrangement of alternate routing can realize these flows. The reason is that, in order to realize the first carried flow, all of the external flow of 10 Erlangs must be offered to the first path. The overflow from this path is only 2 Erlangs, insufficient to produce the flow carried on the second path.

As can be seen from the example, this situation arises because the prescribed carried flow on the first path is too large, not leaving enough overflow to meet the requirements of the other paths. This explains why the upper bounds of Eq. (9.38) are added to the multicommodity model. The calculation of these upper bounds depends on the particular technique used to realize the flows after the optimization is terminated.

For instance, consider the example of the skip-one-path method for realizing a set of flows. Given a value for the traffic carried on a path and the blocking probability, one of two cases can occur. The traffic available to realize the prescribed carried traffic is the sum of the overflow from the immediately preceding path and the traffic skipped from the next-to-last preceding path. If this traffic is sufficient to realize the carried flow, the linear programming bound is set at the value of the carried traffic that would be produced by this total offered traffic, thus increasing the potential value of the linear programming solution at the next iteration. If the traffic is insufficient to realize the flow, then the bound is set at the value that can be realized with the current overflow. This will decrease the bound on the amount of traffic that can be carried on the path in question, thus making the linear programming solution closer to a solution that can be realized by the skip-one-path method.

Heuristic for Routing Optimization

Most of the computational effort goes into the routing-optimization phase. Although a linear program, it still requires a very large amount of computation because of its large size. For this reason, this portion of the Unified Algorithm would benefit most from simplifying the model or the solution technique; a heuristic has been proposed to replace the exact linear programming solution of the routing phase. The heuristic is described here for the path formulation since, in this form, it is an application of the flow-deviation method discussed in Chapter 7. The method operates by rerouting flows from one path to another one whenever the marginal cost of the operation appears favorable. This procedure is carried out one period at a time, as follows.

First, for each link s, we can determine the set of periods where the traffic offered a_s^t is maximum. Let τ_s be this set for link s, and $|\tau_s|$ be its cardinality. The effect on the network cost of a variation of traffic on a link in a given period depends on the nature of the variation and on the period. For traffic increments, the link size must be increased in the periods of maximum flow; the size need not be changed if the period is not a saturation period. If the change is a decrease, it has no effect on the link size if the period is not a saturation period. If it is a saturation period, and there are other periods where the link traffic is maximum, then the link size cannot be decreased in the current period, even though the offered traffic is decreased, and the change in offered traffic has no effect. If, on the other hand, the current period is the only period of maximum traffic, then a decrease in traffic can induce a decrease in group size. This is summarized by the notion of marginal cost of a reroute for each link in each period:

$$\gamma_{s,t}^{+} = \begin{cases} M_s & \text{if } t \in \tau_s \\ 0 & \text{otherwise} \end{cases}$$

$$\gamma_{s,t}^{-} = \begin{cases} M_s & \text{if } t \in \tau_s \text{ and } |\tau_s| = 1 \\ 0 & \text{otherwise} \end{cases}$$

where $\gamma_{s,t}^{+}$ and $\gamma_{s,t}^{+}$ represent the marginal cost of an increase or a decrease, respectively, in the traffic offered to the link.

Having defined the marginal costs of all links in all periods, we can use them to decide on flow deviations in a particular period t for a given commodity k. Consider two paths (k,j) and (k,l), where the notation indicates the jth path available to commodity k. The question is whether some of the flow currently on (k,j) should be rerouted on (k,l) and, if so, in what amount. To answer the first question, we define the marginal reroute cost for each path in period t as

$$\Gamma_t^{k,l,(+,-)} = \sum_{s \in (k,l)} \gamma_{s,t}^{(+,-)},$$

where $\Gamma_t^{k,l,(+)}$ and $\Gamma_t^{k,l,(-)}$ correspond to an increase or a decrease in traffic, respectively. Flow is rerouted from (k,j) to (k,l) if $\Gamma^{k,l,-} - \Gamma_t^{k,j,+} < 0$. Once the pair of paths is chosen, we must compute the amount of flow to reroute. This is determined by two conditions: (1) each flow must remain within its assigned bounds and (2) as the reroute is performed, changes that can occur in the Γs must be taken into account in the rerouting process.

Consider path (k,j), where the flow is decreasing, and some link with $\gamma_{s,t}^{-} > 0$. As the flow is decreased on this link, it eventually reaches a point where the current period is no longer the unique saturation period for the link. This occurs when the offered traffic reaches the level of the next-highest offered traffic in other periods. At this point, the marginal cost of the link vanishes, and the path marginal cost changes abruptly (see Fig. 9.6). Similar behavior occurs for path (k,l), where the flow is increasing. At some point, one of the links with zero marginal cost will have so much flow that the current period becomes the saturation period, and its marginal cost becomes positive; the increase in network cost will have a change in slope (see Fig. 9.7 for an example).

Because the desirability of the reroute is based on the marginal costs at the current solution, the flow deviation should not be extended beyond these break points — the basis on which the reroute was decided (i.e., the marginal costs for the paths) has changed, and may not be accurate. This is the rule used in the heuristic optimization version of the Unified Algorithm; its validity is discussed in the next section.

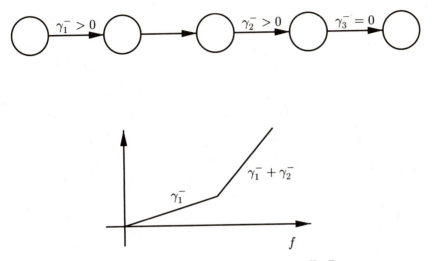

Figure 9.6 Marginal-Cost Change for Traffic Decrease

Numerical Results

Numerical results are related to the computational efficiency of the method, as well as to the accuracy of the results measured by the economies that DNHR provides over more conventional routing techniques.

   Computational Efficiency.   The numerical efficiency of the Unified Algorithm is determined to a large extent by the solution of the large linear program corresponding to Eqs. (9.34) and (9.35). Although standard linear programming techniques can be used, the computational times are such that large networks cannot be optimized in reasonable amounts of time. Because an exact solution is not required in this phase, Ash, Cardwell, and Murray [18] have proposed a heuristic for solving the routing optimization. With this heuristic, solutions within a few percentage points of the linear programming optimum can be obtained hundred of times faster than required with simplex-like algorithms. With this heuristic, it is estimated that a 190-node network with six periods could be designed in less than four hours on a large computer.

   Accuracy of the Solution.   We have not discussed the question of the accuracy of the solution with respect to the exact solution of (9.31) and (9.32), mainly because no method currently solves this problem exactly in a

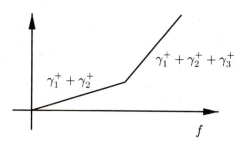

Figure 9.7   Flow Increment and Marginal Costs

Routing	Cost	GOS	Savings(%)
Hierarchical	5.949	.009	
Progressive	5.567	.004	6.4
Multilink	5.511	.005	7.4
Two-link	5.556	.005	6.6

Table 9.4   Single-Hour Design, 10-Node Network

reasonable time. Instead, the accuracy of the method is estimated by comparing its cost with the cost of the equivalent hierarchical network, dimensioned to the usual grade of service on the finals. Three types of nonhierarchical routings have been used for comparison. *Progressive routing* is the standard sequential office control described in Chapter 4. Routes are generated with some restrictions on long paths in order to avoid inefficient use of trunks. *Multilink routing* is nonhierarchical routing with originating office control, also described in Chapter 4, without restrictions on the number of tandems in a path. Finally, *two-link routing*, as indicated by its name, is multilink routing restricted to a single tandem in each path. Savings of approximately 7% have been realized for long distance networks with a single-hour design (see Table 9.4), and savings of approximately 15% for a three-hour design (see Table 9.5). Comparable results have been obtained for metropolitan networks [19].

Routing	Cost	Savings(%)	GOS
Hierarchical	7.160		
Progressive	6.043	15.6	.003
			.002
			.003
Multilink	5.980	16.5	.002
			.001
			.002
Two-link	6.064	15.3	.003
			.002
			.003

Table 9.5   Three-Hour Design, 10-Node Network

This routing technique has been implemented in the long distance telephone network of the United States, where integration was expected to be completed by the end of 1989 [20].

9.5   Dimensioning of Adaptive Routing Networks

Proposals for implementing adaptive routing methods are fairly recent, and thus comparatively little work has been done on the dimensioning of networks operating with these routing techniques. The general formulation (9.7) is also valid for networks operating with adaptive routing, and general-purpose mathematical programming techniques can be used to obtain a solution, provided there is an algorithm to evaluate the blocking constraints. In practice, the evaluation of the grade of service is often too difficult, and methods based on standard mathematical programming techniques do not appear feasible except for small networks.

For this reason, we limit the discussion here to a single published heuristic, designed specifically to dimension networks using adaptive routing based on residual capacity such as DCR. The algorithm, described in [21,22], tries to capture the main features of the routing as proposed for the long distance network of Canada, at the same time attempting to produce a network with minimum cost. It is modular, in the sense that the trunk groups are sized in terms of modules of 24 circuits, and is also a multihour method, using the fact that more than one traffic matrix represents the demand on the network. Because there is no published mathematical model of the method, most of the description of the dimensioning algorithm presented here is qualitative. Even though implementation details have not been published, the overall operation of the method is clear (see Fig. 9.8).

Recall that networks operating with residual-capacity adaptive routing are made of two types of offices: I-offices, which participate in the adaptive routing but cannot operate as tandems, and T-offices, which have this tandem capability. The algorithm is based on a classification of trunk groups into three categories: (1) I-I groups, which receive first-offered traffic only, (2) I-T groups, which receive first-offered and overflow traffic from the I-I groups, and (3) T-T groups. Each group is dimensioned on a distinct principle.

Dimensioning I-I Groups

Because I-I groups receive only first-offered traffic, they play the role of a first-choice high-usage group in hierarchical networks. For this reason, I-I groups are sized on the basis of an ECCS criterion defined by an equilibrium condition between the cost of routing traffic on the direct route versus a comparable cost for the alternate network. The actual equation used in the algorithm, although not given in [22], probably has a form similar to the ECCS equation (9.16). Note, however, that the heuristic is not a dual method and that the Kuhn-Tucker multipliers are not constructed by the dimensioning algorithm. Since the multipliers represent the marginal cost of violating the constraints, the precise form of the marginal cost of alternate routing depends on the nature of the constraints defined for the problem. As we shall see, these constraints are not the end-to-end blocking probability, but rather a simpler expression related to the blocking on each of the clusters.

Dimensioning I-T Groups

The dimensioning of groups that can receive alternate-routed traffic is more complex, precisely because of the mutual overflow present in the network. The dimensioning principle is expressed in terms of bundle blocking, where a bundle is defined as the set of all trunk groups originating from a particular office, and is considered as a single entity. The trunk groups are offered both first-offered and overflow traffic from the I-I groups. The calls in the first category are allowed to overflow onto T-T groups, while the others are lost whenever they are blocked. From this point of view, the I-T bundles play the role of final groups for I-I calls, and of intermediate high-usage groups for the I-T calls. Both interpretations of the role of the I-T groups are used in the dimensioning.

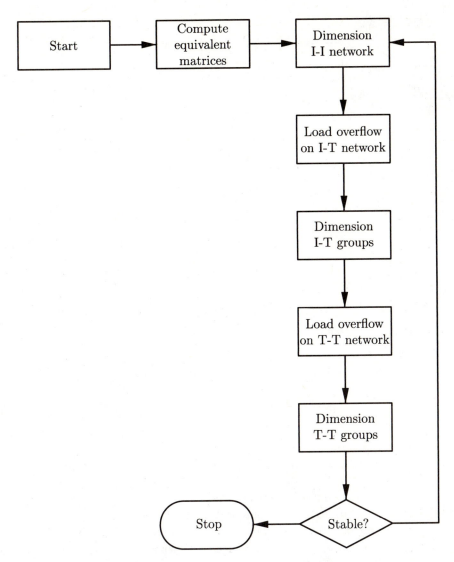

Figure 9.8 Dimensioning Heuristic for DCR Networks

First, the bundle as a whole is dimensioned to meet a blocking grade-of-service constraint — the only place in the algorithm that uses the notion of grade of service. Also, the multihour engineering aspect of the method is used here. Each bundle is dimensioned for the hour when the total bundle traffic

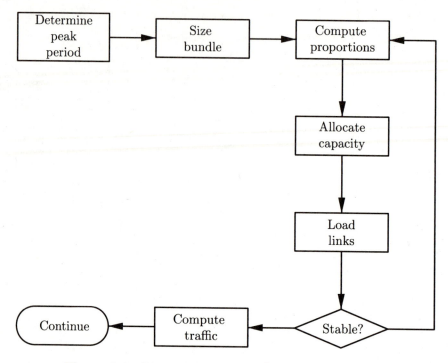

Figure 9.9   Dimensioning the Groups in an I-T Bundle

is largest. This technique bears a strong resemblance to the cluster busy-hour method, which is frequently used for the multihour engineering of classical hierarchical routing networks. Note that the constraints are imposed on the *total bundle blocking*, not on the end-to-end blocking, as would be expected. The mapping between these two measures of grade of service is quite complex, as shown in Chapter 6, and computing it can be time consuming. This is the main reason why the resulting grade of service as measured by the end-to-end blocking probability of a network dimensioned with a set of bundle constraints must be evaluated *after* the dimensioning ends.

After the bundle is sized, each individual group within the bundle must be sized. At this stage, the groups play the role of intermediate high-usage groups, and thus are sized using an economic criterion. Qualitatively, the rule is that the incremental cost of carried traffic should be equal on all groups in the bundle — similar to the ECCS principle for ordinary dimensioning. No calculation of the marginal cost of alternate routing has been published, however, and a number of plausible heuristics could be used.

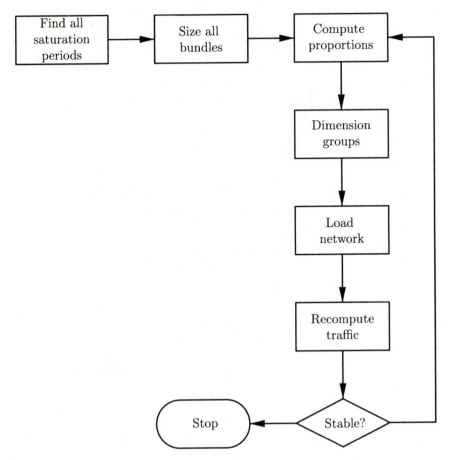

Figure 9.10 Dimensioning the Groups in a T-T Bundle

Dimensioning T-T Groups

T-T groups are dimensioned similarly, except that the bundles cannot be sized independently. Because of the mutual overflow that occurs between alternate routes, an iterative procedure must be used to find a set of consistent bundle sizes and traffic patterns. Each time a bundle is sized, individual groups must be computed, requiring another level of iteration, just as for the case of I-T groups (see Fig. 9.10 for the corresponding flowchart).

Network Loading

Whenever the groups are dimensioned, the external traffic flows must be loaded in the network to determine the amount of traffic offered to each group. In principle, this is determined uniquely by the routing method used in the network. In the present case, a traffic stream is normally split among the various alternate paths according to the residual capacity available on each path; it is necessary to compute some measure of the expected residual capacity on all paths available to a stream. An approximate value can be computed by assuming that the traffic carried on each link is known, that the number of free circuits on each link is a random variable with uniform distribution, and that these variables are independent on the two links in a path. If we let $\overline{N}_s$ be the average number of free trunks on link s, then we have, with the usual definitions, $\overline{N}_s = N_s - \overline{a}_s$. If $P(x)$ is the number of free connections on an alternate path composed of links a and b going through tandem k, then

$$P_k(x = l) = Pr\left\{(a = l \text{ and } b \geq l) \text{ or } (a \geq l \text{ and } b = l)\right\}$$
$$= \frac{2\overline{N}_a + 2\overline{N}_b + 1 - 2k}{(2\overline{N}_a + 1)(2\overline{N}_b + 1)},$$

and the expected value is

$$\overline{P}_k = \overline{N}_a - \frac{\overline{N}_a^2}{3\overline{N}_b} - \frac{\overline{N}_a}{2\overline{N}_b}. \tag{9.39}$$

This last quantity should be used in loading the network by partitioning each stream in proportion to the expected value $\overline{P}_k$. In practice, in addition to the residual-capacity factor provided by the routing, an economic factor is introduced into the link-loading process. The rationale for this extra element is that capacity should not be added to the network to permit the alternate routing of traffic in nonpeak periods if the capacity has not already been provided for routing in some peak period. If the residual capacity rule (9.39) had the effect of separating the traffic to take advantage of this spare capacity, perhaps more capacity would have to be provided at the next iteration, with a detrimental effect on the network cost. For this reason, Huberman, Hurtubise, Le Nir, and Drwiega suggest that alternate routing on expensive paths should be avoided, and the path loading be done in proportion to a modified rule of the form $\overline{P}_k^{\beta_P} / C_k^{\beta_C}$, where C_k is the marginal cost of alternate routing on the path through tandem k. The exponents β_C and β_P can be chosen to give more weight to one or the other of the two factors, depending on the emphasis placed on cost versus efficiency.

Results

The only numerical results for this dimensioning algorithm can be found in [22] for a 38-node network, which was dimensioned taking into account six traffic matrices. Two dimensioning methods for the case of hierarchical routing, as well as the multihour heuristic for adaptive routing, were used. In the latter case, the network was loaded using the mixed rule with both residual capacity and cost. The results of the comparison are summarized in Table 9.6.

Routing	No. Trunks	Network Cost	Trunk Miles
Hierarchical	16560	10.38	5.72
Method of [21]	15120	9.70	5.26
Method of [22]	14736	9.09	4.87

Table 9.6 Cost Comparison of Dimensioning Algorithms

It is difficult to interpret these results since the networks are dimensioned to different constraints. The DCR network of [22] is calculated with a constraint on the bundle blocking, while the hierarchical network used for the comparison is computed with a constraint on final groups. Although each network meets its own constraint, it is not obvious how one constraint is related to the other, and to what extent the cost difference found in Table 9.6 stems from this difference in grade of service or from the intrinsic merits of the routing method. If, on the other hand, one uses a common measure of grade of service, such as the end-to-end blocking probability, the networks would probably not have the same loss value. Table 9.7 displays some values for the average end-to-end blocking obtained by simulating the same traffic load on the network operating with hierarchical routing and with DCR. We note from the table that the adaptive routing network has a higher end-to-end blocking than the hierarchical network.

Routing	Load 1	Load 2	Load 3	Load 4
Hierarchical	.41	.65	.41	.39
HPR	.76	.89	.46	.60

Table 9.7 End-to-End Blocking for 38-Node Network

Because no analysis of the sensitivity of cost to grade of service has been published, it is impossible to decide whether the cost reductions found by the dimensioning algorithm arises from a better network utilization, or simply from different constraints. In the present case, the DCR network is more economical, but has a poorer grade of service than the hierarchical network. It is not clear how this cost benefit would change if the constraints were made identical. The answer cannot be given until a more rigorous dimensioning method is found, based on a mathematical model that explicitly contains optimality conditions and grade-of-service constraints.

Summary

The heuristic proposed in [22] is a first step toward a practical dimensioning method for adaptive routing networks. Although the heuristic can handle moderately large networks, its accuracy is still open to question. This matter will be resolved when a more accurate dimensioning model is proposed, which in turn will probably require a more efficient performance-evaluation model.

Problems

9.1. Reformulate Moe's model for a single user with blocking constraints on the traffic that must be carried. Show that, if the optimal decision is to install just enough capacity to meet the constraint, then the marginal cost of construction is strictly greater than the marginal revenue generated by the minimal amount of traffic carried on the link.

9.2. One solution for the case in which it is not economical to install any capacity on a link is to attempt to modify the revenues generated by the calls to make the installation profitable. Consider now the situation where there are k independent customers. Assume that the demand for service in Moe's model depends on the price charged for the service, as well as the revenue generated by the calls. Assume that the revenue is linear in the number of calls, but that the demand function is arbitrary, decreasing in the price per call. Recompute the optimality equations for the optimal dimensioning equations, and show that if the *same* price per call is charged to all users, then it is still possible that some users will not be given any service.

9.3. Derive the optimality conditions for the user-optimal and game-theoretic formulation of the dimensioning problem described in Section 9.1.

9.4. Write Eq. (9.13) for the case of two-link alternate routing with SOC.

9.5. Write the ECCS equations for the case of multihour dimensioning for nonhierarchical alternate routing.

9.6. Define a relaxation procedure for solving the dimensioning problem in the one-parameter Berry model. Be sure to state what precautions are needed to ensure that the algorithm remains within the feasible domain.

9.7. Write the Kuhn-Tucker equations for the subproblems of the decomposition model for multihour engineering, when the link-blocking probabilities are taken as the independent variables, as defined in Eq. (9.21). Discuss in detail the solution of the subproblem for the N_s variables in the case where the cost functions are linear. In particular, explain why a subgradient method could not be used to resolve the dual.

9.8. Define a routing and dimensioning model of the multicommodity type where the routing is over least-cost paths, such that the link metric is precisely the one used in the Unified Algorithm (see Section 9.4).

References

[1] Jensen, A., *Moe's principle: an econometric investigation intended as an aid in dimensioning and managing telephone plants*, Copenhagen Telephone Company, 1950.

[2] Basu, K.K., "Optimizing telephone network with alternate routes: an integer programming solution," *International Teletraffic Congress*, vol. 9, pp. Basu1–Basu5, 1979.

[3] Harris, R.J., "Concepts of optimality in alternate routing networks," *Australian Telecommunication Research*, vol. 7, pp. 3–8, 1973.

[4] Harris, R.J., "A comparison of system and user optimised telephone networks," *Australian Telecommunication Research*, vol. 11, pp. 125–132, 1977.

[5] Gill, P.E., Murray, W., and Wright, M., *Practical Optimization*, Academic Press, 1981.

[6] Luenberger, D.G., *Linear and Nonlinear Programming*, Addison-Wesley, 1984.

[7] Girard, A., and Pagé, R., "Dimensioning of telephone networks with nonhierarchical routing and trunk reservation," *Network Planning Symposium*, vol. 3, pp. 85–93, June 1986.

[8] Cameron, H., Galloy, P., and Graham, W.J., "Report on the Toronto advanced routing concept trial," *Network Planning Symposium*, vol. 1, pp. 228–236, 1980.

[9] Pióro, M.P., "A uniform approach to the analysis and optimization of circuit switched communication networks," *International Teletraffic Congress*, vol. 10, pp. 4.3A:1–4.3A:7, 1983.

[10] Minoux, M. and Serreault, J.Y., "Subgradient optimization and large scale programming: an application to optimum multicommodity network synthesis with security constraints," *Revue d'automatique, informatique et recherche opérationnelle (R.A.I.R.O–Operations Research)*, vol. 15, pp. 185–203, 1981.

[11] Minoux, M. and Serreault, J.Y., "Optimal synthesis of a telecommunication network with security constraints," (in French), *Annales des télécommunications*, vol. 36, pp. 1–19, 1981.

[12] Katz, S., "Trunk engineering of nonhierarchical networks," *International Teletraffic Congress*, vol. 6, pp. 142.1–142.8, 1971.

[13] Knepley, J.E., "Minimum cost design for circuit switched networks," Report No. AD–A014 101, Defense Communications Agency Systems, Engineering Facility, Reston, Virginia, July 1973.

[14] Berry, L.T.M., *A mathematical model for optimizing telephone networks*, Ph.D. Thesis, University of Adelaide, 1971.

[15] Berry, L.T.M., "An explicit formula for dimensioning links offered overflow traffic," *Australian Telecommunication Research*, vol. 8, pp. 13–17, 1974.

[16] Harris, R.J., "The modified reduced gradient method for optimally dimensioning telephone networks," *Australian Telecommunication Research*, vol. 10, pp. 30–35, 1976.

[17] Berry, L., and Harris, R.J., "Modular design of a large metropolitan telephone network: a case study," *International Teletraffic Congress*, vol. 11, pp. 2.3A-5-1–2.3A-5-7, 1985.

[18] Ash, G.R., Cardwell, R.H., and Murray, R.P., "Design and optimization of networks with dynamic routing," *Bell System Technical Journal*, vol. 60, pp. 1787–1820, 1981.

[19] Field, F.A., "The benefits of dynamic nonhierarchical routing in metropolitan traffic networks," *International Teletraffic Congress*, vol. 10, pp. 3.2.1.1–3.2.1.6, June 1983.

[20] Ash, G.R., Kafker, A.H., and Krishnan, K.R., "Intercity dynamic routing architecture and feasibility," *International Teletraffic Congress*, vol. 10, pp. 3.2.2.1–3.2.2.7, June 1983.

[21] Cameron, H., and Régnier, J., "Dynamic routing for intercity telephone networks," *International Teletraffic Congress*, vol. 10, pp. 3.2.1–3.2.8, June 1983.

[22] Huberman, R., Hurtubise, S., Le Nir, S.A., and Drwiega, T., "Multihour dimensioning for a dynamically routed network," *International Teletraffic Congress*, vol. 11, September 1985.

CHAPTER 10

Future Networks

As mentioned in Chapter 1, the nature of telecommunication networks is rapidly changing, driven by the evolution of switching and transmission technologies toward digitization, as well as the requirements for new kinds of services. While it is feasible to plan and maintain two separate networks, as now the case for telephony and computer communications, developing additional specialized networks will be increasingly inefficient and difficult as services such as video, inter-LAN communications, and bulk data transfer are offered. Cost, of course, is an important factor. A multiplicity of networks require separate managements, equipment bases, and operational procedures. Also, a completely separate set of networks cannot benefit from the economies of scale in these functions achieved if all the networks were integrated.

Communication among networks will also be needed. There is a tendency to limit the range of capabilities of each system to make interconnection easier. The development of separate networks could follow such a course, with a corresponding lack of functionality. Add the inconvenience of having different terminal equipment, connection protocols, and operation and administrative procedures such as billing, and the case for integration becomes even more compelling.

Perhaps the most important argument for integration is that currently no good estimate exists, even within an order of magnitude, of the future demand for different types of new services. Worse, some of these services, such as video teleconferences, have very large bandwidth requirements. Building a separate network for each service becomes risky: A small error in forecasting the number of customers can affect the network operation catastrophically. In view of this uncertainty, a multiservice network that can serve a wide variety of demands using a single installed base of equipment is certainly more attractive. This equipment can be planned for on the basis of forecasts for overall demand, not of individual service demands, as would be the case for separate networks.

Given the arguments for an integrated network, let us discuss the future of circuit-switching techniques in this context, considering how these techniques should be modified to meet the new requirements that are behind the evolution toward integration. To do this, we must examine the characteristics of the new services to be carried by the networks, as well as the requirements imposed by these characteristics on network structure and operation. This leads to a short review of current transmission and switching technology, for both packet switching and circuit switching, which we see are insufficient for the foreseen needs of integrated networks. We then review current promising proposals for improved transmission and switching methods. Finally, we discuss the impact of these new services and techniques on the routing and dimensioning techniques reviewed previously, indicating the magnitude of the work necessary to arrive at adequate methods for the integrated services digital network (ISDN).

10.1   Characteristics of ISDN Networks

Even though a truly integrated services network does not exist, we can state what such a network should provide. Basically, an ISDN should have three capabilities: (1) message signaling, (2) uniform access to *all* telecommunication services, and (3) digital end-to-end connectivity for user data. In the following discussion, we describe the capabilities of the ordinary telephone and packet-switched data networks.

Message Signaling

The information carried in a network can be divided into two broad classes: (1) the actual user information and (2) the control information necessary for network operation. The second kind of information, called *signaling*, is found in both the access loop and the transport network between switches. This information can be carried either on a separate channel with distinct messages — called *message signaling* — or within the network, where it is mixed with the user information — in which case we talk of *in-band signaling*.

Because of the nature of packet switching, message signaling was the first signaling technique implemented in packet networks — an advantage of these networks over the telephone network, where interswitch signaling is of two types. The supervision of lines, such as the signaling required for call set-up, call termination, and busy/idle status of lines, is done on a support distinct from the lines that carry user data (in this case, the telephone conversation). The other type of information, used for routing, consists of the representation of the digits of the called number, either by electrical pulses or by pairs of carefully defined tones. The important fact about this information is that it is carried *in-band*, that is, on the same channel that carries the voice conversation. The first requirement of an ISDN network is that such information be carried on a support distinct from the user data, and be implemented through the exchange of messages between switches. The CCITT has issued two recommendations for this type of signaling, systems 6 and 7. System 6 has already been implemented in North America and Japan, while system 7 is gradually being introduced all over the world. In this sense, the ordinary telephone network does meet the requirement of message signaling, at least as far as interswitch communication is concerned.

The message-signaling requirement, however, is also an end-to-end requirement. This means that message signaling should be available between the user terminal and its local switch — a capability well beyond the current access telephone network, which is made up of a single analog loop; the only signaling available is the on-hook/off-hook condition of the receiver. The first efforts toward standardization have been made here, providing improved access to the network by means of the message-signaling capability required of a truly integrated network.

Access Standards

The access standard for low-speed services, such as voice and interactive data, is summarized in the so-called 2B+D interface, defined by the CCITT. The user is provided three access channels, two of type B and one of type D. The B channels are 64 kb/sec channels, typically one for digitized voice and the other for low-speed data. The D channel, a 16 kb/sec channel used for signaling purposes, has its own protocol.

Defining the user access in terms of separate B and D channels also meets the requirement of message signaling on the user access, at least for low-speed services [1,2,3]. Protocols for wide-band and multimedia calls are currently being defined.

Digital End-to-End Connectivity

The requirement for digital end-to-end connectivity is partly met by the message-signaling condition of the access portion of the network. Because most telephone networks are evolving toward a digital-transmission medium, the requirement for digital connectivity is also well on the way toward being met in the current telephone network. Packet networks, on the other hand, have used digital transmission from the beginning, and thus already provide an adequate transmission technique. In fact, this requirement for digital end-to-end connectivity will impose some of the more drastic changes in the way the networks operate. To understand the nature of these changes and available solutions, we must now examine three aspects of digital transmission as they currently exist in the network: (1) the digitization of sources, (2) digital multiplexing, and (3) transmission and digital switching.

10.2   Digital Sources

The nature of the future ISDN will be determined to a large extent by the nature of the services that must be provided. Although it is unclear at this time precisely which services will become commercially viable, let us examine those that could become the driving force behind the conversion to the ISDN. Such services are either narrow band or wide band.

Narrow-Band Sources

Voice is the traditional source for the telephone network, and the techniques of voice digitization are well understood. Uncoded voice with pulse-code modulation normally yields a 64 kb/sec stream, explaining the rate chosen for the B channel for ISDN access. Using adaptive techniques, another standard can produce a stream of 32 kb/sec with comparable quality. The weight of invested PCM equipment, however, means that the standard B channel will remain for a long time.

There is no question that voice will remain a dominant component of any integrated network for quite some time. The importance of voice traffic as a source of narrow-band data is often underestimated. As an example, consider the values taken from [4], where it is pointed out that four minutes of voice conversation digitized at 64 kb/sec generates the same amount of data as the transmission of *War and Peace* using 8-bit ASCII. Although each voice channel operates at a comparatively low rate, the huge number of sources makes voice the dominant factor in terms of total volume generated, a much greater volume than that of any alphanumeric source currently in use.

Bulk data transfer can generate large amounts of data per call. The number of users for these services is much smaller than for voice, however, keeping the total effect on network traffic far below that of voice. Whether this situation will continue and, if not, when the change will become significant, is one of the unknowns that make the planning of ISDN so difficult.

Wide-Band Sources

Video services make up the other class of users that could affect traffic volume significantly. For the system currently normalized by the comité consultatif international pour la radio (CCIR), the corresponding uncoded rates yield a channel operating at 216 Mbits/sec. Coding techniques allow bandwidth reduction to values between 140 Mbits/sec and 34 Mbits/sec, depending on picture quality. The services in this class are standard real-time point-to-point video, video conferences, either coded or uncoded, and broadcast video in a pay-channel system. Although users of video services generate very high bit rates, significantly higher than voice channels, the same remark can be made for them as for bulk data transfer: Because terminal cost is quite high, it is not known which of these services will become commercially attractive; hence the traffic volume that will have to be transported by the network is also unknown.

It is possible to conceive of even higher bandwidth requirements. An interesting case is the need for communication between local area networks, that is, private networks of terminals attached to one or more computers. The need to transfer files between two such networks could yield huge bit rates — for instance, when computer-generated graphics produced on a computer at one site are required at another site, in which case peak rates could be in the Gbit/sec range. Typical users of such a service would be remote sites that access supercomputers, requiring graphical output of the results of ongoing iterative computations as they are produced in order to select the parameters of the next iteration.

The implication is that the traffic sources for the ISDN may be very different from current homogeneous networks, which are characterized by many independent, low-speed customers with smooth inputs. Wide-band ISDN will undoubtedly continue to have these customers also, but also a few, very high-rate customers with very bursty utilization patterns that compete for the same transmission and switching resources. Current tools may not be well suited for this new pattern of demand.

Although it is possible to identify some services with potential effects on the structure of the ISDN, the whole area is uncertain: The penetration of these services depends not only on technical issues, such as the cost of a high-speed video terminal, but also on other aspects such as tariffs, the evolution policy from the current network to the ISDN, and the availability of service providers to attract subscribers. It is therefore essential that the network be capable of carrying any of these services without major technological change. Thus the transmission and switching techniques must be sufficiently flexible to carry any of these services, but must also provide a smooth evolution path from the current telephone network to the future ISDN. As we shall now see, these are conflicting requirements. We show this by examining the current network transmission and switching methods, and why they are insufficiently flexible. We then review the current proposals, seeing why most of them fail to provide a smooth evolutionary path — with one possible exception, the subject of Section 10.4.

10.3   Digital Transmission and Switching

The impact of new services will be felt most strongly in the area of transmission and switching. To see the magnitude of the required changes, we must know how these functions are implemented in the network as it exists today. Digital transmission and switching each constitute an area of specialization well beyond the scope of this book, and thus we give only the bare essentials required to understand the limitations of the current networks and how they have to be extended to provide the wide-band services required by future ISDN. The interested reader can find many excellent references [5,6,7] that cover digital transmission and switching in depth.

Digital Transmission and Multiplexing

Transmission systems for the ISDN will have to use multiplexing, obviously some form of time multiplexing. The only possible exception is optical fiber-based networks, which operate in a frequency multiplexing mode — necessary because switching still must be done electronically, at rates of an order of magnitude smaller than the transmission rates available in the optical part of the network. Thus each user, although it may be using a high-bandwidth transmission system, has in effect a very limited (relatively speaking) bandwidth available. Frequency multiplexing is then used to allow the fiber network to be used simultaneously at different frequencies, permitting an overall throughput significantly higher than the individual throughput available to a single user [8]. Because this technique will probably become obsolete when truly optical switching elements become available, we limit the discussion on digital systems to the time-division case. A time-multiplexed transmission system can be operated either synchronously or asynchronously.

Synchronous Mode.   In the synchronous mode, time is divided into equal intervals called *frames*, typically of 125 μsec. Users transmit cyclically once per frame, and thus this type of multiplexing is called *synchronous transfer mode* (STM). Each frame is further subdivided into subintervals, called *slots*. There are 24 slots per frame in North America and Japan, and 30 in Europe. Each user of the line is given a slot number, determining the time at which it is allowed to transmit relative to the beginning of the frame. The length of this slot is sufficient to permit a single byte to be transmitted for each user; thus the basic system is said to be *byte interleaved*. The great advantage of the synchronous mode of operation is that the user's identity is implicitly known from the slot number. Conversely, a very accurate clock must be maintained on the link because a timing error may mean that data is delivered to the wrong user, or corrupted in some unpredictable way. In current systems, this synchronization is maintained separately for each link.

We have defined circuit switching as the real allocation of resource to a user at call-connect time. In older analog systems, this could be a frequency band, or even a metallic path through the network. For time-division systems, the resource in question is the slot in each frame, which is reserved for the user and cannot be used by anyone else.

The basic rate for the North American system is the so-called DS0 rate, 64 kb/sec. The first level, the DS1 level, operates at 1.544 Mb/sec; this level multiplexes 24 DS0 channels onto a single DS1 channel by the byte-interleaving process just described. The apparent difference between the total bandwidth of the 24 DS0 channels and the DS1 bandwidth is taken up by signaling and control information. Note that this byte interleaving is possible because all the DS0 signals are derived from the same clock. Thus these signals are both synchronized and aligned, permitting the byte interleaving.

Higher transmission speeds are often desirable, in which case four DS1 channels can be multiplexed into a DS2 channel operating at 6.312 Mb/sec. Because the DS1 signals may be on different links in a network, they are neither aligned nor synchronized. For this reason, the next stage in the multiplexing hierarchy is really asynchronous. Since the DS2 system must operate in a synchronous mode, however, the DS1 streams must be somehow aligned and synchronized. This is done by buffering the data of each DS1 stream, reading out the bits at a rate higher than that normally required. The effect is to provide more slots than needed to output the buffers; the extra slots are filled with dummy pulses called *stuffing bits*. Because this technique of bit stuffing causes no loss of information, and only a slight increase in transmission rate, it is quite acceptable for use in the current network. Note, however, that the users are not byte interleaved anymore, but rather *bit interleaved*. Thus more information must be carried by the system to enable it to recognize the owner of each bit in the frame. This asynchronous process makes the current system unsuitable for wide-band applications, as we shall see shortly.

The transmission rates are built up in a hierarchical system, where a level multiplexes a number of systems of the lower level into a single entity by the bit-interleaving technique. This transmission hierarchy is well defined up to approximately 45 Mb/sec, with one system for North America and Japan, and another for Europe. Currently the standards committees are considering whether to extend the hierarchy to higher rates, for both the electronics transmission system [9] and the future optical networks [10]. Table 10.1 summarizes the current hierarchy and some of the proposals.

All digital telephone networks use some form of STM. The large capital investment in these systems has a considerable influence on the transition toward an ISDN. Most importantly, a complete initial replacement of the transmission infrastructure is excluded. Any transmission format for the ISDN must evolve from the current system — efficiently, it is hoped. This constraint will also profoundly influence the switching techniques that can be realistically used in the future ISDN, as we shall see later.

Asynchronous Mode.   In the asynchronous transmission mode, time is not divided into frames. Messages of variable length can arrive on a link at arbitrary points in time. There is no unique time at which a message must start or end, as for synchronous transmission. Instead, the start and end of a message are determined by transmitting a specific bit pattern. Thus it is necessary to ensure that no message can contain one of these patterns as data, an added

	North America & Japan		Europe	
	Rate (Mb/sec)	Factor	Rate (Mb/sec)	Factor
DS0	0.064		0.064	
DS1	1.544	24	2.048	30
DS1C	3.152	2		
DS2	6.312	2	8.448	4
DS3	44.736	7	34.368	4
H2	30-45			
H3	60-70			
H4	120-140			

Table 10.1 Current and Proposed Transmission Hierarchies

complexity of the asynchronous mode of transmission. Also, the identity of the owner of the message must be explicitly contained in the message, generally in an address field. The advantage, of course, is that the transmission capacity can be allocated only when needed, operating the system much more efficiently than synchronous transmission whenever utilization is low.

Note that the two modes of transmission are completely separate, each with its own advantages and disadvantages. Because most of the transmission systems in the telephone network operate synchronously, it is not easy to put asynchronous traffic on these systems without complex multiplexing and de-multiplexing schemes. This requirement is even more stringent for wide-band services, and some attempts have been made to define modes of transmission that lie between the pure synchronous and pure asynchronous modes. This is discussed further in Section 10.4, along with other improvements required by the new wide-band services.

Digital Switching

The other function required of a digital system is the switching of channels from an incoming multiplex to the appropriate channels of the outgoing multiplex. Here the fundamental differences between switching techniques come to light. In the synchronous mode, we examine space and time switches, also reviewing the operation characteristics of asynchronous switching as currently used for data networks.

Space Switching.   Let us examine first the operation of a space switch for a synchronous multiplex. Space switching is illustrated in Fig. 10.1, which shows the switching of n input lines to a particular output line. We assume

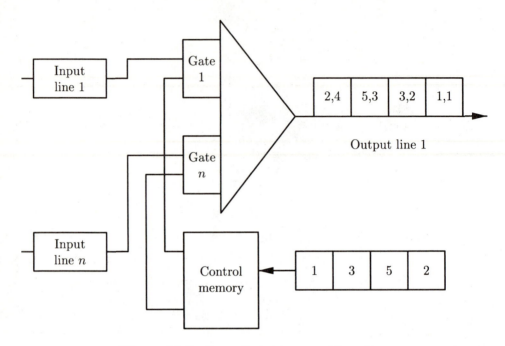

Figure 10.1   Space Switching to a Given Line

that the frames in the input lines have been aligned and synchronized. Each output line has a control memory that contains the number of the input line that will be connected to this particular output line in each time slot. This connection is implemented by closing the appropriate gates between input and output during the appropriate slot interval. The net result is shown in the figure, where the contents of the control memory are read from left to right. The contents of the frame on the output line are denoted by a pair of symbols (l, k), where l is the number of the line from which this slot comes, and k is the slot number in the frame on this line.

Space switches have a number of important features. An advantage is that the switch operates at the basic frame rate, requiring relatively cheap electronic components. On the other hand, the position of a slot in the frame is the same in the input and output lines, although the slots appear in different output lines. For this reason, space switches can exhibit internal blocking when a call must be set up from line i to line j, but there is no free path connecting these lines because of previously established connections. If line j happens to be free at that time, the call is lost because of the blocking inside the switch. Although combinations of space switches can be made nonblocking, this is expensive, and truly nonblocking space switches are seldom used as the sole component of large switching machines.

Time Switching.   Truly nonblocking switches can be realized more economically if the slot position within the frame can be changed by the switch. This is done by time switches, using a technique called *time-slot interchange* (TSI).

The switch consists of two types of memories, one for data and one for control. Conceptually we can assume that there is one data buffer for each input line and one control memory for each output line, although in practice memory may be organized quite differently. First a complete incoming frame is stored in the data memory of each line. (The control memory is responsible for the actual switching.) During slot interval i, all the slots of input line i are transferred to the appropriate output lines. The output lines are scanned in their numerical order, from first to last, but the input buffer is not scanned sequentially. Instead, the order of scanning of the input buffer is contained in the control memory for this input buffer. In Fig. 10.2, an example of the switching of four slots of two lines, each row of the control memory corresponds to an input line. Each column corresponds to a slot number in the output lines. In this organization, all the elements of row 1 are read out first, then placed in the first slot of the frame of each of the output lines. Line 2 is then read out, and so on until the last row, corresponding to the last input line, is read, and the corresponding input slots placed in the last slot of the output lines.

Time switches can be shown to be nonblocking, in the sense that, whenever a call arrives at the switch, it can always be connected if the output port is free. Note, however, that the whole operation of writing the data buffers and reading out to the output buffers must occur within a single frame interval. Because each input buffer is read sequentially, and since it operates at the basic frame rate, the whole switch element must operate at a rate n times faster than the basic rate, where n is the number of lines being switched. This in turn implies faster operating electronics, with a correspondingly higher cost.

A final feature of time switches worth mentioning is that the order of slots in a frame is not preserved. Although of no consequence for ordinary calls, this becomes important when we consider switching wide-band calls, as we shall see.

For the reasons presented, large-scale switches are seldom of a single type. The switch is built out of a sequence of space and time stages, the most frequent combination being the time-space-time (TST) configuration. The actual design of these switches in an important area of network planning; the interested reader is referred to the specialized literature on the subject.

Asynchronous Switching.   Synchronous switching is not well suited for transmission systems operating in the asynchronous mode. Asynchronous data is more easily handled by asynchronous switches. All current asynchronous switches have the same centralized architecture, and all have a single connection

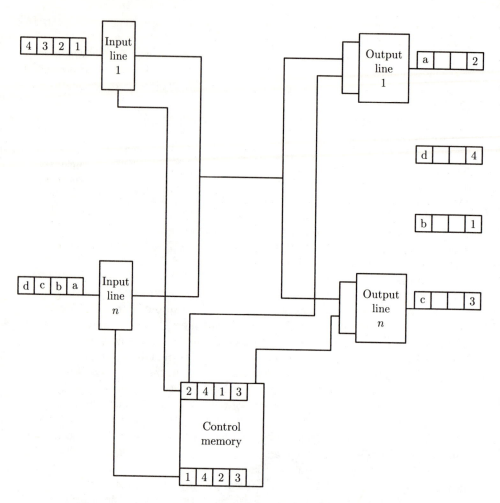

Figure 10.2 Data and Control Memory for a Time Switch

path between input and output ports. This organization is a consequence of the need to examine each packet to obtain its destination address and also of the need to buffer messages in the case of contention for lines arising from the asynchronous nature of the arrivals. The common channel can take many forms — for instance, a common memory, a single bus, or a ring. In the first case, incoming packets are stored in the order of their arrival and read out in some order, generally first-in, first-out. The control memory lists the output port for each user address, which is contained in the packet header. This memory is under the control of a single processor, which is also responsible for carrying out the level-2 and level-3 functions of the protocol. This type of centralized processing severely limits the throughput of current packet switches to many orders of magnitude below that of circuit switches.

Summary

Let us emphasize some fundamental differences between synchronous and asynchronous switching in relation to blocking and architecture. In the synchronous mode, once a call is set up, no blocking is possible in the switch, since slots arriving at an input port have a path through the switch to a reserved output port. In this mode, blocking can occur only at call set-up time. Furthermore, circuit switches can be arranged in such a way that they are nonblocking. "Nonblocking" can be understood in two ways. In the strict sense, a switch is said to be nonblocking if an incoming call can always be connected to an output port whenever this output port is not busy. This strict nonblocking property is a consequence of the switch structure, as well as of the connection algorithm used to establish connections. In the broad sense, a switch is said to be nonblocking if an incoming call can always be connected to a free output port, under the assumption that some previously established connections are rerouted on other paths within the switch. In practice, strictly nonblocking space switches are seldom used because they are too expensive, and thus nonblocking switches in the broad sense are impractical. The increased use of time switches is making this issue less important for circuit switching, and the assumption of nonblocking switches will become more realistic as this technique spreads more widely.

The problem of blocking in an asynchronous switch takes a different meaning because of the asynchronous mode of operation. Strictly speaking, there can be no call blocking since virtual calls use no physical resources in the switch. Thus it is perfectly possible to connect two virtual calls that have the same output port, something impossible for a circuit-switched connection.

Even if virtual calls are set up in the same way as real circuits — that is, by avoiding routing more than one call on a given output port — blocking can still occur in the switch, an event impossible in an STM switch. This can occur because of the asynchronous arrival of packets — when two packets arrive at two different input ports with the same output-port destination. This is a fundamental problem of asynchronous switching, and the protocol used in such cases of collisions largely determines the performance of the switch. All currently existing packet switches resolve the collision by making one of the packets wait in a queue. This is necessary because of the implementation of the data-link level in the switch, which guarantees error-free delivery of all packets through the link between two switches. A consequence is that some form of queue management must be implemented in the switch, limiting the number of packets processed per unit time. The other option in case of collision is simply to drop one of the packets, relying on some other level to detect this loss, and initiating a retransmission if necessary. In this case, the switch must be configured such that the probability of losing a packet is small enough for the application considered. As we shall see, both these strategies for collision resolution are currently envisaged for fast switches.

Another fundamental difference between the two types of switches is that synchronous switches are always multipath switches, while current asynchronous switches are single path. Building multipath switches for synchronous transmission systems is fundamentally easier than for asynchronous systems because processing each slot is reduced to the smallest possible amount. Multipath switches can then be implemented with simple technology, as done with early telephone switches. In fact, the simplest synchronous switches are made up of cross-points and wired-logic memory, both available long before computers began to be used in communication networks. In contrast, in asynchronous systems, a multipath architecture is not really feasible without sophisticated switching matrices because of the need to process addresses within the switch. For this reason, the packet switches under development are quite different in concept from currently existing ones.

10.4   Switching and Transmission for ISDN

Current switching and transmission technologies do permit some form of integration in the transport network, at least for low-speed services. For some time, the telephone network has been used for low-speed data communication through the use of modems, and fast circuit switching has also been examined for this purpose [11]. Integration of speech and data in packet networks, which has also been investigated, has given rise to a form of narrow-band ISDN. In these systems, the stringent time requirement for voice is met by giving high priority to the voice packets over the data packets. This leads to traffic models with different priority classes, and to networks where packet loss, at least for voice calls, can be tolerated. Finally, a hybrid packet/circuit switching technique has been proposed that reserves part of the frame for circuit-switched voice, using the rest for data in a packet-switched mode. This asynchronous portion of the frame may be of fixed length or may vary according to the number of circuit-switched calls present in the frame. A good summary of this work, and some simple analytical models, can be found in [12]. Because the performance of these systems has been the object of widespread attention over the last 10 years, the theoretical, if not economic, reasons for integrating these services are well understood.

The picture changes radically when wide-band services must be provided. Currently these services, such as bulk data transfer and video, are supported by private networks allocated to each customer individually. The set-up time for these special networks is usually long, sometimes of the order of days. This mode of operation is totally unsuitable for certain types of services. As a case in point, it is currently impossible to consult a remote video database on demand. A transmission facility with the required bandwidth, which must be set up in advance, is allocated to the user on a semipermanent basis. It would be much more efficient to set up a circuit-switched call of the appropriate bandwidth for the duration of the consultation, typically a few minutes, and then to release the call. Another possibility is to set up a virtual call on a semipermanent basis, within which a number of accesses would be possible. The first technique requires fast wide-band circuit switching; the second, fast packet switching. Unfortunately, neither option is feasible in present networks.

Circuit-Switched Services

There are a number of problems with providing wide-band services using current transmission hierarchies and circuit-switching techniques. Most important are the lack of flexibility imposed by the fixed transmission hierarchy with respect to the widely different bandwidth requirements expected in the ISDN, the difficulty of switching calls of different rates within the same switch fabric, and the problem of time-slot sequence integrity (TSSI).

In a pure synchronous transfer mode, the only bandwidths available to the user are those used in the transport network. If users were permitted to have any arbitrary input rate to the synchronous network, some form of asynchronous multiplexing would be needed, going against the definition of a pure end-to-end synchronous network. This lack of flexibility, an intrinsic feature of the synchronous mode, is often cited as the main reason why it should be abandoned in favor of the asynchronous technique.

The second problem arises from the fact that current switches can operate only on DS0 channels. This poses some difficulties in the wide-band environment because a wide-band call is implemented by allocating many slots in a frame to a particular call. This means that a multiplexed frame, say at the DS3 level, may have a number of DS0 and DS1 calls. To switch these calls, the switch must recognize which slots belong to which calls, impossible for current switches. Even after the beginning of a frame is detected, it is not possible to know to which DS0 or even to which DS1 the first bit, or any other bit, belongs simply by its position in the frame [13]. This situation arises from the asynchronous multiplexing of lower-level frames into the DS3 formats by the use of bit stuffing. This is an essential feature of asynchronous multiplexing, and the reason it is not possible to identify a particular DS0 channel inside a higher-level frame without going through the inverse of the process used to create the frame in the first place. Thus the whole operation is uneconomical; for this reason, current switches cannot easily accommodate multirate circuit switching.

The third problem is also related to the switching methods currently used in circuit-switched networks. In some applications, such as video, the conservation of the precise order between some slots, is critical — the time-slot sequence integrity (TSSI) problem. If multiple slots belong to the same call, these slots may arrive at the other end of the network in an order different from that in which they were sent at the origin. This can happen both inside and outside switches. Inside switches, slots can be interchanged in the time stage of the switch, which, as we have seen, works by time-slot interchange. Also, if various slots of the same calls are switched individually through different parts of the switch, different delays may be incurred. This problem of different delays through the switch is similar to another problem — that is, different delays through the network because call components are routed on different paths.

Flexibility, invisibility of lower-level channels in the higher levels of the transmission hierarchy, and TSSI are the main factors limiting the use of circuit switching for wide-band ISDN.

Packet-Switched Services

The other option, that of packet switching, is not possible with existing packet switches. Their implementation as a single-channel switch fabric imposes an inherent throughput limitation. Also, the need to implement the full three lower levels of the OSI protocols is also a limitation. Current packet switches operating under the X25 protocol have a throughput of the order of 10^4 packets/sec, while the requirement for a typical wide-band service would be of the order of 10^8 packets/sec, unfeasible with available techniques.

This technical problem is not the only obstacle to a packet-switched ISDN. The telephone network represents such an enormous financial investment that the question of transition from the current system to the ISDN is also of utmost importance, although often neglected in the technical literature. Pure packet switching with asynchronous transmission and variable-length packets cannot easily be integrated within the network as it currently exists. Current packet networks use separate switches precisely for this reason. Thus an evolution from the current network to the future ISDN via the packet technology would have to occur by means of an overlay strategy, with a large initial capital outlay. This is perhaps the most important factor that could prevent packet switching from being implemented as the universal ISDN transport method.

For all these reasons, the implementation of wide-band ISDN is impossible in current networks, and radical changes must be made to the transmission and switching techniques before truly integrated networks can be achieved. This evolution is currently in progress; because of the speed at which it is occurring, it is not yet possible to determine the precise solution that will meet all the requirements of the services envisaged. We can, however, review some of the more promising proposals to improve the transmission and switching capabilities of networks. For circuit-switched networks, the issue is multirate circuit switching and its relation to the transmission hierarchy. For packet switching, the issue is the introduction of self-routing, multipath switch fabrics. Finally, we review a recent proposal that may be the required compromise between the two extreme cases and provide a smooth evolutionary strategy to the ISDN.

Multirate Circuit Switching

Circuit switching has three fundamental defects when it comes to providing wide-band services. First is the lack of flexibility in the bandwidth available to users. Recall, however, that the degree of flexibility required depends on the population of users, the volume of traffic they generate, and the relative cost of transmission bandwidth with respect to switching. After all, if the network is dominated by a single user class, it should be designed to fit the characteristics of these users [4,14]. Also, if bandwidth is cheap, relatively little penalty is incurred in providing only a few bandwidths, forcing the users to subscribe to the next higher bandwidth that will meet their requirements. Unfortunately for this argument, the relative importance of these different classes of users is unknown. The case for asynchronous transfer is generally based on the apparent flexibility it provides in the face of uncertainty, more than on actual service requirements or cost factors.

The second problem lies with the need to switch calls of different rates in the same switch. The fundamental change required by all transmission techniques is that the identity of channels at all levels in the transmission hierarchy must be completely determined by the position of the channels in the frame. In other words, the multiplexing scheme must be truly synchronous throughout the network. The implication is that the network will be completely isochronous, with a single master clock defining the slot intervals, and that all frames will be constructed by interleaving at rates derived from this single clock, with all frames aligned. Although this may seem quite difficult, a number of proposals in this direction have been made, and a standard is emerging for a fully synchronous hierarchy [9,13]. Within this universal hierarchy, proposals have been made to allow wide-band and narrow-band users to coexist, eventually sharing the same switching equipment.

These proposals are closely linked to new transmission hierarchies, to the point that the distinction between transmission and switching rates is becoming less and less relevant. In some proposals, the distinction no longer exists,

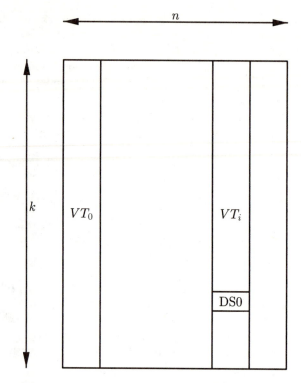

Figure 10.3   Rectangular Frame for DS3 switching

and one speaks of a trans-switching format that is identical for transmission and switching [15]. The impact of these new formats on switching can best be explained in the framework of a single time switch. The fundamental assumption is that the various rates present in the system are all fixed multiples of one another. A frame is built by interleaving the bytes, or in some cases the bits, of the input channels, called *virtual tributaries*, to obtain a completely synchronized superframe. This frame is now represented by a rectangle, as shown in Fig 10.3, where the transmission sequence is from left to right and top to bottom. Each column corresponds to a single virtual tributary, for instance transmitting at the DS1 rate, and a single element in each column can be identified with a precise DS0 channel in that tributary. Typically the beginning of each row contains an extra tributary for control, denoted VT_0.

The advantage of such a synchronous byte-interleaved frame is evident when one considers the requirement for switching a full tributary to a particular destination. With a normal time switch, it is necessary to store the full frame in the input buffer before interchanging the time slots to effect the switching.

The memory and speed requirements then increase with the transmission rate of the system. With the synchronous technique, however, it is not necessary to store the complete frame, but only a single row. Because of the complete synchronization, the position of a particular tributary in this row is always the same and the switching can be done one row at a time. Each line is read into the input buffer of the switch, and read out according to the control memory, just as in ordinary switching. It is this feature that makes multirate circuit switching a practical possibility for the ISDN.

In case of higher bandwidth systems, these rectangular structures can be stacked via a synchronous interleaving technique to form cubes, and the same method used to switch tributaries by storing only one row of the cube at a time. The gains in memory requirements, and consequently in speed and cost, can be as high as 800 to 1 over individual switching of DS0 channels [15].

Finally, the preservation of time-slot sequence integrity may be guaranteed, but at the cost of added complexity in the switching. It is possible to enforce a uniform slot sequence in a time switch either by buffering or by allowing the relative position of frame boundaries to change [4]. If the position of the frame boundaries must be maintained, then it is necessary to add another time stage to preserve TSSI. This can also be achieved by switching the call as a single entity, ensuring that all the slots are switched together both in the switch and on the trunks between the switches [16]. It is not yet clear which of these two methods will be more cost effective for implementation in multirate circuit-switched networks, should this technique be used for some ISDN.

Fast Packet Switching

The use of multirate circuit switching requires some major changes in current transmission and switching techniques. Pure asynchronous transmission can be used for wide-band ISDN without major changes in the transmission technique. The only difference is that packets are generated at a much higher rate than for current services, depending on the instantaneous requirements of the users. The difficulty is that some very bursty users may temporarily saturate the transmission facilities on some paths, a situation that can be prevented by the use of flow control and buffering.

The impact on switching is even more fundamental than for circuit switches. To understand the essential features of fast packet switching, recall the OSI model discussed in Chapter 1. As we saw there, the actual transmission of data through a number of telecommunication systems in series is the responsibility of layers 1 through 3. Given the current implementation of these layers, each and every packet that goes through the switch must go through these three layers.

Another important feature of current packet switches is that the actual routing from the input to the output ports of the switch is done by queuing in a common buffer, which in turn means that *all* packets must be processed by the control unit, and that the amount of processing is quite large. The main consequence of this organization is that the throughput of current packet switches is severely limited. No packet switch in existence today could possibly process all of the data that goes through an ordinary circuit switch carrying telephone traffic.

A significant advance in the area of switching is the development of architectures for packet switches that remove this throughput limitation, at least in principle, and that could permit switching at very high rates. This is achieved by the following simplifications. First, all packets are of fixed lengths, another way of saying that time is slotted to some basic rate. This simplifies the processing at the nodes, also offering the possibility of doing the switching much faster than with variable-length packets.

Also recall that the data-link layer, the network layer, and the transport layer duplicate a number of functions. For instance, the data-link layer is responsible for providing a reliable channel, which it does by error checking and perhaps error correcting. The network layer, however, also responsible for the reliable delivery of packets through the network, implements some form of end-to-end error checking on the packets. Another simplification required for fast packet switching is to remove all these redundancies and to simplify the data-link layer as much as possible. All error-correction mechanisms are pushed back to the upper layers, thus avoiding the need to perform error checking and window control on each packet that goes through the switch.

A third element of the new switches, and the most important one, is that they are multipath, as opposed to single-path conventional packet switches. This is made possible by introducing self-routing networks as the cross-point elements in the switch. In their simplest form, these networks are composed of 2×2 switch elements that switch up or down according to the value of a single bit in the address field of the packet. By combining these elements in an array, it is possible to construct $n \times n$ switching matrices that in effect require no centralized control to do the switching (see Fig. 10.4 for a simple example). The packet arriving on input line i for output line j is given an internal address corresponding to j, after which the fabric will route it correctly to j by reading one bit at a time in each stage of the switch. These self-routing fabrics are nonblocking in the absence of collision, and can also be used in a circuit-switching mode if the packets represent slots in an STM system.

Note the similarity of these switches to circuit switches. The main difference is that the packet address is used for routing, as opposed to the slot position in ordinary time switches. In fact, self-routing switches can be used as circuit switches by simply adding an address field in front of the slots when frames arrive at the input ports. In practice, the distinction between packet and circuit switches tends to decrease — understandable if an integrated fabric is used to switch both types of users.

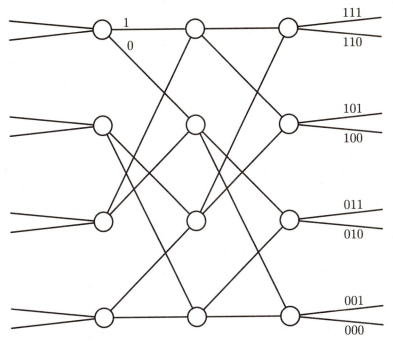

Figure 10.4   8 × 8 Self-Routing Switch

When the switches are used in an asynchronous mode, however, there is still the possibility of collision, which can occur in two ways. Internal collisions is possible if two packets arrive at the same time that are going to the same output port of a *particular switching element*. This can be prevented if the packets are sorted by increasing address at the entry of the switch [17]. Most proposals for fast packet switches are of this variety, where a sorting network is used as a prefiltering stage before the actual self-routing network. The other type of collision occurs when two or more packets are destined for the same *switch output port* at the same instant. This cannot be prevented inside the switch because it involves networkwide features that are generally unknown to the switch. Proposals for fast packet switches differ according to the policy used for collision resolution.

In one method of collision management, packets that have undergone collision are recirculated back to the input port, as in the Starlite switch [17]. In effect, this is equivalent to resolving the collision by queuing, although the queuing is not done in some memory, but in the switch buffers. A counter is added to the recirculated packets to ensure that older packets are given higher priority for the output ports, and the packets are retransmitted in the same sequence that they were received. The switch has constant latency, also an important feature for some services with timing requirements. A similar technique is used in the Knockout switch [18,19], where packets that do not manage to exit from the switch after a fixed number of cycles are simply lost. The possibility of packet loss is a radical departure from traditional packet switching, in which guaranteed transmission of packets between nodes is a fundamental characteristic. In practice, it is possible to construct switches that will have a very small loss probability with a small increment in buffer size, and little added complexity in the management of the switch.

Another technique has been proposed in the Prelude switch [20,21]. This switching technique is a form of cut-through switching, where part of a packet may leave the switch before all of it has been received. The high throughput of the Prelude switch is obtained by effectively decoupling the address-translation process from the packet storing and switching. When a packet arrives, its header is analyzed immediately, and the appropriate translation into the output channel number made. During that time, the packet is stored in a data buffer as it arrives; after it is completely stored, the calculated output address is added to it, and the address of this complete packet is placed in the output queue of the appropriate output buffer. The packet is read out of the data memory when this address reaches the head of the queue. The cut-through nature of the switch results from the possibility of writing out a packet as soon as the address translation is completed, even if all of the packet is not written in the data memory.

Dynamic Time-Division Multiplexing

The purely technical problems raised by the wide-band ISDN can be overcome, in either a circuit-switched or a fast packet-switched environment. These solutions do not address the issue of transition, however, and are not well suited to a smooth evolution from the current structure to the proposed ISDN. Current proposals for the ISDN still have fundamental differences in the transmission system, and to some degree in the accompanying switching technique. Thus both the multislot circuit-switched and the fast packet-switched networks require an evolution via an overlay strategy. Such a strategy would add new transmission and switching equipment on top of the present network to provide services to a few special customers, while the majority of users would continue to use the normal network. As more and more special networks were put in place, more users would find it profitable to migrate to these systems, and the old network would gradually be phased out. These scenarios are required because of the incompatibility of new ISDN systems with the telephone network. The scenarios have the obvious disadvantage that the capital outlay for the special networks must be quite large, and that a reasonably large customer base is required before the initial overlay can be started.

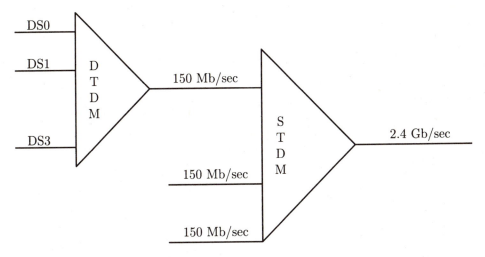

Figure 10.5 Dynamic Time-Division Multiplexing

One proposal that offers the possibility of achieving the evolution toward ISDN via a more gradual replacement strategy is called dynamic time-division multiplexing (DTDM) [22,23]. The most interesting aspect of this method is that it can handle both asynchronous users and synchronous users operating at different rates in the *same* transmission and switching format. Furthermore, it has the capability of merging smoothly into the transmission hierarchy currently existing in the network.

The basic transmission element of the DTDM method, called a *block*, has a constant length. For synchronous users, the block plays the role of a frame in a standard synchronous transmission mode; for asynchronous users, it can be viewed as a fixed-length packet. The block has a fixed control field; the remainder is the payload (typical values are 130 bytes with 10 bytes header). The transmission system is a two-level hierarchy, where the level is crossed at a given transmission rate. The authors of [23] suggest 150Mb/sec; we show this value in the examples, although of course it is an engineering parameter that can be optimized. Below 150mb/sec, both synchronous and asynchronous users are multiplexed *asynchronously* according to the dynamic time-division multiplexing technique. Above this threshold, users are multiplexed in the standard synchronous time-division multiplexing (STDM) mode (see Fig. 10.5 for an example).

This separation between asynchronous and synchronous modes corresponds to the characteristics of the access and backbone networks. Users in the access network typically have different rates and burstiness, for which the asynchronous mode is more flexible and efficient. In the backbone portion of the network, on the other hand, a large number of independent users are merged on the communication channels, with the result that the traffic stream is close to continuous. In this case, the synchronous mode is more appropriate.

The DTDM stage of multiplexing requires that a variety of independent asynchronous sources be multiplexed into a synchronous channel. To do this, the streams corresponding to synchronous users are packetized by the insertion of a header field in the stream at the appropriate point. A very important point is that, once this packet conversion is done, no further header information is added to the packet in any subsequent multiplexing stage. As a consequence, it is possible to observe each individual channel at each point in the multiplexing hierarchy, which, as we have seen, is an important element required for ISDN circuit switches.

After the packets are labeled, all tributaries can be viewed as asynchronous packet streams that must be merged into a synchronous stream. Multiplexing asynchronous sources into a synchronous format requires some form of buffering in the multiplexer, and the possibility exists that a synchronous block may be empty because no input block is available at the time. From these considerations, it follows that the header should contain at least the following information. First, a word is required to signal the beginning of the block. Then, a flag field must appear somewhere to indicate whether the block is empty or full. Finally, the identity of the owner (the virtual- or real-circuit number) must be present, since, because of the asynchronous multiplexing, this identity is no longer defined by the slot position.

The input stream is actually merged into the output stream by *block* stuffing and interleaving, as opposed to the bit or byte stuffing used in more conventional multiplexing systems. As a consequence, the output channel is never fully used unless all the input tributaries are fully synchronized streams, in which case the system operates like a standard STDM multiplex. Figure 10.6 compares this extreme case with ordinary single-rate and multirate time-division multiplexing (MTDM). For asynchronous sources, the utilization of the output channel will be less than 100%, depending on the characteristics of the inputs.

The actual order of merging is not an intrinsic feature of the DTDM method. A simple FIFO method or a more sophisticated "train" scheduling can be used, in which the synchronous tributaries have first access to the available synchronous frames, thus preserving the transparency required of synchronous channels.

The dynamic time-division transmission technique offers the opportunity of having a single switch fabric able to handle both circuit- and packet-switched communications. The switch fabric, a self-routing network, operates with its own set of output-port addresses to route in the cross-point elements. The arriving slots have their own address, necessary because of the asynchronous nature of the multiplexing, and this address must be translated into the proper

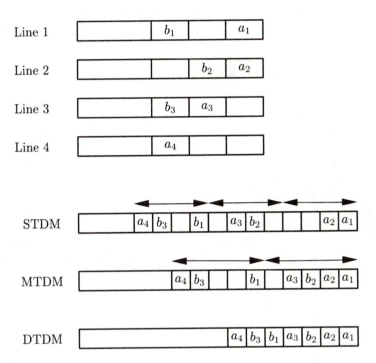

Figure 10.6 Use of a Frame under Various Transmission Modes

internal format. This can be done on-the-fly by the line interface, with the reverse operation performed at the output port. The system can be made to operate as a pure TDM system by putting a single packet per frame for each user, with empty packets in the case of an unused slot. It can also operate as a pure asynchronous system: assigning as many packets as needed to satisfy the current needs of a bursty user and filling unused slots that would belong to someone else in the pure TDM environment. The important point is that the *same* switch and *same* transmission system are capable of supporting either mode of operation, and any intermediate use.

This flexibility is probably the single most important feature of the DTDM scheme. The technique obviates the need for an overlay evolution since it allows a smooth transition from the current voice network by a replacement strategy. Obsolete portions of the ordinary network can be taken out and replaced by DTDM portions; the change would be transparent because the transmission format is compatible with the current system. Also, the technique is ideally suited for implementation both in the backbone transport network and in the local part of the network. This flexibility is a result of the synchronous-asynchronous mode of operation. The asynchronous mode is better suited to the local network, where users tend to have bursty traffic, while the synchronous mode is better suited to the backbone network, where multiplexing of a large number of sources tends to produce nearly continuous streams. The DTDM technique can thus provide a unified transport mode across the user-network interface, another strong point in its favor.

10.5   Impact on Network Routing and Dimensioning

The integration of services in the transport network will require some major changes in the way information is currently carried and switched in the telephone and data networks. These changes will in turn affect the techniques used for planning and evaluating these new networks [24]. Although some major aspects of the ISDN are still changing rapidly, we can already see in what directions these changes must be made. They will affect virtually all aspects of routing and dimensioning: teletraffic models, routing, network performance evaluation, dimensioning, and flow control.

Teletraffic

Some fundamental changes must be made to the teletraffic models currently used to represent network traffic. The new traffic sources are non-Poisson to a much larger degree than was the case for voice. This applies equally well to the sources of calls and to the generation of data within a call. As an example of the first case, consider a video teleconference service. In a given integrated network, the arrival process for such calls will be nowhere near the rate for voice calls. In fact, most likely a finite-source model will be more appropriate for these services than the infinite-source model generally used for voice. Also, it is quite possible that some of these services will operate on a reservation, as opposed to a demand, basis. The analysis of reservation systems is much more difficult [25,26,27], requiring some important advances in traffic models.

As for the second point, the generation of data within, say, a video call is far from Poisson. This effect is even more important if the video channel is coded because most coding techniques operate by sending the difference between two pictures instead of each picture separately. Thus the bit rate can be relatively low during a scene but jump to a very high value when a scene changes, since then a complete picture must be transmitted. In some systems, the output of the coder is buffered to make it smoother; this may not occur in other cases. In any event, the pattern of transmission for these calls may be very different from a call supporting other services such as voice or file transfer, and the modeling must be correspondingly more complex.

Another issue that will become relevant is that switches can influence the statistical characteristics of traffic. This is true for fast packet switches, which operate as constant-time servers. It is not clear at this time to what extent the behavior of the switches must be taken into account in evaluating network performance. This issue must be investigated before attempts are made to design network algorithms.

Not only is the source model different in the ISDN, but so is the link-utilization protocol, especially for multirate circuit switching. In this case, calls of different rates must use the same set of circuits; the question is how to partition this pool of servers among the different classes of users. It is known that unrestricted sharing has undesirable characteristics [28], while complete segregation may not be the most efficient way to effect the integration. The more interesting models are those in which each class has an upper and lower limit to the bandwidth it can use, sharing the rest with other customers [29]. Unfortunately these models are generally multidimensional, and it is generally impossible to compute an exact solution with sufficient accuracy and speed for use in network models. Approximations are required that are not trivial extensions of the exact Markov model, and the selection of optimal sharing parameters requires some consideration.

Routing

The first characteristic that emerges from almost all of the predicted forms of ISDN is that they will use either multirate circuit switching or virtual-call packet switching. In either case, circuit-switching methods will become even more important than they are now, and the theoretical models described in this book and similar ones in the literature will form the basis of the new design methods. For example, alternate routing based on bandwidth has been proposed for integration of voice and data [30], as well as for integrated DNHR networks with two classes of users with segregated bandwidth [31]. It is expected that these kinds of routing methods will become more prevalent as the usefulness of integration is acknowledged more widely.

Network-Performance Evaluation

Virtually all practical network-evaluation methods rely on some form of decomposition method; link decomposition is used most frequently. Certain types of services may not be well represented under the independence assumption. A case in point is multimedia teleconference. In this case, setting up a conference call induces many simultaneous point-to-point calls, each of which can further be divided into correlated calls for each component of the multimedia session. Similar effects may appear for broadcast video, where identical transmission patterns may occur in different portions of the network receiving the same program.

More generally, the independence assumption may not be valid for the portions of a given call on a single path. This could happen in a network where a small number of wide-band sources compete with a large number of narrow-band sources. In a homogeneous network, the independence assumption is often acceptable because a call on a given path represents only a small fraction of the path's capacity; the rest of the path is occupied by other calls that belong to different traffic relations and that are independent. Connecting a wide-band call on a path, in either a real- or virtual-circuit mode, means that the links comprising this path have a significant amount of their capacity occupied by this one call; this effect may be important enough that it is not masked by other narrow-band calls occupying the links in question, thereby making the link-decomposition method useless.

Although link-decomposition methods are not the only methods available, they are by far the most frequently used; they also yield the fastest algorithms. If the link-independence assumption is not valid in some types of ISDN, other, more complex decomposition techniques must be used. Even so, it is not clear that path decomposition will be acceptable in the presence of multipoint calls. This issue is perhaps the most difficult one to be faced: Giving up the link-independence assumption would certainly complicate the task of performance evaluation substantially.

Finally, most network evaluation algorithms are of the relaxation type. The convergence and stability of these algorithms depend to a large extent on the particular traffic model used to represent internal traffic flows. Using these newer models may have a significant effect on the convergence of the relaxation algorithms, a possibility not yet investigated.

Dimensioning

One important difference between the dimensioning of current networks and that of ISDN networks is the way in which performance is characterized — in other words, how to define the grade of service. While average measures of performance, such as expected delay, are often sufficient for current networks, this may no longer be true for some services. Real-time applications may require a performance measure expressed in terms of percentile delay or the distribution of busy circuits [32]. Also, throughput requirements may be imposed, and the peak throughput may be more significant that the average, for instance in video services. The definition of what constitutes an appropriate measure of performance, not to mention its computation, appears to be a difficult problem, one that will require a more detailed understanding of the behavior of the network.

Most practical dimensioning methods are based on some form of relaxation technique. We know that there is no guarantee that these methods will converge, and, if they do, is the final value of the process. The convergence rate, or even the existence of convergence, depends on a number of factors, such as the particular form of the traffic model and constraints. Changing the latter implies that some verification of the relaxation procedures is required, at least to the extent that there is a reasonable assurance of no systematic deviation from a reasonably good solution. Preliminary results have been reported for the extension of the Unified Algorithm to the dimensioning of DNHR networks with two classes of customers and segregated link utilization [31]. The method appears to be well behaved. The more complex cases of shared bandwidth, however, have not yet been examined.

Flow Control

Finally, access and policy control becomes an even more important issue in the wide-band ISDN than was the case for ordinary data or voice networks. The decision to accept a customer with a high bandwidth requirement, in either the real- or the virtual-circuit mode, should be evaluated carefully, since this customer can have a large impact on the operation of the network. For this reason, it will probably be necessary to study the issue of access control much more carefully than was the case for ordinary homogeneous networks. Once a call from a customer with high peak bandwidth is accepted, this customer must not be allowed to swamp the network with data beyond the rate agreed on at connect time. This may be difficult because of the very high speed at which information flows across the network; little time is available to choose and implement a control. Also, the "knee" in the delay-throughput curve for these networks may become very sharp as the service time becomes small, as can be seen from the simple $M/M/1$ queue. The implication of such a behavior is that delay measurements may not give any indication that the network is becoming saturated until it nears the actual saturation point, at which time it will become congested very rapidly. In other words, a high-throughput network may not degrade very gracefully if transit delay is used as the input parameter for congestion control; other, better-behaved parameters may be required. From the point of view of the network, these controls change the statistical characteristics of the source; this effect, if significant, must be taken into account in the network models used for the ISDN.

Summary

As we have seen, most areas of routing and dimensioning must be reviewed to take into account the changes required by an integrated transport network. These changes will require a basic understanding of the mathematical models underlying the current methods. It is the hope of the author that this book serves this purpose to some degree, in some small way helping in the design of these interesting and difficult planning methods.

References

[1] Stallings, W., *Data and Computer Communications*, Macmillan, 1985.

[2] Green, P.E., *Computer Network Architectures and Protocols*, Plenum, 1982.

[3] Green, P.E., "Protocol conversion," *IEEE Transactions on Communications*, vol. 34, pp. 257–268, 1986.

[4] Roberts, J.W., and Van, A.H., "Characteristics of services requiring multi-slot connections and their impact on ISDN design," *ITC Seminar*, vol. 5, 1987.

[5] Inose, H., *An Introduction to Digital Integrated Communication Systems*, University of Tokyo Press, 1979.

[6] Bellamy, J.C., *Digital Telephony*, Wiley, 1982.

[7] McDonald, J.C., ed., *Fundamentals of Digital Switching*, Plenum, 1983.

[8] Acampora, A.S., Karol, M.J., and Hluchyj, M.G., "Terabit lightwave networks: the multihop approach," *AT&T Technical Journal*, vol. 66, pp. 21–34, 1987.

[9] Minzer, S.E., "Toward an international broadband ISDN," *Telecommunications*, pp. 94–112, October 1987.

[10] Boehm, R.J., Ching, Y.C., Griffith, C.G., and Saal, F.A., "Standardized fiber optic transmission system — a synchronous optical network view," *IEEE Journal on Selected Areas in Communications*, vol. SAC-4, pp. 1424–1431, 1986.

[11] Harrington, E.A., "Voice-data integration using circuit switched networks," *IEEE Transactions on Communications*, vol. COM–32, pp. 781–793, 1980.

[12] Schwartz, M., *Telecommunication Networks: Protocols, Modeling and Analysis*, Addison-Wesley, 1987.

[13] Ritchie, G.R., "SYNTRAN—A new direction for digital transmission terminals," *IEEE Communications Magazine*, vol. 23, pp. 20–24, 1985.

[14] Lubacz, J., Jarocinski, M., and Dabrowski, M., "Traffic and economic aspects of voice-data integration," *Network Planning Symposium*, vol. 3, pp. 16–19, June 1986.

[15] Graves, A.F., Littlewood, P.A., and Carlton, S., "An experimental cross-connect system for metropolitan applications," *IEEE Journal on Selected Areas in Communications*, vol. 5, pp. 6–18, 1987.

[16] Niestegge, G., "Nonblocking multirate switching networks," *ITC Seminar*, vol. 5, 1987.

[17] Huang, A., and Knauer, S., "Starlite: a wideband digital switch," *Globecom 84*, vol. 84, pp. 121–125, 1984.

[18] Yeh, Y.S., Hluchyj, M.G., and Acampora, A.S., "The knockout switch: a simple, modular architecture for high-performance packet switching," *IEEE Journal on Selected Areas in Communications*, vol. SAC-5, pp. 1274 –1283, 1987.

[19] Eng, K.Y., Hluchyj, M.G., and Yeh, Y.S., "A knockout switch for variable-length packets," *International Conference on Communications*, vol. 1987, pp. 794–799, 1987.

[20] Thomas, A., Coudreuse, J.P., and Servel, M., "Asynchronous time-division techniques: an experimental packet network integrating video-communications," *International Switching Symposium*, 1984.

[21] Gonet, P., Adam, P., and Coudreuse, J.P., "Asynchronous time-division switching: the way to flexible broadband communications networks," *IEEE International Zurich Seminar on Digital Communication*, 1986.

[22] Wu, L.T., Lee, S.H., and Lee, T.T., "Dynamic TDM: a packet approach to broadband networking," *International Conference on Communications*, pp. 1585–1592, 1987.

[23] Lee, S.H., "An integrated transport technique for circuit and packet switched traffic," *Infocom*, pp. 110–118, 1988.

[24] Kuehn, P.J., "Traffic engineering for ISDN design and planning," *ITC Seminar*, vol. 5, 1987.

[25] Roberts, J.W., "A service system with heterogeneous user requirements: application to multi-services telecommunications systems," in *Performance of Data Communication Systems and Their Applications*, Pujolle, G., ed., pp. 423–431, North-Holland, 1981.

[26] Roberts, J.W., "Teletraffic models for the Telecom 1 integrated services network," *International Teletraffic Congress*, vol. 10, 1983.

[27] Van, A.H., and Roberts, J.W., "Dynamic resource allocation in the Telecom 1 satellite system," *International Conference on Communications*, 1983.

[28] Kaufman, J.S., "Blocking in a shared resource environment," *IEEE Transactions on Communications*, vol. COM-29, pp. 1474–1481, 1981.

[29] Mason, L., Deserres, Y., and Meubus, C., "Circuit-switched multipoint service performance models," *International Teletraffic Congress*, vol. 11, pp. 2.1A-5-1–2.1A-5-6, September 1985.

[30] Gerla, M., "Routing and flow control in ISDN's," in *New Communication Services: A Challenge to Computer Technology*, Kühn, P., ed., pp. 643–647, Elsevier Science Publishers B.V., 1986.

[31] Ash, G.R., "Traffic network routing, control and design for the ISDN era," *ITC Seminar*, 1987.

[32] Ackerly, R.G., Macfayden, N.W., and Songhurst, D.J., "The study of network performance in relation to ISDN," *ITC Seminar*, 1987.

Probability Theory

This appendix briefly reviews some elements of probability theory. The review is short because there is an abundance of excellent references on the subject [1]. The topics included here either are not widely known outside the teletraffic community or are of fundamental importance for the traffic analysis presented in this book. This second category is limited to the fundamental results of birth-and-death equations and of the $GI/M/N/\infty/N$ queue. Applications of the general theory to the particular queues of interest in traffic theory are found in the main text.

A.1 Some Functions Used in Probability Models

The following definitions and simple properties are either used extensively in the text or are not well known outside the teletraffic community.

Binomial Coefficients and Related Polynomials

The binomial coefficients are defined for positive integer n as the coefficients of x in the expansion of

$$(1 + x)^n = \sum_{k=0}^{n} x^k \binom{n}{k}$$

and are given by

$$\binom{n}{k} = \frac{n!}{(n-k)!k!},$$

which can be written

$$= \frac{n(n-1)\ldots(n-k+1)}{k!}.$$

This definition can be extended to nonnegative real a by defining the binomial coefficient as the coefficient of x in the expansion of

$$(1 + x)^a = \sum_{k=0}^{\infty} x^k \frac{a(a-1)\ldots(a-k+1)}{k!},$$

from which we get

$$\binom{a}{k} \overset{\triangle}{=} \frac{a(a-1)\dots(a-k+1)}{k!} \quad \forall a \in \Re, \quad \binom{a}{0} \overset{\triangle}{=} 1 \quad \text{(A.1)}$$

From this, we define the *factorial polynomials*:

$$(a)_k \overset{\triangle}{=} a(a-1)\dots(a-k+1). \quad \text{(A.2)}$$

The binomial coefficients can be extended to arbitrary real a by looking at the power series of

$$(1+x)^{-a} = \sum_{k=0}^{\infty} x^k (-1)^k \frac{a(a+1)\dots(a+k-1)}{k!}, \quad a \geq 0$$

By defining the extended binomial moment as the coefficient of $-x^k$, we get

$$\binom{-a}{k} = \frac{a(a+1)\dots(a+k-1)}{k!}.$$

A useful relation is obtained if we note that the polynomial $a(a+1)\dots(a+k-1)$ can also be viewed as a factorial polynomial starting at $a+k-1$. Rewriting the identity for the polynomial, we get

$$\binom{-x}{k} = \binom{x+k-1}{k}, \quad x > 0$$

The binomial coefficients also have the following useful inversion property:

$$a_n = \sum_{j=n}^{N} \binom{j}{n} b_j$$

$$b_j = \sum_{n=j}^{N} (-1)^{n-j} \binom{n}{j} a_j$$

The factorial polynomials are related to the $a(a+1)\dots(a+k-1)$ polynomials by the functions

$$(1-x)^{-a} = \sum_{k=0}^{\infty} \frac{a(a+1)\dots(a+k-1)x^k}{k!} \quad \text{(A.3)}$$

$$(1+x)^a = \sum_{k=0}^{\infty} \frac{(a)_k x^k}{k!} \quad \text{(A.4)}$$

Factorial polynomials have a double representation that is related by the so-called *Stirling numbers* [2] $s_{q,i}$ and $S_{q,i}$ of the first and second kind, respectively. We have

$$(x)_q = \sum_{i=0}^{q} s_{q,i} x^i$$

$$x(x+1)\ldots(x+q-1) = \sum_{i=0}^{q} S_{q,i}(x)_i$$

with the Stirling numbers defined recursively by

$$s_{q+1,i} = s_{q,i-1} - qs_{q,i}$$
$$S_{q,i+1} = S_{q,i-1} + iS_{q,i}$$
$$s_{0,0} = S_{0,0} = 1$$
$$s_{q,i} = S_{q,i} = 0 \quad i > q \text{ and } i < -1$$

The Kosten and Brockmeyer Polynomials

The Brockmeyer polynomials [3] are defined as

$$S(l,k) = \sum_{i=0}^{l} \frac{A^{l-i}}{(l-i)!}\binom{k-1+i}{i}, \quad S(l,k) = 0 \text{ if } l < 0 \text{ or } m < 0 \quad \text{(A.5)}$$

and the closely related Kosten polynomials [4] by

$$R(k,l) = e^{-A}S(k,l). \tag{A.6}$$

These functions have some useful properties, such as

$$S(k,l) = S(k-1,l) + S(k,l-1)$$
$$kS(k,l) = (A+k-1+l)S(k-1,l) - AS(k-2,l)$$
$$kS(k,l) = AS(k-1,l) + lS(k-1,l+1)$$

$$S(k,l) = \sum_{j=0}^{i}(-1)^{i-j}\binom{i}{j}S(k-i+j,l+i)$$

$$S(k,l) = \sum_{i=0}^{k} S(i,l-1)$$

These polynomials are frequently useful in analyzing queuing systems with loss.

Moments of a Distribution

The various moments of a distribution ranging from 0 to $N \leq \infty$ are defined as

$$\alpha_q = \sum_{j=0}^{N} j^q p_j \tag{A.7}$$

for the ordinary moments;

$$\mu_q = \sum_{j=0}^{N}(j-\alpha_1)^q p_j \tag{A.8}$$

for the central moments;

$$M_q = \sum_{j=q}^{N} (j)_q p_j \tag{A.9}$$

for the factorial moments; and

$$\beta_q = \sum_{j=q}^{N} \binom{j}{q} p_j = \frac{M_q}{q!} \tag{A.10}$$

for the binomial moments.

The various types of moments are interrelated in such a way that, given one set, the other sets can be computed directly. In particular, we have the mean and variance of a given distribution directly from the moments by

$$M \stackrel{\triangle}{=} \alpha_1 = M_1 = \beta_1 \tag{A.11}$$

$$V \stackrel{\triangle}{=} \mu_2 = \alpha_2 - \alpha_1^2 = M_2 - \alpha_1(\alpha_1 - 1) = 2\beta_2 + \beta_1(\beta_1 - 1) \tag{A.12}$$

Generating Functions and Transforms

The generating function, or the z-transform, of a function defined over the nonnegative integers is given by

$$G(z) = \sum_{k=0}^{\infty} p_k z^k, \quad |z| \le 1$$

This sum converges if p_k does not grow faster than geometrically; the generating function is analytic in the disk $|z| \le 1$. For instance, the binomial coefficients have the generating function

$$(1 + z)^n = \sum_{k=0}^{n} \binom{n}{k} z^k.$$

The generating function contains all the information about a distribution. From this function, we can recover either the probabilities or the moments, as needed. We have

$$G(0) = \sum_{n=0}^{N} p_n$$

$$p_n = \frac{1}{n!} \left(\frac{d^n G(z)}{dz^n} \right)_{z=0}$$

$$\beta_n = \frac{1}{n!} \left(\frac{d^n G(z)}{d^n z} \right)_{z=1}$$

and, in particular, the mean and variance of a distribution:

$$M = G'(1)$$
$$V = G''(1) + G'(1) - (G'(1))^2$$

For example, we have the expression of the distribution in terms of the factorial moments as

$$p_j = \sum_{k=0}^{\infty} (-1)^{k-j} \binom{k}{j} \frac{M_k}{k!}. \tag{A.13}$$

For continuous distributions $F(t)$, we define the Laplace-Stieltjes transform $\Phi(s)$ as follows:

$$\Phi(s) = \int_0^{\infty} e^{-st} dF(t)$$

and, if $F(t)$ is differentiable everywhere, the ordinary Laplace transform

$$\phi(s) = \int_0^{\infty} e^{-st} f(t) dt$$
$$\Phi(s) = s\phi(s)$$

Here too, we can get the moments of the distribution $F(t)$ directly from the Laplace-Stieltjes transform:

$$\int_0^{\infty} t^n dF(t) = (-1)^n \left(\frac{d^n \Phi(s)}{ds^n} \right)_{s=0}$$

Also, if we define the generating function for the binomial moment,

$$F(z) = \sum_{k=0}^{N} \beta_k z^k,$$

it is not hard to show that this function is related to the probability generating function by

$$F(z) = G(z + 1).$$

A.2   Birth-and-Death Processes

Birth-and-death (BD) processes are the simplest type of processes that can be used to analyze queuing systems [5]. BD processes are characterized uniquely by their state-dependent arrival and departure rates. For one-dimensional processes, the state is represented by k, the number of customers present in the system. The arrival rate when the system is in state k is λ_k; the departure rate is given by μ_k. The time-dependent state equation is then given by

$$\frac{dp_k}{dt} = -(\lambda_k + \mu_k)p_k + \lambda_{k-1}p_{k-1} + \mu_{k+1}p_{k+1}, \qquad \text{(A.14)}$$

and the stationary form

$$0 = -(\lambda_k + \mu_k)p_k + \lambda_{k-1}p_{k-1}p + \mu_{k+1}p_{k+1}. \qquad \text{(A.15)}$$

The general solution for the stationary state probabilities is given by

$$p_k = p_0 \prod_{j=0}^{k-1} \frac{\lambda_j}{\mu_{j+1}}, \qquad \text{(A.16)}$$

which satisfies the useful recurrence

$$p_{k+1} = \frac{\lambda_k}{\mu_{k+1}} p_k$$

and the normalization condition

$$\sum_{k=0}^{\infty} p_k = 1.$$

As we saw in Chapter 3, a large number of queuing systems of interest can be modeled by a suitable choice of λ_k and μ_k.

A.3   Renewal Processes and the $GI/M/N/\infty/N$ Queue

A general analysis of overflow processes is based on the $GI/M/N/\infty/N$ queue. In such a queue, the arrival process is of the renewal type, and the service periods have a negative exponential distribution. A complete description of the results available on the $GI/M/N$ system can be found in [6,7]. Here we briefly summarize the derivation of the general equations that can be used to describe this queue.

Distribution of Arrivals in a Fixed Interval

When considering the sequence of requests for service on a particular link, we are naturally led to consider the random variable that represents the length of time that separates two successive arrivals. Following Syski [7], we denote this variable by L_r, calling it the *life* of the interval between the $r-1^{\text{th}}$ and r^{th} calls. The arrival process is a *renewal process* if the L_r variables are independent, nonnegative, identically distributed variables. Although the theory is explained in terms of call arrivals, it applies equally well to the call-departure process, or to any other type of event that is of interest.

We denote the distribution of L_r by $F(t)$, and its density by $f(t)$. For an arbitrary interval $(0, t]$ two quantities are of interest: (1) $N(t)$, the number

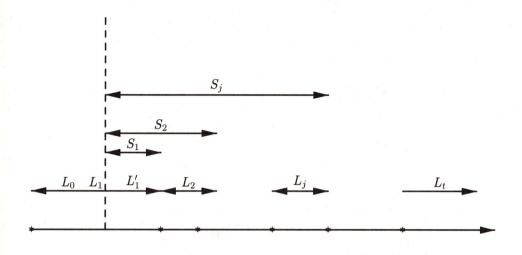

$t = 0$

Figure A.1   Definition of Variables Related to a Renewal Process

of arrivals during this interval, and (2) $L(t)$, the time since the last arrival before time t, called the *age* of the interval, with the distribution $Y(s,t) \triangleq Pr\{L(t) \le s\}$. Note that Y is not simply the value of t because we can select the origin of time at an arbitrary instant, which need not be the time of an arrival.

Calculating the distribution of these random variables require some auxiliary variables. Let S_j be the total lifetime of j calls that arrive in this interval. The distribution functions of the S_js are denoted $F_j(t) = Pr\{S_j \le t\}$. This is the total duration of the j intervals, and it is obviously given by $S_j = L'_1 + L_2 + \ldots + L_j$. Note the special notation for the first interval. Because we wish to be able to select the origin at an arbitrary point, this origin generally does not coincide with an arrival. In this case, the time origin is inside an interarrival period, and the age of the first interval as measured from the origin is different from the ages of the other intervals. This first partial interval is denoted $L'_1 = L_1 - L_0$; this term appears in the definition of S_j. In other words, L'_1 is residual life of the first interval after we start looking at the system. Note also that we have

$$L_t = \begin{cases} t - S_{N(t)} & \text{if } N(t) \ge 1 \\ t + L_0 & \text{if } N(t) = 0 \end{cases}$$

The meaning of these variables is shown in Fig A.1.

Our main concern here is with calculating the statistical properties of $N(t)$. Let $p_j(t)$ be the probability of having j arrivals in the interval $(0, t]$. The number of arrivals in the interval is larger than j if and only if the total duration of the first j calls in the interval is not larger than t. This is expressed by

$$Pr\{N(t) \geq j\} = Pr\{S_j \leq t\}$$
$$= F_j(t),$$

and we have, by the definition of F_j,

$$\sum_{k=j}^{\infty} p_k(t) = F_j(t).$$

Taking partial sums from j and $j + 1$ and subtracting, we have

$$p_j(t) = F_j(t) - F_{j+1}(t). \tag{A.17}$$

We now need the F_js, the distribution of the cumulative intervals S_j. All these intervals are similar, except for the first one, which depends on the position of the time origin. Let $B(t)$ be the distribution of L_1'. We then have

$$B(t) = \int_0^{\infty} \frac{F(t+s) - F(s)}{1 - F(s)} dY(s, t) \tag{A.18}$$

$$F_0(t) = 1$$
$$F_1(t) = B(t)$$
$$F_j(t) = \int_0^{\infty} F(t - \tau) dF_{j-1}(\tau) \tag{A.19}$$
$$F_{\infty}(t) = 0$$

The first equation can be understood as follows. We know that the time origin is inside the first interval. The probability that this interval lasts for another period s after t, given that the time origin is in this interval, is called the *remaining lifetime distribution*; it is given by

$$Pr\{L \leq t + s \mid L \geq t\} = \frac{F(t+s) - F(t)}{1 - F(t)}. \tag{A.20}$$

(Solving this equation is left to the reader.) S_1, then, is the lifetime of the first interval after the origin of the time axis; it is given by the convolution of the distribution of the two events: (1) the residual life must be at least as large as s and (2) there must be no further arrival until t, the density of which is given by dY. The convolution of these two events is the distribution $B(t)$. Similarly, Eq. (A.19) follows from the convolution theorem when we note that $S_j = S_{j-1} + L_j$. Using Eq. (A.19) in Eq. (A.17), we obtain

$$p_j(t) = \int_0^{\infty} [1 - F(t - \tau)] dF_j(\tau). \tag{A.21}$$

The expectation of $N(t)$ is then given by

$$\sum_{j=0}^{\infty} jp_j(t) = \sum_{j=1}^{\infty} F_j(t).$$

From this, we get the fundamental integral equation of renewal theory concerning $G(t)$, the expected number of arrivals in the interval,

$$G(t) \overset{\triangle}{=} E\{N(t)\}$$
$$= B(t) + \int_0^{\infty} F(t-\tau)dG(\tau), \qquad (A.22)$$

and the corresponding integral equation for the density,

$$g(t) = b(t) + \int_0^t f(t-\tau)g(\tau)d\tau,$$

where $g(t)$ is defined as

$$G(t) = \int_0^t g(\tau)d\tau.$$

The intuitive interpretation of $g(t)$ is the renewal rate of the process — in other words, the probability that there is a renewal in a short interval dt at time t is precisely $g(t)dt$. More important, however, is the stationary behavior of the density. It is known that $\lim_{t \to \infty} g(t) = 1/m$, where $m = E\{L\}$ is the expected lifetime of an interval.

All that remains to be computed is the distribution of the age of the interval $Y(s,t)$ or, equivalently, of its density $y(s,t)$. This is needed because of the arbitrary position of the first interval with respect to the time origin, which appears in Eq. (A.18), the distribution of the residual life of the first interval. Two cases must be considered, depending on whether or not the interval started before the origin of time. If not, the interval started at $t-s$, with probability density $g(t-s)$. It lasts up to time s, with probability $1-F(s)$. Thus the probability of having age s at time t has the density

$$y(s,t) = g(t-s)\left[1-F(s)\right]ds, \quad t > s$$

If, on the other hand, the interval started before the time origin, then it had age $t-s$ at time 0 with probability $y(s-t,0)ds$. Further, the probability that the life of the interval will continue until s, given that it has already lasted $s-t$, is given by $(1-F(s))/(1-F(s-t))$. Hence we have, in this case, from the residual-life formula (A.20),

$$y(s,t) = y(s-t,0)\frac{1-F(s)}{1-F(s-t)}ds, \quad t \le s \qquad (A.23)$$

This completes the derivation for the distribution of $N(t)$ for a given interval of size s. In the case of telecommunication networks, we are not particularly interested in the exact time dependence of Y, but rather in its asymptotic, stationary value. Under suitable conditions, there exists such a stationary distribution of age that is independent of t and of the initial distribution. It is given by

$$Y(s, \infty) = \int_0^s \frac{1 - F(\tau)}{m} d\tau \qquad \text{(A.24)}$$

for finite m. In fact [7], the process $L(t)$ is Markov, has stationary probabilities, and, under suitable conditions, is also ergodic. This expression is the explanation of the so-called *renewal paradox*, a discussion of which is proposed in Problem 3.10.

Distribution of Interarrival Times in a Random Interval

The results obtained so far deal with the number of arrivals during a given interval $(0, t]$. In many cases, we are interested in the number of arrivals during an interval whose length is also a random variable. The application we shall consider is the number of call terminations in the interval between two arrivals in a group of servers. Because of the random nature of the arrivals, the time during which we count the terminations is a random variable, which explains the interest in these processes. These processes are called *compound process*.

Let $N(t)$ be the number of arrivals in a random interval starting at t. It would be useful to relate quantities of interest about $N(t)$ to corresponding quantities about $N(s, t)$, the number of arrivals in an interval of given length s starting at t, since we already have many results in this case. To do this, let the length of time we are considering be a random variable L with distribution $U(t)$. The relation between the distribution of $N(t)$ and $N(s, t)$ is straightforward if we view the distribution of N as conditional on L. We can write

$$Pr\{N = n\} = \int_0^\infty Pr\{N(s, t) = n \mid L = s\} dU(s) \qquad \text{(A.25)}$$

In many cases, the N and L processes are independent, and $U(s)$ is independent of the starting point of the interval t and is unrelated to the distribution of N. Thus, using Eq. (A.25), we can readily obtain the distribution of N for a random interval if we have this distribution for a fixed interval of size s.

Similar relations exist between other functions of the random variables $N(t)$ and $N(s, t)$. Two important cases are the z transform and the expectations. To get the z transform $G(z, t)$ of $N(t)$, we multiply both sides of Eq. (A.25) by z^n, taking the sum from 0 to ∞. We get the required relation

$$G(z, t) = \int_0^\infty dF(s) G(z, s, t) dz.$$

From this equation, we obtain a similar equation for the expectation,

$$E\{N\} = \int_0^\infty E\{N(s,t)\}dF(s).$$

Eq. (A.25) is of fundamental importance for the discussion in Chapter 3. Most of the results that we will derive for teletraffic are applications of this equation or of one of its variants.

Compound Process in the $GI/M/N/\infty/N$ Queue

Consider now the process by which calls in service in a group terminate. We are interested in $p_{i,j}$, the probability that there are j calls in progress at the end of a single interarrival period, given that there were i calls in progress at the beginning. If we assume that the calls in progress are independent, and have the same holding time distribution $H(s)$ with mean $1/\mu$, then the termination process has all the characteristics of a renewal process, and we can use the results that we previously derived — in particular, Eq. (A.25). First we must compute the probability that j calls are in progress at the end of a given interval of size s, given that i calls were present at the beginning of the interval. Consider first a particular call in progress. The probability that it still exists at time s is just the probability that its age exceeds s. But we know from Eq. (A.24) that this is given by

$$y(s) = \mu \int_s^\infty [1 - H(\tau)]d\tau \qquad (A.24)$$

The probability $p_{i,j}$ that there are j calls in progress at the end of the period, given that there were i calls at the beginning, is a Bernouilli distribution with parameter $y(s)$ and is given by

$$p_{i,j} = \binom{i}{j} y^i (1-y)^{i-j}.$$

Because the length of an interval is the time between two arrivals to the queue, it is a random variable. Thus we must use Eq. (A.25) with $U(t) = F(t)$, which yields

$$p_{i,j} = \int_0^\infty \binom{i}{j} y^j (1-y)^{i-j} dF(s), \quad i \geq j \qquad (A.26)$$

where y stands for $y(s)$ and $F(s)$ is the distribution of the interarrival times.

When the holding time distribution is negative exponential, $y(s) = e^{-\mu s}$. If $F(s)$ is also negative exponential with parameter λ, then we get

$$p_{i,j} = \binom{i}{j} \frac{\lambda}{\mu} B\left(j + \frac{\lambda}{\mu}, i - j + 1\right), \qquad (A.27)$$

where $B(m,n)$ is the Beta function.

References

[1] Feller, W., *An Introduction to Probability Theory and Its Applications*, Wiley, 1957.

[2] Abramowitz, M., and Stegun, I.A., *Handbook of Mathematical Functions*, Dover, 1970.

[3] Brockmeyer, E., "The simple overflow problem in the theory of telephone traffic," (in Danish), *Teleteknik*, vol. 5, pp. 361–374, 1954.

[4] Kosten, L., "On the blocking probability of graded multiples," (in German), *Elektr. Nachr.-Techn.*, vol. 14, pp. 5–12, 1937.

[5] Kleinrock, L., *Queuing Systems*, Wiley, 1975.

[6] Takács, L., *Introduction to the Theory of Queues*, Oxford University Press, 1962.

[7] Syski, R., *Introduction to congestion theory in telephone systems*, North-Holland, 1986.

Optimization Theory

An enormous literature exists on the subject of optimization, too large to be summarized in a short discussion like this one. Here we can present only a brief review of the more elementary results used in the text. The discussion is on optimization of differentiable functions in subsets of R^n, in the spirit of [1,2]. We leave aside combinatorial optimization and integer programming, which play a relatively minor role here. Good references on these topics are [3,4,5].

After reviewing some definitions related to convexity, we state the necessary conditions for optimality and give a short review of nonlinear duality theory. We then discuss some frequently used methods for computing numerical solutions. We end the appendix by presenting some well-known results of the general theory when it is applied to linear programs, emphasizing network flows.

B.1   Convexity

Convex sets and convex functions play a central role in optimization theory. Let us recall some useful definitions and properties in relation to convexity.

Convex Sets

Let $\mathbf{x}_1, \mathbf{x}_2$ be two points in some set S. We define a convex linear combination (clc) of these points as the vector $\alpha\mathbf{x}_1 + (1 - \alpha)\mathbf{x}_2$ where $0 < \alpha < 1$. This notion can be generalized to l points by

$$\mathbf{y} \stackrel{\triangle}{=} \sum_{k=1}^{l} \alpha_k \mathbf{x}_k$$

$$\sum_{k=1}^{l} \alpha_k = 1$$

$$\alpha_k \geq 0$$

A set S is said to be *convex* if any clc of any two of its points is also in S. Geometrically, this means that any point on the line segment between $\mathbf{x}_1$ and $\mathbf{x}_2$ is also a point of S. Examples of convex sets are a triangle, a circle, the half-space defined by $<\mathbf{a}, \mathbf{x}> \leq b$, and the positive quadrant in R^2. It is not hard to show that the intersection of any number of convex sets is also convex. From this theorem we get the important class of convex sets called *polytopes*, defined by the set of m linear inequalities $A\mathbf{x} \leq \mathbf{b}$, where A is an $m \times n$ matrix and $\mathbf{b}$ is an m-vector. A bounded polytope is called a *polyhedron*.

Although any clc of points of a convex S is in S, it does not follow that any element of S is a clc of some set of points (think of the summits of the triangle). We call those points that cannot be written as a clc of some other elements *extreme points* of the set. Extreme points of the circle are the points on the perimeter, and the positive quadrant has only one extreme point, that is, the origin.

This last set, which is unbounded, has two other interesting elements: the semi-axes. This notion is generalized to the concept of *rays*. We say that $\mathbf{d}$ is a ray of the convex set S if $\mathbf{x} + \alpha\mathbf{d} \in S$ for any $\mathbf{x} \in S$ and $\forall \alpha \geq 0$. A vector $\mathbf{d}$ is an *extreme ray* if there does not exist any $\mathbf{d}_1$, $\mathbf{d}_2 \in S$ and $\mathbf{d}_2 \neq \mathbf{d}_1$ such that $\mathbf{d} = \alpha\mathbf{d}_1 + (1 - \alpha)\mathbf{d}_2$ for some $0 \leq \alpha \leq 1$. Note the analogy with extreme points. We also need the notion of a *cone*. We say that a set S is a cone if, for every $\mathbf{d} \in S$ and every $\alpha \geq 0$, the vector $\mathbf{y} = \alpha\mathbf{d} \in S$. Note that the positive quadrant is a cone.

With these definitions, we are ready to state a fundamental theorem of geometry. Given a convex set S, any point in S can be expressed as a clc of extreme points and extreme rays. From this theorem, we see that the extreme points and rays are in this sense sufficient to characterize the convex set. This property is used extensively in many areas of optimization, especially in decomposition methods for large problems.

Convex Functions

Let f be some function defined on some convex set S. We say that f is a *convex function* if

$$f(\alpha\mathbf{x}_1 + (1 - \alpha)\mathbf{x}_2) \leq \alpha f(\mathbf{x}_1) + (1 - \alpha)f(\mathbf{x}_2) \qquad \text{(B.1)}$$
$$\forall \mathbf{x}_1, \mathbf{x}_2 \in S$$
$$0 \leq \alpha \leq 1$$

The function is said to be strictly convex if the inequality is strict in the definition. Examples of convex functions are x^2 and $|x|$. The second function is an example of a convex function that is not differentiable at the origin.

We recall some elementary properties of convex functions defined over a convex set S. If f_1 and f_2 are convex functions, then so are $f_1 + f_2$ and

αf_1 for $\alpha > 0$. From this follows the general property that a positive linear combination of convex functions is also convex. Also note that the set defined as $S = \mathbf{x} \mid f(\mathbf{x}) \leq b$ is a convex set whenever f is a convex function. From this, we see that a set defined by the nonlinear inequalities $g_i(\mathbf{x}) \leq b_i$ is also a convex set whenever all the g functions are convex.

The notion of convexity can be made more explicit if f is differentiable. Recall that the *gradient* of f is the vector ∇f with components $\partial f / \partial x_i$, and that the Hessian matrix is the one with component $H_{i,j} = \partial^2 f / \partial x_i \partial x_j$.

We can characterize a convex function that is differentiable once by the property that

$$f(\mathbf{y}) \geq f(\mathbf{x}) + <\nabla f(\mathbf{x}), \mathbf{y} - \mathbf{x}>, \quad \forall\, \mathbf{x}, \mathbf{y} \in S$$

Geometrically, this means that the function f lies above its tangent plane at some point $\mathbf{x}$, and that this holds for all points $\mathbf{x}$.

If the function is twice differentiable, it is not hard to show that f is convex at some point $\mathbf{x}$ inside S if $H(\mathbf{x})$ is positive semidefinite at that point. Also, f is globally convex if it is convex at all points in S. This condition reduces to the familiar condition $d^2 f / dx^2 > 0$ for one-dimensional functions. Note, however, that extending this condition to many variables by the rule $\partial^2 f / \partial x_i^2 > 0$ is *not* sufficient to ensure convexity at some point.

Finally, we say that f is *concave* if $-f$ is convex. Concave functions are often used in cost models where economies of scale are present, and optimization problems with concave functions occur quite frequently.

B.2   Optimality Conditions for Optimization Problems

We are now ready to examine the general optimization problem

$$\min\ f(\mathbf{x}) \tag{B.2}$$
$$\mathbf{x} \in S \subseteq R^n$$

In what follows, we say that a point $\mathbf{x} \in S$ is *feasible*; we denote the solution of this problem by $\mathbf{x}^*$, and the value of f at this point by $f^* \stackrel{\triangle}{=} f(\mathbf{x}^*)$ whenever it is necessary to distinguish these values from more general ones. Otherwise we omit the superscript, simply using $\mathbf{x}$ for the optimal solution and so indicating in the text. We define the local minimum of the function first for unconstrained problems, then for constrained ones. By unconstrained problems, we mean those where either $S = R^n$ or the minimum occurs at an interior point of S, in which case we might as well have extended the domain to R^n in the first place.

A point $\mathbf{x}$ is an *unconstrained local minimum* of f if there is a neighborhood ϵ of $\mathbf{x}$ such that, for any displacement $\mathbf{d}$ from $\mathbf{x}$ in this neighborhood, the function is not increasing. Algebraically, this is written

$$f(\mathbf{x} + \mathbf{d}) \geq f(\mathbf{x}), \quad |\mathbf{d}| \leq \epsilon \tag{B.3}$$

The minimum is said to be *global* if $\epsilon = \infty$, that is, if the neighborhood in question extends to the whole space.

For constrained problems, where $S \subset R^n$ and the minimum occurs on the boundary, definition (B.3) is no longer valid: The displacement from $\mathbf{x}$ may lead outside S, in which case the solution is no longer feasible. The definition can be amended to take care of this case by adding that condition (B.3) must hold for any *feasible* displacement $\mathbf{d}$. We have

$$f(\mathbf{x} + \mathbf{d}) \geq f(\mathbf{x}), \quad |\mathbf{d}| \leq \epsilon, \ \mathbf{x} + \mathbf{d} \in S \tag{B.4}$$

First-Order Conditions

The definition of a local minimum is usually not easy to check because it involves conditions on *all* feasible displacements. When the problem functions are differentiable, it is possible to derive more easily verifiable conditions from Eq. (B.3). Here we state the first-order necessary conditions, expressed in terms of the first derivatives only. From this point on, we assume that the set S is given by the inequalities $g_i(\mathbf{x}) \leq 0$, $i = 1, \ldots m$. Theoretically, the case of equality constraints $h_i(\mathbf{x}) = 0$ can be included by replacing h_i by two inequality constraints of the form $g_i(\mathbf{x}) \leq 0$ and $-g_i(\mathbf{x}) \leq 0$. Also, we say that a constraint i is *active*, or *tight*, at point $\mathbf{x}$ if $g_i(\mathbf{x}) = 0$. Otherwise, the constraint is said to be inactive, or slack.

For the unconstrained case, the necessary condition reduces to the familiar case $\nabla f = 0$, which can easily be derived by expanding f to first order in the neighborhood of the optimal point $\mathbf{x}$.

For the constrained case, this condition is no longer necessary. The necessary conditions for optimality have been stated by Kuhn and Tucker as follows. Assume that $\mathbf{x}$ is a minimum. Then there exist a set of quantities called the Kuhn-Tucker multipliers u_i such that

$$\nabla f(\mathbf{x}) = -\sum_{i=1}^{m} u_i \nabla g_i(\mathbf{x}) \tag{B.5}$$

$$g_i(\mathbf{x}) \leq 0 \quad i = 1 \ldots m \tag{B.6}$$

$$u_i \geq 0 \quad i = 1 \ldots m \tag{B.7}$$

$$u_i g_i(\mathbf{x}) = \quad i = 1 \ldots m \tag{B.8}$$

The first condition states that, at an optimal solution $\mathbf{x}$, the direction opposite to that of the gradient must lie in the cone of the gradients of active constraints at that point. The second set, called the *primal feasibility* condition, states that the point $\mathbf{x}$ must be feasible for the original problem. The third set, called the *dual feasibility* conditions, defines the domain of the dual problem (see Section B.3). The last set, called the *complementary slackness* condition, states that, if a constraint is slack, then the corresponding multiplier must vanish. Note, however, that the inverse statement is not necessarily true, and that there can be tight constraints with zero multipliers.

These conditions hold if the functions are differentiable, and also if certain regularity conditions hold on f and g. Although these regularity conditions are theoretically important, they have no effect in practice, and can be ignored for the purpose of this discussion. In the case of equality constraints, the equations are the same, except that condition (B.7) is no longer present. This is easy to check by replacing the equality constraints by a pair of inequality constraints of opposite sign, using conditions (B.5–B.8).

The first condition can be expressed more concisely by defining the *Lagrange function*, or Lagrangian, as a function of both the $\mathbf{x}$ and the $\mathbf{u}$ variables

$$\mathcal{L}(\mathbf{x}, \mathbf{u}) \triangleq f(\mathbf{x}) + \sum_{i=1}^{m} u_i g_i(\mathbf{x}) \tag{B.9}$$

This function is built by incorporating the constraints linearly into the objective function, using the multipliers as coefficients. The first optimality condition then reduces to

$$\nabla_x \mathcal{L}(\mathbf{x}, \mathbf{u}) = 0, \tag{B.10}$$

where ∇_x denotes the gradient with respect to the $\mathbf{x}$ variables.

Second-Order Conditions

The Kuhn-Tucker conditions are necessary but not sufficient for an optimal solution. A sufficient but not necessary condition for a minimum is that f and g_i all be convex functions at that point. For unconstrained problems, this is equivalent to saying that the Hessian is positive semidefinite at the solution. In the constrained case, the condition is somewhat more complex; the interested reader should consult the appropriate references [1].

Global Optimality

The discussion so far has covered conditions for a local optimum. In general, we are often interested in having a global optimum, that is, a solution with the lowest value over all possible solutions in the set, not only in the neighborhood of some point.

Although there exist methods for finding a global solution of an arbitrary optimization problem, they are extremely time consuming and are limited to very small problems with only a few constraints and variables. The only useful result on the question of global optimality is in the case of convex problems, where both the objective function and the domain are convex. In this case, one can show that any local minimum of the problem is also a global one. In practice, this condition is often not easy to verify, and we must be content to find a local solution.

When it is not know whether the problem is convex, some measure of reassurance about the global nature of the solution can be obtained by starting the solution algorithm from widely different initial solutions. If at least two of the final solutions have different values, then we have demonstrated that the problem is not convex. If all the solutions are identical, we have an indication that the minimum *may* be global. The degree of confidence in this conclusion, however, depends largely on the nature of the domain and the function.

Finally, we recall an important theorem concerning the minimization of concave function over convex sets. The theorem states that the global minimum can be found on at least one of the extreme points of the set. In cases when this set is finite, this reduces the optimization to a search over a finite set that may be easier to perform than the search in R^n.

B.3   Duality Theory

To verify that a solution $\mathbf{x}$ satisfies the necessary conditions for optimality, the Kuhn-Tucker multipliers must be known. Of course, these multipliers usually are not known, and calculating them leads us into the subject of duality.

We start by remarking that the Lagrange function can be viewed as a function of two vectors, that is, $\mathbf{x}$ and $\mathbf{u}$. Since we are interested in $\mathbf{u}$, we may think of eliminating the other vector. This defines the *dual function*

$$w(\mathbf{u}) \stackrel{\triangle}{=} \min_{\mathbf{x} \in S} \mathcal{L}(\mathbf{x}, \mathbf{u}) \qquad (B.11)$$

which is a function of $\mathbf{u}$ only. This function has a number of interesting properties:

1. It is continuous over its domain.

2. It is concave everywhere over its domain.

3. It is not necessarily differentiable everywhere.

4. Let $\mathbf{x}^*(\mathbf{u})$ be the solution of the minimization (B.11) for some value of $\mathbf{u}$. Suppose also that w is differentiable everywhere. The gradient of w at this point is given by $\nabla w = \mathbf{g}(\mathbf{x}^*)$. When w is not differentiable, the constraint vector is a subgradient of w.

5   The function w satisfies the weak duality theorem. For any pair of feasible solutions $\mathbf{x} \in S$ and $\mathbf{u} \geq 0$, we have $w(\mathbf{u}) \leq f^* \leq f(\mathbf{x})$.

These properties hold under very general assumptions about S, which need not be convex, or for that matter may be finite or denumerably infinite. This is why the theory of duality plays such an important role in combinatorial optimization and also in optimization methods for large systems.

As we said at the beginning of this section, we are interested in calculating the multipliers. This leads us into the definition of the *dual problem*

$$\max w(\mathbf{u}) \qquad \qquad \text{(B.12)}$$
$$\mathbf{u} \geq 0$$

where problem (B.2) is now called the *primal problem*. Let $\mathbf{u}^*$ be the optimal solution of the dual. The difference $f(\mathbf{x}^*) - w(\mathbf{u}^*)$ is called the *duality gap*. One question of interest is the size of this gap. It turns out that in general the duality gap does not vanish. If, on the other hand, the primal is a convex problem, at least in a small neighborhood of the solution, then we can show that the duality gap does vanish, and that the optimal value of the dual is precisely equal to the optimal value of the primal. Furthermore, the optimal solution $\mathbf{u}^*$ is precisely the set of multipliers required by the Kuhn-Tucker equations for the primal at that point.

Even when this is not the case, duality has great practical importance in relation to property 5, called the *weak duality* theorem, which states that the value of *any* feasible dual solution is a lower bound on the optimal value. Because many problems are intrinsically difficult to solve, sometimes the calculation of a solution must be terminated before the optimal solution is reached. In such cases, knowing the value of a dual solution can be a useful bound on the error made because of this premature termination.

B.4   Numerical Methods for Unconstrained Problems

Virtually all methods for obtaining a numerical solution to an optimization problem are iterative. Because unconstrained optimization methods are conceptually simpler, and also because they are used as subalgorithms in constrained problems, we first explain several such methods. Most are of the descent type and operate as follows. A starting point $\mathbf{x}^0$ is chosen by some unspecified technique. Let $\mathbf{x}^k$ be the current point at iteration k:

1. Check some optimality condition. In general, we use $|\nabla f(\mathbf{x}^k)| \leq \epsilon$. If the condition is met, stop. If not, proceed to the next iteration.

2. Compute a new value $\mathbf{x}^{k+1}$:

    a. Compute a direction of displacement $\mathbf{d}^k$. This a vector such that for sufficiently small $\epsilon > 0$, we have $f(\mathbf{x} + \epsilon \mathbf{d}) < f(\mathbf{x})$.

    b. Compute α^k, the amount of displacement in this direction. Called the *line search*, this consists of finding a minimum of f on the half-line $\mathbf{x}^k + \alpha \mathbf{d}^k$, where $\alpha \geq 0$. The value of α^* at this minimum, called the *step size*, becomes α^k.

    c. Compute a new position $\mathbf{x}^{k+1} = \mathbf{x}^k + \alpha^k \mathbf{d}^k$.

We now examine some algorithms frequently used to perform the line search and to calculate directions.

Line Search

The line search is a one-dimensional optimization problem of the form

$$\min_{\alpha \geq 0} \; g(\alpha) = f(\mathbf{x} + \alpha \mathbf{d}) \qquad (B.13)$$

where we have dropped the iteration index k for simplicity of notation. Because of this simplified structure, efficient techniques can be used to solve (B.13). The methods are classified according to the type of information used in the minimization, as measured by the order of the derivatives of g that are used.

    Zeroth-order methods, also called *interval methods*, do not use any derivative information. The basic assumption is that an initial interval has been determined in which the function is unimodal, that is, has a single minimum. This happens when three increasing values α_0, α_1, and α_2 have been found such that $g(\alpha_1) < g(\alpha_2)$ and $g(\alpha_1) < g(\alpha_0)$. The uniqueness of the minimum is always assumed; if the algorithm fails, this is taken as a sign that the assumption was unjustified. The interval is then reduced at each iteration, while ensuring that it always contains the minimum. We now reintroduce an iteration index l, but with a different meaning. Here l denotes the number of the current iteration when a minimum in the direction $\mathbf{d}$ is being searched for; it must not be confused with the iteration index k, used to denote the iteration number in the search for a minimum in R^n. The particular method used for this interval reduction defines the technique. Simple bisection of the current interval into two equal parts can be used, as can the so-called *golden section method* and the Fibonnaci search, where the interval is divided into unequal parts. This last technique produces the largest relative decrease in the interval for a given number of function evaluations. The golden section method, while not quite optimal, will achieve as good a reduction as that of the Fibonnaci search method, with one additional function evaluation at most.

    Other methods construct a quadratic interpolation through the three points, selecting the minimum of the interpolation as the third point required to construct a smaller interval. The convergence rate of these methods is generally linear, often with a rather slow rate near the solution.

First-order methods use the information contained in the first derivative of g. A frequently used technique is the *secant method*, where an iteration is calculated by

$$\alpha^{l+1} = \alpha^l - g'(\alpha^l)\frac{\alpha^l - \alpha^{l-1}}{g'(\alpha^l) - g'(\alpha^{l-1})}. \tag{B.14}$$

Second-order methods use the information contained in the second derivative of g. The most widely known, Newton's method, uses the iteration

$$\alpha^{l+1} = \alpha^l + \frac{g'(\alpha^l)}{g''(\alpha^l)} \tag{B.15}$$

Provided the initial value is close enough to the solution, the convergence is quite rapid when expressed as the number of iterations required to meet some stopping rule. Because each iteration requires the calculation of second derivatives, however, the total time to reach the solution may still be quite large. The method is also subject to oscillation whenever the initial value is not close enough to the solution, and there is no easily computable rule to determine when this is the case.

For all these reasons, in practice the derivative methods and interval-reduction methods are often combined. The latter are used to safeguard against a lack of convergence in the early iterations, while the faster secant or Newton methods are used in the final iterations to obtain an accurate solution faster than can the interval techniques. Also, the line search is generally not performed very accurately, at least in the first stages of the calculation: There is not much point in computing a very accurate solution to the line search since the current value of $\mathbf{x}$ may be far from the optimal solution in any case. Theoretical results state the minimum decrease in f that must be achieved in each line search to guarantee that the overall algorithm will still converge.

Direction Calculation

The second element of descent methods is the computation of a search direction. A number of techniques are available, depending on the order of the derivatives used. All these techniques meet the obvious requirement that the chosen direction must allow a decrease of the objective function in the neighborhood of the current solution. In the following, we denote $\nabla f(\mathbf{x}^k) = \mathbf{g}^k$.

First-order methods use only the gradients, either those at the current iteration or some of the values of preceding iterations. The simplest direction, using $\mathbf{d}^k = -\mathbf{g}^k$, is called the *steepest-descent method*. The reason for this name is that, at the point $\mathbf{x}^k$, the direction $-\mathbf{g}^k$ gives the direction of largest decrease of f, *at least in the neighborhood of* $\mathbf{x}$. Although this method appears simple, it can exhibit an extremely slow convergence near the solution, and thus is almost never used in practice.

The most frequently used first-order method, called the *conjugate-direction method*, uses values of the gradient at the present iteration, modified with the directions used at the previous iteration. The direction is given by

$$\mathbf{d}^0 = -\mathbf{g}^0$$
$$\mathbf{d}^k = -\mathbf{g}^k + \beta_k \mathbf{d}^{k-1} \tag{B.16}$$

where the choice of β_k determines the particular type of conjugate-direction method used. The most frequent choices are

$$\beta_k = \begin{cases} \dfrac{<\mathbf{g}^k, \mathbf{g}^k>}{<\mathbf{g}^{k-1}, \mathbf{g}^{k-1}>} & \text{for the Fletcher-Reeves method} \\[2ex] \dfrac{<\mathbf{g}^k - \mathbf{g}^{k-1}, \mathbf{g}^k>}{<\mathbf{g}^{k-1}, \mathbf{g}^{k-1}>} & \text{for the Polak-Ribière method} \end{cases}$$

The conjugate-direction methods have a number of interesting properties. First, given exact arithmetic, they find the minimum of a quadratic function of n variables in precisely n iterations. This feature is not present in the steepest-descent method; for some quadratic functions, the algorithm converges extremely slowly near the solution. Although this result does not apply to general functions, convergence of the conjugate-direction method is often quite good near a minimum since, at this point, the function is well approximated by its second-order term, and looks very much like a quadratic function. Also, the storage requirements are relatively modest, and, because only vector multiplications are involved, the calculation can be vectorized quite easily, also lending itself to a sparse representation when the problem data is sparse. For these reasons, conjugate-direction methods are currently the only realistic methods for truly large-scale optimization problems that do not have some special structure to be exploited.

Second-order methods achieve faster convergence rates than the conjugate-direction techniques by using information contained in the Hessian matrix of f. The prototype for second-order methods is Newton's method, which can be stated as

$$\mathbf{x}^{k+1} = \mathbf{x}^k - H^{-1}(\mathbf{x}^k)\mathbf{g}^k. \tag{B.17}$$

Note that the method has no line search, but computes a new solution directly from the Hessian matrix and the current point. It is possible to show that the algorithm converges quadratically to the solution, provided it is started close enough to the solution, but there is no computational test to determine this radius of convergence. Even if such a test were possible, the amount of work required per iteration is quite large, since it involves computing the Hessian matrix and inverting it. Unless the function has a simple analytic form, the computation must be done by finite differences, with a corresponding loss of accuracy, and the inversion can become time consuming as the problem size increases. Although seldom used, Newton's method has been the source of more practical algorithms that can achieve rapid convergence with moderate computation times.

All quasi-Newton methods are based on the fact that, when far from the solution, the exact computation of the inverse of the Hessian matrix is really unnecessary, and that an approximate value for this inverse would probably be quite sufficient. Such methods use the general iteration scheme

$$\mathbf{x}^{k+1} = \mathbf{x}^k - \alpha^k S^k \mathbf{g}^k, \qquad (\text{B}.18)$$

where S^k is some symmetric, positive-definite matrix that may depend on the iteration. If $S^k = I$, we have the steepest-descent method; if $S^k = H^{-1}$, Newton's method. The quasi-Newton methods lie between these two extremes since they construct successive approximations F^k of the inverse Hessian matrix in such a way that the amount of computation at each iteration is relatively small and that the exact Hessian inverse is obtained after n iterations for a quadratic function of n variables. These methods differ in the way the inverse is updated at each iteration; the two techniques are called *rank-one* and *rank-two* updates — so named because the approximation is updated at each iteration by matrices of rank one or two, respectively. Some frequently used update formulas are as follows:

$$F^{k+1} = F^k + \frac{(\mathbf{p}^k - F^k \mathbf{q}^k)(\mathbf{p}^k - F^k \mathbf{q}^k)^T}{\mathbf{q}^{k^T}(\mathbf{p}^k - F^k \mathbf{q}^k)} \qquad (\text{B}.19)$$

or

$$F^{k+1} = F^k + \frac{\mathbf{p}^k \mathbf{p}^{k^T}}{\mathbf{p}^{k^T} \mathbf{q}^k} - \frac{F^k \mathbf{q}^k \mathbf{q}^{k^T} F^k}{\mathbf{q}^{k^T} F^k \mathbf{q}^k}, \qquad (\text{B}.20)$$

where

$$\mathbf{p}^k = \mathbf{x}^k - \mathbf{x}^{k-1}$$
$$\mathbf{q}^k = \mathbf{g}^k - \mathbf{g}^{k-1}$$

Eq. (B.19) is called the Davidon-Fletcher-Powell rank-one update formula, while Eq. (B.20) is known as the Broyden-Fletcher-Goldfarb-Shanno rank-two update. In practice, second-order methods can solve problems with a few hundred variables and perhaps tens of nonlinear constraints; the major limitation is the storage requirements of the partial inverse Hessian matrix. It is quite obvious that second-order techniques are inadequate for network problems, where the number of variables can range in the thousands and where the number of constraints is of the same order of magnitude unless some particular simplification related to the problem structure can be used.

B.5   Numerical Methods for Constrained Problems

We now consider numerical algorithms for computing the solution of problems of the type

$$\min f(\mathbf{x})$$
$$g_i(\mathbf{x}) \leq 0$$

We concentrate on the more difficult case, that with inequality constraints; most methods can readily be adapted to the case of equality constraints. Numerical methods for constrained problems fall into two classes: (1) primal methods and (2) relaxation methods. There is a wide variety of each type, and since our purpose is not to give an exhaustive survey, we concentrate on a few successful techniques, those with the best computation times for small and medium problems.

Primal Methods

Primal methods assume an initial feasible solution and maintain feasibility throughout the calculation by ensuring that all the constraints are met at all stages. The obvious advantage is that, if the algorithm must be terminated prematurely, the current solution, being feasible, can be used. The disadvantage is that an initial feasible solution must be found; maintaining feasibility at all times means that the algorithm must follow the boundary of the domain — quite difficult if the constraints are nonlinear. These methods operate as unconstrained algorithms as long as none of the constraints is active — that is, as long as the current solution is inside the domain. The presence of active constraints affects both elements of the descent algorithms: the line search and the direction calculation.

In this section, we assume for ease of exposition that the constraints are linear, of the form

$$<\mathbf{a}^i, \mathbf{x}> \leq b_i,$$

or, in matrix form,

$$A\mathbf{x} \leq \mathbf{b},$$

where A is an $m \times n$ matrix with $m > n$. We assume that A is of rank n, again for simplicity. The theory can be extended to the nonlinear case by considering the tangent plane at the current point, but in practice the numerical solutions are generally much more difficult. Because our interest lies in the conceptual nature of the method, the limitation to linear constraints is not really important; using it clarifies the exposition.

The basic notion underlying primal techniques is that of the *active set*, which is, as indicated by its name, the set of constraints active at the current point. For a given active set defined by l equality constraints, define A_l as the $l \times n$ matrix of the rows $\mathbf{a}^i$, $i = 1, \ldots l$ of the active constraints. Assume also that the A_l matrix is of rank l. Each active constraint $<\mathbf{a}^i, \mathbf{x}> = b_i$ defines a hyperplane in R^n. The vector $\mathbf{a}^i$ is orthogonal to this plane, and the set of vectors $\mathbf{a}_i = (\mathbf{a}^i)^T$, $i = 1, \ldots l$ defines a subspace $R^l \subset R^n$. The set of hyperplanes can be characterized as the set of vectors $\mathbf{d}$ orthogonal to all of the $\mathbf{a}^i$; it also forms a subspace R^{n-l} of R^n and is the orthogonal complement of R^l. This is expressed by the set of linear equations $<\mathbf{d}, \mathbf{a}^i> = 0$, or, in matrix form, $A_l \mathbf{d} = 0$.

All active-set methods proceed in the same manner:

1. Determine, at the current point, a suitable active set that can be a subset of the active constraints.

2. Minimize f on this active set.

3. At the minimum of f, test some stopping rule. One of three cases can occur:

   a. A previously inactive constraint has become active. In this case, add it to the active set and start another iteration.

   b. It is possible to decrease f by moving away from the surface defined by the current active set. In this case, drop one or more constraints from the set, and start another iteration.

   c. Neither of these cases is true. We have found a point that satisfies the first-order necessary conditions.

Primal methods differ in the way that the first two steps are actually carried out. Two of the most widely used methods are gradient projection and reduced gradient.

The Gradient-Projection Method.   In the gradient-projection technique, the gradient of the objective function at the current solution is projected onto the surface defined by the active set, becoming the search direction in this subspace. The direction $\mathbf{d}$ is a vector that lies in R^{n-l}, the subspace orthogonal to the $\mathbf{a}^i$ vectors that define the active set. Recall that any vector of R^n can be expressed as a linear combination of vectors in R^l and its orthogonal complement. This means that we have

$$\mathbf{g} = \mathbf{d} + A^T \mathbf{u} \tag{B.21}$$

for some vector $\mathbf{u} \in R^n$. Because $\mathbf{d}$ is on the surface, we must have $A\mathbf{d} = 0$; replacing in Eq. (B.21), we can solve for $\mathbf{u}$,

$$\mathbf{u} = -(A_l A_l^T)^{-1} A_l \mathbf{g},$$

and replacing in Eq. (B.21), we get for the projection of the gradient on the plane

$$\mathbf{d} = -\left[I - A_l^T (A_l A_l^T)^{-1} A_l\right] \mathbf{g},$$

where the projection operator is defined

$$P_l \stackrel{\triangle}{=} I - A_l^T (A_l A_l^T)^{-1} A_l.$$

This direction is then used to search for a minimum *on the surface*. The line-search algorithm must be modified to recognize two kinds of outcomes:

1. A displacement in the direction would lead outside the domain; in other words, a new constraint has become active.

2. A minimum has been reached on the surface.

In the first case, a new active set is constructed, and the procedure is restarted. The situation is somewhat more complex in the second case, where a minimum has been found on the surface. This happens whenever $\mathbf{d} = 0$. In this case, from Eq. (B.21), we have the conditions

$$\mathbf{g} + \mathbf{u}^T A_l = 0.$$

If $\mathbf{u} \geq 0$, then the Kuhn-Tucker conditions are satisfied, and a point has been found that satisfies the first-order necessary conditions. If, on the other hand, one or more components of $\mathbf{u}$ is negative, then it is possible to find a direction of motion where the function decreases and remains feasible. In this case, constraints corresponding to negative u_is are dropped from the active set, and the procedure is restarted.

Reduced-Gradient Method.   The reduced-gradient method is currently the most efficient primal method for linearly and nonlinearly constrained problems. It is best explained in the context of a problem of the form

$$\min f(\mathbf{x}) \tag{B.22}$$
$$A\mathbf{x} = \mathbf{b}$$
$$\mathbf{x} \geq 0$$

where A is an $m \times n$ matrix with $m < n$. Here too, we assume for simplicity that A is of full rank. Being a primal method, the reduced-gradient method ensures that the optimization proceeds on the constraint surfaces. This is equivalent to saying that, of the n components of $\mathbf{x}$, only $n - m$ are truly independent variables, and that the other m are determined by the requirement that the point $\mathbf{x}$ must satisfy the constraints.

Given a feasible point, the vector $\mathbf{x}$ is partitioned into two parts $\mathbf{y}$ and $\mathbf{z}$, corresponding, respectively, to the dependent and independent variables. This partition is reflected by a similar partition of the constraint matrix into two parts B and D, the first matrix being $m \times m$ and regular, and the second $m \times n - m$. The B matrix is called the *basis*; the $\mathbf{y}$ variables are thus called the *basic variables*.

The original problem can be rewritten

$$\min \ f(\mathbf{y}, \mathbf{z})$$
$$B\mathbf{y} + D\mathbf{z} = \mathbf{b}$$
$$\mathbf{y}, \mathbf{z} \geq 0$$

For a given basis, however, the problem can also be viewed as a minimization on the $\mathbf{z}$ variables only, and can be written

$$\min \ F(\mathbf{y}(\mathbf{z}), \mathbf{z}) \tag{B.23}$$
$$\mathbf{y} = B^{-1}(\mathbf{b} - D\mathbf{z})$$
$$\mathbf{y}, \mathbf{z} \geq 0$$

F is minimized over $\mathbf{z}$ by a gradient-search method; the search direction requires the calculation of $\mathbf{G}$, the gradient of F, which is called the *reduced gradient* of the problem. It is not hard to see that

$$\mathbf{G} = \nabla_z f(\mathbf{y}, \mathbf{z}) - \nabla_y f(\mathbf{y}, \mathbf{z}) B^{-1} D \tag{B.24}$$

and that a point satisfies the first-order optimality conditions if

$$G_i \begin{cases} = 0 & \text{if } z_i > 0 \\ \geq 0 & \text{if } z_i = 0 \end{cases}$$

The search proceeds in the space of independent variables as in the gradient-projection method.

The method can be extended to nonlinear equality constraints of the form $\mathbf{h}(\mathbf{x}) = 0$ by assuming that the Jacobian matrix of the transformation $\nabla_y \mathbf{h}(\mathbf{y}, \mathbf{z})$ is regular at the current point. In this case, the reduced gradient has the form

$$\mathbf{G} = \nabla_z f(\mathbf{y}, \mathbf{z}) + \mathbf{u}^T \nabla_z \mathbf{h}(\mathbf{y}, \mathbf{z}), \tag{B.25}$$

where $\mathbf{u}$ satisfies

$$\nabla_y f(\mathbf{y}, \mathbf{z}) + \mathbf{u}^T \nabla_y \mathbf{h}(\mathbf{y}, \mathbf{z}) = 0.$$

In practice, the procedure is similar to the linear case, but computationally is much more difficult. The $\mathbf{z}$ variables change in the direction of the reduced gradient, but the $\mathbf{y}$ variables must move *nonlinearly* to ensure that the constraints $\mathbf{h}(\mathbf{y}, \mathbf{z}) = 0$ are continually met while $\mathbf{z}$ changes. Procedures exist for doing this efficiently, either by moving temporarily away from the surface and then projecting back onto it, or by iteratively resolving the constraint equations by an approximate Newton method at each step during the line search. This last procedure, implemented in one of the most efficient existing codes for nonlinear programming, allows the solution of problems with a few hundred variables and tens of nonlinear constraints.

Relaxation Methods

Relaxation methods attempt to solve a constrained problem by using the well-established algorithms for unconstrained minimization. This is done by constructing a sequence of unconstrained problems whose sequence of solution converges to the solution of the original constrained problem. Relaxation methods differ depending on the way the unconstrained, or relaxed, problems are constructed. Most frequently used are the penalty and barrier methods, the dual methods, and the multiplier method.

Penalty and Barrier Methods.   Penalty and barrier techniques are the oldest used to solve constrained problems. They were developed in the 1960s, when the theory of constrained optimization was relatively undeveloped and almost no practical algorithmic implementations existed. The main difference between penalty techniques and barrier techniques is that the former may leave the domain, while the latter are strictly feasible throughout the calculation.

In the case of the penalty method, each unconstrained problem is constructed by removing the constraints and adding a penalty term $P(\mathbf{x})$ to the objective function that somehow represents the "cost" of violating the constraints. Intuitively, it is clear that, if this penalty becomes large enough, the solution of the unconstrained problem should be feasible; if the penalty term was chosen correctly, the solution should be close to that of the original problem. At iteration k, the unconstrained problem is of the form

$$\min f(\mathbf{x}) + C^k P^k(\mathbf{x}),$$

where the penalty function must satisfy the following requirements:

1. P is continuous.

2. $P(\mathbf{x}) \geq 0$ for all $\mathbf{x}$ outside the domain.

3. $P(\mathbf{x}) = 0$ if and only if $\mathbf{x}$ is inside the domain.

A typical penalty function could be of the form $P(\mathbf{x}) = \sum_i \max [0, g_i(\mathbf{x})]^2/2$. Given a set of weights $C^{k+1} > C^k$, it is possible to show that the limit of the sequence of solutions to the unconstrained problems converges to the solution of the original problem.

Barrier methods operate on the same principle but are limited to domains with an interior. The subproblems are of the form

$$\min f(\mathbf{x}) + \frac{1}{C^k} B(\mathbf{x}),$$

where $C^k \to \infty$ and the barrier term $B(\mathbf{x})$ is now defined in such a way that

1. $B(\mathbf{x})$ is continuous.

2. $B(\mathbf{x}) \geq 0$.

3. $B(\mathbf{x}) \to \infty$ as $\mathbf{x}$ approaches the boundary of the domain.

For a domain defined by the set of inequalities $g_i(\mathbf{x}) \leq 0$, a typical barrier function could be $B(\mathbf{x}) = -\sum_i 1/g_i(\mathbf{x})$. Clearly, if the initial solution to the first subproblem is feasible, then all solutions will remain feasible. Here again, the appropriate choice of the barrier term guarantees that the limit point of the unconstrained solutions converges to the optimal solution of the original problem.

Penalty and barrier methods have the advantage that they are easy to program, given the existence of an unconstrained minimization algorithm. Because the weight of the penalty or barrier term must increase with the number of iterations, individual problems become increasingly ill conditioned and difficult to solve numerically. As a consequence, the number of iterations is generally small, and the accuracy of the final solution may not be very high.

Dual Methods and the Subgradient Algorithm.   The process by which the constraints are incorporated in the objective function to construct the subproblems is strongly reminiscent of the way the Lagrange function is built. In fact, the only difference is that the coefficients of the penalty or barrier terms are not the multipliers, but some increasing value more or less arbitrarily chosen.

The theory of duality can be used to compute the solution of a convex constrained problem by solving the dual, taking the solution obtained in the minimization of the Lagrangian as the solution of the primal. More precisely, we solve

$$\max w(\mathbf{u})$$
$$\mathbf{u} \geq 0$$

Calculating the value of the dual function for some value of the multipliers $\mathbf{u}$ by

$$w(\mathbf{u}) = \min \ \mathcal{L}(\mathbf{x}, \mathbf{u})$$
$$\mathbf{x} \in S$$

we let $\mathbf{x}^*(\mathbf{u})$ be the optimal solution of the minimization for the current value of $\mathbf{u}$. It is possible to show that if $\mathbf{u}^*$ is the optimal solution of the dual, then $\mathbf{x}^*(\mathbf{u}^*)$ is the optimal solution of the primal.

This method is not generally useful for an arbitrary problem because evaluating the dual function can be quite difficult, and also because $w(\mathbf{u})$ may not be differentiable everywhere. In this case, the solution of the dual can be computed only by methods of nondifferentiable optimization, which require long computation times. The approach has some advantages when a special structure can be exploited.

One such case is the so-called *separable* problem. Typically, a separable problem is of the form

$$\min \sum_{j=1}^{l} f_j(\mathbf{x}_j)$$

$$\sum_{j=1}^{l} \mathbf{g}_j(\mathbf{x}_j) \leq 0$$

$$\mathbf{h}_j \leq 0$$

The structure is such that the vector of variables $\mathbf{x}$ can be partitioned in l sets of vectors $\mathbf{x}_j$; similarly, each constraint function is the sum of constraint functions defined over these sets. In this case, the calculation of the dual function becomes

$$w(\mathbf{u}) = \sum_{j=1}^{l} \min \ f_j(\mathbf{x}_j) + <\mathbf{u}_j, \mathbf{g}_j(\mathbf{x}_j)>$$

$$\mathbf{h}_j \leq 0$$

In other words, the evaluation of the dual function separates into l independent minimization problems. In many cases, this reduction in complexity may justify recourse to the dual approach, even though the dual problem itself may be harder to solve.

Another frequent situation in this context occurs when a very precise solution is not required — for instance, when the actual data for the problem is not known with high accuracy. It thus does not make much sense to compute a solution to many significant digits; an approximate solution is often sufficient. In this case, the dual problem is not solved very accurately; rather, a crude search technique is used. In this method, called the *subgradient* method, a direction of ascent is given by $\mathbf{g}(\mathbf{x})$ at each value of $\mathbf{u}$, where $\mathbf{x}$ is the solution obtained in calculating the dual function. Instead of trying to find a maximum of w in this direction, a single step is taken, given by

$$\mathbf{u}^{k+1} = \mathbf{u}^k + \alpha_k \mathbf{g}^k$$

$$\alpha_k = \frac{\lambda_k [w^* - w(\mathbf{u})]}{||\mathbf{g}(\mathbf{x})||^2}$$

$$0 < \epsilon_1 < \alpha_k \leq 2 - \epsilon_2$$

$$\epsilon_2 > 0$$

Although no attempt is made to find a maximum in the direction, it is still possible to prove convergence of the method under the conditions stated. In practice, w^* is not known, and an approximation is used. The method is particularly useful when the dual calculation is separable, as explained earlier, and when there exists a fast algorithm to compute a feasible solution to the primal $\mathbf{x}'$. In this case, we have, by the weak theorem of duality, $w(\mathbf{u}) \leq f^* \leq f'$. We can use f' to approximate w^* in the step-size calculation, and use the gap $f' - w$ as a stopping rule. The value of this gap is an upper bound on the error made by stopping the algorithm before optimality is reached; if small enough, it indicates that the suboptimal solution thus computed may be sufficient for practical purposes. This method has found widespread application in the areas of integer programming and of large-scale nonlinear problems with structure, for which it is probably the most efficient technique.

Multiplier Method.   The preceding ideas have been extended to the multiplier method, a synthesis of the penalty and barrier methods on the one hand, and of Lagrangian techniques on the other, without the drawbacks of either approach. The multiplier method does not suffer from the stability problems of the standard penalty method; all the minimization subproblems are differentiable and can be solved by standard unconstrained techniques.

In the multiplier method, a penalty is added to the Lagrangian instead of to the function itself. The general formulation for problems with equality constraints

$$\min f(\mathbf{x})$$
$$h_i(\mathbf{x}) = 0$$

is to solve a sequence of subproblems of the form

$$\min \; L(C^k, \mathbf{x}, \mathbf{u}^k) = f(\mathbf{x}) + \sum_i u_i^k h_i(\mathbf{x}) + \frac{1}{2} C^k \sum_i [h_i(\mathbf{x})]^2. \qquad \text{(B.26)}$$

The advantage is that one can prove convergence with a *finite* weight of the penalty term, making the subproblems much easier to solve. The case with inequality constraints can be reduced to formulation (B.26) through the use of slack variables.

Multiplier methods, along with the reduced-gradient technique, have the best numerical performance for small- to medium-size problems.

B.6   Linear Programming

The theory and practice just described take a particularly simple form when the objective and constraint functions are linear. Linear programming dates back to the beginning of operations research during the 1940s; there exists a very large literature on the subject. We thus do not pursue the subject in any depth, but instead point out certain features that are used in this text. The problem is written

$$\min \; z = \, <\mathbf{c}, \mathbf{x}> \qquad\qquad\qquad \text{(B.27)}$$
$$A\mathbf{x} = \mathbf{b}$$
$$\mathbf{x} \geq 0$$

which is known as the standard form of linear programming. Here, A is an $m \times n$ matrix with $m < n$ and of rank m.

The domain of the linear program is convex, since it is the intersection of m half-planes and the positive orthant. In the discussion that follows, we assume that the set of constraints is feasible, that the minimum is finite, and that the constraints are not redundant. In practice this is unnecessary, but it simplifies the exposition of the basic principles required here.

The objective function, being linear, is both convex and concave. For this reason, we know that any local minimum of the problem is also a global minimum and that this minimum occurs on at least one of the extreme points of the domain. At such a point, the m inequalities are tight, which means that m of the variables are determined by this system of equations and that $n - m$ are undetermined. The partition of the vector $\mathbf{x}$ in these two sets determines what is called a *basis*, where $\mathbf{x}$ is the concatenation of two vectors: (1) a vector of *basic variables* $\mathbf{x}_B$ of m components and (2) a vector of *nonbasic variables* $\mathbf{x}_D$ of $n - m$ components. The coefficient matrix A is partitioned in the same way by regrouping the columns corresponding to $\mathbf{x}_B$ into an $m \times m$ regular submatrix B, and the other columns in an $n - m \times n$ matrix D. A similar partition can be made for the cost vector, which is written $\mathbf{c}_B$, $\mathbf{c}_D$. The system of equations corresponding to the constraints can then be written

$$B\mathbf{x}_B + D\mathbf{x}_D = \mathbf{b}. \tag{B.28}$$

A *basic solution* is defined as a solution of the linear system where $\mathbf{x}_D = 0$. In this case, the basic variables are simply given by

$$\mathbf{x}_B = B^{-1}\mathbf{b}, \tag{B.29}$$

which is always possible since B is regular by definition. Note, however, that the solution may have negative components $x_i < 0$. A basic solution is said to be *feasible* if it does meet the inequality constraints $\mathbf{x} \geq 0$.

This concept of a basic feasible solution is central to the theory of linear programming. The fundamental theorem states that to each extreme point of the constraint polytope there corresponds a basic feasible solution, and that the converse is also true. Two extreme points are said to be *adjacent* if they differ by a single component of their basic vector. Because of the concave nature of the objective function, we know that it is possible to find an optimal solution by examining only the extreme points; this theorem gives a simple algebraic characterization of them. The solution of a linear program is therefore reduced to the search over the basic feasible solutions — a considerably easier task than a full search over the domain.

A simple enumeration algorithm would not be practical since the number of bases is of the order of $\binom{n}{m}$, which grows very rapidly with the number of variables and constraints. The most widely used algorithm for finding an optimal solution, called the *simplex algorithm*, can be viewed as the application of the steepest-descent method to the linear program (B.27). The simplex method explores the set of extreme points of the polytope, but proceeds in directions of steepest descent at each iteration, remaining feasible at all times once a feasible solution is found. Given a basic feasible solution $\mathbf{x}_B$, $\mathbf{x}_D = 0$, the algorithm computes another basic feasible solution with a lower value of the objective function. It does this by replacing one of the current basic variables x_i with one of the nonbasic variables x_j.

The first step consists of choosing the nonbasic variable x_j, called the *candidate* variable. It is chosen such that the marginal decrease of the objective function is the largest possible at the current point. In this sense, the simplex algorithm behaves as the steepest-descent method for general nonlinear programming. Recall that the current solution is a basic feasible one. Hence $x_j = 0$ at the beginning, and making it basic means that its value *increases*. Because the solutions must remain feasible, the linear system (B.28) must always be verified. It can be written as

$$\mathbf{x}_B = B^{-1}\mathbf{b} + \sum_j x_j B^{-1}\mathbf{a}_j.$$

Since only one nonbasic variable is being changed, it becomes

$$\mathbf{x}_B = B^{-1}\mathbf{b} - x_j B^{-1}\mathbf{a}_j, \tag{B.30}$$

where $\mathbf{a}_j$ is the column of A corresponding to x_j. By replacing the basic variables, the objective function can also be written as a function of x_j, yielding

$$z(x_j) = <\mathbf{c}_B, B^{-1}\mathbf{b}> + \left[c_j - <\mathbf{c}_B, B^{-1}\mathbf{a}_j>\right] x_j. \tag{B.31}$$

The term $c_j - <\mathbf{c}_B, B^{-1}\mathbf{a}_j>$, called the *reduced cost* for the nonbasic variable x_j, is denoted r_j. This reduced cost can also be written

$$\begin{aligned} r_j &= c_j - <\mathbf{c}_B, B^{-1}\mathbf{a}_j> \\ &= c_j - <\mathbf{c}_B B^{-1}, \mathbf{a}_j> \\ &= c_j - <\mathbf{u}, \mathbf{a}_j>. \end{aligned} \tag{B.32}$$

The vector $\mathbf{u} \overset{\triangle}{=} \mathbf{c}_B B^{-1}$, called the *shadow-price* vector for the current basis, is intimately related to the dual of the linear program. The objective function changes linearly with the nonbasic variable at the rate r_j. Now, since we want to minimize z, we should choose the nonbasic variable that has the smallest such reduced cost. If the smallest $r_j \geq 0$, then all nonbasic variables have a nonnegative rate, and the current solution is a local — and by the convexity of the problem, a global — minimum. If some $r_j < 0$, then the j for which the minimum occurs is chosen as the variable that will become basic, and is called the *entering* variable.

Having decided which nonbasic variable will become basic, we must now decide what value it should take. This is determined again by the requirement that the system (B.28) must remain feasible as x_j increases. Rewriting the system (B.30) for the ith component, we have

$$x_i = (B^{-1}\mathbf{b})_i - x_j \left(B^{-1}\mathbf{a}_j\right)_i, \tag{B.33}$$

where the subscript i indicates that we are interested in the ith component of the vector in question. Here again, we see that each basic variable varies linearly with the nonbasic variable, with coefficient $z_i = -\left(B^{-1}\mathbf{a}_j\right)_i$. Clearly, if $z_i \geq 0$ for all values of i, all basic variables will increase as x_j is increased, and x_j can be increased without limit. Since the effect of increasing x_j is to decrease z, however, the value of the linear program is unbounded. If, on the other hand, some of the z_is are positive, then some of the basic variables will decrease when x_j increases. Because we want to maintain feasibility of the solution, the basic variables can only decrease to zero. In this case, the value of x_j is limited by Eq. (B.33), which must be maintained for all i. Setting $x_i = 0$ in this equation, we get the largest value for x_j permitted by this basic variable, which is

$$x_j(i) = \frac{\left(B^{-1}\mathbf{b}\right)_i}{\left(B^{-1}\mathbf{a}_j\right)_i}.$$

The value of x_j will be given by $\min_i x_j(i)$. At this value, $x_i = 0$ and becomes the nonbasic variable, and $x_j > 0$ becomes the new basic variable.

The third and final step is to recompute the inverse basis B^{-1}, which is needed for the next iteration. In theory, this poses no difficulty since the columns of the basis are known from the set of basic variables. In practice, very efficient numerical methods can be used to compute the new value of B^{-1} since this is the inverse of a matrix that differs from the basis of the previous iteration by the interchange of a single column. Given the inverse of the basis at the previous iteration, it is possible to recompute a new inverse much more efficiently than by standard Gaussian elimination, with corresponding efficiency in the numerical solution of linear programs.

Linear Programming Duality

The general theory of duality takes a particularly simple form in the context of linear programming. Given the primal problem (B.27), we can construct the Lagrangian by incorporating the linear constraints into the objective function

$$\mathcal{L}(\mathbf{x}, \mathbf{u}) = <\mathbf{c}, \mathbf{x}> + <\mathbf{u}, \mathbf{b} - A\mathbf{x}>. \tag{B.34}$$

The dual function is then given by

$$w(\mathbf{u}) = <\mathbf{u}, \mathbf{b}> + \min_{x \geq 0} <\mathbf{c} - \mathbf{u}A, \mathbf{x}>.$$

The solution of this minimization is

$$x_i = \begin{cases} 0 & \text{if } (\mathbf{c} - \mathbf{u}A)_i > 0 \\ \infty & \text{if } (\mathbf{c} - \mathbf{u}A)_i < 0 \\ \text{arbitrary} & \text{if } (\mathbf{c} - \mathbf{u}A)_i = 0 \end{cases}$$

The second case is interpreted by saying that the domain of the dual problem should be restricted to the set $\mathbf{u}A \leq \mathbf{c}$ since the value of the dual function is $w(\mathbf{u}) = -\infty$ outside this set. Thus the dual problem becomes

$$\max \ w(\mathbf{u}) = <\mathbf{u}, \mathbf{b}>$$
$$\mathbf{u}A \leq \mathbf{c}$$

The dual problem has a number of symmetries with the primal. Like the primal problem, it is a linear program, and can be solved by the simplex algorithm. In fact, it can be shown that the shadow prices $\mathbf{u}$ at the optimal solution are identical to the optimal values of the variables of the dual problem. The objective is maximization, and the cost and constraint vectors are inverted from one problem to the other. Note also that the number of rows of the dual is the number of variables of the primal, and vice versa. Given that the computation time of the simplex algorithm depends more strongly on the number of constraints than on the number of variables, it may be preferable to solve the dual rather than the primal problem whenever the latter has a large number of constraints.

Network Flows

One class of linear problems has a special structure that can be exploited in numerical algorithms. These problems are related to the transportation of material in a network from a given source node to another destination, or *sink node*. In practice, the same structure may appear in contexts totally unrelated to transportation. Whenever possible, it is advantageous to transform a particular linear problem to exhibit the presence of network flows.

In this case, the variables, denoted f_{ij}, represent the amount of material carried on the arc (i, j) in the network. The flow domain $\mathcal{F}$ is defined by the constraints

$$\sum_j f_{ij} - \sum_j f_{ji} = \begin{cases} v & \text{if } i \text{ is the source} \\ -v & \text{if } i \text{ is the sink} \\ 0 & \text{otherwise} \end{cases}$$
$$f_{ij} \geq 0 \qquad\qquad\qquad (\text{B.35})$$

The conservation equations can be put in matrix form $\mathcal{I}\mathbf{f} = \mathbf{v}$ by using the node-arc incidence matrix $\mathcal{I}$, defined as

$$\mathcal{I}_{i,j} = \begin{cases} +1 & \text{if arc } (i, j) \text{ goes out of node } i \\ -1 & \text{if arc } (i, j) \text{ goes into node } i \\ 0 & \text{otherwise} \end{cases}$$

In this expression, the sum over j is taken over all arcs having their origin at i and their end node at j. The first set of equations is called the *conservation constraints*.

In practice, some physical limitation is often imposed on the amount of material that can go through an arc. This is modeled by the set of capacitated flows $\mathcal{F}_c$, which is given by

$$\mathbf{f} \in \mathcal{F}$$
$$f_{ij} \leq C_{ij}$$

Typical problems that arise in this context are the maximum-flow problem,

$$\max v(\mathbf{f})$$
$$\mathbf{f} \in \mathcal{F}_c$$

and the minimum-cost flow problem

$$\min \sum_{ij} a_{ij} f_{ij}$$
$$\mathbf{f} \in \mathcal{F} \quad \text{or} \quad \mathbf{f} \in \mathcal{F}_c$$

where $a_{i,j}$ is the transportation cost per unit flow on arc (i, j). The obvious solution to the uncapacitated minimum-cost flow problem is to have all the flow on the path with minimum cost from source to sink. This can be computed easily by using any one of the many shortest-path algorithms, with the unit costs a_{ij} as the length of the arc. Since the problem is a linear problem, its solutions lie on extreme points of the uncapacitated-flow domain $\mathcal{F}$. For this reason, we see that the extreme points of $\mathcal{F}$ are defined by the shortest paths from source to sink.

Although the constrained problems are more difficult to solve, there are specialized versions of the simplex algorithm [6] that allow solutions to be calculated for networks with tens of thousand of nodes and arcs — substantially larger than can be solved by the general-purpose simplex algorithm.

The single-commodity flow problems also have an important property that is not present in linear programs in general. Assume that all the data (capacities, costs, and requirement) is integer. For a general linear program, this is no guarantee that the solution of the simplex algorithm will have only integer values; in general, it will not. In the case of network flow, however, integer solutions appear naturally from the simplex method, without the necessity of using special integer programming techniques. This is very important in the many cases where the flow variables represent technical systems that must be represented by whole numbers.

Flow models are useful to represent the transportation of a single item in a network, but are generally insufficient in many applications. This happens whenever more than one item, or commodity, must use the network. In this case, a set of flows must be defined, one for each commodity k. The equations that define the domain of multicommodity flows $\mathcal{F}_m$ are quite similar:

$$\sum_j f_{ij}^k - \sum_j f_{ji}^k = \begin{cases} v^k & \text{if } i \text{ is the origin of commodity } k \\ -v^k & i \text{ is the sink of commodity } k \\ 0 & \text{otherwise} \end{cases}$$

$$f_{ij}^k \geq 0$$

The capacitated version $\mathcal{F}_{mc}$ has the additional constraints that link the commodities together:

$$\sum_k f_{ij}^k \leq C_{ij}.$$

The most frequent optimization problem is that of minimum cost,

$$\min \sum_{ij} \sum_k a_{ij}^k f_{ij}^k$$

$$\mathbf{f} \in \mathcal{F}_m \quad \text{or} \quad \mathbf{f} \in \mathcal{F}_{mc}$$

where the unit transportation cost $a_{i,j}^k$ is different for each link and each commodity. The solution of the uncapacitated version is once again to route each commodity on the least-cost path from its source to its sink; this can be calculated by a shortest-path algorithm. In the capacitated version, however, the solution is much more difficult. In fact, there is currently no specialized algorithm that will perform substantially better than the simplex method when it is tailored to sparse problems (which is the case for the minimum-cost multicommodity flow). Also, the integrality of solutions no longer holds, and special integer programming methods must be used whenever these integer requirements are important.

References

[1] Luenberger, D.G., *Linear and Nonlinear Programming*, Addison-Wesley, 1984.

[2] Shapiro, J. F., *Mathematical Programming: Structures and Algorithms*, Wiley, 1979.

[3] Lawler, E., *Combinatorial Optimization, Networks and Matroids*, Holt, Rinehart & Winston, 1976.

[4] Papadimitriou, C.H., and Steiglitz, K., *Combinatorial Optimization: Algorithms and Complexity*, Prentice-Hall, 1982.

[5] Salkin, H.M., *Integer Programming*, Addison-Wesley, 1975.

[6] Grigoriadis, M.D., and Hsu, T., "RNET: Rutgers minimal cost network flow subroutines — user documentation," Report No. V 3.61, Department of Computer Science, Rutgers University, October 1979.

Notation and List of Symbols

In this appendix we collect the main conventions for notation used in this book. We also include an alphabetic list of symbols used most frequently.

C.1   Notation

Vectors are denoted in boldface $\mathbf{x}$, and matrices in uppercase italic A. Unless absolutely necessary, we do not explicitly distinguish between row and column vectors, and do not use the transpose notation to simplify notation. Thus the expression $A\mathbf{x}$ denotes the product of the vector $\mathbf{x}$ by the matrix A; we assume that the matrix and vectors have the adequate dimensions. In this case, the assumption is that $\mathbf{x}$ is a column vector.

It is sometimes necessary to use row vectors, especially for matrix multiplications. Most such cases are recognizable because the vector appears on the left of the matrix, as in $\mathbf{x}A$, which represents the left multiplication of the row vector $\mathbf{x}$ by the matrix A. This is equivalent to $A^T\mathbf{x}$, where now $\mathbf{x}$ is a column vector, but avoids the need for yet another superscript in situations where the vector may already have many others.

The ith component of $\mathbf{x}$ is denoted by x_i, the jth column of matrix A by $\mathbf{a}_j$, and the ith row by $\mathbf{a}^i$. Recall that the product $A\mathbf{x}$ can be read $\sum_i x_i \mathbf{a}_i$ — that is, as the linear combination of the columns of A, with the components of $\mathbf{x}$ as the coefficients. When it is necessary to identify a particular component of the vector $A\mathbf{x}$, we denote this by $(A\mathbf{x})_i$. The inner product of two vectors is denoted $<\mathbf{x},\mathbf{y}>$. Vector inequalities or equalities hold component-wise.

Many variables appear in a network context, where it is often necessary to indicate to which arc the variable belongs, which commodity it represents, or both. This is simplified as much as possible by the following convention for indices. Many variables in networks are double-index variables, referring either to arcs in a graph or to some matrix element. The double-index notation is sometimes essential, and sometimes too cumbersome. Something described by two indices may be described equally well with a single index if we assume that there is a mapping from one representation to the other. For instance, we may denote the flow on the arc (i, j) of a graph by $f_{i,j}$, or, if we know that arc (i, j) is the kth in some given list of arcs, by f_k. In the text, we assume that such a unique transformation always exists, and we use the single and double indices freely according to the needs of the exposition.

In general, superscripts refer to a commodity, and subscripts to a link. Thus $f_{i,j}^{k,l}$ denotes the flow of commodity having its source at k and its sink at l on the link (i, j). This same quantity could as well have been denoted f_s^m, or $f_s^{k,l}$ if it is important for the discussion to know the origin and destination of the flow, but not the origin and extremity of the arc in question.

A similar simplification is made for denoting paths in networks. A path from i to j can be specified by giving the list of nodes encountered on the path, as in $(i, k_1, k_2, \ldots k_l, j)$, or the list of arcs $((i, k_1), (k_1, k_2), \ldots (k_l, j))$. Using the simplified notation for arcs, we could denote it as well by $(s_1, s_2, \ldots s_l)$. In many cases, it is not useful to know the precise composition of the path. In this case, we assume that all paths have been placed in a list, referring to the kth path between i and j as (i, j, k). Even more generally, if the particular origin and destination nodes are not needed, we may assume that there is a global list of all paths in the network, (or of all paths of interest in the particular situation) and refer to the kth path.

There is another convention regarding traffic and the relation between offered, carried, and overflow traffic. If x is a symbol representing traffic, then the variable x by itself denotes offered traffic, $\overline{x}$ denotes carried traffic, and $\hat{x}$ denotes blocked, or overflow, traffic. This convention applies to link, path, or route traffic, with the appropriate notation in each case.

C.2   List of Symbols

Here we list the symbols that occur regularly throughout the text. A particular symbol may be used with a different meaning in some short section, in which case this is indicated in the text. The reason is the convenience of conforming with specialized notations that are customary in certain areas.

$A^{i,j}$ = The value of the external traffic from i to j. This is the intensity of the Poisson process that describes the arrival of new calls into the network.

$A_k^{i,j}$ = The value of the external traffic from i to j that is offered to the kth path available to this stream.

$a_{s,t}$ = The total traffic offered to link s, t. This is generally made up of two components, direct trafic $A^{s,t}$ and internal traffic, that is, calls that either originate at a node other than s or terminate at a node other than t.

$a_{s,t}^{i,j}$ = The traffic offered to link (s,t) that belongs to the stream (i,j). This is often called a traffic *parcel*.

B_s = The blocking probability of link s. This is the probability that all circuits on link s are occupied.

B_s' = The probability of reaching or exceeding the protection threshold on link s. This is the probability that m or more circuits on link s are occupied.

C = A cost (most often). It can be a function of the group size, or a constant when the cost model is linear. It is also used occasionally in the discussion of flow models to denote the arc capacity.

$d(k)$ = The destination (sink) node of commodity k.

$E(A, N)$= The Erlang B function.

f = A flow variable or a generic function.

$F(t)$ = A distribution of interarrival times. Its density is represented by $f(t)$.

H = The marginal occupancy on a link. This is the incremental amount of traffic that can be carried on a link for a small increment of capacity, given a constant offered traffic.

L^k = The end-to-end blocking probability for stream k. This is the probability that a k-call cannot be connected.

M = The mean of a traffic. In some cases, this can also be represented by the lowercase m.

m = The protection level of a link. This is the number of busy circuits at which some calls begin to be blocked.

N_s= The number of circuits on link s.

$o(k)$ = The origin (source) of commodity k.

$P_k^{i,j}$ = The probability of overflow to the kth path in the route tree of stream (i,j).

Q = The connection probability; $1 - P$.

p_k = The probability of being in state k for a stochastic process.

r_s = The reservation level for link s. We always have $r = N - m$.

$r_{i,j}$ = The reward for the transition from state i to state j in a Markov model.

R_s = The residual capacity of link s. This can also be used for paths, with the appropriate change in indices.

V = The variance of a traffic. In some cases, this is represented by the lowercase variable v.

$\mathbf{x}$ = A path-flow vector. This is the flow carried on all paths in a network.

$\mathbf{u}, \mathbf{v}, \mathbf{w}$ = Vectors of Kuhn-Tucker multipliers.

$\mathcal{I}$ = The incidence matrix of a network.

$\mathcal{L}$ = The Lagrange function, also called the Lagrangian.

$\mathcal{P}_k^{i,j}$ = The probability that the kth path available to stream (i, j) is blocked.

$\alpha_k^{i,j}$ = The load-sharing coefficient for the kth path available to stream (i, j). This is also the tandem selection probability in residual capacity adaptive routing.

β = The marginal capacity of a link. This is the increment of traffic that can be offered to a link for a small increment in the link size such that the blocking probability remains constant.

γ = The marginal overflow of a link. This is the increment of overflow traffic corresponding to a small increase in the offered traffic, for a given constant link size.

$\delta_{i,j}$ = The Kroenecker symbol. $\delta_{i,j} = 1$ if $i = j$, and 0 otherwise.

λ_k = The arrival rate when the system is in state k for an arrival process.

μ_k = The average service rate when the system is in state k. In other words, $1/\mu$ is the average service time.

$\Phi(s)$ = The Laplace-Stieltjes transform of the distribution $F(t)$. The corresponding transform for the density is denoted by $\phi(s)$.

Numerical Data

In Figs. D.1–D.7, this appendix provides the information necessary to do those exercises that require numerical calculations. The information is by no means intended for real design problems. The reason is that the data is applicable only to the case of Poisson traffic — not a realistic approximation for all hierarchical networks and some nonhierarchical networks. Also, as cheap microcomputers are being introduced, manual network design is rapidly becoming obsolete; such design should be done only for educational purpose, as in the present case.

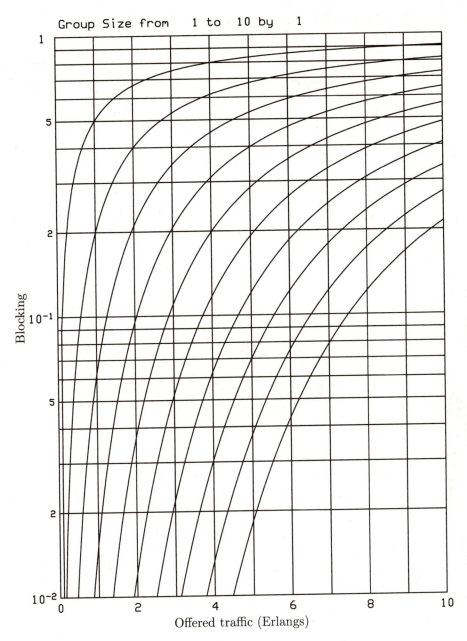

Figure D.1 Erlang B Function

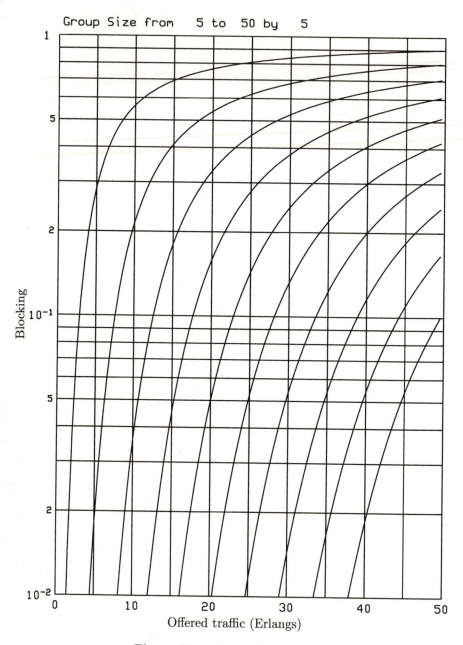

Figure D.2 Erlang B Function

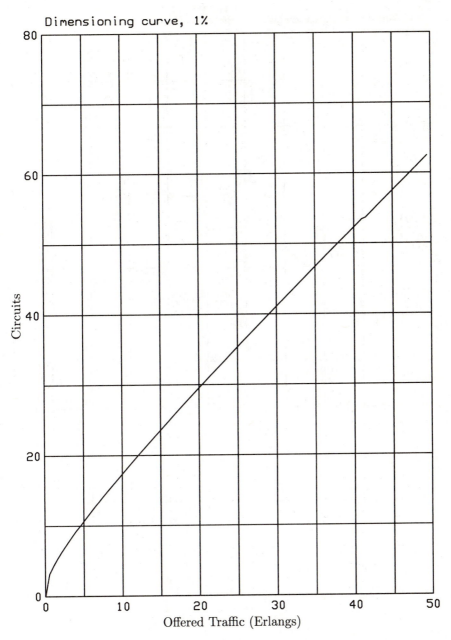

Figure D.3 Dimensioning Curve

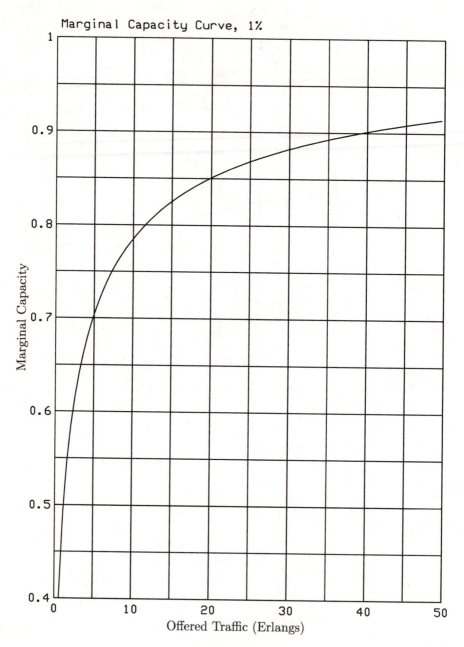

Figure D.4   Marginal Capacity Curve

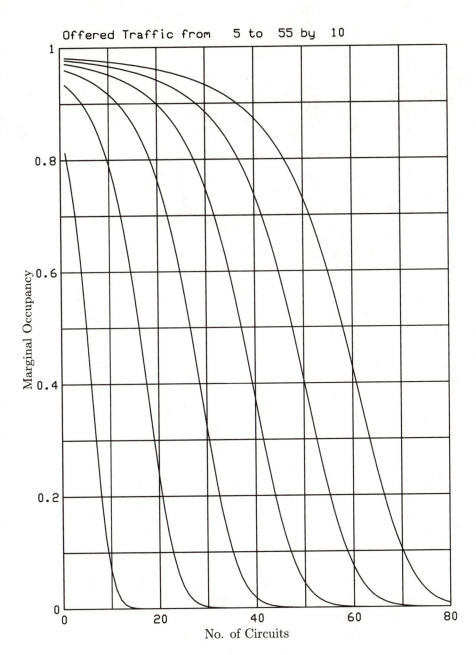

Figure D.5 Marginal Occupancy

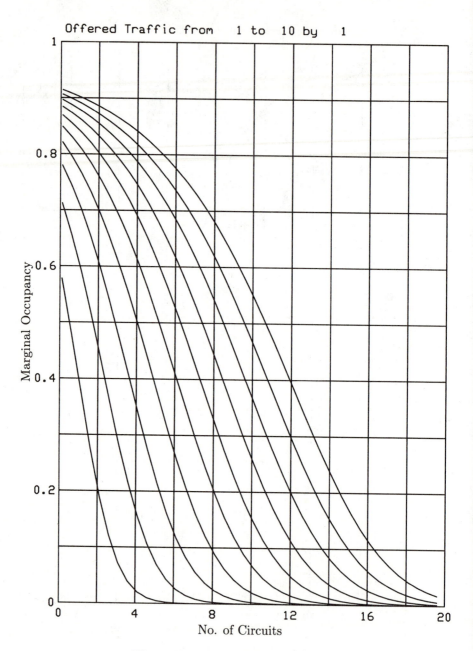

Figure D.6   Marginal Occupancy

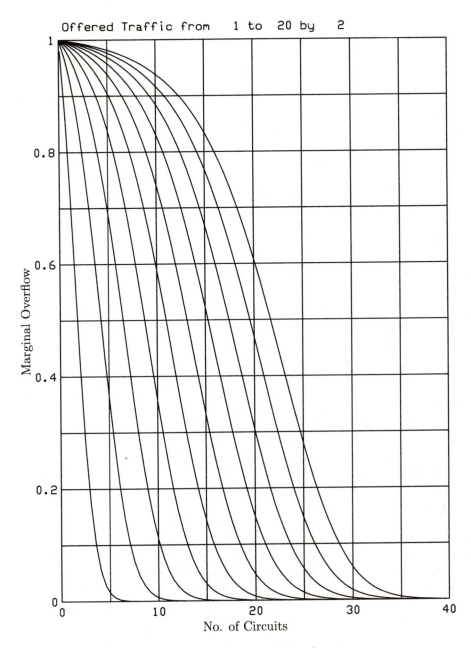

Offered Traffic from 1 to 20 by 2

Figure D.7 Marginal Overflow

Answers to
Some Problems

We give in this section the solution to some of the problems suggested. The problems were chosen because they either provide insight into a particularly important theoretical point or are related to an important application.

Problem 2.1

State i is defined by a vector $\mathbf{n}_i = n_1, n_2 \ldots$, where n_l is the number of busy circuits on link l. We want to compute $p_{i,j}$, the probability of a transition from state i to state j. Note that a transition occurs only when a call arrives or terminates. We consider both cases.

Assume that the event is a call arrival. Let state i be defined by $\mathbf{n}_i$ and state j by $\mathbf{n}_j = n_1 + 1, n_2, n_3 + 1, \ldots$, that is, some links have an additional circuit busy. Since the event is an arrival, the set of links with an increment defines a path between some origin-destination pair (o, d). By an argument similar to that of Section 2.2, Eq. (2.4) gives the transition probability conditional on the event being an arrival.

Similarly, if the event is a call departure, state j is defined by a vector $\mathbf{n}_j = n_1, n_2 - 1, n_3 - 1, \ldots$, where some of the groups have one busy circuit less. This set of links defines a path between some $(o - d)$ pair, and the conditional transition probability is given by Eq. (2.2).

To compute the true probability, we must know the number of calls in progress in state i, either to determine the probability that an event is a call arrival or termination, or to compute the fraction of calls in progress that belong to (o, d). This number, however, cannot be computed from the current description of state i. To do this, it is necessary to recall the complete history of the process up to the current time. That is, we would lose the memoryless character of the process and not be able to use the theory of Markov processes.

Problem 2.3

Figure E.1 is the Hasse diagram for direct-link only routing. The Hasse diagram for alternate routing with the direct link as first choice is shown in Fig. E.2, and the Hasse diagram for alternate routing with the direct link as second choice is shown in Fig. E.3.

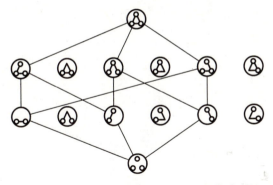

Figure E.1   Hasse Diagram for Direct-Only Routing

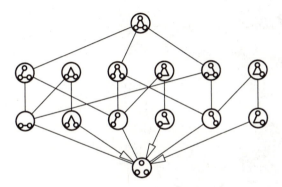

Figure E.2   Hasse Diagram for Alternate Routing with Direct
Link as First Choice

Problem 2.8

Label the nodes from A to F, starting from the origin node at left to
the destination node at right, and following the hierarchical path. With this
notation, the augmented route tree is shown in Fig. E.4.

Problem 2.9

Using the same notation for the nodes as in Problem 2.8, we obtain the
influence graph shown in Fig. E.5.

Problem 3.1

First, we note that, by simple derivation of the sum,

$$\frac{d}{dz} e_n(Az) = A e_{n-1}(Az).$$

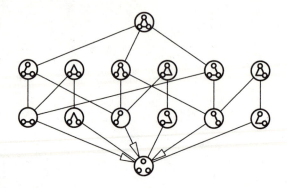

Figure E.3 Hasse Diagram for Alternate Routing with Direct Link as Second Choice

The mean of the distribution is given by

$$M = G'(1)$$
$$= A \frac{e_{N-1}(A)}{e_N(A)}$$
$$= A \frac{e_N(A) - A^N/N!}{e_N(A)}$$
$$= A(1 - E(A, N)).$$

Similarly, the variance is given by

$$V = G''(1) + G'(1) - (G'(1))^2$$
$$= A^2 \frac{e_{N-2}(A)}{e_N(A)} + M - M^2$$
$$= A^2 \frac{e_N(A) - A^N/N! - A^{N-1}/(N-1)!}{e_N(A)} + M - M^2$$
$$= A^2 \left[1 - E(A, N) - \frac{N}{A} E(A, N) \right] + M - M^2,$$

which, after terms are rearranged, gives

$$= M + AE(A, N)(M - A).$$

Problem 3.2

Write

$$\frac{1}{E(A, N)} = \frac{\sum_{j=0}^{N} A^j/j!}{A^N/N!}$$

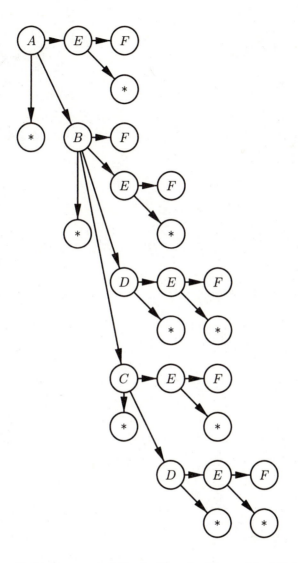

Figure E.4 Augmented Route Tree for Hierarchical Network

$$= \frac{\sum_{j=0}^{N-1} A^j/j! + A^N/N!}{A^N/N!}$$

$$= 1 + \frac{N}{A} \frac{\sum_{j=0}^{N-1} A^j/j!}{A^{N-1}/(N-1)!},$$

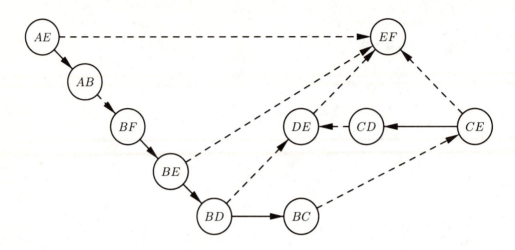

Figure E.5   Influence Graph for Hierarchical Network

which is the required relation.

Problem 3.3

Integrate by parts.

Problem 3.4

Replace the values for the arrival and departure rates in Eq. (A.16). We get

$$
p_k = \begin{cases} p_0 \left(\dfrac{\lambda}{\mu}\right)^k \dbinom{n}{k} & \text{if } k \le n \\ 0 & \text{otherwise} \end{cases} \tag{E.1}
$$

The normalization is straightforward, yielding, by the binomial theorem,

$$
p_0^{-1} = \left(1 + \frac{\lambda}{\mu}\right)^n .
$$

Simple algebraic manipulations bring this form into the required solution. The generating function can be computed simply by the binomial theorem; after setting $A = \lambda/\mu$, we obtain

$$
G(z) = \frac{(1 + Az)^n}{(1 + A)^n} .
$$

From this expression, it is not difficult to derive the value of the mean and variance of the distribution,

$$M = n\left(\frac{A}{1+A}\right)$$

$$V = n\frac{A}{(1+A)^2}$$

$$Z = \frac{1}{1+A}$$

which shows that the distribution has the required smoothness property. The model has a number of defects, as a representation of both offered and carried traffic [1]. First note that because of the finite population model underlying the derivation, the distribution cannot extend beyond n. If we want to use the model to represent an arbitrary smooth traffic, this restriction seems somewhat restrictive, since it would be surprising that the number of busy servers in the infinite group never exceeds n. Thus the straightforward use of the binomial distribution may introduce an inaccuracy stemming from the hard limit on the busy-server distribution.

Also, for arbitrary values of M and $V < M$, A is fixed by the value of Z, and we have $n = M/1 - Z$, which is not necessarily an integer. In this case, interpreting n as the number of sources does not hold any longer. Although the distribution could be extended to noninteger n by using the relation

$$\binom{n}{k} = \frac{(n)_k}{k!},$$

here again, we must have $p_k = 0$ for $k > \lfloor n+1 \rfloor$ to guarantee that the probability does not become negative.

Finally, we would like to use this distribution in calculating blocking probability. In the spirit of the BPP model, we would then assume that the busy-circuit distribution in the finite group is given by Eq. (E.1), but properly normalized to the group size N instead of normalized to the source population n. We can then compute the blocking probability of a group of size N by the recurrence

$$E_N = \frac{A(n-N+1)E_{N-1}}{N + A(n-N+1)E_{N-1}}$$

$$E_0 = 1$$

If n is an integer, this probability will eventually become equal to zero. If not, then care must be taken that the values do not become negative. This is impossible if $M/(1-Z) \geq N$, a condition likely to be satisfied in practice. Nevertheless, this condition limits the use of the binomial model as a representation of smooth traffic in networks, and the vanishing of E_N for certain values of N when n is an integer can also be the cause of problems in numerical calculations, especially if derivatives are needed.

Problem 3.5

Let n be the size of the primary group, and l the size of the secondary group. We have, by inspection of the transition diagram,

$$(a + n + m)p_{n,m} = p_{n-1,m} + (n + 1)p_{n+1,m} + (m + 1)p_{n,m+1}$$

$$n = 0, \ldots N - 1, \; m = 0, \ldots L$$

$$(a + N + m)p_{N,m} = p_{N-1,m} + (m + 1)p_{N,m+1} + Ap_{N,m-1} \quad m = 0, \ldots L$$

$$(N + L)p_{N,L} = Ap_{N-1,L} + Ap_{N,L-1}$$

Problem 3.9

Use the independence of the interarrival times and Baye's rule.

Problem 3.10

The interarrival distribution is given by $F(t) = 1 - e^{-\lambda t}$. Integrating, we get

$$Y(s) = 1 - e^{-\lambda s}$$

and

$$E\{Y\} = \int_0^\infty s \, dY(s)$$

$$= \lambda \int_0^\infty s e^{-\lambda s} ds.$$

Integraging by parts,

$$= \int_0^\infty e^{-\lambda s} ds$$

$$= \frac{1}{\lambda}.$$

The paradox is due to the fact that the probability of intercepting an interval of length l depends on l, and that the larger l, the larger is the probability of intersecting this interval.

Problem 3.11

We have

$$\psi(z) = \sum_{i=0}^{N-1} P_i \int_0^\infty (1 - a + az)^{i+1} dF(t) + P_N \int_0^\infty (1 - a + az)^N dF(t)$$

$$\frac{d^n \psi(z)}{dz^n} = \sum_{i=0}^{N-1} P_i \int_0^\infty (i + 1)i(i - 1) \ldots (i + 1 - n + 1)a^n (1 - a + az)^{i+1-n} dF(t) +$$

$$P_N \int_0^\infty (1 - a + az)^{N-n} N(N - 1) \ldots (N - n + 1) dF(t)$$

and, setting $z = 1$,

$$= \sum_{i=0}^{N-1} P_i \int_0^\infty (i+1)i(i-1)\dots(i+1-n+1)a^n dF(t) +$$

$$P_N \int_0^\infty N(N-1)\dots(N-n+1)dF(t)$$

and, dividing by $n!$,

$$\beta_n = \sum_{i=0}^{N-1} P_i \binom{i+1}{n} \int_0^\infty a^n dF(t) + P_N \binom{N}{n} \int_0^\infty a^N dF(t).$$

Since

$$\int_0^\infty a^n dF(t) = \int_0^\infty e^{-n\mu t} dF(t)$$

$$= \Phi(n\mu),$$

we finally get

$$\beta_n = \Phi(n\mu) \left[\sum_{i=0}^{N-1} P_i \binom{i+1}{n} + P_N \binom{N}{n} \right],$$

as required.

Problem 3.13

From Eq. (3.77), we have

$$\pi_{k0} = \frac{\gamma}{s+\omega} \pi_{k1}.$$

We can use this value to replace in Eq. (3.76) to get an equation for the states $(k1)$ only. We have

$$\left[s + \lambda + \gamma - \frac{\omega\gamma}{s+\omega} \right] \pi_{k1} = \lambda\pi_{k-1,1},$$

which can be solved by

$$\pi_{k,1} = \left[\frac{\lambda(s+\omega)}{s^2 + s(\lambda+\gamma+\omega) + \omega\lambda} \right]^k \pi_{01}$$

$$= \left[\frac{\lambda(s+\omega)}{g(s)} \right]^k \pi_{01}.$$

We now use Eqs. (3.75) and (3.76) at $k = 0$ to obtain the two equations for the initial values

$$(s+\omega)\pi_{00} = \gamma\pi_{01}$$

$$(s+\lambda+\gamma)\pi_{01} = \omega\pi_{00} + 1$$

From these, we get

$$\pi_{00} = \frac{\lambda}{g(s)}$$

$$\pi_{01} = \frac{s+\omega}{\gamma}\pi_{00}$$

Having defined

$$\pi_k = \pi_{k0} + \pi_{k1},$$

we get

$$\pi_k = \frac{s+\omega+\gamma}{s+\omega}\pi_{k1}.$$

This, along with the normalization constants π_{00}, gives the required value for the transform.

Problem 3.15

Letting $A = k\mu$, we have

$$
\begin{aligned}
Z &= 1 - \frac{A}{k} + \frac{A^k}{(1+A)^k - A^k} \\
&= 1 - \frac{A}{k} + \frac{A^k}{\displaystyle\sum_{j=0}^{k-1}\binom{k}{j}A^j} \\
&\leq 1 - \frac{A}{k} + \frac{A^k}{\binom{k}{k-1}A^{k-1}} \\
&\leq 1
\end{aligned}
$$

Problem 3.16

For the Poisson process, $\Phi(s) = A/(A+s)$. From this, we get

$$k_r(\mu) = \frac{r!(A+r+1)}{A^r(A+1)}.$$

This can then be used directly in Eq. (3.64) to compute the mean of the overflow. For the variance, rewrite Eq. (3.54) as

$$V = M\left(1 - M + \frac{\hat{\Phi}(\mu)}{1 - \hat{\Phi}(\mu)}\right)$$

and use

$$\frac{\hat{\Phi}(\mu)}{1 - \hat{\Phi}(\mu)} = \frac{\displaystyle\sum_{r=0}^{N-1}\binom{N-1}{r}k_r(\mu)}{\displaystyle\sum_{r=1}^{N}\binom{N-1}{r-1}k_r(\mu)}$$

$$= \frac{A \sum_{m=0}^{N} \dfrac{A^m}{m!}}{(N+1) \sum_{m=0}^{N} \dfrac{A^m}{m!} - A \sum_{m=0}^{N-1} \dfrac{A^m}{m!}}$$

$$= \frac{A}{N+1+m-A},$$

which is the required expression.

Problem 3.17

After multiplying by $z^n/n!$ and summing, keeping the term $j = 0$ apart, we have

$$\sum_{n=0}^{\infty} \frac{z^n}{n!} \sum_{j=1}^{n+1} \Phi_j(s) \int_0^{\infty} e^{-st} \binom{n+1}{j} (1-a)^{n+1-j} a^j \, dF(t) +$$

$$\sum_{n=0}^{\infty} \frac{z^n}{n!} \sum_{j=1}^{n+1} \Phi_j(s) \int_0^{\infty} e^{-st} \binom{n+1}{j} (1-a)^{n+1-j} a^j \, dF(t),$$

which we rewrite as $T_1 + T_2$. First we concentrate on T_2. We have

$$\sum_{n=0}^{\infty} \frac{z^n}{n!} \Phi_0(s) \int_0^{\infty} e^{-st} (1-a)^{n+1} \, dF(t)$$

$$= \int_0^{\infty} e^{-st} \Phi_0(s)(1-a) \sum_{n=0}^{\infty} \frac{z^n}{n!} (1-a)^n \, dF(t)$$

$$= \int_0^{\infty} e^{-st} \Phi_0(s)(1-a) e^{z(1-a)} \, dF(t).$$

Now let us consider T_1. Recall the identity

$$\sum_{n=0}^{\infty} \sum_{j=1}^{n+1} f(j,n) = \sum_{l=0}^{\infty} \sum_{k=0}^{\infty} f(k+1, k+l).$$

Replacing in the expression, we have

$$T_1 = \sum_{l=0}^{\infty} \sum_{k=0}^{\infty} \frac{z^{k+l}}{(k+l)!} \Phi_{k+1}(s) \int_0^{\infty} e^{-st} \binom{k+l+1}{k+1} (1-a)^l a^{k+1} \, dF(t).$$

Since

$$\binom{k+l}{k} = \binom{l+k}{l}$$

we can replace and can change the limits on the sum over k to get

$$= \sum_{k=1}^{\infty} z^k \Phi_k(s) \sum_{l=0}^{\infty} \int_0^{\infty} e^{-st} z^{l-1} \frac{(k+l)}{k!l!} (1-a)^l a^k dF(t)$$

$$= \sum_{k=1}^{\infty} \frac{z^k \Phi_k(s) a^k}{k!} \int_0^{\infty} e^{-st} \sum_{l=0}^{\infty} (1-a)^l \frac{z^{l-1}(l+k)}{l!} dF(t)$$

$$= \sum_{k=1}^{\infty} \frac{z^k \Phi_k(s) a^k}{k!} \int_0^{\infty} e^{-st} \sum_{l=0}^{\infty} (1-a)^l \frac{1}{k!} \frac{dz^{l+k}}{dz}.$$

Taking the derivative outside the summation,

$$= \sum_{k=1}^{\infty} \frac{z^k \Phi_k(s) a^k}{k!} \int_0^{\infty} e^{-st} \frac{d}{dz} z^k \sum_{l=0}^{\infty} (1-a)^l \frac{z^k}{k!}$$

$$= \sum_{k=1}^{\infty} \frac{z^k \Phi_k(s) a^k}{k!} \int_0^{\infty} e^{-st} \frac{d}{dz} z^k e^{z(1-a)}$$

$$= \int_0^{\infty} e^{-st} \frac{d}{dz} \sum_{k=1}^{\infty} \frac{z^k \Phi_k(s) a^k}{k!} z^k e^{z(1-a)}.$$

Adding T_2 to this last equation, we obtain the desired result.

Problem 3.18

The parameters of the equivalent system A^* and N^* are given by the solution of

$$M = A^* E(A^*, N^*)$$

$$V = M \left[1 - M + \frac{A^*}{N^* + 1 - A^* + M} \right]$$

We assume that $A^* \geq 0$, but allow N^* to take any value. Rewrite the equation for the variance as

$$V - M(1 - M) = \frac{MA^*}{N^* + 1 - A^* + M}. \tag{E.2}$$

The sign of this quantity is the sign of $N^* + 1 - (A^* - M)$. We examine two cases. First, if $N^* > 0$, then $A^* - M$ denotes the traffic carried on the equivalent group, and is never negative. If, on the other hand, $N^* < 0$, then we use the well-known relation for the Erlang B function

$$N + 1 + AE(A, N) = \frac{AE(A, N)}{E(A, N+1)}.$$

Replacing in Eq. (E.2), we get

$$V - (1 - M)M = \frac{MA^*}{\dfrac{A^* E(A^*, N^*)}{E(A^*, N^*+1)} - A^*}$$

$$= \frac{ME(A^*, N^* + 1)}{E(A^*, N^*) - E(A^*, N^* + 1)}.$$

The right-hand side is always positive since $E(A, N)$ is a nonnegative, monotone-decreasing function for any real N. As a consequence, there will be no solution if

$$V \le M(1 - M).$$

Problem 3.20

For the general renewal process, we have

$$\frac{\beta^*_{n+1}}{\beta^*_n} = \frac{h_n}{h_{n-1}}$$

$$= \frac{\Phi(n\mu)}{1 - \Phi(n\mu)}$$

and the limit as $n \to \infty = 0$. For the Pascal distribution, we can get the moments from the generating function of the distribution

$$G(z) = \left(\frac{1-q}{1-zq} \right)^n$$

for some value of n that depends on the parameters. Taking the lth derivative at $z = 1$, we get

$$\frac{\beta^*_{n+1}}{\beta^*_n} = \frac{(n+l)(1-q)}{(l+1)q},$$

which does not go to zero as $l \to \infty$ — the required contradiction. This means that it is not possible to get an arbitrarily accurate representation of a Pascal distribution by a renewal process. It is still possible, however, to match a finite number of moments to an accuracy sufficient for the purpose at hand. In fact, such matching is done all the time, providing very good results.

Problem 3.24

The term $m_1^{j\,*}/E$ is the average of the number of busy circuits given that the group is blocked. But N is also the average of $\sum_{j=1}^{k} X_j$ under the same condition. The equation states that the ratio of these two conditional averages should be equal to the corresponding ratio of the offered traffics.

Problem 4.1

Assume there are l alternate paths through nodes $k_1, k_2, \ldots k_l$. Then

$$L = \sum_{m=1}^{l} B_{k_m, d}(1 - B_{o, k_m}) \prod_{j=1}^{m-1} B_{o, k_j} + B_{o, d} \prod_{j=1}^{l} B_{o, k_j}$$

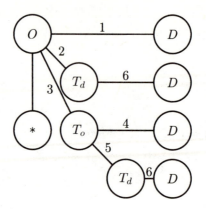

Figure E.6 Augmented Route Tree for Double-Sector Tandem Network

Problem 4.2

Assume that the arcs are labeled in the order of the influence graph. In the route tree shown in Fig. E.6, we see that arc 6 is repeated in the graph. We have

$$Q(U_1) = 1 - B_1$$
$$Q(U_2) = B_1(1 - B_2)(1 - B_6)$$
$$Q(U_3) = (1 - B_3)(1 - B_4)B_1\left[1 - (1 - B_2)(1 - B_6)\right]$$
$$Q(U_4) = (1 - B_3)(1 - B_5)(1 - B_6)B_1 B_2 B_4$$
$$L = 1 - [Q(U_1) + Q(U_2) + Q(U_3) + Q(U_4)]$$

If we neglect the conditional probability, we get

$$Q(U_1) = 1 - B_1$$
$$Q(U_2) = B_1(1 - B_2)(1 - B_6)$$
$$Q(U_3) = [1 - (1 - B_3)(1 - B_4)] B_1 \left[1 - (1 - B_2)(1 - B_6)\right]$$
$$Q(U_4) = B_1 \left[1 - (1 - B_2)(1 - B_6)\right] \times$$
$$[1 - (1 - B_3)(1 - B_4)] (1 - B_5)(1 - B_6)B_1 B_2 B_4$$

Problem 4.3

The repeated arcs are arcs 3 and 6. In each case, we must compute P, and the corresponding weighting factor in the sum that represents the end-to-end blocking. We get the results indicated in Table E.1.

The end-to-end probability is given by

$$L = B_1 \{B_2 B_4 B_5(1 - B_3)(1 - B_6) + B_4 B_6(1 - B_3) + B_2 B_3(1 - B_6) + B_3 B_6\}.$$

3	6	P	Factor
Free	Free	$B_1B_2B_4B_5$	$(1-B_3)(1-B_6)$
Free	Blocked	B_11B_41	$(1-B_3)B_6$
Blocked	Free	B_1B_211	$B_3(1-B_6)$
Blocked	Blocked	B_1111	B_3B_6

Table E.1 Calculation for Double-Sector Tandem Network by the Method of Butto, Colombo, and Tonietti

Problem 4.4

For the first two paths, we get

$$Q^1 = 1 - \mathcal{P}^1 = (1 - B_{o,a})(1 - B_{a,d})$$
$$Q^2 = 1 - \mathcal{P}^2 = (1 - B_{o,b})(1 - B_{b,e})(1 - B_{e,d}) \times \mathcal{P}^1$$

The calculation becomes more complex for the third path; it contains arc (A, D), which also appears in the first path, and link (O, B), which is part of the previous path. In this case, we must take into account the probability that these links are free in the calculation of the path blocking. We get

$$Q^3 = B_{o,a}(1 - B_{o,b})(1 - B_{b,a})(1 - B_{a,d}) \times$$
$$[1 - (1 - B_{b,e})(1 - B_{e,d})].$$

The other paths can be computed similarly because they do not contain any repeated arc.

Problem 4.7

Assume that there are l alternate paths. We have

$$L = Q(U_1, U_2, \ldots U_{l+1})$$
$$= 1 \times \left[1 - \sum_{k=1}^{l} Q\left(U_{1(l)}, U_{2(l)}, \ldots U_{k(l)}\right)\right]$$

since the only loss path is the one after the lth path, and its blocking probability is always zero. Because of the structure of the route tree (no repeated arcs), we have

$$U_{j(m)} = U_j - U_m = U_j$$

so that

$$L = 1 - \sum_{k=1}^{l} Q(U_1, U_2, \ldots U_k)$$
$$= 1 - Q(U_1) - Q(U_1, U_2) \ldots - Q(U_1, U_2, \ldots U_l), \quad (\text{E.3})$$

where

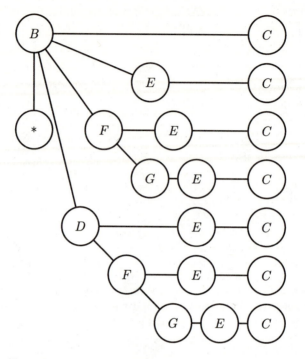

Figure E.7 Route Tree for Stream (B, C) in Seven-Node Network

$$Q(U_1, U_2, \ldots U_l) = Q^l \left[1 - Q(U_1) - Q(U_1, U_2) - \ldots - Q(U_1, \ldots U_{l-1})\right]. \quad \text{(E.4)}$$

The connection probability on path l is given by

$$Q^l = (1 - B_{o,k_l})(1 - B_{k_l,d})$$
$$= 1 - \mathcal{P}^l$$

and, replacing Eq. (E.4) in Eq. (E.3), we get

$$L = (1 - Q^l) \left[1 - Q(U_1) - Q(U_1, U_2) - \ldots Q(U_1, U_2 \ldots U_{l-1})\right].$$

By repeating the calculation, we get

$$= \mathcal{P}^l \mathcal{P}^{l-1} \ldots \mathcal{P}^1,$$

which is the required result.

Problem 4.8

The route tree is shown in Fig. E.7; we give the solution for the last path, the most complex case. The link set U_7 is the set of arcs on this path. We want to compute the probability of using U_7, which is given by

$$Q(U_1, \ldots U_7) = \prod_{s \in U_7} (1 - B_s) \left[1 - \sum_{k=1}^{6} Q(U_{1(7)}, \ldots U_{k(7)}) \right].$$

This means that we must compute the connection probabilities for the partial link sets

$$U_{1(7)} = \{(B, C)\}$$
$$U_{2(7)} = \{(B, E)\}$$
$$U_{3(7)} = \{(B, F), (F, E)\}$$
$$U_{4(7)} = \{(B, F)\}$$
$$U_{5(7)} = \{(D, E)\}$$
$$U_{6(7)} = \{(F, E)\}$$

The first five terms in the computation of the probabilities are straightforward, and are given by

$$Q(U_{1(7)}) = 1 - B_{b,c}$$

$$Q(U_{1(7)}, U_{2(7)}) = (1 - B_{b,e}) \left[1 - \sum_{k=1}^{1} Q(U_{1(7)(2(7))}) \right]$$
$$= (1 - B_{b,e}) \left[1 - (1 - B_{b,c}) \right]$$
$$Q(U_{1(7)}, U_{2(7)}, U_{3(7)}) = B_{b,c} B_{b,e} (1 - B_{b,f})(1 - B_{f,e})$$
$$Q(U_{1(7)}, \ldots, U_{4(7)}) = B_{b,c} B_{b,e} \left[1 - (1 - B_{b,f})(1 - B_{f,e}) \right]$$
$$Q(U_{1(7)}, \ldots, U_{5(7)}) = B_{b,c} B_{b,e} \left[1 - (1 - B_{b,f})(1 - B_{f,e}) \right] (1 - B_{d,e})$$

For the last case, we want to compute $Q(U_{1(7)}, \ldots, U_{6(7)})$. This is because link sets $U_{3(7)}$ and $U_{6(7)}$ still have one link in common, that is, link (F, E). This is shown in Fig. E.8, where the route tree is redrawn, but with the arcs already removed (as indicated by dotted lines). We can see that the third and sixth "paths" still have a link in common; this must be taken into account when computing the probability of using the last link set. The application of the standard recurrence yields in this case

$$Q(U_{1(7)}, \ldots, U_{6(7)}) = B_{b,c} B_{b,f} B_{b,e} B_{d,e} (1 - B_{f,e}),$$

which is the last term remaining for the calculation of the probability of using the last path.

Problem 4.12

See [2].

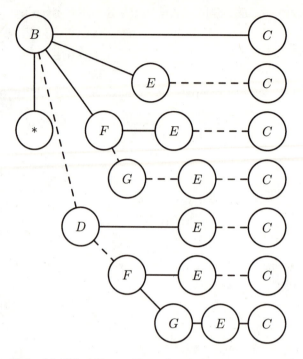

Figure E.8   Modified Route Tree, Seven-Node Network, Blocking
Calculation

Problem 4.14

For one-way circuits, the problems separate into two independent problems, each corresponding to one direction of the (o, d) traffic. We consider the
network that carries the traffic from o to d, and the corresponding high usage.
Let $B_1 = B_{o,d}$ be the blocking on the direct group, $B_2 = B_{o,T}$, and $B_3 = B_{T,d}$,
and use the same notation for the traffics A^i, $i = 1, 2, 3$. From the route tree
for (o, d) traffic, we get

$$\bar{a}_2 = A^2(1 - B_2) + A^1 B_1(1 - B_2)(1 - B_3)$$
$$a_2 = A^2 + A^1 B_1(1 - B_3)$$
$$\bar{a}_3 = A^3(1 - B_3) + A^1 B_1(1 - B_2)(1 - B_3)$$
$$a_2 = A^3 + A^1 B_1(1 - B_2)$$
$$B_2 = E(a_2, N_2)$$
$$B_3 = E(a_3, N_3)$$

From the symmetry of the data, the system reduces to

$$a = A\left[1 + B_1(1 - B)\right]$$
$$\dot{B} = E(A, N)$$

where $B = B_2 = B_3$, and similarly $N = N_2 = N_3$ and $A = A^2 = A^3$, which can be solved by relaxation. From the value of B, the end-to-end blocking is

$$L = \frac{A^2 B_2 + A^3 B_3 + A^1 B_1\left[1 - (1 - B_2)(1 - B_3)\right]}{A^1 + A^2 + A^3}.$$

For the two-way circuit case, the approach is similar. The system to be solved is given by

$$a = 2A\left[1 + B_1(1 - B)\right]$$
$$B = E(a, N)$$

which is solved in the same manner. The expression for the end-to-end blocking probability is identical. For the values given in the problem, we get the results indicated in Table E.2.

	One-Way	Two-Way	Nonhierarchical
$B_{o,d}$	.2145	.2145	.36737
$B_{o,T}$	.2828	.2207	.36737
$a_{o,T}$	11.54	22.48	29.30
$L^{o,d}$	.1042	.0489	.22034
$\overline{L}$	.22353	.16796	.22034

Table E.2 Results for Three-Node Network

Problem 4.15

Because of the symmetry of the data, the problem reduces to a single equation that determines the blocking probability. The fixed-point equation to be solved is given by

$$a = 2\left[A + 2BA(1 - B)\right]$$
$$B = E(a, N)$$
$$L = B\left[1 - (1 - B)^2\right]$$

Solving for the given values of traffic and group sizes, we get $L = 0.22034$. The values of the other parameters are indicated in Table E.2. Note the large increase in the values of the offered traffic and blocking probabilities on the links to the node that was used as tandem in the hierarchical routing.

Problem 4.17

Let A be the value of the total external traffic offered to each link, that is, the sum of the traffic in both directions. Define also $\mathcal{P} = 1 - (1 - B)^2$, the probability that a path is blocked, and m as the number of overflows for each stream. The traffic carried on each path is given by

$$A(1 - B) \text{ for the direct link}$$
$$2AB(1 - \mathcal{P}) \text{ for the first overflow path}$$
$$2AB(1 - \mathcal{P})\mathcal{P} \text{ for the second overflow}$$
$$2AB(1 - \mathcal{P})\mathcal{P}^{l-1} \text{ for the } l^{\text{th}} \text{ overflow}$$

The factor 2 in each value for the overflow paths appears because the link appears exactly once as the first and second segment in this path in all the route trees. Taking the sum over all alternate paths, and dividing each element by $(1 - B)$ to get the offered traffic, we get, for the total traffic offered to the link,

$$a = A \left[1 + \frac{2B}{1 - B}(1 - \mathcal{P}^m) \right].$$

Problem 4.20

We have, from Problem 4.17 in the case of a finite network, that

$$a = A \left[1 + \frac{2B}{1 - B}(1 - \mathcal{P}^m) \right],$$

and that, as $m \to \infty$,

$$a = A \left[1 + \frac{2B}{1 - B} \right]. \tag{E.5}$$

We know that the fixed-point equation is

$$E(a, N) = B.$$

Solving for B in Eq. (E.5), we get the required equation

$$E(a, N) = \frac{a - A}{a + A} \tag{4.49}$$

First note that there always exists an asymptotic solution at $a \to \infty$. The left-hand side is the Erlang function, which increases monotonically from zero to one as a increases from A to infinity. The right-hand side has the same characteristics, and because of the shape of the curves, they can intersect at more than one point.

The solutions are analyzed by rewriting Eq. (4.49) as a polynomial $\sum_{k=1}^{N} b_k a^k = 0$, examining the sign of the coefficients as A and N vary. This equation becomes

$$(a - A) \sum_{j=0}^{N} \frac{a^j}{j!} - (a + A)\frac{a^N}{N!} = 0$$

and we have the coefficients

$$b_N = 1 - \frac{2A}{N}$$

$$b_k = 1 - \frac{A}{k}, \quad 1 \le k < N$$

$$b_0 = -A$$

Because there is at least one negative coefficient, we can be sure that there are no other solutions besides the asymptotic one if all coefficients are negative. This amounts to having $A > \max\{N, 1\}$. For other values of A, there can be other solutions. One such numerical value is for $A = 0.5$ and $N = 2$, which has a solution near the origin.

Problem 5.2

We are computing the probability that there are exactly m background calls on the path. This event happens when there are m visible calls on a link. Call $N_i - N_0$ the excess capacity on link i. There are m visible calls on a link only if there are m calls above the excess capacity, that is, if the event $X_i = m + (N_i - N_0)$ happens.

The formula computes the probability of the event $X_e = m$ by assuming that link i is the *first* link on the path where the level of visible calls reaches m. This means that there cannot be more than $m + (N_n - N_0) - 1$ visible calls *before* link i, but that there can be at least $m + (N_n - N_0)$ visible calls *after* link i, but no more, since the event we are considering is $X_e = m$.

The total probability is the sum of probabilities corresponding to having the first link i in all possible positions on the path.

Problem 6.1

The event that there are f free paths on the two groups can be decomposed as follows. There can be either exactly $N_s - f$ busy circuits on s and any number of busy circuits less than $N_t - f$ on t, or exactly $N_t - f$ busy circuits on t, and less than $N_s - (f + 1)$ busy circuits on s. Note that we must have $f + 1$ in this last term for the same reasons that were explained in problem 5.2.

Problem 6.2

Simply note that $Q_e(x) = P(N^* - f)$ from the definition of the equivalent system

Problem 6.3

Let

$$p = \frac{1}{Z}$$

$$q = 1 - p$$

$$n = \frac{M^2}{V - M}$$

Replacing in the equation, we get the recurrence

$$Q(x) = \frac{[nq + (x - 1)q]Q(x - 1)}{x},$$

from which it is not difficult to get

$$Q(x) = \binom{n + k - 1}{k} \frac{q^k}{k!} Q(0)$$

and the normalization condition imposes

$$Q(0) = p^n,$$

which is the definition of the Pascal distribution.

Problem 7.3

Recall that

$$\mathcal{L}(A, \mathbf{u}, \mathbf{v}) = \sum_{l,n} a_{l,n} B_{l,n} + \sum_{n,m} a_{n,m} B_{n,m}$$

$$+ \sum_{l,m} v^{l,m} \left(\sum_n A_n^{l,m} - A^{l,m} \right) - \sum_{l,m,n} u_n^{l,m} A_n^{l,m}.$$

Taking the derivative with respect to $A_k^{i,j}$, we get

$$u_k^{i,j} = v^{i,j} + \sum_{l,n} \frac{\partial a_{l,n}}{\partial A_k^{i,j}} \left[B_{l,n} + a_{l,n} \frac{\partial B_{l,n}}{\partial a_{l,n}} \right]$$

$$+ \sum_{n,m} \frac{\partial a_{n,m}}{\partial A_k^{i,j}} \left[B_{n,m} + a_{n,m} \frac{\partial B_{n,m}}{\partial a_{n,m}} \right] \qquad \text{(E.6)}$$

Now use the fact that

$$\frac{\partial a_{l,m}}{\partial A_k^{i,j}} = \sum_m \frac{\partial A^{l,m}}{\partial A_k^{i,j}} = \delta_{i,l} \delta_{k,n},$$

and similarly that

$$\frac{\partial a_{n,m}}{\partial A_k^{i,j}} = \sum_l \frac{\partial A^{l,m}(1 - B_{l,n})}{\partial A_k^{i,j}}$$

$$= \sum_l \left[(1 - B_{l,n}) \delta_{j,m} \delta_{n,k} \delta_{i,l} - A_n^{l,m} \frac{\partial B_{l,n}}{\partial a_{l,n}} \frac{\partial a_{l,n}}{\partial A_k^{i,j}} \right]$$

$$= (1 - B_{i,n}) \delta_{j,m} \delta_{k,n} - A_n^{i,m} \frac{\partial B_{i,n}}{\partial a_{i,n}} \delta_{k,n}.$$

Replacing these derivatives in Eq. (E.6) and doing the appropriate sums, we get the desired result.

Problem 7.6

The second term of Eq. (7.14) goes to zero as fast as $B_{i,k}$. We must therefore show that the last term goes to zero at least as fast as B — in other words, that $\partial B_{i,k}/\partial a_{i,k}$ goes to zero as fast as B. Note that because B goes to zero the derivatives do not necessarily vanish. In the present case, however, we can use the relation $\partial B/\partial a = (1-B)(B_{N-1}-B_N)$, which is valid for the Erlang B function, to see that indeed the derivative vanishes as $O(B_N)$. This means that the correction term is of the same order of magnitude as the part that was dropped in the second term of the equation.

Problem 7.7

First we must compute the partial derivatives of the traffic offered to the links with respect to the decision variables. We get

$$\frac{\partial a_{l,n}}{\partial A_k^{i,j}} = (1-B_{n,j})\delta_{l,i}\delta_{n,k} - \sum_m A_n^{l,m} \frac{\partial B_{n,m}}{\partial a_{n,m}} \frac{\partial a_{n,m}}{\partial A_k^{i,j}}$$

$$\frac{\partial a_{n,m}}{\partial A_k^{i,j}} = (1-B_{i,n})\delta_{m,j}\delta_{n,k} - \sum_l A_n^{l,m} \frac{\partial B_{l,n}}{\partial a_{l,n}} \frac{\partial a_{l,n}}{\partial A_k^{i,j}}$$

Consider now a particular origin-destination pair (i,j). For this stream, on all the paths where there is some positive flow, we have

$$v^{i,j} = (1-B_{k,j})\gamma_{i,k} + (1-B_{i,k})\gamma_{k,j}$$

$$- \sum_{l,m,n} A_n^{l,m} \left[\gamma_{l,n} \frac{\partial B_{n,m}}{\partial a_{n,m}} \frac{\partial a_{n,m}}{\partial A_k^{i,j}} + \gamma_{n,m} \frac{\partial B_{l,n}}{\partial a_{l,n}} \frac{\partial a_{l,n}}{\partial A_k^{i,j}} \right].$$

The structure of these equations suggests the following (yet untested) two-stage solution algorithm. First assume some value for the traffic offered to each link. From this, solve the linear system, thus obtaining the correct values for the derivatives. Note that all the parameters of the system are quantities that are related to individual links and that can be computed independently for each link.

In the second stage, use the values of the derivatives just computed in the optimality equations, routing the traffic such that all the right-hand sides will be equal on the paths that carry traffic. In theory, the coefficients would change as we load the traffic on the paths. To make the method usable, we assume that the coefficients that appear in the equation are fixed, not changing as we vary the traffic. In this case, we have a straightforward flow-deviation problem, which can be solved easily. After this second stage, we have new values for the link-offered traffic, from which we can start another iteration.

Problem 7.9

If we eliminate the last tandem in position $k+1$, we have

$$\delta_1 = -A^{i,j} p_{k+1}^{i,j} (1-B_{i,k+1})(1-B_{k+1,j})$$

$$\delta_2 = a_{i,k+1} \Delta B_{i,k+1}$$

where

$$\Delta B_{i,k+1} = E(a_{i,k+1}, N_{i,k+1}) - E(a_{i,k+1} + \delta_1, N_{i,k+1})$$

and, similarly,

$$\delta_3 = a_{k+1,j}\Delta B_{k+1,j},$$

with the corresponding expression for ΔB. In case of a permutation of two adjacent nodes, say k_1 and k_2, we have

$$\delta_1 = D_1 + D_2$$
$$\delta_2 = a_{i,k_1}\Delta B_{i,k_1} + a_{k_1,j}\Delta B_{k_1,j}$$

where

$$\Delta B_{i,k_1} = E(a_{i,k_1} + D_1, N_{i,k_1}) - E(a_{i,k_1}, N_{i,k_1})$$

and a similar expression for δ_3, with k_1 replaced by k_2, and D_1 by D_2. In these expressions, D_1 and D_2 stand for the net increase in carried traffic on the path through k_1 and k_2, respectively. Note that, for OOC, we have $D_1 = -D_2$. This can be seen by assuming that the initial order is k_1 and then k_2, and that k_1 is at level l in the tree. Omitting the (i,j) superscript for simplicity, we then have

$$D_1 = AP_{l-1}\left[(1 - \mathcal{P}_{k_1}) - (1 - \mathcal{P}_{k_2})\right]$$
$$D_2 = AP_{l-1}\left[\mathcal{P}_{k_1}(1 - \mathcal{P}_{k_2}) - \mathcal{P}_{k_2}(1 - \mathcal{P}_{k_1})\right]$$

from which it is not difficult to see that the net change is zero. As a consequence, $\delta_1 = 0$, which is to be expected with an OOC control since any difference in overflow on one path will be taken up by the following one.

Problem 7.8

Write the Lagrange function

$$\mathcal{L} = \sum_m L^m(B)A^m + \sum_t w_t\left[B_t - E(a_t, N_t)\right] + \sum_t z_t\left[a_t - \sum_{m|t\in m} A^m \prod_{\substack{r\in m \\ r\neq t}}(1 - B_r)\right]$$
$$+ \sum_{i,j} v^{i,j}\left[\sum_k A_k^{i,j} - A^{i,j}\right] - \sum_{i,j,k} u_k^{i,j} A_k^{i,j}$$

We take the derivative with respect to a_t and get the first set of optimality equations:

$$z_s = w_s \frac{\partial E}{\partial a_s}$$

The simplicity of this equation is a sign that the variables a_s and B_s are very closely related. In fact, we might as well have taken only one of these as the relaxation variable, just as for the case of revenue optimization. Next we take the derivative with respect to $a_k^{i,j}$. We get

$$0 = L_k^{i,j} - \sum_{t\in(i,j,k)} z_t \frac{1 - L_k^{i,j}}{(1 - B_t)} + v^{i,j} - u_k^{i,j}.$$

Consider now a particular origin-destination pair (i, j). On all paths (i, j, k) where $A_k^{i,j} > 0$, we have by the complementarity conditions $u_k^{i,j} = 0$. For these paths, the Kuhn-Tucker equation becomes

$$v^{i,j} = -L^{i,j} - (1 - L^{i,j}) \sum_{t \in (i,j,k)} w_t \eta_t.$$

Finally, consider the derivative with respect to B_s. We have

$$\frac{\partial \mathcal{L}}{\partial B_s} = -\sum_m A^m \frac{\partial}{\partial B_s} \prod_{t \in m} (1 - B_t) + w_s - \sum_t z_t \sum_{m|t \in m} A^m \frac{\partial}{\partial B_s} \prod_{\substack{r \in m \\ r \neq t}} (1 - B_r)$$

$$= -\sum_{m|s \in m} A^m (-1) \prod_{\substack{t \in m \\ t \neq s}} (1 - B_t) + w_s - \sum_{t \neq s} z_t \sum_{\substack{m|t \in m \\ m|s \in m}} A^m (-1) \prod_{\substack{r \in m \\ r \neq t \\ r \neq s}} (1 - B_r)$$

$$= \frac{1}{(1 - B_s)} \sum_{m|s \in m} A^m \prod_{\substack{t \in m \\ t \neq s}} (1 - B_t) + w_s$$

$$+ \frac{1}{(1 - B_s)} \sum_{t \neq s} z_t \sum_{\substack{m|t \in m \\ m|s \in m}} A^m \frac{1}{(1 - B_t)} \prod_{r \in m} (1 - B_r)$$

$$= \frac{1}{(1 - B_s)} \sum_{m|s \in m} \overline{A}^m + w_s + \frac{1}{(1 - B_s)} \sum_{t \neq s} \frac{1}{(1 - B_t)} z_t \sum_{\substack{m|t \in m \\ m|s \in m}} \overline{A}^m$$

$$= \frac{1}{(1 - B_s)} \sum_{m|s \in m} \overline{A}^m + w_s + \frac{1}{(1 - B_s)} \sum_{t \neq s} w_t \eta_t \sum_{\substack{m|t \in m \\ m|s \in m}} \overline{A}^m,$$

which is the required equation.

Problem 7.12

From the recurrence equations, we have, after rearranging terms,

$$g = \lambda [v(k + 1) - v(k)] - k [v(k) - v(k - 1)], \quad 0 \leq k \leq N - 1$$
$$= \lambda - N [v(N) - v(N - 1)].$$

Let $\delta_k = v(k + 1) - v(k)$. These equations can be rewritten as

$$\delta_{N-1} = \frac{\lambda - g}{N} \tag{E.7}$$

$$\delta_k = \frac{k \delta_{k-1} + g}{\lambda} \tag{E.8}$$

This last equation is reminiscent of the recurrence relation for the Erlang B function,

$$\frac{1}{E_N} = \frac{N}{A} \frac{1}{E_{N-1}} + 1, \tag{E.9}$$

and we assume that $\delta_k = \alpha 1/E_k$, where the constant α is to be chosen to verify the recurrence. Replacing in Eq. (E.9), we have

$$\frac{1}{E_k} = \frac{k}{\lambda}\frac{1}{E_{k-1}} + \frac{g}{\alpha\lambda},$$

from which we conclude that

$$\alpha = \frac{g}{\lambda}$$

$$= \frac{1}{1 + \dfrac{N}{\lambda E_{N-1}}}$$

$$= E_N.$$

Problem 8.1

We solve

$$\min z = \sum_i C_i(N_i)$$

$$B_i \le \overline{B}_i, \quad i = 2, 3$$

$$N_i \ge 0$$

Writing the Lagrangian, we have

$$\mathcal{L} = \sum_i C_i(N_i) + \sum_{j=2}^{3} u_j(B_j - \overline{B}_j).$$

The first-order optimality conditions are

$$u_i = -\frac{C_i}{\partial B_i/\partial N_i}, \quad i = 2, 3$$

$$\frac{\partial \mathcal{L}}{\partial N_1} = C_1 + \sum_{j=2}^{3} u_j \frac{\partial B_j}{\partial N_1}$$

Using $\hat{a}_1 = a_2$ and $a_3 \approx \bar{a}_2 \approx a_2$, we get for the optimality condition for the high-usage case

$$C_1 = \frac{\partial \bar{a}_1}{\partial N_1}\left(-C_2\frac{\partial B_2/\partial a_2}{\partial B_2/\partial N_2} - C_3\frac{\partial B_3/\partial a_3}{\partial B_3/\partial N_3}\right),$$

which gives

$$C_1 = H_1\left(\frac{C_2}{\beta_2} + \frac{C_3}{\beta_3}\right).$$

The two-link alternate path can be replaced by a single path if $C_2/\beta_2 = C_3/\beta_3$, in which case we get the standard ECCS equation for the two-path network.

Otherwise, one must use the precise composition of the alternate path to get the optimality equation.

Problem 8.2

The first three iterations of the ECCS method yield the values shown in Table E.3.

Iteration	β	N_D
1	0.5	13.017
2	0.7235	11.287
3	0.7364	11.184
4	0.7372	11.179

Table E.3   Iterations of ECCS Method

Problem 8.3

The problem being solved is

$$\min_{N} C_D N_D + C_T N_T$$

$$B_T \leq \overline{B}$$

$$N_D, N_T \geq 0$$

Assuming $N_T > 0$ at the optimal solution, the optimality condition for the high-usage case is

$$v_D = C_D + u \frac{\partial B_T}{\partial N_D}.$$

Using the optimal value for u,

$$= C_D - C_T \frac{H_D(N_D)}{\beta_T(N_D)}.$$

If $\beta(N_D = 0)/CR \geq H_d(0)$, then the right-hand side is positive, and so is v_D. It satisfies the Kuhn-Tucker conditions and thus solves the problem. If, on the other hand, the condition is not true, then we have

$$H_D(0) > \frac{\beta_T(0)}{CR}$$

so that, at the origin, the curve corresponding to H is above the curve corresponding to β/CR. But we know that $H(N_D)$ decreases much more rapidly that $\beta(N_D)$ as N_D increases. Thus there is a point $N_D > 0$ where these two curves will cross, which is the required solution.

Problem 8.4

The problem is to determine the behavior of the β function as B changes, for a given value of a. This is because, if we fix a on the plot, we can see how the curves intersect the vertical line representing this constant value and thus determine which curve corresponds to the higher blocking values.

To do this, consider the following argument. Assume that we increase the number of circuits by one unit. We know that the corresponding change in the carried traffic $\Delta\bar{a}$ cannot be larger than one. We then have

$$\Delta a = \frac{\Delta\bar{a}}{(1 - B)}.$$

If $B \approx 1$, then the increase in a can be very large, and hence the value of β will be large. Correspondingly, if $B \approx 0$, Δa will be of the order of $\Delta\bar{a}$, which is bounded by one. Hence β increases as B increases, which means that the upper curve corresponds to the higher blocking value.

This also shows that β is *not* bounded above by one, contrary to what is often stated. The origin of this mistake is probably due to the fact that an analogy is drawn between H and β, from which it is concluded that they should behave in the same way. In fact, H is a marginal *carried* traffic, which is bounded by one, while β is a marginal *offered* traffic, which can take any positive value if the blocking probability is sufficiently large. Of course, in most dimensioning applications, B is small, and β is generally below one.

Problem 8.5

We give the derivation for the case of overflows. The argument is the same for the case of carried traffic. We want to examine the effect of a small variation of the size of group i on the traffic of stream k offered to some other group m. Because of the ordered nature of the hierarchical network, this can happen only if m follows i in the link sequence. We consider two cases, depending on whether m is the first group following i or not. If m is the first group, then we have $a_m^k = a_i^k B_i^k$. We must assume that the blocking is independent of the stream — in other words, that $B_i^k = B_i$. In this case, for overflow, we have the first case, since the traffic offered to i is independent of N_i. If m is further down from i, then we must take into account that the traffic offered to m also depends on N_i, presumably by a sequence of overflow and carried traffics. Assuming again that the blocking probability is independent of k, we have

$$\frac{\partial a_m^k}{\partial N_i} = \frac{\partial(a_{m-1}^k B_{m-1})}{\partial N_i},$$

and, by the derivation of a product,

$$= B_{m-1}\frac{\partial a_{m-1}^k}{\partial N_i} + a_{m-1}^k\frac{\partial B_{m-1}}{\partial N_i}.$$

We know that B_{m-1} depends on a_{m-1}. We want to compute the variation of B_{m-1} when the effect of a change in N_i is made through the stream k — that is, through the path in the influence graph that leads from i to $m-1$ for the stream k. In this case, the variation with respect to a_{m-1} is in fact a variation with respect to a_{m-1}^k. Because we have assumed that all streams experience the same blocking, we can write

$$\frac{\partial B_{m-1}}{\partial N_i} = \frac{\partial B_{m-1}}{\partial a_{m-1}} \frac{\partial a_{m-1}^k}{\partial N_i}.$$

Replacing, we get

$$\frac{\partial a_m^k}{\partial N_i} = \frac{\partial a_{m-1}^k}{\partial N_i} \left[B_{m-1} + a_{m-1}^k \frac{\partial B_{m-1}}{\partial a_{m-1}} \right],$$

which is the required expression.

Problem 8.8

Recall that Eq. (8.29) applies when we know that the optimal solution lies inside a region — that is, when the constraints at the optimal solution are saturated in only one period each. In this case, we know the period and the t^*s. For this reason, we can reformulate the dimensioning problem by dropping the constraints that are slack at the solution, keeping only the tight ones. To simplify the notation, we dispense with the t^* notation, assuming that the terms corresponding to the appropriate period are used in each case. The dimensioning problem is then a standard hierarchical dimensioning, with the extra term representing the switching cost. We must solve

$$\min \ z = \sum_{i,j} C_{i,j}(N_{i,j}) + C_s a_s(N_{i,j}, N_{i,T}) + C_{i,T}(N_{i,T}) + \sum_j C_{T,j}(N_{T,j})$$

$$B_{i,T} \leq \overline{B}_{i,T} \quad (u_T)$$
$$B_{T,j} \leq \overline{B}_{T,j} \quad (u_j)$$
$$N \geq 0$$

We can write the Lagrangian as usual and take the gradient with respect to the various variables. First, taking the components corresponding to the $N_{T,j}$s, we obtain the usual expression for the multipliers:

$$u_j = -\frac{C'_{T,j}}{\partial B_{T,j}/\partial N_{T,j}}.$$

We first examine the component with respect to $N_{i,T}$. Note that, in this case, there will be an extra term because of the presence of the switching cost. We get

$$\frac{\partial \mathcal{L}}{\partial N_{i,T}} = C'_{i,T} + C_s \frac{\partial a_s}{\partial N_{i,T}} + u_T C'_{i,T} + \sum_j u_j \frac{\partial B_{T,j}}{\partial N_{i,T}}.$$

We can make the usual assumption that blocking probabilities are independent on the finals, and drop the sum over the terminating final groups. Note, however, the presence of the term $\partial a_s / \partial N_{i,T}$. We know that a_s depends only on $N_{i,T}$ and on the $N_{i,j}$s. Here we must make some further assumptions about the behavior of the network. In principle, a_s is the traffic going through the switch. It must be $\bar{a}_{i,T}$, the traffic carried on (i, T). We have $\bar{a}_{i,T} = a_{i,T}(1 - B_{i,T})$. If we cannot neglect the blocking probability, then we must include the effect of B in the derivative. If, on the other hand, we assume that the blocking is small, then we might as well also assume that $\bar{a}_{i,T} = a_{i,T}$; since the traffic offered to (i, T) is independent of $N_{i,T}$, the term corresponding to the switching cost disappears, and we have the equation

$$ u_T = -\frac{C'_{i,T}}{\partial B_{i,T} / \partial N_{i,T}}, $$

which is the standard equation for a final group. Turning now to the high-usage case, we have the equation

$$ \frac{\partial \mathcal{L}}{\partial N_{i,j}} = C'_{i,j} + C_s \frac{\partial a_s}{\partial N_{i,j}} + \sum_j u_j \frac{\partial B_{T,j}}{\partial N_{i,j}} $$

$$ C'_{i,j} = -C_s \frac{\partial a_{i,T}}{\partial N_{i,j}} - C'_{i,T} u_T \frac{\partial B_{i,T}}{\partial N_{i,j}} - \sum_j u_j \frac{\partial B_{T,j}}{\partial N_{i,j}} $$

We can replace the multipliers u_T and u_j by their values, getting

$$ C'_{i,j} = C_s H_{i,j} - \sum_j C'_{T,j} \frac{1}{\beta_{T,j}} - C'_{i,T} \frac{1}{\beta_{i,T}} H_{i,j}. $$

This equation has been obtained by noting that, under the usual assumptions,

$$ \frac{\partial a_{T,j}}{\partial N_{i,j}} = -H_{i,j} \frac{\partial a_{T,j}}{\partial \hat{a}_{i,j}} $$

$$ = -H_{i,j} $$

$$ \frac{\partial a_{i,T}}{\partial N_{i,j}} = -H_{i,j} \frac{\partial a_{i,T}}{\partial \hat{a}_{i,j}} $$

$$ = -H_{i,j} $$

It would seem that we should be able to factor out the $H_{i,j}$ term, but in fact we must be careful about interpreting the optimality equation. Recall that we dropped the time index from the notation for the sake of simplicity. In fact, each of the three terms is evaluated in a single period, but there is no assumption that this saturation period is the same for all components of the network. This means that the β and H terms are evaluated at different periods, that is, with different traffic values. Hence the numerical values of H, in particular, will not be the same in the three terms. For this reason, we must keep the $H_{i,j}$ terms separate, writing the optimality equation as stated in Eq. (8.29).

Problem 9.1

We have the problem

$$\min_{\overline{A},N} z = C(N) - D(\overline{A})$$

$$\overline{A} \geq \overline{A}_0 \quad (\nu)$$
$$N \geq 0 \quad (\mu)$$
$$\overline{A} = A[1 - E(A, N)] \quad (\lambda)$$

Write the corresponding Lagrangian:

$$\mathcal{L} = C(N) - D(\overline{A}) + \nu \left[\overline{A}_0 - \overline{A}\right] - \mu N + \lambda \left[\overline{A} - A[1 - E(A, N)]\right].$$

Taking the derivatives with respect first to N and then to $\overline{A}$, we get the two optimality equations

$$\mu = \frac{\partial C}{\partial N} + \lambda A \frac{\partial E}{\partial N}$$

$$\nu = \lambda - \frac{\partial D}{\partial \overline{A}}$$

Because of the constraint on carried traffic, any feasible solution must have $n > 0$, which in turn means that $\mu = 0$. Replacing in the first equation, we get

$$\frac{\partial C}{\partial N} = -\lambda A \frac{\partial E}{\partial N}$$
$$= \lambda H(N),$$

where $H(N)$ is the marginal carrying capacity of the group, as defined in Chapter 8. Replacing in the second equation, we finally get

$$\nu = \frac{1}{H} \frac{\partial C}{\partial N} - \frac{\partial D}{\partial \overline{A}} \geq 0,$$

or

$$\frac{1}{H} \frac{\partial C}{\partial N} \geq \frac{\partial D}{\partial \overline{A}}.$$

Unless the problem is degenerate, which does not normally happen with reasonable functions, the inequality will be strict, which proves the statement.

Problem 9.2

Let d be the revenue generated by each carried call, and assume that the revenue generated by some traffic $\overline{A}$ is $\overline{A}d$. Assume also that the offered traffic at system i is given by some known function $A_i(d)$. Note that there is a single d for all sites. We want to solve

$$\min_{d,N_i} z = \sum_i C_i(N_i) - d \sum_i A_i(d)\left[1 - E(A_i, N_i)\right]$$

$$N_i \geq 0 \quad (\mu_i)$$

$$d \geq 0 \quad (\nu)$$

Using the standard procedure, we get, after taking the derivative with respect to the N_is,

$$\mu_i = \frac{\partial C_i}{\partial N_i} + dA_i \frac{\partial E}{\partial N_i},$$

which is the dimensioning equation for customer i, if we know the correct price d and the appropriate multiplier μ_i. The optimal price is determined by

$$\nu = -\frac{\partial}{\partial d}\left[d \sum_i A_i\left[1 - E(A_i, N_i)\right]\right],$$

which is an equation on the marginal revenue generated by the calls. This equation in turn determines the optimal price, and this level may be low enough that some customers will not get service.

Problem 9.4

Recall that the loss probability can be written as

$$L^k = B_{i,j}\left[\sum_n (1 - B_{i,n})B_{n,j}\prod_{m=1}^{n-1} B_{i,m} + \prod_{m=1}^{l} B_{i,m}\right],$$

where we assume that there are l tandem nodes and that stream k is from i to j. The derivation is not difficult if we consider the three possible cases for s: (1) as the first link, (2) as an (i,r) link, and (3) as a (r,j) link. We immediately get

$$\frac{\partial L^k}{\partial B_s} = \frac{L^k}{B_s} \quad s = (i,j)$$

$$= B_{i,j}\left[-B_{r,j}\prod_{m=1}^{r-1} B_{i,m} + \sum_{n>r}(1 - B_{i,n})B_{n,j}\prod_{\substack{m=1\\m\neq r}}^{n-1} B_{i,m}\right.$$

$$\left. + \prod_{\substack{m=1\\m\neq r}}^{n-1} B_{i,m}\right] \quad s = (i,r)$$

$$= B_{i,j}(1 - B_{i,r})\prod_{m=1}^{r-1} B_{i,m} \quad s = (r,j),$$

where the sum over $k > r$ means that the sum is taken over all arcs that occur after the path where the link s appears in the tree.

Problem 9.6

Choose some value $a_s < \bar{a}_s$. Note that the inequality is strict. Then compute the link blocking by $\bar{a}_s = a_s(1 - B_s)$. Using Eq. (9.25), recalculate an new value for the offered traffics. The procedure stops when the a_ss stabilize to some constant value. Having the correct link-blocking probabilities and the offered traffic, size the groups using Eq. (9.24).

One must be careful to ensure at each iteration that we have $a_s > \bar{a}_s$. Given a set of B_ss computed in the first part of the algorithm, it is not clear whether the resulting a_ss satisfy this condition. If not, they must be reduced strictly below the value of the carried traffic. It is not clear how this should be done, since reducing by a fixed amount may prevent convergence of the algorithm for the groups that have a high load.

Problem 9.7

The dimensioning problem decomposes into $T + 1$ independent subproblems, where the multipliers are known in each case. The subproblem for the N_s variables, the real dimensioning variables, is

$$\min \sum_s C_s(N_s) - U_s N_s,$$

where

$$U_s \triangleq \sum_t u_s^t.$$

Note that, except for the nonnegativity constraints on N_s, this is an unconstrained minimization. The Kuhn-Tucker equations are then

$$\mu_s = \frac{dC_s}{dN_s} - U_s,$$

and, given the value of μ_s and U_s, we can solve the equation and obtain the current optimal value for N_s. From this, and from the resolution of the other subproblems, we can construct a search direction in the space of multipliers by using the constraints $N_s = N_s^t$ as the direction vectors. Consider now the case where C_s is a linear function. Assume that $N_s > 0$. Then we have

$$C_s = U_s,$$

and the N_ss have disappeared from the original problem and from the optimality equation. The resolution of the equation no longer gives a value for N_s at the current multipliers. Instead, this equation is now a constraint on the multipliers since it is equivalent to

$$C_s = \sum_t u_s^t.$$

If we do not have the current value for N_s, however, we cannot use the coupling constraints $N_s = N_s^t$ as a search direction in the space of multipliers. This means that the simplifying feature of the subgradient method will not be available, and that another, presumably more complex method must be found to compute a search direction.

References

[1] Delbrouck, L.E.N., "A unified approximate evaluation of congestion functions for smooth and peaky traffics," *IEEE Transactions on Communications*, vol. COM–29, pp. 85–91, 1981.

[2] Dewdney, A.K., "Probing the strange attraction of chaos," Computer Recreations, *Scientific American*, July 1987.

Index